NEW COMPLETE BOOK OF
COLLECTIBLE
CARS 1930-80

by Richard M. Langworth, Graham Robson,
and the Auto Editors of CONSUMER GUIDE®

BEEKMAN HOUSE
New York

Contents

Copyright© 1987 by Publications International, Ltd. All rights reserved. This book may not be reproduced or quoted in whole or in part by mimeograph or any other printed means or for presentation on radio, television, videotape, or film without written permission from:

Louis Weber, President
Publications International, Ltd.
3841 West Oakton Street
Skokie, Illinois 60076

Permission is never granted for commercial purposes.

Manufactured in Yugoslavia.

h g f e d c b a

This edition published by Beekman House, distributed by Crown Publishers, Inc., 225 Park Avenue South, New York, New York 10003.

ISBN 0-517-64744-3

Photo Credits

Henry Austin Clark, Jr.
John A. Conde
George Domer
Jeffrey I. Godshall
Asa Hall
Phil Hall
Bob Hovorka
Richard M. Langworth
Richard Quinn
Graham Robson
Nicky Wright
American Motors Corporation
Avanti Motor Corporation
Chrysler Historical Collection
Excalibur Automobile Corporation
Ford Motor Company

General Motors Corporation
Motor Vehicle Manufacturers Association
Special thanks to Donald R. Peterson

Color Photography

William L. Bailey
Roland Flessner
David Gooley & Associates
Bert E. Johnson
Bud Juneau
Vince Manocchi
Douglas J. Mitchel
Andre Van De Putte
Bob Welnetz
Nicky Wright

Acknowledgements

The editors gratefully acknowledge the following owners whose cars appear in the color sections: Mike Abbott (1969 Pontiac Firebird), Dr. Barbara Atwood (1933 Pierce-Arrow), Les Aubol (1939 Graham Supercharger), Jim Barrington (1963 Porsche Carrera 2), Ed Barwick (1941 Studebaker President), Blackhawk Automobile Collection (1936 Mercedes-Benz 500K), Joseph E. Bortz (1952 Muntz Jet), R.G. Brelsford (1950 Oldsmobile 88 Holiday), Kathy Crasweller (1954 Hudson Italia), Al DeFabrizio (1949 Willys Jeepster), Larry Desenville (1936 DeSoto Airflow), Joe Eder (1941 Plymouth), Bev Ferreira (1948 Tucker), Gary Gettleman (1953 Cadillac Eldorado), Pete Haldiman (1970 Dodge Challenger R/T Hemi), Julian J. Jaraqosky (1951 Henry J), Jerry Johnson (1954 Kaiser-Darrin), Lowell Johnson (1952 Allstate), Jay B. Jonagan (1954 Mercury Monterey), Robert Joynt (1934 Chrysler Imperial Airflow), Larry Klein (1930 LaSalle), Tom & Diane Korbas (1966 Chevrolet Corvette Sting Ray 427), Phillip Kuhn III (1936 Hudson Custom Eight), Chris LaPorte (1957 Ferrari 410 Superamerica), Cecil S. Madaus (1939 American Bantam), Richard O. Matson (1948 DeSoto), Burnell Mills (1949 Cadillac), Stephen M. McCarthy (1951 Lincoln Cosmopolitan), Gordon McGregor (1953 Nash-Healey), W.A. McKnight (1962 Facel Vega Facel II), Ray L. Menefee (1940 LaSalle), Richard Monaco (1963 Ford Galaxie 500XL), Ken Nelson (1966 Oldsmobile Toronado), Walter Neumeyer (1950 Alfa Romeo 6C2500), Len Nowosel (1955 Ford Thunderbird), Leo Oser (1936 Auburn 852 Supercharged), Bob Patrick (1957 Studebaker Golden Hawk), Donald W. Peters (1951 Ford Crestliner), Dick Pyle (1939 Chevrolet Master DeLuxe), Vincent Rufolo (1948 Nash Ambassador), Arthur Sabin (1948 Frazer Manhattan), David Schramm (1956 Continental Mark II), John Shulze (1955 Packard Clipper), David P. Smith (1960 Ferrari 250GT), Walter Sprague (1931 Reo Royale), Danny Stine (1949 Crosley Hotshot), Chris Terry (1966 Pontiac GTO), Unique Motorcars (1947 Ford Sportsman), Neil Vedder (1957 Dodge Custom Royal Lancer), Dean Watts (1955 Mercedes-Benz 300SL), Harry Wynn (1941 Lincoln Continental), Dennis Yauger (1954 Kaiser Manhattan), Ray Zeman (1966 Buick Riviera).

COVER CREDITS

Michael L. Berzenye (1958 Buick Limited), Jim Bowersox (1941 Buick), Frank Capolupo (1969 Chevrolet Corvette), Raymond E. Dade (1947 Studebaker), Dr. Gerard Depersio (1958 Cadillac), Joanne Fisher (1962 Facel III), William Goodsell (1957 Triumph TR3), Jerry Johnson (1951 Henry J), Jack Karleskind (1970 Mercury Cougar), Phil Lagerquist (1970 Plymouth Superbird), Barry Norman (1963 Ford), Frederick J. Roth (1954 Hudson), Samuel and Wanda Roth (1969 AMC Javelin), S.H. Sanger (1937 Cord 812), Ted Sattler (1935 Ford), Ernest J. Toth, Jr. (1933 Stutz DV-32), Brian H. Williams (1955 Imperial), Harry Woodnorth (1955 Aston Martin DB2/4).

CONTENTS

CONTENTS

CONTENTS

1961 Oldsmobile Starfire convertible

1956 Packard Caribbean 2-door hardtop

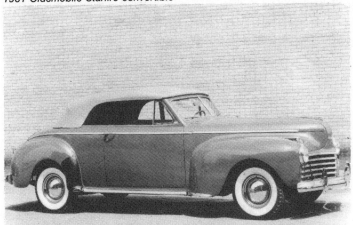

1941 Chrysler Windsor Highlander convertible

1934 Terraplane DeLuxe Six convertible coupe

Introduction

Welcome to the updated and expanded version of a first-edition sellout, now spannig the full 50-year period that accounts for the bulk of old-car enthusiasm today. That original work, *The Complete Book of Collectible Cars 1940-1980,* appeared some ten years ago as the only book of its kind on the market. This was undoubtedly as much a factor in its high success as America's continuing love affair with the automobile, which has only grown stronger in the years since. Continuing demand for that book, plus pleas for coverage of Thirties models and the inevitable need to adjust price information for inflation and changing market trends, are the main reasons behind this "revised and updated" edition. Moreover, the Auto Editors of CONSUMER GUIDE® had recently completed a similar revision of our highly acclaimed *Encyclopedia of American Cars,* so it made eminent sense to make this companion volume conform to the same chronological scope.

In the Introduction to the original book, we stated that "there are, conservatively speaking, a quarter-million people in all walks of life who like to acquire, restore, and exhibit their older cars—not to mention the thousands in the specialized industry that supports the old-car hobby." The only thing we'd change in that statement is the number, which is now probably more like a half-million. And, of course, that doesn't include the millions of non-collector enthusiasts who buy books like this one for their reference and/or nostalgia value and those who simply like to reminisce about cars that are very different from today's offerings.

Few hobbies attract a more varied group of enthusiasts than the old-car avocation. Some collectors amass old cars—and, increasingly, commercial vehicles too—the way some folks gather up antique furniture or old coins, owning five, 10, or more. Others diligently search only for particular models, often those they remember from their youth, while others specialize in rare or obscure makes and models, a particular type of car—Classics of the early Thirties or Sixties "muscle cars," for example. They look in newspaper classifieds, advertisements in a growing number of hobby periodicals, on the fringes of used-car lots, in junkyards, at auctions, and in places like the proverbial old barns where, as legend would have it, you might find anything from a Duesenberg to an Edsel just waiting to be snapped up for a song from some owner totally unaware of the treasure he has.

And that's just the beginning. Typically, collectors want to restore their prizes, perhaps even drive them regularly. A lot depends on the car in question, how old or rare it is, its condition, and the individual's personal interests. For some the object may simply be to get the thing running again. Others may settle for nothing less than a complete teardown and rebuild involving lots of money, considerable time in tracking down authentic replacement parts—whether "new-old stock" leftovers or brand-new reproductions—locating specialists to do the work where necessary and, finally, deciding where to keep the like-new machine—and how much it's worth to insure. Like enthusiasts of any kind, car collectors often belong to clubs that stage regular meetings, social gatherings, and shows. And it doesn't take much to encourage many owners to enter their cars in general

1934 Studebaker President "Year Ahead" Land Cruiser sedan

1930 Ruxton roadster

"open" shows, where they vie for trophies and plaques, public approval (in the form of "people's choice" balloting), and sometimes money.

Of course, not every older car is worth collecting or even preserving. Deciding which ones are and which aren't is often a highly subjective matter, especially since most anything can be collectible if it's rare enough, whether by dint of attrition or original scarcity. Nevertheless, there are several standards on which knowledgeable car fans agree and that can be applied with a fair degree of consistency and objectivity.

That's the purpose of this book. Like its predecessor, *The Complete Book of Collectible Cars 1930-80* has been compiled by the Auto Editors of CONSUMER GUIDE® together with two of the most widely recognized experts in the field, noted historian Richard M. Langworth (whose legion of credits includes the aforementioned *Encyclopedia*) and veteran British journalist Graham Robson. As before, entries are divided into American and Foreign Collectible Cars and follow the popular CONSUMER GUIDE® magazine new-car format. Each includes a capsule **History** of the model or models covered, a summary of characteristics **For** and **Against** collectibility, pertinent **Specifications**, and current collector market **Prices**. Also provided are two items of particular interest to collectors: original **Production**—broken down where possible by model year, body style, engine, or other factors and an indicator of current availability—and a unique **5-year Projection** of the percentage value increase (or, in a few cases, decrease) that can be expected based on previous market performance.

There's very little else you need to know as you delve into the listings. However, three areas deserve a few words of explanation: the factors that entered into our selections, the way we arrived at the prices and projections, and notes about technical data.

Selection Criteria

Entries are arranged alphabetically by make and chronologically by initial production or model year. The product of considerable culling and thought, they're based on contemporary accounts and "standard works" as modified by the seasoned judgments of the authors, contributors, and the editors. Of course, no two people will agree completely on the full roster. There will doubtless be some models you think we should have included and some you think we should have left out. As before, the book is aimed mainly at American and Canadian readers, so original availability on the North American market was a first consideration. However, you will find some rare models and foreign marques not widely known here, mainly because other factors make these cars too historically significant and/or valuable to ignore.

One factor that weighed heavily for a given model was whether or not it has been recognized as a Milestone. This designation, born in 1972 with the founding of the Milestone Car Society (MCS), has become a widely accepted indicator of a postwar car's collectibility, both historically and monetarily. By the MCS definition, a car must be judged superior relative to its contemporaries in at least two of five categories to be accorded Milestone status. These are summarized by the acronym SEPIC: Styling (both good *and* bad), Engineering (ditto), Performance ("roadability" as well as quick acceleration and/or high top speed), Innovation (in concept or some pioneering new feature), and Craftsmanship. As you might imagine, this very broad umbrella can cover a multitude of sins. Some cars, like the Mercedes-Benz 300SL or the Continental Mark II, would arguably qualify in all five. Others, the Rolls-Royce Silver Dawn or the Frazer Manhattan for example, barely make it in two, and one of those is often Craftsmanship. We also considered the similar list of Classics recognized by the Classic Car Club of America (CCCA), which was especially important in narrowing down the many possible choices from the Thirties, though eligibility for this designation runs only to 1948 models.

But the MCS and CCCA lists were only starting points, mainly because a good many newer cars have already generated high collector interest. This suggested another criterion that helped us single out desirable models not honored by either group. In some cases we've included an entire model line, noting individual versions as more or most collectible. These typically consist of, but are not limited to, those body styles traditionally favored by enthusiasts: convertible sedans and convertible coupes, structural wood-body station wagons, early hardtop coupes (1949-50), and some hardtop sedans (1955-56). It was neither possible nor reasonable to give more than a few lines such "across the board" endorsements for more than a handful of years. Where we chose to do so, it was because collector interest in the make for that period was high enough to render distinctions between models, body styles, engines, etc. more or less meaningless. This applies as much to 1930-38 Duesenberg Model Js as to 1955-57 Chevys.

Limited-production models or special packages were obvious candidates, and you'll find a great many of them here. But we also looked around them to see if there were linemates that also satisfied the MCS criteria. In some instances there were. Thus, for example, you'll find the limited-production 1956-58 Plymouth Fury and its more common convertible and hardtop coupe counterparts in the standard Belvedere series for these years, treated as separate entries.

Prices and Projection

Here you may be in for a few surprises. Unlike various "old-car price guides," we do not attempt to make hairline distinctions between individual models, body styles or equipment, except where the market makes them or the gulf is obviously wide. Nor have we set up a complicated system of grading values based on a vehicle's condition or equipment. Instead, you'll find a more common-sense approach that covers three states of condition:

Restorable: This is what buffs mean by a car that's "all there." It has a body, a chassis, an engine, even an interior (or at least part of one). However, it may not be running and always needs considerable work at the very least. This definition does *not* refer to "basket cases" or total rust-outs that are clearly unsalvageable. To be restorable, a car must have enough of its original "self" left so an owner can bring it back to life, even if it breaks a bank account.

Good: This is either a "stock" original or an older restoration that is completely driveable and serviceable in its present state but needs obvious mechanical and cosmetic work. It's not a show winner by any means. It may need paint, new chrome, interior work, and some mechanical ministerings—but not a whole *new* interior or engine. This description also applies to a combination of, say, amateur mechanical work and a professional body rebuild.

Excellent: Here we mean a car in fine original or restored condition, capable of scoring at least 85 out of 100 points in typical show judging. Everything on it works as intended and nothing major has to be done, though there may be a small thing or two that isn't completely perfect, as there always is.

The **Prices** shown for each of these conditions are ranges that are sometimes wide. There are also some gaps and/or overlaps between conditions, so that a particular specimen you might be interested in buying could fall between them. The **5-year Projection** is based solely on a model's change in value over time and does not consider outside forces, such as the onset of a deep economic recession.

The rationale for this pricing system is that it's simply impossible to peg collector cars as close to the mark as "used cars." There, values are usually quoted down to $10 and $50 increments based on whether or not a given unit has air conditioning, radio, automatic, or other equipment and how old it is or how many miles it's done. Now common sense will tell you that a 1953 Packard Patrician with factory air will be worth more than one without, because it's an early example of a factory-installed option that was uncommon at the time, even among Packards. On the other hand, A/C won't affect the value of, say, a 1967 Lincoln Continental, because it was standard.

Another element that influences collector market but not used car prices is "interest value." For example, with a few notable exceptions, cars of the Seventies just aren't collectible at present, and most may never be no matter how scarce they might become through attrition. Enthusiasts tend to regard most Detroit products in these years as more boring and thus less desirable than corresponding Sixties models, usually blaming the presence of federally mandated safety and emissions equipment for taking away much of the fun, fire, and flair they knew in earlier cars. Fortunately, the American industry is again turning out machinery that car lovers can get excited about. And though it's too early to predict just when, Eighties iron like the third-generation Chevrolet Camaro/Pontiac Firebird, the Dodge Daytona Turbo Z, and the aerodynamic 1983 Ford Thunderbird will undoubtedly be the collector cars of the 21st century. Judgments on those, however, will have to await a future edition of this book.

But the main reason we cannot draw razor-sharp price distinctions is that they just don't exist. Compared to ordinary used cars, even those that are 10 or more years old, collector cars change hands far less often. Used-car value books track hundreds of thousands of sales made in the course of a few months, and can thus average prices with a fair degree of accuracy. Collector-car guides cover far fewer transactions that may take place over a year or more, and thus can't be anywhere near as precise.

This isn't to deny the value of the various old-car guides, which serve a very useful function in recording these longer-term price fluctuations, thus indicating demand changes (or lack thereof) for specific models. For example, a Porsche fancier can gain a very

clear idea of what a 911S is worth to other Porschephiles by following it in a good price guide over a couple of years. On the other hand, that doesn't necessarily mean that you'll be able to buy one at those prices at auction or from a private seller or a used-car dealer, where almost anything can be touted as a "classic," especially if it's in good condition. Then again, you might get it for less depending on when and where you buy. As most of us know, convertibles are always worth more in the spring than in the winter.

Our purpose is more limited in a way, but it's also more realistic. The ranges shown are merely a guide. You have to take it from there, factoring in your own knowledge, local and current market conditions, and a particular car you may be considering.

Notes on Specifications

Besides the development and technical background found in the **History** section, each entry also contains major specifications of the sort most important to enthusiasts. These include overall length, wheelbase (the longitudinal distance between front and rear wheel centers), vehicle weight (manufacturer's quoted curb weight with base equipment), and original selling price in contemporary U.S. dollars. Multiple figures are provided in entries that cover more than one model year or model variation. For broader entries, like the 1939-40 Ford DeLuxe line, ranges are shown where appropriate.

Note that **Price (new)** means base price. For some foreign entries, lack of information on currency exchange rates at the time of manufacture rendered it impossible to calculate dollar values. Where known, advertised list prices for U.S. export models are shown regardless of the number of cars actually sold. Contemporary dollar equivalents, again where known, are listed for those foreign models not officially imported.

Following the dimensions and prices in each entry is a chart listing available **Engines** for the model or models covered. Each is shown with its displacement in cubic inches (cid) or cubic centimeters (cc), type of valvetrain and/or head arrangement (L-head, F-head, overhead valve, overhead camshaft, etc.), block configuration (inline, vee, etc.), bore and stroke dimensions (in English or metric units as appropriate), rated horsepower, and the years available.

As an aid for "unmetricated" Americans, the cid equivalent for a cc displacement is shown directly below it (this applies mostly to the foreign entries). Unless otherwise noted, horsepower figures are always expressed by the customary American rating method in force through the early Seventies, the SAE (Society of Automotive Engineers) gross measurement. DIN stands for *Deutsche Industrie Normen*, and virtually all German engines are rated by this standard, which is also used by some manufacturers in other European countries. It is closer to the "truth" than SAE gross, though a shade more flattering than the current SAE net rating. A simple "net" bhp refers to a European measurement of horsepower developed at the flywheel with most engine accessories installed. However, this is *not* the same as the SAE net rating. Similarly, European gross horsepower is a bit more realistic than SAE gross figures.

Foreign automakers traditionally have not—and a few still don't—observe formal model years like American manufacturers. Engine substitutions and mechanical and styling modifications were frequently made as running changes within a model's life without regard to the calendar or a selling period, whereas most Detroit producers saved such alterations for the coming year's models, which usually go on sale a few months before a new calendar year begins, a practice that gained acceptance in the Thirties. Therefore, headings and engine availability for American entries almost always reflect *model year* production. Assume *calendar year* production for foreign entries unless otherwise noted. This will be evident from both the engine chart and the comments in the **History**.

A Final Word

The editors warmly welcome your comments, corrections, and additions (some of those received from the first edition are reflected in this second one). Nothing is forever "cast in concrete," and there will undoubtedly be yet another version of this book in the future. Address: Automotive Editor, CONSUMER GUIDE® Publications, 3841 W. Oakton St., Skokie, IL 60076.

The Auto Editors of CONSUMER GUIDE®

1970 Chevrolet Camaro Rally Sport coupe

American Collectible Cars

Allstate Four
1952-53

1952 DeLuxe Four 2-door sedan

PRODUCTION

1952 900 (est.) **1953** 425 (est.)

HISTORY

Four-cylinder version of the Allstate Six. Offered in basic, standard, and Deluxe trim for 1952, standard and Deluxe for 1953. Like the Six, the Four used a Kaiser-Frazer L-head engine, obtained from Willys-Overland in this case.

FOR

As for Allstate Six, with the addition of outstanding gas mileage, up to 35 mpg

AGAINST

As for Allstate Six, plus lackluster performance

SPECIFICATIONS

Length (in.) 176.6 **Wheelbase (in.)** 100.0
Weight (lbs.) 2300-2405 **Price (new)** $1395-1589

ENGINES

cid/type	bore x stroke	bhp	years
134.2/L4	3.11×4.38	68	1952-53

PRICES/PROJECTION

Restorable $1000-2500 **Good** $2000-4000 **Excellent** $3500-5000
5-year projection 10% lower than for Allstate Six

Allstate Six
1952-53

PRODUCTION

1952 666 **1953** 372 (est.)

HISTORY

Sears, Roebuck's version of the Henry J, built by Kaiser-Frazer. Sold nationwide through the Sears catalog, but confined to the Southeast in actual promotion. Styled by Alex Tremulis, with a more distinctive front end than the Henry J's, special Allstate badges, and many Sears-produced components such as tires, battery, spark plugs. A "basic" and Deluxe 2-door sedan were offered for 1952, but only the Deluxe was listed for '53. Lack of public response caused Sears to drop the car in early 1953, thus ending the first and last Sears automobile experiment since 1912. (See also Henry J.)

FOR

More unique and desirable than Henry J •Definite rarity •Quality interior •Good performance

AGAINST

Indifferent styling •Distinctively Allstate body parts (grilles, hood ornaments, badges, etc.) now in very short supply

SPECIFICATIONS

Length (in.) 176.6 **Wheelbase (in.)** 100.0
Weight (lbs.) 2325-2455 **Price (new)** $1594-1785

ENGINES

cid/type	bore x stroke	bhp	years
161/L6	3.13×3.50	80	1952-53

PRICES/PROJECTION

Restorable $1250-2750 **Good** $3000-4500
Excellent $4000-6500 **5-year projection** +25%

American Austin
1930-34

PRODUCTION

1930 8558 **1931** 1279 **1932** 3846 **1933** 4725 **1934** 1300 (est.)
(calendar year figures)

HISTORY

Produced in Butler, Pennsylvania by Sir Herbert Austin. An early attempt at tariff-busting via local assembly, prefiguring today's U.S. VW and Honda operations. Based on the British Austin Seven design and powered by a two-main-bearing L-head four. Offered in roadster, runabout, cabriolet and coupe models, of which the first three are far more desirable. The American Austin failed because the economy began picking up soon after it was introduced, and because Americans didn't really take to cars this small. Though few survive today, those that do are increasingly admired. Continued as the American Bantam (see entry).

FOR

As whimsical and cute as a 1930s car ever got • Low purchase and operating costs • Parts usually inexpensive

1930 2-door sedan

AGAINST

Underpowered and underbraked • Parts increasingly scarce, particularly sheetmetal

SPECIFICATIONS

Length (in.) 105.0 **Wheelbase (in.)** 75.0
Weight (lbs.) 1020-1175 **Price (new)** $275-550

ENGINES

cid/type	bore x stroke	bhp	years
46/L4	2.20×3.00	13/14	1930-34

PRICES/PROJECTION

Restorable $2500-4000 **Good** $4500-8500
Excellent $9000-12,000 **5-year projection** +25%

American Bantam
1938-41

1938 four-passenger Speedster

PRODUCTION

1936 under 500* **1937** 3500 (est)* **1938** 2000 (est) **1939** 1229
1940 800 **1941** 138 *Recorded from industry sources. Factory produced no cars in 1935-36; these may have been leftovers or assembled from parts. 1939-41 figures are calendar year.

HISTORY

American Austin built in Butler, Pennsylvania under Roy S. Evans. Abandoned for Jeep production during World War II and never revived afterward. Evans hired racing engineer Harry Miller to consult with his own engineers, and Alexis de Sakhoffsky, who

designed a new body with smooth hood, rounded grille, and curvy fenders. (He charged Evans a mere $300 and the line was retooled for only $7000!) Bantam engine had full pressure lubrication, cars had new three-speed transmission and cam-and-lever steering. Engines had three main bearings after 1939, making the 1940-41 models the best of Butler mechanically. These last cars also had improved brakes, Monroe shocks, Goodyear "air-form" seat cushions (deluxe models) and headlamps mounted in fenders.

FOR

Cute and attractive • Outstanding operating economy

AGAINST

Still underpowered • Parts problems • Engine durability questionable through 1939

SPECIFICATIONS

Length (in.) 105.0 **Wheelbase (in.)** 75.0
Weight (lbs.) 1130-1434 **Price (new)** $399-565

ENGINES

cid/type	bore x stroke	bhp	years
46/L4	2.20×3.00	20	1938-39
50.1/L4	2.26×3.13	22	1940-41

PRICES/PROJECTION

OPEN MODELS **Restorable** $2500-4000 **Good** $4500-8500
Excellent $9000-12,000 CLOSED MODELS
Restorable $1500-3000 **Good** $3500-6000
Excellent $6500-9000. Add 15% for wagons.
5-year projection +25%

AMC Metropolitan
1958-62

1959 Metropolitan 1500 2-door coupe

PRODUCTION

1958 13,128 **1959** 22,309 **1960** 13,103 **1961** 853
1962 412 (based on shipments from England)

HISTORY

Continuation of the 1954-57 Nash/Hudson Metropolitan (see entries) under the AMC badge. Still powered by Series 56 1500cc Austin four. The tiny "Met" hit its all time peak of 22,309 importation in 1959, after which Detroit's compacts overwhelmed it in the economy-car market and sales plummeted drastically. In mid-1959, AMC added an opening trunklid for the first time, along with more comfortable seats, vent wings, and tubeless tires.

FOR

The most refined Met • Very economical

AGAINST

Dumpy styling • Serious ruster

SPECIFICATIONS

Length (in.) 149.5   **Wheelbase (in.)** 85.0
Weight (lbs.) 1850-1890   **Price (new)** $1626-1697

ENGINES

cid/type	bore x stroke	bhp	years
90.9/L4	2.88×3.50	52	1958-62

PRICES/PROJECTION

COUPES Restorable $800-2000 **Good** $2000-3000
Excellent $3000-4000 **CONVERTIBLES Restorable** $1000-2250
Good $2500-4000 **Excellent** $3000-5000
5-year projection +10%

AMC Marlin 1966-67

1967 Marlin 2-door fastback hardtop

PRODUCTION

1966 4547   **1967** 2545

HISTORY

Continuation of the 1965 Rambler Marlin. Marketed under the AMC badge for these two years. An attempt to cash in on the temporary boom in fastbacks, the Marlin was based on the intermediate Rambler Classic chassis. Its swooping roofline was styled by AMC design chief Richard A. Teague. Luxuriously furnished with vinyl bucket seats and deep carpeting, it was billed as a sports car, which it definitely wasn't. For 1967 the car was switched to the longer Ambassador platform, which better suited the long roof. Though it offered some sporty options (4-speed shift, tachometer and up to 280 bhp), the Marlin never enjoyed the success of the Big Three ponycars, and was accordingly dropped to make way for AMC's entry in that field, the Javelin. (See also 1965 Rambler Marlin.)

FOR

Has status as a lost cause • Unique looks • Smooth V8 power • Rarity

AGAINST

Unique looks • Limited appreciation potential • Visible, but not distinctive

SPECIFICATIONS

Length (in.) 195 (1966), 201.5 (1967)
Wheelbase (in.) 112 (1966), 118 (1967)
Weight (lbs.) 3050 (1966), 3342 (1967)
Price (new) $2601 (1966), $2963 (1967)

ENGINES

cid/type	bore x stroke	bhp	years
232/ohv I6	3.75×3.50	145/155	1966-67
287/ohv V8	3.75×3.25	198	1966
327/ohv V8	4.00×3.25	250/270	1966
290/ohv V8	3.75×3.28	200	1967
343/ohv V8	4.08×3.28	235/280	1967

PRICES/PROJECTION

Restorable $1000-1500 **Good** $2000-3500
Excellent $3000-4500 **5-year projection** +10%

AMC AMX 1968-70

1968 AMX 2-seat fastback coupe

PRODUCTION

1968 6725   **1968** 8293   **1970** 4116

HISTORY

Short-wheelbase two-seater cleverly produced by carving a foot out of the Javelin body. Introduced mid-1968 model year, and brought AMC's new 390 V8 (boasting forged steel crankshaft and connecting rods) as an option. Crisp, if chunky, styling coupled with taut suspension, comprehensive instruments, bucket seats, and optional four-speed gearbox made it a genuine sports car. Saw some success in competition. The AMX name was applied to all manner of post-1970 AMC sporty models from Javelins to Concords to

Spirits, and was thereby diluted. The 1968-70 models are the "true" AMXs, and thus have greatest collector appeal.

FOR

Exciting performance • No-nonsense, two-seats-only layout • Still relatively inexpensive • Good parts sources • Active club

AGAINST

390 version has more engine than the chassis can handle • Tends to rust unless given care • Spotty construction quality

SPECIFICATIONS

Length (in.) 177.2 (1968-69), 179.0 (1970)
Wheelbase (in.) 97.0 **Weight (lbs.)** 3097-3126
Price (new) $3245-3395

ENGINES

cid/type	bore x stroke	bhp	years
290/ohv V8	2.75×3.28	225	1968-69
343/ohv V8	4.08×3.28	280	1968-69
360/ohv V8	4.08×3.44	290	1970
390/ohv V8	4.17×3.57	315-340	1968-70

PRICES/PROJECTION

Restorable $1500-2000 **Good** $3500-5000
Excellent $5000-8000 **5-year projection** +10%

AMC Javelin 1968-70

1968 Javelin 2-door fastback hardtop

PRODUCTION

1968 56,462   **1969** 40,675   **1970** 28,210

HISTORY

Dick Teague's finely styled and still underrated answer to the Mustang and Camaro, beautifully sculpted and clean lined. With the standard six could cruise effortlessly at 70 mph; with one of the optional V8s was capable of much higher cruising speeds and a top end of around 110. Optional "Go Package" with four-barrel 343 V8, dual exhausts, power front disc brakes, heavy-duty suspension, and wide tires quite desirable. A minor facelift for '69 was followed by more radical sheetmetal surgery for 1970, but the original 1968 edition strikes us as the cleanest Javelin. The same bodyshell was continued through 1974, but clothed in more bulbous, less attractive sheetmetal. Despite the aura of competition success (the Penske/Donohue Trans-Am effort) and big-inch engines, the later Javelins are less desirable.

FOR

A bargain compared to contemporary Mustangs and Camaros, offering much the same kind of style and spirit • Good mileage with the six • Reasonable blend of performance and economy from V8s

AGAINST

Tends to rust • Limited appreciation potential • Not much of a following at present among collectors

SPECIFICATIONS

Length (in.) 182.2 (1968-69), 191.0 (1970)
Wheelbase (in.) 109.0 **Weight (lbs.)** 2826-3340
Price (new) $2482-3995

ENGINES

cid/type	bore x stroke	bhp	years
232/ohv I6	3.75×3.50	145/155	1968-70
290/ohv V8	3.75×3.28	225	1968-69
343/ohv V8	4.08×3.28	280	1968-69
390/ohv V8	4.17×3.15	315/325/340	1968-70
304/ohv V8	3.75×3.44	210	1970
360/ohv V8	4.08×3.44	245/290	1970

PRICES/PROJECTION

Restorable $1000-2000 **Good** $1500-2500
Excellent $2500-4000 (Deduct 15% for sixes)
5-year projection +10%

AMC Rebel SST 1968-70

1968 Rebel SST convertible

PRODUCTION

Specific breakdown not available from factory; 1968 SST convertibles: 823

HISTORY

Launched as the Rambler Rebel in 1967 to replace the staid Classic as AMC's mid-size line. Shared some styling points with the larger Ambassador. AMC badge substituted for '68, when Rebel was only AMC series to offer a convertible. The SST was the sportiest Rebel, with standard bucket seats and a 290 V8. Many handling and performance options along Javelin lines were also available. Though it has yet to achieve significant "collectibility," the '68 convertible should gain in importance as the last of AMC's ragtops. Wagons and sedans joined the SST hardtop for 1968-70, but the two-doors are the only models with any collector appeal.

1969 Rebel SST 2-door hardtop

FOR

Very low prices •Reasonable availability •Excellent performance and good economy with small-block V8

AGAINST

Little collector recognition •Dwindling parts supplies •Rust tendencies •Clean but mundane styling

SPECIFICATIONS

Length (in.) 197 (1968-69), 199 (1970) **Wheelbase (in.)** 114.0 **Weight (lbs.)** 3140-3375 **Price (new)** $2598-2999

ENGINES

cid/type	bore x stroke	bhp	years
290/ohv V8	3.75×3.28	200	1968
343/ohv V8	4.08×3.28	235/280	1968-69
390/ohv V8	4.17×3.57	315/325/340	1968-69
232/ohv I6	3.75×3.50	145/155	1969-70
304/ohv V8	3.75×3.44	210	1970
360/ohv V8	4.08×3.44	245/290	1970

PRICES/PROJECTION

Restorable $1000-2000 **Good** $2000-3000 **Excellent** $3000-4000 Convertibles add 25% **5-year projection** +10%

AMC Rebel Machine 1970

1970 Rebel Machine 2-door hardtop

PRODUCTION

2326

HISTORY

Successor to the '69 SC/Rambler as AMC's factory hot rod. Based on the intermediate Rebel, and offered only for 1970. Standard hardware included AMC's 390 V8 with 340 bhp, a 4-speed manual transmission with Hurst shifter, and 3.54:1 rear axle ratio. Body decor comprised a Ram-Air hood scoop, special red white and blue paint, and 15-inch magnesium alloy wheels with raised white letter tires. An 8000 rpm tach, dual exhausts, low back pressure mufflers, and a definite front end rake completed the package. First shown at the NHRA World Championship Drag Finals, but too heavy to be competitive in that kind of racing, or any other.

FOR

Increasing interest and price as early ponycars become more expensive •Blistering straightline performance •Distinctive appearance •Rarity

AGAINST

"Greasy kid car" styling •Shocking fuel consumption •Indifferent fit and finish •Rust potential •Limited parts supply

SPECIFICATIONS

Length (in.) 199.0 **Wheelbase (in.)** 114.0 **Weight (lbs.)** 3650 **Price (new)** $3475

ENGINES

cid/type	bore x stroke	bhp	years
390/ohv V8	4.17×3.57	340	1970

PRICES/PROJECTION

Restorable $1000-1500 **Good** $2000-3000 **Excellent** $3000-4500 **5-year projection** +10%

AMC Hornet SC/360 1971

1971 Hornet SC/360 2-door sedan

PRODUCTION

784

HISTORY

Short-lived performance version of American Motors' new compact Hornet introduced for 1970. Offered only as a two-door sedan, the SC/360 was named for its 360-cid derivative of AMC's big-block 343 V8. With standard two-barrel carb it pumped out 245 horses while a four-barrel option yielded 285. Both versions ran on regular gas. A large hood scoop was provided to assist the hotter engine's breathing, and both models were decked out with tape striping, heavy-duty handling package, styled steel wheels, and fat tires. An optional four-speed gearbox with Hurst linkage was offered. Not very well accepted by AMC's traditional economy-oriented clientele, and went against the "economy experts" image the company was trying to re-establish as the performance market waned in the early '70s. Far from a bona fide collectible right now, but a spirited little car that makes a good daily-driver for enthusiasts looking for something different.

FOR

Neat if innocuous styling •Good performance and handling balance •Low-production appeal •Cheap to buy

AGAINST

Difficult to find •Thirsty •Unit-construction rust propensity

SPECIFICATIONS

Length (in.) 184.9   **Wheelbase (in.)** 108.0   **Weight (lbs.)** 3105
Price (new) $2663

ENGINES

cid/type	bore x stroke	bhp	years
360/ohv V8	4.08×3.44	245/285	1971

PRICES/PROJECTION

Restorable $750-1800 **Good** $2200-2800
Excellent $3000-4000 **5-year projection** +10%

AMC Javelin 1971-74

1971 Javelin AMX 2-door fastback hardtop

PRODUCTION

1971 26,866 (inc. 2054 AMX)   **1972** 32,850 (inc. 5000 AMX) (est.)
1973 26,782 (inc. 4635 AMX)   **1974** 27,536 (inc. 4980 AMX)

HISTORY

The restyled second-generation AMC ponycar. Longer, lower, wider, and slightly more aerodynamic than its 1968-70 predecessor. Rode a 1-inch longer wheelbase, though basic inner body structure was unchanged. The more curvaceous styling featured marked bulges over the front wheel arches, something like the then-current Corvette's. The AMX badge was transferred to the Javelin line as the new top model, with base and SST versions continuing as before. Inside was a new dash that curved inward in the middle to give a "cockpit" feel for the driver. Engine choices ran from mild-mannered sixes to AMC's largest-ever V8, a new 401-cid

enlargement of the 343/390 block, rated at 330 horses. It would be the last AMC mill to require premium gas. By now, the performance and ponycar markets were on the downturn, so the Javelin's days were numbered. The base model was deleted for 1972, and the big-block V8 detuned to run on regular. Still, the 401 was available right on through the last of the line, the '74s, unlike some other ponycars that lost their big-inch options. Limited production makes the AMX versions the most desirable models in this bunch, though none of these Javelins has yet to achieve a significant collector following.

FOR

Penske/Donohue race-image ruboff •Last of the line •High performance •Unique styling •Relatively cheap •Nice interior

AGAINST

Less graceful than earlier Javs •Hard to find in pristine condition •Thirsty with big-inch engines •Rust-prone

SPECIFICATIONS

Length (in.) 192.3   **Wheelbase (in.)** 110.0
Weight (lbs.) 2900-3350   **Price (new)** $2890-3400 (approx.)

ENGINES

cid/type	bore x stroke	bhp	years
232/ohv I6	3.75×3.50	145	1971-74
304/ohv V8	3.75×3.44	210	1971-74
360/ohv V8	4.08×3.44	245/290	1971-74
401/ohv V8	4.17×3.68	330*	1971-74

*rated 255 bhp SAE net from 1972 on; approx. 270-280 bhp gross

PRICES/PROJECTION

Restorable $500-1000 **Good** $1000-2000
Excellent $2000-3000 Add 20% for AMX model
5-year projection +10%

Apollo 3500GT 1963-65

1964 3500GT 2-door coupe

PRODUCTION

Coupes (incl. 5000 GT) 39 (1963-65)   **Convertibles** 1 (1964)
An additional 5 cars were built later with leftover bodies. An additional 17 coupes and 7 convertibles constructed as Vetta Venturas, of which 14 were completed; 10 bodies were left over.

HISTORY

Sleek, beautiful American *gran turismo*. Powered by light, efficient Buick engines, the vast majority the aluminum block 3.5-liter V8 from the early-'60s Special. The body, styled by Ron Plescia, was bolted to a simple, ladder-type frame with modified Buick suspension and a Borg-Warner T-10 four-speed gearbox (also used on Corvette). Apollo founder Milt Brown set up assembly facilities at Pasadena, California. Bodies were supplied by Frank Reisner's Intermeccanica firm in Turin, Italy. A convertible version, styled by Scaglione, numbered 11 in all, of which 10 were called Vetta Ventura.

FOR

Smoother, more nimble than Corvette • Real exclusivity • Familiar mechanical components • Strong appreciation potential

AGAINST

Variable assembly quality, though it improved as production progressed • Not quite as quick as a Corvette off the line

SPECIFICATIONS

Length (in.) 177.0 **Wheelbase (in.)** 97.0 **Weight (lbs.)** NA
Price (new) $6797 (coupe), $7347 (convertible)

ENGINES

cid/type	bore x stroke	bhp	years
215/ohv V8	3.50×2.80	200	1963-65

PRICES/PROJECTION

Restorable $2500-5000 **Good** $4500-7000
Excellent $7500-10,000 Add 20% for roadster.
5-year projection +10%

Apollo 5000GT
1964-65

PRODUCTION

See 1963-65 Apollo 3500 GT

HISTORY

A big-engine version of the 3500GT, featuring Bendix power front disc brakes. While the 3500 would do 0-60 mph in 8-9 seconds and had 130 mph on tap, the 5000GT cut the 0-60 sprint time by 1.5 to 2 seconds, and offered another 15-20 mph.

FOR

More potent and desirable variant of widely sought after grand touring car • Reasonably easy servicing due to mass production components • Very high performance

AGAINST

As for 3500GT

SPECIFICATIONS

Length (in.) 177.0 **Wheelbase (in.)** 97.0 **Weight (lbs.)** NA
Price (new) $7965 (coupe), $8950 (convertible)

ENGINES

cid/type	bore x stroke	bhp	years
300/ohv V8	3.75×3.40	250	1964-65

PRICES/PROJECTION

Restorable $3000-5000 **Good** $5000-8000
Excellent $8000-12,000 **5-year projection** +10%

Auburn Eight
1931-36

1932 Custom Eight 2/4-passenger cabriolet

PRODUCTION

1931 36,148 **1932** 6000* **1933** 4000* **1934** 3500*
1935-36 3000* *Estimated from reported factory production by calendar year

HISTORY

A glamorous era was ushered in by the sleek, long Auburn Eights of 1931 with their big 268.6-cid Lycoming engines, bored to 280 cid for 1934. Two series, Standard and Custom. Capable of nearly 90 mph with the lighter open bodies, terrific for the time. A truncated speedster (not the later supercharged model) was available in 1932-33. The most expensive range was the 1933 Salon (Series 8-105), which reappeared as the unblown 851/852 Salon line for 1935-36. Auburn Eights had a reputation for size, luxury and performance far beyond their price: the most expensive Custom Eight Dual Ratio in 1932 cost only $1005. Auburn finally collapsed in 1936, one of the saddest deaths in auto history.

FOR

Like the Twelve, a CCCA Classic • Superb roadability and performance • Still a good buy among certified Classics

AGAINST

Traditionally a wallflower compared to the 1935-36 Speedsters and Twelves • Closed models slow to appreciate • High operating costs

SPECIFICATIONS

Length (in.) NA **Wheelbase (in.)** 127.0, 136.0
Weight (lbs.) 3320-4125 **Price (new)** $945-1448

ENGINES

cid/type	bore x stroke	bhp	years
268.6/L8	3.00×4.75	98/100	1931-33
280.0/L8	3.06×4.75	100/115	1934-36

PRICES/PROJECTION

SPEEDSTER (1932-33) **Restorable** $20,000-40,000
Good $40,000-60,000 **Excellent** $75,000-100,000 OTHER OPEN
MODELS 75% of above. CLOSED MODELS
Restorable $7500-10,000 **Good** $10,000-18,000
Excellent $15,000-25,000 **5-year projection** OPEN MODELS
+25% CLOSED MODELS +10%

Auburn Twelve
1932-34

1933 Custom Twelve 4-door sedan

PRODUCTION

Under 2000 for the three years; 305 Salon Twelves for 1933

HISTORY

The least expensive V12 ever at $975 for the Standard coupe and
$1275 for the top-of-the-line Custom Speedster. Power by Lycoming
in a huge double-braced frame. Custom Twelves had a Columbia
dual-ratio rear axle with 3.04 and 4.55 gearing, interchangeable
under 40 mph. The magnificent V12 boattail Speedsters, so rare
today, were the finest expressions of Classic-era styling. Unfortunately for Auburn, its unprecedented value didn't impress a
public adamant for economy cars, and the firm scrubbed all its
Twelves after 1934.

FOR

One of the most balanced and best engineered 1930s Classics
• Stunning design, especially open models • Values still
appreciating

AGAINST

Prices already formidable • Operating costs and parts commensurately expensive • Lacks "blue chip" aura of Cord and
Duesenberg stablemates

SPECIFICATIONS

Length (in.) NA **Wheelbase (in.)** 133.0
Weight (lbs.) 4135-4870 **Price (new)** $945-1745

ENGINES

cid/type	bore x stroke	bhp	years
391.6/V12	3.13 × 4.25	160	1932-34

PRICES/PROJECTION

SPEEDSTERS **Restorable** $25,000-45,000
Good $45,000-65,000 **Excellent** $80,000-120,000. OTHER
OPEN MODELS **Restorable** 75% of above.
Add 5% for Dual Ratio Custom/Salon models.
CLOSED MODELS **Restorable** $10,000-12,500
Good $12,000-20,000 **Excellent** $20,000-35,000
5-year projection +10%

Auburn Supercharged
851/852
1935-36

1936 Supercharged Eight Dual Ratio 4-door sedan

PRODUCTION

Approx. 500

HISTORY

One of the quintessential recognized Classis, with prices and demand to suit. Styling by Gordon Buehrig, engineering by August
Duesenberg, both directed by Auburn-Cord-Duesenberg president
Harold T. Ames. Buehrig's absolutely splendid design was a budget
package based on leftover Twelves, but all new and glamorous from
the cowl forward, with beautiful pontoon fenders and outside exhausts. Duesenberg's engine was an extension of the 1934 six, but
with 150 bhp courtesy its Schwitzer-Cummins blower. Speedsters
claimed an honest 100 mph off the showroom floor and were among
the most breathtakingly beautiful automobiles of all time, yet in 1935
they sold for just $2245. Most Classic enthusiasts wish they had a
time machine for cars like these.

FOR

Speedster among the top blue chip Classics • Stunning looks and
great vintage performance • A legend among motorcars

AGAINST

Price, price and price • High operating costs • Rarity

SPECIFICATIONS

Length (in.) NA **Wheelbase (in.)** 127.0
Weight (lbs.) 3565-3729 **Price (new)** $1445-2245

ENGINES

cid/type	bore x stroke	bhp	years
280.0/L8	3.06×4.75	150	1935-36

PRICES/PROJECTION

SPEEDSTER **Restorable** $25,000-40,000
Good $45,000-80,000 **Excellent** $80,000-120,000 CABRIOLET/
PHAETON deduct 25% from above. CLOSED MODELS
Restorable $5000-8000 **Good** $9000-12,000
Excellent $12,000-18,000 **5-year projection** OPEN MODELS
+15% CLOSED MODELS +10%

Avanti II
1966-80

1979 Avanti II sport coupe

PRODUCTION

1966 98 **1967** 60 **1968** 89 **1969** 103 **1970** 111
1971 on approx. 200 per year

HISTORY

Handbuilt continuation of Studebaker's 1963-64 Avanti. Retained
Studebaker convertible frame initially, but updated to Corvette
power. Offered with a limitless choice of paint colors and interior
trim materials — anything the customer wanted. Differences from
the original include reduced-radius wheel openings, less forward
rake, a slightly higher hoodline to accommodate the Corvette engine, and "Avanti II" script. A great buy for the money in its early
years ($6550 in late 1965), but price has gone up steadily since
(though at about $25,000 the new ones aren't overpriced by con-
temporary standards). Low production guarantees every Avanti II is
collectible. Spotty quality control has been a problem throughout
the car's history.

FOR

Smooth performance •Drivetrains familiar to any Chevy dealer
•Sensational styling •Individuality •Factory can still refurbish
every one made

AGAINST

Poor finish, especially paint and chrome •Gas mileage falls off on
1970s models •Lower appreciation potential than original Avanti

SPECIFICATIONS

Length (in.) 192.5 **Wheelbase (in.)** 109.0 **Weight (lbs.)** 3217
Price (new) $6550 (1966), $7500 by 1970

ENGINES

cid/type	bore x stroke	bhp	years
327/ohv V8	4.00×3.25	300	1966-69
350/ohv V8	4.00×3.48	300	1969 on

PRICES/PROJECTION

Restorable $3000-6000 **Good** $6000-12,000
Excellent $10,000-18,000 **5-year projection** +10%

Blackhawk
1930

PRODUCTION

1930 280 (calendar year)

HISTORY

One of the several junior makes launched in the heady late Twenties
and quietly dropped shortly after the Wall Street crash. Introduced in
1929 as a companion to Stutz and based on the 1928 Model BB.
Offered with an advanced 85-bhp overhead-cam six or a more
conventional L-head eight by Continental. First-year production was
a disappointing 1310 units. Although sixes were listed for 1930, it is
believed that only eights were built. Priced in the $2000-2800 range
and thus an upper-medium car, though one wonders how it came to
be rated a Classic. No relation to the famous Stutz Black Hawk (two
words) speedster.

FOR

Solid, four-square Classic styling, recognizably Stutz up front
• Wide range of body types including three Weymann styles each
model • CCCA Classic • Rare

AGAINST

Leisurely performance from the fairly modest powerplants • Parts
dicey • High operating costs

SPECIFICATIONS

Length (in.) NA **Wheelbase (in.)** 127.5 **Weight (lbs.)** NA
Price (new) $2000-2800

ENGINES

cid/type	bore x stroke	bhp	years
NA/L6	NA	85	1930
NA/L8	NA	90	1930

PRICES/PROJECTION

SPEEDSTERS **Restorable** $10,000-20,000 **Good** $20,000-30,000
Excellent $30,000-50,000 CABRIOLET/WEYMANNS
Restorable $7500-10,000 **Good** $12,000-18,000
Excellent $20,000-30,000. OTHERS **Restorable** $5000-7500
Good $7500-12,500 **Excellent** $15,000-25,000
5-year projection +15%

Buick Series 60 Century 1936-42

1941 Series 60 Century business coupe

PRODUCTION

1936 sedan 4d 18,203 **conv cpe** 766 **spt cpe** 1078 **spt cpe R/S** 1018 **victoria cpe** 3799 **chassis** 1115 **1937 sedan 4d** 25,911 **conv cpe** 843 **spt cpe** 2873 **chassis** 1026 **sedan 2d** 4015 **phaeton** 425 **1938 sedan 4d** 14,189 **conv cpe** 694 **spt cpe** 2030 **chassis** 762 **sedan 2d** 1393 **phaeton** 219 **1939 sedan 4d** 18,783 **conv cpe** 850 **spt cpe** 3470 **chassis** 518 **phaeton** 269 **1940 sedan 4d** 8708 **bus cpe** 44 **conv cpe** 550 **spt cpe** 96 **phaeton** 203 **1941 sedan 4d** 15,136 **bus cpe** 222 **sedanet** 5547 **1942 sedan 4d** 3319 **sedanet** 1232

HISTORY

With remarkably low production aside from the conventional four-door and coupes, the Century appeared in 1936 as part of a whole new line with all-steel "Turret-Top" construction. Always powered by the 320-cid ohv straight-eight, which gained 45 horsepower in seven years. The Century's traditional combination of light body and big-Buick power was established during this period. Among the more desirable body styles are the 1937-38 two-door sedans and the sleek fastback sedanet of 1941-42, which vie in popularity with the rare open phaetons and convertibles. Many bare chassis (1936-39) were fitted with custom coachwork and can thereby qualify as CCCA Classics. One of the best all-around Buicks of the period.

FOR

Good styling • Reasonable parts supplies • Fine straightline performance • Higher appreciation potential than comparable lower-line Buicks

AGAINST

Undistinguished handling • Fairly thirsty • Not a certified Classic

SPECIFICATIONS

Length (in.) NA **Wheelbase (in.)** 122.0(1936); 126.0(1937-42) **Weight (lbs.)** 3195-4065 **Price (new)** $1035-1620

ENGINES

cid/type	bore x stroke	bhp	years
320.2/L8	3.44×4.31	120-165	1936-42

PRICES/PROJECTION

OPEN CARS **Restorable** $5000-10,000 **Good** $10,000-20,000 **Excellent** $18,000-30,000. CLOSED CARS Deduct 50%. **5-year projection** +10%

Buick Series 70/80 Roadmaster 1936-41

1936 Series 80 Roadmaster 4-door trunkback sedan

PRODUCTION

1936 conv phaeton 1230 **sedan 4d** 15,328 **chassis** 534 **1937 conv phaeton** 1155 **sedan 4d** 14,981 **chassis** 606 **formal sedan** 489 **1938 conv phaeton** 411 **sedan 4d** 4704 **chassis** 223 **formal sedan** 296 **spt sedan** 466 **1939 conv phaeton** 367 **sedan 4d** 5619 **chassis** 143 **formal sedan** 340 **spt sedan** 20 **1940 conv phaeton** 238 **sedan 4d** 13,733 **conv cpe** 612 **1941 conv phaeton** 326 **sedan 4d** 10,553 **conv cpe** 1869 **spt cpe** 2834

HISTORY

Born with the redesign of 1936, the Roadmaster went on to become the most prestigious Buick after the Limited was dropped following World War II. Big and luxurious, the ultimate owner-driver Buick of the period. Also well styled and solidly engineered. Still a smooth highway-driver. Aside from the four-door sedan, the production figures speak for themselves: all the other body styles are highly collectible. Not a Classic, except for the odd custom body from 1936-39 production.

FOR

Luxury and grace • Strong club and parts support • Smooth if not vivid performance

AGAINST

Thirsty on gas, of course • Lacks Classic status

SPECIFICATIONS

Length (in.) NA **Wheelbase (in.)** 131.0(1936-37); 133.0(1938-39); 126.0(1940); 128.0(1941) **Weight (lbs.)** 3990-4469 **Price (new)** $1255-1983

ENGINES

cid/type	bore x stroke	bhp	years
320.2/L8	3.44×4.31	120-165	1936-41

PRICES/PROJECTION

As for comparable 1936-41 Century

Buick Series 80/90 Limited 1936-42

1938 Series 90 Limited 8-passenger touring sedan

PRODUCTION

All body styles under 1000 per year except 1936-37 sedans and 1941 sedan; 1942 production extremely low: 365 sedans, 250 limousines, 85 formals. Series 80 Limited (1940 only): 3898 sedans, 270 formals, 250 phaetons, 28 "Streamlined" models (of which 7 were open).

HISTORY

Cadillac didn't like the idea of Buick's 1930s prestige models with Brunn custom bodies, so Flint dropped them and put all its luxury emphasis on the long-wheelbase Limited from 1936 on. A smaller Series 80 Limited appeared on a shorter 130-inch wheelbase for 1940 only. Production was low, the cars were huge, and quality and workmanship were exceptional. All Series 90s are recognized Classics. Fully restyled with pontoon fenders for 1942, but only a handful were built. Not revived until 1958 but was merely a glorified Roadmaster.

FOR

Luxurious interiors • Outstanding craftsmanship, quality

AGAINST

Ponderous road manners (the six-passenger sedan is an exception) • High operating costs.

SPECIFICATIONS

Length (in.) NA **Wheelbase (in.)** 138.0 (1936-37); 140.0 (1938-40); 139.0 (1941-42); 133.0 (1940 Series 80) **Weight (lbs.)** 4400-4765 **Price (new)** $1695-2545

ENGINES

cid/type	bore x stroke	bhp	years
320.2/L8	3.44 × 4.31	120-165	1936-42

PRICES/PROJECTION

Restorable $2500-5000 **Good** $5000-7500
Excellent $8000-13,000. Add 10% for limousines. 1940 SERIES 80 LIMITED As above except for Phaeton:
Restorable $5000-12,000 **Good** $15,000-22,000
Excellent $20,000-30,000 **5-year projection** +15%

Buick Eight 1931-35

1933 Series 60 Century Victoria coupe

PRODUCTION

1931 138,695 **1932** 56,790 **1933** 46,924 **1934** 71,009 **1935** 53,249

HISTORY

Increasing scarcity and high fluctuation in values among a wide variety of models make it difficult to supply hard and fast guidelines for pre-1936 Buicks. All Series 90s from 1931 on are recognized Classics; no other models are, although individual custom bodies may be certified. Open styles in all series are worth up to $40,000 in perfect show condition. Restorable examples will rarely be priced below $4000 if they can be found at all. Closed models run about half that much. The usual rule that open cars far surpass closed models in value applies; likewise, coupes are more sought-after than sedans. Prices remain more moderate among 1934-35 Buicks. The most desirable models are undoubtedly the Series 90 convertible coupe and phaeton ($35,000 maximum in top condition).

FOR

Straight-eight smoothness • Senior models' posh and panache

AGAINST

Open models' scarcity • Lack of status for all but Series 90s.

SPECIFICATIONS

Length (in.) NA **Wheelbase (in.)** 132.0 (1931); 134.0 (1932); 138.0 (1933); 136.0 (1934-35) **Weight (lbs.)** 4010-4876 **Price (new)** $1610-2175

ENGINES

cid/type	bore x stroke	bhp	years
344.8/L8	3.13 × 5.00	104-116	1931-35

PRICES/PROJECTION

See History

Buick Roadmaster 1942-48

PRODUCTION

| 1942 4d sedan 5418 | convertible 511 | sedanet 2475 |
| 1946 4d sedan 20,864 | convertible 2587 | sedanet 8292 |

1942 Series 70 Roadmaster convertible coupe

1947 4d sedan 47,152 **convertible** 12,074 **sedanet** 19,212
4d wagon 529 **1948 4d sedan** 47,569 **convertible** 11,503
sedanet 20,649 **4d wagon** 350

HISTORY

Buick's luxury standard bearer, and especially attractive in these years. The Harley Earl styling was distinguished by long, tapering pontoon front fenders; a wide, vertical grille; and gunsight hood ornament (postwar models only). The convertible is the most prized body style, but the sleek sedanet is a better buy. The partially wood-bodied Estate Wagon is very rare and desirable.

FOR

Large and luxurious, a fine touring car ● Dynaflow automatic available on 1948s

AGAINST

A hefty armful to drive ● High fuel consumption ● Sluggish acceleration with Dynaflow

SPECIFICATIONS

Length (in.) 217.5 **Wheelbase (in.)** 129.0
Weight (lbs.) 4075-4460 **Price (new)** $1395-3433

ENGINES

cid/type	bore x stroke	bhp	years
320.2/L8	3.44×4.31	144/165	1942-48

PRICES/PROJECTION

SEDAN/SEDANET **Restorable** $1000-3500 **Good** $4000-7000
Excellent $8000-11,000. Add 300% for convertible, 250% for wagon. **5-year projection** +10%

Buick Roadmaster Riviera 1949

PRODUCTION

4343

HISTORY

The Milestone designation for this model stems mainly from its two-door "hardtop convertible" body style (also pioneered by the '49 Cadillac Coupe de Ville and Oldsmobile Holiday). Also significant for collectors is its quality, leather-accented interior, bright color schemes, and clean, streamlined styling. The big Roadmaster straight eight gives vivid performance for a standard-size car of this period. Hardtop styling gives the Riviera a slight edge over the Roadmaster convertible as the most desirable '49 Buick.

1949 Roadmaster Riviera 2-door hardtop

FOR

Pioneer hardtop ● Clean styling ● Very posh ● Fine road car

AGAINST

Some body parts increasingly hard to find ● Limited availability ● High prices if you find one

SPECIFICATIONS

Length (in.) 214.1 **Wheelbase (in.)** 126.0 **Weight (lbs.)** 4420
Price (new) $3203

ENGINES

cid/type	bore x stroke	bhp	years
320.2/L8	3.44×4.31	150	1949

PRICES/PROJECTION

Restorable $2500-4000 **Good** $4000-8000
Excellent $9000-15,000 **5-year projection** +10%

Buick Skylark 1953

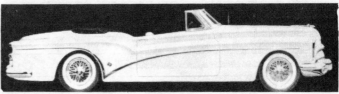

1953 Skylark convertible

PRODUCTION

1690

HISTORY

An exciting, limited production convertible in the Roadmaster series. Styled by Harley Earl, and prefigured some appearance features of later production Buicks. A cutdown version of the standard convertible with sectioned windshield and bodysides. Lacked trademark portholes, but had Kelsey-Hayes chrome wire wheels as standard. Also had the hottest Buick V8, tinted glass, "Selectronic" radio with power antenna, and whitewall tires. One of the all-time great Buicks.

FOR

Limited production ● Ultra-clean, distinctive styling ● Performance ● Luxury ● Built in Buick's Golden Anniversary year

AGAINST

Price will always be forbidding ●Some Skylark-only parts scarce
●Wire wheels can cost $750 a set

SPECIFICATIONS

Length (in.) 207.6 **Wheelbase (in.)** 121.5 **Weight (lbs.)** 4315
Price (new) $5000

ENGINES

cid/type	bore x stroke	bhp	years
322/ohv V8	4.00×3.20	188	1953

PRICES/PROJECTION

Restorable $4000-6000 **Good** $7500-12,000
Excellent $15,000-25,000 **5-year projection** +10%

Buick Skylark
1954

1954 Skylark convertible (prototype)

PRODUCTION

836

HISTORY

A separate Buick model this year. Few were sold because of high
price, so Skylark was discontinued for 1955. Unlike the '53 model,
1954's body was not sectioned, but wheel wells were still full cutouts, ornamentation was unique, and touches like rear fender
sculpture and large chrome tailfins set the Skylark apart from other
'54 Buicks. Kelsey-Hayes wires remained part of the standard
package.

FOR

Lower-priced alternative to the '53 Skylark ●Unique styling features
●Performance ●Quite rare (not many survive)

AGAINST

Less distinguished than its predecessor ●Styling dated now

SPECIFICATIONS

Length (in.) 206.3 **Wheelbase (in.)** 122.0 **Weight (lbs.)** 4260
Price (new) $4483

ENGINES

cid/type	bore x stroke	bhp	years
322/ohv V8	4.00×3.20	200	1954

PRICES/PROJECTION

Restorable $3000-4500 **Good** $5000-9000
Excellent $10,000-15,000 **5-year projection** +25%

Buick Century
1954-55

1955 Century 2-door hardtop

PRODUCTION

1954 convertible 2790 **2d hardtop** 45,710
1955 convertible 5588 **2d hardtop** 80,338
4d hardtop 55,088

HISTORY

Buick's hot rod in the mid-'50s. These more sporty models are
still-affordable collector's items with fair appreciation potential. The
Century formula of a short wheelbase body with a more potent than
average V8 worked particularly well in these years. Styling good
despite massive size, construction and quality also good. Very fast
despite bulk—a genuine 100-mph cruiser. A cheaper alternative to
Skylarks for fanciers of '50s Buicks, and superb on the highway.

FOR

Reasonably affordable now ●Outstanding performance ●More
maneuverable chassis ●Readily available ●Period styling

AGAINST

High fuel (and, some collectors say, oil) consumption ●Relatively
slow to appreciate in value

SPECIFICATIONS

Length (in.) 206.3 (1954), 206.6 (1955) **Wheelbase (in.)** 122.0
Weight (lbs.) 3795-3995 **Price (new)** $2490-3470

ENGINES

cid/type	bore x stroke	bhp	years
322/ohv V8	4.00×3.20	200/236	1954-55

PRICES/PROJECTION

CONVERTIBLES Restorable $2500-5000 **Good** $5000-10,000
Excellent $10,000-15,000 Hardtops approx. 40% lower
5-year projection +15%

Buick Limited
1958

1958 Limited 2-door hardtop

PRODUCTION

2d hardtop 1026   **4d hardtop** 5571   **convertible** 839

HISTORY

All the styling excesses of the decade are wrapped up in this bloated, overdecorated kitsch-wagon. Has a sort of reverse snob appeal for some (a Detroit stylist commutes to work in a pink convertible). Fine craftsmanship and high-quality interiors. Relatively immune to rust, though chrome plating bills will be high if all that brightwork ever needs attention. Not for everyone, but there's no bigger or flashier example of the best and worst in late-'50s American cars.

FOR

One-year-only styling and series

AGAINST

Dreadful styling ●High thirst ●Gargantuan size ●Barge-like handling ●Limited appreciation potential

SPECIFICATIONS

Length (in.) 227.1   **Wheelbase (in.)** 127.5
Weight (lbs.) 4603-4710   **Price (new)** $5002-5125

ENGINES

cid/type	bore x stroke	bhp	years
364/ohv V8	4.13×3.40	300	1958

PRICES/PROJECTION

CONVERTIBLES **Restorable** $2500-5000 **Good** $8000-10,000
Excellent $10,000-15,000 CLOSED MODELS deduct 50% for coupe, 65% for sedan. **5-year projection** +10%

Buick Special
Skylark 1961-63

PRODUCTION

1961 sport coupe 12,683   **1962 sport coupe** 34,060
convertible 8913   **1963 sport coupe** 32,109
convertible 10,212

1962 Special Skylark 2-door hardtop

HISTORY

Highly underrated pioneer of the sporty compact idea. Ideal transportation now for those collectors who'd prefer to drive a pleasant everyday car that can be sold for more than they paid for it. Values should keep pace with the rate of inflation, and may even exceed it slightly. Convertibles naturally more desirable than the coupes. Buick's aluminum V8 gives decent go. An efficient V6 was available for 1962-63 and delivers good economy. Quality and luxury surprisingly good. Great attention paid to soundproofing for that big-car feel so beloved by Detroit. Still quite contemporary compared to much newer designs.

FOR

Attractive, if busy, styling ●Good gas mileage ●Compact size
●Posh (look for optional leather bucket seats)

AGAINST

Not recognized yet as collectible ●Some susceptibility to body rot
●Body parts now scarce

SPECIFICATIONS

Length (in.) 188.4 (1961-62)   192.1 (1963)
Wheelbase (in.) 112.0 (1961) 112.1 (1962-63)
Weight (lbs.) 2687-2871   **Price (new)** $2621-3012

ENGINES

cid/type	bore x stroke	bhp	years
215/ohv V8	3.50×2.80	155/185/200	1961-63
198/ohv V6	3.63×3.20	135	1962-63

PRICES/PROJECTION

Restorable $1000-2000 **Good** $2000-4000
Excellent $4000-6000 Deduct 50% for coupes
5-year projection +10%

Buick Wildcat
1962

PRODUCTION

2000

HISTORY

Buick's initial entry in the full-size bucket-seats-and-console market. Officially part of the Invicta line. Had vinyl color-keyed interior and top, special side trim and emblems. It was well re-

1962 Wildcat 2-door hardtop

ceived. The '62 remains a "comer" among collector cars because of low production, and has a good shot at high value appreciation. Expanded into a series of hardtops and convertibles beginning with 1963, which diminishes the collector appeal of the later models.

FOR

Sleek, crisp styling ●High-output V8 ●Snazzy interiors ●Comfortable long-haul touring capability

AGAINST

Wicked fuel consumption ●Limited collector acceptance at present ●Quite big for around-town use

SPECIFICATIONS

Length (in.) 215.7   **Wheelbase (in.)** 123.0   **Weight (lbs.)** 4150
Price (new) $3927

ENGINES

cid/type	bore x stroke	bhp	years
401/ohv V8	4.19×3.64	265/280	1962

PRICES/PROJECTION

Restorable $1000-2000 **Good** $2500-4000
Excellent $4000-6000 **5-year projection** +10%

Buick Riviera 1963-65

1963 Riviera 2-door hardtop

PRODUCTION

1963 40,000   **1964** 37,658   **1965** 34,586

HISTORY

Bill Mitchell's magnificent anti-Thunderbird, offered as a hardtop coupe only. Originally intended for Cadillac as a new LaSalle, but awarded to a flagging Buick Division as it neared production. One of the outstanding GM designs of the '60s, respected by an army of

industrial designers. Has already gained high repute among collectors for its beautiful lines, personal-luxury character, and smooth performance. Definitely one of the big guns among collectible Buicks, and high on the list of every serious investor in the marque. Hidden headlights the main styling change for '65. The 1963 original seems to have a slight lead in collector preference.

FOR

Landmark design, virtually flawless ●Outstanding construction quality ●Buckets-and-console appeal ●Performance

AGAINST

Bulk ●Greedy fuel consumption

SPECIFICATIONS

Length (in.) 208.0   **Wheelbase (in.)** 117.0
Weight (lbs.) 3988-4036   **Price (new)** $4333-4408

ENGINES

cid/type	bore x stroke	bhp	years
401/ohv V8	4.19×3.64	325	1963,65
425/ohv V8	4.31×3.64	340/360	1964-65

PRICES/PROJECTION

Restorable $1000-2000 **Good** $2500-4500
Excellent $4000-7000 Add 15% for Gran Sport package (1965)
5-year projection +20%

Buick Skylark Gran Sport 1965-67

PRODUCTION

1965 2d coupe 11,877   **2d hardtop** 47,034
2d convertible 10,456   **1966 2d coupe** 1835
2d hardtop 9934   **2d convertible** 2047
1967 2d coupe 1014   **2d hardtop** 10,659
2d convertible 2140

HISTORY

Buick's mid-size hot rod of the mid-'60s. Introduced as an option package for the Skylark coupe, hardtop, and convertible, then graduated to separate-series status for 1966. Power in the first two years came from the big-block 401 V8 from the full-size Buicks, the pentroof engine that dated from Buick's original 1953 "Fireball" ohv V8. For 1967, an all-new block arrived with semi-wedge heads, and model designation changed to GS400. That same year, Buick introduced a junior muscle car, the GS340, powered by an enlarged version of its small-block V8, and front disc brakes were added to the option list. All Gran Sports were built on the heavier convertible chassis, and had heavy-duty suspension and the requisite scoops, stripes, and bulges as battle dress. Quite quick (0-60 mph came up in as little as 6.0 seconds flat according to one contemporary road test), the GS was also one of the better-handling performance machines of the era, and had Buick's customary luxury and solid construction quality. Not a high-appreciation collectible at present, but a good alternative to an Olds 4-4-2 or Pontiac GTO. The low-production convertibles are naturally the most desirable models.

FOR

Fast ●Very roadable ●Not oversized for today ●Solid Buick quality ●Handsome furnishings ●Deft GM styling

AGAINST

Very thirsty (high octane a must) ●Juvenile "go-faster" add-ons ●Body parts supplies drying up

SPECIFICATIONS

Length (in.) 203.4 (1965), 204.0 (1966), 205.0 (1967)
Wheelbase (in.) 115.0 **Weight (lbs.)** 3283-3505
Price (new) $2845-3167

ENGINES

cid/type	bore x stroke	bhp	years
340/ohv V8	3.75×3.85	260	1967
401/ohv V8	4.19×3.64	325/340	1965-66
400/ohv V8	4.04×3.90	340/360	1967

PRICES/PROJECTION

Restorable $1000-2000 **Good** $2500-3500
Excellent $3500-5000 Convertibles add 75%
5-year projection +5%

Buick Riviera 1966-67

1967 Riviera GS 2-door fastback hardtop

PRODUCTION

1966 45,348 **1967** 42,799

HISTORY

Rarely does Detroit follow one design triumph with another, but the second-generation Riviera was an exception. Larger than the original 1963-65 series, it was nonetheless deftly executed, with flowing lines that also managed to incorporate the traditional British "razor edge" school exemplified by Hooper-bodied Rolls-Royces. Particularly desirable is the GS (Gran Sport), a package option that included Positraction rear axle, cast aluminum rocker covers, chrome air cleaner, whitewalls, road wheels, and special trim.

FOR

Less costly than 1963-65 Riviera ●Beautiful styling ●Quickness ●Roadability (GS) ●Not a Milestone, but should be

AGAINST

Extreme thirst (down to single digits at times) ●Too large for its four-passenger capacity

SPECIFICATIONS

Length (in.) 211.3 **Wheelbase (in.)** 119.0
Weight (lbs.) 4180-4190 **Price (new)** $4424-4469

ENGINES

cid/type	bore x stroke	bhp	years
401/ohv V8	4.19×3.64	340	1966
430/ohv V8	4.19×3.80	360	1967

PRICES/PROJECTION

Restorable $1000-2500 **Good** $2500-4000
Excellent $4000-6000 Add 10% for Gran Sport package
5-year projection +15%

Buick GS 1968-72

1970 GS455 2-door hardtop

PRODUCTION

1968 GS350 2d hardtop 10,530 **GS400 2d hardtop** 10,743
GS400 2d convertible 2454 **1969 GS350 2d hardtop** 4933
GS400 2d hardtop 6456 **GS400 2d convertible** 1776
1970 GS 2d hardtop 9948 **GS455 2d hardtop** 8732
GS455 2d convertible 1416 **1971-72** NA

HISTORY

Continuation of Buick's mid-size stormer, with all-new styling on GM's split-wheelbase (112 inches on two-doors, 116 on four-doors) A-body platform. A slight bore increase on the Buick small-block V8 made the previous GS340 into the GS350. The GS400 continued as before, augmented at mid-1968 model year by the hot Stage I option for the big-block, which included a high-lift cam, reworked carb, and free-flow exhaust system. For 1970, GM rescinded its unwritten ban on intermediates with less than 10 pounds per horsepower, so Buick bolted in its big-car 455 V8. The GS350 became just plain GS. A mid-season arrival was the GSX, an $888 package option featuring front and rear spoilers, striping, hood-mounted tach, and four-speed manual transmission. Power began to be watered down starting in 1971, but a Stage I 455 could still scamper from rest to 60 mph in 6.5 seconds. The GSX was dropped for 1972, but the 455 carried on, now rated in SAE net horsepower figures. A new-generation Buick intermediate, the Century, debuted for '73. The GS reverted to being a package option, convertibles disappeared, and appearance was more subdued, but it was still fairly hot. However, we think the desirable Buick muscle cars end with the '72s. The low-production convertibles stand to become fairly sought-after in a few years.

FOR

Handsome looks •Great performance •Capable handling •Rag-tops' rarity •Atypical models for Buick

AGAINST

As for 1965-67 Skylark Gran Sport

SPECIFICATIONS

Length (in.) 200.7 (1968-70), 203.3 (1971-72)
Wheelbase (in.) 112.0   **Weight (lbs.)** 3375-3700
Price (new) $2926-5350

ENGINES

cid/type	bore x stroke	bhp	years
350/ohv V8	3.80×3.85	280	1968-72
400/ohv V8	4.04×3.90	340/360	1968-69
455/ohv V8	4.31×3.90	315-360*	1970-72

*rated at 250 bhp SAE net in 1972; Stage I rated at 270 bhp net

PRICES/PROJECTION

Restorable $1000-2000 **Good** $2000-3000
Excellent $3000-5000 Add 50% for convertible; add 25% for 455
5-year projection +20%

Cadillac Eight 1930-35

1932 Series 355B Fleetwood convertible sedan

PRODUCTION

1930 11,005 **1931** 10,709 **1932** 2693 **1933** 2906 **1934** 5080
1935 3209

HISTORY

Certified CCCA Classics and the high point of Cadillac luxury and design in the prewar years, although the Depression caused production to drop drastically after 1932. Not numerous enough now to establish firm price guidelines for individual models. The 353-cid V8 was based on the 341-cid unit introduced in 1928, one of the great eights of the golden age. Square-rigged styling began to disappear in 1932 and was entirely late '30s streamlined by 1934. Notable engineering feats peppered this period: "Syncro-Mesh" transmission in 1929, helical-cut synchronized gears in 1932, "No-Draft Ventilation" and vacuum-assisted brakes in 1933, independent front suspension in 1934, all-steel bodies in 1935. Aside from a switch to a

new L-head eight in 1936, there were other quality downgrades which have prevented post-1935 models from being cited as Classics across-the-board. In all, very fine cars—connoisseurs' pieces through 1933—but only for the wealthy today.

FOR

Classic status • Superb styling through 1933, excellent through 1935 • 353-cid V8 one of the great Classic powerplants • High appreciation potential

AGAINST

Extremely expensive, especially open models • Costly to restore • Hard to find even if you have the money

SPECIFICATIONS

Length (in.) NA **Wheelbase (in.)** 140.0 (1930); 134.0, 140.0 (1931-33); 128.0 Series 10; 136.0 Series 20; 146.0 Series 30 (1934-35) **Weight (lbs.)** 4355-5650 **Price (new)** $2645-5695

ENGINES

cid/type	bore x stroke	bhp	years
353.0/V8	3.63×4.94	95/130	1930-35

PRICES/PROJECTION

OPEN MODELS **Restorable** $7500-15,000
Good $20,000-45,000 **Excellent** $50,000-80,000 Add 30% for Fleetwood bodies. CLOSED MODELS **Restorable** $4000-7500 **Good** $10,000-18,000 **Excellent** $20,000-30,000 Add 15% for Fleetwood bodies. **5-year projection** +15%. Because of the wide variety in body styles and a lack of sales, it is impossible to state more precise value ranges. Potential buyers should consult a qualified appraiser.

Cadillac Sixteen 1930-37

1933 Series 452C Victoria convertible coupe

PRODUCTION

1930-31 3250 **1932** 296 **1933** 125 **1934** 60 **1935** 50 **1936** 52
1937 49

HISTORY

The all-time great among Cadillacs, with a gem of an overhead valve V16 engine producing 165 bhp and 320 lb-ft of torque. Initially available in 33 different models, sub-models or trim variations, it returned eight miles per gallon and would do 90 mph. The division used its longest wheelbases and most elaborate bodies and accoutrements for the Sixteens, which sold for $4700 and up—usually far up. Cadillac described its performance fairly accurately as "a continuous flow … constantly at full-volume efficiency … flexible … instantly responsive."

FOR

A great locomotive of a car and avidly admired • Very high investment and appreciation potential • Scarcity of all body styles makes each car a rarity

AGAINST

Towering purchase price and running costs • Restorations should not be undertaken unless the individual model is very special

SPECIFICATIONS

Length (in.) NA **Wheelbase (in.)** 148.0 (1930-31); 143.0, 149.0 (1932-33); 154.0 (1934-37) **Weight (lbs.)** 5115-6450
Price (new) $4695-9250

ENGINES

cid/type	bore x stroke	bhp	years
452.0/V16	3.00×4.00	165	1930-37

PRICES/PROJECTION

OPEN MODELS **Restorable** $25,000-50,000
Good $60,000-100,000 **Excellent** $100,000-200,000 CLOSED MODELS deduct 50%. MADAME X BODIES (1930-31) Fleetwood four-doors and two coupe types with 18-degree windshield rake have only a 5% lead on comparable standard bodies but are considered more desirable by connoisseurs. As is usual with stratospherically priced Classics, the scarcity of cars, infrequency of sales, and the natural reticence of buyers/sellers prevents more specific pricing. Potential purchasers are urged to seek the advice of a qualified appraiser.
5-year projection +25%

Cadillac Twelve 1930-37

1936 Series 80 Fleetwood convertible sedan

PRODUCTION

1930-31 5725 **1932** 1709 **1933** 952 **1934** 683 **1935** 377 **1936** 901 **1937** 474

HISTORY

A multi-cylinder companion to the Sixteen and announced nine

months later. Basically the V16 with four fewer cylinders and commensurately less power in smaller bodies mounted on a chassis shared with the Eights. Though not as fast as the Sixteen, the free-revving Twelve was well known for its smooth, even power, and it cost considerably less. The light roadster ($3945 in 1930) would approach 85 mph with standard rear axle and can still cruise a modern Interstate at 70. As with the Sixteen, sales never recovered from the Depression, and the Twelve lingered on in diminishing volume until it was scrubbed from the Cadillac line in 1938.

FOR

Full Classic status • Elegant, luxurious body styles • High investment value

AGAINST

Expensive to buy and own • Not quite a Sixteen, and always takes a back seat in comparisons—unfairly

SPECIFICATIONS

Length (in.) NA **Wheelbase (in.)** 140.0, 7P-143.0 (1930-31); rdstr., cpe., conv. cpe.—134.0, others 140.0 (1932-33); 146.0 (1934-35); 131.0, 138.0 (1936-37) **Weight (lbs.)** 4800-6040
Price (new) $3145-6495

ENGINES

cid/type	bore x stroke	bhp	years
368.0/V12	3.13×4.00	135/150	1930-37

PRICES/PROJECTION

OPEN MODELS & AERO COUPE **Restorable** $15,000-30,000
Good $30,000-60,000 **Excellent** $75,000-150,000 CLOSED MODELS Deduct 50%. FISHER BODIES Deduct 25%. Scarcity and few sales make exact pricing a fool's game. Consult club experts and/or qualified appraisers. **5-year projection** +25%

Cadillac Series 60 Special 1938-41

1938 Series 60 Special 4-door sedan

PRODUCTION

1938 3703 **1939 sedan** 5219 **sunroof sedan** 225 **sunroof imperial** 55 **chassis** 7 **1940 sedan** 4472 **division sedan** 110 **town car** 15 **1941 sedan** 3878 **division sedan** 220 **town car** 1 **chassis** 1

HISTORY

A motoring masterpiece with watershed styling by young William L.

Mitchell, later to relieve Harley Earl as GM design chief. Ranked by Cadillac enthusiasts as the marque's leading design accomplishment in the late '30s. Aimed at owner-drivers and sweepingly modern with pontoon fenders but no running boards or nonfunctional ornamentation. Notable was the distinct delineation of lower body from greenhouse using elegant, thin-frame side windows. Also a smooth performer thanks to the low-revving, high-torque L-head eight. Handsomely facelifted for 1941 on a revised chassis with more power and newly optional Hydra-Matic Drive. A fixture at Cadillac through the early '70s, but much less special after '41.

FOR

One of the late-1930s greats • All are CCCA-rated Classics • A historic styling *tour de force* that looks as lovely as ever today • Still a fine investment

AGAINST

Very expensive and still climbing • High operating costs • More expensive to repair/restore than other models of the same year

SPECIFICATIONS

Length (in.) 208.8 approx. **Wheelbase (in.)** 127.0 (1938-40); 126.0 (1941) **Weight (lbs.)** 4070-4485 **Price (new)** $2090-3820

ENGINES

cid/type	bore x stroke	bhp	years
346.0/V8	3.50 × 4.50	135	1938-40
346.0/V8	3.50 × 4.50	150	1941

PRICES/PROJECTION

Restorable $5000-7000 **Good** $9000-12,500
Excellent $15,000-25,000. Add 10% for sunroof/division sedans. Prices for sunroof imperials and town cars higher but not determinable. Consult club experts and appraisers.
5-year projection +20%

Cadillac Series 90 Sixteen 1938-40

1940 Series 90 Sixteen Town Sedan

PRODUCTION

1938 311 **1939** 136 **1940** 61

HISTORY

Sixteen production was never more than a few hundred per year after 1933. Both the V12 and original V16 engines were dropped

after 1937. Cadillac offered a new L-head V16 for three more model years. At 431 cid and 185 bhp, this powerplant was smaller and lighter but more powerful than the earlier jewel-like engine, but it's never received collector acclaim. The advent of precision-insert con rod bearings helped eliminate the traditional knock and engine wear of eights and sixes, which had occasioned multi-cylinder engines. Cadillac found it uneconomical to continue this Sixteen past 1940 even though it shared wheelbase and many body styles with the Series 75. Few open models were built. Most were Imperial and formal sedans.

FOR

Despite lesser reputation, flathead V16 was smooth and near silent • All models have full Classic status • Luxury, refinement • Good roadability • A bit easier to acquire than pre-1938 models

AGAINST

Still very expensive • Hard to find • Colossal restoration costs

SPECIFICATIONS

Length (in.) NA **Wheelbase (in.)** 141.3
Weight (lbs.) 4830-5330 **Price (new)** $5140-7175

ENGINES

cid/type	bore x stroke	bhp	years
431.0/V16	3.25 × 3.25	185	1938-40

PRICES/PROJECTION

OPEN MODELS **Restorable** $20,000-30,000
Good $30,000-60,000 **Excellent** $60,000-80,000 COUPES, FORMALS & TOWN CARS **Restorable** $8000-12,000
Good $15,000-30,000 **Excellent** $35,000-50,000 OTHER CLOSED CARS Deduct 10% from preceding prices. Appraisal strongly recommended. **5-year projection** +15%

Cadillac Series 75 1942-49

1946 Series 75 7-passenger imperial sedan

PRODUCTION

1941 cars 1949 **chassis** 155 **1942 cars** 1100 **chassis** 426 **1946 cars** 635 **chassis** 1292 **1947 cars** 2410 **chassis** 2626 **1948 cars** 1260 **chassis** 2069 **1949 cars** 1501 **chassis** 1861

HISTORY

A long-running (because of low production) design, but happily so good in the first place that nobody felt any need for change. The 75 remained basically in its prewar form for two years after the rest of the Cadillac line was restyled for 1948. Very well-built, solid cars with all the luxury one expects in a long-wheelbase limousine or formal sedan. Offered in a wide variety of body types, though most of those produced were variations of the seven-passenger sedan. A "Godfather" car for collectors who like their machines high, wide, handsome, and heavy.

FOR

Conservative design for the period ●Quality ●Luxury

AGAINST

Too much bulk for many garages ●High running costs

SPECIFICATIONS

Length (in.) 225.8 **Wheelbase (in.)** 136.0 (chassis: 163.0)
Weight (lbs.) 4750-4959 **Price (new)** $2895-5199

ENGINES

cid/type	bore x stroke	bhp	years
346/LV8	3.50×4.50	150	1941-48
331/ohv V8	3.81×3.63	160	1949

PRICES/PROJECTION

Restorable $1000-2500 **Good** $3000-5000
Excellent $5000-8000. Add 15% for 1949 models, 25% for special noncommercial bodies and 10% for division window sedan. **5-year projection** +10%

Cadillac Series 62 convertible/sedanet 1948-49

1949 Series 62 sedanet

PRODUCTION

1948 convertible 5450 **sedanet** 4764
1949 convertible 8000 **sedanet** 7515

HISTORY

Elegantly beautiful Cadillacs, part of the first postwar redesign, and among the most graceful cars of the era. The fastback sedanet (also known as the club coupe) had the aura of the Classic boat-tail about it. The significant mechanical difference between the two model years is engines: the '48s had the last of the 346-cid flathead V8s, while the '49s had the first of the pioneering 331-cid overhead valve units. Some collectors prefer the earlier engine, saying it is smoother and quieter, though the ohv unit provides more power

and returns better mileage. Both years are almost identical in styling, though the '49 looks a little heavier in front. The '48 possesses a fine one-year-only drum-style instrument cluster; the '49 dash is more conventional.

FOR

One of the great postwar American designs ●High-demand item ●Widely recognized for excellence

AGAINST

Fairly high running costs ●Uninspired interiors

SPECIFICATIONS

Length (in.) 213.9 **Wheelbase (in.)** 126.0
Weight (lbs.) 4125-4449 **Price (new)** $2912-3442

ENGINES

cid/type	bore x stroke	bhp	years
346/LV8	3.50×4.50	150	1948
331/ohv V8	3.81×3.63	160	1949

PRICES/PROJECTION

CONVERTIBLES **Restorable** $4000-8000 **Good** $8000-15,000 **Excellent** $15,000-20,000, add 20% for 1949 model. SEDANET **Restorable** $1500-4000 **Good** $4000-6500 **Excellent** $7000-9000 Add 20% for 1949 model.
5-year projection +15%

Cadillac Series 61 sedanet 1948-49

1949 Series 61 sedanet

PRODUCTION

1948 3521 **1949** 6409

HISTORY

Slightly detrimmed (no front splash guard, for instance) parallel line to the Series 62, originally priced about $200 lower and lacking a convertible. The 61 sedanet has the same fine styling attributes of its upper class cousin.

FOR

Somewhat rarer than the 62 sedanet ●A bit less costly on today's collector market

AGAINST

Slightly less flashy than the 62 (though some might consider that a plus) •Interior very plain for a Cadillac

SPECIFICATIONS

Length (in.) 213.9 **Wheelbase (in.)** 126.0
Weight (lbs.) 3838-4068 **Price (new)** $2728-2788

ENGINES

cid/type	bore x stroke	bhp	years
346/LV8	3.50×4.50	150	1948
331/ohv V8	3.81×3.63	160	1949

PRICES/PROJECTION

As for 1948-49 Series 62 sedanets

Cadillac Series 62 Coupe de Ville 1949

1949 Series 62 Coupe de Ville

PRODUCTION

2150

HISTORY

Rare and highly desirable milestone. Shares status with the 1949 Buick Roadmaster Riviera and Oldsmobile 98 Holiday as the first "hardtop convertibles." Lavishly upholstered in leather and vinyl; bright metal strips on headliner simulated convertible top bows. The 1950 and later models are collectible, too, but only the '49 holds Milestone status. Also, post-1949 Cadillacs were more ornate, especially in front.

FOR

Pioneer hardtop •Loads of luxury •Rarity and consequent desirability •Modern ohv V8

AGAINST

Pricey and getting pricier •Hard to find now

SPECIFICATIONS

Length (in.) 213.9 **Wheelbase (in.)** 126.0 **Weight (lbs.)** 4033
Price (new) $3497

ENGINES

cid/type	bore x stroke	bhp	years
331/ohv V8	3.81×3.63	160	1949

PRICES/PROJECTION

Restorable $2000-4000 **Good** $5000-7500
Excellent $8000-12,000 **5-year projection** +15%

Cadillac Series 62 Eldorado 1953

1953 Series 62 Eldorado convertible

PRODUCTION

532

HISTORY

Like the contemporary Buick Riviera and Oldsmobile Fiesta, a limited production show car, and widely sought after because of this. Quite a few have survived in proportion to those built. Cut-down body and windshield, metal convertible boot, ultra-luxurious upholstery, and chrome plated wire wheels made it the sportiest Cadillac ever. Created quite a stir despite an eye-opening price.

FOR

Historical importance •Exclusive styling features •Very desirable in Cadillac circles •High performance

AGAINST

Heavier-looking than the smooth 1948-49 models •Many body parts now virtually unobtainable •High price on today's market

SPECIFICATIONS

Length (in.) 215.8 **Wheelbase (in.)** 126.0 **Weight (lbs.)** 4800
Price (new) $7750

ENGINES

cid/type	bore x stroke	bhp	years
331/ohv V8	3.81×3.63	210	1953

PRICES/PROJECTION

Restorable $5000-10,000 **Good** $10,000-18,000
Excellent $20,000-28,000 **5-year projection** +10%

Cadillac Series 62 Eldorado 1954-55

1955 Series 62 Eldorado convertible

PRODUCTION

1954 2150   **1955** 3950

HISTORY

Continuation of the successful limited production 1953 Eldorado, but priced quite a bit less and built in greater quantity. Like the 1954 Buick Skylark, far less "custom" in these years, sharing the basic 62 convertible body but with exclusive shark fin rear end and round taillights. For 1955, the standard engine was a special high-performance version of the Cadillac V8, offered on no other model that year.

FOR

More affordable than the '53 ●Lots of luxury ●Comparative rarity ●Good investment ●Parts not normally a problem

AGAINST

Larger and thirstier than the '53, too ●Also less unique in appearance and engineering ●The '54 curiously lacks Milestone status

SPECIFICATIONS

Length (in.) 223.4   **Wheelbase (in.)** 129.0
Weight (lbs.) 4809-4815   **Price (new)** $4738-6286

ENGINES

cid/type	bore x stroke	bhp	years
331/ohv V8	3.81×3.63	230/270	1954-55

PRICES/PROJECTION

Restorable $5000-8000 **Good** $7000-12,000
Excellent $12,000-20,000 **5-year projection** +15%

Cadillac Series 62 Eldorado Biarritz 1956-57

PRODUCTION

1956 2150   **1957** 1800

1957 Series 62 Eldorado Biarritz convertible

HISTORY

Revised editions of the Eldorado convertible that did not sell particularly well. Biarritz designation new for '56. Cadillac's 331 V8 was bored out to 365 cid for 1956, with a special tuned version reserved for Eldorados. Comments on mechanical and design features of companion Seville hardtop also apply here. After 1960, the Seville was dropped from the Eldorado line, which had been separated from the Series 62 the year before. For now, the 1956-57 models are the last highly collectible Eldorado convertibles through 1971. The 1958 version was a chrome-plated monster, and the '59 took tailfins to a new level of absurdity. Styling was gradually improved on the early-'60s models, but they were never as "special" as the 1953-57 cars.

FOR

Unique rear-end appearance ●Smooth, high-speed performance ●Luxurious interiors ●Somewhat rare

AGAINST

Heavy gas drinker ●Less interesting than 1953-55 Eldos

SPECIFICATIONS

Length (in.) 222.2 (1956), 222.1 (1957)
Wheelbase (in.) 129.0 (1956), 129.5 (1957)
Weight (lbs.) 4880-4930   **Price (new)** $6556-7286

ENGINES

cid/type	bore x stroke	bhp	years
365/ohv V8	4.00×3.63	305/325	1956-57

PRICES/PROJECTION

Restorable $2500-5000 **Good** $5000-9000
Excellent $10,000-15,000 **5-year projection** +10%

Cadillac Series 62 Eldorado Seville 1956-57

PRODUCTION

1956 3900   **1957** 2100

HISTORY

A variation of the Eldorado format in an expensive limited-edition spinoff of the standard 62 hardtop. (Seville was simultaneously used by DeSoto for one of its four-door hardtops, but only for '56.)

1957 Series 62 Eldorado Seville 2-door hardtop

As in 1954-55 convertibles, the '56 Seville shared the basic 62 shell adorned with prominent tailfins. For 1957, the whole Cadillac line was redesigned. Eldorados retained their tailfin shape, but gained softer lines front and rear and a lower stance. Specially tuned V8s were again exclusive to Eldorados in these years.

FOR

Sedan comfort with hardtop styling ●Cadillac amenities and furnishings ●Better than average performance

AGAINST

A symbol of Cadillac's mid-'50s preference for flamboyance over taste ●Very thirsty

SPECIFICATIONS

Length (in.) 222.2 (1956), 222.1 (1957)
Wheelbase (in.) 129.0 (1956), 129.5 (1957)
Weight (lbs.) 4665-4810   **Price (new)** $6556-7286

ENGINES

cid/type	bore x stroke	bhp	years
365/ohv V8	4.00×3.63	305/325	1956-57

PRICES/PROJECTION

Restorable $2000-5000 **Good** $5000-7000
Excellent $10,000-15,000 **5-year projection** +10%

Cadillac Series 70 Eldorado Brougham 1957-58

1957 Series 70 Eldorado Brougham 4-door hardtop

PRODUCTION

1957 400   **1958** 304

HISTORY

Cadillac's answer to the Continental Mark II, and priced at the same stratospheric level (equivalent to $40,000 today). While the Mark II stressed conservative looks and engineering, the Brougham was radical: center-opening doors, brushed stainless steel roof, quad headlights (a 1957 first shared with Nash and Lincoln), and problem-laden air suspension. Because of severe leaks, the air suspension was often replaced with conventional coil springs by disgruntled owners, making original Broughams fairly scarce today. Full of high-roller accoutrements, right down to a matched set of silver tumblers and special lipstick and cologne.

FOR

One-of-a-kind concept ●Advanced engineering ●The ultimate in luxury ●Fine road manners with or without air suspension

AGAINST

Very expensive on today's market ●Many body and component parts (like those silver tumblers) now impossible to find ●High running costs

SPECIFICATIONS

Length (in.) 216.3   **Wheelbase (in.)** 129.0   **Weight (lbs.)** 5315
Price (new) $13,074

ENGINES

cid/type	bore x stroke	bhp	years
365/ohv V8	4.00×3.63	310/325	1957-58

PRICES/PROJECTION

Restorable $3000-6000 **Good** $7500-12,500
Excellent $14,000-20,000 **5-year projection** +10%

Cadillac Eldorado Brougham 1959-60

1959 Eldorado Brougham 4-door hardtop

PRODUCTION

1959 99   **1960** 101

HISTORY

After limited success with the 1957-58 original (and Continental's departure from the super-luxury market), Cadillac farmed out Eldorado Brougham production to Pininfarina in Italy. PF handled body styling (a mild modification of standard 1959-60 lines marked by less outlandish tailfins) and assembly (using stock Cadillac components) in Turin. Though the 1959-60 Brougham was more closely related to the standard Cadillacs, price remained the same as for previous models, and sales were few. Name and high status makes these models collectible now, though they lack the prestige and interest value of the 1957-58.

FOR

Priced less than 1957-58 Broughams on today's market ●One-upmanship value of Pininfarina badges ●High luxury

AGAINST

Less different from ordinary Cadillacs than earlier Broughams ●Much lower appreciation potential than 1957-58 models ●High running costs

SPECIFICATIONS

Length (in.) 225.0 **Wheelbase (in.)** 130.0 **Weight (lbs.)** NA
Price (new) $13,075

ENGINES

cid/type	bore x stroke	bhp	years
390/ohv V8	4.00×3.88	345	1959-60

PRICES/PROJECTION

Restorable $1500-3000 **Good** $3000-4500
Excellent $6000-12,000 **5-year projection** +10%

Cadillac Series 62 De Ville/Eldorado 1959

1959 Coupe deVille 2-door hardtop

PRODUCTION

62 70,736 **DeVille** 53,390 **Eldorado Seville** 975 **Convertible 62** 11,130 **Eldorado Biarritz** 1320

HISTORY

Depending on your taste, the most outlandish or magnificent of all tailfinned Detroiters, beloved and despised by equally large and vociferous armies of collectors. There's more unanimity over the powerplant, the 390 being among Cadillac's better V8s (it debuted in 1959). Glitzy chrome trim, especially on the Eldo, and lavish color-keyed interiors with a jukebox dash made this the epitome of late-50s kitch. Tailfins never grew larger even on Chrysler products, but Cadillac cropped them drastically for 1960. By 1965 they'd vanished. A big, powerful highway cruiser with better economy and more competent handling than you'd expect.

FOR

Distinction—one way or the other ● Smooth performance ● Series 62 ragtops still in good supply

AGAINST

Very controversial—"I'd be embarrassed to be seen in one," says one longtime Cadillac collector ● Workmanship not good ● Tends to rust ● Biarritz now scarce ● Costly body and interior restoration (find a good original)

SPECIFICATIONS

Length (in.) 225.0 **Wheelbase (in.)** 130.0
Weight (lbs.) 4690-4855 **Price (new)** $4892-7401

ENGINES

cid/type	bore x stroke	bhp	years
390.0/V8	4.00×3.88	325/345	1959

PRICES/PROJECTION

HARDTOP SEDANS **Restorable** $1000-2000 **Good** $2000-4000 **Excellent** $4000-6000. Add 5% for 4-window version. HARDTOP COUPES **Restorable** $900-2000 **Good** $2500-4500 **Excellent** $5000-8000. Deduct 10% for 62, add 10% for Eldorado Seville. CONVERTIBLE **Restorable** $3000-5000 **Good** $5000-8000 **Excellent** $9000-12,000. Add 40% for Eldorado Biarritz. **5-year projection** open cars +20%, closed cars +10%.

Cadillac Eldorado 1967-70

1967 Fleetwood Eldorado 2-door hardtop

PRODUCTION

1967 17,930 **1968** 24,528 **1969** 23,333 **1970** 28,842

HISTORY

One of the more interesting cars of the late '60s, essentially Cadillac's heavily re-engineered version of Oldsmobile's front-wheel-drive Toronado. An exceptional road machine considering its size, with outstanding handling and surprising get-up-and-go. Finely honed body styling in the Cadillac idiom, somewhat less radical and aggressive than the Toronado's. Growing collector interest in all fwd Eldorados means that "collectibility" doesn't end with the 1970s, though the boom demand for 1976's "last convertible" petered out several years ago. The first-generation cars are still the best investment and the most satisfying to drive.

FOR

Engineering excellence ●A big luxurious car that can really go, stop, and handle ●Graceful styling has aged well

AGAINST

Driveability problems progressively worse on post-'67 models as emission controls tighten • High running costs

SPECIFICATIONS

Length (in.) 220.0 (approx.) **Wheelbase (in.)** 120.0
Weight (lbs.) 4500-4630 **Price (new)** $6277-6903

ENGINES

cid/type	bore x stroke	bhp	years
429/ohv V8	4.13×4.00	340	1967
472/ohv V8	4.30×4.06	375	1968-69
500/ohv V8	4.30×4.30	400	1970

PRICES/PROJECTION

Restorable $750-1500 **Good** $1500-2500
Excellent $3000-5000 Add 20% for 1967 model
5-year projection +10%

Cadillac Eldorado convertible 1971-76

1976 Fleetwood Eldorado convertible

PRODUCTION

1971 6800 **1972** 7975 **1973** 9315 **1974** 7600
1975 8950 **1976** 14,000

HISTORY

A dubious collectible at best. The '76 seemed destined to go down in history as the last factory-built American convertible. But that status has been rendered obsolete now that Detroit is getting back into ragtops again, at least on a small scale. So, the question of whether these Eldos are truly collectible is certainly open to debate. Cadillac's second-generation personal-luxury front-driver was certainly a big, impressive package. But the proportions were embarassingly outsized, styling lacked the clean distinction of the first-generation 1968-70 models, and there was virtually nothing innovative or technically interesting about it. Our guess is that it may not be until the year 2000 that the '76 Eldo convertible becomes scarce enough to be noticed by serious collectors — about the only reason it would be desirable even then. And because many owners have already mothballed their cars as future investments, mint-condition '76s may actually be a lot more commonplace in a few years than the lower-production, less "worthy" 1971-75 models, which aren't all that different anyway. All of which argues for choosing one of the earlier models over the '76 if you plan to acquire one of these barges anytime soon.

FOR

Minor historical interest • As big and luxurious as they come • In reasonable supply yet

Very high running costs • Hardly a great Cadillac

SPECIFICATIONS

Length (in.) 220.0-224.1 **Wheelbase (in.)** 126.3
Weight (lbs.) 5275 (average) **Price (new)** $8500-14,000 (approx.)

ENGINES

cid/type	bore x stroke	bhp	years
500/ohv V8	4.30×4.30	235-365*	1971-76

*SAE net

PRICES/PROJECTION

Restorable $1000-3000 **Good** $3000-6000
Excellent $7000-13,000 **5-year projection** +15%

Cadillac Seville 1976-79

1976 Seville 4-door sedan

PRODUCTION

1976 60,127 **1977** 45,060 **1978** 56,985 **1979** 53,487

HISTORY

First-generation "baby" Cadillac and the division's smallest car since the last LaSalle of 1940. Partly a trial balloon for General Motors' revolutionary downsizing program that began in earnest with its 1977 full-size cars. As such, a complete reversal of Detroit's time-honored notions about size and price: the smallest Caddy in living memory yet costlier than any other model in the line save the big Series 75 sedans and limos. A heavy rework of the corporate X-body four-door compact, with typical GM rear-drive chassis and front-coil/rear-leaf suspension, but crisper, more formal styling on a 3.3-inch longer wheelbase, Cadillac-assembled Olds engine with exclusive electronic fuel injection system, and full-house standard equipment. A very successful transformation aesthetically, mechanically, and commercially, and still with us in an even smaller third-generation guise. Four-wheel disc brakes from 1977, but avoid trouble-prone 1978-79 Olds-built diesel V8 option.

FOR

A '70s sleeper • Cadillac cachet and equipment • Clean lines • Good go (10-11 sec. 0-60 mph) • Decent economy • Handy size • Widely available • Very affordable • Parts plentiful

AGAINST

Not widely recognized yet • A Jag/M-B/BMW rival in size but not status • Tight cabin • Dismal diesel engine • Humble design origins

SPECIFICATIONS

Length (in.) 204.0 **Wheelbase (in.)** 114.3
Weight (lbs.) 4179-4232 **Price (new)** $12,479-14,710

ENGINES

cid/type	bore x stroke	bhp	years
350.0/ohv V8	4.06×3.39	170/180*	1976-79
350.0/ohv V8	4.06×3.39	125**	1978-79

*SAE net; electronic fuel injection
**diesel; Olds-built

PRICES/PROJECTION

1976-77 Restorable $1000-3000 **Good** $3000-5000
Excellent $5000-6000 1978-79 Governed more by used-car than collector-market forces at present. Approximate average values: $4800-8000 Deduct 35% for diesel engine.
5-year projection +5%

Chevrolet open models 1932-36

1932 Confederate Series BA DeLuxe Sports Roadster

PRODUCTION

1932 Del. rdstr 8552 **Del. phaeton** 1000* **Std. rdstr** 1118 **Std. phaeton** 600* **1933 Del. rdstr** 2876 **Del. phaeton** 543 **Del. cabriolet** 4276 **1934 Del. rdstr** 1974 **Del. cabriolet** 3276 **Std. rdstr** 1038 **Std. Phaeton** 234 **1935 Std. rdstr** 1176 **Std. phaeton** 217 **1936 Std. cabriolet** 3629
*estimates

HISTORY

All Chevys of this period are collectible, but the open models are, as usual, more collectible than the others. Topless cars were fast going out of fashion in the threadbare '30s as all-steel bodies began to appear around mid-decade, so the above production figures are not as astonishing as they may appear. Top-notch styling arrived with the 1932s, reminiscent of Harley Earl's earlier LaSalles. Streamlining began with the '33s, became more radical on the '34s. Desirability not so high on 1936-40 models. All Chevys from 1932 on had the long-lived and reliable "Blue Flame" six. Open cars began shifting to the Standard series for 1934. The longer-wheelbase Deluxe versions are more desirable, but the trick is to find one at all.

FOR

Simple to fix, relatively easy to restore • Excellent parts situation

including some body/trim bits • An all-round nifty rig • Strong club support

AGAINST

Doesn't rival early-30s Ford V8s among enthusiasts, thus relatively lower investment potential • Hard to find • Easy to over-restore

SPECIFICATIONS

Length (in.) NA **Wheelbase (in.)** 109.0 (1932); 110.0 (1933); 107.0, 112.0 (1934); 107.0 (1935); 109.0 (1936)
Weight (lbs.) 2380-2815 **Price (new)** $445-640

ENGINES

cid/type	bore x stroke	bhp	years
194.0/L6	3.13×3.75	60	1932
181.0/L6	3.31×3.50	60/74	1933-35
206.8/L6	3.31×4.00	65/80	1933-36

PRICES/PROJECTION

1932 Restorable $3500-6500 **Good** $7500-15,000
Excellent $20,000-28,000 **1933-35 Restorable** $3000-5000
Good $6000-10,000 **Excellent** $12,000-20,000
1936 Restorable $2500-4000 **Good** $5000-9000
Excellent $9000-14,000 **5-year projection** 1932 models +15%, others +10%

Chevrolet Special DeLuxe 1941

1941 Special DeLuxe Town Sedan

PRODUCTION

2d Town Sedan 288,458 **business coupe** 17,602
coupe 155,889 **convertible coupe** 15,296
4d Sport Sedan 148,661 **4d wagon** 2045
4d Fleetline sedan 34,162

HISTORY

A classic prewar Chevy, though not a designated Classic. An elegant refinement of the 1940 design, with a special Fleetline sedan with more formal styling added to the lineup. Well-proportioned and solidly built, the '41s are prized among Chevrolet fanciers. The top-of-the-line Special DeLuxe commands naturally greater attention than the cheaper Masters. Typically, the rarer body styles are more desirable; the Fleetline receives good marks for its stylish blind rear roof quarters.

FOR

Good styling •Construction quality •A vintage Chevy year •Unbreakable six

AGAINST

No performance vs. Ford V-8 • Very common

SPECIFICATIONS

Length (in.) 196.0 **Wheelbase (in.)** 116.0
Weight (lbs.) 3040-3410 **Price (new)** $769-995

ENGINES

cid/type	bore x stroke	bhp	years
216.5/L6	3.50×3.75	90	1941

PRICES/PROJECTION

Restorable $800-1200 **Good** $1500-3000
Excellent $3000-6500 Add 150% for convertible; add 75% for wagon **5-year projection** +15%

Chevrolet Fleetline 1942

1942 Fleetline 2-door Aerosedan

PRODUCTION

2d Aerosedan 61,885 **4d Sportmaster sedan** 14,530

HISTORY

Buyer acceptance of the 1941 Special DeLuxe Fleetline led to this offshoot of the '42 Fleetmaster line. Curiously, only the two-door Aerosedan continued the fastback styling from '41; the Sportmaster was a more conventional notchback. Both models were distinguished by triple chrome bands on the front and rear fenders.

FOR

Aerosedan relatively easy to find (highest production of any '42 Chevy) • Top-of-the-line trim • Sleek styling • Bulletproof six

AGAINST

Not much go

SPECIFICATIONS

Length (in.) 196.0 **Wheelbase (in.)** 116.0
Weight (lbs.) 3105-3165 **Price (new)** $880 (Aerosedan); $920 (Sportmaster)

ENGINES

cid/type	bore x stroke	bhp	years
216.5/L6	3.50×3.75	90	1942

PRICES/PROJECTION

Restorable $1100-2000 **Good** $2000-3300
Excellent $4500-6000 Deduct 10% for Sportmaster
5-year projection +5%

Chevrolet Fleetmaster 1942

PRODUCTION

2d Town Sedan 39,421	**2-pass. coupe** 1716
4d Sport Sedan 31,441	**convertible coupe** 1182
5-pass. coupe 22,187	**4d wagon** 1057

HISTORY

A further development of the pretty 1941 styling, with extended front fenders similar to those on the more expensive GM makes. Abbreviated production in February 1942 to make way for defense work makes the '42 marginally more desirable than the '41. Only a handful of convertibles and wagons were built; the two-passenger coupe is also extremely scarce. No mechanical changes from 1941.

FOR

Rarity, desirability • Surprising body parts availability today • Others as for 1941 models

AGAINST

Some models virtually impossible to find • Plodding performance

SPECIFICATIONS

Length (in.) 196.0 **Wheelbase (in.)** 116.0
Weight (lbs.) 3070-3425 **Price (new)** $815-1095

ENGINES

cid/type	bore x stroke	bhp	years
216.5/L6	3.50×3.75	90	1942

PRICES/PROJECTION

Restorable $1000-1400 **Good** $2000-3000
Excellent $3300-6100 Add 300% for convertible; add 75-100% for wagon; add 20% for coupes **5-year projection** +5%

Chevrolet Fleetline 1946-48

PRODUCTION

1946 2d Aerosedan 57,932	**4d Sportmaster sedan** 7501
1947 2d Aerosedan 159,407	**4d Sportmaster sedan** 54,531
1948 2d Aerosedan 211,861	**4d Sportmaster sedan** 64,217

HISTORY

Chevy's top-line fastback and formal notchback sedans in warmed-over postwar guise. As with other models, grille became full width for 1947 and more "important" looking for '48. Production increased dramatically each year. The 1947-48 Aerosedan is still

1948 Fleetline 2-door Aerosedan

easy to find and swoopy-looking despite its age. A handful had wood side panels a la Chrysler Town & Country and Nash Suburban of the same years. However, this was not factory equipment but a dealer installation.

FOR

Readily available • Extremely popular with collectors • Aerosedan's dramatic styling (more so with wood paneling)

AGAINST

Sportmaster's chunky looks • Both types fairly slow to appreciate

SPECIFICATIONS

Length (in.) 197.8 **Wheelbase (in.)** 116.0
Weight (lbs.) 3100-3240 **Price (new)** $1249-1492

ENGINES

cid/type	bore x stroke	bhp	years
216.5/L6	3.50×3.75	90	1946-48

PRICES/PROJECTION

Restorable $700-1500 **Good** $2000-3500
Excellent $3500-6000 Add 10% if wood paneled. Deduct 20% for Sportmaster **5-year projection** +10%

Chevrolet Fleetmaster 1946-48

1947 Fleetmaster 4-door sedan

PRODUCTION

1946 4d sedan 73,746 **2d sedan** 56,538 **coupe** 27,036 **convertible** 4508 **4d wagon** 804 **1947 4d sedan** 91,440 **2d sedan** 80,128 **coupe** 59,661 **convertible** 28,443 **4d wagon** 4912 **1948 4d sedan** 93,142 **2d sedan** 66,208 **coupe** 58,786 **convertible** 20,471 **4d wagon** 10,171

HISTORY

Postwar continuation of the basic 1942 design. Grille went to full width for 1947, became more ornate for '48. Because of its wide availability, attractive styling, and use of precision-type engine main bearings (formerly rough cut), the '48 is clearly more popular than the 1946-47 models. The styling was beginning to age, but these well-built Chevys were no less the quality cars they were in 1942.

FOR

Plentiful • Wide availability of body and mechanical parts • Strong club activity and interest

AGAINST

Commonplace by any yardstick • Slower to appreciate than the 1941-42 models

SPECIFICATIONS

Length (in.) 197.8 **Wheelbase (in.)** 116.0
Weight (lbs.) 3090-3465 **Price (new)** $1212-2013

ENGINES

cid/type	bore x stroke	bhp	years
216.5/L6	3.50×3.75	90	1946-48

PRICES/PROJECTION

Restorable $750-1500 **Good** $1200-3200
Excellent $3000-7000 Add 100% for convertible; and 75% for wagon **5-year projection** +10%

Chevrolet Fleetline DeLuxe 1949-52

1950 Fleetline DeLuxe 2-door sedan

PRODUCTION

1949 4d sedan 130,323		**2d sedan** 180,251	
1950 4d sedan 124,187		**2d sedan** 189,509	
1951 4d sedan 57,693		**2d sedan** 131,910	
1952 2d sedan 37,164			

HISTORY

Here's a car almost everybody's missed, the last of the "torpedo" Chevys. Look at one from the rear three-quarters and you may do a double-take, for there is a close similarity here to the fabulous Bentley R-type Continental. (Or was the Continental a copy of the Chevy? We doubt it, but some buffs insist it was.) Both the 2- and 4-door models are truly elegant but have been overlooked by collectors and so could be an inexpensive yet worthy addition to your garage. Built with all the Swiss-watch quality for which Chevy was noted at the time, and trimmed with the best the make had to offer. If you have a choice, the '51 two-door with its more nicely integrated grille would be the one to take.

FOR

Low asking prices •Fine construction quality •Rakish good looks

AGAINST

A "sleeper"—slow appreciation seems certain

SPECIFICATIONS

Length (in.) 197.0-197.8 **Wheelbase (in.)** 115.0
Weight (lbs.) 3095-3155 **Price (new)** $1482-1707

ENGINES

cid/type	bore x stroke	bhp	years
216.5/L6	3.50×3.75	90/92	1949-52
235.5/L6	3.56×3.94	105	1950-52

PRICES/PROJECTION

Restorable $500-1500 **Good** $1800-2200 **Excellent** $2500-5000
5-year projection +10%

Chevrolet Styleline DeLuxe 1949-52

1949 Styleline DeLuxe 4-door sedan

PRODUCTION

1949 4d sedan 191,357 **2d sedan** 147,347 **coupe** 78,785
convertible 32,392 **4d wagon** 9348
1950 4d sedan 316,412 **2d sedan** 248,567 **coupe** 81,536
convertible 32,810 **4d wagon** 166,995
1951 4d sedan 380,270 **2d sedan** 262,933 **coupe** 64,976
convertible 20,172 **4d wagon** 23,586
1952 4d sedan 319,736 **2d sedan** 215,417 **coupe** 36,954
convertible 11,975 **4d wagon** 12,756

HISTORY

Harley Earl and company attended to Chevrolet's first postwar restyle after all other GM cars except Pontiac, so these two makes used prewar shells through 1948. But when change did come it was dramatic: the '49 Chevys were some of the best looking GM products ever, and were precision built as well. Power finally went up for 1950 with arrival of Powerglide two-speed automatic, for which the Chevy six was given increased displacement and 15 percent more

horsepower. Mundane then and now, the '49s nevertheless make a good choice for routine transportation, and a good, clean original will never lose its value.

FOR

Wide availability •1949 production includes 3342 very desirable wood-body wagons, the last of this type •High construction quality

AGAINST

Slow to appreciate in value •Ordinary by any standard

SPECIFICATIONS

Length (in.) 197.0-197.8 **Wheelbase (in.)** 115.0
Weight (lbs.) 3065-3485 **Price (new)** $1482-2297

ENGINES

cid/type	bore x stroke	bhp	years
216.5/L6	3.50×3.75	90/92	1949-52
235.5/L6	3.56×3.94	105	1950-52

PRICES/PROJECTION

Restorable $800-1800 **Good** $1800-3000
Excellent $3000-5100 **Add 75-100% for convertible**
5-year projection +10%

Chevrolet Styleline DeLuxe Bel Air 1950-52

1952 Styleline DeLuxe Bel Air 2-door hardtop

PRODUCTION

1950 76,662 **1951** 103,356 **1952** 74,634

HISTORY

Due to styling priorities favoring higher-priced GM makes, Chevy was a Johnny-come-lately to the hardtop ranks, though it beat both Ford and Plymouth by a year. The smoothly executed Bel Air had the standard GM treatment: a convertible-like deluxe interior, simulated top bows on the headliner, and a price just shy of the real convertible's. But buyers loved the hardtop Chevy. Sales shot up in 1951, only to drop when the industry lost momentum during the Korean War's opening stages.

1951 Styleline DeLuxe Bel Air 2-door hardtop

FOR

The best-looking, most interesting Chevy of these years • Very high quality for its class • Available Powerglide

AGAINST

Not much movement on the collector market • Poor performance

SPECIFICATIONS

Length (in.) 197.5-197.8 **Wheelbase (in.)** 115.0
Weight (lbs.) 3215-3225 **Price (new)** $1741-2206

ENGINES

cid/type	bore x stroke	bhp	years
216.5/L6	3.50×3.75	92	1950-52
235.5/L6	3.56×3.94	105	1950-52

PRICES/PROJECTION

Restorable $1000-2000 **Good** $2000-4000
Excellent $4000-8000 Add 10% for 1950 model
5-year projection +10%

Chevrolet Bel Air hardtop/convertible 1953-54

1953 Bel Air convertible

PRODUCTION

1953 convertible 24,047 **hardtop** 99,028
1954 convertible 19,333 **hardtop** 66,378

HISTORY

Another group of Chevys for the budget-minded collector. The 1953-54 models had transitional styling that was not as expertly drawn as that of 1949-52. Chevrolets grew shorter, wider, and taller and lacked their predecessor's purity of line, yet they were as well built as ever. Color started to enter the picture. Two-tones were commonplace, the contrasting color applied to a sweep panel on the rear fenders and, on hardtops, to the roof. Engine power took a jump in each year, though no V8 would be offered until 1955.

FOR

Easy on the wallet • Fairly easy to come by as a good number have survived • More colorful paint and interiors than before

AGAINST

Little collector interest • Less integrated styling

SPECIFICATIONS

Length (in.) 195.0-195.5 **Wheelbase (in.)** 115.0
Weight (lbs.) 3310-3470 **Price (new)** $2051-2185

ENGINES

cid/type	bore x stroke	bhp	years
235.5/L6	3.56×3.94	105/115	1953
235.5/L6	3.56×3.94	115/125	1954

PRICES/PROJECTION

HARDTOP **Restorable** $1000-2000 **Good** $2500-3500
Excellent $4000-6500. Add 10% for convertible.
5-year projection no change

Chevrolet Corvette 1953-55

1954 Corvette roadster

PRODUCTION

1953 300 **1954** 3640 **1955** 700

HISTORY

The first of Chevrolet's fiberglass bodied sports cars. Disappointing sales for these years nearly killed it after 1954. Helped tremendously in performance and sales appeal by new V-8 option for 1955 (fewer than a dozen six-cylinder models were built that year). Styling by GM Art & Colour under Harley Earl: a toothy grille, stone guards over inset headlamps, "twin pod" rear fenders, "rocketship" taillights. Powerglide two-speed automatic was standard; a 3-speed manual was offered late in '55. The first-generation cars were considered boulevardiers though they did handle reasonably well and the modified "Stovebolt" six delivered good power for its size.

FOR

Very scarce, for obvious reasons ● High collector demand, with extremely strong appreciation potential ● Adequate performance ● Large club following ● Historical interest

AGAINST

Expensive ● Mixed reputation among non-Corvette owners ● Questionable styling ● Indifferent fit and finish

SPECIFICATIONS

Length (in.) 167.0 **Wheelbase (in.)** 102.0
Weight (lbs.) 2650-2705 **Price (new)** $2799-3513

ENGINES

cid/type	bore x stroke	bhp	years
235.5/L6	3.56×3.94	150	1953-55
265/ohv V8	3.75×3.00	195	1955

PRICES/PROJECTION

1953 Restorable $10,000-20,000 **Good** $20,000-30,000
Excellent $30,000-40,000 **1954 Restorable** $8000-12,000
Good $14,000-20,000 **Excellent** $20,000-28,000
1955 Restorable $9000-14,000 **Good** $15,000-22,000
Excellent $25,000-30,000 Add 15% for 1955 factory 3-speed
transmission **5-year projection** +15%

Chevrolet Bel Air (exc. wagons) 1955-57

1956 Bel Air 4-door Sport Sedan

PRODUCTION

1955 4d sedan 345,372 **2d sedan** 168,313
2d hardtop 185,562 **convertible** 41,292
1956 4d sedan 269,798 **2d sedan** 104,849
4d hardtop 103,602 **2d hardtop** 128,382
convertible 41,268 **1957 4d sedan** 254,331
2d sedan 62,751 **4d hardtop** 137,672 **2d hardtop** 166,426
convertible 47,562

HISTORY

Top-of-the-line "classic Chevy," and the most desirable standard Chevrolets on today's market. Outstanding styling, high-performance potential, and fine build quality have created a huge collector following. As with the downmarket models, Bel Air values vary considerably with year. The 1955s and '57s are more in demand than the 1956s. Interest apparently relates to original sales, and 1956 was not a record year for Detroit. Stylewise, the 1955 is the purest and finest; the '56 has a reasonable if ordinary facelift; the '57 is the boldest (a quality collectors either despise or

applaud). All mid-'50s Bel Airs are still very hot items, so time is of the essence. If you find one for sale and don't take it, rest assured someone else quickly will.

FOR

One of the most desirable collector cars around, and *the* collectible Chevy passenger car ● Classic styling ● Great V8 performance ● Tremendous investment

AGAINST

Styling gets busier each year ● Strong buyer competition for good ones now, so expect steep asking prices

SPECIFICATIONS

Length (in.) 195.6 (1955), 197.5 (1956), 200.0 (1957)
Wheelbase (in.) 115.0 **Weight (lbs.)** 3140-3409
Price (new) $1888-2511

ENGINES

cid/type	bore x stroke	bhp	years
235.5/ohv I6	3.56×3.94	123/136/140	1955-57
265/ohv V8	3.75×3.00	162-225	1955-56
283/ohv V8	3.88×3.00	185-283	1957

PRICES/PROJECTION

Restorable $2000-4000 **Good** $4000-6000
Excellent $8000-10,000 Add 100-150% for 2d hardtop or convertible, 25% for A/C, 15% for Power-Pak V8s, 50% for fuel-injected 1957 model. Deduct 20% for six
5-year projection +20%

Chevrolet Bel Air Nomad 1955-57

1955 Bel Air Nomad 2-door wagon

PRODUCTION

1955 8530 **1956** 8103 **1957** 6534

HISTORY

The prettiest station wagon ever, and the least practical. Only two doors and raked B-pillars made interior access clumsy, especially to the rear. Slanted tailgate was subject to rain leaks and consequent rust. Sales never lived up to expectations, and Chevy dropped the model (but not the name) after 1957. But there's no way to fault the superb looks, especially in 1955 form. Low production guarantees the Nomad's continued collector appeal and high appreciation potential.

FOR

Perhaps the most desirable 1955-57 Chevy ● Large following in National Nomad Club ● Sure-fire appreciation ● Show car styling ● Performance

AGAINST

Expensive to buy now; some reproduction Nomad-only parts now available, but are quite costly (same for used and NOS) ● Leaks and rust around tailgate

SPECIFICATIONS

Length (in.) 197.1 (1955), 200.8 (1956), 202.8 (1957)
Wheelbase (in.) 115.0 **Weight (lbs.)** 3285-3465
Price (new) $2471-2757

ENGINES

cid/type	bore x stroke	bhp	years
235.5/ohv I6	3.56×3.94	123/136/140	1955-57
265/ohv V8	3.75×3.00	162-225	1955-56
283/ohv V8	3.88×3.00	185-283	1957

PRICES/PROJECTION

Restorable $2500-4000 **Good** $6000-10,000
Excellent $12,000-16,000 Add 25% for air conditioning, 15% for Power-Pak V-8, 50% for fuel injection (1957). Deduct 20% for six. **5-year projection** +10%

Chevrolet One-Fifty (exc. wagons) 1955-57

1957 One-Fifty 2-door Utility sedan

PRODUCTION

1955 4d sedan 29,898 **2d sedan** 66,416
Utility sedan 11,196 **1956 4d sedan** 51,544
2d sedan 82,384 **Utility sedan** 9879
1957 4d sedan 52,266 **2d sedan** 70,774 **Utility sedan** 8300

HISTORY

Bottom-of-the-line doesn't mean undesirable when it comes to mid-'50s Chevys. Excellent styling and V8 engines offering up to 1 hp per cubic inch by 1957 make even the plain-Jane One Fiftys definite collector's items. But you've got to have the "right" equipment, which usually means a hairy engine and stick shift. Chevrolet offered a wide assortment of engine tunes and two different V8 displacements, and even the milder versions provide sparkling performance. All Chevys in these years are the right size, too—not

too small for six passengers, not too big to get out of their own way. The two-door Utility sedan is too bare, the four-door too "practical." We'd take the standard 1957 two-door with a 283 V8, a leadfoot's temptation if ever there were one.

FOR

Priced less than corresponding 210s and Bel Airs ● Broad powerplant choice ● Exceptional styling ● Readily available parts

AGAINST

Spartan interiors ● Minimal flash (though that's not all bad)

SPECIFICATIONS

Length (in.) 195.6 (1955), 197.5 (1956), 200.0 (1957)
Wheelbase (in.) 115.0 **Weight (lbs.)** 3070-3236
Price (new) $1593-2048

ENGINES

cid/type	bore x stroke	bhp	years
235.5/ohv I6	3.56×3.94	123/136/140	1955-57
265/ohv V8	3.75×3.00	162-225	1955-57
283/ohv V8	3.88×3.00	185-283	1957

PRICES/PROJECTION

Restorable $600-1200 **Good** $1000-2000
Excellent $2700-6000 Add 25% for A/C, 15% for Power-Pak V8s, 50% for fuel-injected 1957 model. Deduct 20% for six
5-year projection +10%

Chevrolet Two-Ten (exc. wagons) 1955-57

1957 Two-Ten 4-door sedan

PRODUCTION

1955 4d sedan 317,724 **2d sedan** 249,105
2d hardtop 11,675 **Delray coupe** 115,584
1956 4d sedan 283,125 **2d sedan** 205,545
4d hardtop 20,021 **2d hardtop** 18,616
Delray coupe 56,382 **1957 4d sedan** 260,401
2d sedan 162,090 **4d hardtop** 16,178 **2d hardtop** 22,631
Delray coupe 25,644

HISTORY

Midrange series in the enormously popular 1955-57 Chevy lineup, boasting a higher trim standard than the One-Fifty but less sparkle than the Bel Air. The latter had more appeal when new, and does today. The sporty Two-Tens are more affordable than their Bel Air counterparts, however, and offer the same attractive styling, features, and performance. Fewer were sold new, so fewer are around now. Though Chevy's full range of engines was available, most Two-Tens were equipped for workaday duty only.

FOR

Cheaper than Bel Air • Hardtops quite rare • Lovely looks • Parts plentiful • Reasonable appreciation potential

AGAINST

Far behind Bel Air in collector esteem • Few equipped with performance engines or exotic accessories (though it's easy to add both)

SPECIFICATIONS

Length (in.) 195.6 (1955), 197.5 (1956), 200.0 (1957)
Wheelbase (in.) 115.0   **Weight (lbs.)** 3130-3320
Price (new) $1775-2270

ENGINES

cid/type	bore x stroke	bhp	years
232.5/ohv I6	3.56×3.94	123/136/140	1955-57
265/ohv V8	3.75×3.00	162-225	1955-57
283/ohv V8	3.88×3.00	185-283	1957

PRICES/PROJECTION

Restorable $1200-2400 **Good** $3000-4800
Excellent $4800-7200 Add 150% for hardtop, 400% for convertible, 25% for air conditioning, 15% for Power-Pak V-8, 50% for fuel injection (1957). Deduct 10% for 1956 model, 5% for 1957 model, 20% for six. **5-year projection** +10%

Chevrolet Corvette 1956-57

1956 Corvette convertible

PRODUCTION

1956 3467   **1957** 6339

HISTORY

A dramatic improvement on the first-generation 'Vette. More rakish, better integrated styling featured concave bodyside sculpture, semi-frenched taillights, optional hardtop, neater front end. Chevy made V8 engine standard, and had various optional stages of tune ranging up to the 283 bhp fuel-injected 283 for '57. Fine performance and aggressive good looks. Literally saved Corvette from an early demise, so this is an historic car apart from its other virtues.

1956 Corvette with optional hardtop

FOR

Prime investment, especially the fuelie • Good all-around roadability on straights or curves • Better weather protection • Roll-up windows and hardtop • Styling • Rust-free body

AGAINST

Expensive today • High-performance models can cost a bundle to maintain • Can be overpowered and underbraked, depending on equipment

SPECIFICATIONS

Length (in.) 168.0   **Wheelbase (in.)** 102.0
Weight (lbs.) 2730-2764   **Price (new)** $3149-3465

ENGINES

cid/type	bore x stroke	bhp	years
265/ohv V8	3.75×3.00	225	1956
283/ohv V8	3.88×3.00	220-283	1957

PRICES/PROJECTION

Restorable $5000-8000 **Good** $10,000-17,500
Excellent $19,000-25,000 Add $1000 for twin four-barrel carbs, $1500 for factory hardtop, $3000-4000 for fuel injection.
5-year projection +10%

Chevrolet Bel Air Impala 1958

1958 Bel Air Impala 2-door Sport Coupe

PRODUCTION

2d hardtop 43,000   **convertible** 17,000 (approx.)

HISTORY

The 1958 Chevrolets used an all-new, one-year-only bodyshell (body sharing with other GM divisions began with the 1959 model year). The '58s were longer, lower, wider, and heavier than the 1955-57s. Styled in the Harley Earl idiom, they were "round" where their predecessors had been "straight." Though not as important as the "classic" Chevys, they expressed commendable restraint in an era of tailfin excesses, and were solidly built. The limited-production Impala, a package option for the Bel Air hardtop and convertibles, featured special trim, deluxe interiors, and the steepest price in the lineup. A good reception caused Chevy to expand Impala offerings into a separate series for '59.

FOR

Smooth if somewhat bulky styling • Good performance • Luxurious for a Chevy

AGAINST

Far less recognition than 1955-57 models • 348 V8 addicted to gasoline • Handling sacrificed to smooth ride

SPECIFICATIONS

Length (in.) 209.1 **Wheelbase (in.)** 117.5
Weight (lbs.) 3458-3523 **Price (new)** $2586-2841

ENGINES

cid/type	bore x stroke	bhp	years
235.5/ohv I6	3.56×3.94	145	1958
283/ohv V8	3.88×3.00	185/230/250	1958
348/ohv V8	4.13×3.25	250/280	1958

PRICES/PROJECTION

Restorable $2000-4000 **Good** $5000-7500
Excellent $6500-9000 Add 15% for convertible.
5-year projection 10%

Chevrolet Corvette 1958-60

1959 Corvette convertible

PRODUCTION

1958 9168 **1959** 9670 **1960** 10,261

HISTORY

A bulkier extension of the 1956-57 Corvette design, with rather more ornate styling based on previous themes. Increased use of aluminum on the 1960 models, which also featured a new rear anti-sway bar to improve handling. A Corvette running under the Briggs Cunningham colors finished eighth overall at the 1960 Le-Mans 24-Hour race. A washboard hood (simulated louvers) and twin decklid chrome strips identified the '58; the '59 and '60 were shorn of these doo-dads, and look almost identical to one another. Redesigned cockpit featured new dash with all gauges grouped in a cluster directly ahead of the driver plus a passenger grab bar.

FOR

Good value appreciation • Somewhat less expensive than 1956-57 models • Sizzling performance • Much improved handling

AGAINST

Busy styling (the quad lights don't look happy) • Needless chrome on the '58

SPECIFICATIONS

Length (in.) 177.2 **Wheelbase (in.)** 102.0
Weight (lbs.) 2793-2840 **Price (new)** $3631-3934

ENGINES

cid/type	bore x stroke	bhp	years
283/ohv V8	3.88×3.00	230-315	1958-60

PRICES/PROJECTION

Restorable $1000-9000 **Good** $9000-14,000
Excellent $14,000-22,000 **5-year projection** +10%

Chevrolet Corvair Monza 1960-64

1964 Corvair Monza coupe

PRODUCTION

1960 coupe 11,926	**1961 coupe** 109,945	**4d sedan** 33,745
1962 coupe 144,844	**convertible** 13,995	**4d sedan** 48,059
1963 coupe 117,917	**convertible** 36,693	**4d sedan** 31,120
1964 coupe 88,440	**convertible** 31,045	**4d sedan** 21,926

HISTORY

Introduced midway through the 1960 model year, the sporty Monza coupe pushed Corvair sales upward dramatically. Before then, Chevy's compact with the aircooled rear mounted flat six had not sold well against the very conventional Ford Falcon. Monza quickly revealed an untapped market for bucket seat compacts with deluxe interiors and, preferably, stick shifts. Chevrolet quickly brought out a convertible version, and began offering performance options (better brakes, handling packages, and more horsepower). A solid hit, Monza was the best-selling Corvair by 1961, and would remain so right up to the end in 1969.

FOR

Trend setter • Affordable today • Nice styling • Deluxe interiors • Milestone

CHEVROLET

AGAINST

Twitchy handling on pre-1963 models (tire pressures critical) • Oil leaks • Tends to rust • Indifferent assembly quality

SPECIFICATIONS

Length (in.) 180.0 **Wheelbase (in.)** 108.0
Weight (lbs.) 2280-2555 **Price (new)** $2238-2492

ENGINES

cid/type	bore x stroke	bhp	years
140/ohv flat 6	3.38×2.60	80/95	1960
145/ohv flat 6	3.44×2.60	80/98	1961-63
164/ohv flat 6	3.44×2.94	95/110	1964

PRICES/PROJECTION

Restorable $1000-1500 **Good** $1000-2000
Excellent $3000-5000 Add 35% for convertible, 10% for 1960 model. **5-year projection** +10%

Chevrolet Corvette 1961-62

1962 Corvette convertible

PRODUCTION

1961 10,939   **1962** 14,531

HISTORY

The 1958-60 Corvette, mildly "facelifted" with Bill Mitchell's ducktail rear end first shown on the racing Stingray and the XP-700 show car. Increased performance from new 327 V8 for the 1962, which also de-emphasized the bodyside cove sculpture and had a blacked-out grille. Both models retained quad headlamps but used a simplified mesh grille without previous 'Vettes' trademark teeth. Corvette won the SCCA's A-production championship in 1962.

FOR

Neater rear end styling • Significant performance boost on '62s • Last of the third-generation design

AGAINST

Same bulky frontal look • Fuel thirst

SPECIFICATIONS

Length (in.) 176.7 **Wheelbase (in.)** 102.0
Weight (lbs.) 2905-2925 **Price (new)** $3934-4038

ENGINES

cid/type	bore x stroke	bhp	years
283/ohv V8	3.88×3.00	230-315	1961
327/ohv V8	4.00×3.25	250-360	1962

PRICES/PROJECTION

Restorable $3000-7000 **Good** $8000-12,000
Excellent $12,000-18,000 Add 10% for 1962 model, $1000 each for fuel injection or factory hardtop. **5-year projection** +15%

Chevrolet Corvair 500 Lakewood 1961

1961 Corvair 500 Lakewood 4-door wagon

PRODUCTION

5591

HISTORY

The stripped version of the Corvair wagon, with the same general qualities of the midrange 700-series model but a plainer, cheaper interior. The only year for the wagon in this trim level. Like 700 models, wagon styling was derived from that of the original Corvair sedan.

FOR

As for 700 Lakewood, plus rarity and one-year model status

AGAINST

As for 700 Lakewood • Little collector interest

SPECIFICATIONS

Length (in.) 180.0 **Wheelbase (in.)** 108.0 **Weight (lbs.)** 2530
Price (new) $2266

ENGINES

cid/type	bore x stroke	bhp	years
145/ohv flat 6	3.44×2.60	80/98	1961

PRICES/PROJECTION

Restorable $500-1000 **Good** $1000-2000
Excellent $2500-3500 **5-year projection** no change

Chevrolet Corvair 700 Lakewood/wagon 1961-62

1962 Corvair 700 4-door wagon

PRODUCTION

1961 20,451   **1962** 3716

HISTORY

Before the Monza coupe started selling so spectacularly, Chevy's marketing plan for Corvair called for practical vehicles for the second model year. That included these wagons (called Lakewood only for 1961). The Monza's image rubbed off on this little hauler, making it a sort of sport wagon. With a stick shift and various aftermarket performance and handling accessories, it could be exactly that. The pancake six allowed a flat, though high, cargo bed and the basic Corvair styling suited the wagon body style well. Not important historically, but a car with great character and potential appeal to collectors, especially those who need something distinctive for carrying loads to flea markets.

FOR

Good looks ● Scarcity ● Very affordable ● Low operating costs

AGAINST

The usual early Corvair problems (oversteer, oil leaks, rust) ● Mundane interior ● Wagons dropped before the advent of factory performance options, unfortunately

SPECIFICATIONS

Length (in.) 180.0   **Wheelbase (in.)** 108.0
Weight (lbs.) 2555-2590   **Price (new)** $2331-2407

ENGINES

cid/type	bore x stroke	bhp	years
145/ohv flat 6	3.44×2.60	80/98	1961-62

PRICES/PROJECTION

Restorable $1000-1500 **Good** $1500-2500
Excellent $2500-4000 **5-year projection** +10%

Chevrolet Impala Super Sport V8 1961-64

1963 Impala Super Sport 2-door hardtop

PRODUCTION

1961 453   **1962** approx. 100,000   **1963** 153,271
1964 185,325   **With 409 engine 1961** 142   **1962** 15,091

HISTORY

The sporty compact concept applied to the full-size Chevrolet; worked remarkably well. Sixes were available for 1962-64 though not many were built. SS equipment, introduced mid-1961, was available only for the top-line Impala. The V8 hardtop and convertible are the center of collector interest today. The Chevy 283/327 offered a good combination of power and efficiency, while the big-block (348 in 1961, 409 in 1961-64) provided neck-snapping performance. The typical SS also had handling and brake options and 3- or 4-speed manual gearbox besides regular items like bucket seats, console, and deluxe interior. Big, but more competent on twisty back roads than many sports car drivers suspect.

FOR

Still relatively inexpensive ● Perhaps the next hot collector items after 1955-57 ● Crisp styling ● High performance ● Reproduction parts available

AGAINST

All the faults with which big cars have been cursed for so long ● Fuel thirst ● Indifferent construction quality

SPECIFICATIONS

Length (in.) 209.3-210.4   **Wheelbase (in.)** 119.0
Weight (lbs.) NA   **Price (new)** approx. $3,000
(1961) $3200 (1964) with base engines

1964 Impala Super Sport 2-door hardtop

ENGINES

cid/type	bore x stroke	bhp	years
283/ohv V8	3.88×3.00	170-195	1962-64
327/ohv V8	4.00×3.25	250/300	1962-64
348/ohv V8	4.13×3.25	205/340/350	1961
409/ohv V8	4.31×3.50	340-425	1961-64

PRICES/PROJECTION

Restorable $500-1500 **Good** $1500-3000
Excellent $4000-7000 Add 50% for convertible
5-year projection +10%

Chevrolet Corvair Monza Spyder 1962-64

1963 Corvair Monza Spyder convertible

PRODUCTION

1962 coupe 6894	**convertible** 2574	**1963 coupe** 11,627
convertible 7472	**1964 coupe** 6480	**convertible** 4761

HISTORY

Chevy's "other" sports car in the early '60s, with a big increase in power over other Corvairs from a carefully engineered turbo-supercharger. Strong performance, multi-gauge instrumentation set in a brushed aluminum panel, numerous handling and sports accessories, and a choice of coupe or convertible made the Spyder an ideal domestic alternative to the cramped and uncomfortable low-bucks foreign sports cars of the period. Unfortunately, it was introduced right as Corvair sales peaked, and its relatively high base price and mechanical complexity kept sales modest.

FOR

The most desirable pre-1965 Corvair (especially the convertible) ● Good parts supplies (except for blower) ● Outstanding performance and handling

AGAINST

Not the "poor man's Porsche" some claimed it to be ● Difficult to find in an unmodified state ● Blower parts may prove scarce

SPECIFICATIONS

Length (in.) 180.0   **Wheelbase (in.)** 108.0
Weight (lbs.) 2440-2650   **Price (new)** $2589-2811

ENGINES

cid/type	bore x stroke	bhp	years
145/ohv flat 6	3.55×2.60	150	1962-63
164/ohv flat 6	3.44×2.94	150	1964

PRICES/PROJECTION

Restorable $1250-1750 **Good** $2250-3000
Excellent $3500-4000 Add 50% for convertible; add 10% for 1964 models **5-year projection** +10%

Chevrolet Corvair Monza wagon 1962

1962 Corvair Monza 4-door wagon

PRODUCTION

2362

HISTORY

The most desirable—and scarcest—Corvair wagon. Had the full Monza treatment: full carpeting, bucket seats, color-keyed upholstery. Most often found with automatic transmission, sad to say, which makes manual models that much more highly prized. Like most sporty wagons, not very popular new, as indeed were all Corvair wagons, which lived for only two model years.

FOR

The best buy and highest investment potential among Corvair wagons ● Others as for 1961-62 700 models ● Monza trim and equipment

AGAINST

Extremely rare ● Likely to command fairly stiff price if the owner knows it

SPECIFICATIONS

Length (in.) 180.0   **Wheelbase (in.)** 108.0   **Weight (lbs.)** 2590
Price (new) $2569

ENGINES

cid/type	bore x stroke	bhp	years
145/ohv flat 6	3.44×2.60	80/102	1962

PRICES/PROJECTION

Restorable $1500-2500 **Good** $3000-4000
Excellent $4000-5000 **5-year projection** +10%

Chevrolet Chevy II Nova Super Sport 1963-67

1963 Chevy II Nova Super Sport 2-door hardtop

PRODUCTION

1963 42,432   **1964** 10,576   **1965** 9100   **1966** 21,000
1967 10,100

HISTORY

The compact Falcon-beater wasn't immediately seen as a candidate for the SS treatment, but with the rapid expansion in high-performance small cars Chevrolet offered a bucket-seat SS package for the 1963 Chevy II Nova. These were all six-cylinder cars; a factory V8 didn't appear until 1964. The latter made this humdrum compact quite a stormer, and won it enthusiastic, if limited, appreciation by performance buyers in its day. Unfortunately, Chevy couldn't get this act completely together. The convertible disappeared after 1963, before the factory V8 was offered, and the 1966-67 facelift was clumsy. Nevertheless, the V8 versions in the last two years of this generation are highly prized today.

FOR

Low-priced ●1963 and 1966-67 models in fairly good supply at present ●Still contemporary in size ●Light and fast

AGAINST

Not yet a prime collectible ● Fit and finish debatable ● Big-engine models overpowered for brakes, suspension

SPECIFICATIONS

Length (in.) 183.0-184.7   **Wheelbase (in.)** 110.0
Weight (lbs.) approx. 2600-2870   **Price (new)** $2430-2487 (six); approx. $2500 (base V-8 hardtop)

ENGINES

cid/type	bore x stroke	bhp	years
194/ohv I6	3.56×3.25	120	1963-67
230/ohv I6	3.88×3.25	140/155	1964-66
250/ohv I6	3.88×3.53	155	1967
283/ohv V8	3.88×3.00	195/220	1964-67
327/ohv V8	4.00×3.25	250-350	1964-67

PRICES/PROJECTION

Restorable $1000-2000 **Good** $2000-4000
Excellent $4500-6000 Add 20% for convertible, 25% for 350-bhp V8 (1966). **5-year projection** +10%

Chevrolet Corvette Sting Ray Coupe 1963-67

1965 Corvette Sting Ray coupe

PRODUCTION

1963 10,594   **1964** 8304   **1965** 8186   **1966** 9958   **1967** 8504

HISTORY

A genuine grand touring car in every sense of the word, nicely hung together with a vast range of drivetrain options. One of the best styling efforts of the decade, the '63 in particular by virtue of its split rear window (stylist Bill Mitchell felt that deleting it on the '64 "spoiled the whole car"). No changes to the engine lineup for 1963, but rear suspension was now a three-link independent setup with a single transverse leaf spring. Styling became generally cleaner in successive years. The shortest-lived Corvette design, and probably the most sought-after apart from the 1953-57 models.

FOR

One of Chevrolet's greats, with high historical significance ●Tremendous investment potential ●Outstanding ride, handling, performance

AGAINST

Commands high prices today

SPECIFICATIONS

Length (in.) approx. 175.5   **Wheelbase (in.)** 98.0
Weight (lbs.) 2859-3000   **Price (new)** $4252-4353

ENGINES

cid/type	bore x stroke	bhp	years
327/ohv V8	4.00×3.25	250-365	1963-67
396/ohv V8	4.09×3.76	425	1965
427/ohv V8	4.25×3.76	390-435	1966-67

1965 Corvette Sting Ray coupe

PRICES/PROJECTION

Restorable $4000-8000 **Good** $10,000-15,000
Excellent $15,000-22,000 Add 10% each for 1963 model,
396/427 V8s, $500 for air, $1000 for knock-off wheels, $2500 for
fuel injection. **5-year projection** +15%

Chevrolet Corvette Sting Ray convertible 1963-67

1964 Corvette Sting Ray convertible

PRODUCTION

1963 10,919   **1964** 13,925   **1965** 15,376   **1966** 17,762
1967 14,436

HISTORY

Convertible counterpart to the Sting Ray coupe, with the same
stunning appearance and blistering performance. Larger and more
powerful engines including the big-block Mark IV unit beginning
with 1965, which was the last year for the fuel-injection small-block
V8. Offered like earlier Corvette roadsters with optional lift-off
hardtop. Shares Sting Ray coupe's independent rear suspension
and interior design with interesting "twin cowl" dash.

FOR

Less important than coupe, but still highly desirable ●Open-air
allure with Sting Ray looks, go ●Roadability

AGAINST

Expensive now, like coupe

SPECIFICATIONS

Length (in.) 175.5 **Wheelbase (in.)** 98.0
Weight (lbs.) 2881-3020 **Price (new)** $4037-4141

1964 Corvette Sting Ray convertible

ENGINES

cid/type	bore x stroke	bhp	years
327/ohv V8	4.00×3.25	250-375	1963-67
396/ohv V8	4.09×3.75	425	1965
427/ohv V8	4.25×3.76	390-435	1966-67

PRICES/PROJECTION

Deduct 10% from Sting Ray coupe prices.
5-year projection +30%

Chevrolet Chevelle Malibu SS V8 1964-67

1964 Chevelle Super Sport 2-door hardtop

PRODUCTION

1964 76,860   **1965** 101,577 (201 SS396s)
1966 72,300 (all SS396)   **1967** 63,000 (all SS396)   (Figures
include sixes)

HISTORY

Chevrolet's attractive intermediate Super Sport, introduced with the
new 1964 Chevelle line as a special series of six-cylinder (not
widely collected) and V8 hardtop coupes and convertibles. GM
policy at the time prohibited engines over 400 cid from being used
in anything smaller than standard-size cars save Corvettes, but the
396 option for 1966 and the maximum-power 327s before it gave
dazzling pickup in the lighter Chevelle shell.

FOR

Crisp, clean styling ●Reasonable overall size ●Less costly than
comparable Impala SS ●Excellent roadability

AGAINST

Limited collector recognition to date ●Some body parts scarce now
●Big-engine models predictably gas-hungry

SPECIFICATIONS

Length (in.) 197.0 **Wheelbase (in.)** 115.0
Weight (lbs.) 3000-3485 **Price (new)** $2646-3033 (with
base V8)

ENGINES

cid/type	bore x stroke	bhp	years
283/ohv V8	3.88×3.00	195/220	1964-65
327/ohv V8	4.00×3.25	250/300/350	1964-65
396/ohv V8	4.09×3.76	325-375	1966-67

PRICES/PROJECTION

Restorable $1000-1500 **Good** $1500-3000
Excellent $4000-7000 Add 25% for convertible
5-year projection +20%

Chevrolet Corvair Corsa 1965-66

1965 Corvair Corsa 2-door hardtop

PRODUCTION

1965 coupe 20,291 **convertible** 8353 **1966 coupe** 7330
convertible 3142

HISTORY

All the good points of the 1962-64 Monza Spyder, plus the sensational styling of the second Corvair generation, and even more horsepower. The standard unblown 140-bhp flat 6 delivered fine getaway, but the turbocharged version was now up 20 percent in output, and could deliver 115 mph tops and an 18-second quarter-mile time. This was perhaps the most sophisticated (certainly one of the most ambitious) cars ever to come from Detroit: gobs of power, world-class handling, and looks that simply couldn't be better.

FOR

The most desirable Corvair •High appreciation guaranteed

AGAINST

As for Monza Spyder

SPECIFICATIONS

Length (in.) 183.3 **Wheelbase (in.)** 108.0
Weight (lbs.) 2475-2720 **Price (new)** $2519-2665

1966 Corvair Corsa convertible

ENGINES

cid/type	bore x stroke	bhp	years
164/ohv flat 6	3.44×2.94	140/180	1965-66

PRICES/PROJECTION

Restorable $1000-1750 **Good** $2250-3000
Excellent $3000-$4000 Add 25% for convertible, 10% for 1966 models, 10% for turbocharger **5-year projection** +50%

Chevrolet Corvair Monza 1965-69

1967 Corvair Monza 4-door hardtop

PRODUCTION

1965 2d hardtop 88,954 **4d hardtop** 37,157
convertible 26,466 **1966 2d hardtop** 37,605
4d hardtop 12,497 **convertible** 10,345
1967 2d hardtop 9771 **4d hardtop** 3157 **convertible** 2109
1968 2d hardtop 6807 **convertible** 1386
1969 2d hardtop 2717 **convertible** 521

HISTORY

A design triumph from the Bill Mitchell studios. Ironically destined to slip away because of too-strong competition from the conventional but very attractive Mustang, and because of bad publicity about handling problems of the 1960-63 Corvairs. The first postwar American car (other than Corvette) with fully independent rear suspension via upper and lower control arms and coil springs (even Corvette lacked the latter), which banished handling ills completely. Remains underappreciated and underrated today, but certain to be regarded more highly in the future. The kind of cars we should have had in the 1970s, and didn't.

FOR

Styling •Sophisticated ride and roadability from all-independent suspension •Still affordable •Great fun to drive

AGAINST

Post-1967 models, though rare, suffer driveability problems as stiffer emission controls took effect •Can rust unless properly cared for

SPECIFICATIONS

Length (in.) 183.3 **Wheelbase (in.)** 108.0
Weight (lbs.) 2440-2770 **Price (new)** $2347-2641

ENGINES

cid/type	bore x stroke	bhp	years
164/ohv flat 6	3.44×2.94	95/110/140	1965-69

PRICES/PROJECTION

Restorable $700-1200 **Good** $1500-2000
Excellent $3000-4500 Add 30% for convertible, 10% for 1969 models. Deduct 10% for 4d hardtop **5-year projection** +10%

Chevrolet Impala Super Sport V8 1965-69

1966 Impala Super Sport convertible

PRODUCTION

1965 243,114 **1966** 119,314 **1967** 76,055 (2124 SS427)
1968 38,210 (1778 SS427) **1969** 2455 (all SS427)

HISTORY

The SS edition of the larger, more ponderous full-size Chevy introduced for 1965. The separate Impala SS series vanished for 1968-69, and the equipment reverted to option status, just as in 1961. The 1969 model was officially designated the Impala SS427. As with earlier models, interest centers mainly on the V8 cars. Six-cylinder versions were offered through '68, but were really a contradiction in terms. "Hi-po" big Chevy production tapered off rapidly after 1965, and was only a fraction of division output by the end of the decade.

FOR

Less costly than pre-1965 models ●Later editions quite rare ●High performance for the period ●Luxury interior ●SS427 may be a sleeper

AGAINST

Bulky, big, and (to many eyes) indifferently styled ●Low mileage ●Limited collector recognition

SPECIFICATIONS

Length (in.) 213.2 (1966-67), 214.7 (1968), 215.9 (1969)
Wheelbase (in.) 119.0 **Weight (lbs.)** 3570-3835
Price (new) $2950-3650 (base engine)

ENGINES

cid/type	bore x stroke	bhp	years
283/ohv V8	3.88×3.00	195/220	1965-67
307/ohv V8	3.88×3.25	200	1968
327/ohv V8	4.00×3.25	250-350	1965-68
396/ohv V8	4.09×3.76	325	1966-68
427/ohv V8	4.25×3.76	385/390/425	1966-69

PRICES/PROJECTION

Restorable $1500-2500 **Good** $2500-4000
Excellent $4000-5500 Add 50% for convertible, 30% for SS427.
5-year projection +10%

Chevrolet Camaro 1967-69

1967 Camaro Sport coupe

PRODUCTION

1967 total six 58,808	**total V8** 162,109	**Z-28 (V8)** 602
1968 total six 50,937	**total V8** 184,178	**Z-28 (V8)** 7199
1969 total six 65,008	**total V8** 178,087	**Z-28 (V8)** 19,014

HISTORY

Chevrolet's answer to the Mustang, offering a similarly long and detailed options sheet. An early ponycar that can still be satisfying in everyday use. Clean styling (GM's interpretation of the long-hood/short-deck Mustang theme) and practical size in hardtop or convertible models. And don't forget the formidable Z-28, which went on to become champion of SCCA's Trans-Am "sedan" series. High production and that plethora of extra-cost equipment makes hunting for a specific first-generation Camaro time-consuming but interesting. Very limited production makes the '67 Z-28 the prize pick in these years; naturally, it will cost the most.

FOR

Tremendous appreciation potential ●Strong collector and club interest ●Good performance ●Tidy package size ●Many reproduction parts now available

AGAINST

Variable assembly quality ●Cramped in back ●Meager trunk space

SPECIFICATIONS

Length (in.) 184.7 **Wheelbase (in.)** 108.1
Weight (lbs.) 2770-3295 **Price (new)** $2466-5000

ENGINES

cid/type	bore x stroke	bhp	years
230/ohv I6	3.88×3.25	140	1967-68
250/ohv I6	3.88×3.53	155	1967-69
302/ohv V8	4.00×3.00	290	1967-69
327/ohv V8	4.00×3.25	210/275	1967-69
350/ohv V8	4.00×3.48	255/295/300	1967-69
396/ohv V8	4.09×3.76	325	1968-69
427/ohv V8	4.25×3.76	425	1969

PRICES/PROJECTION

HARDTOP **Restorable** $800-1200 **Good** $1500-2500
Excellent $3000-5500
CONVERTIBLE **Restorable** $1250-1850 **Good** $2000-5000
Excellent $5000-7000 Add 75% for Z-28, 15% for RS or SS
equipment; deduct 25% for sixes **5-year projection** +10%
(+75% for Z-28)

Chevrolet Chevelle SS396/SS454 1968-70

1968 Chevelle SS396 2-door hardtop

PRODUCTION

1968 62,785   **1969** 86,307   **1970** 53,599 (3733 SS454)

HISTORY

The hairiest of the intermediate Super Sport Chevelles, marketed despite increasingly stringent government regulations that discouraged high performance and, by 1970, a fading market. Continued through 1973, but were performance shadows of the late-'60s models and are far less collectible. Following division trends, styling was rounder and bulkier than in earlier years, but deluxe bucket-seat interiors and flashy paint and striping still set these Chevelles apart. (The 350-cid V8 was brought in for the '71, and the designation changed to Chevelle SS.)

FOR

Very high performance • Manageable size • Styling has held up reasonably well

AGAINST

Piggish at the pump • Slow to appreciate at present compared to other SS Chevys

SPECIFICATIONS

Length (in.) 197.1-200.9 **Wheelbase (in.)** 112.0
Weight (lbs.) 3550-3700 (approx.) **Price (new)** $2899-3200
(base V8)

ENGINES

cid/type	bore x stroke	bhp	years
396/ohv V8	4.09×3.76	325/350/375	1968-69
402/ohv V8	4.13×3.76	350/375	1970
454/ohv V8	4.25×4.00	360/450	1970

PRICES/PROJECTION

Restorable $1000-2000 **Good** $1000-3000
Excellent $3000-7000 Add 25-30% for convertible, 25-50% for SS454 **5-year projection** +15%

Chevrolet Chevy II/ Nova SS 1968-70

1968 Chevy II Nova SS 2-door coupe

PRODUCTION

1968 5571   **1969** 17,564   **1970** 19,558

HISTORY

Engineered alongside the 1967 Camaro, Chevrolet's second-series compact (the Chevy II name was officially dropped in favor of Nova after 1968) was offered with some of its hefty engines, including the big 396 with up to 375 bhp. But the Super Sport was reduced to an option package in these years, and was not the separate series it had been previously. The Nova SS continued to be listed as late as 1976, though as with Chevy's other performance models it was not the hell-for-leather machine we knew in the late '60s. Clean, if somewhat anonymous, styling in the then-current GM mold bore a familial relationship to the contemporary Chevelle. Modest production numbers make these high-powered coupe/sedans likely climbers on the collector-car value scale in the future.

FOR

A definite "comer" • Still affordable • Fairly scarce • Zip • Sedan practicality

AGAINST

Undistinguished sedan styling • Overpowered • Thirsty • Indifferent construction quality

SPECIFICATIONS

Length (in.) 189.4 **Wheelbase (in.)** 111.0
Weight (lbs.) 2995-3048 **Price (new)** approx. $2600 (350 V8)

ENGINES

cid/type	bore x stroke	bhp	years
350/ohv V8	4.00×3.48	295/300	1968-70
396/ohv V8	4.09×3.76	325/350/375	1968-69
402/ohv V8	4.13×3.76	350/375	1970

1970 Nova SS 2-door coupe

PRICES/PROJECTION

Restorable $350-750 **Good** $1000-1750
Excellent $2000-3500 **5-year projection** +10%

Chevrolet Corvette 1968-70

1969 Corvette Stingray 2-door coupe

PRODUCTION

1968 coupe 9936 **convertible** 18,630 **1969 coupe** 22,154
convertible 16,608 **1970 coupe** 10,668 **convertible** 6648

HISTORY

Rebodied successor to the 1963-67 Sting Ray with all-new styling (predicted by the Mako Shark II show car) by David Holls of the Chevrolet studio. Engines and chassis design carried over pretty much intact from 1967. No model designation for 1968, but it came back as one word (Stingray) on 1969 and subsequent models. Curiously enough, these gadget-filled 'Vettes were more highly regarded by Europeans than Americans, though the design certainly captivated buyers here. Sales were extraordinary, and the coupe outsold the previous top-selling roadster for the first time in 1969. Professionals view the styling as less distinctive than the Sting Ray's, yet it was good enough to be retained through 1982 with only minor adjustments to meet federal bumper regulations. The relatively free-breathing 1968-70 engines give these models a definite edge over later Corvettes for performance and collector appeal.

FOR

Show car styling • Tremendous go from big-block engines • Decent construction quality • Rot-free body (but not the chassis)

AGAINST

Appreciating more slowly than earlier Corvettes • Bulkier, less sporting to drive, too • Fuelishness • Cramped cabin

SPECIFICATIONS

Length (in.) 182.5 **Wheelbase (in.)** 98.0
Weight (lbs.) 3055-3196 **Price (new)** $4320-5192

ENGINES

cid/type	bore x stroke	bhp	years
327/ohv V8	4.00×3.25	350	1968
350/ohv V8	4.00×3.48	300/350/370	1969-70
427/ohv V8	4.25×3.76	400/430/435	1968-69
454/ohv V8	4.25×4.00	390/465	1970

PRICES/PROJECTION

Restorable $3000-6000 **Good** $6000-9000
Excellent $9000-12,000 Deduct 10% for 1969-70 models.
5-year projection +10%

Chevrolet Camaro 1970

1970 Camaro Sport Coupe

PRODUCTION

sixes 12,566 **V8s** 112,323 (including 8733 Z-28)

HISTORY

A stunning rework of the Chevrolet ponycar, and so good that this second generation would last a dozen years. Sad to say, the convertible body style was dropped; it would have looked stunning. Collector interest in Camaros thus far has generally been in the 1967-69s, but the 1970 and newer examples are certain to gain in appeal. At what model year the detuned engines of the '70s will take its toll on collectibility is unclear, but post-1970 cars were certainly not in the same performance league with earlier Camaros. Styling didn't suffer as much as on many other cars of the '70s, due to soft-nose facelifts (1974 and '78) that were skillfully blended with the basic 1970 body lines. As the first of the breed, however, the '70 is the one to have.

FOR

Still reasonably inexpensive • Landmark styling • High appreciation potential (particulary Z-28)

AGAINST

Bulkier than 1967-69 • High operating costs with big engines • Not half as roadable as it looks without proper suspension and brake options

SPECIFICATIONS

Length (in.) 188.0 **Wheelbase (in.)** 108.1
Weight (lbs.) 3076-3300 (approx.) **Price (new)** $2749-5000+;
average V8: $3500

ENGINES

cid/type	bore x stroke	bhp	years
250/ohv I6	3.88×3.53	155	1970
307/ohv V8	3.88×3.25	200	1970
350/ohv V8	4.00×3.48	250/300/360	1970
396/ohv V8	4.13×3.76	350/375	1970

PRICES/PROJECTION

Restorable $700-1000 **Good** $1000-3000
Excellent $3000-5000 **Add** 200% for Z-28
5-year projection +50%

Chevrolet Monte Carlo SS454 1970-71

1971 Monte Carlo SS454 2-door hardtop

PRODUCTION

1970 3823   **1971** 1919

HISTORY

Chevy's fling at a red-hot personal-luxury car. Introduced for 1970, the Monte Carlo was based on the intermediate Chevelle platform, but had a different roofline and the longest hood ever riveted onto a Chevy. Equipped with the mild 307 and 350 V8s, it offered luxury and smoothness, and was a solid sales hit. A few buyers checked RPO Z20 on the order form, however, and got the 360-bhp 454 big-block V8, square-tip dual exhausts, and a chassis fortified with automatic-level-control rear shocks, stiffer-than-stock front shocks, and power front disc brakes. Only discreet SS454 badges and thin black rocker panel accents gave a clue as to what was under the hood. Acceleration was vivid: 0-60 mph in 7.7 seconds, the quarter-mile in 16.2 seconds at 90-plus mph. A handful of non-standard options found their way onto SS Montes, too, such as the 450-bhp LS-6 engine and M-series four-speed manual gearbox (Turbo Hydra-matic was standard). The '71 rendition was little changed except for slightly bolder ornamentation and eye-catching Rally wheels. Altogether, a rare and interesting Chevy from the twilight years of the performance age. We predict it will ultimately be the highest appreciating investment among all Chevy's SS models.

FOR

A different sort of Chevy: an adult hot rod • Very fast • Subdued good looks • Good roadability • Cushy cabin • Low-production appeal • Sure-fire appreciator

AGAINST

A gas hog • Difficult to find now • Indifferent construction quality

SPECIFICATIONS

Length (in.) 205.8 **Wheelbase (in.)** 116.0 **Weight (lbs.)** 3600 (approx.) **Price (new)** $3543/3757 (approx.)

ENGINES

cid/type	bore x stroke	bhp	years
454/ohv V8	4.25×4.00	360/425/450	1970-71

PRICES/PROJECTION

Restorable $1000-2000 **Good** $2000-3500
Excellent $4000-6000 **5-year projection** +10%

Chevrolet Camaro Z-28 1971-72

1971 Camaro Z-28 Sport Coupe

PRODUCTION

1971 4862   **1972** 2575

HISTORY

Continuation of Chevy's beautifully styled second-generation ponycar in its sportiest guise. Little changed from the "1970½" version, except for new high-back bucket seats and various mechanical changes that marked the start of the performance decline going on throughout Detroit. Because Camaro wasn't spared GM's self-imposed, corporate-wide drop in compression ratios for '71 (along with the Corvette and Pontiac's Firebird), output of the Z's 350 V8 tumbled from 360 to 330 bhp gross. The following year, use of SAE net horsepower figures made for a more dramatic apparent drop, down to 255. Still, this was one mean machine, offering taut, assured handling combined with very brisk straightline pickup and nearly flawless appearance. The main reason these particular Camaros warrant inclusion is their low production. The '72s are particularly scarce, reflecting a crippling auto workers strike that shut down the Norwood, Ohio plant for 174 days.

FOR

As for 1970 Camaro, plus greater exclusivity

AGAINST

As for 1970 Camaro, plus lower Z-28 performance in these years

SPECIFICATIONS

Length (in.) 188.0 **Wheelbase (in.)** 108.1 **Weight (lbs.)** 3300
Price (new) $4000 (approx.)

ENGINES

cid/type	bore x stroke	bhp	years
350/ohv V8	4.00×3.48	275/255*	1971-72

*SAE net; rated at 330 bhp gross in 1971

PRICES/PROJECTION

Restorable $1500-2500 **Good** $3000-4500
Excellent $5000-7500 **5-year projection** +20%

Chevrolet Corvette roadster 1975

PRODUCTION

4629

HISTORY

The last of the traditional fully open Corvettes (until 1986, that is) desirable now because of low production and the evergreen appeal of "America's only true sports car." The only engine available this year was the small-block 350 V8, detuned to 165 or 205 bhp net to satisfy Washington's clean-air mandates. Aside from adoption of GM's High Energy Ignition system and the industry-wide catalytic converter, little changed from previous years. The last of the big-block engines had appeared for 1974, along with a rear-end restyle to match the revised front end on the 1973s. The public's continued preference for closed-cabin comfort and security plus the threat of government-imposed standards for rollover protection were doing in ragtops throughout Detroit in the early '70s, and Chevy saw little reason to continue the open Corvette.

FOR

Nothing like a convertible 'Vette • Others as for 1968-70 Corvette

AGAINST

As for 1968-70 Corvette, plus greater rarity

SPECIFICATIONS

Length (in.) 185.5 **Wheelbase (in.)** 98.0 **Weight (lbs.)** 3530 (approx.) **Price (new)** $5499

ENGINES

cid/type	bore x stroke	bhp	years
350/ohv V8	4.00×3.50	165/205*	1975
*SAE net			

PRICES/PROJECTION

Restorable $5000-7000 **Good** $6500-8500
Excellent $9000-16,000 **5-year projection** +25%

Chevrolet Cosworth-Vega 1975-76

1975 Cosworth-Vega hatchback coupe

PRODUCTION

1975 2061 **1976** 1447

HISTORY

Chevrolet's unsuccessful try at shoring up the sagging image of its trouble-plagued economy car with this enthusiast-oriented model. The main attraction of the "CosVeg" was its engine. It was a de-stroked version of the regular aluminum-block, 2.3-liter (140-cid) Vega four with a twincam, 16-valve aluminum head designed by Cosworth Engineering in England. Bendix electronic fuel injection fed the cylinders, actuated by a glovebox-mounted "computer." Chevy had originally planned to introduce the Cosworth engine as an option for 1974, but problems in meeting emissions standards pushed back the actual launch to April 1975. The result was somewhat disappointing: only 21 more horsepower than the "cooking" Vega (111 versus the 150 bhp rumored earlier) and a total price of well over $6000. The engine package was available only for the hatchback in only one color—black. It included special gold body-side striping and cast aluminum wheels, wider radial tires, full instrumentation set in an engine-turned dash appliqué, anti-roll bars front and rear, specific gear ratios for the four-speed manual transmission, free-flow exhaust system, quick steering, and a special vehicle identification plate on the dash. Alas, the Cosworth engine didn't make the Vega into a BMW or Alfa beater. The problem was too little power for too much weight. Despite a planned production run of 5000 units annually, Chevy built less than half that number in 1975. The model continued into the 1976 season, available in any standard Vega color and offered with an optional five-speed gearbox. Many of the cars were still unsold at model year's end. The Vega itself would die after 1977, a victim of a poor reliability/durability record.

FOR

Technical interest • Very rare • Fine handling • Decent performance (0-60 mph in 9 seconds) • Neat looks

AGAINST

The premature rusting common to all Vegas • Difficult to find in good condition • Little collector interest at present

SPECIFICATIONS

Length (in.) 175.4 **Wheelbase (in.)** 97.0 **Weight (lbs.)** 2523
Price (new) $6000 (approx.)

ENGINES

cid/type	bore x stroke	bhp	years
122/dohc I4	3.50×3.16	111*	1975-76
*SAE net			

PRICES/PROJECTION

Restorable $1000-2000 **Good** $2000-3500
Excellent $4000-6000 **5-year projection** no change

Chevrolet Camaro Z-28 1977

PRODUCTION

14,349

HISTORY

The sportiest Camaro redefined. Brought back at the middle of the 1977 model year after a two-year hiatus, mainly to cash in on the

1977 Camaro Z-28 Sport Coupe

excellent publicity Camaro had earned as the car of the International Race of Champions. Also, Chevy was envious of Pontiac's unbroken sales success with its Trans Am Firebird. Though cars like the Z-28 had been almost unsaleable following the Arab oil embargo of 1973-74, the market was picking up a bit by 1977. All this encouraged Chevy to revive the Z, but this time with the emphasis on grand touring road manners instead of raw acceleration to fit the spirit of the times. Engineer Jack Turner took a straightforward approach to the chassis: tighter springs at each corner, a thicker front anti-roll bar, a more flexible rear bar, and larger wheels and tires. All this was announced by bold exterior graphics and bright colors that admirably suited the basic 1970 bodyshell with its 1974 facelift. Because of the mid-year introduction, the '77 Z-28 saw fairly limited production. But it had served its purpose, and sales took off in 1978 and '79. Low numbers plus its status as the "first of the last" performance Camaros make this Z a natural future collectible.

FOR

Fairly rare among late-model Camaros ● Peerless handling/roadholding ● Other second-generation Camaro virtues

AGAINST

Second-generation Camaro vices, including heavy thirst, shoebox-size trunk ● Too new for stable collector prices to be established

SPECIFICATIONS

Length (in.) 195.4　**Wheelbase (in.)** 108.1　**Weight (lbs.)** 3600 (approx.)　**Price (new)** $6000 (approx.)

ENGINES

cid/type	bore x stroke	bhp	years
350/ohv V8	4.00×3.48	185*	1977
*SAE net			

PRICES/PROJECTION

Restorable $1500-2000　**Good** $2000-3500
Excellent $4000-6000　**5-year projection** +10%

Chevrolet Corvette Pace Car Replica 1978

PRODUCTION

6502

HISTORY

One of two limited editions issued in the 25th birthday season of Chevrolet's plastic-body sports car. This facsimile of the 'Vette that paced the 62nd annual Indy 500 was decked out with a black upper body and silver-metallic lower body, plus the nice-looking alloy wheels and fat Goodyear tires worn by the Silver Anniversary model. The Pace Car Replica also carried front and rear spoilers. A novel touch was that the identifying "Pace Car" decals were supplied separately so the owner could apply them if desired. Upholstery was your choice of silver leather or a silver leather/grey cloth combination. The seats were a new design scheduled for all '79 Corvettes. Standard equipment included power windows, electric rear window defroster, air conditioning, sport mirrors, and other features, which boosted the Pace Car's price over $4000 above that of the standard Corvette. Because of the announced limited production run, however, the Replicas fetched upwards of $28,000 as would-be collector's items when new. This tempted some owners of standard 'Vettes to paint their cars to match to pass them off as "factory" Pace Cars. All this created much anguish for dealers and buyers alike. In fact, it still does. More than with any other factory special, it will pay to make sure that a '78 Corvette Pace Car is, in fact, the genuine article. The clue is the seats: similar to, but not exactly the same as, the ones used in production '79s. Chevrolet would remember this experience when it issued the Collector Edition 1982 model to mark the last of the "big" 'Vettes. The '78 Replicas came with the L-48 or L-82 V-8. Thus, apart from those seats, about the only way to tell a bogus car from the real thing is by serial number (numbers 900001-906502).

FOR

Uniqueness ● The Corvette's usual performance and sex appeal ● Fine handling ● More luggage space than earlier fifth-generation models

AGAINST

Verifying authenticity takes more than usual effort ● Not easily found ● Quite thievable ● Costs a mint to insure

SPECIFICATIONS

Length (in.) 185.2　**Wheelbase (in.)** 98.0　**Weight (lbs.)** 3500
Price (new) $13,653 original list price

ENGINES

cid/type	bore x stroke	bhp	years
350/ohv V8	4.00×3.48	185/220*	1978
*SAE net			

PRICES/PROJECTION

Difficult to establish accurately at present. The following should be considered estimates only: **Restorable** $5000-6000
Good $10,000-12,000　**Excellent** $13,000-17,000
5-year projection no change

1978 Corvette Pace Car Replica coupe

Chevrolet Corvette Silver Anniversary Edition 1978

1978 Corvette Silver Anniversary Edition coupe

PRODUCTION

NA

HISTORY

"America's Only True Sports Car" was 25 years old in 1978, and Chevy observed the milestone by fitting special commemorative emblems to all Corvettes that year. In one sense, all '78s can be considered "Silver Anniversary Editions," but one special option makes some more collectible today than others. This was the "25th Anniversary Paint," option B2Z. It was described in the catalog as "a distinctive two-tone silver paint treatment. . .Upper body color is silver metallic with charcoal silver on lower body. Pin stripes accentuate front upper profiles, wheel openings, front fender vents, hood, and rear license cavity. Available aluminum wheels and dual sport mirrors required..." All Corvettes got a new fastback roofline with large, wraparound backlight for '78. Four-speed manual shift was reinstated as standard, and a higher-output 350 V8 was optional (with automatic only).

FOR

As for 1978 Corvette Pace Car Replica

AGAINST

As for 1978 Corvette Pace Car Replica

SPECIFICATIONS

Length (in.) 185.2 **Wheelbase (in.)** 98.0 **Weight (lbs.)** 3400 (approx.) **Price (new)** $9600 (approx.)

ENGINES

cid/type	bore x stroke	bhp	years
350/ohv V8	4.00×3.48	175/185/220*	1978
*SAE net			

PRICES/PROJECTION

Deduct 20% from 1978 Corvette Pace Car Replica prices
5-year projection no change

Chrysler Imperial Series CG/CH/CL 1931-33

1932 Series CL Custom Imperial convertible sedan

PRODUCTION

1931 (CG) 3228 **1932** (CH) 1402 **1932** (CL) 220 **1933** (CL) 151

HISTORY

All Imperials of this period are full Classics except for the 1933 Series CX (why it isn't mystifies us). It's not hard to understand why. These were Chrysler's most magnificent cars of the golden era, massive, built on the longest wheelbases, powered by the largest engines, often fitted with custom bodywork. Powered by nine-bearing straight eights, these 2½-ton giants could hit over 95 mph and rack up 0-60 mph in 22 seconds. But it was styling that makes them so memorable: long, low, gracefully curved, and with a rakish grille reminiscent of Duesenberg's. Many fitted with available coachwork from the cream of the custom houses—Locke, Derham, Murphy, Waterhouse and LeBaron. Flawless in every way for their time and the most beautiful Chryslers ever built, bar none.

FOR

Magnificent cars widely respected • All rated Classic by the Classic Car Club of America

AGAINST

Formidable prices • Hard to come by; when they change hands it's usually seldom, and without any advertising fanfare.

SPECIFICATIONS

Length (in.) NA **Wheelbase (in.)** 145.0 (1931); 146.0 (1932-33 CL); 135.0 (1933 CH) **Weight (lbs.)** 4480-5330
Price (new) $1925-3995

ENGINES

cid/type	bore x stroke	bhp	years
384.8/L8	3.50×5.00	125/135	1931-33

PRICES/PROJECTION

Infrequent sales makes reliable prices hard to establish. Most desirable of all is the 1933 CUSTOM CONVERTIBLE SEDAN: **Restorable** $30,000-60,000 **Good** $75,000-110,000 **Excellent** $125,000-150,000. Other open models deduct 10-15%. 1932 individual customs, same prices, semi-customs deduct 10-15%. NON-CUSTOM CLOSED BODIES

Restorable $8000-15,000 **Good** $18,000-25,000
Excellent $30,000-40,000. Club expertise and/or appraisal services strongly recommended. **5-year projection** open cars +15%, closed cars +5%.

Good $10,000-18,000 **Excellent** $20,000-40,000 OTHERS
Restorable $2000-5000 **Good** $5000-10,000
Excellent $10,000-15,000 **5-year projection** Cust. Imp. +20%, others +10%

Chrysler Airflow 1934-37

1935 C2 Imperial Airflow 4-door sedan

PRODUCTION

1934 Eight (CU) 8389 **Imperial (CV)** 2277 **Custom Imperial (CX)** 106 **1935 Eight (C-1)** 4996 **Imperial (C-2)** 2598 **Custom Imperial (C-3)** 125 **1936 Eight (C-9)** 4500 **Imperial (C-10)** 1700 **Custom Imperial (C-11)** 75 **1937 Eight (C-17)** 4600

HISTORY

Chrysler's unsuccessful bid to steal the styling initiative historically significant for pioneering construction and engine placement in the modern sense. Looks failed to catch on, and the company put more emphasis on conventional models the year following the Airflow's debut. Wind tunnel tests suggested the shape: a teardrop altered to allow for a hood and windshield. Solidly built and an excellent performer with Chrysler straight-eight engines that gave it remarkable speed for a car weighing up to two tons.

FOR

Unique concept • Relatively available • Reasonable operating costs • Good club support

AGAINST

An "ugly duckling" reputation has followed it since birth • Limited appreciation potential • No open body styles

SPECIFICATIONS

Length (in.) NA **Wheelbase (in.)** 123.0 (CU, C-1, C-9); 128.0 (CV, C-2, C-10, C-17); 137.5 (CX, C-3, C-11)
Weight (lbs.) 3823-6000 **Price (new)** $1245-2575

ENGINES

cid/type	bore x stroke	bhp	years
298.7/L8	3.25×4.50	122	1934*
323.5/L8	3.25×4.88	115/138	1934-37

*CU

PRICES/PROJECTION

CUSTOM IMPERIAL **Restorable** $3500-8000

Chrysler Custom Imperial Airflow Series CW 1934-36

1934 Series CW Custom Imperial Airflow 4-door sedan

PRODUCTION

1934 22 **1935** 32 **1936** 10

HISTORY

The only Airflows rated as Classic and the most opulent of the company's senior models converted to this controversial styling for 1934. All are sedans and limousines on the longest wheelbase. Conceived by engineer Carl Breer and designed by Oliver Clark, the highly advanced Airflows had ultra-wide seats, vast interior space, a forward-mounted engine, and solid construction in addition to their "aero" styling. The public didn't take to it, but interesting and predictive for the period.

FOR

The longest and thus prettiest Airflow • CCCA Classic status • Novel and worth owning despite history's bum rap • Opulent interiors • Progressive engineering

AGAINST

Remains the 1930's Edsel for many • Very scarce • No open body styles

SPECIFICATIONS

Length (in.) NA **Wheelbase (in.)** 146.0 (1934); 146.5 (1935-36)
Weight (lbs.) 4750-6250 **Price (new)** $5000-5145

ENGINES

cid/type	bore x stroke	bhp	years
384.8/L8	3.50×5.00	150	1934-35
323.5/L8	3.25×4.88	130	1936

PRICES/PROJECTION

Restorable $10,000-18,000 **Good** $20,000-30,000
Excellent $35,000-50,000. Add 10% for limousines.
5-year projection +10%

Chrysler New Yorker Highlander 1940-42

New Yorker Highlander interior

PRODUCTION

Not available, but no more than 1000 per year.

HISTORY

Chrysler revamped its cars for 1940, and there are many collectible two-door models in this design generation, which lasted into 1949. By far the most interesting are the special-trim two-door (and, rarely, the occasional four-door) New Yorker models with Scottish plaid cloth and leatherette upholstery. This option cost $20-25 extra, and cars so equipped carried "Highlander" script, although Chrysler listed a distinct Highlander model in 1940 only. On convertibles, the plaid fabric was also used for the top boot. Highlander plaid has been recently reproduced for restorers.

FOR

Eye-catching interior ● Smooth ride ● Comfort

AGAINST

Nondescript styling (though rear fender skirts help) ● Drunkardly thirst ● Fluid Drive transmission may prove troublesome to maintain

SPECIFICATIONS

Length (in.) 216.0 **Wheelbase (in.)** 128.5 (1940); 127.5 (1941-42) **Weight (lbs.)** 3570-4033 **Price (new)** $1255-1548

ENGINES

cid/type	bore x stroke	bhp	years
323.5/L8	3.25×4.88	135/137/140	1940-42

New Yorker Highlander interior

PRICES/PROJECTION

Restorable $2500-3500 **Good** $4000-6000
Excellent $6000-8500 Add 100% for convertible.
5-year projection +10%

Chrysler New Yorker Navajo 1940-42

PRODUCTION

Not available; rare model

HISTORY

Even more exclusive and unusual than the Highlander, this trim option consisted of broadcloth upholstery woven to simulate the design of Navajo Indian blankets. Vertical stripes on 1941s, horizontal with "Thunderbird" motif on '42s.

FOR

Rarity and high desirability ● Others as for Highlander

AGAINST

As for Highlander

SPECIFICATIONS

Length (in.) 216.0 **Wheelbase (in.)** 127.5
Weight (lbs.) 3570-4033 **Price (new)** $1255-1548

ENGINES

cid/type	bore x stroke	bhp	years
323.5/L8	3.25×4.88	135/137/140	1940-42

PRICES/PROJECTION

Restorable $2700-4200 **Good** $4800-7300
Excellent $7300-10,400 Add 100% for convertible.
5-year projection +10%

Chrysler Windsor Highlander 1940-42

PRODUCTION

Not available; no more than 1500 per year

1941 Windsor Highlander convertible

HISTORY

The Highlander trim package applied to the smaller six-cylinder Chrysler. Higher production makes this version somewhat more plentiful today.

FOR

As for New Yorker Highlander

AGAINST

Lower collector demand (convertibles are the best buys) ● Others as for New Yorker Highlander

SPECIFICATIONS

Length (in.) 210.0 **Wheelbase (in.)** 122.5 (1940), 121.5 (1941-42) **Weight (lbs.)** 3135-3661 **Price (new)** $1020-1420

ENGINES

cid/type	bore x stroke	bhp	years
241.5/L6	3.38×4.50	108/112	1940-41
250.6/L6	3.44×4.50	120	1942

PRICES/PROJECTION

Restorable $1000-2500 **Good** $2500-4000
Excellent $4000-7000 Add 100% for convertible.
5-year projection +25%

Chrysler Windsor Town & Country 1941-42

1941 Windsor Town & Country 9-passenger wagon

PRODUCTION

1941 9-pass. 796 **6-pass.** 200 **1942 9-pass.** 849
6-pass. 150

HISTORY

A significant step toward the modern station wagon and away from the boxy woody. Somewhat sedan-like in appearance, with a streamlined steel roof and tailgate doors that opened like a clam shell via outboard hinges. The concept was floated by Chrysler Division general manager David Wallace, who was also noted for the "Superfinish" engine process.

FOR

High appreciation potential ● Unique body style

AGAINST

'41 almost impossible to find ● Wood structure difficult, though critical, to maintain

SPECIFICATIONS

Length (in.) 210.0 **Wheelbase (in.)** 121.5
Weight (lbs.) 3540-3699 **Price (new)** $1412-1685

ENGINES

cid/type	bore x stroke	bhp	years
241.5/L6	3.38×4.50	112	1941
250.6/L6	3.44×4.50	120	1942

PRICES/PROJECTION

Restorable $4000-8000 **Good** $10,000-18,000
Excellent $18,000-25,000 Deduct 15% for 1942 model.
5-year projection +10%

Chrysler Crown Imperial 1946-48

1947 Crown Imperial limousine

PRODUCTION

sedans 750 **limousines** 650

HISTORY

The largest and most impressive of the harmonica-grille postwar Chryslers. Built to the high fit-and-finish standard expected at the price, which was close to $5000 new, quite a bit of dough in those days. Every bit the luxury cars the big Packard Customs and Cadillac Series 75s were. All Crowns in this period offered eight-passenger seating; two extra persons were accommodated on fold-down jump seats. Plentiful room for all thanks to the long wheelbase.

FOR

Chrysler's highest luxury in this period ● Beautifully built, formal cars

AGAINST

Ponderous road manners, so no picnic to drive • Fuel thirst • Too long for many garages (and some parking spaces)

SPECIFICATIONS

Length (in.) 234.8 **Wheelbase (in.)** 145.5
Weight (lbs.) 4814-4875 **Price (new)** $3875-4767

ENGINES

cid/type	bore x stroke	bhp	years
323.5/L8	3.25×4.88	135	1946-48

PRICES/PROJECTION

Restorable $800-2000 **Good** $2000-3500
Excellent $4000-6000 **5-year projection** +10%

Chrysler Town & Country 1946-48

1947 Town & Country 4-door sedan

PRODUCTION

1946 6-cyl. sedan 124 **8-cyl. sedan** 100
8-cyl. convertible 1935 **1947 6-cyl. sedan** 2651
8-cyl. convertible 3136 **1948 6-cyl. sedan** 1175
8-cyl. convertible 3309 (figures do not include 1946 factory prototypes)

HISTORY

The "classic" Town & Country models most people associate with the name. The eight-cylinder convertible built on the New Yorker chassis is the most common. All carried the Wallace idea of wood trim on a conventional steel body one step further, putting them in the "glamor" class with Chrysler's big top-line convertibles. Alas, the mahogany-veneer panels gave way to Di-Noc decals in late 1947. The eight-cylinder sedan was discontinued early, and its six-cylinder counterpart departed at mid-year 1948. A few 1948 convertibles were reserialed as part of Chrysler's stopgap "first series" 1949 lineup.

FOR

High collector recognition • Prime investment • Striking looks

AGAINST

Difficulty of wood maintenance and restoration • High asking prices • Sporty to look at, not to drive

SPECIFICATIONS

Length (in.) 221.8 (6-cyl. sedan), 216.8 (8-cyl. models)
Wheelbase (in.) 121.5 (6-cyl. sedan), 127.5 (8-cyl. models)
Weight (lbs.) 3917-4332 **Price (new)** $2366-3395

ENGINES

cid/type	bore x stroke	bhp	years
250.6/L6	3.44×4.50	114	1946-48
323.5/L8	3.25×4.88	135	1946-48

PRICES/PROJECTION

CONVERTIBLE Restorable $8000-11,000 **Good** $10,000-20,000
Excellent $25,000-35,000 **SEDAN (6) Restorable** $6000-9000
Good $10,000-12,000 **Excellent** $13,000-17,000 Add 25% for 8 cyl. sedan **5-year projection** +100%

Chrysler Imperial 1949-54

1954 Imperial Newport 2-door hardtop

PRODUCTION

1949 4d sedan 50 **1950 4d sedan** 10,650*
1951 4d sedan 13,678** **club coupe** 2226**
2d hardtop 749 **convertible** 650 **1952 4d sedan** 8033**
club coupe 1307**; **2d hardtop** 440**
1953 4d sedan 7793 **2d hardtop** 823 **limousine** 243
1954 4d sedan 4324 **2d hardtop** 1249 **convertible** 1
limousine 85
*Includes 1150 Deluxe models
**Est. 1951-52 breakdown

HISTORY

With the new boxy body style for 1949, Chrysler decided to field a line of "owner-driver" Imperials. The sedan came first, followed briefly by a convertible and club coupe. The Newport hardtop arrived to stay for 1951. These were the top of the Chrysler line—beautifully built and thoroughly engineered but drably designed and dull on the road. Then as now, they appealed mainly to those who liked Chryslers in general. Though they were an engineering match for Cadillac and Lincoln, they were not as well styled, and styling was almost everything in those years. Sales lagged accordingly. (See also "Imperial," the separate make launched for 1955.)

FOR

Engineering excellence • Craftsmanship • Luxury

AGAINST

Underwhelming looks • Fuel thirst • Some body parts in short supply now

SPECIFICATIONS

Length (in.) 212.5 (1949), 213.6 (1950), 212.6 (1951-52),
219.0 (1953-54) **Wheelbase (in.)** 131.5 (1949-52),
133.5 (1953-54; '53 hardtop: 131.5) **Weight (lbs.)** 4220-5295
Price (new) $3055-7044

ENGINES

cid/type	bore x stroke	bhp	years
323.5/L8	3.25×4.88	135	1949-50
331.1/ohv V8	3.81×3.63	180/235	1951-54

PRICES/PROJECTION

Restorable $1500-2500 **Good** $2500-4000
Excellent $4000-6000 Add 10% for hardtop, 50% for
convertible, 10% for 1953-54 limousine. **5-year projection**
+10%

Chrysler Town & Country 1949

1949 Town & Country convertible

PRODUCTION

1000

HISTORY

A continuation of the T&C idea, but confined strictly to a New Yorker-based convertible, the highest-priced T&C yet. (A Newport hardtop was also planned, but not produced.) As before, the wood trim with Di-Noc "mahogany" inserts adorned doors, rear bodysides (above the fenders), and trunk deck, but only the latter was structural. Craftsmanship was as good as ever, and the Town & Country was still the best-looking Chrysler by a long way.

FOR

As for previous models • Just as desirable

AGAINST

Fairly scarce now • Less investment potential than 1946-48 convertibles

SPECIFICATIONS

Length (in.) 212.5 **Wheelbase (in.)** 131.5 **Weight (lbs.)** 4630
Price (new) $4665

ENGINES

cid/type	bore x stroke	bhp	years
323.5/L8	3.25×4.88	135	1949

PRICES/PROJECTION

Restorable $3000-4500 **Good** $6000-10,000
Excellent $12,000-20,000 **5-year projection** +20%

Chrysler Town & Country Newport 1950

1950 Town & Country Newport 2-door hardtop

PRODUCTION

700

HISTORY

The final year for a non-wagon T&C. Chrysler now went the other way, abandoning the ragtop for a pillarless hardtop, still powered by the L-head straight eight. A noteworthy mechanical feature was four-wheel disc brakes, among the first applications for a production model. Frontal styling was cleaned up somewhat over '49, and there were tidier taillights, too. A very pretty car, nicely upholstered, comfortable on the highway, beautifully constructed.

FOR

As for earlier Town & Country models, plus snob appeal as the last of a breed • Quite rare, then and now

AGAINST

Wood upkeep difficult • Disc brake problems • Few now left

SPECIFICATIONS

Length (in.) 222.5 **Wheelbase (in.)** 131.5 **Weight (lbs.)** 4670
Price (new) $4003

ENGINES

cid/type	bore x stroke	bhp	years
323.5/L8	3.25×4.88	135	1950

PRICES/PROJECTION

Restorable $3000-5000 **Good** $6000-10,000
Excellent $12,000-18,000 **5-year projection** +20%

Chrysler Saratoga club coupe 1951

PRODUCTION

5355 (est.)

HISTORY

The Saratoga was the lightest Chrysler series available with the revolutionary new V8 with hemispherical combustion chambers, then in its first year of production. But the hemi alone is not enough to qualify the whole series as collector items. Regrettably, Chrysler decided not to offer Saratoga hardtops or convertibles this year, although one experimental Newport hardtop was built. So, the best choice is the sporty club coupe. The lookalike 1952 Saratoga would be an alternative, though it lacks "first year" status for the hemi. For those who like the smoother 1953-54 models, there's the Windsor Deluxe, which took over for the Saratoga in that period.

FOR

Chrysler's "hot rod," with the lighter Windsor body and the powerful hemi V8 instead of a six

AGAINST

Limited collector interest • Dowdy styling detracts from a brilliant powerplant

SPECIFICATIONS

Length (in.) 207.8 **Wheelbase (in.)** 125.5 **Weight (lbs.)** 3948
Price (new) $3348

ENGINES

cid/type	bore x stroke	bhp	years
331.1/ohv V8	3.81×3.63	180	1951

PRICES/PROJECTION

Restorable $1000-1500 **Good** $1500-3500
Excellent $3000-5000 **5-year projection** +25%

Chrysler New Yorker hardtop/convertible 1955-56

1955 New Yorker Deluxe Newport 2-door hardtop

1955 New Yorker Deluxe convertible

PRODUCTION

1955 Newport 2d hardtop 5777
St. Regis 2d hardtop 11,076   **convertible** 946
1956 Newport 2d hardtop 4115   **St. Regis 2d hardtop** 6686
convertible 921   **Newport 4d hardtop** 3599

HISTORY

If you can't afford a 300 or simply want a more available luxury Chrysler, these handsome Virgil Exner creations of the mid-'50s may be just the ticket. The 1955 had that "hundred million dollar look," with a split eggcrate grille and tall, chrome-encased taillights, plus attractive cloth and vinyl interiors and the ever potent hemi-head V8. The 1956s acquired a more massive and unified grille and more prominent (though still conservative) tailfins housing larger vertical taillights. New that year was the Newport hardtop sedan, which offered four-door practicality with pillarless construction. PowerFlite two-speed automatic was standard (three-speed TorqueFlite became available for mid-'56) controlled by a menacing chrome wand jutting from the dash on '55s and by the famous pushbuttons on '56s. The more plushly trimmed St. Regis two-door proved quite popular. Bargain hunters, but not serious collectors, might also consider the less expensive Windsor equivalents, which had their own distinct front and rear styling for '56. Though not as fast then or as desirable now, they were still every inch a Chrysler.

FOR

Attractiveness • Still reasonably priced • Fast • Luxurious

AGAINST

Slower to appreciate than 300s • A bit heavy on the chrome • Large in today's context

SPECIFICATIONS

Length (in.) 218.6 (1955), 220.4 (1956) **Wheelbase (in.)** 126.0
Weight (lbs.) 4125-4360 **Price (new)** $3652-4243

ENGINES

cid/type	bore x stroke	bhp	years
331.1/ohv V8	3.81×3.63	250	1955
354/ohv V8	3.94×3.63	280	1956

PRICES/PROJECTION

Restorable $1000-2000 **Good** $2500-3500
Excellent $3000-5000 Add 40% for convertible
5-year projection +10%

Chrysler C300/300B
1955-56

ENGINES

cid/type	bore x stroke	bhp	years
331.1/ohv V8	3.81×3.63	300	1955
354/ohv V8	3.94×3.63	340/355	1956

PRICES/PROJECTION

Restorable $2500-5000 Good $4000-7500
Excellent $7500-10,000 5-year projection +10%

Chrysler 300C/300D
1957-58

1955 C300 2-door hardtop

PRODUCTION

1955 1725 **1956** 1102

HISTORY

The first of what writer Karl Ludvigsen called the "Beautiful Brutes," and two of the most memorable performance cars ever made. Unabashedly created for NASCAR racing which they dominated until the Automobile Manufacturers Association shied away from factory competition support in early 1957. Powered by the most potent hemi-head V8s yet, the 1955 C300 (as it was officially designated) and 1956 300B had Virgil Exner's fine body styling, a New Yorker Newport (hardtop) body with an Imperial eggcrate grille. Though primarily a showroom attention-getter, off the track the big 300 was more than just performance. It also offered luxurious accommodations (including leather upholstery), though it was naturally harder-riding and noisier than a New Yorker.

FOR

One of the very important Milestones • Prime investment • Very fast • Satisfying to drive

AGAINST

Scarcity • High prices • Fuel thirst (and a taste for high-octane gas now hard to come by)

SPECIFICATIONS

Length (in.) 218.6 (1955), 220.4 (1956) **Wheelbase (in.)** 126.0
Weight (lbs.) 4005-4145 **Price (new)** $4110-4419

1955 C300 2-door hardtop

1957 300C 2-door hardtop

PRODUCTION

1957 2d hardtop 1918 **convertible** 484
1958 2d hardtop 618 **convertible** 191

HISTORY

Restyled, even more potent extensions of Chrysler's brawny hot rod. The 1957 300C and 1958 300D were the last of the hemi-powered letter series, and were sold in hardtop or new convertible form. On 9.25:1 compression the 1957 hemi delivered 375 bhp, and 390 bhp (maybe more) was available with special 10:1-compression heads. Three-speed TorqueFlite automatic or manual transmission was offered. Shared new torsion-bar front suspension with New Yorker (and other Chrysler products) but had beefier bars. Quality control declined, but the leather-trimmed interior now had individual seats. For 1958, the optional "hi-po" engine was a fuel-injected 392, conservatively rated at 390 bhp. The only differences in Virgil Exner's dramatic styling between the two models are minor: shorter taillights that didn't entirely fill the fin, and a modified windshield header for the 300D.

FOR

The best-looking tailfin Mopars ever • High appreciation potential • Great long-haul road car

AGAINST

As for 1955-56 300s, plus definitely susceptible to rust

SPECIFICATIONS

Length (in.) 219.2 (1957) 220.2 (1958) **Wheelbase (in.)** 126.0
Weight (lbs.) 4235-4475 **Price (new)** $4929-5603

ENGINES

cid/type	bore x stroke	bhp	years
392/ohv V8	4.00×3.90	375/380/390	1957-58

PRICES/PROJECTION

Restorable $2000-4000 **Good** $4000-7000
Excellent $7000-10,000 Deduct 20% for hardtop.
5-year projection +10%

Chrysler 300E 1959

1959 300E 2-door hardtop

PRODUCTION

2d hardtop 550 **convertible** 140

HISTORY

The fifth edition of the letter-series 300. Basically the same car as the 1958 300D, but sported a horizontal-bar grille instead of the previous eggcrate and a 413-cid wedgehead V8 instead of the fabled hemi. The E's reputation for sluggishness is undeserved: most contemporary road tests pegged it a good second quicker than the D up to 60 mph and up to three seconds faster to 90 mph. Rear-end styling was altered in line with other '59 Chryslers. A difficult sales year for the industry as a whole limited production, making this model a real find today.

FOR

More rare than other 300s •Styling (still good) •Performance •Roadability •Magnificent mile-eater •Interior luxury

AGAINST

A "bum rap" for "doing in the hemi" •Magnificent fuel-eater •Rust-prone

SPECIFICATIONS

Length (in.) 220.6 **Wheelbase (in.)** 126.0
Weight (lbs.) 4290-4350 **Price (new)** $5319-5749

ENGINES

cid/type	bore x stroke	bhp	years
413/ohv V8	4.18×3.75	380	1959

PRICES/PROJECTION

Restorable $1000-1500 **Good** $2500-4000

Excellent $5000-6000 Add 35% for convertible
5-year projection +10%

Chrysler 300F/300G/ 300H 1960-62

1961 300G 2-door hardtop

PRODUCTION

1960 2d hardtop 964 **convertible** 248
1961 2d hardtop 1280 **convertible** 337
1962 2d hardtop 435 **convertible** 123

HISTORY

Despite styling generally seen as retrograde, the 1960 300F offered some important improvements: unit construction, optional 400-bhp ram-manifold wedgehead V8, standard bucket seats and center console front and rear, optional Pont-á-Mousson four-speed manual gearbox (fitted to no more than 15 examples), and a choice of axle ratios from 2.93 to 3.73. The embossed decklid "spare tire" was deleted on the tidier 1961 300G, which introduced an upside-down trapezoid grille and canted, vertical quad headlights. A heavy-duty three-speed manual was reinstated as an option to replace the French four-speeder, and the 300 reverted to 15-inch wheels for the first time since 1956. The 1962 300H retained the same basic look aside from being shorn of its fins (which led stylist Virgil Exner to refer to it later as the "plucked chicken"), and rode a 4-inch shorter wheelbase.

FOR

Less costly now than earlier 300s • Aggressive good looks •300H's finless rear •Good assembly quality •Speedy and well-furnished as ever

AGAINST

Definite ruster •Very thirsty •Requires high octane

SPECIFICATIONS

Length (in.) 219.7 (1960-61), 215.3 (1962)
Wheelbase (in.) 126.0 (1960-61), 122.0 (1962)
Weight (lbs.) 4010-4315 **Price (new)** $5090-5841

ENGINES

cid/type	bore x stroke	bhp	years
413/ohv V8	4.18×3.75	375-405	1960-62

PRICES/PROJECTION

1960-61 Restorable $1000-2000 **Good** $2000-3000
Excellent $4500-7000 Add 30% for convertible
1962 Restorable $800-1000 **Good** $1500-3000
Excellent $3500-6000 Add 30% for convertible
5-year projection +10%

Chrysler 300J/300K 1963-64

1963 300J 2-door hardtop

PRODUCTION

1963 2d hardtop 400 **1964 2d hardtop** 3022
convertible 625

HISTORY

All-new styling by Virgil Exner characterized Chryslers of this period, billed as having "the crisp, clean custom look." Whether it was good or not is debatable, but the 300 letter-series was the cleanest of the range, with a blacked-out grille and conservative side treatment. The 1963 300J (Chrysler skipped the letter "I" in the alphabetical sequence) was offered as a hardtop only and in just one state of tune. It lacked the traditional emblem and bright spear that had graced 300 rear fenders since 1957. Few '63s were sold. Sales rebounded with the 1964 300K to set a record. The convertible was reinstated, and a choice of two power stages was offered, including a ram-induction 413 boasting 390 bhp.

FOR

Even more affordable than earlier 300s ●300Ks in good supply ●Higher-than-average performance ●Low-production appeal

AGAINST

Bulky, controversial styling ●Rust-prone

SPECIFICATIONS

Length (in.) 215.5 **Wheelbase (in.)** 122.0
Weight (lbs.) 3965-4000 **Price (new)** $4056-5184

ENGINES

cid/type	bore x stroke	bhp	years
413/ohv V8	4.19×3.75	360/390	1963-64

PRICES/PROJECTION

300J Restorable $1500-2500 **Good** $2500-5000
Excellent $5000-7500 **300K Restorable** $750-1500
Good $2000-3000 **Excellent** $3000-4000 Add 20% for convertibles **5-year projection** +20%

Chrysler 300L 1965

1965 300L 2-door hardtop

PRODUCTION

2d hardtop 2405 **convertible** 440

HISTORY

Last gasp (and a bit of a wheeze) for the letter-series 300. Shared Elwood Engel's new styling with other '65 Chryslers, but was more a trim option than on a separate model in its own right. Handling and performance were only marginally better than on other Chryslers, and it was hardly the stormer its predecessors had been. A single 360-bhp powerplant was offered. After 1965, Chrysler abandoned the big-car performance market, and the letter-series was dropped. The non-letter 300, which had replaced the Windsor in the 1962 line, continued on into the 1970s.

FOR

More distinctive than other '65 Chryslers ●300 designation

AGAINST

Little that makes it a thoroughbred ●Questionable assembly quality ●Thirsty ●Big

SPECIFICATIONS

Length (in.) 218.2 **Wheelbase (in.)** 124.0
Weight (lbs.) 4170-4245 **Price (new)** $4153-4618

ENGINES

cid/type	bore x stroke	bhp	years
413/ohv V8	4.19×3.75	360	1965

PRICES/PROJECTION

Restorable $1500-2500 **Good** $2500-4000
Excellent $3500-5000 Add 50% for convertible, 10% for 4-speed manual. **5-year projection** +10%

Chrysler 300-Hurst 1970

1970 300-Hurst 2-door hardtop

PRODUCTION

501 (inc. 1 convertible)

HISTORY

Not a return of the fabled letter-series 300s, but a specially produced non-letter 300 hardtop built by Hurst Performance Products and sold through Chrysler dealers. Features included special road wheels, wider-than-stock tires, the 375-bhp version of Chrysler's big-block 440 V8, heavy-duty suspension, and, of course, a Hurst shifter for the standard TorqueFlite automatic. The exterior was dressed up by a snazzy gold and white paint job, twist-lock hood tiedowns, a subtle scoop at the rear of the hood near the cowl, and a loop-type rear spoiler.

FOR

Rarity • Good performance • Clean styling

AGAINST

Heavy and thirsty • Rust-prone unless looked after

SPECIFICATIONS

Length (in.) 224.7 **Wheelbase (in.)** 124.0 **Weight (lbs.)** 4135 (approx.) **Price (new)** $4400 (approx.)

ENGINES

cid/type	bore x stroke	bhp	years
440/ohv V8	4.32×3.75	375	1970

PRICES/PROJECTION

Restorable $1500-2000 **Good** $2500-4000
Excellent $4000-7000 **5-year projection** +20%

Clipper Custom Constellation 1956

1956 Custom Constellation 2-door hardtop

PRODUCTION

1466

HISTORY

When James J. Nance became Packard president in 1952, one of his immediate marketing objectives was to divorce the marque from the medium-priced field, which had hindered the luxury Packards' sales performance since the war. Nance reinvoked the Clipper name as a Packard series for 1953. It was then formally registered as a separate make for 1956. But by then it was too late; the Clipper "make" lasted only a year. The Constellation hardtop was the flashiest and easily the most desirable of the '56s, nicely trimmed and finished, and offered with Packard's innovative Torsion-Level suspension. (See also "Packard.")

FOR

Good styling (compromised by bizarre two-toning) • Fine ride • Adequate performance • Historical interest

AGAINST

A low-profile collectible • Thirsty

SPECIFICATIONS

Length (in.) 214.8 **Wheelbase (in.)** 122.0 **Weight (lbs.)** 3860 **Price (new)** $3164

ENGINES

cid/type	bore x stroke	bhp	years
352/ohv V8	4.00×3.50	275	1956

PRICES/PROJECTION

Restorable $600-1000 **Good** $1000-2500
Excellent $3500-4500 **5-year projection** +5%

Continental Mark II 1956-57

PRODUCTION

1956 1325 **1957** 444

1956 Mark II 2-door hardtop

HISTORY

Mid-'50s successor to the original Continental of the '40s. Magnificently styled by a team including John Reinhart, William Clay Ford, and Gordon Buehrig. Engineer Harley Copp's unique "cowbelly" frame dipped low to permit high seating without a tall body. With Multi-Drive three-speed automatic and balanced, individually tested Lincoln V8, the Mark II was marketed as an image leader intended to steal Cadillac's thunder in the ultra-luxury class. Despite beautiful styling, it didn't sell well; probably because its price was so close to the (then) breathtaking $10,000 mark. Ford had not originally seen the Mark II as a profit-maker. Yet because the firm lost $1000 on each one sold, the urge to cheapen the car for 1958 proved irresistible. A Mark II cabriolet was contemplated, but never actually produced on a series basis.

FOR

One of the all-time American postwar greats • Timeless, elegant styling • High-quality materials inside and out • High appreciation potential

AGAINST

Not nearly so elegant in motion, especially compared to post-1960 Continentals • Interiors rather plain for the class • High operating costs

SPECIFICATIONS

Length (in.) 218.5 **Wheelbase (in.)** 126.0
Weight (lbs.) 4800-4825 **Price (new)** $9695-9966

ENGINES

cid/type	bore x stroke	bhp	years
368/ohv V8	4.00×3.66	285/300	1956-57

PRICES/PROJECTION

Restorable $3000-5500 **Good** $7000-12,000
Excellent $12,000-20,000 **5-year projection** +20%

Continental Mark III
1958

PRODUCTION

4d sedan 1283 **2d hardtop** 2328 **convertible** 3048
Landau 4d hardtop 5891

HISTORY

The successor to the upper-crust Mark II, but far less exclusive. Essentially a high-line version of 1958's new unit-body Lincoln, with

1958 Mark III Landau 4-door hardtop

a finer eggcrate grille texture, repeated on the rear panel, which also featured triple-element taillight clusters. A Mercury cost expert had been brought in during the Mark III's early planning stages, and list price was cut by 40 percent compared to the Mark II in order to pick up more sales. The line was expanded to include pillared and pillarless sedans and a convertible. Horsepower increased 25 percent. Greatly enlarged and completely different in concept from the Mark II, the Mark III had contemporary styling that would quickly become dated. There was liberal use of bright metal, plus prominent tailfins and canted quad headlamps. Continued for 1959-60 as the Mark IV and V, both of which were officially tagged Lincolns following demise of the separate Continental Division.

FOR

More affordable than Mark II • Powerful • Luxurious • Impressive size

AGAINST

Controversial styling • Prone to mechanical and electrical failures • Much lower investment potential than Mark II • Very heavy • Gargantuan proportions • Extremely thirsty

SPECIFICATIONS

Length (in.) 229.0 **Wheelbase (in.)** 131.0
Weight (lbs.) 4800-5040 **Price (new)** $5825-6283

ENGINES

cid/type	bore x stroke	bhp	years
430/ohv V8	4.30×3.70	375	1958

PRICES/PROJECTION

Restorable $500-1500 **Good** $1500-2500
Excellent $3000-5000 Add 150% for convertible.
5-year projection +15%

Continental Mark III
1968-71

PRODUCTION

1968 7770	**1969** 23,088	**1970** 21,432	**1971** 27,091

HISTORY

The model that revived Continental as a separate marque in the '60s. Never officially listed as a Lincoln (it was an L-M Division product since there was no separate Continental Division as in

1968 Mark III 2-door hardtop

1956-58). Another of Ford's attempts to upstage Cadillac, the Mark III was aimed squarely at the Eldorado and other large personal-luxury cars. Sales rarely trailed Eldorado's by more than 2000 units, so the Mark III must be considered a success. Handsome if a bit baroque in appearance, the "new" Mark has lately begun to take hold with collectors, who seem to prefer it to the later Mark IV and V of 1972-79.

FOR

Crisp, traditional styling • Elegance and luxury • Smooth long-haul road car

AGAINST

Extreme thirst • A little early to predict its ultimate worth as a collectible

SPECIFICATIONS

Length (in.) 216.1 **Wheelbase (in.)** 117.2
Weight (lbs.) 4739-4762 **Price (new)** $6585-7281

ENGINES

cid/type	bore x stroke	bhp	years
460/ohv V8	4.36 × 3.75	365	1968-71

PRICES/PROJECTION

Restorable $800-1500 **Good** $2000-4000
Excellent $5000-7000 **5-year projection** +15%

Cord L-29
1930-32

1930 L-29 cabriolet

PRODUCTION

1930 1700* **1931** 1433 **1932** 335* *registrations (total production about 5000; began 1929)

HISTORY

Errett Lobban Cord's front-drive masterpiece. Designed by Harry Miller and Cornelius Van Ranst, but underpowered with its adopted Auburn engine. Three-speed sliding-pinion transmission was sandwiched between clutch and differential, brakes were inboard hydraulics, shocks Houdaille-Hershey all around, and the front halfshafts used Cardan constant-velocity joints—all very advanced. But the result was tail-heavy for a front-driver, so handling was skittish and the U-joints wore out with fervor. Al Leamy designed the beautiful cowl-forward ensemble, which announced some of the most stunning styling of the day. High initial price limited sales in a competitive field. Cord cut it drastically in 1931, but it didn't help. Sadly, the L-29 could have been a wonderful car with enough development time, but time wasn't on its side.

FOR

Some of the most majestic bodywork among full Classics • Novel, predictive engineering • The magic of a name

AGAINST

High price • Extreme scarcity • Complicated mechanicals

SPECIFICATIONS

Length (in.) NA **Wheelbase (in.)** 137.5
Weight (lbs.) 4300-4560 **Price (new)** $2395-3295

ENGINES

cid/type	bore x stroke	bhp	years
298.6/L8	3.25 × 4.50	125	1930-32

PRICES/PROJECTION

CABRIOLET **Restorable** $20,000-40,000 **Good** $50,000-75,000
Excellent $75,000-100,000 PHAETON Add 10% to above.
SEDAN & BROUGHAM Deduct 40% from above.
5-year projection +20%

Cord 810/812
1936-37

PRODUCTION

Said to be nearly 3000 by some sources; reported registrations were only 1174 in 1936 and 1146 in 1937.

HISTORY

One of the most important automobiles of all time. Predictive "coffin nose" styling by Gordon Buehrig, Dale Cosper, Dick Roberson and Paul Laurenzen. Powered by a Lycoming V8 connected to a four-speed electric pre-selector gearbox (set the next gear, then stab the clutch to shift). More compact engine set relatively farther back in the chassis gave better fore/aft weight balance than the L-29, and front suspension was independent. Offered with a supercharger option in 1937 that yielded 0-60 mph in 13 seconds and nearly 110 mph maximum. Design now world famous: wrapped radiator louvers,

1937 812 Supercharged Beverly 4-door sedan

exposed pipes on blown 812, turned-metal dash, and concealed headlamps (a first). Bustle-trunk Westchester and fastback Beverly sedans plus cabriolet and phaeton joined by long-wheelbase Custom sedans in 1937. Cheap when first introduced at $2195 tops. Prices then went up and have hardly ever depreciated since.

FOR

Perhaps the most recognized single model in history • Design and engineering brilliance • Fine road manners • "Can't miss" investment

AGAINST

Unreliable mechanically • High operating costs • Rarely offered for sale • Costs a fortune when it is

SPECIFICATIONS

Length (in.) NA **Wheelbase (in.)** 125.0; 132.0 Custom
Weight (lbs.) 3715-4170 **Price (new)** $1995-3575

ENGINES

cid/type	bore x stroke	bhp	years
288.6/V8	3.50×3.75	115	1936-37
288.6/V8	3.50×3.75	190*	1937
*supercharged			

PRICES/PROJECTION

SEDANS **Restorable** $5000-10,000 **Good** $15,000-20,000 **Excellent** $22,000-40,000. Add 10% for lwb Customs. OPEN MODELS Add 100%. **5-year projection** sedans +20%, open models +30%

Crosley Hotshot 1949-52

PRODUCTION

1949 752 **1950** 742 **1951** 646 **1952** 358 (incl. Super Sports 1950-52)

HISTORY

The open version of Powel Crosley, Jr.'s economy car, and one of the outstanding early postwar sports cars. Could do about 85 mph right off the showroom floor despite the little 44-cid cast-iron four, which was more than adequate for the tiny 1300-pound curb weight. Semi-elliptic/coil front and quarter-elliptic rear suspension gave very nimble handling. Set up for racing, it was even better: a

Hotshot won the Index of Performance at Sebring in 1951, and fared well in many road races. But in an age of horsepower and cubic inches, it was overwhelmed in the marketplace, and the company quit the car business in 1952.

FOR

Vastly underrated Milestone car • Outstanding performance and handling • Easy on fuel • Not difficult to restore

AGAINST

Spot-disc brakes subject to freeze-ups due to dirt • Fair ability to rust • Some parts now in very short supply

SPECIFICATIONS

Length (in.) 137.0 **Wheelbase (in.)** 85.0
Weight (lbs.) 1175-1240 **Price (new)** $849-952

ENGINES

cid/type	bore x stroke	bhp	years
44/I4	2.50×2.25	25.5/26.5	1949-52

PRICES/PROJECTION

Restorable $300-1000 **Good** $1000-2500
Excellent $2500-4500 **5-year projection** +5%

Crosley Super Sports 1950-52

1952 Super Sports roadster

PRODUCTION

1950 742 **1951** 646 **1952** 358 (figures include Hotshot)

HISTORY

A more deluxe version of the Hotshot, with built-in doors (auxiliary doors were available as an option for the Hotshot). Better trimmed, but otherwise the same.

FOR

As for Hotshot

AGAINST

As for Hotshot

SPECIFICATIONS

Length (in.) 137.0 **Wheelbase (in.)** 85.0
Weight (lbs.) 1175-1240 **Price (new)** $925-1029

ENGINES

cid/type	bore x stroke	bhp	years
44/L4	2.50×2.25	25.5/26.5	1950-52

PRICES/PROJECTION

Restorable $500-1200 **Good** $1200-2800
Excellent $2800-5000 **5-year projection** +5%

Cunningham C-3
1953-55

1954 C-3 coupe by Vignale

PRODUCTION

coupe 19 **convertible** 9

HISTORY

Briggs S. Cunningham conceived his original C-1 sports car in 1951 with racing in mind, and his later models were definite contenders. The C-4R finished fourth at Le Mans '52; the following year a C-5R was third, outclassed (and outbraked) by a pair of Jaguars. The C-3, elegantly styled by Giovanni Michelotti of Carrozzeria Vignale in Turin, was Cunningham's "production" model, high-priced and blindingly fast with its Chrysler hemi-head V8 engine. It was one of two American cars (the other was the '53 Studebaker Starliner) named among the world's ten best designs by Arthur Drexler of the New York Museum of Modern Art. Cunningham lost money on every car he built, however, and halted C-3 production after two years.

FOR

One of the greats—a thoroughbred by any yardstick • Tremendous hemi power • Fine handling

AGAINST

Cost • Body parts now very scarce

SPECIFICATIONS

Length (in.) 168.0 **Wheelbase (in.)** 107.0 (105.0 on first coupe built) **Weight (lbs.)** 3500 (approx.) **Price (new)** $10,000 ($11,500 in 1955)

1953 C-3 coupe by Vignale

ENGINES

cid/type	bore x stroke	bhp	years
331.1/ohv V8	3.81×3.63	220-235	1953-55

PRICES/PROJECTION

Restorable $5000-10,000 **Good** $10,000-17,000
Excellent $15,000-23,000 **5-year projection** +10%

DeSoto Airflow
1934-36

1934 Series SE Airflow coupe

PRODUCTION

1934 coupe 1584 **brougham** 522 **sedan 4d** 11,713 **Town sedan** 119 **chassis** 2 **1935 coupe** 418 **sedan 4d** 6269 **Town sedan** 40 **bus coupe** 70 **1936 coupe** 250 **sedan 4d** 4750

HISTORY

Smaller, less expensive running mate to Chrysler's Airflow, and even less saleable. Only one series with fewer body styles and six-cylinder power. Production varied widely, so the above indicates which models are most desirable. DeSoto mainly built conventional cars from 1935 on, with Airlows diminishing through the end of this design in 1936. Built on a shorter wheelbase, so not as nice-looking as their Chrysler counterparts.

FOR

Aerodynamics pioneer • Good workmanship and materials • Relatively inexpensive to own and operate

AGAINST

Styling as lumpy and controversial as ever • Not a great deal of collector recognition • Low appreciation potential

SPECIFICATIONS

Length (in.) NA **Wheelbase (in.)** 115.5
Weight (lbs.) 3323-3400 **Price (new)** $995-1095

ENGINES

cid/type	bore x stroke	bhp	years
241.5/L6	3.38×4.50	100	1934-36

PRICES/PROJECTION

Restorable $2000-3000 **Good** $3000-4000
Excellent $5000-7000. Add 10% for Town sedan. Deduct 10% for four-door sedans. **5-year projection** +10%

DeSoto Custom 1942

1942 Custom convertible coupe

PRODUCTION

4d sedan 7974 **club coupe** 2236 **town sedan** 1084
2d sedan 913 **convertible coupe** 489
business coupe 120 **7-pass. sedan** 79
7-pass. limousine 20

HISTORY

One styling feature makes the '42 DeSoto collectible: hidden headlights. This gimmick, probably inspired by earlier Cords, was unique for 1942 and was far ahead of the "eyelid" styles in the 1960s. DeSoto called them Airfoil headlamps, and they added a new dimension to the cars' styling, allowing the entire grille to be carried smoothly below. Also new for 1942 was the streamlined lady hood mascot, a trademark DeSoto would retain until 1950.

FOR

Solid construction • High quality • Relatively affordable • Hidden headlamps

AGAINST

Very ordinary apart from the headlamps • Hard to find now

SPECIFICATIONS

Length (in.) 206.0 **Wheelbase (in.)** 121.5 (139.5 on 7-pass. models) **Weight (lbs.)** 3205-3820 **Price (new)** $1046-1580

ENGINES

cid/type	bore x stroke	bhp	years
236.6/L6	3.44×4.25	115	1942

PRICES/PROJECTION

Restorable $1000-2000 **Good** $3000-5000
Excellent $5000-7000 Add 25% for long-wheelbase models and 100% for convertible. **5-year projection** +25%

DeSoto Deluxe 1942

PRODUCTION

4d sedan 6463 **club coupe** 1968 **2d sedan** 1781
business coupe 469 **town sedan** 291
convertible coupe 70 **7-pass. sedan** 49

HISTORY

The lower-priced and less elaborately trimmed DeSoto series for '42, also distinguished by the unusual Airfoil hidden headlamps.

FOR

As for 1942 Custom

AGAINST

As for 1942 Custom, plus less deluxe furnishings

SPECIFICATIONS

Length (in.) 206.0 (exc. 7-pass.) **Wheelbase (in.)** 121.5 (139.5 on 7-pass. models) **Weight (lbs.)** 3190-3705
Price (new) $1010-1455

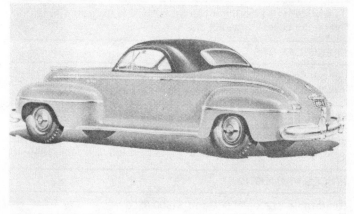

1942 Deluxe business coupe

ENGINES

cid/type	bore x stroke	bhp	years
236.6/L6	3.44×4.25	115	1942

PRICES/PROJECTION

About 10% lower than for comparable Custom models
5-year projection +10%

DeSoto Custom Suburban 1946-48

1946-48 Custom Suburban 8-passenger sedan

PRODUCTION

7500

HISTORY

Like the Chrysler Town & Country, this large sedan used woody-wagon timber as decoration for a standard steel body. This 139.5-inch-wheelbase, eight-passenger sedan was also equipped with a fold-down rear seat, and no trunk partition. A favorite of livery services for hauling a great deal of luggage along with their passengers. Fine wood trim was found inside too, and wood combined with metal in the standard roof rack.

FOR

One of the more unique DeSotos, and among the more interesting early-postwar models • Well built

AGAINST

Dowdy styling • Wood trim can be expensive to restore • Hard to find on the collector market

SPECIFICATIONS

Length (in.) 225.3   **Wheelbase (in.)** 139.5
Weight (lbs.) 3974-4012   **Price (new)** $2093-2631

ENGINES

cid/type	bore x stroke	bhp	years
236.6/L6	3.44×4.25	109	1946-48

PRICES/PROJECTION

Restorable $1200-2000   **Good** $1800-3500
Excellent $4000-6000   **5-year projection** +10%

DeSoto Custom Sportsman 1950

1950 Custom Sportsman 2-door hardtop

PRODUCTION

4600

HISTORY

Although Chrysler built seven experimental Town & Country hardtops for 1946, mass-produced pillarless Mopars didn't begin until the 1950 model year. DeSoto's version was the Sportsman, upholstered to convertible standards and built with all the integrity that distinguished Chrysler products of this period. Of the several interesting DeSotos from the 1950-51 styling generation, the Sportsman hardtop is the most important historically.

FOR

Pioneer DeSoto hardtop • Robust construction • Not prone to rust

AGAINST

Lackluster six-cylinder performance • Underwhelming looks

SPECIFICATIONS

Length (in.) 207.0   **Wheelbase (in.)** 125.5   **Weight (lbs.)** 3735
Price (new) $2489

ENGINES

cid/type	bore x stroke	bhp	years
236.6/L6	3.44×4.25	112	1950

PRICES/PROJECTION

Restorable $500-1000   **Good** $1500-2500
Excellent $3000-4500   **5-year projection** no change

DeSoto Fireflite 1955-56

PRODUCTION

1955 4d sedan 26,637   **2d Sportsman hardtop** 10,313
convertible 775   **1956 4d sedan** 18,207*   **2d hardtop** 8475
convertible 1385**   **4d hardtop** 3350   *Includes Coronado
**Includes Pacesetter

1955 Fireflite Sportsman 2-door hardtop

HISTORY

The first DeSotos completely styled by Virgil Exner, and among the division's most striking cars. Featured lush upholstery and trick design features like a "gullwing" dash and a toothy grille. Performance more than ample from hemi-head V8 engines. Buyers had a choice between solid and wild two-tone colors (the latter with contrasting color in a chrome trimmed bodyside sweep-spear). (See also Fireflite Coronado, Pacesetter, and Adventurer.)

FOR

Good styling for the period ● Quality construction ● Performance

AGAINST

Limited collector appeal ● Debatable design details

SPECIFICATIONS

Length (in.) 217.9 **Wheelbase (in.)** 126.0
Weight (lbs.) 3890-4075 **Price (new)** $2727-3615

ENGINES

cid/type	bore x stroke	bhp	years
291/ohv V8	3.72×3.34	200	1955
330.4/ohv V8	3.72×3.80	255	1956

PRICES/PROJECTION

Restorable $400-1000 **Good** $1500-3100
Excellent $3500-5000 Add 25% for Sportsman 2d hardtop, 50% for convertible **5-year projection** +25%

DeSoto Fireflite Coronado 1955

1955 Fireflite Coronado 4-door sedan

PRODUCTION

500 (est.)

HISTORY

A springtime trim option offered for the Fireflite four-door sedan. Marked by an arresting three-tone paint job (black top, turquoise body, white color sweep) and an interior to match. Identified by small "Coronado" label under Fireflite script on front fenders. Soon abandoned, although DeSoto had produced a less collectible Coronado package for 1954 as well.

FOR

As for other 1955-56 Fireflite ● Striking paint ● Rarity

AGAINST

Extremely scarce now

SPECIFICATIONS

Length (in.) 217.9 **Wheelbase (in.)** 126.0 **Weight (lbs.)** 3940
Price (new) $3500 (est.)

ENGINES

cid/type	bore x stroke	bhp	years
291/ohv V8	3.72×3.34	200	1955

PRICES/PROJECTION

Restorable $650-1900 **Good** $1900-3100
Excellent $3200-5000 **5-year projection** +10%

DeSoto Fireflite Adventurer 1956

1956 Fireflite Adventurer 2-door hardtop

PRODUCTION

996

HISTORY

The first of DeSoto's supercars, the Division's equivalent to the Chrysler 300. Part of the Fireflite series in this first year, and offered only as a hardtop. Equipped with a specially tuned version of the DeSoto hemi and firm suspension as standard, it was the fastest DeSoto yet. It was also one of the most visible, with stock gold-and-white paint job and anodized-gold blade-type wheel covers.

FOR

Perhaps the most desirable postwar DeSoto ● Tremendous performance ● Rarity

AGAINST

Busy styling • Expensive to operate • Some Adventurer-only parts now in short supply

SPECIFICATIONS

Length (in.) 217.9 **Wheelbase (in.)** 126.0 **Weight (lbs.)** 3870
Price (new) $3728

ENGINES

cid/type	bore x stroke	bhp	years
341.4/ohv V8	3.78×3.20	320	1956

PRICES/PROJECTION

Restorable $1800-2500 **Good** $3000-5000
Excellent $5500-9300 **5-year projection** +20%

DeSoto Fireflite Pacesetter 1956

1956 Fireflite Pacesetter convertible

PRODUCTION

100 (est.)

HISTORY

A near replica of the Fireflite convertible that paced the Indy 500 this year. Had a stock Fireflite drivetrain, but a firmer suspension. Wore Adventurer-style finned wheel covers and color scheme, and offered many standard features, including power seat and windows.

FOR

Low production, so a sought-after rarity • Others as for 1955-56 Fireflite

AGAINST

Gaudiness • Scarcity • Others as for 1955-56 Fireflite

SPECIFICATIONS

Length (in.) 217.9 **Wheelbase (in.)** 126.0 **Weight (lbs.)** 4070
Price (new) $3615

ENGINES

cid/type	bore x stroke	bhp	years
330.4/ohv V8	3.72×3.80	255	1956

PRICES/PROJECTION

Restorable $1800-3700 **Good** $3700-6200
Excellent $6200-11,000 **5-year projection** +20%

DeSoto Adventurer 1957-59

1957 Adventurer 2-door hardtop

PRODUCTION

1957 2d hardtop 1650 **convertible** 300
1958 2d hardtop 350 **convertible** 82 **1959 2d hardtop** 590
convertible 97

HISTORY

DeSoto's limited-edition performance series, now separate from Fireflite. A declining market cut hard into Adventurer production and DeSoto sales as a whole. As a result, collector demand for these fast, aggressive-looking, heroically tailfinned cars is fast outstripping supply, as the production figures suggest. Continued to offer exceptional performance, and boasted the hottest V8s available from DeSoto (two power choices were offered for 1958). Like Chrysler, DeSoto switched to the wedgehead V8 for 1959. Road manners also very capable. Of the three model years, the '57 is arguably the nicest in appearance.

FOR

Very desirable • Good appreciation potential • Fine performance • Great on the highway

AGAINST

The first in a long line of Mopar rusters • Many body parts now hard to find • High operating costs

SPECIFICATIONS

Length (in.) 218.0-221.1 **Wheelbase (in.)** 126.0
Weight (lbs.) 3980-4235 **Price (new)** $3997-4749

ENGINES

cid/type	bore x stroke	bhp	years
345/ohv V8	3.80×3.80	345	1957
361/ohv V8	4.13×3.38	345/355	1958
383/ohv V8	4.25×3.38	350	1959

PRICES/PROJECTION

Restorable $650-2500 **Good** $2500-4300
Excellent $3700-6000 Add 75% for convertible.
5-year projection +15%

DeSoto Adventurer 1960

1960 Adventurer 4-door hardtop

PRODUCTION

4d sedan 5746   **2d hardtop** 3092   **4d hardtop** 2759

HISTORY

DeSoto's upper series for 1960, and a kissin' cousin to that year's midrange Chrysler. Both shared a new unitized bodyshell and similar styling with a more integrated trapezoidal grille and sweeping, flared tailfins. The Adventurer was no longer a limited edition, and pushed the former top-line Fireflite down the price-and-prestige ladder. The medium-priced Firedome line vanished, as did the Dodge-based low-line Firesweep series. As "standard" cars, the '60 Adventurers used a milder engine than before, and were in no way related to the hot models of yore. If it has any significance it is that the Adventurer was the best DeSoto had to offer in its last full model year.

FOR

Affordable • Strong engine • Decent "period" styling

AGAINST

Severe rust problems • Fuel thirst • Limited appreciation potential

SPECIFICATIONS

Length (in.) 217.0   **Wheelbase (in.)** 122.0
Weight (lbs.) 3895-3940   **Price (new)** $3579-3727

ENGINES

cid/type	bore x stroke	bhp	years
383/ohv V8	4.25×3.38	305	1960

PRICES/PROJECTION

4-DOORS **Restorable** $500-1000   **Good** $1000-2000
Excellent $2000-3000 2-doors add 25%.
5-year projection +10%

DeSoto 1961

PRODUCTION

4d hardtop 2123   **2d hardtop** 911

1961 DeSoto 2-door hardtop

HISTORY

The token, end-of-the-line models from Chrysler's traditional lower-medium-priced make, a victim of a changed market by the turn of the decade. For 1961, the DeSoto line was whittled down to just two offerings, neither of which bore a series name. A clumsy facelift on the 1960 bodyshell brought a grotesque two-tier grille (neither of which related to the other), curious side sculpturing, and heavy taillights. Production was halted before the end of calendar 1960, about a year after another medium-priced casualty, Edsel. It was a sad finale for a make that, though not among the greats, had always stood for quality—and occasionally performance.

FOR

They didn't make any more • Rarity • Good engine

AGAINST

Ugly • Thirsty • Rust-prone

SPECIFICATIONS

Length (in.) 215.8   **Wheelbase (in.)** 122.0
Weight (lbs.) 3760-3820   **Price (new)** $3102-3167

ENGINES

cid/type	bore x stroke	bhp	years
361/ohv V8	4.13×3.38	265	1961

PRICES/PROJECTION

Restorable $500-1000   **Good** $1200-2500
Excellent $3000-4000   **5-year projection** no change

Dodge Deluxe convertible 1940

PRODUCTION

2100

HISTORY

Dodge doesn't enjoy the large following of Ford or Chevrolet, so the money-minded collector must pick and choose models more carefully. The obvious ones in the 1940-48 styling generation are the convertibles — and good ones can command staggering prices. This body design was mainly the work of Raymond H. Dietrich, who had left Chrysler by the time it was in production. The flathead

1940 Deluxe convertible

Dodge six was no performance engine, but it was known for its reliability and longevity. Accompanying the new rounded styling were sealed beam headlamps (with parking lights in the bezels) and a delete-option running board.

FOR

Open-air appeal • Solid construction • Quality leather interior

AGAINST

Little styling distinction • Limited collector recognition

SPECIFICATIONS

Length (in.) 203.0 **Wheelbase (in.)** 119.5 **Weight (lbs.)** 3190
Price (new) $1030

ENGINES

cid/type	bore x stroke	bhp	years
217.8/L6	3.25×4.38	87	1940

PRICES/PROJECTION

Restorable $2500-3500 **Good** $4500-7500
Excellent $8500-13,000 **5-year projection** +25%

Dodge Custom convertible 1941-42

1941 Custom convertible

PRODUCTION

1941 3554   **1942** 1185

HISTORY

A facelift on the 1940 body, featuring a more massive divided grille. The distinctive Dodge ram mascot was now unrecognizable. No-cost Custom features included foam seat cushions, dual electric wipers, and a passenger's door armrest. For 1942, the dull six was stroked to 230.2 cubic inches, a size that would be continued at Dodge all the way up through 1959.

FOR

As for 1940 convertible, and more affordable

AGAINST

As for 1940 convertible • '42 is scarce

SPECIFICATIONS

Length (in.) 203.3 **Wheelbase (in.)** 119.5
Weight (lbs.) 3384-3476 **Price (new)** $1162-1245

ENGINES

cid/type	bore x stroke	bhp	years
217.8/L6	3.25×4.38	91	1941
230.2/L6	3.25×4.63	102	1942

PRICES/PROJECTION

Restorable $3000-6000 **Good** $8000-12,000
Excellent $12,000-18,000 **5-year projection** +20%

Dodge Custom convertible 1946-49

1946-48 Custom convertible

PRODUCTION

9500

HISTORY

Postwar continuation of the Dietrich-styled bodywork. Lasted through the spring of 1949, at which point Dodge's restyled "second series" '49s appeared (along with its Chrysler Corporation companion lines). Mechanically and bodily unchanged in these years. A mild facelift of the '42 styling featured an eggcrate grille (slightly heavy on the chrome) incorporating square parking lights.

FOR

Priced lower than prewar counterparts (higher production) • Open-air fun

AGAINST

Very ordinary by any standard

SPECIFICATIONS

Length (in.) 204.6 **Wheelbase (in.)** 119.5 **Weight (lbs.)** 3461
Price (new) $1649-2189

SPECIFICATIONS

Length (in.) 204.6 **Wheelbase (in.)** 119.5 **Weight (lbs.)** 3461
Price (new) $1649-2189

ENGINES

cid/type	bore x stroke	bhp	years
230.2 L6	3.25×4.63	102	1946-49

PRICES/PROJECTION

Restorable $3000-4000 **Good** $5000-8000
Excellent $7500-12,000 **5-year projection** +20%

Dodge Wayfarer Roadster 1949

1949 Wayfarer roadster

PRODUCTION

5420

HISTORY

An intriguing Dodge, part of the first all-new postwar series. Sort of Detroit's farewell to the genuine roadster, with removable plastic side curtains instead of conventional roll-up glass. The Wayfarer's interest value belies its unassuming nature, and despite its economy format it's the most sought-after '49 Dodge. Roll-up windows and wing vents replaced the side curtains during the model year, but some purists prefer the original style, suggesting it may be worth marginally more than the later version.

FOR

Strong collector interest • Novelty • Good construction quality • Scarcity

AGAINST

Ho-hum styling • Minimal performance

SPECIFICATIONS

Length (in.) 196.0 **Wheelbase (in.)** 115.0 **Weight (lbs.)** 3145
Price (new) $1727

ENGINES

cid/type	bore x stroke	bhp	years
230.2/L6	3.25×4.63	103	1949

PRICES/PROJECTION

Restorable $2500-4000 **Good** $5000-7500
Excellent $8000-10,000 **5-year projection** +20%

Dodge Coronet Diplomat 1950

1950 Coronet Diplomat 2-door hardtop

PRODUCTION

3600

HISTORY

Dodge's first pillarless hardtop. Little to recommend it as a collectible apart from that. Styling was dumpy despite the hardtop's natural sportiness, and the low-suds Dodge six provided sedate pickup at best. Well-built, though.

FOR

Pioneer hardtop • Robust construction • Sturdy engine

AGAINST

The same crashing boredom that characterized the entire 1950 line

SPECIFICATIONS

Length (in.) 202.9 **Wheelbase (in.)** 123.5 **Weight (lbs.)** 3515
Price (new) $2233

ENGINES

cid/type	bore x stroke	bhp	years
230.2 L6	3.25×4.63	103	1950

PRICES/PROJECTION

Restorable $500-1000 **Good** $1500-2300
Excellent $3000-4000 **5-year projection** +25%

Dodge Coronet wood-body wagon 1950

PRODUCTION

600

1950 Coronet wood-body wagon

HISTORY

Although the all-steel Sierra wagon is rarer (only 100 built), Dodge's last woodie wagon is better-looking and far more sought-after by collectors. Quality birch framing was used on doors and superstructure; the "mahogany" graining on the doors was not veneer but merely a decal.

FOR

Wood-body looks ●Fine carpentry ●Last of a type

AGAINST

Wood's susceptibility to rot and surface wear ●A crashing bore

SPECIFICATIONS

Length (in.) 197.4 **Wheelbase (in.)** 123.5 **Weight (lbs.)** 3850
Price (new) $2865

ENGINES

cid/type	bore x stroke	bhp	years
230.2 L6	3.25×4.63	103	1950

PRICES/PROJECTION

Restorable $1000-2000 **Good** $2000-5000
Excellent $5000-7500 **5-year projection** +35%

Dodge Wayfarer Sportabout 1950-51

1950 Wayfarer Sportabout 2-seat roadster

PRODUCTION

1950 2903   **1951** 1002

HISTORY

A continuation of the 1949 roadster with its own special name. Shared somewhat cleaner styling with other 1950-51 Dodge models. Should have sold better than it did at the low price, but remember that just another $100 bought a much more rakish Chevy convertible in these years.

FOR

As for 1949 Wayfarer roadster, plus low production

AGAINST

As for 1949 Wayfarer roadster

SPECIFICATIONS

Length (in.) 196.3 **Wheelbase (in.)** 115.0
Weight (lbs.) 3155-3175 **Price (new)** $1727-1924

ENGINES

cid/type	bore x stroke	bhp	years
230.2 L6	3.25×4.63	103	1950-51

PRICES/PROJECTION

Restorable $2300-3600 **Good** $4500-6800
Excellent $7200-9000 **5-year projection** +15%

Dodge Coronet Eight convertible 1953

1953 Coronet Eight convertible

PRODUCTION

4100

HISTORY

The collectible soft-top model in the series that ushered in Dodge's first V8. The famous Red Ram was essentially a scaled-down version of the Chrysler hemi, with smooth manifolding and porting, jumbo valves set well apart, excellent thermal efficiency, and considerable high-performance potential. The '53 Dodge line was restyled by Virgil Exner (who'd come to Chrysler from Studebaker in 1949), and looked lighter and less stodgy than earlier models. The V8 cars performed well, yet offered good economy. One returned 23.4 mpg in the 1953 Mobilgas Economy Run, while other Red Rams were in the process of breaking 196 AAA stock car speed records at Bonneville.

FOR

First V8 •Top-down allure •Acceptable styling •High performance •Reasonable price

AGAINST

Slow to gain collector recognition •Modest appreciation potential

SPECIFICATIONS

Length (in.) 189.6 **Wheelbase (in.)** 114.0 **Weight (lbs.)** 3438
Price (new) $2494

ENGINES

cid/type	bore x stroke	bhp	years
241.3/ohv V8	3.44×3.25	140	1953

PRICES/PROJECTION

Restorable $1500-2500 **Good** $3000-5000
Excellent $6000-8500 **5-year projection** +20%

Dodge Royal 500 1954

1954 Royal convertible (Royal 500 similar)

PRODUCTION

701

HISTORY

A pretty and quite desirable Dodge. A package model fashioned after the Royal convertible that paced the 1954 Indianapolis 500. Not a separate model, but a souped-up derivative of the standard Royal ragtop, which numbered 2000 in all. The 500 package included Kelsey-Hayes chrome plated wire wheels, an exterior spare tire mount, special trim, and a 150-bhp version of the Red Ram V8. For a little more money, an Offenhauser manifold and special carburetion that raised output to over 200 bhp was available as a dealer option.

FOR

Very desirable •Good styling •Sizzling performance

AGAINST

The most expensive collector Dodge of the 1950-70 era

SPECIFICATIONS

Length (in.) 196.0 **Wheelbase (in.)** 114.0 **Weight (lbs.)** 3575
Price (new) $2632

ENGINES

cid/type	bore x stroke	bhp	years
241.3/ohv V8	3.44×3.25	150	1954

PRICES/PROJECTION

Restorable $2500-3500 **Good** $4500-6500
Excellent $7500-9500 **5-year projection** +25%

Dodge Custom Royal two-doors 1955-56

1956 Custom Royal convertible

PRODUCTION

1955 2d hardtop 30,499 **convertible** 3302
1956 2d hardtop 26,000 (est.) **convertible** 2900 (est.)

HISTORY

Dodge's top-line 2-door hardtop and convertible, part of Chrysler Corporation's company-wide redesign in these years, the one that turned its fortunes around after the lean early-'50s period. Styling, evolved by Exner lieutenant Murray Baldwin, featured a bold divided grille and flashy side trim. The '55 Custom Royal prefigured 1956 Chrysler products in having small, chrome-plated bolt-on fins. A neat asymmetrical dash and plush interior were also provided. Lancer hardtops shared another new idea with the '55 DeSoto Coronado — three-tone paint jobs. A four-door Custom Royal hardtop also dubbed Lancer was added for 1956, but the two-doors have the edge in collector appeal.

FOR

Distinctive looks •Fine performance from standard V8 (higher power options available)

AGAINST

A certain flashiness that has not worn well

SPECIFICATIONS

Length (in.) 212.1 **Wheelbase (in.)** 120.0
Weight (lbs.) 3480-3630 **Price (new)** $2543-2913

ENGINES

cid/type	bore x stroke	bhp	years
270.1/ohv V8	3.63×3.25	183/193	1955
315/ohv V8	3.63×3.80	218/260	1956

PRICES/PROJECTION

HARDTOP **Restorable** $500-1000 **Good** $1000-2000
Excellent $3500-5000 CONVERTIBLE **Restorable** $1500-2500
Good $3500-5500 **Excellent** $5500-7500 Deduct 5-10% for
1956 models **5-year projection** +35%

Dodge Custom Royal
Lancer LaFemme 1955-56

1956 Custom Royal Lancer LaFemme 2-door hardtop

PRODUCTION

1000 (est.)

HISTORY

What the male chauvinists at Dodge thought women would die for
in the mid-'50s. Appeared as a trim option for the Lancer hardtop in
the spring of 1955. Included a pink and white color scheme and
a raft of interior accessories like a cosmetic kit and color-keyed
umbrella.

FOR

Unique limited edition • Others as for 1955-56 Custom Royal
Lancer

AGAINST

Ask Betty Friedan

SPECIFICATIONS

Length (in.) 212.1 **Wheelbase (in.)** 120.0
Weight (lbs.) 3480-3505 **Price (new)** $2843-2993

ENGINES

cid/type	bore x stroke	bhp	years
270.1/ohv V8	3.63×3.25	183/193	1955
315/ohv V8	3.63×3.80	218/260	1956

PRICES/PROJECTION

Restorable $2000-3000 **Good** $4500-6000
Excellent $6500-8500 **5-year projection** +50%

Dodge D-500
1956

1956 D-500 Royal 2-door hardtop

PRODUCTION

2500 (est.)

HISTORY

Not a distinct model, but a performance package available for any
'56 Dodge V8, Coronet, Royal, or Custom Royal. Consisted mainly
of a 260-bhp version of the Dodge 315 V8, plus appropriately stiffer
suspension settings. Most D-500s were based on the Custom
Royal, but a few Coronets were ordered this way by racers, and
were definitely wolves in sheep's clothing.

FOR

Terrific performance for the period • Rare

AGAINST

High operating costs

SPECIFICATIONS

Length (in.) 212.1 **Wheelbase (in.)** 120.0
Weight (lbs.) 3250-3630 **Price (new)** $2200-3000 (approx.)

ENGINES

cid/type	bore x stroke	bhp	years
315/ohv V8	3.63×3.80	260	1956

PRICES/PROJECTION

For Custom Royal add 25% to hardtop/convertible prices (see
1955-56 Dodge Custom Royal). On other models,
approximately the same as for Custom Royal hardtop

Dodge Custom Royal
two-doors 1957

PRODUCTION

2d hardtop 32,000 **convertible** 4000 (est.)

1957 Custom Royal Lancer 2-door hardtop

HISTORY

All-new "Swept-Wing" styling from the Virgil Exner studio, with bold fins and a glittery front end, marked the '57 Dodge. Despite a busy look and the Custom Royal's flashy paint job, the overall result was graceful and well integrated, and the '57 line sold well. The basic design was modestly facelifted for 1958, then became more bloated and garish for '59. Perhaps as a result of this, collector interest in these later models is not as strong. Like other '57 Chrysler products, Dodge acquired the firm's new torsion bar front suspension and optional three-speed pushbutton TorqueFlite automatic transmission. The new lower body featured greatly increased glass area, with compound-curve windshield on the convertible.

FOR

Decisively improved roadability • High performance

AGAINST

Seriously rust-prone • Sloppy construction quality • High operating costs

SPECIFICATIONS

Length (in.) 212.2   **Wheelbase (in.)** 122.0
Weight (lbs.) 3670-3810   **Price (new)** $2920-3146

ENGINES

cid/type	bore x stroke	bhp	years
325/ohv V8	3.69×3.80	260	1957

PRICES/PROJECTION

As for 1955-56 Dodge Custom Royal

Dodge D-500 1957-59

PRODUCTION

3000 (est.)

HISTORY

Continuation of Dodge's high-performance package in the late '50s, with a choice of conventional carburetor or fuel injection. The latter delivered 310, 333, and 345 bhp respectively for the three model years. Fast but less distinctive than the 1955-56 versions. Comparatively more scarce, however.

1957 D-500 convertible

DODGE D-500 continued

FOR

As for 1957 Custom Royal Lancer • Sensational go • Rarity

AGAINST

More expensive to run than standard Custom Royal • '59 styling • Others as for 1957 Custom Royal Lancer

SPECIFICATIONS

Length (in.) 212.2 (1957), 213.8 (1958), 217.4 (1959)
Wheelbase (in.) 122.0   **Weight (lbs.)** 3444-4000
Price (new) $2200-3500 (approx.)

ENGINES

cid/type	bore x stroke	bhp	years
325/ohv V8	3.69×3.80	285/310	1957
354/ohv V8	3.94×3.63	340	1957
361/ohv V8	4.12×3.68	305/333	1958
383/ohv V8	4.25×3.38	320/345	1959

PRICES/PROJECTION

Restorable $1500-2500   **Good** $3500-5000
Excellent $5000-7500   **5-year projection** +20%

Dodge Lancer GT 1962

PRODUCTION

13,683

HISTORY

Chevy's Corvair Monza proved that bucket seats, floorshift, high-trim interiors, and sporty styling made compacts much more saleable than as low-line economy small cars, and everybody rushed to copy it. At Dodge this meant a tricked-up version of the compact Lancer, introduced for 1961 as a badge-engineered divisional sibling of the Plymouth Valiant. Based on 1961's new two-door hardtop, the Lancer GT for '62 was hardly a grand tourer in the accepted sense, but it was a pleasant little car, and shared Virgil Exner's interesting Valiant styling. In basic design and appointments it paralleled the '62 Valiant Signet hardtop. For its 1963 compacts Dodge discarded the Lancer name in favor of Dart, making this a one-year-only model.

1962 Lancer GT 2-door hardtop

FOR

Rugged slant-six engine (still built today), with a 225-cid "big-block" available • Right size for today's driving • Cheap

AGAINST

Styling a bit bulgy • Rust-prone • Indifferent fit and finish

SPECIFICATIONS

Length (in.) 188.8 **Wheelbase (in.)** 106.5 **Weight (lbs.)** 2560
Price (new) $2257

ENGINES

cid/type	bore x stroke	bhp	years
170/ohv I6	3.40×3.13	101	1962
225/ohv I6	3.40×4.13	145	1962

PRICES/PROJECTION

Restorable $300-800 **Good** $1000-2000
Excellent $2000-3000 **5-year projection** +35%

Dodge Dart GT 1963-66

1964 Dart GT 2-door hardtop

PRODUCTION

1963 sixes 34,227 **1964 sixes** 37,660 **V8s** 12,170
1965 sixes 35,000* **V8s** 10,000* **1966 sixes** 20,000*
V8s 10,000*
*estimated

1965 Dart GT convertible

HISTORY

Successor to the Lancer GT as Dodge's sporty compact. Slightly upsized with a new body. Styling by Elwood Engel has a minimum of fussiness (except maybe grilles) that has worn well. The GTs offered the most deluxe Dart trim and several sporty mechanical options. From 1964, Chrysler's fine 273-cid V8 (from which the revised 1967 318 was derived) was listed as an option. Up to 235 bhp was available for '65, making this one of the hotter compacts around. The same basic package was continued for 1966 in a rather effective facelift with more squared-off lines.

FOR

Affordable • Wide powerteam choice • Available as hardtop and convertible • Attractive styling • Decent road manners

AGAINST

Limited collector interest • Limited appreciation potential • Body-rot tendency

SPECIFICATIONS

Length (in.) 196.4 **Wheelbase (in.)** 111.0
Weight (lbs.) 2670-2995 **Price (new)** $2289-2828

ENGINES

cid/type	bore x stroke	bhp	years
170/ohv I6	3.40×3.13	101	1963-66
225/ohv I6	3.40×4.13	145	1963-66
273.5/ohv V8	3.63×3.31	180/235	1965-66

PRICES/PROJECTION

Restorable $500-1000 **Good** $1000-2500
Excellent $3000-4500 Deduct 25% for hardtop and 15% for six-cylinder engines **5-year projection** +10%

Dodge Coronet Hemi-Charger 1965

PRODUCTION

500 (est.)

HISTORY

A lightweight, high-powered two-door sedan riding a special 2-inch shorter wheelbase than other '65 Dodge intermediates. Built strictly for the Division's stock-car and drag racing programs, and one of the most formidable street cars you could buy (not an easy chore as most were snapped up by the pros). Base price included heavy-duty suspension, anti-roll bar, four-speed gearbox, "police" brakes, and the mighty 426-cid street/stock hemi V8 pumping out 365 bhp (and 425 was optional). The Hemi-Charger could turn 0-60 mph in seven seconds flat and hit 120 mph. Non-street versions cleaned up on the strips during the '65 season.

FOR

One of the more unique performance cars of the decade ● Clean styling ● Rarity ● Gobs of power

AGAINST

Poor fit and finish ● Very expensive to run or restore ● Hard to find one, let alone one that hasn't been thrashed

SPECIFICATIONS

Length (in.) 204.2 **Wheelbase (in.)** 115.0 **Weight (lbs.)** 3165
Price (new) NA

ENGINES

cid/type	bore x stroke	bhp	years
426/ohv V8	4.25×3.75	365/425	1965

PRICES/PROJECTION

Restorable $2000-3500 **Good** $3500-6000
Excellent $7000-10,000 **5-year projection** +25%

Dodge Charger 1966-67

PRODUCTION

1966 37,344　**1967** 15,788

HISTORY

Dodge's response to the fastback fad started by Plymouth's Barracuda and the Mustang 2+2, but on a larger scale. Launched at mid-model year 1966, but originally scheduled for introduction to preview the '66 Coronet, with which it shared most sheetmetal below the beltline. Because it was an intermediate like the Rambler Marlin, the Charger could have been an esthetic disaster, but long side windows prevented its sweeping roof from looking too heavy. Unique touches included hideaway headlamps, a standard V8, and

1967 Charger fastback 2-door hardtop

a split fold-down rear seatback with trunk partition *a la* Barracuda. Power options ran from the 361 and 383 V8s up to the 426 hemi, and manual transmission and Rally suspension were also available. With automatic and the 383, the car timed out at 9 seconds in the 0-60 mph dash, and could reach 110mph (or more with longer gearing). Not a big sales winner in these years, but the fuselage-shaped '68 design would change all that.

FOR

Handsome in its way (better looking than a Marlin) ● Wide power-team choices (but 383 or hemi fidgety for the street) ● Cargo-carrying versatility ● Busy but fully instrumented dash

AGAINST

Styling won't win awards ● Mediocre construction quality ● High running costs

SPECIFICATIONS

Length (in.) 208.0 **Wheelbase (in.)** 117.0
Weight (lbs.) 3480-3499 **Price (new)** $3122-3130

ENGINES

cid/type	bore x stroke	bhp	years
318/ohv V8	3.91×3.31	230	1966-67
361/ohv V8	4.13×3.38	265	1966
383/ohv V8	4.25×3.38	325	1966-67
426/ohv V8	4.25×3.75	425	1966-67
440/ohv V8	4.32×3.75	375	1967

PRICES/PROJECTION

Restorable $500-1300 **Good** $2000-3000
Excellent $3000-4500 Add 25% for hemi V8, 10% for 1967 R/T model **5-year projection** +10%

Dodge Coronet R/T 1967-70

1968 Coronet R/T 2-door hardtop

PRODUCTION

1967 10,000 (est.)　**1968** 10,849　**1969** 7238　**1970** 2615

HISTORY

Offered in 2-door hardtop or convertible form, the R/T (for Road/Track) version of the mid-size Dodge was a crisply styled, luxurious, high-speed machine. It packed the "Magnum" 440 V8 as standard and offered the 426 hemi as an option. Features included heavy-duty suspension, bucket seats, special identification, and Dodge's bumblebee tail striping. A vast styling improvement occurred for 1968, and this design continued through the final Coronet R/T of 1970. For '71 Coronet became more mundane, and Dodge performance buyers had to look to other models.

FOR

Good styling (very good from 1968 on) • Outstanding performance

AGAINST

Little collector following • Fuelishness • Mediocre quality control

SPECIFICATIONS

Length (in.) 209.2 **Wheelbase (in.)** 117.0
Weight (lbs.) 3530-3721 **Price (new)** $3199-3785

ENGINES

cid/type	bore x stroke	bhp	years
426/ohv V8	4.25×3.75	425	1967-69
440/ohv V8	4.32×3.75	375/390	1967-70

PRICES/PROJECTION

Restorable $1500-2500 **Good** $2500-5000
Excellent $4500-7000 **5-year projection** +25% Deduct 25% for hardtop or 1969-70 models

Dodge Charger R/T 1968-70

1970 Charger R/T 2-door hardtop

PRODUCTION

1968 20,000 (est.) **1969** 20,057 **1970** 10,337 (includes Daytona model)

HISTORY

All-new notchback replacement for Dodge's fastback sports/specialty mid-size. A styling sensation then, and still looks great today. The R/T was the more sporting of the two versions initially offered, identified by its "Scat Pack" bumblebee-striped tail, and comprehensively equipped for grand touring American-style. The usual plethora of powerplants was available, including the hemi. In these cars Dodge achieved a combination rare in Detroit: classic lines, outstanding performance, and better-than-average quality control. It was a good one. Unfortunately, it wouldn't last long. Styling deteriorated, and more emphasis was placed on luxury than performance after 1970, a reflection of sky-high insurance rates and dwindling customer demand for hot cars. The name continued through the '70s until it was completely watered down for Dodge's duplicate of the Chrysler Cordoba. It's currently in use on a "performance" version of the front-drive 024 coupe.

FOR

Underrated and probably undervalued in today's market

AGAINST

Only its basic character; high-compression, high-octane engines don't cope well with today's low-calorie gas

SPECIFICATIONS

Length (in.) 208.0 **Wheelbase (in.)** 117.0
Weight (lbs.) 3575-3610 **Price (new)** $3506-3711

ENGINES

cid/type	bore x stroke	bhp	years
318/ohv V8	3.91×3.31	230	1968-70
383/ohv V8	4.25×3.38	290/330/335	1970
426/ohv V8	4.25×3.75	425	1968-70
440/ohv V8	4.32×3.75	375/390	1968-70

PRICES/PROJECTION

Restorable $1000-1250 **Good** $1500-3000 **426** +250%
Excellent $3500-5500 **5-year projection** +10%

Dodge Coronet Super Bee 1968-70

1968 Coronet Super Bee 2-door coupe

PRODUCTION

1968 20,000 (est.) **1969** 27,846 **1970** 15,506

HISTORY

The budget version of the Coronet R/T, much in the mold of the Plymouth Road Runner. Packed the Mopar 383 V8 as standard. Available as a pillared coupe in its first year like Road Runner, with a two-door hardtop alternative for 1969 and '70. However, unlike Plymouth, Dodge never offered a convertible version of its low-bucks muscle car. Roughly comparable in interior appointments to the Coronet 440, and marked externally by the bumblebee tail striping Dodge used in those years on all its hotter models, which formed the "Scat Pack." In its final season, the Super Bee was listed with the big hemi V8 as an option, as well as the 390-bhp 440 "six-pack" V8 with three two-barrel carbs.

FOR

As for Coronet R/T

AGAINST

As for Coronet R/T

SPECIFICATIONS

Length (in.) 209.2 **Wheelbase (in.)** 117.0
Weight (lbs.) 3200-3535 **Price (new)** $3027-3138

ENGINES

cid/type	bore x stroke	bhp	years
383/ohv V8	4.25×3.38	335	1968-70
426/ohv V8	4.25×3.75	425	1970
440/ohv V8	4.32×3.75	390	1970

PRICES/PROJECTION

Restorable $1000-2000 **Good** $2000-3000
Excellent $3500-4500 **5-year projection** +15%

Dodge Dart GTS 1968-69

1968 Dart GTS 2-door hardtop

PRODUCTION

1968 8745 **1969** 6702

HISTORY

Dodge's answer to the Chevrolet Nova SS, and based on the rebodied 1967 design by Elwood Engel. Darts in general have yet to achieve collector status, with one exception: the hot GTS, with a standard 340-cid V8 or Chrysler's potent 383 offered optionally. Available as a hardtop or convertible, both luxuriously and comprehensively equipped. At about 3000 pounds, these were tremendously powerful, often greatly underrated by opponents on the dragstrip.

FOR

Low-cost performance ● Neat styling

AGAINST

Indifferent quality ● Growing parts scarcity ● Low appreciation

SPECIFICATIONS

Length (in.) 195.4 **Wheelbase (in.)** 110.0
Weight (lbs.) 3065-3210 **Price (new)** $3189-3419

ENGINES

cid/type	bore x stroke	bhp	years
340/ohv V8	4.04×3.31	275	1968-69
383/ohv V8	4.25×3.38	300/330	1968-69

PRICES/PROJECTION

Restorable $500-1500 **Good** $2000-3000
Excellent $3000-5000 Deduct 10% for hardtop.
5-year projection +10%

Dodge Charger Daytona 1969

1969 Charger Daytona 2-door hardtop

PRODUCTION

between 501 and 507 (factory figure 505)

HISTORY

Aerodynamic weapon to help Dodge take the NASCAR title away from Ford, and built by Creative Industries in Detroit. Featured a smooth droop-snoot (with hidden headlights) bolted to the front frame members and a huge rear stabilizer wing supported by struts mounted from inside the trunk. "Street" Daytonas scored 14.5-second quarter-mile times at around 95 mph when equipped with the Mopar 440 V8. Won 80 percent of the races it entered, and helped Dodge take 22 Grand Nationals, four less than Ford. Dodge built only enough to qualify it for NASCAR, and production ceased after 1969. Instead, a Daytona performance version of the 1970 Charger R/T was fielded while Plymouth's Superbird took up where the winged Dodge left off.

FOR

An important contributor to performance and racing history ● Wild looks ● Outstanding performance

AGAINST

Nervous in daily use ● Slack quality control ● Cop-baiting appearance ● Probably won't have been pampered

SPECIFICATIONS

Length (in.) 220.0 **Wheelbase (in.)** 117.0
Weight (lbs.) approx. 3900 **Price (new)** approx. $4000

ENGINES

cid/type	bore x stroke	bhp	years
440/ohv V8	4.32×3.75	375	1969
426/ohv V8	4.25×3.75	425	1969

PRICES/PROJECTION

Restorable $2000-3500 **Good** $3500-5000
Excellent $5000-7500 **5-year projection** +30%

Dodge Challenger
1970-74

1970 Challenger R/T convertible

PRODUCTION

1970 83,032 (19,938 R/T) **1971** 29,883 (4630 R/Ts)
1972 26,658 (8123 Rallyes) **1973** 32,596 **1974** 16,437

HISTORY

Dodge's belated answer to the Camaro/Mustang and a near-cousin to Plymouth's contemporary Barracuda apart from external skin and a two-inch-longer wheelbase. Too late to do Dodge much good in the declining ponymarket, and sales tapered off rapidly. All models have lately become valid collectibles, but the lower-volume specialty models like the R/T and its 1970-only T/A offshoot (equivalent to the AAR 'Cuda) continue to command the most interest. A good solid convertible is worth looking at, because ragtops were so few: 4243 for 1970 (1070 R/T), 2165 total for 1971, and none after that. Just 4630 R/Ts were sold for '71, while the last "special" Challenger was the slick-looking 1972 Rallye (8123 units). Among R/Ts the 340 and 383 V-8s are the best choices (the available 440 and Hemi simply overwhelmed the chassis).

FOR

Uncommon ponycar • Muscle models' high performance • Smooth styling • Still cheap

AGAINST

Poor construction/material quality • Rust-prone • Heavy and thirsty • Real room only for two

SPECIFICATIONS

Length (in.) 191.3 **Wheelbase (in.)** 110.0
Weight (lbs.) 3028-3495 **Price (new)** $2727-3273

ENGINES

cid/type	bore x stroke	bhp	years
225.0/L6	3.40×4.13	110/145	1970-72
318.0/V8	3.91×3.31	150/230	1970-74
340.0/V8	4.04×3.31	240/275	1970-73
360.0/V8	4.00×3.58	245	1974
383.0/V8	4.25×3.38	275/335	1970-71
426.0/V8	4.25×3.75	425	1970-71
440.0/V8	4.32×3.75	375/390	1970-71

PRICES/PROJECTION

STANDARD **Restorable** $500-1500 **Good** $2000-3000
Excellent $2800-4000 R/T add 10%, T/A add 25%, convertibles add 15%, Rallye & S.E. add 5% **5-year projection** convertibles and T/A +10%, others +5%

Dual-Ghia
1956-58

1957 convertible

PRODUCTION

117 (includes 13 prototypes; two cars were converted to hardtops)

HISTORY

Conceived by auto transport contractor Eugene Casaroll, who formed Dual Motors in Detroit to build this limited-production convertible based on Virgil Exner's Dodge Firebomb/Firearrow show cars of the early '50s. When Chrysler decided not to put the basic design into production, Casaroll bought the original Firebomb show car, had it reengineered, and contracted to buy complete Dodge chassis, including the hot D-500 V8. The plan was to build 150 Dual-Ghias per year. Chassis were shipped to Turin, Italy where the Ghia coachworks hammered out the steel bodies by hand over aluminum dies. Designer Paul Farago had added extra passenger and cargo space to enhance liveability. Quality was the watchword: body moldings were held in place with chrome-plated brass clips, and interiors were swathed in genuine Connolly hides. Ghia fitted body to chassis, and the completed assembly was returned to Detroit where Dual Motors installed the drivetrain and the interior trim. Despite all its custom craftsmanship, the D-G was priced less than a contemporary Cadillac Eldorado and Continental Mark II. Hollywood personalities (notably Frank Sinatra, Peter Lawford, and other members of the "Rat Pack") vied with one another to get on the waiting list. But mounting costs combined with Casaroll's refusal to compromise quality lost the company money on every car. Distinctive and quite fast, with a top speed of 120 mph reported in a contemporary road test. The first-generation D-G venture wound down in 1958.

FOR

Exclusivity • Handsome good looks • Strongly built • Excellent performance

AGAINST

Very costly now • Body hardware extinct • Multi-piece Italian body seriously rust-prone

SPECIFICATIONS

Length (in.) 203.0 **Wheelbase (in.)** 115.0 **Weight (lbs.)** 3800
Price (new) $7741

ENGINES

cid/type	bore x stroke	bhp	years
315/ohv V8	3.63×3.80	230-285	1956-58

PRICES/PROJECTION

Restorable $5000-8000 Good $7000-12,000
Excellent $14,000-18,000 5-year projection no change

Dual-Ghia L6.4 1961-63

1961 L6.4 2-door hardtop

PRODUCTION

26

HISTORY

A comeback attempt by Casaroll and company. Built only as a glassy two-door hardtop with new styling by Ghia, though frontal appearance was quite similar to that of the earlier D-G. The model designation relates to the displacement, in liters, of the Chrysler 383-cid wedgehead V8, but there were fewer Mopar components (including the separate chassis, which was now a special design as Chrysler had switched to unit construction for all its cars except Imperial in 1960). Twice as costly as its predecessor and faster but softer riding, with handling not as taut as that of the earlier cars. But svelte good looks made up for a lot, and everybody who was anybody wanted one. Again, however, incredibly high overhead costs plagued the project, and Casaroll called it quits after a mere handful of cars were built. He would go on to play a role in the project that led to a new Stutz, born out of Virgil Exner's proposal for a modern Duesenberg.

FOR

As for 1956-58 Dual-Ghia, and even more desirable

AGAINST

As for 1956-58 Dual Ghia, but even costlier and harder to find

SPECIFICATIONS

Length (in.) 210.0 Wheelbase (in.) 115.0 Weight (lbs.) 4200
Price (new) $13,500

ENGINES

cid/type	bore x stroke	bhp	years
383/ohv V8	4.25×3.38	335	1961-63

PRICES/PROJECTION

Restorable $5000-8000 Good $8000-15,000
Excellent $15,000-20,000 5-year projection +10%

Duesenberg Model J/SJ/ SSJ/JN 1930-37

Model SJN "Twenty Grand" sedan by Rollson

PRODUCTION

470 incl. 36 Model SJ, 2 Model SSJ, 10 Model JN; total engines: 480 (began 1928)

HISTORY

The undisputed "King of the Classics," announced in 1928 by E.L. Cord and engineered by Fred Duesenberg. Powered by an exquisite 32-valve Lycoming straight eight with 200 horsepower (ads claimed 265) and capable of 90 mph in second gear and about 115 mph in top, aided by extensive use of weight-saving materials that made these mammoths surprisingly light. Bodywork was anything the customer desired—and could afford—so "standard" examples were few. Supercharged SJ bowed in 1932 with 320 bhp or, with August Duesenberg's "ram's horn" manifolds, a smashing 400 bhp. A stock SJ could hit 104 mph in second and 140 flat-out, and racing great Ab Jenkins recorded 160 mph on one trial lap. Tremendous in size and presence, Duesies nevertheless had balance, precision, and finesse, and were remarkably docile at low speeds. Two short-chassis SJ roadsters, designated SSJ, were built for and purchased by actors Gary Cooper and Clark Gable. The lithe LeGrand bodywork was symbolic more of Gable's personality than Coop's. Both cars have survived. Comparatively plain Model JN appeared in 1935 as a last gasp, built only on the long wheelbase but equipped with smaller 17-inch-diameter wheels. E.L. Cord built "the world's finest motor car" with no real plan to make money, and Duesenberg didn't. What killed it, however, was not the Depression but the collapse of Cord's business empire in 1937.

FOR

Everything (to quote Ken Purdy: "With his mind and his two good hands [Fred Duesenberg] had created something new and good and, in its way, immortal.")

AGAINST

The near-impossible odds of owning one

SPECIFICATIONS

Length (in.) NA (variable with body) Wheelbase (in.) 142.5, 153.5 (JN, lwb J), 125.0 (SSJ) Weight (lbs.) 4800-5200
Price (new) from $11,000; average $15,000-18,000 depending on body (J chassis $8500)

ENGINES

cid/type	bore x stroke	*bhp	**years
420.0/dohc I8	3.75×4.75	200, 320/400	1930-37
*J	**SJ		

PRICES/PROJECTION

It would take a small book to analyze Duesenberg values completely. Even then it would probably be obsolete after the next major auction. The scarcity and desirability of all these cars render all the usual rules meaningless. For instance, a very special closed model may sell for as much as a phaeton. A quarter million dollars may be assumed as a starting point for open cars, $175,000 for closed cars (most Duesenbergs have been restored at least once). Buyers should be particularly aware of the increasing number of counterfeit bodies (there are now more open Duesies around than were originally built) and should consult qualified appraisers.

Du Pont Models G & H
1930-32

PRODUCTION

Model G (including 1929) 273 **Model H** 3

HISTORY

Built by E. Paul DuPont (not Pierre S. of GM) and among the finest luxury cars of its day. The dashing and beautiful Model G appeared in 1929, powered by a 140-bhp Continental side-valve eight. Most bodies were by Merrimac, with a handful from Waterhouse and Derham. The Model H of 1931 was essentially a long-wheelbase G but only three were built: a sedan, a limousine, and a magnificent sport phaeton "with tonneau cowl." Painted black and white, the latter is well known among Classic enthusiasts today. Production ceased at the Moore, Pennsylvania plant in January 1932. Mr. DuPont considered carrying on with a lower-priced product, but ultimately decided to rest on his laurels.

FOR

High exclusivity • Vivid styling with a highly recognizeable front-ispiece • Strong investment potential • The magic of a famous name

AGAINST

Expensive to buy and restore (although most restorations have been done) • Difficult parts situation

SPECIFICATIONS

Length (in.) NA **Wheelbase (in.)** 144.0 (Model G), 146.0 (Model H) **Weight (lbs.)** NA **Price (new)** NA

ENGINES

cid/type	bore x stroke	bhp	years
322.1/L8	3.38×4.50	140	1930-32

PRICES/PROJECTION

CLOSED MODELS **Restorable** $6000-18,000 **Good** $18,000-24,000 **Excellent** $24,000-36,000. Phaeton & touring add 100%. Other open models add 30%. Model H add 70%. **5-year projection** +20%

Edsel Citation
1958

1958 Citation 4-door hardtop

PRODUCTION

4d hardtop 5112 **2d hardtop** 2535 **convertible** 930

HISTORY

The brightest and the best in the debut year of what would turn out to be Ford Motor Company's biggest flop. The most interesting and luxurious of the '58 Edsel line, and not cheap when new. Despite considerable size and weight, quite speedy thanks to torquey big-block V8. Shared chassis and bodyshell with the '58 Mercury. Featured a full array of late-'50s gadgetry, such as "Teletouch" automatic transmission (pushbuttons in the steering wheel hub), a rotating drum speedometer that changed color as speed rose (a throwback to the '30s), and every power accessory known to the civilized world. The Citation convertible would be the most expensive Edsel ever built, and was also the second lowest in production this year, making it a highly coveted commodity. In all, Edsel showed that even the best market research can mislead if you don't ask the right questions. "Do we really *need* another medium-priced car?" was the one Ford should have asked in the first place.

FOR

Looks like no other car on the road • Power • Luxury • Large club following • "Lost cause" panache • Better quality control than on smaller Ford-based Edsels

AGAINST

Retains its "loser" image to this day • Styling more panned than praised • Gulps gas • Electrical maladies

SPECIFICATIONS

Length (in.) 218.9 **Wheelbase (in.)** 124.0 **Weight (lbs.)** 4136-4311 **Price (new)** $3535-3801

ENGINES

cid/type	bore x stroke	bhp	years
410/ohv V8	4.25×3.70	345	1958

PRICES/PROJECTION

HARDTOPS **Restorable** $500-1000 **Good** $2000-3500 **Excellent** $3500-5000 CONVERTIBLE **Restorable** $1200-2000 **Good** $2500-4500 **Excellent** $6000-8500 **5-year projection** +10%

Edsel Corsair
1958

1958 Corsair 4-door hardtop

PRODUCTION

4d hardtop 5880   **2d hardtop** 3312

HISTORY

The next step down on the Edsel price-and-luxury ladder for '58, a slightly detrimmed version of the Citation. Aside from front fender script, marked externally by absence of the contrasting color insert used on the Citation's concave rear fender "spears." No convertible offered, but based on the same Mercury platform and powered by the larger of Edsel's two V8s.

FOR

As for 1958 Citation, but more affordable

AGAINST

As for 1958 Citation

SPECIFICATIONS

Length (in.) 218.9   **Wheelbase (in.)** 124.0
Weight (lbs.) 4134-4235   **Price (new)** $3346-3425

ENGINES

cid/type	bore x stroke	bhp	years
410/ohv V8	4.20×3.70	345	1958

PRICES/PROJECTION

Restorable $500-1000 **Good** $1500-2750
Excellent $3000-5000 **5-year projection** +10%

Edsel Pacer
1958

PRODUCTION

2d hardtop 6139   **4d sedan** 6083   **4d hardtop** 4959
convertible 1876   **Bermuda 6-pass. wagon** 1456   **Bermuda
9-pass. wagon** 779

1958 Pacer 2-door hardtop

HISTORY

The more expensive and better equipped of Edsel's two junior series for '58, based on the 118-inch-wheelbase (116 for wagons) platform introduced with the 1957 Ford. Shared basic styling and interior design with the Citation/Corsair, but had a notably lighter "greenhouse." The lineup included the Bermuda wagon with simulated wood side trim *a la* Ford's Country Squire. The 9-passenger version is the rarest of the '58 Edsels. Like the cheaper companion Ranger series, available only with a 361 V8 based on Ford's FE-series Y-block engine, and, with its light body, was probably the most agile Edsel. Also like Ranger, built alongside Fords at the firm's Louisville assembly plant where quality control was more lax than on the senior cars built by Lincoln-Mercury.

FOR

Cheaper than Citation/Corsair ● Speedy ● "Distinctive" looks

AGAINST

Less power and sheer luxury than the bigger models ● Piggish thirst ● Construction quality borders on slipshod

SPECIFICATIONS

Length (in.) 213.1 (wagons: 205.5)   **Wheelbase (in.)** 118.0
(wagons: 116.0)   **Weight (lbs.)** 3773-3919
Price (new) $2375-3247

ENGINES

cid/type	bore x stroke	bhp	years
361/ohv V8	4.05×3.50	303	1958

PRICES/PROJECTION

Restorable $500-1000 **Good** $1500-2250
Excellent $3000-4500 CONVERTIBLE **Restorable** $1000-2000
Good $2500-4000 **Excellent** $5500-7500
5-year projection +10%

Edsel Ranger
1958

PRODUCTION

4d sedan 6576   **2d hardtop** 5546   **2d sedan** 4615
4d hardtop 3077   **Villager 6-pass. wagon** 2294   **Villager
9-pass. wagon** 978   **Roundup 2d wagon** 963

HISTORY

The bottom end of the '58 Edsel line, using the shorter wheelbase

1958 Ranger 4-door hardtop

and smaller engine of the Pacer. Same basic styling, but simplified side trim and interior decor. Body styles unique to this series were the 2-door sedan and Roundup wagon.

FOR

Affordable (and likely to remain so) ● Others as for other 1958s

AGAINST

The slowest appreciation rate among '58 Edsels ● The least exciting, too

SPECIFICATIONS

Length (in.) 213.1 (wagons: 205.5) **Wheelbase (in.)** 118.0 (wagons: 116.0) **Weight (lbs.)** 3729-3900
Price (new) $2519-2990

ENGINES

cid/type	bore x stroke	bhp	years
361/ohv V8	4.05×3.50	303	1958

PRICES/PROJECTION

Restorable $500-1000 **Good** $1000-2000
Excellent $2500-4500 **5-year projection** no change

Edsel Corsair 1959

1959 Corsair 4-door hardtop

PRODUCTION

4d sedan 3301 **2d hardtop** 2315 **4d hardtop** 1694
convertible 1343

HISTORY

The uppermost series for the second year of Dearborn's million-dollar baby. Now based exclusively on the Ford chassis and body-

shell, the Edsel lineup was consolidated around three series (wagons were broken out from other body styles). The pre-ordained facelift was shared by all: a more unified grille still dominated by the central "horse collar" motif, restyled taillights, and revised side trim. As a result, the '59s were chromier than the '58s. Prices were slashed in an effort to attract customers back into near-deserted showrooms. The costliest model, the Corsair convertible, listed at just $3072 versus the $3801 of the comparable '58 Citation. Ford's 332 V8 was standard for Corsair, and the 361 unit from the previous year's smaller models was optional across the board. There was also a reduction in gimmickry, such as the troublesome Teletouch transmission pushbuttons that were replaced by a conventional column lever control.

FOR

Less unique appearance, but possibly more successful ● All models still in good supply, including convertibles

AGAINST

Less distinctively "Edsel" than the '58s ● Won't ever appreciate as much, either

SPECIFICATIONS

Length (in.) 210.9 **Wheelbase (in.)** 120.0
Weight (lbs.) 3696-3790 **Price (new)** $2812-3072

ENGINES

cid/type	bore x stroke	bhp	years
332/ohv V8	4.00×3.30	225	1959
361/ohv V8	4.05×3.30	303	1959

PRICES/PROJECTION

CONVERTIBLE **Restorable** $2000-3500 **Good** $3500-5000
Excellent $5000-7000 Deduct 50% for other models.
5-year projection +10%

Edsel Ranger hardtops 1959

1959 Ranger 4-door hardtop

PRODUCTION

2d hardtop 5474 **4d hardtop** 2352

HISTORY

The '59 Ranger four-door sedan set the Edsel production record for a single model (12,814 units), which makes it comparatively plentiful today. But it's the scarcer hardtops that should concern the collector. Less elaborately trimmed and equipped than Corsairs, they were available with an optional six, Ford's well-known 223-cid unit, as well as a standard 292 V8. The Corsair's standard 332-cid powerplant and the carryover 361 V8 were also offered. Most comments for the '59 Corsair also apply here.

FOR

As for '59 Corsair, but priced less

AGAINST

As for '59 Corsair, but slower to appreciate and less luxurious

SPECIFICATIONS

Length (in.) 210.9   **Wheelbase (in.)** 120.0
Weight (lbs.) 3591-3682   **Price (new)** $2691-2756

ENGINES

cid/type	bore x stroke	bhp	years
223/ohv I6	3.62×3.60	145	1959
292/ohv V8	3.75×3.30	200	1959
332/ohv V8	4.00×3.30	225	1959
361/ohv V8	4.05×3.50	303	1959

PRICES/PROJECTION

Restorable $500-1000 **Good** $1500-2500
Excellent $2750-4500 **5-year projection** +10%

Edsel Ranger
1960

1960 Ranger 4-door sedan

PRODUCTION

4d sedan 1288   **2d sedan** 777   **2d hardtop** 295
4d hardtop 135   **convertible** 76

HISTORY

The last of the Edsels, and obviously related to this year's Ford with which it shared a brand-new bodyshell. Though much more conventional in appearance, the '60 was short-lived: by now it was too late to save Edsel. Production ceased after only 3000 units had been built, making these the rarest (and therefore the most desirable) Edsels. The Ranger was one of two series (Villager wagons was the other). Front end styling abandoned the much-joked-about

"Olds-sucking-a-lemon" vertical motif in favor of a neat, horizontal split grille quite similar to the '59 Pontiac's (though this was purely a coincidence). Heavy chrome accents appeared on a full-length crease along the upper bodysides, and a drooping thinner chrome molding was used below. At the rear, twin vertical oval pods housed taillights and backup lamps either side, and looked distinctive if a bit out of place on a rear panel clearly designed for the Ford's half-square units. The six was still a no-cost extra, while a 352 V8 was offered at $58 extra.

FOR

Last of the line ● Very rare ● Strong appreciation

AGAINST

Little distinction ● Parts in short supply

SPECIFICATIONS

Length (in.) 216.4   **Wheelbase (in.)** 120.0
Weight (lbs.) 3601-3836   **Price (new)** $2643-3000

ENGINES

cid/type	bore x stroke	bhp	years
223/ohv I6	3.62×3.50	145	1960
292/ohv V8	3.75×3.30	185	1960
352/ohv V8	4.00×3.50	300	1960

PRICES/PROJECTION

CONVERTIBLE **Restorable** $1200-2000 **Good** $2500-4000
Excellent $5500-8000 OTHERS **Restorable** $500-1500
Good $1500-2500 **Excellent** $2750-4500 **5-year projection** +10%

Edsel Villager
1960

1960 Villager 6-passenger wagon

PRODUCTION

6-pass. 216   **9-pass.** 59

HISTORY

Edsel wagons are not as desirable as other body styles, but these two 1960 Villagers are so rare as to be an exception. With less than 300 built, they are hot in Edsel circles, and probably undervalued. Shared basic styling and mechanicals with the 1960 Ranger models, and comments about them also apply here.

FOR

Rarity • Interesting styling (a Ford that took pep pills?) • Others as for 1960 Ranger

AGAINST

As for 1960 Ranger

SPECIFICATIONS

Length (in.) 214.8 **Wheelbase (in.)** 120.0
Weight (lbs.) 4029-4046 **Price (new)** $2989-3072

ENGINES

cid/type	bore x stroke	bhp	years
223/ohv I6	3.62×3.50	145	1960
292/ohv V8	3.75×3.30	185	1960
352/ohv V8	4.00×3.50	300	1960

PRICES/PROJECTION

Restorable $500-1000 **Good** $1800-2500
Excellent $2500-4000 **5-year projection** no change

Excalibur Series I/II/III 1965-69

1975-79 Series III Phaeton

PRODUCTION

Series I (1965-69) 359 (incl. 168 SSKs) **Series II (1970-74)** 342
Series III (1975-79) 1141 (incl. 76 roadsters)

HISTORY

First and most successful of the neoclassics. Conceived as the SS for Studebaker on the Lark Daytona convertible chassis, but switched to Corvette power in independent production. The initial two-seat SSK was a handsome brute styled much in the image of the early-'30s Mercedes SSK that inspired it. A bulkier roadster and phaeton were available from 1966. With introduction of the longer-wheelbase Series II in 1970, the phaeton came to dominate sales. The Series II discarded the old Lark frame for a purpose-designed chassis with all-independent suspension. This was continued for the Series III, basically the II modified to meet federal safety and emissions standards. This in turn gave way to the much plusher and larger Series IV of 1980, which followed Mercedes' own move toward streamlining in the late Thirties. Though certainly collectible, it is too soon to make judgments and value guesses on the Series IV. Originally designed by Brooks Stevens and carried forward by his sons David and Steve, the Excalibur shows what devoted enthusiasts with plentiful talent can accomplish. After a 1985 brush with Chapter 11 bankruptcy, Acquisition Company reorganized Excalibur in 1986 to market Series V cars, and in 1987 added a four-door sedan and limo.

FOR

High fun quotient • Crowd-pleasing looks • Goes and handles with competence • SSK roadster a magnificent replica if not absolutely exact • Parts, service, factory support all good

AGAINST

Collector bias against all replicas • Phaeton's hulky coachwork • Series I rather spartan

SPECIFICATIONS

Length (in.) 170.0 (Series I) **Wheelbase (in.)** 109.0 (Series I); 111.0 (Series II); 112.0 (Series III) **Weight (lbs.)** 2100-2650 (Series I); 2900-3000 (Series II); 4350 (Series III)
Price (new) $7250-10,000 (Series I); $12,500-17,000 (Series II); $18,900-28,600 (Series III)

ENGINES

cid/type	bore x stroke	bhp	years
327.0/V8	4.00×3.25	300/435	1966-69
350.0/V8	4.00×3.48	300	1970-74
454.0/V8	4.25×4.00	180-215	1975-79

PRICES/PROJECTION

SSK Restorable $5000-10,000 **Good** $10,000-18,000
Excellent $20,000-25,000 OTHER MODELS
Restorable $4000-8000 **Good** $10,000-15,000
Excellent $18,000-30,000. **5-year projection** SSKs +25%, others +10%

Ford Model A 1930-32

1931 Model A DeLuxe rumble-seat roadster

PRODUCTION

1930 1,261,053 **1931** 626,579 (some sold through April 1932)

HISTORY

Superficially the same as the early 1928-29 models but considerably altered in detail. Changes include lower, wider fenders, higher hoodline, stainless-steel instead of nickel-plated radiator and headlamp shells, smaller wheels, higher steering ratio, and standard vacuum wipers and balloon tires. New body styles were the DeLuxe two-door phaeton and, from autumn 1930, the Victoria coupe. Packed more value for the money than just about any other car on the road, and the public responded: Ford again led Chevrolet in production for 1929-31. Though its suspension was the same as that of the long-lived Model T, the Model A was superior in every way and far more sophisticated. It would do 65 mph, had a modern gearbox and electrical system, and stopped much better with its four- (instead of two-) wheel mechanical brakes.

FOR

For years the most popular single collector car • Strong support from two large clubs • Supply of both mechanical and structural parts almost endless • Wide variety of body styles, most of which are readily available • Reasonable prices

AGAINST

Indifferent and inaccurate restorations common • Tends to be over-restored

SPECIFICATIONS

Length (in.) NA **Wheelbase (in.)** 103.5
Weight (lbs.) 2155-2462 **Price (new)** $$430-660

ENGINES

cid/type	bore x stroke	bhp	years
200.5/L4	3.88 × 4.25	40-50	1930-32

PRICES/PROJECTION

OPEN MODELS **Restorable** $3000-5000 **Good** $7000-10,000 **Excellent** $12,000-18,000. VICTORIA Deduct 50%. DEL SPT COUPE & PHAETON Deduct 30%. OTHERS Deduct 50%
5-year projection open cars +20%, closed cars +10%

Ford Model B/C 1932-33

1932 Model B wood-body station wagon

PRODUCTION

1932 (Model B) 75,945 **1933 (Model C)** 7560. For 1932, about 56,000 units were Tudor coupes/sedans, 10,000 were Fordors/Deluxe Tudors and 3719 were DeLuxe roadsters. Other styles

were under 1000 units each. For 1933, 5000 were Standard 5-window coupes or Tudors; others were under 1000 each. Fewer than 30 units each of the Cabriolet, DeLuxe coupe and Victoria were built for 1933.

HISTORY

Extension of the Model A, sharing the new 1932 Model 18 V8 body (except for badging). The V8's strong public reception prompted Ford to abandon four-cylinder cars after 1933, resulting in extreme scarcity of certain models today, particularly Model Cs.

FOR

Worth collecting; the Model C must be one of the few 1930s "sleepers" left—extremely scarce • Priced no more than comparable Model As, and as a result, in our opinion, underpriced.

AGAINST

More difficult to find except for the common Tudor and Fordor sedans

SPECIFICATIONS

Length (in.) NA **Wheelbase (in.)** 106.5
Weight (lbs.) 2021-2505 **Price (new)** $$410-600

ENGINES

cid/type	bore x stroke	bhp	years
200.5/L4	3.88 × 4.25	50	1932-33

PRICES/PROJECTION

RDSTR/PHTN/CONV SDN **Restorable** $3500-6000
Good $10,000-15,000 **Excellent** $15,000-22,000 CABRIOLET VICTORIA Deduct 25%. OTHERS Deduct 50%
5-year projection open cars +30%, closed cars +20%

Ford V-8 1932-38

1932 V-8 DeLuxe 3-window coupe

PRODUCTION

1932 2d Del. rdstr 6893 **2d Std. rdstr** 520 **4d Del. phaeton** 923 **4d Std. phaeton** 483 **cabriolet** 5499 **conv. sedan** 842 **1933 2d Del. rdstr** 4223 **2d Std. rdstr** 126 **4d Del. phaeton** 1483 **4d Std. phaeton** 232 **cabriolet** 7852 **wagon** 1654 **1934 4d Del. phaeton** 3128 **4d Std. phaeton** 373 **cabriolet** 14,496 **wagon** 2905 **1935 2d Del. rdstr** 4896 **4d Del. phaeton** 6073 **cabriolet**

1937 V8 DeLuxe Fordor touring sedan

17,000 **conv. sedan** 4234 **wagon** 4536 **1936 2d Del. rdstr** 3862 **4d Del. phaeton** 5555 **cabriolet** 4616 **conv. sedan** 5601 **conv, 3/5 pass. wagon** 7044 **1937 2d Del. rdstr** 1250 **4d Del. phaeton** 3723 **cabriolet** 18,184 **conv. sedan** 4378 **wagon** 9304 **1938 4d Del. phaeton** 1169 **conv. sedan** 2703 **conv, 3/5 pass. wagon** 6944

HISTORY

All these Ford V8s are collectible, and the general remarks applied to wagons and open cars apply. Typically, however, the former are the ones to look for. Hoping to leap-frog Chevy's six, Ford brought the wonderful little V-8 out only four years after the Model A debuted, and it was a tremendous buy for the money. The cast-iron flathead gave at least 78 mph. Streamlining began with the much swoopier 1933 models, which also had a longer wheelbase. Horsepower was 85 by 1934 and the cars even sleeker. A much smaller V8 was added beginning with 1937, when styling took another turn, now very rounded and smooth indeed. The early V8 years brought fairly swift change by Ford standards, with body design evolving dramatically (it was all-steel by 1937), engines growing in power, and time-honored styles like the roadster and convertible sedan being phased out.

FOR

Open models and the beautiful woody wagons are among the most desirable standard production cars of the 1930s • Strong, competent national support from the Early Ford V8 Club • Plentiful parts original and repro • Excellent investment potential

AGAINST

Can often be over-restored • Easy to overspend on a restoration • Some V8 experts say open models like phaeton and convertible sedan are grossly overpriced • Later Fordors very dowdy; rounded streamlined styling didn't "take" as well as on the Tudors and open cars.

SPECIFICATIONS

Length (in.) NA **Wheelbase (in.)** 106.5 (1932) 112.0 (1933-38) **Weight (lbs.)** 2217-2543 (1932); 2337-3020 (1933-38) **Price (new)** $425-900

ENGINES

cid/type	bore x stroke	bhp	years
221.0/V8	3.06×3.75	65/85	1932-38
136.0/V8	2.60×3.20	60	1937-38

PRICES/PROJECTION

1932 OPEN Restorable $4500-8500 **Good** $10,000-20,000 **Excellent** $20,000-30,000 VICTORIA Deduct 30% OTHERS Deduct 60%. **1933-36 OPEN Restorable** $4000-8000 **Good** $9000-18,000 **Excellent** $18,000-27,500. WAGON/

VICTORIA Deduct 50%, OTHERS Deduct 75%. 1937-38 OPEN **Restorable** $3500-7000 **Good** $8000-12,000 **Excellent** $12,000-20,000. WAGON Deduct 30%, others deduct 60%. **5-year projection** open models +20%, closed models +10%

Ford V8 DeLuxe 1939-40

1940 V8 DeLuxe convertible coupe

PRODUCTION

1939 conv coupe 10,422 **conv sedan** 3561 **coupe** 37,326 **Tudor sedan** 144,333 **wagon** 6155 **Fordor sdn** 90,551 **1940 conv coupe** 23,704 **coupe** 27,919 **Tudor sedan** 171,368 **wagon** 8730 **Fordor sedan** 91,756 **bus cpe** 20,183

HISTORY

Among the prettiest Fords ever built, thanks to deft design work by Bob Gregorie and the keen aesthetic sense of Edsel Ford. The legendary '40s have been favored by many enthusiasts for three generations. Our choice would be the 1940 85-bhp convertible, but the serious investor would want to look for the scarce 1939 convertible sedans—and the woodies are hardly common. The Standard series offered the same body styles except for convertibles but were somewhat dumpier in appearance.

FOR

Superb styling • Vast following and club support • Good performance • Fine construction

AGAINST

Increasingly expensive • Open models almost overpriced now

SPECIFICATIONS

Length (in.) 195.0 **Wheelbase (in.)** 112.0 **Weight (lbs.)** 2752-3262 **Price (new)** $702-947

1939 V8 DeLuxe convertible coupe

ENGINES

cid/type	bore x stroke	bhp	years
221.0/V8	3.06×3.75	85	1939-40

PRICES/PROJECTION

OPEN MODELS **Restorable** $4500-8000 **Good** $10,000-14,000
Excellent $15,000-20,000. WAGONS **Restorable** $2500-3500
Good $4000-8000 **Excellent** $9000-14,000. OTHERS
Restorable $750-2000 **Good** $2500-5000
Excellent $5000-7500. **5-year projection** +10%

Ford V8 Super DeLuxe 1941-42

1942 V8 Super DeLuxe coupe sedan

PRODUCTION

1941 350,000 **1942** 80,000 (est.)

HISTORY

An all-new Ford arrived for 1941 on a two-inch-longer wheelbase,
but it lacked the clean-lined beauty of the '40. The top series was
now designated Super DeLuxe, and came in much the same body
styles as the previous DeLuxe. A more integrated lower grille was
the main appearance change for 1942, the model year that ended
in February as Ford shifted to defense production.

FOR

Popular ●Well-built ●Good performance

AGAINST

Very ordinary in appearance and feel

SPECIFICATIONS

Length (in.) 198.2 **Wheelbase (in.)** 114.0
Weight (lbs.) 2969-3419 **Price (new)** $777-1013

ENGINES

cid/type	bore x stroke	bhp	years
221/LV8	3.06×3.75	85/90	1941-42

PRICES/PROJECTION

CONVERTIBLE **Restorable** $3000-5000 **Good** $7500-12,000
Excellent $15,000-23,000 Deduct 10% for wagon, 65% for other
models. **5-year projection** +20%

Ford V8 Super DeLuxe Sportsman 1946-48

1946 V8 Super DeLuxe Sportsman convertible

PRODUCTION

1946 1209 **1947** 2250 **1948** 28

HISTORY

A convertible in the mold of Chrysler's Town & Country, with
wooden framing and mahogany or decal inserts helping to jazz up
what was basically a prewar design. Essentially fielded as a showroom traffic-builder. The most expensive Ford in these years, and
as such not too saleable. Collectors have changed all that though,
not to mention boosting the asking prices. A very pretty car despite
its outmoded styling, and packed traditional Ford V8 performance.

FOR

Good performance ●Nice looks ●Rarity ●It's a convertible

AGAINST

Pricey today ●Structural wood demands periodic maintenance

SPECIFICATIONS

Length (in.) 198.2 **Wheelbase (in.)** 114.0
Weight (lbs.) 3340-3366 **Price (new)** $1982-2282

ENGINES

cid/type	bore x stroke	bhp	years
239.4/LV8	3.19×3.75	100	1946-48

PRICES/PROJECTION

Restorable $3500-5500 **Good** $6000-10,000
Excellent $10,000-18,000 **5-year projection** no change

Ford Custom V8 (exc. sedans) 1949

PRODUCTION

club coupe 150,254 convertible 51,133
wagon 31,412

1949 Custom V8 wagon

1950 Custom Crestliner 2-door sedan

HISTORY

Should be a Milestone because of its adroit styling (albeit the work of moonlighting Studebaker people) and solid craftsmanship combined with the traditional performance of Ford's flathead V8. It was great stuff for 1949, good enough to rejuvenate the firm's failing corporate health. The company's successes in the '50s were made possible by the success of this car, the first all-new Ford in a decade or more. We single out the non-sedan body styles as having more than average interest and especially good styling.

FOR

Historical importance • Fine styling • Good driver's cars

AGAINST

Moderately rust-prone • Less deftly designed than concurrent Chevys

SPECIFICATIONS

Length (in.) 196.8 **Wheelbase (in.)** 114.0
Weight (lbs.) 2948-3543 **Price (new)** $1511-2119

ENGINES

cid/type	bore x stroke	bhp	years
239.4/LV8	3.19×3.75	100	1949

PRICES/PROJECTION

CONVERTIBLE/WAGON **Restorable** $2000-5000
Good $5000-10,000 **Excellent** $10,000-18,000
Deduct 75% for other models **5-year projection** no change.

Ford Custom Crestliner 1950-51

PRODUCTION

1950 17,601 **1951** 8703

HISTORY

A gussied-up version of the regular Tudor sedan added late in the 1950 model year. Designed to fill in for a true "hardtop convertible" pending arrival of the Victoria for 1951. Styling by Gordon Buehrig featured a contrasting color sweep panel on the bodysides and a padded top. Arresting two-tone paint jobs were offered with black as the main color. Priced $200 upstream of the Custom Tudor, which may explain why sales were not impressive. Perhaps the most interesting of the 1950-51 Fords, and well worth considering.

FOR

Minor historical significance, but rather unique • Others as for 1949 Custom

AGAINST

As for 1949 Custom

SPECIFICATIONS

Length (in.) 196.7 (1950), 197.3 (1951) **Wheelbase (in.)** 114.0
Weight (lbs.) 3050-3065 **Price (new)** $1711-1595

ENGINES

cid/type	bore x stroke	bhp	years
239.4/LV8	3.19×3.75	100	1950-51

PRICES/PROJECTION

Restorable $750-1500 **Good** $2500-4500
Excellent $4000-6500 **5-year projection** +25%

Ford Custom Victoria 1951

1951 Custom Victoria 2-door hardtop

PRODUCTION

110,286

HISTORY

Ford's first hardtop, offered only in V8 guise. Appeared in the last year of the 1949 styling generation, but proved immensely popular (it outsold Chevrolet's Bel Air by about 7000 units this year). Pillarless superstructure was styled by Gordon M. Buehrig (of Auburn-Cord-Duesenberg fame), who had come to Dearborn after leaving the Loewy team at Studebaker. With clean lines, relatively posh interior, and good performance from the reliable flathead V8, the first Victoria has been somewhat overlooked by collectors.

FOR

Historical significance ● One of the best-looking 1949-51 Fords ● Reasonable parts supplies ● Decent performance from sturdy engine

AGAINST

As for 1950-51 Custom Crestliner

SPECIFICATIONS

Length (in.) 197.3 **Wheelbase (in.)** 114.0 **Weight (lbs.)** 3188
Price (new) $1925

ENGINES

cid/type	bore x stroke	bhp	years
239.4/LV8	3.19×3.75	100	1951

PRICES/PROJECTION

Restorable $1000-2000 **Good** $2500-4000
Excellent $3500-6500 **5-year projection** +15%

Ford Crestline Skyliner 1954

1954 Crestline Skyliner 2-door hardtop

PRODUCTION

13,344

HISTORY

The first of Ford's production "bubbletops" (along with this year's Mercury Sun Valley equivalent) featuring a transparent Plexiglas forward roof section. An idea of designer L. David Ash, it has modern counterparts in the moonroof and flip-up sunroof. An ac-

---

cessory sunshade was offered to keep interior heat levels reasonable on bright days, and it was needed. Otherwise, not much different from other models. Despite only a $109 price premium over the regular Victoria hardtop, it scored but a fourth of that model's sales. Available with Ford's first ohv V8, the new Y-block unit introduced for '54, which gave much better performance than the venerable flathead. The see-through roof continued as an option for the 1955-56 Fairlane Crown Victoria, but sales were again miniscule compared to the steel-topped version. The Skyliner name was revived for Ford's retractable hardtop of 1957-59, another model with a fanciful roof and similarly short-lived.

FOR

Interesting and ahead of its time ● Good construction quality ● Performance ● Clean if bland styling

AGAINST

A sweatbox in summer ● Some rust tendencies

SPECIFICATIONS

Length (in.) 198.3 **Wheelbase (in.)** 115.5 **Weight (lbs.)** 3265
Price (new) $2164

ENGINES

cid/type	bore x stroke	bhp	years
223/ohv I6	3.62×3.60	115	1954
239/ohv V8	3.50×3.10	130	1954

PRICES/PROJECTION

Restorable $750-1500 **Good** $2500-3500
Excellent $4000-5500 **5-year projection** +25%

Ford Fairlane 1955-56

1955 Fairlane 4-door Town Sedan

PRODUCTION

1955 2d Club Sedan 173,311 **4d Town Sedan** 254,437
Victoria 2d hardtop 113,372 **Crown Victoria**
2d sedan 33,165 **Crown Victoria (plastic top)** 1999
Sunliner convertible 49,966 **1956 2d Club Sedan** 142,629
4d Town Sedan 224,872 **Victoria 2d hardtop** 177,735
Victoria 4d hardtop 32,111 **Crown Victoria 2d sedan** 9209
Crown Victoria (plastic top) 603 **Sunliner convertible** 58,147

HISTORY

In all the hoopla about mid-'50s Chevys over the years, most people seem to have forgotten these Fords, which were pretty nice,

1955 Fairlane Crown Victoria 2-door sedan

1955 Thunderbird 2-seat convertible (prototype)

too. Fairlane was the new top-of-the-line series for '55, equivalent to the Chevy Bel Air, and came in six flavors; a four-door hardtop was added for '56. All featured fine styling with the rakish "Fairlane stripe" side trim, and were solidly built and quick in V8 form. Low production makes the plastic-top Crown Victoria the most collectible model in this group, with the steel-top version and the Sunliner ragtop next in importance and desirability.

FOR

Clean, colorful styling • Performance • Construction quality

AGAINST

Despite fine design, not the solid investment a 1955-56 Chevy is

SPECIFICATIONS

Length (in.) 198.5 **Wheelbase (in.)** 115.5
Weight (lbs.) 3155-3315 **Price (new)** $1914-2272

ENGINES

cid/type	bore x stroke	bhp	years
223/ohv I6	3.62×3.60	120/137	1955-56
272/ohv V8	3.62×3.30	162-182	1955-56
292/ohv V8	3.75×3.30	200	1956
312/ohv V8	3.80×3.44	215/225	1956

PRICES/PROJECTION

Restorable $1000-2000 **Good** $2000-4500
Excellent $4000-6000 Add 100% for Victoria, 150% for Crown Victoria or convertible, 200% for plastic-roof Crown Victoria.
5-year projection +20%

Ford Thunderbird 1955-57

PRODUCTION

1955 16,155 **1956** 15,631 **1957** 21,380

HISTORY

One of the earliest collectibles among postwar cars, the two-seat T-Bird has, if anything, gained in popularity as the years have passed (as the recent spate of Pinto-powered replicas suggests). Its original sales triumph over the Chevrolet Corvette was the result of clean styling, creature comforts, and V8 refinement rather than novel fiberglass construction and sports-car starkness. Even so, sales volume didn't impress Ford's then-conservative management (headed by Robert S. McNamara). A four-seat replacement was in the works for 1958 even as the first Birds rolled off the line, thereby

making them collector's items almost immediately. To many eyes, the heavily facelifted '57 is the most desirable because of its arguably more "together" styling. It's also the most numerous owing to an extended model year, and was offered with the widest array of powerteams. Most surviving two-seaters were spoken for long ago, however, so acquiring one now will require a hefty bank account—and a lot of patient looking.

FOR

Outstanding styling; still looks great • Good performance • High-value appreciation • Large club support • Two-seat, open-air mystique

AGAINST

Handling uninspired • Pricey • Some rust susceptibility

SPECIFICATIONS

Length (in.) 175.3 (1955-56), 185.2 (1957)
Wheelbase (in.) 102.0 **Weight (lbs.)** 2980-3145
Price (new) $2944-3408

ENGINES

cid/type	bore x stroke	bhp	years
292/ohv V8	3.75×3.30	193-212	1955-57
312/ohv V8	3.80×3.44	215-340	1956-57

PRICES/PROJECTION

Restorable $6000-8000 **Good** $8000-14,500
Excellent $15,000-23,000 Add 5-10% for 1957 models, 10% for factory hardtop **5-year projection** +25%

1957 Thunderbird 2-seat convertible with hardtop

Ford Fairlane 500 Skyliner 1957-59

1957 Fairlane 500 Skyliner retractable hardtop-convertible

PRODUCTION

1957 20,766   **1958** 14,713   **1959** 12,915

HISTORY

The world's first—and only—production retractable hardtop-convertible. Seemed like a good idea at the time (and a typically '50s one at that), but proved to be a complicated beast with a lot to go wrong. It was also expensive, $400 more than the conventional Sunliner soft-top. Both factors put the crimp in sales. Stylists did the best they could to provide enough room for that big roof to slide back into the trunk area. But even though the roof was shorter than on other models and its front section hinged for more compact storage, the Skyliner still ended up with a higher rear deck and bulgier "bustle" rear panel. Also differed from other Fords in having a standard V8, a relocated gas tank (behind the back seat instead of under the trunk floor), and virtually no luggage space. Heavily restyled and re-engineered for 1959, and officially part of that year's new top-line Galaxie series though it continued to wear Fairlane 500 script. An interesting car, and a reminder of that age when Detroit thought it could do anything.

FOR

Technical fascination • A crowd-pleaser • Good appreciation potential

AGAINST

Mechanical/electrical gremlins • Clumsy rear styling • Shares a great deal with ordinary Fords

SPECIFICATIONS

Length (in.) 210.8 (1957-58), 208.1 (1959)
Wheelbase (in.) 118.0   **Weight (lbs.)** 3916/4069/4064
Price (new) $2942/3163/3346

ENGINES

cid/type	bore x stroke	bhp	years
272/ohv V8	3.62×3.30	190	1957
292/ohv V8	3.75×3.30	200/205/212	1957-59
312/ohv V8	3.80×3.44	245	1957
332/ohv V8	4.00×3.30	225/240/265	1958-59
352/ohv V8	4.00×3.50	300	1958-59

PRICES/PROJECTION

Restorable $2500-5000 **Good** $4000-8000
Excellent $8000-12,000 **5-year projection** +10%

Ford Thunderbird 1958-60

1958 Thunderbird 2-door hardtop

PRODUCTION

1958 2d hardtop 35,758   **convertible** 2134
1959 2d hardtop 57,195   **convertible** 10,261
1960 2d hardtop 78,447*   **convertible** 11,860
"Gold Top" 2d hardtop 2536
*includes approx. 2500 sunroof models

HISTORY

The first of the four-seat Thunderbirds, and nicknamed "Squarebird" because of its boxy lines and wide-pillar roof (which would be applied to other Ford models from Galaxies to Falcons in the '60s). Started slow in collector circles, but has come of age now, and enjoys a fairly wide following. Underrated for years because of its immediate predecessors, this T-Bird series was, in fact, quite unorthodox: unit construction, low build, and the pioneering bucket-seats-and-console interior that established the personal-luxury concept. A retractable hardtop had been planned, but was shelved because of the Skyliner experience and the McNamara regime's high-profit approach to design. Prize picks here are the '58 convertible (rare because of initial production delays), the special "golden edition" 1960 hardtop, and a limited-production 1960 hardtop with the country's first postwar sliding steel sunroof (about 2500 built). Few mechanical changes in these years apart from the Lincoln 430 V8, added as an option for 1959 and '60.

FOR

Luxurious • Reasonably compact • Strong club support • Nice looks • Personal-luxury pathfinder • Great highway cruiser

AGAINST

Rusts too easily • Thirsty • Variable construction quality • Clumsy in corners

SPECIFICATIONS

Length (in.) 205.3   **Wheelbase (in.)** 113.0
Weight (lbs.) 3799-3944   **Price (new)** $3631-4222

ENGINES

cid/type	bore x stroke	bhp	years
352/ohv V8	4.00×3.50	300	1958-60
430/ohv V8	4.30×3.70	350	1959-60

PRICES/PROJECTION

Restorable $2000-3000 **Good** $3000-5000
Excellent $6000-9000 Add 50% for convertible, 35% for gold-top 1960 hardtop **5-year projection** +25%

Ford Falcon Futura
1961-63

1962 Falcon Futura 2-door sedan

PRODUCTION

1961 44,470   **1962** 17,011   **1963 2d sedan** 27,018
2d hardtop 28,496   **convertible** 31,192

HISTORY

Ford's contender in the bucket-seat compact market opened up by the Chevrolet Corvair Monza. Debuted as a two-door sedan only for 1961. A choice of two rooflines (regular and T-Bird style) was offered for '62. Expanded into a separate series for '63, when a four-door sedan, two-door hardtop, and convertible were added, and you could get much the same interior treatment on the Squire wagon as well. Limited to two sturdy six-cylinder engines until the V8 Sprint arrived for mid-1963. Probably the prettiest of the Falcons, as only minor grille and ornamentation changes were made to the clean simplicity of the original 1960 styling. The '63 convertibles and "slantback" hardtops are especially attractive and the most desirable models in this group.

FOR

Low-bucks collectible •Handsome interior •Styling •Surprising ride and roadability

AGAINST

Can rust •Only fair assembly quality •Sedate performance

SPECIFICATIONS

Length (in.) 181.1   **Wheelbase (in.)** 109.5
Weight (lbs.) 2308-2645   **Price (new)** $2116-2470

1962 Falcon Futura 2-door sedan

ENGINES

cid/type	bore x stroke	bhp	years
144.3/ohv I6	3.50×2.50	85	1961-63
170/ohv I6	3.50×2.94	101	1961-63

PRICES/PROJECTION

Restorable $800-1200 **Good** $1200-2500
Excellent $2500-4500 Add 30% for convertible
5-year projection +25%

Ford Thunderbird
1961-63

1961 Thunderbird 2-door hardtop

PRODUCTION

1961 2d hardtop 62,335   **convertible** 10,516
1962 2d hardtop 69,554*   **convertible** 7030
1963 2d hardtop 42,806   **convertible** 5913
Landau 2d hardtop 14,139
*inc. Landau hardtop

HISTORY

The third-generation Thunderbird, successor to the 1958-60 "Squarebird." Chassis design was much as before, but reworked slightly for a smoother ride and better handling. All-new bodyshell featured a severely pointed front "prow," modest fins above huge renditions of Ford's traditional round taillights, and softer roof contours on hardtops. Cowl was shared with the new Lincoln Continental, and some similarity in grille styling is evident, particularly the quad headlamps recessed in oblong housings. Interior design featured a dash that curved at its outboard ends to blend in with the door panels, and the first "Swing-Away" steering wheel. Great attention to quality control and soundproofing made this the most comfortably quiet T-Bird to date. Ford's burly 390 V8 was the only engine offered for '61, but a higher-output "M" unit was cataloged for 1962-63. A new Landau hardtop with simulated top irons on its rear roof pillars introduced a T-Bird styling gimmick that would be retained for several years. Models to look for are the M-engine versions and 1963's Limited-Edition Landau with special trim.

FOR

Good styling •High quality •Smoothness • Refinement

AGAINST

Rust problems •Thirst

SPECIFICATIONS

Length (in.) 205.0 **Wheelbase (in.)** 113.0
Weight (lbs.) 3958-4370 **Price (new)** $4172-4912

ENGINES

cid/type	bore x stroke	bhp	years
390/ohv V8	4.05×3.78	300/340	1961-63

PRICES/PROJECTION

Restorable $2000-3000 **Good** $3000-4500
Excellent $6000-10,000 Add 50% for convertible
5-year projection +25%

Ford Galaxie 500XL
1962-64

1964 Galaxie 500XL convertible

PRODUCTION

1962 2d hardtop 28,412 **convertible** 13,183
1963 2d hardtop 134,370 **convertible** 29,713
4d hardtop 39,154* **1964 2d hardtop** 58,306
convertible 15,169 **4d hardtop** 14,661
*inc. non-XL Galaxie 500s

HISTORY

The first of the big performance Fords, with bucket seats, console, and posh interior trim. Introduced for mid-1962 as a subseries in the Galaxie 500 lineup (named after the 500-mile NASCAR races in which Ford was doing so well). Numerous drivetrain options were available from the start, including a four-speed manual transmission and up to 425 bhp. At mid-season 1963, the XL hardtop gained a sloping semi-fastback roofline (shared with equivalent Mercurys), and a four-door version was added. For 1964, styling was more sculptured and busier than the straight-lined 1962-63. Deemphasized as a performance car after Ford's winningest NASCAR year ever, 1965, in which the division's full-size cars cleaned up on the supertracks against smaller, lighter intermediate competition. However, the XL remained part of the Ford line through 1970, though engines were progressively detuned to comply with federal emissions mandates. Quality control was a strong point on these cars, particularly the '64s.

FOR

Historical interest • Race image rub-off • Straightline performance • Luxury • Refinement • Robust construction

AGAINST

Fuelishness • A handful in corners

SPECIFICATIONS

Length (in.) 209.0 (1962-63), 210.0 (1964)
Wheelbase (in.) 119.0 **Weight (lbs.)** 3672-3722
Price (new) $2268-3495

ENGINES

cid/type	bore x stroke	bhp	years
289/ohv V8	4.00×2.87	195	1963-64
292/ohv V8	3.75×3.30	170	1962
352/ohv V8	4.00×3.50	220	1962-64
390/ohv V8	4.05×3.78	300/330	1962-64
406/ohv V8	4.13×3.78	385/405	1962
427/ohv V8	4.23×3.78	410/425	1963-64

PRICES/PROJECTION

Restorable $1000-2000 **Good** $2000-3000
Excellent $3000-5500 Add 25% for convertible
5-year projection +10%

Ford Thunderbird
Sports Roadster
1962-63

1962 Thunderbird Sports Roadster

PRODUCTION

1962 1427 **1963** 455

HISTORY

A gesture toward buyers still pining for the two-seat Thunderbird in the early '60s. A fiberglass tonneau cover, designed by Bud Kaufman, fit over the rear seat area of the normal four-seat convertible to give the appearance of a two-seater with a very long rear deck. Twin headrests at the cover's forward edge fit over the regular front bucket seats, and were raised so as to flow back to the rear, thus avoiding a too-flat appearance. The cover was designed so as not to interfere with the convertible top's operation. Kelsey-Hayes chrome plated wire wheels were standard, and the stock rear fender skirts were deleted to provide clearance for their knock-off centers. Offered by the factory for these two years only, but a few tonneau covers found their way onto the restyled '64 convertible (minus the wire wheels) at the dealer level. In all, a clever idea (usually attributed to Lee Iacocca), but it didn't take hold, probably because the cover was cumbersome to remove or replace. Rarity and distinctive good looks make this *the* prime collectible among T-Birds of these years.

FOR

Attractiveness • Unique equipment • Rarity • Others as for 1961-63 Thunderbird

AGAINST

Body rust • Fuel thirst • Tonneau won't fit the trunk • Wire wheels costly and scarce

SPECIFICATIONS

Length (in.) 205.0 **Wheelbase (in.)** 113.0
Weight (lbs.) 4471-4396 **Price (new)** $5439-5563

ENGINES

cid/type	bore x stroke	bhp	years
390/ohv V8	4.05×3.78	300/340	1962-63

PRICES/PROJECTION

Restorable $7000-10,000 **Good** $10,000-15,000
Excellent $15,000-20,000 **5-year projection** +30%

Ford Falcon Futura Sprint V8 1963-65

1964 Falcon Futura Sprint V8 convertible

PRODUCTION

1963 2d hardtop 10,479 **convertible** 4602
1964 2d hardtop 13,830 **convertible** 4278
1965 2d hardtop 2806 **convertible** 300

HISTORY

The most important collector Falcon. Introduced for mid-1963, and quite successful in a short international rally career that was part of Ford's Total Performance competition program in the '60s. Available with the outstanding 260-cid small-block V8 as an option for 1963-64, and a very lively performer. A 170-cid six was standard. Also featured a slightly tweaked suspension, the bucket-seats-and-console interior from the "cooking" Futura, and more complete instrumentation including tachometer. A four-speed manual gearbox was listed at extra cost. Continued as part of the Futura series for 1964, when all Falcons were reskinned with bulkier, more sculpted sheetmetal. Only a handful were built in its final year, when the 260 was replaced by the 289-cid version of the small-block. The '65s are worth looking for because of low production, but the '63s are the nicest looking.

FOR

Fine handling and performance • Fun to drive • Not too gas-greedy • '63 styling • '65s rarity

AGAINST

Variable construction quality • Rust-prone • Manual steering

SPECIFICATIONS

Length (in.) 181.1 (1963), 181.6 (1964-65)
Wheelbase (in.) 109.5 **Weight (lbs.)** 2438-3008
Price (new) $2320-2671

ENGINES

cid/type	bore x stroke	bhp	years
260/ohv V8	3.80×2.87	164	1963-64
289/ohv V8	4.00×2.87	200	1965

PRICES/PROJECTION

Restorable $750-1250 **Good** $1500-2500
Excellent $3000-5000 Add 25% for convertible, 10% for 1963 models **5-year projection** +15%

Ford Mustang 1965-66

1965 Mustang GT 2+2 fastback coupe

PRODUCTION

1965 2d hardtop 501,965 **convertible** 101,945
fastback 77,079 **1966 2d hardtop** 499,751
convertible 72,119 **fastback** 35,698

HISTORY

Ford's biggest success of the '60s, originator of the "ponycar" concept. Essentially a sporty compact with long-hood/short-deck proportions based on Falcon and Fairlane chassis and drivetrain components. Phenomenally successful a generation ago, it is still avidly pursued by collectors today, many of whom grew up with the car and are now reaching their peak earning years. Introduced in advance of the 1965 model year in April 1964. The fastback was added six months after launch, at which time some engine and equipment shuffling took place. Modest appearance and options alterations marked the carryover '66 version. Despite cramped rear seat accommodations, still a practical everyday car for the '80s, particularly with one of the thrifty sixes. A plethora of available factory accessories and option packages mean there's no "typical" example of the breed, but cars with the "hi-po" 289 V8, manual shift, the GT package, or all three are worth searching for. Unfortunately, they're also in greater demand than tamer models, and bring correspondingly higher asking prices.

FOR

Vast following • High appreciation potential • Good styling • Fine V8 performance • Good six-cylinder economy • Practical size

1965 Mustang 2+2 fastback coupe

AGAINST

Indifferent quality control •Some rust problems •Wildly fluctuating prices

SPECIFICATIONS

Length (in.) 181.6 **Wheelbase (in.)** 108.0
Weight (lbs.) 2583-2650 **Price (new)** $2372-2653

ENGINES

cid/type	bore x stroke	bhp	years
170/ohv I6	3.50×2.94	101	1965
200/ohv I6	3.68×3.13	120	1965-66
260/ohv V8	3.80×2.87	164	1965
289/ohv V8	4.00×2.87	200/225/271	1965-66

PRICES/PROJECTION

Restorable $1000-2500 **Good** $2500-5000
Excellent $5500-9000 Add 35% for convertible, 15% for fastback, 15% for 271 bhp V8, 15% for GT, 5% for Pony interior. Deduct 15% for six, 20% minimum for non-factory modifications.
5-year projection V8s +50%, sixes +25%

Ford Fairlane 500XL GT 1966-67

1967 Fairlane 500XL 2-door hardtop (GT similar)

PRODUCTION

1966 2d hardtop 33,015 **convertible** 4327
1967 2d hardtop 18,670 **convertible** 2117

HISTORY

The sportiest of the mid-size Fords of the mid-'60s. Shared the normal XL's bucket-seats-and-console interior and distinguishing exterior striping, but had a standard 315-bhp 390-cid V8 with a 335 bhp option for blistering straightline go. Ford's mighty 427 V8 was also listed as an option starting at mid-model year 1966, though it's

likely only a few found their way into these models. Appearance was notably leaner and tauter in these years compared to previous Fairlanes. Cars with automatic were designated GT/A on exterior emblems. The small-block 289 V8 became the standard GT powerplant for '67, but 270- and 320-bhp versions of the big-block 390 were intermediate power options just below the 427. Far less numerous than the "cooking" XLs, but only modest appreciation potential despite this.

FOR

Sensible size •High performance •Good construction quality •Nice lines

AGAINST

Thirsty •Some body parts becoming scarce

SPECIFICATIONS

Length (in.) 197.0 **Wheelbase (in.)** 116.0
Weight (lbs.) 3070-3607 **Price (new)** $2843-3068

ENGINES

cid/type	bore x stroke	bhp	years
289/ohv V8	4.00×2.87	200	1967
390/ohv V8	4.05×3.78	270/320/335	1966-67
427/ohv V8	4.23×3.78	410/425	1967

PRICES/PROJECTION

Restorable $750-1500 **Good** $1000-3000
Excellent $3000-5000 Add 35% for convertible.
5-year projection +10%

Ford Mustang 1967-68

1967 Mustang 2-door hardtop

PRODUCTION

1967 2d hardtop 356,271 **convertible** 44,808
fastback 71,042 **1968 2d hardtop** 249,447
convertible 25,376 **fastback** 42,581

HISTORY

The heavily facelifted continuation of Ford's 1965-66 ponycar design. The main styling changes for 1967 were bulkier sheetmetal below the beltline, a more aggressive grille, concave tail panel (with the three-element taillight clusters now separated), and a full fastback roofline for that body style. The big-block 390 V8 was available for the first time as the top power option. It gave blinding acceleration, but made the car a piggish handler. Chassis engineers tweaked suspension attachment bushings for reduced noise, vibration, and harshness. The '68s were marked by a simpler grille and side trim, and the hulking 427 V8 was made available on a very limited basis. Overwhelming collector interest right now is in the 1965-66 Mustang, but comparable models in these last two years of the first generation can be had at half the price. However, the prospect of strong value appreciation is unclear at the moment. An interesting Shelbyesque derivative, the 1968 California Special hardtop, may be the exception because of limited production.

FOR

More affordable than 1965-66s, and much the same qualities

AGAINST

As for 1965-66 Mustang, plus the first emissions controls on '68s and poor handling with big-inch engines

SPECIFICATIONS

Length (in.) 183.6   **Wheelbase (in.)** 108.0
Weight (lbs.) 2568-2745   **Price (new)** $2461-2814

ENGINES

cid/type	bore x stroke	bhp	years
200/ohv I6	3.68×3.13	115/120	1967-68
289/ohv V8	4.00×2.87	195-271	1967-68
302/ohv V8	4.00×3.00	230	1968
390/ohv V8	4.05×3.78	320/325	1967-68
427/ohv V8	4.23×3.78	390	1968

PRICES/PROJECTION

Restorable $750-1500   **Good** $2000-3500
Excellent $4000-8000 Add 50% for convertible, 15% for fastback, 20% for California Special (1968), 15% for performance V8, 10% for GT package. Deduct 10% for six, 20% minimum for non-factory modifications. **5-year projection** +25%

Ford Torino GT 1968-69

1968 Torino GT 2-door fastback hardtop

PRODUCTION

1968 2d fastback 74,135   **2d hardtop** 23,939
convertible 5310   **1969 2d fastback** 61,319
2d hardtop 17,951   **convertible** 2552

HISTORY

Ford's sporting intermediates in these years, part of the newly named upper series in the restyled Fairlane line. The usual buckets-and-console interior treatment and a more muscular chassis continued to set these GTs apart from the "family" Torinos and

Fairlanes just like the previous Fairlane 500XLs. New this year was a sleek fastback two-door hardtop that proved very slippery—and very successful—in long-distance stock car races. Restyled for 1970 with sleeker-looking lines that actually proved less aerodynamic on the supertracks.

FOR

As for 1966-67 Fairlane 500XL GT ● Convertible rarity ● Neat if not timeless styling

AGAINST

Spotty assembly quality ● Thirsty with performance engines

SPECIFICATIONS

Length (in.) 201.0   **Wheelbase (in.)** 116.0
Weight (lbs.) 3173-3356   **Price (new)** $2747-3090

ENGINES

cid/type	bore x stroke	bhp	years
302/ohv V8	4.00×3.00	210/220/230	1968-69
351/ohv V8	4.00×3.50	250/290	1969
390/ohv V8	4.05×3.78	265/335	1968-69
427/ohv V8	4.23×3.78	390	1968
428/ohv V8	4.13×3.98	335	1969

PRICES/PROJECTION

Restorable $700-1500   **Good** $1000-2500
Excellent $2000-4000 Add 10% for fastback, 25% for convertible. **5-year projection** +10%

Ford Mustang Boss 302/429 1969-70

1969 Mustang Boss 302 fastback coupe

PRODUCTION

1969 302 1934   **429** 858   **1970 302** 6318   **429** 498

HISTORY

Ford's purpose-built contender for the Sports Car Club of America's Trans-Am sedan road racing series, and similar in concept to Chevy's Camaro Z-28 package. Exciting graphics by ex-GM stylist Larry Shinoda such as backlight louvers, front under-bumper lip spoiler, trunklid wing spoiler, and distinctive bodyside striping marked this near race-ready version of the Mustang fastback. Underneath were a stiff suspension, four-speed gearbox, power front disc brakes, wide tires, and a much-fortified, high-winding 302 V8. From mid-1969, a very limited-production Boss 429 was also available, created mainly for dragstrip duels. Has tremendous appeal because of "factory racer" exclusivity, but a rare bird on today's market.

FOR

Tremendous performance ● Handling/roadholding ● Rarity

AGAINST

Not very tractable for street use ● High running costs ● Hard to find in original condition

SPECIFICATIONS

Length (in.) 187.4 **Wheelbase (in.)** 108.0
Weight (lbs.) 3210-3227 **Price (new)** $3588-3720

ENGINES

cid/type	bore x stroke	bhp	years
302/ohv V8	4.00×3.00	290	1969-70
429/ohv V8	4.36×3.59	360	1969-70

PRICES/PROJECTION

Restorable $2000-4000 **Good** $5000-7000
Excellent $8000-12,000. **5-year projection** +35%

Ford Mustang Mach 1 1969-70

1969 Mustang Mach 1 fastback coupe

PRODUCTION

1969 72,458   **1970** 40,970

HISTORY

The high-performance leader in the second-series Mustang line. Based on the "SportsRoof" fastback, with individual styling touches like matte-black hood paint, twist hood locks, bodyside striping, and special wheel trims. The base engine was a 351 V8, but power options up to the 335-bhp 428 Cobra Jet (complete with shaker hood scoop) were offered. Interiors could be as plain or fancy as you liked thanks to Ford's practice of allowing customers to specify almost any combination of performance and luxury features. The model continued in the much larger third-generation 1971-73 series. It's too early to say much about the collectibility of these, though it's likely they will be in some demand down the road.

FOR

Performance with a capital P ● Exciting styling

AGAINST

Doesn't like low-octane gas ● A heavy drinker ● "Gee-whiz" styling fillips may be too juvenile for some

SPECIFICATIONS

Length (in.) 187.4 **Wheelbase (in.)** 108.0
Weight (lbs.) 3175-3240 **Price (new)** $3139-3271

ENGINES

cid/type	bore x stroke	bhp	years
351/ohv V8	4.00×3.50	250/290/300	1969-70
390/ohv V8	4.05×3.78	320	1969
428/ohv V8	4.13×3.98	335	1969-70
429/ohv V8	4.36×3.59	360	1969-70

PRICES/PROJECTION

Restorable $1000-2500 **Good** $2000-4500
Excellent $4500-8000 **5-year projection** +20%

Ford Torino Cobra 1969-70

1969 Torino Cobra 2-door fastback hardtop

PRODUCTION

1969 Torino GT option NA   **1970** 7675

HISTORY

Ford's answer to the Plymouth Road Runner, a low-bucks mid-size muscle machine based on the Fairlane/Torino platform. Originally a package option for any Torino GT, but virtually all the '69s built were fastbacks. Became a separate model the following year, when Ford upped its intermediate wheelbase by one inch and adopted more flowing body lines. The 1970 Cobra was identified by its louvered rear window, blackout exterior trim, and fat tires. Standard power initially was a big-block 428 available with or without Ram Air induction (at $133 extra). Other equipment: four-speed gearbox, heavy-duty suspension, hood lock pins, special decals (a cartoon snake), and no-nonsense interior. Capable of astonishing acceleration, with a quarter-mile time of less than 15 seconds at a terminal speed close to 100 mph. NASCAR versions could achieve 190 mph given enough room. Continued in the lineup for 1971, but downgraded to a standard four-barrel 351-cid small-block V8 (though the 429 was still optional in four versions with up to a claimed 370 bhp). By then, however, performance cars were becoming passé in Detroit, and the following year brought a heavier, more luxury-oriented Torino line, minus the Cobra. Of the two model years here, the '69 is preferred for its lighter weight and less emissions-throttled powerplants, not to mention the racing image of its NASCAR relatives, which continued to be campaigned after the restyled 1970s appeared.

FOR

As for 1968-69 Torino GT, plus staggering performance and capable handling

AGAINST

As for 1968-69 Torino GT, plus high operating costs and limited street tractability

SPECIFICATIONS

Length (in.) 197.0-198.5 **Wheelbase (in.)** 116.0 (1969), 117.0 (1970) **Weight (lbs.)** 3200-3774
Price (new) $3000-3500 (approx.)

ENGINES

cid/type	bore x stroke	bhp	years
428/ohv V8	4.13×3.98	335	1969
429/ohv V8	4.36×3.59	360/370/375	1970

PRICES/PROJECTION

Restorable $1000-2000 **Good** $2000-4000
Excellent $4000-7000 **5-year projection** +30%

Ford Mustang II King Cobra 1978

1978 Mustang II King Cobra hatchback coupe

PRODUCTION

5000 (est.)

HISTORY

An interesting low-production "paint-on performance" edition of Ford's pudgy little compact ponycar in its last season. Designed under the auspices of Ford styling chief Eugene Bordinat, and given impetus by the sales success of the earlier Cobra II option package. Available only as a three-door fastback, the King Cobra had almost every racy styling touch a kid could want. There was a giant snake decal and bold scoop on the hood and tape stripes on the roof, rear deck, rocker panels, around the windshield and wheel arches, and on the deep front air dam that was also part of the package. The words "King Cobra" appeared on each door and on the standard decklid spoiler. A black-finished grille, window moldings, headlamp bezels, and wiper arms plus a brushed aluminum instrument panel applique completed the cosmetics. Functionally, the King Cobra was built around the Mustang II's optional small-block V8, bolstered by standard power steering, "Rallye" handling package, and Goodrich raised white letter 70-series radial tires. Capable of 17 second quarter-mile times — not high performance like in the '60s, but good for an emissions-throttled, safety-certified 1970s car. Much less numerous than the

Cobra II models (which earned hoots of derision from Shelby-Mustang lovers), but seems likely to remain a low-appreciation item on the collector market for some time yet.

FOR

"Macho" appearance features ●Good performance/economy balance ●A decent handler ●Hatchback practicality ●Cheap-to-buy, sensible everyday driveable

AGAINST

Muscle-car doodads look silly on this scale to some eyes ●Collectibility questionable at present

SPECIFICATIONS

Length (in.) 175.0 **Wheelbase (in.)** 96.2 **Weight (lbs.)** 2950 (approx.) **Price (new)** $5075

ENGINES

cid/type	bore x stroke	bhp	years
302/ohv V8	4.00×3.00	140*	1978

*SAE net

PRICES/PROJECTION

Difficult to establish accurately at present. Consider the following as estimates only: **Restorable** $2000-2500 **Good** $2500-3500
Excellent $3500-4500 **5-year projection** no change

Ford Mustang Pace Car Replica 1979

1979 Ford Mustang Pace Car Replica hatchback coupe

PRODUCTION

11,000

HISTORY

Ford's totally redesigned third-generation ponycar was chosen to pace the 1979 Indianapolis 500, just as the original Mustang had 25 years earlier. A few weeks before the race, Ford issued these pace-car replicas, which introduced styling features adopted the following year for the optional Cobra package. While the one-off '79 pace car was powered by a much-modified 302 V8 and had a T-bar roof (which caused a few construction headaches), the replicas were offered with either the stock-tune V8 or Ford's interesting turbocharged 2.3-liter four-cylinder engine. Everything else was the same, though: distinctive pewter and black paint treatment with orange and red tape striping, aerodynamic slatted grille above a deep chin spoiler, special hood scoop, plus multi-adjustable Recaro racing-type bucket front seats. The usual pace car regalia adorned the bodysides, and included a multi-image running horse logo. All the replicas were the three-door hatchback equipped with four-speed manual shift and flip-up glass sunroof. A very nice limited edition of a well-balanced, stylish, latterday ponycar.

FOR

Fairly exclusive • Tasteful performance-look styling • Fine handling • Nice interior • Basic body and mechanical pieces still as close as your local dealer

AGAINST

Not that much different mechanically from stock '79s • Watch out for bogus replica conversions of standard Mustangs • Too recent to be a high-demand item just yet

SPECIFICATIONS

Length (in.) 179.1 **Wheelbase (in.)** 100.4 **Weight (lbs.)** 2800 (approx.) **Price (new)** NA

ENGINES

cid/type	bore x stroke	bhp	years
140/ohc I4T	3.78×3.13	131*	1979
302/ohv V8	4.00×3.00	140*	1979
*SAE net			

PRICES/PROJECTION

Restorable $3000-4000 **Good** $4000-5000
Excellent $5000-7000 **5-year projection** −10%

Franklin Supercharged Twelve 1932-34

PRODUCTION

Approx. 400

HISTORY

While all the Franklins are historic and collectible, the great Supercharged Twelve represented the company's finest hour and is easily the most significant model of its later years. At nearly 400 cid this engine was the largest in Franklin history, and with traditional air-cooling and aluminum construction it was unique and technically fascinating. Coachwork was hand-built by Franklin itself in Syracuse to a LeBaron design, distinguished by a sharply vee'd grille and a long, shapely hood extending back to a rakishly angled windshield. Imposingly beautiful but, like so many of its ilk, it just didn't sell in the depressed market of the day.

FOR

Spectacular engineering to a unique specification • Magnificent coachwork • CCCA Classic status yet not too pricey

AGAINST

Scarcity of available models • Significant parts shortage • High

1933 Supercharged Twelve 5-passenger sedan

maintenance/operating costs • No open body styles

SPECIFICATIONS

Length (in.) NA **Wheelbase (in.)** 144.0
Weight (lbs.) 5515-5900 **Price (new)** $2885-3185

ENGINES

cid/type	bore x stroke	bhp	years
398.0/V12	3.25×4.00	150*	1932-34
*Supercharged			

PRICES/PROJECTION

Restorable $4000-8000 **Good** $10,000-15,000
Excellent $15,000-25,000 **5-year projection** +10-15%

Frazer Manhattan 1947-48

1948 Manhattan 4-door sedan

PRODUCTION

1947 32,655 **1948** 18,591

HISTORY

Top-of-the-line Kaiser-Frazer product, the first entirely new postwar body style, and a never before equalled array of interior and exterior colors are points that distinguish these Howard Darrin-designed four-door sedans. The bulbous body and long wheelbase gave enormous interior space, and combined with an economical six-cylinder engine to provide smooth highway travel with surprising gas mileage. Colors and fabrics selected by designer Carleton Spencer, a genius whose efforts predicted industry-wide practice.

FOR

Historical importance: the first straight-through fenderlines and advanced color/trim combinations • High quality • Parts supplies still good

AGAINST

Underwhelming styling • Engine subject to cooling problems, enjoys blowing head gaskets.

SPECIFICATIONS

Length (in.) 203.0 **Wheelbase (in.)** 123.5 **Weight (lbs.)** 3375
Price (new) $2712-2746

ENGINES

cid/type	bore x stroke	bhp	years
226.2/L6	3.31×4.38	112	1947-48

PRICES/PROJECTION

Restorable $600-1000 **Good** $1000-2000
Excellent $3000-5000 **5-year projection** 10%

Frazer Standard 1947

1947 4-door sedan

PRODUCTION

8940

HISTORY

The first Frazers, built by Graham-Paige Motors under a work-sharing agreement with Kaiser-Frazer. Costs of operations proved more than G-P could bear, so the firm sold its interests to K-F. Standard (non-Manhattan) Frazers bearing serial numbers up to F47-009940 (1001 was the first number) are G-P products, and bear the nameplates of that old-line company. That historical aspect plus rarity puts these models in a class apart from K-F-built Frazers this year.

FOR

Extremely rare • Historical interest • New styling for the time

AGAINST

Not pretty • Mundane interiors • Almost impossible to find, yet not a high-potential investment

SPECIFICATIONS

Length (in.) 203.0 **Wheelbase (in.)** 123.5 **Weight (lbs.)** 3340
Price (new) $2295

ENGINES

cid/type	bore x stroke	bhp	years
226.2/L6	3.31×4.38	100	1947

PRICES/PROJECTION

Restorable $500-1000 **Good** $1000-2000
Excellent $2500-5000 **5-year projection** +10%

Frazer Manhattan 1949-50

1949 Manhattan 4-door sedan

PRODUCTION

4d sedan 9950 **4d convertible sedan** 70 (figures approximate; includes some reserialed 1949s sold as 1950 models)

HISTORY

The last Frazer authorized by Joseph W. Frazer before he was replaced as K-F president by Edgar Kaiser. These cars retained the previous bodyshell, spruced up with a new honeycomb grille and large vertical taillamps. The convertibles required a heavily reinforced X-braced frame to provide torsional stiffness for the pillarless body, which was virtually handbuilt from the sedan shell.

FOR

Same good qualities of 1947-48 • More glittery look • Posh interior • Unusual postwar convertible sedan style, scarce and desirable

AGAINST

As for 1947-48 Manhattan • Convertibles likely to become the costliest collector K-F products • Convertible trim, particularly interior, nearly impossible to find

SPECIFICATIONS

Length (in.) 207.5 **Wheelbase (in.)** 123.5
Weight (lbs.) 3391-3726 **Price (new)** $2595-3295

ENGINES

cid/type	bore x stroke	bhp	years
226.2/L6	3.31×4.38	112	1949-50

PRICES/PROJECTION

SEDAN As for 1947-48 Manhattan CONVERTIBLE
Restorable $2000-4000 **Good** $5500-8000
Excellent $9000-15,000 **5-year projection** no change

Frazer Manhattan 1951

1951 Manhattan 4-door hardtop sedan

PRODUCTION

4d hardtop sedan 152   **4d convertible sedan** 131

HISTORY

The last of the Frazers. Marked by an extreme facelift from the cowl forward by K-F stylist Herb Weisinger, who also raised the rear fenders and gave them shallow, faired-in taillights. Also new was Hydra-Matic transmission, "imported" from General Motors, as standard. Despite styling that generally provoked all-or-nothing reaction, more '51s could have been sold than were built, but the main reason for offering them at all was to use up leftover Kaiser convertible and hardtop bodies. When they were gone (by mid-1951), so was the Frazer.

FOR

Scarce and desirable • High-quality materials and body construction • Smooth runners (though no hot rods)

AGAINST

Debatable styling • Body parts in short supply • Same engine drawbacks as other 226-cid K-F models

SPECIFICATIONS

Length (in.) 211.4   **Wheelbase (in.)** 123.5
Weight (lbs.) 3771-3941   **Price (new)** $3075 (either model)

ENGINES

cid/type	bore x stroke	bhp	years
226.2/L6	3.31×4.38	115	1951

PRICES/PROJECTION

CONVERTIBLE **Restorable** $2500-4500   **Good** $6000-8500
Excellent $9500-15,000   HARDTOP SEDAN
Restorable $1250-2750   **Good** $3000-4500
Excellent $5000-7500   **5-year projection** +10%

Frazer Standard 1951

1951 4-door sedan

PRODUCTION

9931 (includes approx. 3000 Vagabond 4d utility sedans)

HISTORY

The base series in Frazer's last model year, with the same styling as the '51 Manhattan. Includes the intriguing Vagabond utility sedan, a carryover of the 1949-50 Kaiser model featuring a double rear hatch and fold-down rear seatback that opened up an enormous load bed. The Vagabond was K-F's halfway solution to the problem of how to offer wagon-like cargo carrying capacity and versatility without the tooling expense for a separate wagon body. The regular sedan was more luxurious than previous base Frazers, being trimmed to 1949-50 Manhattan levels.

FOR

Good quality • Smooth road cars • Vagabond's versatility, unusual design

AGAINST

As for 1951 Manhattan

1951 Vagabond 4-door utility sedan

SPECIFICATIONS

Length (in.) sedan: 211.4; Vagabond: 207.7
Wheelbase (in.) 123.5   **Weight (lbs.)** 3456-3556
Price (new) $2359-2999

ENGINES

cid/type	bore x stroke	bhp	years
226.2/L6	3.31×4.38	115	1951

PRICES/PROJECTION

Restorable $500-1000   **Good** $1500-2500
Excellent $2500-4500 Add 10% for Vagabond
5-year projection no change

Graham Supercharger 1938-40

1940 Supercharger Custom 4-door sedan

PRODUCTION

1938 2410   **1939** 2479   **1940** under 1000

HISTORY

The remarkable, radical "Spirit of Motion," better known as the "sharknose." Introduced for 1938 and underwhelmed the market. First offered only as a four-door sedan in two trim levels, expanded to include two-door coupe and sedan for 1939-40 in Standard and Custom versions. The Graham-built centrifugal supercharger was the only blower available in a popular-priced car and boosted horsepower on the Continental six from about 90 to 116 for 1938-39 and 120 for 1940. Quietly dropped in 1940 in favor of the Hollywood based on the Cord 810 dies. A year later, Graham-Paige abandoned the car business altogether for $20 million worth of defense contracts. Joseph W. Frazer gained control of G-P in 1944 and briefly returned to the field with the 1946 Frazer, but soon sold its automotive interests to Kaiser-Frazer Corporation.

FOR

Exotic, if bizarre, styling • Good performance • Rarity

AGAINST

Body parts very scarce • Good examples hard to find

SPECIFICATIONS

Length (in.) NA   **Wheelbase (in.)** 120.0
Weight (lbs.) 3250-3370   **Price (new)** $1070-1295

ENGINES

cid/type	bore x stroke	bhp	years
217.8/L6	3.25×4.38	116-120*	1938-40
*supercharged			

PRICES/PROJECTION

Restorable $1000-2000   **Good** $2000-4000
Excellent $4000-9000   **5-year projection** +10%

Graham Hollywood 1940-41

1940 Hollywood Custom 4-door sedan (prototype)

PRODUCTION

1959 (some sources list 1597)

HISTORY

Companion to the Skylark from Hupp, part of a last-ditch comeback attempt by two moribund automakers trying to survive together instead of singly. Both based on a modified version of the 1936-37 Cord Beverly sedan body but with rear drive instead of front drive and a different front end treatment that shaved several inches from the Cord's overall length. The Hollywood was powered by Graham's own supercharged six-cylinder engine, with an offset carburetor and air cleaner to clear the low Beverly hoodline. Horsepower was increased slightly for 1941 (mostly by the stroke of a pen), when an unblown version was also listed. The complexity of the old Cord dies delayed Hollywood/Skylark production, and the project never really got off the ground apart from these pilot-assembly units. Main appeal here is for "underdog" fans interested in the uncommon.

FOR

Pretty • Pretty unusual • Cheaper than a Cord • Historical interest

AGAINST

A challenge to restore because of body complexity • Expect rust

- Body parts (especially those unique to these models) very scarce
- Not plentiful

SPECIFICATIONS

Length (in.) 190.0 **Wheelbase (in.)** 115.0
Weight (lbs.) 2915-2965 **Price (new)** $968-1250

ENGINES

cid/type	bore x stroke	bhp	years
217.8/L6	3.25×4.38	93-124	1940-41

PRICES/PROJECTION

Restorable $3500-5000 **Good** $5500-7500
Excellent $9000-11,000 **5-year projection** +10%

Henry J DeLuxe 1951

1951 DeLuxe 2-door sedan

PRODUCTION

43,400 (est.)

HISTORY

Pioneer American compact, the attempt by tycoon Henry J. Kaiser to reach less affluent buyers who could only afford a used car. A good idea messed up with dumpy styling (selected over several better-looking proposals, including one by Howard Darrin with a familial relationship to the stunning '51 Kaiser), very plain interior decor, sparse standard equipment, and a steep price (not much less than that of a full-size Chevy, Ford, or Plymouth). Total model year production was only 81,942 units, with the six-cylinder DeLuxe slightly leading the four-cylinder standard version.

FOR

Surprising performance and handling • Reliable engine • Low operating costs

AGAINST

Low-buck finish inside and out • Rust-prone • Dumpy styling

SPECIFICATIONS

Length (in.) 174.5 **Wheelbase (in.)** 100.0 **Weight (lbs.)** 2341
Price (new) $1499

ENGINES

cid/type	bore x stroke	bhp	years
161/L6	3.13×3.50	80	1951

PRICES/PROJECTION

Restorable $300-600 **Good** $750-1500
Excellent $2000-3000 **5-year projection** +10%

Henry J Standard 1951

1951 2-door sedan

PRODUCTION

38,500 (est.)

HISTORY

Four-cylinder running mate to the Henry J DeLuxe, intended for the bottom end of the market. Same comments apply here except for the engine, which sacrificed performance for remarkable fuel economy (up to 35 mpg when driven conservatively).

FOR

Mileage • Easy on the collector's budget • Others as for 1951 DeLuxe

AGAINST

Underpowered • Heavy steering • Choppy ride • Others as for 1951 DeLuxe

SPECIFICATIONS

Length (in.) 174.5 **Wheelbase (in.)** 100.0 **Weight (lbs.)** 2293
Price (new) $1363

ENGINES

cid/type	bore x stroke	bhp	years
134.2/L4	3.13×4.38	68	1951

PRICES/PROJECTION

Restorable $500-1000 **Good** $1000-2500
Excellent $2500-4000 **5-year projection** no change

Henry J Vagabond 1952

1952 Vagabond DeLuxe 2-door sedan

PRODUCTION

7017

HISTORY

An interim version of Kaiser's compact, actually a leftover '51 fitted with "continental" outside spare tire and slightly upgraded interior. Available with both four- and six-cylinder engines, and identified by appropriate front fender script.

FOR

The outside spare did a little for the dumpy looks ● Others as for 1951 models

AGAINST

Otherwise, it was the same package ● Others as for 1951 models

SPECIFICATIONS

Length (in.) 179.4 **Wheelbase (in.)** 100.0
Weight (lbs.) 2365-2385 **Price (new)** $1407-1552

ENGINES

cid/type	bore x stroke	bhp	years
134.2/L4	3.13×4.38	68	1952
161/L6	3.13×3.50	80	1952

PRICES/PROJECTION

Restorable $600-1000 **Good** $1000-2500
Excellent $2500-5000 **5-year projection** +10%

Henry J Corsair 1952-54

PRODUCTION

1952 7600 **1953** 8500 **1954** 800 (all est.)

1953 Corsair 2-door sedan

HISTORY

As before, the four-cylinder companion to the DeLuxe, and sharing the same improvements. Also see 1951 Henry J standard.

FOR

As for 1953-54 Corsair DeLuxe, but with better economy and poorer performance

AGAINST

As for 1953-54 Corsair DeLuxe

SPECIFICATIONS

Length (in.) 181.5 **Wheelbase (in.)** 100.0
Weight (lbs.) 2370-2405 **Price (new)** $1399-1517

ENGINES

cid/type	bore x stroke	bhp	years
134.2/L4	3.13×4.38	68	1952-54

PRICES/PROJECTION

Restorable $500-1000 **Good** $1000-3000
Excellent $3000-5000 Add 10% for overdrive, 10% for 1954 model **5-year projection** +10%

Henry J Corsair DeLuxe 1952-54

PRODUCTION

1952 8900 **1953** 8100 **1954** 300 (all est.)

HISTORY

An attempt to improve the Henry J's sales appeal. Marked externally by a full-width grille and taillamps set into the tips of the little rear fender fins. Interiors became a bit less spartan, the dash was revised slightly, and prices were higher (though they were reduced a little as time went on). As before, DeLuxe signified the six-cylinder engine. None of this was enough to halt the sales downslide. Total production (including the four-cylinder versions) was 23,658, 16,672, and 1123 for these model years, respectively.

1953 Corsair DeLuxe 2-door sedan

FOR

Better looking (but not much) •Improved workmanship •Good economy •Sprightly performance (0-60 mph in 16 seconds)

AGAINST

The same dull styling

SPECIFICATIONS

Length (in.) 181.5 **Wheelbase (in.)** 100.0
Weight (lbs.) 2405-2455 **Price (new)** $1566-1664

ENGINES

cid/type	bore x stroke	bhp	years
161/L6	3.13×3.50	80	1952-54

PRICES/PROJECTION

Restorable $500-1000 **Good** $1000-2500
Excellent $2500-5000 Add 10% for all-vinyl or leather interior, 10% for overdrive, 10% for 1954 model **5-year projection** +10%

Hudson Eight 1930-33

1931 Greater Eight boattail Sport Roadster by Murray

PRODUCTION

1930 85,407 **1931** 22,156 **1932** 8,000 (est) **1933** 1890

HISTORY

Coupled with the closure of the famous Biddle & Smart coachbuilders, the Depression severely hurt sales of Hudson's premium models, and none are rated Classics after 1929. Perhaps some should be. Hudson Eights were often luxurious, and usually smooth, effortless performers, thanks to the firm's new 1930 L-head engine, which would run through 1952. The Greater Eight and Major Eight lines of 1931-33 offered a number of stylish open body types, including speedsters, roadsters, and phaetons with coachwork by LeBaron, Murray, and Briggs. Designer Frank Spring began his long Hudson career with the pretty '32s, whose beautiful vee'd grille and flowing fenderlines carried over on the 1933s. Four-square styling was then abandoned for Hudson's new generation of 1934.

FOR

Strong club support • Handsome styling • Snob appeal of the occasional custom body • Good tourers

AGAINST

A mite underpowered • Parts problems

SPECIFICATIONS

Length (in.) NA **Wheelbase (in.)** 119.0, 126.0 (1930-32); 119.0 (1933); 132.0 (1932-33 Major) **Weight (lbs.)** 2675-3650
Price (new) $735-1595

ENGINES

cid/type	bore x stroke	bhp	years
213.5/L8	2.75×4.50	80	1930
233.7/L8	2.88×4.50	87	1931
254.0/L8	3.00×4.50	101	1932-33

PRICES/PROJECTION

ROADSTERS/PHAETONS **Restorable** $10,000-17,000
Good $22,000-33,000 **Excellent** $35,000-44,000
SPEEDSTERS/CUSTOM OPEN add 20%. CLOSED BODIES
Restorable $3300-5500 **Good** $5500-7800
Excellent $8500-12,000 **5-year projection** +10%

Hudson Custom Eight 1935-38

PRODUCTION

1935 NA **1936** NA **1937** 6926 **1938** NA

HISTORY

After a series of shorter, smaller Eights in 1934, Hudson released the big Custom for 1935, with a new all-steel body—an industry first—in brougham and sedan styles on an extra-long wheelbase. Chassis spans varied from 120 to 129 inches on an expanding line of bodies through 1938, during which time Hudson gradually evolved toward more enveloping, curvy bodywork. Styling was all-new for 1936 but not as radical as most of the competition's. Big, handsome cars that deserve a close look, if you can find one in good shape.

FOR

Innovative and contemporary for the time • Handsome styling, more streamlined in each successive year • Solidly built • Good performance

1938 Custom Eight Country Club 4-door sedan

AGAINST

Not many open bodies available • Relatively high operating costs • Parts supplies short, so consider only top-condition examples

SPECIFICATIONS

Length (in.) NA **Wheelbase (in.)** 124.0 (1935); 120.0/127.0 (1936); 122.0/129.0 (1937-38) **Weight (lbs.)** 2950-3275
Price (new) $845-1299

ENGINES

cid/type	bore x stroke	bhp	years
254.5/L8	3.00 × 4.50	113-128	1935-38

PRICES/PROJECTION

OPEN BODIES **Restorable** $3300-7800 **Good** $7800-13,500
Excellent $13,000-20,000. CLOSED BODIES
Restorable $2200-3400 **Good** $3300-5500
Excellent $5500-9000 **5-year projection** +10%

Hudson Eight 1939-40

1940 Eight convertible coupe

PRODUCTION

1939 9000 (est.) **1940** 10,620

HISTORY

Handsomely restyled for 1939, extensively facelifted for 1940, these Hudsons shared the sharp-nosed look of concurrent Fords and Studebakers and are among the nicest-looking Detroit cars of these years. Called Country Club (the Big Boy name appeared on two long-wheelbase 1940 models), the top-of-the-line Eights used Hud-

son's longest chassis, carried its highest prices and were the most lavishly equipped cars ever to bear the White Triangle logo. Except for larger displacement, the company's big, smooth-running L-head eight continued largely unchanged from its original 1930 form. Total 1939 production is not available but was probably a shade lower than the 1940 figure.

FOR

Slick styling • Excellent go off the line • Good roadability

AGAINST

Rust-prone • Somewhat clumsy handling • Thirsty

SPECIFICATIONS

Length (in.) NA **Wheelbase (in.)** 122.0, 129.0 (1939); 118.0, 125.0 (1940) **Weight (lbs.)** 3003, 3400 **Price (new)** $860-1430

ENGINES

cid/type	bore x stroke	bhp	years
254.5/L8	3.00 × 4.50	122-128	1939-40

PRICES/PROJECTION

CONVERTIBLE (incl. 1940 CONV. SEDAN)
Restorable $2800-5000 **Good** $6000-9200
Excellent $11,000-15,500. CLOSED MODELS
Restorable $1100-2200 **Good** $2200-3800
Excellent $3800-5500. Add 20% for coupe or victoria.
5-year projection +10%

Hudson Commodore Eight 1941-42

1942 Commodore Eight 4-door sedan

PRODUCTION

1941 9718   **1942** 6592

HISTORY

Continuation of the smooth-performing big Eights. Hudson facelifted again for these last prewar models, and changed wheelbase lengths. A wide range of body styles was catalogued: convertible sedans (an estimated 200 and 100 built) and wagons (80 and 40, respectively). Appearance changes for 1942 included hiding the running boards and lowering and cleaning up the grille.

FOR

Pleasing good looks • Solid construction • Good performance • Avid club support

AGAINST

Heavy handling • Thirsty • Somewhat rust-prone

SPECIFICATIONS

Length (in.) NA **Wheelbase (in.)** 121.0
Weight (lbs.) 3110-3400 **Price (new)** $1071-1451

ENGINES

cid/type	bore x stroke	bhp	years
254/L8	3.00×4.50	128	1941-42

PRICES/PROJECTION

As for 1940 Hudson Eight

Hudson Commodore Eight 1946-47

1946 Commodore Eight 4-door sedan

PRODUCTION

1946 8193 **1947** 12,593

HISTORY

The top-line series in Hudson's early postwar lineup. Shared body-shell and most design features with other models; all were holdovers of the 1941-42 offerings. Available as a four-door sedan, club coupe, and Brougham convertible coupe. Ragtops were few, probably not exceeding 500 units for both model years here. The big eight gave the Commodore strong performance, and you also got nicer trim than in the Super Six. A companion Super Eight series with slightly less luxurious fittings was also offered in sedan or club coupe body styles only.

FOR

Construction quality • Luxury • Enthusiastic club • Top-line models • Fine performance

AGAINST

Not a styling masterpiece • Heavy steering • Clumsy handling

SPECIFICATIONS

Length (in.) 204.5 **Wheelbase (in.)** 121.0
Weight (lbs.) 3235-3435 **Price (new)** $1760-2196

ENGINES

cid/type	bore x stroke	bhp	years
254/L8	3.00×4.50	128	1946-47

PRICES/PROJECTION

Restorable $900-2000 **Good** $2500-4500
Excellent $5000-7000 Add 100% for convertible
5-year projection +10%

Hudson Super Six 1946-47

1946 Super Six 4-door sedan

PRODUCTION

1946 61,787 **1947** 49,276

HISTORY

The best-selling Hudsons in the early postwar years, and the most readily available today. Body choices were two- and four-door sedans, coupe, club coupe, and convertible. Soft-top production was about 2500 units for the two years. Styling was a little busier than in 1940-42, but was still based on the prewar bodyshell. Three transmissions were offered: overdrive, Drive-Master, and Vacumotive Drive. The last was a semi-automatic and worked the clutch, while Drive-Master eliminated both clutch and shift motions. A Commodore Six sedan and club coupe were also available in these two model years.

FOR

Relatively easy to find • Strong club support • Solid construction

AGAINST

Busy styling • Heavy steering • Plain interiors

SPECIFICATIONS

Length (in.) 204.5 **Wheelbase (in.)** 121.0
Weight (lbs.) 2950-3750 **Price (new)** $1481-2021

ENGINES

cid/type	bore x stroke	bhp	years
212/L6	3.00×5.00	102	1946-47

PRICES/PROJECTION

Restorable $750-2000 **Good** $2500-4000
Excellent $4000-6000 Add 10% for coupes, 100% for
convertible **5-year projection** +10%

Hudson Commodore Eight 1948-49

1948 Commodore Eight 4-door sedan

PRODUCTION

1948 35,315   **1949** 28,687

HISTORY

Hudson's top-of-the-line, offered in three body styles including a convertible. Proved more popular than previous incarnations because of trend-setting Step-Down design, and scored close to 60,000 sales for these two model years, during which no styling or specification changes were made. Smooth and ground-hugging in appearance, and more roadable by far than virtually any other full-size American car.

FOR

Luxury • Performance • Robustness • Roadability • Good appreciation potential

AGAINST

Thirsty • Priciest of the 1948-49s

SPECIFICATIONS

Length (in.) 207.5   **Wheelbase (in.)** 124.0
Weight (lbs.) 3600-3800   **Price (new)** $2448-3198

ENGINES

cid/type	bore x stroke	bhp	years
254/L8	3.00×4.50	128	1948-49

PRICES/PROJECTION

Restorable $1000-2500 **Good** $3000-4500
Excellent $4500-7000 Add 100% for convertible.
5-year projection +10%

Hudson Commodore Six 1948-49

1948 Commodore Six Brougham convertible

PRODUCTION

1948 27,159   **1949** 32,715

HISTORY

Costlier (about $200 more) companion series to the Super Six, available as a Brougham convertible as well as two- and four-door sedan body types in these years. Chief difference from Super Six is a more lushly appointed interior with such amenities as fold-down armrests and a chrome-plated steering column.

FOR

As for 1948-49 Super Six

AGAINST

As for 1948-49 Super Six, but somewhat heavier, so performance poorer

SPECIFICATIONS

Length (in.) 207.5   **Wheelbase (in.)** 124.0
Weight (lbs.) 3540-3780   **Price (new)** $2374-3057

ENGINES

cid/type	bore x stroke	bhp	years
262/L6	3.56×4.38	121	1948-49

PRICES/PROJECTION

As for 1948-49 Super Six

Hudson Super Eight 1948-49

PRODUCTION

1948 5338   **1949** 6365

HISTORY

The cheaper of Hudson's two eight-cylinder series in this period. Offered only in four-door sedan and two-door club coupe guise. More rare than other 1948-49 models, but lack of top-line status makes it less desirable despite that.

1948 Super Eight club coupe

FOR

The great Step-down design, plus eight-cylinder performance

AGAINST

Scarce; hard to find ● No "sporty" body styles

SPECIFICATIONS

Length (in.) 207.5 **Wheelbase (in.)** 124.0
Weight (lbs.) 3495-3550 **Price (new)** $2245-2343

ENGINES

cid/type	bore x stroke	bhp	years
254/L8	3.00×4.50	128	1948-49

PRICES/PROJECTION

As for closed body styles 1948-49 Commodore Eight

Hudson Super Six 1948-49

1948 Super Six Brougham 2-door sedan

PRODUCTION

1948 49,388 **1949** 91,333

HISTORY

One of the truly significant new designs of the early postwar years, the "Step-down" Hudson was low and sleek. It even looks pretty good today. Unit body/chassis construction featured a dropped floorpan (hence the nickname) surrounded by massive chassis girders for a very safe, solid structure. Big instrument dials on a

businesslike dash and armchair-comfortable seats marked the roomy interior. The result of all this was soaring sales, the low-priced Super Six again leading the four-series Hudson line. The same five body styles from 1946-47 were again fielded. Super Six convertible production is estimated at 88 and 1870 for these two years, respectively. No body or mechanical changes for '49. Super Six values currently level-peg those for comparable 1946-47 models, making the first of the six-cylinder Step-downs some of today's best collector buys.

FOR

Design merit ● Excellent roadability ● Solid construction

AGAINST

Very little—one of the greats

SPECIFICATIONS

Length (in.) 207.5 **Wheelbase (in.)** 124.0
Weight (lbs.) 3460-3750 **Price (new)** $2053-2836

ENGINES

cid/type	bore x stroke	bhp	years
262/L6	3.56×4.38	121	1948-49

PRICES/PROJECTION

As for 1946-47 Super Six **5-year projection** +15%

Hudson Hornet 1951-53

1951 Hornet 4-door sedan

PRODUCTION

1951 43,656 **1952** 35,921 **1953** 27,208
(Convertible estimates: 550, 360, 150; Hollywood 2d hardtop estimates: 2100, 2160, 910)

HISTORY

The most remembered Hudson of the postwar years, one of the industry's all-time greats. Virtually unbeatable in stock-car racing through 1954, and continued to compete with some success even after the Step-down line came to an end with the Nash-based '55 Hudsons. Amazingly, this racing success was achieved with a six-cylinder engine — the last performance six before Pontiac's late-'60s overhead-cam engine. "Twin-H Power" for 1953 (twin carbs and dual manifold induction) and the 210-bhp 7-X racing engine late that same year were early examples of factory "prodifying" that helped the likes of Marshall Teague and Herb Thomas dominate NASCAR and AAA tracks against ostensibly much more potent machinery. Positioned just below the top-line Commodore Eight series for 1951-52; moved to the top for '53. The Hornet's legendary performance prowess gives it a big edge in collector appeal over the basically similar Pacemaker, Super Six, and Wasp models of this period.

FOR

One of the great postwar landmarks—a true champion • Fine performance • Surprising handling • Quality • Luxury

AGAINST

Step-down design looking dated by '51 • Interior and some exterior details clumsily executed • Thirsty

SPECIFICATIONS

Length (in.) 208.3 (1951-52), 208.5 (1953)
Wheelbase (in.) 124.0   **Weight (lbs.)** 3530-3780
Price (new) $2543-3342

ENGINES

cid/type	bore x stroke	bhp	years
308/L6	3.81×4.50	145/160/170	1953

PRICES/PROJECTION

Restorable $1100-2800 **Good** $2500-4500
Excellent $4500-6500 Add 100% for convertible, 25% for hardtop, 10% for Twin-H Power, 50% for 7-X engine.
5-year projection +10%

Hudson Wasp 1952-54

1952 Wasp Hollywood 2-door hardtop

PRODUCTION

1952 21,876   **1953** 17,792   **1954** 11,603 (incl. 1953-54 Super Wasp)

HISTORY

Attractively upgraded version of the short-wheelbase 1950-52 Pacemaker, with the larger Commodore six for improved performance. A full line of sedans, club coupe, hardtop, and convertible was offered in the 1952 debut series, then became the Super Wasp offerings for 1953-54. Just three closed bodies were listed for the standard Wasp in those years.

FOR

A bit more compact, easier-to-handle Step-down • Overshadowed by the mighty Hornet, so less expensive • Quality construction and materials

AGAINST

Lower appreciation than Hornet • Not too many around now

SPECIFICATIONS

Length (in.) 201.5   **Wheelbase (in.)** 119.0
Weight (lbs.) 3340-3635   **Price (new)** $2209-3048

ENGINES

cid/type	bore x stroke	bhp	years
232/L6	3.56×3.88	126	1954
262/L6	3.56×4.38	127	1952-53

PRICES/PROJECTION

SEDANS/COUPE **Restorable** $500-1000 **Good** $1250-2200
Excellent $2500-3500 Add 50% for Hollywood hardtop, 100% for convertible **5-year projection** +10%

Hudson Jet 1953-54

1954 Jet Family Club 2-door sedan

PRODUCTION

1953 11,000   **1954** 7000 (both estimated)

HISTORY

Hudson's ill-starred attempt to save itself with a compact at a time when demand for such cars was quite limited and what market there was belonged almost totally to Rambler. Solidly built with traditional Hudson engineering integrity, but styling was dowdy and price uncomfortably close to that of the standard Ford, Chevy, and Plymouth. Production failed to break 40,000 during two model years, and the Jet certainly hastened Hudson's demise as a fully independent automaker. This basic version appeared as a four-door sedan only. A two-door was added the following year along with a stripped "Family Club" two-door late in the season.

FOR

Good quality • Decent performance • Excellent roadability

AGAINST

Dull • Barren interior • Rust-prone

   continued on page 137

△1950 Alfa Romeo 6C2500 Super Sport   ▽1952 Allstate

△1939 American Bantam Riviera ▽1960 Aston Martin DB4GT Zagato

△1936 Auburn 852 Supercharged   ▽1954 Buick Skylark

△1966 Buick Riviera   ▽1933 Cadillac Sixteen

△1949 Cadillac Series 62 ▽1953 Cadillac Eldorado

△1939 Chevrolet Master DeLuxe ▽1966 Chevrolet Corvette Sting Ray

△1934 Chrysler Custom Imperial Airflow   ▽1972 Citroën SM

△1956 Continental Mark II   ▽1930 Cord L-29

△1949 Crosley Hotshot ▽1936 DeSoto Airflow

△1948 DeSoto Custom ▽1957 Dodge Custom Royal Lancer D-500

△1970 Dodge Challenger R/T Hemi   ▽1931 Duesenberg Model J by Murphy

△1962 Facel Vega Facel II ▽1960 Ferrari 250GT by Pinin Farina

△1957 Ferrari 410 Superamerica by Pinin Farina　▽1947 Ford Super DeLuxe Sportsman

△1951 Ford Custom Crestliner   ▽1955 Ford Thunderbird

△1963 Ford Galaxie 500/XL ▽1948 Frazer Manhattan

△1939 Graham Supercharger   ▽1951 Henry J DeLuxe

SPECIFICATIONS

Length (in.) 180.7 **Wheelbase (in.)** 105.0
Weight (lbs.) 2650-2715 **Price (new)** $1621-1858

ENGINES

cid/type	bore x stroke	bhp	years
202/L6	3.00×4.75	104/106/114	1953-54

PRICES/PROJECTION

Restorable $600-1200 **Good** $1200-2200
Excellent $2200-3400 **5-year projection** ±10%

Hudson Super Jet
1953-54

1953 Super Jet 4-door sedan

PRODUCTION

1953 10,000   **1954** 6000 (both estimated)

HISTORY

The upper-class version of Hudson's ho-hum compact, though no different bodily or mechanically from the plain Jet. Offered from the first in two- and four-door sedan styles, with the scrunched-up proportions that gave the Jet the look of a big Hudson that had shrunk at the cleaners.

FOR

As for 1953-54 Jet, but nicer furnishings and easier to live with

AGAINST

As for 1953-54 Jet

SPECIFICATIONS

Length (in.) 180.7 **Wheelbase (in.)** 105.0
Weight (lbs.) 2695-2725 **Price (new)** $1933-1954

ENGINES

cid/type	bore x stroke	bhp	years
202/L6	3.00×4.75	104/106/114	1953-54

PRICES/PROJECTION

Restorable $900-2200 **Good** $2200-2800
Excellent $2800-4000 Add 15% for 1954 model.
5-year projection +10%

Hudson Super Wasp
1953-54

1954 Super Wasp Hollywood 2-door hardtop

PRODUCTION

See 1953-54 Wasp (combined production; no separate figures available)   **Estimated 1953 convertible** 50
Hollywood 2d hardtop 590

HISTORY

Luxury expansion of the shorter-wheelbase Hudson series. A full line including convertible and Hollywood hardtop. As in previous years, there were no Step-down wagons, which would have helped the firm's sales (they declined each year the design continued without significant change). One of its problems was that it was difficult and expensive to alter. Hudson did manage a fairly extensive reskinning operation for the Step-down's final year, however, with a more contemporary square-sided look that did away with the very '40s "torpedo" lines. The Super Wasp was distinguished from the regular Wasp by an air-vent hood ornament and appropriate script on glovebox door, trunklid, and front fenders above the bodyside moldings. The '54 models had a more powerful version of the Hudson six with slightly greater displacement.

FOR

As for 1952-54 Wasp

AGAINST

As for 1952-54 Wasp

SPECIFICATIONS

Length (in.) 201.5 **Wheelbase (in.)** 119.0
Weight (lbs.) 3455-3680 **Price (new)** $2413-3048

ENGINES

cid/type	bore x stroke	bhp	years
232/L6	3.56×3.88	127	1953
262/L6	3.56×4.38	140	1954

PRICES/PROJECTION

As for 1952-54 Wasp

Hudson Hornet
1954

1954 Hornet Special 4-door sedan

PRODUCTION

24,833

HISTORY

Hudson's legendary race winner in the last year of the (by now) aged Step-down design. Featured the most radical facelift to be carried out on the original 1948 body, with raised rear fenders carrying fender-tip taillights and a more aggressive full-width grille. The usual Hornet sedan, coupe, Hollywood hardtop, and convertible were supplemented during the model year by the Hornet Special two- and four-door sedans and club coupe. All were powered by the 160-bhp version of the famous Hornet six. But the buying public was V8 crazy, and despite Hudson's continued race track successes sales dropped appreciably. Temporary salvation came with the Nash-Kelvinator merger in late April 1954.

FOR

As for 1951-53 Hornet

AGAINST

As for 1951-53 Hornet, but styling less distinctive

SPECIFICATIONS

Length (in.) 208.5 **Wheelbase (in.)** 124.0
Weight (lbs.) 3620-3800 **Price (new)** $2742-3288

ENGINES

cid/type	bore x stroke	bhp	years
308/L8	3.81×4.50	160/170	1954

PRICES/PROJECTION

As for 1951-53 Hornet

Hudson Italia
1954-55

PRODUCTION

25; also, one prototype coupe and one prototype four-door (X-161)

1954-55 Italia 2-door coupe

HISTORY

Built by Italy's Carrozzeria Touring on the chassis and mechanicals of the compact Jet, this grand touring coupe styled by Frank Spring might have been the basis for a whole new model line had Hudson remained independent. Advanced styling features included a wraparound windshield, doors cut into the roof, functional fender-mounted air scoops, flow-through ventilation, and form-fitting leather-covered bucket seats. Powered by the higher-output 114-bhp Jet six, the Italia was not fast despite its "Superleggera" (lightweight) construction and aluminum bodywork, but would have undoubtedly been swifter had it been built in mass-production quantity. A tall $4800 price tag put the kabosh on sales, and the Nash/Hudson merger ended whatever chance it had for inspiring Hudson's own models for 1955 and beyond.

FOR

Rare and desirable • Advanced styling and design features • Good road car • Not a Milestone, but should be

AGAINST

Styling gimmicky in places • Flimsy construction • Body parts now unobtainable

SPECIFICATIONS

Length (in.) 200.0 **Wheelbase (in.)** 105.0 **Weight (lbs.)** 2710
Price (new) $4800

ENGINES

cid/type	bore x stroke	bhp	years
202/L6	3.00×4.75	114	1954-55

PRICES/PROJECTION

Restorable $6000-8000 **Good** $8000-13,000
Excellent $16,000-22,000 **5-year projection** +10%

Hudson Jet-Liner
1954

PRODUCTION

2000 (est.)

1954 Jet-Liner 4-door sedan

HISTORY

Certainly the model to look for if a Hudson Jet turns you on. The top-line offering in the car's second and final year, with a choice of two or four doors. Interior decor featured duotone vinyl trim. Most Jet-Liners had the optional 114-bhp version of Hudson's small six-cylinder engine, which actually had been tooled from the old Commodore eight. Designer Frank Spring's proposed styling was much prettier than the shape that emerged, the Jet's kiddy-car proportions being fostered mainly by Hudson president Edward Barit.

FOR

The best of the Jets • Moderately luxurious • Good performance • Fine roadability

AGAINST

As for 1953-54 Jet and Super Jet

SPECIFICATIONS

Length (in.) 180.7   **Wheelbase (in.)** 105.0
Weight (lbs.) 2740-2760   **Price (new)** $2046-2057

ENGINES

cid/type	bore x stroke	bhp	years
202/L6	3.00×4.75	104/106/114	1954

PRICES/PROJECTION

Restorable $750-1200   **Good** $1800-3000
Excellent $3000-5000   **5-year projection** +10%

Hudson Hornet
1955-57

PRODUCTION

1955 4d sedan 10,010   **Hollywood 2d hardtop** 3324
1956 4d sedan 6512   **Hollywood 2d hardtop** 1640
1957 (combined total) 3876

HISTORY

Unflatteringly referred to nowadays as the "Hash," the predictable result of the American Motors merger. Now built as a reskinned Nash on the Kenosha, Wisconsin assembly lines instead of Hudson's old Detroit factory. Styling was individual, but became progressively worse. The '55 was the cleanest model of this trio, with a broad eggcrate grille and distinctive two-toning. For 1956 there was "V-Line Styling" that attempted to put Hudson's traditional triangle logo shape in every nook and cranny, blindingly accented by tacky

1957 Hornet Custom Hollywood 2-door hardtop

tinfoil appliques. The last Hudsons appeared for '57, even more gaudy than before. The Hornet's legendary six, with and without Twin-H Power, was offered through 1956, and AMC's new 320-cid V8 was available in all three years. A 1956-only Hornet Special came with Kenosha's 250 V8 and a lower price. A companion Wasp series was also fielded for 1955-56 based on the shorter wheelbase Nash Statesman platform and with less ornate trim. It was replaced by the Hornet Super for '57, while the more deluxe version was called Hornet Custom.

FOR

The comfy Nash body • Hudson's great six or a new V8 • Good performance • Not too expensive

AGAINST

Dreadful 1956-57 appearance • Thirsty • Rusts easily • Body parts supplies spotty or nonexistent • Not a true Hudson to some

SPECIFICATIONS

Length (in.) 209.3   **Wheelbase (in.)** 121.3
Weight (lbs.) 3467-3826   **Price (new)** $2405-3159

ENGINES

cid/type	bore x stroke	bhp	years
308/L6	3.81×4.50	160/170	1955
308/L6	3.81×4.50	165/175	1956
250/V8	3.50×3.25	190	1956
320/ohv V8	2.81×3.50	208	1955-56
327/ohv V8	4.00×3.25	255	1957

PRICES/PROJECTION

HOLLYWOOD **Restorable** $750-2000   **Good** $2500-4000
Excellent $4500-6500   **Deduct 20% for sedan**   **5-year projection** +10%

Hudson Metropolitan
1955-57

See 1955-57 Nash Metropolitan

Hupmobile Skylark Custom 1940-41

1940 Skylark Custom 4-door sedan (prototype)

PRODUCTION

319 (some sources list 371) plus 35 prototypes constructed 1939

HISTORY

Last gasp of the old Hupp Company in the auto business, after which it became a component supplier to other carmakers. Like the Graham Hollywood (the result of a Hupp-Graham accord) based on the old dies from the front-drive 1936-37 Cord Beverly sedan, but 5.5 inches shorter overall and with rear drive. Appearance differed only slightly from the Hollywood's, and the Skylark's engine was Hupp's four-main-bearing L-head six, about midway in performance between the supercharged and unsupercharged versions of the Graham engine. The complexity of the Cord dies and other problems delayed production startup until May 1940, by which time most of the sizeable number of initial orders had been cancelled. The Skylark was thus even less successful than the Hollywood, itself no great star.

FOR

Almost as pretty as a Cord • Rare and increasingly desirable • Good performance • Uniqueness

AGAINST

Spare parts (especially body pieces) very limited

SPECIFICATIONS

Length (in.) 190.0   **Wheelbase (in.)** 115.0   **Weight (lbs.)** 3000
Price (new) $895-1145

ENGINES

cid/type	bore x stroke	bhp	years
245/L6	3.50×4.25	101	1940-41

PRICES/PROJECTION

Restorable $3500-5000   **Good** $6000-8000
Excellent $9500-11,500   **5-year projection** no change

Imperial 1955-56

1955 Newport 2-door hardtop

PRODUCTION

1955 4d sedan 7840	**Newport 2d hardtop** 3418
1956 4d sedan 6821	**Southampton 2d hardtop** 2094
Southampton 4d hardtop 1543	

HISTORY

Chrysler's finest, spun-off as a separate make beginning with the 1955 models, which were terrific. Styled by Virgil Exner along the lines of his 1954 Parade Phaeton show cars. A big split eggcrate grille was used in front, distinctive gunsight taillights adorned the rear, and sculpted, flowing body lines (with fully radiused rear wheel openings) appeared in between. The '56s gained tailfins of good taste, plus a slightly longer wheelbase and overall length. Power was supplied by Chrysler's hemi-head V8, with a displacement and power boost for '56. Also that year a four-door hardtop sedan was added to the line in common with other Chrysler divisions.

FOR

Fine styling • Good quality control • Great road car • One of the more affordable luxury Milestones

AGAINST

Thirsty • Handling and braking not up to the horsepower

SPECIFICATIONS

Length (in.) 223.0 (1955), 226.0 (1956)
Wheelbase (in.) 130.0 (1955), 133.0 (1956)
Weight (lbs.) 4565-4680   **Price (new)** $4483-5225

ENGINES

cid/type	bore x stroke	bhp	years
331/ohv V8	3.81×3.63	250	1955
354/ohv V8	3.94×3.63	280	1956

1955 Newport 2-door hardtop

PRICES/PROJECTION

Restorable $1200-2200 **Good** $2200-3400
Excellent $3400-5000 Add 40% for 2-door hardtop, 20% for 4-door hardtop. **5-year projection** +10%

Crown Imperial
1955-56

1955 limousine

PRODUCTION

1955 4d sedan 45   **limousine** 127   **1956 4d sedan** 51
limousine 175

HISTORY

Continuation of the long Imperials of the early '50s, with Exner styling and sybaritic furnishings. The last cars of their type built in Detroit (after which Chrysler farmed out assembly to Ghia in Turin, Italy). These eight-passenger models replaced all the previous long-wheelbase offerings bearing Dodge, DeSoto, and Chrysler nameplates. Styling and mechanical changes parallel those made to the standard Imperials of these years.

FOR

As for 1955-56 Imperial, but less roadable because of extra size and weight

AGAINST

Thirsty • Large and cumbersome • Body parts unique to these models now very scarce

SPECIFICATIONS

Length (in.) 242.5 **Wheelbase (in.)** 149.5
Weight (lbs.) 5145-5205 **Price (new)** $6973-7737

ENGINES

cid/type	bore x stroke	bhp	years
331/ohv V8	3.81×3.63	250	1955
354/ohv V8	3.94×3.63	280	1956

PRICES/PROJECTION

Restorable $1000-1800 **Good** $2000-3400
Excellent $3300-5000 Add 50% for limousine.
5-year projection +10%

Imperial Crown
1957-60

1957 Crown convertible

PRODUCTION

1957 4d sedan 3642		**Southampton 4d hardtop** 7843	
Southampton 2d hardtop 4199		**convertible** 1167	
1958 4d sedan 1240		**Southampton 4d hardtop** 4146	
Southampton 2d hardtop 1939		**convertible** 675	
1959 4d sedan 1335		**Southampton 4d hardtop** 4714	
Southampton 2d hardtop 1728		**convertible** 555	
1960 4d sedan 1594		**Southampton 4d hardtop** 4510	
Southampton 2d hardtop 1504		**convertible** 618	

HISTORY

The midrange offerings in Chrysler's flagship line, given a new bodyshell for 1957 along with soaring "Forward Look" styling. The Crown lineup included the first open Imperials since 1953, the only series in which this body style was offered. Like other Chrysler products of the era, featured the firm's new torsion-bar front suspension, which greatly improved ride and handling. Styling was marked by Virgil Exner's heroically sized tailfins, complicated grillework, gunsight taillamps, and large compound-curve windshield. The hemi was ousted in favor of larger wedgehead V8s, with displacement increasing to 413 cid beginning with the '59s. While other Chrysler cars switched to unit construction for 1960, Imperial retained its body-on-frame construction, which would continue through 1966.

FOR

Luxurious and majestic • Comfortable road car

AGAINST

Not as well-built as 1955-56 models • Subject to rust • Thirsty • Grotesque 1960 styling

SPECIFICATIONS

Length (in.) 226.3-228.0 **Wheelbase (in.)** 129.0
Weight (lbs.) 4730-4915 **Price (new)** $5269-5774

ENGINES

cid/type	bore x stroke	bhp	years
392/ohv V8	4.00×3.90	325/345	1957-58
413/ohv V8	4.18×3.75	350	1959-60

PRICES/PROJECTION

Restorable $900-1800 **Good** $1800-3000
Excellent $3000-4500 Add 100-125% for convertible
5-year projection +10%

Crown Imperial by Ghia 1957-65

1958 limousine

PRODUCTION

1957 36	1958 31	1959 7	1960 16	1961 9	1962 0
1963 13	1964 10	1965 10			

HISTORY

Low demand sent Chrysler calling on Ghia of Italy to build its long-wheelbase limousines starting in 1957. Chrysler sent over a two-door hardtop body mounted on the more rigid convertible chassis. Ghia cut the car apart, added 20.5 inches to the wheelbase, reworked the superstructure, and applied posh upholstery and interior accoutrements. Each of these custom Crowns took a month to build, and at $15,075 in 1957 (up to $18,500 by 1965) not many were sold. One problem was that Imperial lacked Cadillac's prestige among heads of state, funeral directors, and corporate executives. Though quite luxurious and having the Ghia name's snob appeal, they just didn't compete well with the Standard of the World's Series 75. Styling generally followed model year changes for the standard Imperial line.

FOR

Very rare • Ride • Luxury • Smooth performance

AGAINST

Enormity • Thirst • Rust threat • Scarce body parts • Mixed construction quality

SPECIFICATIONS

Length (in.) 248.0 (average) **Wheelbase (in.)** 149.5
Weight (lbs.) 5960-6100 **Price (new)** $15,075-18,500

ENGINES

cid/type	bore x stroke	bhp	years
392/ohv V8	4.00×3.90	325	1957-59
413/ohv V8	4.18×3.75	340/350	1960-65

PRICES/PROJECTION

1957-61 Restorable $1800-2800 **Good** $3000-5000
Excellent $5000-6500 **1963-65 Restorable** $1500-2500
Good $3000-5000 **Excellent** $5000-6500
5-year projection +10%

Imperial LeBaron 1957-60

1957 LeBaron Southampton 4-door hardtop

PRODUCTION

1957 4d sedan 1729	**Southampton 4d hardtop** 911
1958 4d sedan 501	**Southampton 4d hardtop** 538
1959 4d sedan 510	**Southampton 4d hardtop** 622
1960 4d sedan 692	**Southampton 4d hardtop** 999

HISTORY

Produced in very small quantities, and worth seeking out. Imperial's premium series, priced $400-500 above comparable Crown models, and not very popular when new because of that. The four-door pillared sedan was priced identically with the Southampton four-door hardtop. Bodily and mechanically identical to the less expensive offerings, the LeBaron (named after the great 1930s coachbuilder) was somewhat more luxurious, Imperial's equivalent to the Cadillac 60 Special.

FOR

Rarity • Luxury • Comfort

AGAINST

Fuelishness • Tends to rust • Hard to find nowadays

SPECIFICATIONS

Length (in.) 226.3-228.0 **Wheelbase (in.)** 129.0
Weight (lbs.) 4760-4940 **Price (new)** $5743-6318

ENGINES

cid/type	bore x stroke	bhp	years
392/ohv V8	4.00×3.90	325/345	1957-58
413/ohv V8	4.18×3.75	350	1959-60

PRICES/PROJECTION

Restorable $1000-2000 **Good** $2000-3500
Excellent $3500-5200 **5-year projection** +10%

Imperial Crown 1961-63

PRODUCTION

1961 Southampton 2d hardtop 1007   **Southampton 4d hardtop** 4769   **convertible** 429   **1962 Southampton 2d**

1961 Crown Southampton 4-door hardtop

hardtop 1010   **Southampton 4d hardtop** 6911
convertible 554   **1963 Southampton 2d hardtop** 1067
Southampton 4d hardtop 6960   **convertible** 531

HISTORY

The last Imperials with all-Exner styling. All were marked by his favored throwback to the classic era, freestanding headlamps (actually headlight pods mounted on short stalks just above the bumper). A significant facelift for '61 brought swollen fins with taillights dangling down underneath them. The fins were shorn for '62, and 1956-style gunsight taillamps appeared on the cropped fenders. Exner's successor, Elwood Engel, put the taillights back in the fenders on the mildly refurbished '63s. Chrysler's wedgehead 413 V8 was the power source in all years, and there were few mechanical or chassis changes from previous Imperials. Interiors continued to be luxurious, set off by a commanding and somewhat gimmick-laden control panel featuring Chrysler's pushbutton controls for transmission and heater/air conditioning system.

FOR

Not as costly as pre-1961 Crowns •Luxury •Roadability

AGAINST

'61 styling •Can rust • Thirsty •Spotty fit and finish

SPECIFICATIONS

Length (in.) 227.1 (1961-62), 227.8 (1963)
Wheelbase (in.) 129.0   **Weight (lbs.)** 4650-4795
Price (new) $5400-5782

ENGINES

cid/type	bore x stroke	bhp	years
413/ohv V8	4.18×3.75	340/350	1961-63

PRICES/PROJECTION

Restorable $1000-1500 **Good** $2000-3000
Excellent $3000-5000 Add 25-35% for convertible
5-year projection +10%

Imperial
LeBaron
1961-63

PRODUCTION

1961 1025   **1962** 1449   **1963** 1537

1963 LeBaron Southampton 4-door hardtop

HISTORY

The costliest standard Imperial, reduced to a single Southampton four-door hardtop in these years. As before, more luxurious than but otherwise the same as the Crown.

FOR

As for 1961-63 Crown, plus greater rarity

AGAINST

As for 1961-63 Crown

SPECIFICATIONS

Length (in.) 227.1 (1961-62), 227.8 (1963)
Wheelbase (in.) 129.0   **Weight (lbs.)** 4725-4830
Price (new) $6422-6434

ENGINES

cid/type	bore x stroke	bhp	years
413/ohv V8	4.18×3.75	340/350	1961-63

PRICES/PROJECTION

Restorable $1000-1750 **Good** $2250-3000
Excellent $3000-5100 **5-year projection** +10%

Imperial Crown
1964-70

PRODUCTION

1964 2d hardtop 5233	**4d hardtop** 14,181	**convertible** 922
1965 2d hardtop 3974	**4d hardtop** 11,628	**convertible** 633
1966 2d hardtop 2373	**4d hardtop** 8977	**convertible** 514
1967 2d hardtop 3225	**4d hardtop** 9415	**convertible** 577
4d sedan 2193	**1968 2d hardtop** 2656	**4d hardtop** 8492
convertible 474	**4d sedan** 1887	**1969 2d hardtop** 224
4d hardtop 823	**4d sedan** 1617	**1970 2d hardtop** 254
4d hardtop 1333	**4d sedan** 1617	

HISTORY

The base Imperial series in these years, and more popular than LeBaron up through 1968. Chrysler's new head stylist, ex-Ford designer Elwood Engel, favored crisp, conservative lines instead of Virgil Exner's baroque curves, and the 1964-66 Imperials are similar in overall theme to Engel's square-cut 1961 Lincoln Continental. To provide extra quietness and road noise isolation in its flagship

1968 Crown 4-door hardtop

1969 LeBaron 4-door hardtop

models, Chrysler retained separate body/frame construction through 1966. Imperial was then redesigned around a unit body/chassis and a shorter wheelbase. It was, in fact, quite similar to then-current Chryslers except for its less sculptured outer body panels. The similarity increased on the "fuselage styled" '69s, by which time Imperial was on the decline as a major luxury-market competitor despite a sizeable drop in prices. The trend continued into the '70s, until Imperial ceased as a separate make after 1975. The '76 "Imperial" was nothing more than a Chrysler New Yorker with different nameplates. The name was dormant until 1981, when it was revived for a high-roller coupe based substantially on the mid-size Cordoba/LeBaron platform.

FOR

Good supply • Convertible's strong appreciation potential • Smooth highway performance

AGAINST

Indifferent fit and finish • Very gas-hoggish • Too big for some

SPECIFICATIONS

Length (in.) 227.8 (1964-66), 224.7 (1967-68), 229.7 (1969-70)
Wheelbase (in.) 129.0 (1964-66), 127.0 (1967-70)
Weight (lbs.) 4555-5345   **Price (new)** $5374-6497

ENGINES

cid/type	bore x stroke	bhp	years
413/ohv V8	4.18×3.75	340	1964-65
440/ohv V8	4.32×3.75	350/360	1966-70

PRICES/PROJECTION

Restorable $1000-1500 **Good** $1500-2500
Excellent $3000-5000 Add 50% for convertible.
5-year projection +10%, convertibles +10%

Imperial LeBaron 1964-70

PRODUCTION

1964 2949   **1965** 2164   **1966** 1878   **1967** 2194
1968 1852   **1969 4d hardtop** 14,821   **2d hardtop** 4592
1970 4d hardtop 8426   **2d hardtop** 1803   **Limousine production** 6 in 1967 and 1968, 6 (est.) 1969 and 1970

HISTORY

Imperial's small-volume (except for the bumper 1969 season) upper-class line, still a more luxurious version of the less expensive

models. Offered only as a four-door hardtop sedan through 1968, then joined by a two-door companion. Priced $600-800 upstream of the comparable Crowns, with more standard accessories and more lavish interior appointments. A half-dozen cars were converted into limousines by the Stageway Coaches company in Arkansas, Chrysler's attempt to keep alive the spirit of the earlier Ghia Crowns. Predictably, comments for 1964-70 Crown models also apply here.

FOR

Reasonably good supply • A daily-driver for big-car collectors • High-grade interior • Power assists galore

AGAINST

Fuel thirst • Bulk • Quality control slips after '68

SPECIFICATIONS

Length (in.) 227.8 (1964-66), 224.7 (1967-68), 229.7 (1969-70);
Limo: 260.7 (1967-68), 265.7 (1969-70)
Wheelbase (in.) 129.0 (1964-66), 127.0 (1967-70);
Limo: 163.0 (1967-70)   **Weight (lbs.)** 4610-5090;
Limo: 6300-6500   **Price (new)** $5898-6596

ENGINES

cid/type	bore x stroke	bhp	years
413/ohv V8	4.18×3.75	340	1964-66
440/ohv V8	4.32×3.75	350/360	1966-70

PRICES/PROJECTION

1964-66 Restorable $1200-2500 **Good** $2500-4000
Excellent $4000-5500 **1967-70 Restorable** $1000-1200
Good $1250-1800 **Excellent** $1800-3300
LIMOUSINE Restorable $1800-2200 **Good** $2500-3800
Excellent $3800-5600 **5-year projection** 1964-66 +20%;
1967-70 +10%; LIMO no change

Jordan Model 8G/90 1930-31

PRODUCTION

No more than 2000

HISTORY

Last gasp of a famous company. These big eight-cylinder cars rode the firm's two longest wheelbases and were almost as glorious as Ned Jordan's famous ads had tried to paint their much less impres-

1931 Model 90 Playboy roadster

sive forebears in the 1920s. A phaeton, convertible and roadster were offered in the 1930 8G line. The following year's Model 90 series included the 125-inch-wheelbase Speedboy sport phaeton and the last of the famous Playboy roadsters, on the 131-inch chassis. Jordan filed for receivership in April 1931. Though always "assembled" cars with proprietary engines and other mechanicals, Jordans remained a cut above the norm even in these final years. Curiously, they have yet to be recognized as Classics.

FOR

Last-of-the-line status • Exclusivity • Beautiful styling • Relatively affordable • The timeless mystique of Ned Jordan's great ads

AGAINST

Extreme scarcity of all models, open ones particularly • Almost impossible parts situation

SPECIFICATIONS

Length (in.) NA **Wheelbase (in.)** 125.0 (8G), 131.0 (90) **Weight (lbs.)** 3700-5000 **Price (new)** $2395-2995

ENGINES

cid/type	bore x stroke	bhp	years
268.5/L8	3.00×4.75	85	1930-31

PRICES/PROJECTION

OPEN MODELS **Restorable** $11,000-15,000 **Good** $20,000-30,000 **Excellent** $35,000-45,000. Add 25% for 1931 Playboy. CLOSED MODELS **Restorable** $9000-14,000 **Good** $12,500-17,000 **Excellent** $19,000-23,000 **5-year projection** +20% NOTE The famous Model Z Speedway Ace sedan and Sportsman roadster were additional models in the line, but only one roadster is known to exist.

Kaiser Custom 1947-48

PRODUCTION

1947 5412 **1948** 1263

HISTORY

More luxurious, top-of-the-line model among early Kaisers, and also more desirable now, though built in smaller quantities and not as easily found. Its price premium over the basic Special was

1947 Custom 4-door sedan

largely due to its more plush, color-keyed interior. Exterior trim was much the same on both models, though Customs carried indentifying fender script.

FOR

Quite rare • Smooth road car • Significant styling for its time

AGAINST

Slab-sided design now looks old • Engine not known for reliability • Interior restoration expensive

SPECIFICATIONS

Length (in.) 203.0 **Wheelbase (in.)** 123.5 **Weight (lbs.)** 3295 **Price (new)** $2456-2466

ENGINES

cid/type	bore x stroke	bhp	years
226.2/L6	3.31×4.38	100/112	1947-48

PRICES/PROJECTION

Restorable $1000-2000 **Good** $2000-2750 **Excellent** $3000-4500 **5-year projection** +10%

Kaiser DeLuxe 1949-50

1949 DeLuxe 4-door convertible sedan

PRODUCTION

4d sedan 38,250 **Vagabond 4d utility sedan** 4500 **Virginian 4d hardtop sedan** 946 **4d convertible** 54 (all est.)

HISTORY

Kaiser's renamed upper series for these years. Shared the 1949 facelift with the cheaper Specials. Leftovers were reserialed but otherwise unchanged for 1950. The DeLuxe lineup included three interesting models. The Vagabond was a spiffier version of the Special Traveler. Both were sedans with a double-hatch rear end and fold-down back seat, giving Kaiser a station wagon-type model without the expense of tooling up for a separate body. The four-door convertible sedan had a counterpart in the Frazer Manhattan line. Both were literally hand-built from sedan bodies (aided by the cutting torch) and mounted on heavier-than-stock frames to preserve some semblance of body rigidity. The Virginian was a fixed-roof convertible with either a painted or padded vinyl top. This trio exemplified Kaiser's innovative thinking in trying to broaden its market.

FOR

Unique body styles • Good quality • Lots of color inside and out

AGAINST

Underpowered • Underbraked • Clumsy handling • Thirstier than earlier Kaisers

SPECIFICATIONS

Length (in.) 206.5   **Wheelbase (in.)** 123.5
Weight (lbs.) 3341-3726   **Price (new)** $2195-3195

ENGINES

cid/type	bore x stroke	bhp	years
226.2/L6	3.31×4.38	112	1949-50

PRICES/PROJECTION

Excellent $5500-7500 **5-year projection** +5%, convertible +100%, Virginian +10%

Kaiser Special Traveler 1949-50

1949 Special Traveler 4-door utility sedan

PRODUCTION

22,000 (est.)

HISTORY

Basic version of the DeLuxe Vagabond, more affordable for collectors, and possibly just the thing for your flea marketing. Sold in reasonable numbers when new, and offered station wagon-style cargo carrying flexibility. Looked just like a conventional Kaiser sedan, but the rear double-hatch doors and flip-down back seat opened up to give a nine-foot load platform.

FOR

More available and affordable than Vagabond • Others as for 1949-50 DeLuxe

AGAINST

Lacks Milestone status • Lower appreciation than Vagabond • Others as for 1949-50 DeLuxe

SPECIFICATIONS

Length (in.) 206.5   **Wheelbase (in.)** 123.5   **Weight (lbs.)** 3456
Price (new) $2088

ENGINES

cid/type	bore x stroke	bhp	years
226.2/L6	3.31×4.38	100	1949-50

PRICES/PROJECTION

Restorable $500-1500 **Good** $1500-2500
Excellent $2750-5000 **5-year projection** +10%

Kaiser DeLuxe 1951

1951 DeLuxe club coupe

PRODUCTION

Traveler 2d utility sedan 10,000   **4d sedan** 70,000
2d sedan 11,000   **4d Traveler utility sedan** 1000
2d club coupe 6000   (estimated breakdowns; total model year production including Specials 139,452)

HISTORY

The more expensive series in Kaiser's all-new second-generation lineup. A daring and successful styling departure for its day, with the lowest beltline and greatest glass area in the industry (a distinction it would retain until Virgil Exner's 1957 Chrysler products appeared). Designed largely by Howard "Dutch" Darrin, assisted by

Duncan McRae, with detail trim applied by Herb Weissinger. Wheelbase was shortened five inches, and the unique Traveler utility sedan/wagon model was continued, bolstered by a two-door running mate. Unfortunately, power continued to be the Kaiser L-head six, which would look increasingly old-hat as time went on and other makes had modern V8s. Kaiser never would get one, though, and this was one factor that caused sales to spiral downward, leading eventually to the death of the Kaiser marque.

FOR

Beautiful styling, perhaps the best among early-'50s domestics • Good quality • Smooth highway performance

AGAINST

Can rust, particularly rocker panels and fenders • Vapor lock a constant problem • Other engine quirks, including overheating

SPECIFICATIONS

Length (in.) 210.4 **Wheelbase (in.)** 118.5
Weight (lbs.) 3111-3345 **Price (new)** $2275-2433

ENGINES

cid/type	bore x stroke	bhp	years
226.2/L6	3.31×4.38	115	1951

PRICES/PROJECTION

Restorable $500-1000 **Good** $2000-3000
Excellent $3000-5000 Add 10% for club coupe, 10% for Traveler or 2-door sedan. **5-year projection** +10%

Kaiser DeLuxe Dragon 1951

1951 DeLuxe Golden Dragon 4-door sedan

PRODUCTION

approximately 1000, mostly 4d sedans

HISTORY

A special-trim version of the Kaiser DeLuxe created by K-F's brilliant color and upholstery specialist Carleton Spencer. The initial models were all called Golden Dragon, and had two-tone paint, embossed "dragon" vinyl, rolled and pleated upholstery, and smooth vinyl headliner. A second series with padded tops and "dinosaur" vinyl upholstery was offered as the Golden (yellow/black), Silver (grey/maroon), Emerald (dark green/light green), and

Jade (metallic green/straw) Dragon (colors indicate paint/upholstery). Quite rare and hard to come by today, these were the most spectacular of the '51 Kaisers.

FOR

Hotly sought-after • Very luxurious • Strong appreciation likely • Others as for 1951 DeLuxe

AGAINST

As for 1951 DeLuxe

SPECIFICATIONS

Length (in.) 210.4 **Wheelbase (in.)** 118.5
Weight (lbs.) 3111-3345 **Price (new)** $2400-2560

ENGINES

cid/type	bore x stroke	bhp	years
226.2/L6	3.31×4.38	115	1951

PRICES/PROJECTION

Restorable $1000-2000 **Good** $2000-3000
Excellent $3000-6000 Add 25% for padded-top models
5-year projection +20%

Kaiser Virginian DeLuxe 1952

1952 Virginian DeLuxe club coupe

PRODUCTION

approx. 3500 (total production including Virginian Special: 5579)

HISTORY

Upper-priced series in Kaiser's interim 1952 line, announced at the start of the model year. Composed of leftover '51s with new serial numbers and badges. Withdrawn after the "genuine" '52s were ready. Most came with standard "continental" exterior-mount spare tire.

FOR

As for 1951 DeLuxe, plus scarcity

AGAINST

As for 1951 DeLuxe

SPECIFICATIONS

Length (in.) 215.7 **Wheelbase (in.)** 118.5
Weight (lbs.) 3111-3345 **Price (new)** $2095-2241

ENGINES

cid/type	bore x stroke	bhp	years
226.2/L6	3.31×4.38	115	1952

PRICES/PROJECTION

Add 10% to comparable 1951 DeLuxe

Kaiser Manhattan 1952-53

1952 Manhattan 4-door sedan

PRODUCTION

1952 4d sedan 16,500 **2d sedan** 2000 **2d club coupe** 500
1953 4d sedan 15,450 **2d sedan** 2500 (breakdowns
estimated; total 1952 production including DeLuxe
models: 26,552 1953 Manhattan: 17,957)
One Traveler 2d utility sedan found; no volume production

HISTORY

The trend-setting '51 Kaiser in its newly named top-line series. A
pleasant facelift included a heavier bumper/grille combination,
smooth teardrop taillights, and little chrome rear fender fins on '53s.
Color was strongly featured for '52, and reemphasized for '53 with
attractive upholstery combinations of bouclé cloth and straw-
pattern vinyl. Among the nicest Kaisers to drive, very roomy, and
remarkably frugal with gas.

FOR

Exceptional styling •Low running costs •Smooth road cars

AGAINST

The tinworm likes rocker panels and floorpans •Cloth upholstery
hard to duplicate •Optional hyper-fast power steering needs constant driver correction

SPECIFICATIONS

Length (in.) 208.5 (1952), 211.1 (1953) **Wheelbase (in.)** 118.5
Weight (lbs.) 3185-3371 **Price (new)** $2601-2654

ENGINES

cid/type	bore x stroke	bhp	years
226.2/L6	3.31×4.38	115/118	1952-53

PRICES/PROJECTION

Restorable $500-1000 **Good** $1500-2500
Excellent $3000-5000 Add 20% for club coupe
5-year projection +10%

Kaiser "Hardtop" Dragon 1953

1953 "Hardtop" Dragon 4-door sedan

PRODUCTION

1277

HISTORY

Rebirth of Carleton Spencer's "designer" model, now a separate
series and built only as a four-door sedan. Featured 14-carat gold-
plated hood ornament, exterior emblems and script, and glovebox
nameplate, along with thick carpeting. "Bambu" vinyl upholstery
was combined with bouclé-grained vinyl if you got the canvas top
or "Laguna" cloth with the "bambu" vinyl-covered roof. Standard
equipment included automatic transmission, radio, heater, trunk
carpeting, and extra sound insulation, also power steering (late in
the production run). The most luxurious Kaiser ever built.

FOR

Desirability, appreciation both high •Very comfortable long-haul
tourer •Sharp looks •Distinctive luxury furnishings

AGAINST

Gold plating expensive to restore •Bambu vinyl difficult to match or
replace •Laguna cloth extinct •Twitchy power steering

SPECIFICATIONS

Length (in.) 211.1 **Wheelbase (in.)** 118.5 **Weight (lbs.)** 3320
Price (new) $3924

ENGINES

cid/type	bore x stroke	bhp	years
226.2/L6	3.31×4.38	118	1953

Kaiser Manhattan 1954-55

1954 Manhattan 4-door sedan

PRODUCTION

1954 4d sedan 3860*   **2d sedan** 250*   **1955 4d sedan** 226
2d sedan 44   (does not include 1021 export 1955 4d sedans)
*(est. breakdown; total 1954 production 4110)

HISTORY

An astonishingly successful facelift on Darrin's 1951 design performed by K-F stylist Herb Weissinger. All-new sheetmetal forward of the cowl featured a concave oval grille reminiscent of the Buick XP-300 show car and curvy front fenders with headlights and parking lights set in chrome-encircled teardrops. At the rear were large "Safety-Glo" taillights with illuminated lenses running atop the fenders, and the rear window was fully wrapped around. The redesigned dash was given large, aircraft-like toggle lever controls. Exclusive to these top-line Kaisers was a supercharged (by McCulloch) version of the staid old L-head six, boasting 22 more horsepower. The blower freewheeled economically when not in use. None of this was enough to save Kaiser, however, and production ceased before the end of the model year. The design was salvaged, though, and built in Argentina as the Kaiser Carabela through the early '60s.

FOR

Last of the line • Advanced styling, interior design • High comfort levels • Quick for a standard-size six-cylinder car

AGAINST

Heavy front end, so steering a bear without power assist • Blower was too much for the engine; reliability suffers

SPECIFICATIONS

Length (in.) 215.6   **Wheelbase (in.)** 118.5
Weight (lbs.) 3265-3350   **Price (new)** $2334-2670

ENGINES

cid/type	bore x stroke	bhp	years
226.2/L6	3.31×4.38	140	1954-55

PRICES/PROJECTION

Restorable $1000-1300 **Good** $1300-2500
Excellent $3000-6200 Add 35-50% for 1955 models, 10% for two-door models **5-year projection** +15%

Restorable $1500-2500 **Good** $2500-4000
Excellent $4000-7500 **5-year projection** +25%

Kaiser-Darrin DKF-161 1954

1954 Darrin DKF-161 roadster

PRODUCTION

435

HISTORY

Howard Darrin's dramatic sliding-door sports car with Willys F-head engine in a fiberglass body laid over the Henry J chassis. Features included three-position "landau" top, full instrumentation, and floorshift (with overdrive a common option). More a boulevardier than an outright sports car, the Darrin could nevertheless do 0-60 mph in about 13 seconds and approach the 100-mph mark. But at its steep price, few were sold. Darrin purchased about 100 leftovers and fitted some with Cadillac V8 engines. The vast majority of Darrins are still around; most have been traced by enthusiasts.

FOR

Swoopy styling • Unique sliding doors • Rare and hotly sought-after • A guaranteed show-stopper

AGAINST

Fiberglass bodywork subject to stress cracks • Hardware and windshields extremely scarce • Not cheap

SPECIFICATIONS

Length (in.) 184.1   **Wheelbase (in.)** 100.0   **Weight (lbs.)** 2175
Price (new) $3668

ENGINES

cid/type	bore x stroke	bhp	years
161/F-head I6	3.13×3.50	90	1954

PRICES/PROJECTION

Restorable $4000-7500 **Good** $7500-10,500
Excellent $10,000-15,000 **5-year projection** +20%

Kaiser Special 1954

1954 Special ("early") 2-door sedan

PRODUCTION

3500 ("early") 919 ("late")

HISTORY

The junior Kaiser for 1954 in two versions. "Early" models were leftover '53 Manhattans (complete with interior trim) sporting the new '54 front and rear styling (except the wraparound rear window). The "late" Specials were true '54s, with the revised dash and greenhouse, but less luxurious interior fittings. Not offered with the supercharger, so power output was the same as in 1953. Both Specials are desirable today because so few were made. Of the two, however, the early ones are preferred for their nicer cabin appointments and the easier handling that goes with the lighter 1953 front end. Offered in both two- and four-door sedan form. The former are much rarer (only an estimated 500 and 125 were built, respectively), and now command a small price premium over the four-doors.

FOR

Less costly than '54 Manhattan •"Early" deluxe interior •"Early" handling ease •Rarity

AGAINST

"Late" plain trim •Lack supercharger's interest value (but engine a bit more reliable)

SPECIFICATIONS

Length (in.) 215.6 **Wheelbase (in.)** 118.5
Weight (lbs.) 3235-3305 **Price (new)** $2334-2389

ENGINES

cid/type	bore x stroke	bhp	years
226.2/L6	3.31×4.38	118	1954

PRICES/PROJECTION

Restorable $500-1500 **Good** $1500-2500
Excellent $3000-5000 Add 10% for "late" models.
5-year projection +15%

Kissel White Eagle 1930-31

PRODUCTION

Not more than 50

HISTORY

The grand last hurrah for a long-running company (since 1907). Favored by film stars, gangsters, politicians, and high-flyers until a deepening Depression wiped out the Hartford, Wisconsin automaker. It had a Lycoming-based eight, at least 132 inches between wheel centers, and a price of over $3000 ($35,000-40,000 in modern dollars). A plethora of gorgeous closed "custom" (they really weren't) and open bodies officially comprised the 8-126 series. All have distinction as the only Kissels rated as Classics by the CCCA.

FOR

Beautiful bodywork • Smooth performance • Exclusivity • Appreciation potential

AGAINST

Extremely scarce (more built in 1929, however) • Ditto parts

SPECIFICATIONS

Length (in.) NA **Wheelbase (in.)** 132.0, 139.0
Weight (lbs.) 4000-5000 **Price (new)** $3185-3885

ENGINES

cid/type	bore x stroke	bhp	years
296.8/L8	3.25×4.25	100	1930-31

PRICES/PROJECTION

ROADSTER/SPEEDSTER **Restorable** $15,000-25,000
Good $25,000-40,000 **Excellent** $45,000-60,000 TOURSTER deduct 20% CLOSED deduct 50% **5-year projection** +20%

Kurtis 1948-49

PRODUCTION

20-34

HISTORY

Race-car builder Frank Kurtis' interesting postwar sports car. The 100-inch-wheelbase chassis was integral with a two-seater body made mainly of aluminum. Power was supplied by a supercharged Studebaker Champion six, though some cars had the Ford flathead V8. Only a few were built (estimates vary on the precise number) when Kurtis sold out to super-salesman Earl "Madman" Muntz, who continued the concept in somewhat altered form as the Muntz Jet (see entry).

1948 Kurtis 2-seat convertible

FOR

Rare and unique • Sprightly (but not amazingly quick) • Ubiquitous engines

AGAINST

You'll pay plenty to own one • Bodywork hard to restore, impossible to replace

SPECIFICATIONS

Length (in.) 169.0   **Wheelbase (in.)** 100.0   **Weight (lbs.)** 2300
Price (new) $5000

ENGINES

cid/type	bore x stroke	bhp	years
169.6/L6	3.00×4.00	105	1948-49
239.4/LV8	3.19×3.75	110	1948-49

PRICES/PROJECTION

Restorable $5000-10,000 **Good** $8000-15,000
Excellent $12,000-18,000 **5-year projection** +10%

La Salle
1930-33

1930 Series 340 convertible coupe

PRODUCTION

1930 14,986 **1931** 10,095 **1932** 3386 **1933** 3482

1932 Series 345B convertible coupe

HISTORY

Continuation of the Classic junior Cadillac introduced in 1927. Reached its apogee as a luxury car in this period of rapidly diminishing sales due to the Depression. The '30s were longer, heavier and costlier than previous LaSalles, and included six *luxus* Fleetwood bodies. Cost cutting began for 1931 when the Cadillac V8 was specified in a rationalization move, but it was at least as good an engine as the LaSalle 340. Prices were also reduced, by about $500. But Cadillac prices were also coming down, and what few people could afford cars in this class tended to opt for the more prestigious senior make, which began to catch up to its junior companion in volume. The last CCCA-recognized Classic LaSalle was the '33. Later models were vastly altered for appeal to the medium-priced market.

FOR

Spectacular styling • Mechanical integrity • Classic status

AGAINST

Expensive • A "junior Cadillac" even in the Classic era

SPECIFICATIONS

Length (in.) NA **Wheelbase (in.)** 134.0 (1930-31), 130.0/136.0 (1932-33) **Weight (lbs.)** 4340-5065 **Price (new)** $2195-3995

ENGINES

cid/type	bore x stroke	bhp	years
340.0/V8	3.31×4.94	90	1930
353.0/V8	3.38×4.94	95/115	1931-33

PRICES/PROJECTION

Restorable $4000-10,000 **Good** $15,000-25,000
Excellent $30,000-40,000. Add 25% for coupes, 100-125% for open models, 125% for Fleetwood customs.
5-year projection +15%

La Salle
1937-40

PRODUCTION

1937 32,000 **1938** 14,675 **1939** 21,127 **1940** 24,130

1937

1937 Series 50 convertible coupe

HISTORY

After a dull period in the mid-Thirties, LaSalle dropped its Oldsmobile straight eight (1934-36) and for 1937 adopted the V8 from the 1936 Cadillac 60. At the same time it acquired a four-inch longer wheelbase. The public responded, and LaSalle production set an all-time record. But a recession hit in 1938, and the 1939-40 models were back on the shorter wheelbase again, though with excellent styling. The 1940 design would be the last LaSalle, and it was one of the year's best. By that time, though, Cadillac had no need for a separate nameplate. Though a '41 LaSalle was planned, the division killed the marque in favor of the downmarket Series 61.

FOR

The final four model years for a well-respected make • Good styling, especially 1940 • Smooth V8s

AGAINST

Body hardware very scarce • Open models quite pricey • Are there any left to find?

1940 Series 52 Special 4-door convertible sedan

1940 Series 52 Special 4-door sedan

SPECIFICATIONS

Length (in.) Wheelbase (in.) 124.0 (1937-38), 120.0 (1939-40)
Weight (lbs.) 3460-4110 **Price (new)** $1155-1895

ENGINES

cid/type	bore x stroke	bhp	years
322.0/LV8	3.38 × 4.50	125/130	1937-40

PRICES/PROJECTION

Restorable $3000-7500 **Good** $10,000-18,000
Excellent $18,000-20,000. Add 100% for open models.
5-year projection +10%

Lincoln V-8 Models L/K/KA 1930-32

1931 Model K convertible roadster

PRODUCTION

1930 (L) 3222 **1931 (K)** 3556 **1932 (KA)** 2224

HISTORY

The long-running Model L had been around since Lincoln's founding but was an anachronism even then. Lincoln replaced it in 1931 with a modernized, though dimensionally identical, Model K that had a new chassis with torque-tube drive, floating rear axle, worm-and-roller steering, and hydraulic shocks. The K's V8 retained the old L engine's "fork-and-blade" rods and three-piece cast-iron block/crankcase assembly. All models rode the same wheelbases, and included a wide variety of semi- and full-custom bodies, the latter supplied by Locke, Judkins, Brunn, LeBaron, Willoughby and Dietrich. Prices ranged as high as $7400, and three long-wheelbase chassis (145/150/155 inches) were offered. The K chassis was given over to the V12 Series KB of 1932. That year's V8 Series KA chassis reverted to the L wheelbase but retained the K's improvements.

FOR

Recognized Classics • Superb coachwork, particularly the custom bodies • Noble Lincoln pedigree

AGAINST

Extremely costly to buy, own, and maintain • Parts problems increasing • Model L not in the same league with other '30s Classics

SPECIFICATIONS

Length (in.) NA **Wheelbase (in.)** 136.0 (1930, 1932); 145.0 (1931) **Weight (lbs.)** 4740-6000 **Price (new)** $4200-7400

ENGINES

cid/type	bore x stroke	bhp	years
385.0/V8	3.50 × 5.00	90-125	1930-32

PRICES/PROJECTION

Infrequent sales of scarce cars makes values difficult to establish. The following are thus guidelines for top-condition examples: MODEL L CUSTOMS from $85,000 for LeBaron cabriolet down to $30,000 for sedans, coupes, berlines by Judkins, Dietrich, and Willoughby. Approx. $55,000 for all Brunn and Locke styles and Willoughby limousines. MODEL L STANDARD CLOSED **Restorable $8500-12,000 Good** $12,000-16,000 **Excellent** $18,000-22,000, add 100% for open models. MODEL K/KA OPEN **Restorable** $9000-16,000 **Good** $27,000-44,000 **Excellent** $44,000-75,000, add 20% for dual cowl phaeton. Figures also apply to standard open bodies as well as customs. MODEL K/KA CLOSED **Restorable** $6000-14,000 **Good** $18,000-22,000 **Excellent** $22,000-38,000. Appraisal services recommended. **5-year projection** +10-20%.

Lincoln V12 models 1932-34

1934 Model K convertible victoria

PRODUCTION

1932 (KB) 1525 **1933 (KA)** 1118 **(KB)** 596 **1934 (KA)** 1679 **(KB)** 752

HISTORY

Lincoln's answer to the multi-cylinder Cadillacs and Packards. The huge KB had more performance than the 1931 Model K yet actually sold for less initially and was offered with a wider array of bodies. Magnificent around town and a fast tourer, renowned for looks, quality, luxury, and performance that defied comparison with most ordinary cars of the day. Greatest of them all was the Murphy dual-cowl sport phaeton, which commands the highest price on today's market. A possible ringer here is the 1933 KA with its smaller one-year-only engine. However, all these V12s are closely related and do not affect value as much as condition and, of course, body style.

FOR

Tremendous presence, grand by any standard • Superb coach-work and "clockwork" • A great touring car even now

AGAINST

Mechanical complexity and resultant headaches • Titanic expense from purchase to sale • As scarce as you'd expect

SPECIFICATIONS

Length (in.) NA **Wheelbase (in.)** 145.0 (1932-34 KB); 136.0 (1933-34 KA) **Weight (lbs.)** 4719-5990 **Price (new)** $2700-7200

ENGINES

cid/type	bore x stroke	bhp	years
448.0/V12	3.25 × 4.50	150	1932-33 (KB)
381.7/V12	3.00 × 4.50	125	1933 (KA)
414.0/V12	3.13 × 4.50	150	1934

PRICES/PROJECTION

As for earlier V8s, but individual model prices almost impossible to establish. Consult auction reports, individual owners, club sources, and appraisers. Maximum near six figures for the Murphy phaeton. Minimum perhaps $28,000 for a Judkins coupe, if you're in the right place at the right time. **5-year projection** +10/25%

Lincoln Model K 1935-40

1939 Model K Non-Collapsible Cabriolet by Brunn

PRODUCTION

1935 1434 **1936** 1013 **1937** 977 **1938** 416 **1939** 133 **1940** NA

HISTORY

The senior Lincoln of the late '30s following the advent of the medium-price Zephyr for 1936 (see entry). All have the K designation and the 414-cid V12 introduced with the 1934 KA/KB. Still very costly, so production dwindled as the lean years wore on. Available to special order only for 1940, built on 1939 chassis. One of these was the famous 160-inch-wheelbase "Sunshine Special" parade car of Presidents Roosevelt and Truman, which now resides at the Henry Ford Museum. Officially replaced for '41 by a long-wheelbase Lincoln Custom based on the Zephyr structure, chassis, and running gear.

1939 "Sunshine Special" (with 1942 frontal styling)

FOR

Quality • Performance • The poor man's K, available at much more down to earth prices

AGAINST

Prices likewise reflect the move from four-square styling to streamlining, not handled particularly well compared to, say, Packard or Cadillac • High running costs

SPECIFICATIONS

Length (in.) NA **Wheelbase (in.)** 136.0/145.0
Weight (lbs.) 5030-6300 **Price (new)** $4200-7400

ENGINES

cid/type	bore x stroke	bhp	years
414.0/V12	3.13×4.50	150	1935-40

PRICES/PROJECTION

1935-36 OPEN Restorable $7000-18,000
Good $20,000-38,000 **Excellent** $38,000-55,000 1935-36
CLOSED Restorable $4500-8500 **Good** $8500-15,000
Excellent $15,000-$22,000. Deduct about 5% a year after 1936.
5-year projection +10%

Lincoln Zephyr
1936-48

PRODUCTION

1936 14,994 **1937** 29,997 **1938** 19,111 **1939** 20,905
1940 21,536 **1941** 20,094 **1942** 6,118 **1946** 16,179
1947 19,891 **1948** 6,470

HISTORY

Lincoln's junior make of the Thirties and its response to the Depression. Predictive and innovative streamlined design suggested by John Tjaarda. Teardrop-inspired styling and unit construction retained for production, but original rear-engine layout was discarded as too radical. Mechanically unique in many ways, especially its new, small V12 derived from the Ford V8, which was dogged by reliability woes for a time. Offered considerable interior space compared to most rivals but no hydraulic brakes until 1939. Two-speed Columbia rear axle was an option through 1942. Structurally revised for 1940, heavily facelifted the following year. Returned after the war as a

1936 Series H Zephyr 4-door sedan

warmed-over 1942 continuation with more glitter and fewer body styles but without the Zephyr name.

FOR

Unique and pioneering design, the first successful streamliner • Very strong club support • Interesting—and often rare—model and trim variations

AGAINST

Medium-price aura • Few open models built (none 1936-37; many late ones scrapped for Continental restorations • Mechanically unreliable and prone to overheating • Underpowered, especially convertibles

SPECIFICATIONS

Length (in.) NA **Wheelbase (in.)** 122.0 (1936-37); 125.0 (1938-48) **Weight (lbs.)** 3289-4245 **Price (new)** $1165-3142

ENGINES

cid/type	bore x stroke	bhp	years
267.3/V12	2.75×3.75	110	1936-39
292.0/V12	3.88×3.75	120	1940-41
305.0/V12	2.94×3.75	130	1942
292.0/V12	2.88×3.75	125	1946-48

PRICES/PROJECTION

OPEN Restorable $5500-12,000 **Good** $14,000-17,500
Excellent $18,000-28,000. Coupes deduct 40% OTHER
CLOSED deduct 60%. **5-year projection** +15%

1946 Series 66 H 4-door sedan

Lincoln Continental
1940-41

1940 Continental club coupe

PRODUCTION

1940 2d coupe 350   **2d cabriolet** 54   **1941 2d coupe** 850
2d cabriolet 400

HISTORY

Originally designed as a custom-bodied special for Edsel Ford, Bob Gregorie's "Mark I" Continental seems to look better and better as the years pass. These first models (identical mainly except for pushbuttons instead of handles on the '41 doors) are the cleanest of the breed. Essentially a sportier version of the contemporary Lincoln Zephyr, powered by the long-stroke V12 derived from Ford's flathead V8. This engine had a history of inadequate water passages and poor oil flow before 1940, though these problems were partly corrected this year. One of the first cars recognized as something more than a mere machine (by New York's Museum of Modern Art and the Classic Car Club of America, among others), and one of the finest examples of the automobile as art.

FOR

Ageless design ● A most coveted Classic

AGAINST

Questionable mechanical reliability ● High running costs ● Not cheap and quite rare

SPECIFICATIONS

Length (in.) 209.8   **Wheelbase (in.)** 125.0
Weight (lbs.) 3740-3890   **Price (new)** $2783-2916

ENGINES

cid/type	bore x stroke	bhp	years
292/LV12	2.88×3.75	120	1940-41

PRICES/PROJECTION

Restorable $5000-12,000 **Good** $12,000-22,000
Excellent $22,000-35,000 Deduct 10% if closed model.
5-year projection +10%

Lincoln Continental
1942

1942 Continental cabriolet

PRODUCTION

2d coupe 200   **2d cabriolet** 136

HISTORY

A facelifted version of the 1940-41 Continental, with a somewhat fussier horizontal bar grille and raised rear fenders. New this year was an enlarged version of Lincoln's flathead V12 that proved more reliable than its predecessor. The restyle increased overall length by seven inches, and weight was up, too.

FOR

As for 1940-41 Continental, but not quite as nice-looking ● Rarity in abbreviated prewar model year

AGAINST

Expensive now ● High running costs

SPECIFICATIONS

Length (in.) 216.8   **Wheelbase (in.)** 125.0
Weight (lbs.) 4000-4020   **Price (new)** $3000

ENGINES

cid/type	bore x stroke	bhp	years
305/LV12	2.94×3.75	130	1942

PRICES/PROJECTION

As for 1940-41 Continental

Lincoln Continental
1946-48

PRODUCTION

1946 2d coupe 265   **2d cabriolet** 201   **1947 2d coupe** 831
2d cabriolet 738   **1948 2d coupe** 847   **2d cabriolet** 452

HISTORY

Postwar continuation of the prewar Continental based on the 1942 body dies and chassis design. Identified by a two-tier eggcrate

1946 Continental club coupe

grille. Only detail changes occurred in these three model years. Interestingly, the V12 reverted to its 1940-41 displacement, though somehow an extra 5 horsepower had been found. Plans for a 1949 successor were shelved as Ford sought to gain badly needed sales with its high-volume models. The Mark II had to wait until 1956, when it appeared without the Lincoln nameplate as the product of an entirely distinct Ford Motor Company division.

FOR

As for 1942 Continental

AGAINST

As for 1942 Continental, but more plentiful

SPECIFICATIONS

Length (in.) 216.8 **Wheelbase (in.)** 125.0
Weight (lbs.) 4090-4135 **Price (new)** $4662-4746

ENGINES

cid/type	bore x stroke	bhp	years
292/LV12	2.88×3.75	125	1946-48

PRICES/PROJECTION

COUPES **Restorable** $3000-7000 **Good** $7000-12,000
Excellent $12,000-18,000
CONVERTIBLES **Restorable** $ 5000-12,000
Good $12,000-20,000 **Excellent** $20,000-30,000
5-year projection +10%

Lincoln Cosmopolitan 1949-51

1949 Cosmopolitan convertible

PRODUCTION

1949 35,123 **1950 2d coupe** 1824 **4d sedan** 8341
2d convertible 536 **1951 2d coupe** 2727 **4d sedan** 12,229
2d convertible 857

HISTORY

The upper series in Lincoln's first all-new postwar lineup, part of Ford's company-wide redesign for '49. No match for Cadillac in sales or performance, but still high-quality luxury cars able to cover long distances quickly and quietly. The '49 Cosmopolitan offerings included both Town and Sport four-door sedans. The 1950-51 range listed the Capri, a high-spec two-door coupe with canvas-covered roof and fine upholstery, intended to fill in for a true pillar-less hardtop as a competitor for Cadillac's Coupe deVille. Styling in these years was similar to Mercury's (the base Lincoln series used the same bodyshell) on a four-inch longer wheelbase. The "bathtub" look then in vogue was accented with frenched head- and taillamps, a low grille, and (unique to the Cosmo) heavy chrome moldings on the fender flares. Power was by a larger version of Ford's faithful flathead V8, and overdrive (1949-50) and GM Hydra-Matic (1949-51) were options.

FOR

Luxury ● Solid build ● Smooth performance

AGAINST

"Pregnant" styling ● No speedster

SPECIFICATIONS

Length (in.) 221.3 (1949-50), 223.5 (1951)
Wheelbase (in.) 125.0 **Weight (lbs.)** 4194-4640
Price (new) $3186-3950

ENGINES

cid/type	bore x stroke	bhp	years
336.7/LV8	3.50×4.38	152/154	1949-51

PRICES/PROJECTION

Restorable $1000-2500 **Good** $2000-4000
Excellent $4000-6000 Add 150% for convertible.
5-year projection +20%

Lincoln Capri 1952-54

1953 Capri 4-door sedan

PRODUCTION

1952 4d sedan 7000 (est.) **2d hardtop** 5681
2d convertible 1191 **1953 4d sedan** 11,352
2d hardtop 12,916 **2d convertible** 2372
1954 4d sedan 13,598 **2d hardtop** 14,000
2d convertible 1951

HISTORY

Replacement for the Cosmopolitan as Lincoln's top of the line, offered in three body styles. Both series rode a new 123-inch-wheelbase chassis with newly designed ball joint front suspension, recirculating-ball power steering, and jumbo drum brakes. In the engine room was Ford Motor Company's first overhead valve V8, which would be extended to Ford and Mercury (with reduced displacement) for 1954. For 1953, the Lincoln V8 produced more power per cubic inch (0.64) than any of its competitors. Styling changed completely too, with a more contemporary squared-off look, clean almost to the point of being plain, and again uncomfortably similar to Mercurys of these years. Extensive sound deadening enhanced refinement, and the optional air conditioning system featured flow-through ventilation. Highly regarded today for their superlative performance in the Mexican Road Race in these years.

FOR

Clean, handsome looks • Fine fit and finish • Performance • Good handling for the class

AGAINST

Some rust likely • Body hardware scarce now

SPECIFICATIONS

Length (in.) 214.1 (1952-53), 214.8 (1954)
Wheelbase (in.) 123.0 **Weight (lbs.)** 4140-4350
Price (new) $3331-4031

ENGINES

cid/type	bore x stroke	bhp	years
317.5/ohv V8	3.80×3.50	160/205	1952-54

PRICES/PROJECTION

Restorable $500-1200 **Good** $1500-2500
Excellent $3000-6000 Add 40% for hardtop, 250% for convertible. **5-year projection** +15%

Lincoln Capri
1955

1955 Custom 2-door hardtop (Capri similar)

PRODUCTION

4d sedan 10,724 **2d hardtop** 11,462 **2d convertible** 1467

HISTORY

One of the few makes (others were Kaiser, Studebaker, and Willys)

to start 1955 without a wraparound windshield, mainly because this year's design was a facelift of the 1952-54 styling. It came off exceptionally well, however—ultra-clean front to rear, with massive taillights housed in enlongated fenders. Solidly built with the best materials. Power and comfort more than ample. Lincoln finally introduced an automatic transmission of its own, dubbed Turbo-Drive. To keep pace in the horsepower race, the ohv V8 was bored out to 341 cid for an extra 20 bhp. Sales overall were down compared to 1954, again going against industry trends, probably because the restyle didn't come across as "new" enough.

FOR

Underrated as a collectible • Clean styling in an ostentatious year • Smooth road performance • Comfort • Luxury

AGAINST

Rust can be a bother • Drinks gas greedily

SPECIFICATIONS

Length (in.) 215.6 **Wheelbase (in.)** 123.0
Weight (lbs.) 4245-4415 **Price (new)** $3752-4072

ENGINES

cid/type	bore x stroke	bhp	years
341/ohv V8	3.94×3.50	225	1955

PRICES/PROJECTION

Restorable $750-1200 **Good** $1500-2500
Excellent $2500-5000 Add 40% for hardtop, 250% for convertible. **5-year projection** +15%

Lincoln Premiere
1956-57

1957 Premiere convertible

PRODUCTION

1956 2d hardtop 19,619 **4d sedan** 19,465
2d convertible 2447 **1957 2d hardtop** 15,185
4d sedan 5139 **2d convertible** 3676 **Landau**
4d hardtop 11,223

HISTORY

Lincoln's new premium series in these years, relegating Capri to second-class status. All-new design featured the longer, lower, wider, and heavier body typical of the '50s, a revised chassis on a three-inch longer wheelbase, and a brand-new "True-power" V8 with 285 horses. Styling was right up to date, inspired by the Futura show car: peaked headlamps, partially covered rear wheel openings, wrapped windshield, and a long rear deck tapering to give the straight-through rear fenders a hint of fin. The 1957 facelift brought stacked quad headlamps, much more prominent fins, and the addition of a four-door hardtop called Landau. A short-lived design, replaced by the even larger, unit construction models for 1958.

FOR

Large and luxurious • Ample power

AGAINST

Thirsty • Vague, imprecise handling • Considerable rust threat

SPECIFICATIONS

Length (in.) 222.8 (1956), 224.6 (1957) **Wheelbase (in.)** 126.0
Weight (lbs.) 4347-4676 **Price (new)** $4601-5381

ENGINES

cid/type	bore x stroke	bhp	years
368/ohv V8	4.00×3.66	285/300	1956-57

PRICES/PROJECTION

Restorable $1000-2000 **Good** $2000-3000
Excellent $4000-7000 Add 200% for convertible.
5-year projection +15%

Lincoln Premiere 1958-60

1958 Premiere Landau 4-door hardtop

PRODUCTION

1958 2d hardtop 3043 **4d sedan** 1660
Landau 4d hardtop 5572 **1959 2d hardtop** 1963
4d sedan 1282 **Landau 4d hardtop** 4606
1960 2d hardtop 1364 **4d sedan** 1010
Landau 4d hardtop 4200

HISTORY

The completely redesigned standard Lincoln. Again, priced higher than Capri, but less than the new companion Continental Marks (III, IV, and V) of these years. About six inches longer and several hundred pounds heavier, which made the new 430-cid big-block "MEL" V8 a must. Output was progressively reduced, however, in the quest for whatever mileage improvement was possible in these giants. Styling was marked by quad headlights in slanted recesses flanking an enormous grille and huge bumpers front and rear. Con-

vertibles were sent over to the new Continental Mark III companion line, which shared the standard Lincoln's unit body/chassis construction and basic appearance. A minor facelift was ordained for '59, and a more thorough redo (including a reworked greenhouse) was accomplished for '60. Collector opinion is very divided on these cars. Some find them hideous, overly complex, and wallowy, while others think they're just the thing for long-haul cruising in '50s-style comfort. Low sales and less of the "more is better" attitude generally in Detroit led to an all-new downsized Lincoln line for '61.

FOR

As for 1956-57 Premiere

AGAINST

As for 1956-57 Premiere, but heavier (with expected consequences for mileage and roadability) • Controversial styling • Not that much different from concurrent Continentals

SPECIFICATIONS

Length (in.) 229.0 (1958), 227.2 (1959-60)
Wheelbase (in.) 131.0 **Weight (lbs.)** 4798-5064
Price (new) $5318-5945

ENGINES

cid/type	bore x stroke	bhp	years
430/ohv V8	4.30×3.70	315-375	1958-60

PRICES/PROJECTION

Restorable $450-750 **Good** $1000-2000
Excellent $2000-4000 **5-year projection** +10%

Lincoln Continental Mark IV 1959

1959 Continetal Mark IV 2-door hardtop

PRODUCTION

4d sedan 944 **2d hardtop** 1703 **2d convertible** 2195
4d hardtop 6146 **4d formal sedan** 78 **limousine** 49

HISTORY

Modestly facelifted continuation of the 1958 Continental Mark III, now with the addition of a town car (formal sedan) and limousine, the latter priced close to the 1956-57 Mark II. Continental officially became a Lincoln again for the first time since 1948 following Continental Division's reabsorption into Lincoln-Mercury (which itself was reconstituted from the previous Mercury-Edsel-Lincoln structure). As on this year's standard Lincoln, the big 430 V8 lost 25 horsepower to detuning. Styling retained its similarity to that of the lower-line models except for the sedan and hardtops' reverse-slanted rear roofline with electrically retractable backlight. The town car and limo both had a more conventional roof with blind C-pillars and padded tops. Interiors wore Ford Motor Company's best fabrics and fittings, and most every popular creature assist was standard.

FOR

As for 1958-60 Lincoln Premiere, plus extra luxury • Also relatively affordable

AGAINST

Appeal diluted by similarity to lesser Lincolns • Rust-prone • Electrical/mechanical gremlins • High running costs (especially fuel)

SPECIFICATIONS

Length (in.) 227.1 **Wheelbase (in.)** 131.0
Weight (lbs.) 4967-5061 **Price (new)** $6598-10,230

ENGINES

cid/type	bore x stroke	bhp	years
430/ohv V8	4.30×3.70	350	1959

PRICES/PROJECTION

Restorable $600-1200 **Good** $1500-2500
Excellent $3000-5500 Add 350% for convertible.
5-year projection +10%

Lincoln Continental Mark V 1960

1960 Continental Mark V 4-door hardtop

PRODUCTION

4d sedan 807   **2d hardtop** 1461   **2d convertible** 2044
4d hardtop 6604   **formal sedan** 136   **limousine** 34

HISTORY

Continuation of the Mark IV, with only detail styling changes and 35 less horsepower from the big-inch Lincoln V8. Comments for 1958-60 Lincoln Premiere as well as the 1959 Mark IV apply here.

FOR

As for 1959 Mark IV

AGAINST

As for 1959 Mark IV

SPECIFICATIONS

Length (in.) 227.2 **Wheelbase (in.)** 131.0
Weight (lbs.) 5044-5481 **Price (new)** $6598-10,230

ENGINES

cid/type	bore x stroke	bhp	years
430/ohv V8	4.30×3.70	315	1960

PRICES/PROJECTION

Restorable $600-1200 **Good** $1500-2500
Excellent $3000-5500 Add 350% for convertible.
5-year projection +10%

Lincoln Continental 1961-63

1963 Continental 4-door hardtop sedan

PRODUCTION

1961 4d hardtop sedan 22,203	**4d convertible sedan** 2857
1962 4d hardtop sedan 27,849	**4d convertible sedan** 3212
1963 4d hardtop sedan 28,095	**4d convertible sedan** 3138

HISTORY

Among the most handsome large Americans ever produced. Chiseled, classic lines from the pen of Elwood Engel stayed the same through these years except for minor grille insert and rear panel changes. Superbly engineered with a rigid unit body/chassis, extensive sound insulation, very close machining tolerances, and an unprecedented number of long-life service components such as fully sealed electrical system and thorough factory-applied corrosion protection. The big Lincoln 430 V8 from previous years was retained in somewhat detuned form. Each was bench tested at 3500 rpm for three hours before installation, and all cars were given individual road tests before shipment, reflecting the strong emphasis given quality control. Reintroduced the convertible sedan body type, the first since Kaiser-Frazer's 1949-51 model. More compact than its immediate predecessors, this Continental rode the same wheelbase as the very roadable 1952-55 Lincolns.

FOR

Styling excellence • High quality • Fast and remarkably agile for the luxury class • Poshness • Convertible sedan's uniqueness, allure

AGAINST

Mechanical complexity • Electrical bothers • Somewhat rust-prone

SPECIFICATIONS

Length (in.) 212.4 (1961), 213.0 (1962), 213.3 (1963)
Wheelbase (in.) 123.0 **Weight (lbs.)** 4927-5370
Price (new) $6067-6916

ENGINES

cid/type	bore x stroke	bhp	years
430/ohv V8	4.30×3.70	300/320	1961-63

PRICES/PROJECTION

Restorable $800-1000 **Good** $1500-2250
Excellent $2500-4500 Add 100% for convertible
5-year projection +10%

Lincoln Continental by Lehmann-Peterson 1961-67

1967 Continental limousine by Lehmann-Peterson

PRODUCTION

NA (limited)

HISTORY

Lincoln's custom-built cars of state, converted from standard models by this respected Chicago coachbuilding firm. Division windows, jump seats, and similar limousine equipment was offered, available to customer order. Wheelbase was lengthened considerably, and chassis were reinforced and suspension pieces beefed up to cope with the extra weight. Some sources list production beginning with 1963 models only.

FOR

Milestone status ● Limousine luxury ● Pretend you're in the White House

AGAINST

Oversized ● Thirsty ● Unique body parts scarce

SPECIFICATIONS

Length (in.) 250.0 **Wheelbase (in.)** 160.0
Weight (lbs.) 6000 (est.; variable) **Price (new)** $10,000 and up (variable with equipment)

ENGINES

cid/type	bore x stroke	bhp	years
430/ohv V8	4.30×3.70	300/320	1961-65
462/ohv V8	4.38×3.83	340	1966-67

PRICES/PROJECTION

Restorable $1500-2000 **Good** $2000-3000
Excellent $3000-5000 **5-year projection** +10%

Lincoln Continental 1964-67

1964 Continental 4-door hardtop

PRODUCTION

1964 4d hardtop 33,369 **4d convertible sedan** 3328
1965 4d hardtop 36,824 **4d convertible sedan** 3356
1966 4d hardtop 35,809 **4d convertible sedan** 3180
2d hardtop 15,766 **1967 4d hardtop** 33,311 **4d convertible sedan** 2276 **2d hardtop** 11,060

HISTORY

After making only detail changes to the Continental through 1963, Lincoln extended the car's wheelbase three inches for '64, but generally left its good looks alone. A two-door hardtop was added for '66, and the unique but slow-selling convertible sedan was dropped after 1967. Also for '66, Lincoln's V8 got its first displacement increase since 1958 and the hood was lengthened. These Continentals continued to emphasize quality furnishings and attention to construction details. Considering their size, they were a pleasure to drive. The elegantly understated styling has generally held up well.

FOR

Classy appearance ● Quality ● Luxury ● Fine handling ● Others as for 1961-63 Continental

AGAINST

As for 1961-63 Continental

SPECIFICATIONS

Length (in.) 216.3 (1964-65), 220.9 (1966-67)
Wheelbase (in.) 126.0 **Weight (lbs.)** 5055-5505
Price (new) $5485-6938

ENGINES

cid/type	bore x stroke	bhp	years
430/ohv V8	4.30×3.70	320	1964-65
462/ohv V8	4.38×3.83	340	1966-67

PRICES/PROJECTION

Restorable $750-1000 **Good** $1400-3000
Excellent $3000-5000 **5-year projection** +10%

Marmon Sixteen 1931-33

1932 Sixteen 5-passenger club sedan

PRODUCTION

350 (est.)

HISTORY

The fabulous, 100-mph grand Classic that evidently had more state-of-the-art engineering than any other multi-cylinder motorcar of the day. Remarkably light for its size (bodies used aluminum extensively) and uncommonly elegant. Styled by pioneer industrial designer Walter Dorwin Teague and his son, Walter Jr. Clean vee'd radiator, deep doors, minimal ornamentation, low roofline, and fender flanges to hide shocks and other chassis bits were common to all models. LeBaron did the standard closed bodies, Waterhouse a couple of tourers, and Hayes a victoria to an Alexis de Sakhnoffsky design; the last cost a formidable $5700. More styles were offered in 1932, but by then the limited demand for multi-cylinder luxury cars had been gobbled up by Cadillac's Sixteen, which arrived on the market a year earlier than Marmon's. The company closed its doors in early 1934 and was fully liquidated three years later after an abortive revival attempt.

FOR

Outstanding performance • Sensational coachwork • A design and engineering paragon that's long been on every knowledgeable historian's "10 Best American Cars" list

AGAINST

Extremely scarce • Stratospheric prices

SPECIFICATIONS

Length (in.) NA **Wheelbase (in.)** 145.0
Weight (lbs.) 5090-5440 **Price (new)** $4825-5900

ENGINES

cid/type	bore x stroke	bhp	years
490.8/V16	3.13×4.00	200	1931-33

PRICES/PROJECTION

CLOSED MODELS **Restorable** $12,000-25,000
Good $30,000-45,000 **Excellent** $55,000-85,000 OPEN
MODELS **Restorable** $30,000-45,000 **Good** $50,000-90,000
Excellent $110,000-150,000 **5-year projection** +25%

Mercury 1939-40

1940 convertible sedan

PRODUCTION

1939 75,000 (est.) **1940** 81,000 (est.)

HISTORY

Ford's medium-priced make in its initial incarnation. Shared Bob Gregorie's sharp styling with contemporary Fords. Hallmarks were curvy contours, clean grille, and flush-mount headlamps. Only one series for 1939, with four models including a convertible. A slick convertible sedan was added for 1940 and is now a very hot collectible. The engine was a slightly larger and more powerful version of the Ford flathead V8. Excellent sales quickly established Mercury as a permanent gap-filler in the Dearborn stable.

FOR

Fine period styling • Good performance • Solid construction

AGAINST

Continues to trail the far more numerous 1939-40 Fords in value, despite generally superior specification

SPECIFICATIONS

Length (in.) 199.0 **Wheelbase (in.)** 116.0
Weight (lbs.) 2995-3249 **Price (new)** $916-1212

ENGINES

cid/type	bore x stroke	bhp	years
239.0/V8	3.19×3.75	95	1939-40

PRICES/PROJECTION

OPEN **Restorable** $4000-10,000 **Good** $10,000-20,000
Excellent $20,000-30,000 CLOSED **Restorable** $750-2500
Good $3000-5000 **Excellent** $5000-7500. Add 25% for coupe.
5-year projection +15%

Mercury
1941-42

1941 4-door sedan

PRODUCTION

1941 82,391   **1942** 22,816 (both est.)

HISTORY

Completely restyled for 1941, with a 2-inch longer wheelbase and a wider selection of models. New were a two-passenger coupe and a four-door wagon, while the romantic convertible sedan was dropped. Mechanically unchanged, though the flathead V8 somehow gained five more horsepower for '42, when a new clutchless transmission called "Liquamatic" was also offered. The '42 facelift saw a two-tier horizontal grille substituted for the vertically split '41 affair, giving a more massive look. Production halted in February 1942, making the last prewar Mercs comparatively rare today.

FOR

Fit and finish ● Good performance

AGAINST

Clumsier styling than 1939-40

SPECIFICATIONS

Length (in.) 202.5   **Wheelbase (in.)** 118.0
Weight (lbs.) 3008-3528   **Price (new)** $910-1260

1942 convertible coupe

ENGINES

cid/type	bore x stroke	bhp	years
239.4/LV8	3.19×3.75	95/100	1941-42

PRICES/PROJECTION

Restorable $1000-2500 **Good** $3000-4500
Excellent $5000-8000 Add 100% for wagon, 400% for convertible. **5-year projection** +10%

Mercury Sportsman
1946

1946 Sportsman convertible

PRODUCTION

205

HISTORY

Mercury's counterpart to the wood-bodied Ford Sportsman convertible, produced in very limited numbers for this model year only. Like the Ford, featured structural wood paneling along the bodysides and on the rear deck, but otherwise identical with other models. All were basically warmed-over '42s as Ford had neither time nor money for a brand-new design in the early postwar period. Priced about $500 above the standard ragtop. Intended to lure buyers back into newly reopened showrooms and to renew interest in what was by then a rather familiar group of cars pending arrival of the all-new models scheduled for 1949.

FOR

The most interesting and sought-after (because of low production) early postwar Merc

AGAINST

High maintenance and/or restoration costs for wood trim ● Extremely scarce and expensive now because of that ● Curiously modest appreciation potential

SPECIFICATIONS

Length (in.) 201.8 **Wheelbase (in.)** 118.0 **Weight (lbs.)** 3407
Price (new) $2209

ENGINES

cid/type	bore x stroke	bhp	years
239.4/LV8	3.19×3.75	100	1946

PRICES/PROJECTION

Restorable $5000-8000 **Good** $10,000-20,000
Excellent $20,000-30,000 **5-year projection** +10%

Mercury Monterey 1950-51

1950 Monterey 2-door coupe

PRODUCTION

NA; 2000 estimated

HISTORY

The most exotic model in Mercury's first postwar generation, the "James Dean" design introduced for 1949 that became a favorite of customizers in the '50s. A counterpart to the Ford Crestliner of these years, and intended as a fill-in for a true pillarless hardtop. In essence, the standard club coupe with a plusher interior and a roof cover made of either canvas or leather. A stroke increase brought rated power of the FoMoCo flathead V8 up to 110 bhp for '50 and 112 the following year. Styling was marked by the smooth but bulky bathtub look popular in the late '40s.

FOR

Rarity •Luxury •Good performance • Styling

AGAINST

Very hard to come by, and not cheap

SPECIFICATIONS

Length (in.) 207.0 **Wheelbase (in.)** 118.0
Weight (lbs.) 3480-3485 **Price (new)** $2116-2157

ENGINES

cid/type	bore x stroke	bhp	years
255.4/LV8	3.19×4.00	110/112	1950-51

PRICES/PROJECTION

Restorable $1000-2000 **Good** $3000-5000
Excellent $6500-8000 Add 5% for leather top
5-year projection +10%

Mercury Monterey 1952-54

1953 Monterey convertible

PRODUCTION

1952 4d sedan 30,000 (est.)	**2d hardtop** 24,453

2d convertible 5261 **1953 4d sedan** 64,038
2d hardtop 76,119 **2d convertible** 8463 **4d wagon** 7719
1954 4d sedan 65,995 **2d hardtop** 79,553
2d convertible 7293 **4d wagon** 11,656

HISTORY

A standout among early '50s Mercurys for exceptional styling and sound engineering coupled with solid construction and high-quality fit and finish. Monterey was top-of-the-line, a subseries in 1952, but broken out into a separate line (with a three-model Custom series further down the price scale) for 1953-54. Ford's flathead V8 continued in the first two years, with its highest horsepower rating ever in Mercury tune. For 1954, the company's new Y-block ohv V8 arrived with a five-main-bearing crankshaft and standard four-barrel carburetor. After being a "little Lincoln" in styling and bodyshell for 1949-51, Mercury again became more Ford-like in these years, with similar styling on a 3-inch longer wheelbase.

FOR

Good looks •Quality •Quite quick for the period

AGAINST

Slower to appreciate than concurrent Fords •Susceptible to rust in underbody areas

SPECIFICATIONS

Length (in.) 202.2 (1952-53), 206.3 (1954)
Wheelbase (in.) 118.0 **Weight (lbs.)** 3375-3735
Price (new) $2115-2776

ENGINES

cid/type	bore x stroke	bhp	years
255.4/LV8	3.19×4.00	125	1952-53
256/ohv V8	3.62×3.10	161	1954

PRICES/PROJECTION

Restorable $500-1500 **Good** $1500-2500
Excellent $2500-4000 Add 60% for hardtop, 250% for convertible, 20% for 1954 model. **5-year projection** 1952-53 no change; 1954 models +10%

Mercury Sun Valley 1954-55

1954 Sun Valley 2-door hardtop

PRODUCTION

1954 9761   **1955** 1787

HISTORY

Sharp Mercury version of the "bubbletop" Ford Skyliner/Crown Victoria, with tinted Plexiglas front roof section and deluxe interior with clip-in sunshade for hot days. In other respects, however, just like the regular steel-topped hardtops. Offered in the top-line series, Monterey for '54 and Montclair for '55. Appearance for '54 was a busier facelift of the original 1952 styling. The following year, wheelbase was lengthened an inch, and sheetmetal became crisper though more massive. Also for '55, the Mercury ohv V8 got a displacement boost, which brought output to 188 bhp for Custom and Monterey models or 198 bhp as standard for Montclair. Despite its greater numbers the '54 has remained the more popular, and is often found with distinctive yellow paint that contrasts nicely with the dark green plastic top. Unlike the Plexi-top Crown Victoria, the Sun Valley was not carried on into 1956.

FOR

Novelty value •Handsome styling •Modern ohv V8 with ample performance

AGAINST

A sweatbox on hot days •1955 restyle was different if not for the better •Rust threat in floor, rocker panels, fenders

SPECIFICATIONS

Length (in.) 204.2 (1954), 206.3 (1955)
Wheelbase (in.) 118.0 (1954), 119.0 (1955)
Weight (lbs.) 3535-3560 **Price (new)** $2582-2712

ENGINES

cid/type	bore x stroke	bhp	years
256/ohv V8	3.62×3.10	161	1954
292/ohv V8	3.75×3.30	198	1955

PRICES/PROJECTION

Restorable $2000-3000 **Good** $3000-5500
Excellent $5500-7500 **5-year projection** +10%

Mercury Turnpike Cruiser 1957-58

1957 Turnpike Cruiser 4-door hardtop

PRODUCTION

1957 2d hardtop 7291   **4d hardtop** 8305
2d convertible 1265   **1958 2d hardtop** 2864
4d hardtop 3543

HISTORY

The top-line offerings in the "dramatic expression of dream car design" cars introduced for 1957. Widely but ineffectually promoted as a separate series for 1957, reduced to a Montclair sub-series for 1958, and quietly forgotten for '59. Styling in these years was a direct takeoff of the XM Turnpike Cruiser show car. The production models simply dripped with the latest in gimmickry: "skylight dual curve windshield," air-intakes-cum-radio-aerials in the upper windshield corners, pushbutton "Merc-O-Matic" drive, a "memory seat" adjustable to any one of 49 positions, and a reverse-slanted retractable rear window on hardtops. Engine displacement and rated power went up in both years throughout the Mercury line. High price, a sluggish market, and a public shift away from "futuristic" styling and gadgets kept sales way below expectations.

FOR

Gadgets galore •Flamboyant looks •Good performance and comfort

AGAINST

Very thirsty •A rust bucket •Preposterous styling in the view of many

SPECIFICATIONS

Length (in.) 211.1 (1957), 213.2 (1958) **Wheelbase (in.)** 122.0
Weight (lbs.) 4015-4230 **Price (new)** $3498-3758

ENGINES

cid/type	bore x stroke	bhp	years
368/ohv V8	4.00×3.66	290	1957
383/ohv V8	4.30×3.30	330	1958

Excellent $1900-3100 Add 30% for hardtop, 50% for convertible
5-year projection +10%

PRICES/PROJECTION

Restorable $300-1500 **Good** $2000-3000
Excellent $3000-5000 Add 15% for hardtop coupe, 100% for convertible. **5-year projection** +10%

Mercury Comet S-22 1961-63

1963 Comet S-22 2-door sedan

PRODUCTION

1961 2d sedan 14,004   **1962 2d sedan** 7500 (est.)   **1963 2d sedan** 6303   **2d hardtop** 5807   **2d convertible** 5757

HISTORY

Mercury's entry in the sporty-compact field of the early '60s, and the division's counterpart to the Falcon Futura. Equipped much the same way, too, with luxury interior and bucket seats. Introduced as a two-door sedan for mid-1961, then expanded into a series of sorts with the 1963 addition of a two-door hardtop and convertible. Like other Comets, longer and more heavily styled than equivalent Falcons. Offered initially with the Falcon/Comet six in two displacements; floorshift manual gearbox was an option. For '63, Ford's outstanding small-block V8 was offered at extra cost in 221- and 260-cid forms. Overall, the S-22 had decent handling and roadholding and adequate to brisk performance depending on engine.

FOR

Cheaper to buy than Falcon Futura ● Compact size suits today's traffic conditions ● Six's good mileage ● V8 go

AGAINST

A serious ruster (check your potential purchase carefully underneath) ● Limited appreciation potential ● Underwhelming styling

SPECIFICATIONS

Length (in.) 194.8   **Wheelbase (in.)** 114.0
Weight (lbs.) 2441-2825   **Price (new)** $2171-2710

ENGINES

cid/type	bore x stroke	bhp	years
144.3/ohv I6	3.50×2.50	85	1961-63
170/ohv I6	3.50×2.94	101	1961-63
221/ohv V8	3.50×2.87	145	1963
260/ohv V8	3.80×2.87	164	1963

PRICES/PROJECTION

Restorable $500-800 **Good** $1000-1600

Mercury Marauder 1963-64

1964 Montclair Marauder 4-door hardtop

PRODUCTION

1963 9617 (incl. 2319 S-55)   **1964 4d hardtop** 17,303
2d hardtop 16,271

HISTORY

Mercury cousin to the Ford Galaxie 500XL. Large luxurious cars, they usually had bucket seats, and were offered with a wide assortment of V8s. The "slantback" Marauder two-door hardtop was introduced for 1963½ in the Monterey Custom series, and was also available in super-sporty S-55 form (a bucket-seat subseries begun in 1962) packing heavy-duty suspension and a 300-bhp 390 V8 as standard. No S-55 version was offered for 1964, but you could get Marauder styling in all of Mercury's big-car series (Monterey, Montclair, and Park Lane) with either two or four doors. Engine options were extended that year (Mercury's 25th anniversary) to include the mighty 425-bhp 427. Interestingly enough, there's little collector movement in other big-Merc performance models of the early '60s, even convertibles, which are far less numerous.

FOR

Lots of room ● Ample, even awesome performance ● Brawny looks

AGAINST

Drinks a lot of gas ● Scarce body parts ● Moderately rust-prone

SPECIFICATIONS

Length (in.) 215.0 (1963), 215.5 (1964)   **Wheelbase (in.)** 120.0
Weight (lbs.) 3887-4056   **Price (new)** $3083-3413

ENGINES

cid/type	bore x stroke	bhp	years
390/ohv V8	4.05×3.78	250/300/330	1963-64
406/ohv V8	4.13×3.78	385/405	1963
427/ohv V8	4.23×3.78	410/425	1964

PRICES/PROJECTION

Restorable $500-1000 **Good** $1000-2500
Excellent $2500-3500 **5-year projection** +10%

Mercury Comet Cyclone 1964-65

1964 Comet Cyclone 2-door hardtop

PRODUCTION

1964 7454   **1965** 12,347

HISTORY

An evolution of the Comet S-22, initially offered with Ford's lively 289-cid small-block V8. Available only as a two-door hardtop sharing most styling and equipment specs with the top-line standard Comet series, the bucket-seat Caliente. Like other Comets in these years, a close relative of the Ford Falcon. The 1964 line was even more heavily facelifted than its Ford counterpart, however, with extra inches tacked onto the rear of the Falcon bodyshell. The reason: Comet had to do double duty as Mercury's entry in both the compact and intermediate fields following the demise of the unsuccessful Fairlane-based 1962-63 Meteor. These Cyclones were more compacts than mid-size cars compared to later models bearing this name, and had decent handling and fine performance thanks to their fairly low weight. Distinguished from Calientes by less exterior brightwork and simulated chrome-reverse wheels with exposed lug nuts.

FOR

A sporty, bucket-seat Merc with V8 power at an affordable price

AGAINST

Rather confused styling • Spotty quality control • Moderately rapid ruster

SPECIFICATIONS

Length (in.) 195.1 (1964), 195.3 (1965)   **Wheelbase (in.)** 114.0
Weight (lbs.) 2860-2994   **Price (new)** $2655-2683

1965 Comet Cyclone 2-door hardtop

ENGINES

cid/type	bore × stroke	bhp	years
289/ohv V8	4.00×2.87	200/210/225	1964-65

PRICES/PROJECTION

Restorable $750-1200   **Good** $1500-2500
Excellent $2500-3500   **5-year projection** +10%

Mercury Cyclone 1966-68

1967 Cyclone GT 2-door hardtop

PRODUCTION

1966 2d hardtop 6889   **2d convertible** 1305   **GT 2d hardtop** 13,812   **GT 2d convertible** 2158   **1967 2d hardtop** 2682   **2d convertible** 431   **GT 2d hardtop** 3419   **GT 2d convertible** 378   **1968 2d hardtop** 7199*   **GT 2d hardtop** 6439**
*includes 6165 fastbacks   **includes 6105 fastbacks

HISTORY

Mercury's smallest hot cars in these years, moved up to the mid-size class by adoption of the Ford Fairlane platform. A distinct four-model line (usually referred to without the Comet handle in 1966-67). All featured bucket-seat interiors and sporty styling touches. The GTs came standard with Ford's big-block 390 V8, and several extra-cost stages of tune were available. The line was heated up for 1968 with a new bodyshell and smoother styling plus a sleek fastback hardtop that quickly became the stock-car racer's choice. The Mercury's front-end styling proved to have slightly better aerodynamics than the equivalent Ford Torino, and veterans like Cale Yarborough quickly established the Cyclone as the car to beat on the supertracks.

FOR

Clean, handsome looks • Exceptional GT performance • Non-GTs and convertibles quite rare, stand to gain value rapidly

AGAINST

Only fair construction quality • Subject to moderate rust • GTs thirsty

SPECIFICATIONS

Length (in.) 203.0 (1966), 203.5 (1967), 206.1 (fastback: 203.1) (1968)   **Wheelbase (in.)** 116.0   **Weight (lbs.)** 3075-3595
Price (new) $2700-3294

ENGINES

cid/type	bore x stroke	bhp	years
289/ohv V8	4.00×2.87	200	1966-67
302/ohv V8	4.00×3.00	210/230	1968
390/ohv V8	4.05×3.78	265-325	1966-68
427/ohv V8	4.23×3.78	390/410/425	1967-68

PRICES/PROJECTION

Restorable $300-1000 **Good** $1000-2500
Excellent $2500-3500 Add 20% for GT, 40% for convertible.
5-year projection +15%

Mercury S-55 1966

1966 S-55 convertible

PRODUCTION

2d hardtop 2916   **2d convertible** 669

HISTORY

Mercury's revived big performance car, returning after a two-year absence as a separate series. Featured "Torque Box" construction (frames individually tuned to minimize noise and harshness), standard 428 big-block V8, heavy-duty chassis, and sporty bucket-seat interior. Styling was square and clean "in the Lincoln Continental tradition," as the ads put it. Few were sold, although Mercury generally had a successful big-car year in 1966.

FOR

Clean looks ● Rarity means high appreciation ● High performance

AGAINST

Low mpg ● Some rust potential ● Body parts scarce now

SPECIFICATIONS

Length (in.) 220.4 **Wheelbase (in.)** 123.0
Weight (lbs.) 4031-4148 **Price (new)** $3292-3614

ENGINES

cid/type	bore x stroke	bhp	years
428/ohv V8	4.13×3.98	345	1966

PRICES/PROJECTION

Restorable $750-1500 **Good** $1500-2000
Excellent $2000-3500 Add 75% for convertible.
5-year projection +25%

Mercury Cougar 1967-68

1968 Cougar 2-door hardtop

PRODUCTION

1967 2d hardtop 116,260   **GT 2d hardtop** 7412   **XR7 2d hardtop** 27,221   **1968 2d hardtop** 81,014*   **XR7 2d hardtop** 32,712
*includes GT/GTE

HISTORY

Lincoln-Mercury's upmarket ponycar, introduced two years behind the Mustang and based on its basic chassis design and bodyshell, except for a 3-inch longer wheelbase. A pretty car with all kinds of performance, and could be optioned for fine handling, too. To our eyes, at least as desirable as contemporary Mustangs, particularly the XR7 version with its woodgrain, fully instrumented dash and leather seat facings. Unlike Mustang, Cougar didn't bother with sixes. FoMoCo's 289 V8 was standard for the base and XR7 models, while the GT had the 390. For 1968 a new GTE version was added packing the 427 V8. A handling package was standard on GT/GTE, and is an important option to look for on lesser versions.

FOR

Clean long-hood/short-deck styling ● Pleasant combination of performance and economy with small-block V8 ● High performance in GT/GTE

AGAINST

Some electrical headaches ● Rocker panel and floorpan rust ● GT/GTE very thirsty

SPECIFICATIONS

Length (in.) 190.3 **Wheelbase (in.)** 111.0
Weight (lbs.) 2988-3174 **Price (new)** $2851-3232

ENGINES

cid/type	bore x stroke	bhp	years
289/ohv V8	4.00×2.87	195/200/225	1967-68
302/ohv V8	4.00×3.00	210/230	1968
390/ohv V8	4.05×3.78	280/320/325	1967-68
427/ohv V8	4.23×3.78	390	1968

PRICES/PROJECTION

Restorable $500-1000 **Good** $1000-2500
Excellent $2500-3500 Add 15% for XR7 or GTE.
5-year projection +20%

Mercury Monterey S-55
1967

1967 Monterey S-55 convertible

PRODUCTION

2d hardtop 570   **2d convertible** 145

HISTORY

Continuation of the S-55 package under the Monterey label. Phased out almost as soon as the model year began, probably because big performance cars were deemed inappropriate for a make with luxury aspirations. Styling was of the new rounded school adopted this year, and somewhat less distinctive than before. Mechanical details as for 1966 S-55.

FOR

Extremely rare, and above-average investment • Good performance • Reasonable handling for size

AGAINST

As for 1966 S-55

SPECIFICATIONS

Length (in.) 218.5   **Wheelbase (in.)** 123.0
Weight (lbs.) 3837-3960   **Price (new)** $3511-3837

ENGINES

cid/type	bore x stroke	bhp	years
428/ohv V8	4.23×3.78	345	1967

PRICES/PROJECTION

As for 1966 S-55   **5-year projection** +50%

Mercury Cougar
1969-70

PRODUCTION

1969 2d hardtop 66,331   **2d convertible** 5796

1969 Cougar CJ 2-door hardtop

XR7 2d hardtop 23,918   **XR7 2d convertible** 4024
1970 2d hardtop 49,479   **2d convertible** 2322
XR7 2d hardtop 18,565   **XR7 2d convertible** 1977

HISTORY

The second-series Cougar, with a longer, wider body on the same 111.0-inch wheelbase and two new convertible offerings. Styling similar to 1967-68, but more ordinary, particularly the grille. XR7s continued to feature a full set of needle gauges and leather-faced seat upholstery as standard, and wore blackout grilles for 1970. The former GT and GTE models were reduced to option packages available with or without XR7 trim, but continued to pack big-block V8s. A new variation was the Eliminator package for the hardtop, sporting appropriate tape striping, a rear decklid spoiler, wide wheels and tires, and a 300-bhp version of Ford's 351 V8. Like concurrent Mustangs, these were the last of the true ponycar Cougars. For 1971, Ford and Mercury both bulked up their ponycars, making them heavier and less agile, though more luxurious, than their predecessors. Cougar styling became more like that of the mid-size Montego. Eventually, Cougar would become a Montego variant.

FOR

As for 1967-68 Cougar

AGAINST

As for 1967-68 Cougar, but less distinctive styling and somewhat lower appreciation potential

SPECIFICATIONS

Length (in.) 193.8 (1969), 196.1 (1970)   **Wheelbase (in.)** 111.0
Weight (lbs.) 3219-3408   **Price (new)** $3016-3692

1969 Cougar Eliminator 2-door hardtop

ENGINES

cid/type	bore x stroke	bhp	years
302/ohv V8	4.00×3.00	290	1970
351/ohv V8	4.00×3.50	250/290/300	1969-70
390/ohv V8	4.05×3.78	320	1969
428/ohv V8	4.13×3.98	335	1969-70

PRICES/PROJECTION

Restorable $300-700 **Good** $900-1750
Excellent $1750-2750 Add 10% for XR7, GT, GTE, Eliminator
5-year projection +25%, convertible +35%

Mercury Cyclone 1969-70

1969 Cyclone CJ428 2-door fastback hardtop

PRODUCTION

1969 2d hardtop 5882* **special 2d hardtop** 3261**
1970 2d hardtop 1695* **special 2d hardtop** 10,170** **Spoiler
2d hardtop** 1631
*fastbacks 1969, semi-fastbacks 1970
**CJ 1969, GT 1970

HISTORY

The rapid intermediates from the "sign of the cat," a limited-production series in these years. The '69 retained the 1968 fastback styling only (notchback versions were dropped), with embellishments like special emblems, racing stripes, and unique rear-end treatment. New to the slate was the CJ, with standard Cobra-Jet 428 V8, four-speed stickshift, heavy-duty suspension, and Ram-Air induction. In January 1969 came the Cyclone Spoiler, which featured a large trunklid wing (not approved for NASCAR racing) and signature fender decals to honor Mercury pilots Cale Yarborough and Dan Gurney. A Spoiler II was also fielded with flush grille and other aerodynamic tweaks clearly intended for the supertracks. The 1970 models were reskinned (along with the Ford Torino), and gained a less slippery semi-fastback roofline. The 429 V8 was now offered in four states of tune and with and without Ram-Air. The Spoiler became a distinct model (still retaining its airfoil), and there was a new midrange Cyclone GT. Basic body-shell was still shared with the more mundane Montego line. Cyclone was mostly unchanged for 1971, the last year for true high-performance engines.

FOR

High performance ●Aggressive styling ●Low production (which promises high appreciation)

AGAINST

Substandard fit and finish ●High running costs ●Subject to wheel well and floor rust

SPECIFICATIONS

Length (in.) 206.2 (1969), 209.9 (1970)
Wheelbase (in.) 116.0 (1969) 117.0 (1970)
Weight (lbs.) 3273-3773 **Price (new)** $2771-3759

ENGINES

cid/type	bore x stroke	bhp	years
302/ohv V8	4.00×3.00	220	1969
351/ohv V8	4.00×3.50	250/290/300	1969-70
390/ohv V8	4.05×3.78	320	1969
428/ohv V8	4.13×3.98	335	1969
429/ohv V8	4.36×3.59	360/370/375	1970

PRICES/PROJECTION

Restorable $750-1500 **Good** $1500-2250
Excellent $2250-3200 Add 15% for CJ, 10% for GT, 35% for Spoiler **5-year projection** +15%

Mercury Marauder 1969-70

1969 Marauder X-100 2-door hardtop

PRODUCTION

1969 2d hardtop 9031 **X-100 2d hardtop** 5635
1970 2d hardtop 3397 **X-100 2d hardtop** 2646

HISTORY

Mercury's last fling with full-size fire breathers, issued at the twilight of the performance age. Built on a shorter 121-inch-wheelbase chassis (versus 123 for other big Mercs except wagons) shared with the Ford XL. Hidden headlights and grille design were as for the luxury Marquis, while quad taillights and flying buttress roof design were exclusive to Marauder in the Mercury line. The X-100 was the hotter version, sporting the big 429 V8 and 360 horses. Changed only in detail for 1970, when production was barely a third of '69 output.

FOR

Terrific go ●Smooth highway cruiser ●Good looks ●Well built ●Luxury ●Comfort ●Last of the "sumo" class hot Mercs ●Pretty rare

AGAINST

Very thirsty ●Special trim nearly extinct

SPECIFICATIONS

Length (in.) 219.1 (1969), 221.8 (1970) **Wheelbase (in.)** 121.0
Weight (lbs.) 3972-4191 **Price (new)** $3503-4136

ENGINES

cid/type	bore x stroke	bhp	years
390/ohv V8	4.05×3.78	265/280	1969-70
429/ohv V8	4.36×3.59	360	1969-70

PRICES/PROJECTION

Restorable $750-1000 **Good** $1200-1850
Excellent $1800-2800 Add 25% for X-100
5-year projection +10%

Muntz Jet 1951-54

1952 Muntz Jet convertible

PRODUCTION

394

HISTORY

A much-modified derivative of the Frank Kurtis sports car (see entry) backed by ace huckster and radio king Earl "Madman" Muntz. His Muntz Jet retained the basic Kurtis styling, but had a more fully outfitted interior (complete with radio mounted in a front center armrest) and full four-passenger seating. A lift-off hardtop was also included. The first 28 cars were built in California with aluminum bodies riding an extended 113.0-inch-wheelbase chassis. All had Cadillac's 331-cid ohv V8. Production was then shifted to Muntz's home base, Evanston, Illinois, where wheelbase was increased to 116 inches and power switched to the L-head Lincoln V8. A numerically lower final drive ratio gave the Jet a higher top speed than the Kurtis, and Muntz claimed a 0-60 mph time of as low as 9 seconds. The Jet was much heavier and far less agile, however. Muntz lost about $1000 on every one he sold, the main reason he gave up on the venture after four years.

FOR

Rarity • Performance • Decent handling • Strong appreciation

AGAINST

Body parts very scarce • Aluminum body restoration expensive • Steel body rust • Costly on today's market

SPECIFICATIONS

Length (in.) 182.0/185.0 **Wheelbase (in.)** 113.0/116.0
Weight (lbs.) approx. 3300 **Price (new)** $5000-6000

ENGINES

cid/type	bore x stroke	bhp	years
331/ohv V8	3.81×3.63	160	1951
336.7/LV8	3.50×4.38	154	1952-54

PRICES/PROJECTION

Restorable $4000-6000 **Good** $6000-8000
Excellent $9000-13,000 **5-year projection** +25%

Nash Twin-Ignition Eight 1930-34

1930 Twin-Ignition Eight long-wheelbase dual-cowl touring

PRODUCTION

1930 12,801 **1931** 6199 **1932** 5791 **1933** 1590 **1934** 5000 (est.)

HISTORY

The largest Nashes in a period of sumptuous, beautiful styling and boasting lots of special features. "Twin-Ignition" meant two sets of plugs/points/condensors/coils operating from a single distributor. The 1930 T-I Eight became the Model 890 in 1931; the same 298.6-cid engine was used on the 1932 Model 990, while that year's 1090 Advanced Eight and Ambassador received a larger bored-out version. The latter was adopted for the 1933 Advanced and Ambassador Eights. The Advanced Eight was scrubbed during the model rationalization of 1934. Riding nice long wheelbases, all these Nashes had outstanding performance and were nicely assembled with quality materials.

FOR

Underrated and thus still quite affordable; look for open models • Looks • Finish • Road manners • Interest value

AGAINST

Lack of hobby recognition • Mechanical complexity • Slow to appreciate

SPECIFICATIONS

Length (in.) NA **Wheelbase (in.)** 124.0/133.0 (1930-32); 128.0/133.0/142.0 (1932-34) **Weight (lbs.)** 3710-4650
Price (new) $1475-2055

ENGINES

cid/type	bore x stroke	bhp	years
298.6/L8	3.25×4.50	100-115	1930-32

322.0/L8	3.38×4.50	125	1932-34

OPEN **Restorable** $5000-9000 **Good** $9000-20,000
Excellent $18,000-28,000 LONG WHEELBASE
Restorable $3000-7000 **Good** $7000-10,000
Excellent $10,000-14,000. CLOSED **Restorable** $1500-3000
Good $3000-6000 **Excellent** $5500-9000.
5-year projection +10%

Nash Ambassador Eight 1939-42

1940 Ambassador Eight 4-door fastback sedan

PRODUCTION

1939 17,052 **1940-42** 33,000 (est.)

HISTORY

Nash's best in its final styling generation before the war. Also the firm's last eight-cylinder offerings until 1954. Marked by a striking front-end design plus the traditional Nash valve-in-head engine with nine main bearings for smoothness and longevity. A variety of closed bodies was offered along with a cabriolet (convertible). The latter was dropped for 1942 when Nash adopted a rather less successful horizontal grille. The 1939-41 models are arguably better-looking.

FOR

Smooth performance • Quality • Easy on the budget; convertibles among the few prewar types you can still buy show-ready for a four-figure price

AGAINST

Limited availability • Club and parts support dicey • Rust-prone • Sedans on the dumpy side

SPECIFICATIONS

Length (in.) 213.2 (1939-40); 210.2 (1941-42)
Wheelbase (in.) 125.0 (1939-40); 121.0 (1941-42)
Weight (lbs.) 3260-3820 **Price (new)** $1084-1295

ENGINES

cid/type	bore x stroke	bhp	years
260.8/L8	3.13×4.25	115	1939-42

OPEN **Restorable** $2000-4000 **Good** $5000-7500
Excellent $8500-13,000 CLOSED **Restorable** $500-2000
Good $2000-3000 **Excellent** $3000-4500. Add 20% for 1942
models. **5-year projection** +5%

Nash Ambassador Six 1939-42

1941 Ambassador Six 4-door trunkback sedan

PRODUCTION

1939 8500 **1940-42** 55,000 (est.)

HISTORY

Six-cylinder counterpart to the Ambassador Eight. Mounted on a four-inch shorter wheelbase for 1939-40. Powered by an L-head engine of ample smoothness, and offered in a similar lineup of body styles.

FOR

As for 1939-42 Ambassador Eight but even less costly

AGAINST

As for 1939-42 Ambassador Eight

SPECIFICATIONS

Length (in.) 209.2 **Wheelbase (in.)** 121.0
Weight (lbs.) 3180-3470 **Price (new)** $925-1130

ENGINES

cid/type	bore x stroke	bhp	years
234.8/L6	3.38×4.38	105	1939-42

PRICES/PROJECTION

As for 1939-42 Ambassador Eight less 10%.
5-year projection +5%

Nash 600 1941-42

PRODUCTION

60,000 (est.)

1942 600 4-door trunkback sedan

HISTORY

Replacement for the 1940 Lafayette as Nash's low-priced product, and much more popular. An important car that introduced unit body/chassis construction. A wheelbase 9 inches shorter than the Ambassadors' and significantly less weight yielded astounding gas economy (hence the designation, which stood for 600 miles on a 20-gallon tank). No convertible offered, but nevertheless helped Nash-Kelvinator to a $4.6 million profit in 1941.

FOR

Low running costs • Solid build

AGAINST

As for 1940-42 Ambassador Eight and Six

SPECIFICATIONS

Length (in.) 199.6 **Wheelbase (in.)** 112.0
Weight (lbs.) 2490-2655 **Price (new)** $730-918

ENGINES

cid/type	bore x stroke	bhp	years
172.6/L6	3.13×3.75	75	1941-42

PRICES/PROJECTION

Restorable $350-1000 **Good** $1000-2500
Excellent $3250-5000 **5-year projection** +10%

Nash Ambassador Suburban 1946-48

PRODUCTION

1946 272 **1947** 595 **1948** 130

HISTORY

The most interesting early-postwar Nash, essentially the prewar Ambassador fastback four-door trimmed with wood *a la* Chrysler Town & Country. Not a hot seller, but useful in getting car-hungry customers back into the showrooms and interested again in the holdover prewar design. Offered only with the prewar L-head six as Nash abandoned its straight eight in these years. Very uncommon today, but a good example of a maker's attempt to spruce up its image in this period.

1946 Ambassador Suburban fastback 4-door sedan

FOR

Scarcity and high appreciation potential • Construction quality • Uniqueness

AGAINST

Only 10-15 known to survive today • Wood trim demands high maintenance • Subject to general underbody and structural rust

SPECIFICATIONS

Length (in.) 209.2 **Wheelbase (in.)** 121.0
Weight (lbs.) 3470-3664 **Price (new)** $1929-2239

ENGINES

cid/type	bore x stroke	bhp	years
234.8/L6	3.38×4.38	112	1946-48

PRICES/PROJECTION

Restorable $1000-2000 **Good** $2500-4000
Excellent $4500-7000 **5-year projection** +35%

Nash Ambassador Custom cabriolet 1948

1948 Ambassador Custom cabriolet

PRODUCTION

1000

HISTORY

The first Nash ragtop since the war (and the last unless you count the Ramblers), an addition to the 1948 line. Has become the most expensive Nash of these years, and is highly prized by collectors. The smooth ohv six, a seven-main-bearing unit developing reasonable horsepower, remained the only engine available in early postwar Ambassadors.

FOR

Good appreciation potential • Historical interest • Fine fit and finish • Scarcity

AGAINST

As for 1946-48 Ambassador Suburban, but no wood trim

SPECIFICATIONS

Length (in.) 209.2 **Wheelbase (in.)** 121.0 **Weight (lbs.)** 3465
Price (new) $2345

ENGINES

cid/type	bore x stroke	bhp	years
234.8/L6	3.38×4.38	112	1948

PRICES/PROJECTION

Restorable $2500-4000 **Good** $5000-10,000
Excellent $9000-13,000 **5-year projection** +15%

Nash Ambassador 1949-51

1949 Ambassador Super 4-door sedan

PRODUCTION

198,000 (est.)

HISTORY

The best in the first entirely new postwar Nash generation. Design began taking shape under chief engineer Nils Erik Wahlberg during the war; actual styling is claimed by Holden Koto and Ted Pietsch. The production car, dubbed Airflyte, had superior aerodynamics but unfortunate looks — the nearest thing to a bathtub on wheels America ever built. Bulbous lines disguised what was a very good car, notable for its "Uniscope" instrument cluster, superior "Weather-Eye" heating system, and monocoque construction. Offered in several trim levels each year, variously designated Super, Custom, and Super Special. Ambassadors used the longer Nash wheelbase and were more luxuriously trimmed than the lower-priced 600 (1949) and Statesman (1950-51) series.

FOR

Not costly at present • A fine road car with high comfort levels

AGAINST

Clumsy looking • Rust potential • Low appreciation

SPECIFICATIONS

Length (in.) 210.0 (1949-50), 211.0 (1951)
Wheelbase (in.) 121.0 **Weight (lbs.)** 3325-3445
Price (new) $2039-2501

ENGINES

cid/type	bore x stroke	bhp	years
234.8/L6	3.38×4.38	112/115	1949-51

PRICES/PROJECTION

Restorable $350-1000 **Good** $1000-2000
Excellent $2000-3500 Add 10% for Custom models, 5% for Brougham sedans **5-year projection** +10%

Nash Rambler 1950-52

1952 Rambler Greenbriar Suburban wagon

PRODUCTION

160,000 (est.)

HISTORY

The most successful early compact. The original Rambler came as a cute convertible (with fixed side window frames) and a two-door wagon (which captured most of the sales). A Country Club hardtop was added for '51. Unit construction made for tightness and relative quiet, while a small, L-head six provided pleasing thrift. Rambler rescued Nash's (and later AMC's) fortunes in the '50s, and laid the basis for the company's soaring success in the '60s.

FOR

Pioneer compact • Practicality • Economy that's liveable today • Very affordable

AGAINST

Low appreciation • Unit-body rust-out always a threat • Enclosed front wheel wells mean unduly wide turning circle

SPECIFICATIONS

Length (in.) 176.0 **Wheelbase (in.)** 100.0
Weight (lbs.) 2420-2515 **Price (new)** $1808-2119

ENGINES

cid/type	bore x stroke	bhp	years
172.6/L6	3.13×3.75	82	1950-52

PRICES/PROJECTION

Restorable $250-600 **Good** $750-1250
Excellent $1750-2500 Add 10% for hardtop, 50% for convertible
5-year projection +15%

Nash-Healey 1951

1951 Nash-Healey roadster

PRODUCTION

104

HISTORY

The result of an agreement between sports-car builder Donald Healey of England and George Mason of Nash-Kelvinator. The first examples of this short-lived series of hybrids featured a dashing aluminum roadster body powered by an ohv Nash six tuned to deliver 125 bhp. Racing versions finished ninth in class in the Mille Miglia and fourth overall at Le Mans. Styling was in the British mold, with divided windshield and side curtains, but a vertical bar grille and prominent emblem preserved Nash identity.

FOR

One of the most desirable (and among the first) postwar American sports cars • Quick on straights, nimble on curves • High appreciation • Exclusivity • Milestone status

AGAINST

Aluminum bodywork flimsy • Body parts scarce now • Expensive

SPECIFICATIONS

Length (in.) 170.8 **Wheelbase (in.)** 102.0 **Weight (lbs.)** 2690
Price (new) $4063 (most built had $96 overdrive option)

ENGINES

cid/type	bore x stroke	bhp	years
234.8/ohv I6	3.38×4.38	125	1951

PRICES/PROJECTION

Restorable $4000-6000 **Good** $7500-12,500
Excellent $12,500-18,000 **5-year projection** +10%

Nash Ambassador 1952-54

1953 Ambassador Custom Country Club 2-door hardtop

PRODUCTION

150,000 (est.)

HISTORY

The much-improved, rebodied successor to the 1949-51 Airflyte, with styling based on Pininfarina concepts. The new squared-off body design continued the curious skirted front wheel openings, a Nash trademark that found little buyer acceptance and created a huge turning circle for a car of fairly compact dimensions for its day. A "Le Mans" power option based on the Nash-Healey engine was offered for 1953-54, and provided 140 bhp via dual carbs and high-compression head. An attractive "floating-bar" grille was adopted for '54. "Country Club" hardtops were offered, but not convertibles. More desirable than the shorter, dumpier Statesman models because of more balanced appearance and a new enlarged version of the big Nash six. Continued to pioneer such comfort features as fully reclining front seats and the effective "Weather Eye" heating/ventilation system.

FOR

Generally attractive looks • Great long-haul car • PF badges

AGAINST

Little collector interest • Parts scarce • Rusts easily • Not many around • Tedious in tight spots

SPECIFICATIONS

Length (in.) 209.3 **Wheelbase (in.)** 121.3
Weight (lbs.) 3410-3575 **Price (new)** $2521-2735

ENGINES

cid/type	bore x stroke	bhp	years
252.6/ohv I6	3.50×4.38	120/130/140	1952-54

PRICES/PROJECTION

Restorable $1000-2000 **Good** $1500-2500
Excellent $2000-3200 Add 20% for Country Club hardtop, 10% for Le Mans option, 5% for Custom models (continental spare).
5-year projection +10%

Nash-Healey 1952-54

1953 Nash-Healey Le Mans coupe

PRODUCTION

1952 150 **1953** 162 **1954** 90

HISTORY

A much revised, second-generation Anglo-American hybrid. Body now made of steel, and shaped by Pininfarina. Identified by headlamps mounted within a simple bar grille and uplifted rear fenders. Surprisingly, curb weight was less than the '51 aluminum-body model. A longer-wheelbase fixed-roof coupe dubbed Le Mans (in honor of the N-H's racing successes) was added for '53, and the roadster dropped for '54. Some leftover '54s were retitled and sold as '55s. The racers continued to do well, particularly at Le Mans 1952 where one finished third overall (led only by two Mercedes). The experimental Rambler Palm Beach might have replaced the N-H as American Motors' sports car for 1956, but very limited sales and tight finances (plus the practical bent of AMC president George Romney) spelled the end of the project.

FOR

Larger-engine models more rapid • Le Mans roomy; a genuine GT • Fine handling • Thoroughbred pedigree

AGAINST

Not cheap • Most survivors are off the market

SPECIFICATIONS

Length (in.) 170.8 (roadster), 177.0 (coupe)
Wheelbase (in.) 102.0 (roadster), 108.0 (coupe)
Weight (lbs.) NA **Price (new)** $4721-5899

ENGINES

cid/type	bore x stroke	bhp	years
234.8/ohv I6	3.38×4.38	125	1952*
252.6/ohv I6	3.50×4.38	140	1952-54

*Through serial #N2309 and N3000-3023

PRICES/PROJECTION

Restorable $3000-5000 **Good** $5000-10,000
Excellent $10,000-15,000 **5-year projection** +15%

Nash Rambler 1953-55

1954 Rambler Custom convertible

PRODUCTION

150,000 (est.)

HISTORY

Nash's sales-winning compact, now restyled along the lines of the contemporary Pininfarina senior cars. Model offerings expanded noticeably for '54 with the addition of two- and four-door sedans (joining the wagon, hardtop, and convertible) plus a new low-priced DeLuxe two-door and returning Custom and Super versions of all body styles. The four-door sedans used a longer 108-inch wheelbase. Rambler was spun off as an individual make for 1956, and later models are found under that heading. The 100-inch-wheelbase two-door sedan and wagon from these years would be resurrected with only detail changes for 1958 as the Rambler American.

FOR

As for 1950-52 Rambler

AGAINST

Slow appreciation ● Not as historically significant, but otherwise as for 1950-52 Rambler

SPECIFICATIONS

Length (in.) 176.5 (4d sedan: 186.4) **Wheelbase (in.)** 100.0 (4d sedan: 108.0) **Weight (lbs.)** 2400-2685
Price (new) $1550-2150

ENGINES

cid/type	bore x stroke	bhp	years
184/L6	3.13×4.00	85/90	1953-54
195.6/L6	3.13×4.25	90/100	1955

PRICES/PROJECTION

Restorable $500-1000 **Good** $1000-2000
Excellent $1800-2800 Add 10% for hardtop, 50% for convertible. **5-year projection** no change

Nash Metropolitan Series 54 1954-56

1954 Metropolitan Series 54 convertible

PRODUCTION

1954 13,095 **1955** 6096 **1956** 3000 (est.) (figures based on shipments from Great Britain)

HISTORY

Nash president George Mason's idea of the ultimate commuter/shopping car. Styling was based on the Bill Frajole design for the NXI show car and bore a resemblance to the big Nash, but the scale was tiny: the Met's wheelbase was shorter than a VW Beetle's. Bodies were built in England by Fisher & Ludlow, and the four-cylinder engines came from Austin, which also did final assembly. A three-passenger convertible and fixed-roof hardtop were offered. Later cars had flashy two-tone paint that reminded one stylist of "Neapolitan ice cream." The Met met with modest success in the U.S., and was continued by AMC even after Nash and Hudson had left the scene (both badges were used on the car so both sets of dealers could sell it). The little 1.2-liter engine was bored out

to 1.5 liters during the 1956 model year to produce the Met 1500, and the car would remain basically unaltered until sales ceased in the early '60s.

FOR

Low-bucks collectible ● Still makes sense for around-town use ● A certain charm ● Mileage

AGAINST

Rusts too easily ● Austin engine not very reliable ● Rather dumpy styling

SPECIFICATIONS

Length (in.) 149.5 **Wheelbase (in.)** 85.0
Weight (lbs.) 1803-1843 (conv/coupe)
Price (new) $1445-1469 (coupe/conv)

ENGINES

cid/type	bore x stroke	bhp	years
73.8/ohv I4	2.56×3.50	42	1954-56

PRICES/PROJECTION

COUPE **Restorable** $600-1000 **Good** $1000-2000
Excellent $2000-3000 CONVERTIBLE **Restorable** $500-1000
Good $1000-2250 **Excellent** $2500-4000 **5-year projection** +10%

Nash Ambassador 1955-57

1955 Ambassador Eight Custom Country Club 2-door hardtop

PRODUCTION

Eight 20,000 (est. total) **Six** 15,000 (est. total) **1956 Eight Special** 4154 **1957 Eight** (incl. Super/Custom) 5000

HISTORY

Extension of the Farina-styled 1952-54 design, with wrapped windshield, inboard headlamps and concave grille (1955-56), and progressively more garish two-toning and chrome trim. Excellent performance from Packard's 320 V8 introduced for '55, and AMC's own 327 V8 on the mid-1956 Special and all '57s. Colorful plush interiors continued, so comfort levels as high as ever. Basic styling was good—better than contemporary Hudsons', though that's not saying much—but details were thoughtless. The '57 pioneered quad

1957 Ambassador Custom Country Club 2-door hardtop

headlamps (along with Lincoln), arranged vertically no less. Still no wagons, convertibles, or hardtop sedans, however. Ambassador Six was dropped after '56, but its longer wheelbase and resulting better proportions make it more desirable than the smaller-engine six-cylinder 1955-56 Statesman. Nash disappeared as a make after '57, but this platform continued with a major reskinning as the 1958-59 Rambler Ambassador, which did not prove successful as a stretched, more luxurious version of George Romney's compact.

FOR

In design, preferred over 1955-57 Hudsons; less desirable than 1952-54 Nashes • Last of the line • Others as for 1952-54 Ambassador

AGAINST

Very rust-prone, so not many left now • Busy styling • Others as for 1952-54 Ambassador

SPECIFICATIONS

Length (in.) 209.3 **Wheelbase (in.)** 121.3
Weight (lbs.) 3538-3839 **Price (new)** $2425-3095

ENGINES

cid/type	bore x stroke	bhp	years
252.2/ohv I6	3.50×4.38	130/140	1955-56
320/ohv V8	3.81×3.50	208	1955-56
327/ohv V8	4.00×3.25	190/225	1956-57

PRICES/PROJECTION

1955 SEDANS Restorable $500-800 **Good** $750-1500 **Excellent** $2000-3100 **1955 HARDTOPS Restorable** $750-1000 **Good** $1250-2500 **Excellent** $2000-4800 Add 20% for 1956 models, 40% for 1957s. Deduct 10% for sixes.
5-year projection +10%

Nash Metropolitan Series 56 1500 1956-57

PRODUCTION

1956 6000 (est.) **1957** 15,317

HISTORY

A revised version of the Nash economy runabout, introduced mid-model year 1956. Features included a larger engine and more horsepower, plus a larger clutch, different paint treatment, Z-

1957 Metropolitan 1500 series 56

shaped bodyside moldings, and a new mesh grille bearing either Nash or Hudson emblems according to the selling dealer. The imitation hood scoop of the previous Met was erased. Top speed went from 70 mph to 80, making the Met somewhat more suitable for higher-speed American driving conditions. Continued to be sold by AMC through 1962, though production ended in mid-1960. (See AMC entry for later models.)

FOR

Somewhat livelier • Otherwise as for 1954-56 Series 54

AGAINST

The same curious looks and doubtful Austin engine (albeit with more robust displacement)

SPECIFICATIONS

Length (in.) 149.5 **Wheelbase (in.)** 85.0
Weight (lbs.) 1803-1843 (conv/coupe) **Price (new)** $1527-1591

ENGINES

cid/type	bore x stroke	bhp	years
90.9/ohv I4	2.88×3.50	52	1956-57

PRICES/PROJECTION

As for 1954-56 Series 54

Oldsmobile Series 90 1940

1940 Series 90 club coupe

PRODUCTION

4d sedan 33,075 **2d club coupe** 10,836
2d convertible coupe 290 **4d convertible phaeton** 50

HISTORY

One of the nicest-looking late prewar Oldsmobiles, and top of the 1940 line. The only Olds series this year powered by an eight, an inline unit developing 110 bhp. Hydra-Matic transmission, pioneered by Olds, was found in most examples. Styling was bold for the times, with semi-flush-mounted headlamps, GM's "Turret-Top" all-steel body construction, and gracefully rounded fenders. A solid car, and one that can still cope well with today's traffic conditions.

FOR

Good styling •Superb workmanship •Fine performance •Open models' rarity

AGAINST

Relatively low appreciation compared to sister makes like Buick •Body parts now scarce

SPECIFICATIONS

Length (in.) 210.0 **Wheelbase (in.)** 124.0
Weight (lbs.) 3440-3750 **Price (new)** $1069-1570

ENGINES

cid/type	bore x stroke	bhp	years
257.1/L8	3.25×3.88	110	1940

PRICES/PROJECTION

Restorable $2000-3000 **Good** $3500-5000
Excellent $5000-7800 Add 35% for coupe, 450% for open model. **5-year projection** +10%

Oldsmobile Custom Cruiser 8 & 98 1941-42

1942 Ninety-Eight convertible

PRODUCTION

1941 2d club coupe 6305 **4d sedan** 22,081
2d convertible coupe 1263 **4d convertible phaeton** 119
1942 2d club coupe 1771 **4d sedan** 4672
2d convertible coupe 216

HISTORY

Evolution of the 1940 design, with the same mechanical features and somewhat busier styling. The '42s received more sweeping pontoon fenders and a two-inch longer wheelbase to go with them. As with other makes, low production makes the '42s (along with the last of Olds' convertible sedans) highly desirable today.

FOR

As for 1940 Series 90

AGAINST

As for 1940 Series 90

SPECIFICATIONS

Length (in.) 210.0 (1941), 213.0 (1942)
Wheelbase (in.) 125.0 (1941), 127.0 (1942)
Weight (lbs.) 3430-3955 **Price (new)** $1079-1450

ENGINES

cid/type	bore x stroke	bhp	years
257.1/L8	3.25×3.88	110	1941-42

PRICES/PROJECTION

As for 1940 Series 90

Oldsmobile Custom Cruiser 98 1946-47

PRODUCTION

1946 2d club sedan 2459 **4d sedan** 11,031
2d convertible 874 **1947 2d club sedan** 8475
4d sedan 24,733 **2d convertible** 3940

HISTORY

Postwar carryover of Oldsmobile's top-line series on the same long chassis. Mechanical specifications unchanged. Improved styling, however, especially up front where the complicated prewar grille was replaced by a simpler bar affair.

FOR

More available and affordable than prewar models •Fine high-speed cruisers

AGAINST

Holdover styling •Body and trim pieces now in short supply

SPECIFICATIONS

Length (in.) 213.0 **Wheelbase (in.)** 127.0
Weight (lbs.) 3680-4075 **Price (new)** $1762-2307

ENGINES

cid/type	bore x stroke	bhp	years
257.1/L8	3.25×3.88	110	1946-47

PRICES/PROJECTION

Restorable $900-1500 **Good** $2250-3500
Excellent $3500-4500 Add 125% for convertible
5-year projection +10%

Oldsmobile Futuramic 98 1948

1948 Futuramic 98 convertible

PRODUCTION

2d club sedan 2000   **Deluxe 2d club sedan** 9000
4d sedan 4000   **Deluxe 4d sedan** 25,000   **Deluxe**
2d convertible 9000 (all estimated)

HISTORY

Oldsmobile's first all-new postwar models, introduced early in calendar 1948. (Early-production Dynamic 98s were essentially continuations of the 1946-47 models.) Fine styling by Harley Earl's Art & Colour Studio was a sensation at the time. Power still supplied by the familiar Olds straight eight, now up slightly in horsepower.

FOR

Superb styling ● Often passed over in favor of '48 Cadillacs ● Smooth road performance ● Solid construction

AGAINST

Relatively limited appreciation potential ● Outmoded engine

SPECIFICATIONS

Length (in.) 213.5   **Wheelbase (in.)** 125.0
Weight (lbs.) 3645-4035   **Price (new)** $2078-2624

1948 Futuramic 98 2-door club sedan

ENGINES

cid/type	bore x stroke	bhp	years
257.1/L8	3.25×3.88	115	1948

PRICES/PROJECTION

Restorable $1000-2000 **Good** $2500-3500
Excellent $3500-4500 Add 400% for convertible.
5-year projection +10%

Oldsmobile Futuramic 98 Holiday 1949

1949 Futuramic 98 2-door hardtop

PRODUCTION

3006

HISTORY

Shares honors with this year's Buick Riviera and Cadillac Coupe deVille as the industry's first "hardtop convertible," a deft creation by GM design under the ever-innovative Harley Earl. Widely overlooked today, possibly because of its low production and consequent rarity. Trimmed to convertible standards, which is to say plush, and featured simulated convertible-top bows on the interior headliner like other early GM hardtops. The year's other big news was shared by other 98s and the new Futuramic 88 series, the now-famous Rocket V8, a modern high-compression ohv unit, amazingly powerful and efficient for its day.

FOR

Historical importance (hardtop and V8) ● Performance ● High-quality materials ● Craftsmanship ● Strong value increase

AGAINST

Guzzles gas ● A bit large for some ● Body parts scarce today

SPECIFICATIONS

Length (in.) 213.0   **Wheelbase (in.)** 125.0   **Weight (lbs.)** 4000
Price (new) 2973

ENGINES

cid/type	bore x stroke	bhp	years
303.7/ohv V8	3.75×3.44	135	1949

PRICES/PROJECTION

Restorable $750-1500 **Good** $2000-2750
Excellent $3000-5500 Add 400% for convertible.
5-year projection +10%

Oldsmobile Futuramic 88 1949-50

1950 Futuramic 88 Deluxe 4-door sedan

PRODUCTION

1949 2d club sedan 28,707 **2d club coupe** 11,591
2d convertible 5434 **4d Town Sedan** 5833
4d sedan 46,386 **4d wagon** 1355
1950 2d club sedan 31,093 **2d club coupe** 21,456
2d convertible 9127 **4d sedan** 141,111 **4d wagon** 2382
2d Holiday hardtop 1366 **2d sedan** 50,561

HISTORY

Designated a Milestone for its outstanding blend of styling and performance. Can legitimately be considered Detroit's first high-volume "muscle car." A last-minute addition to the 1949 line, the 88 (along with the luxury 98) featured the year's new high-compression ohv V8. Lighter than the 98, though, so a real tiger. Dominated NASCAR stock-car racing into 1951. Good looks and sparkling pickup were available in a wide range of body styles, offered in standard and fancier Deluxe trim. Particularly desirable today are the low-production convertibles, the all-steel wagons (with imitation wood trim and the last Olds wagons until 1957), and the Holiday hardtop added for 1950. Continued as the Super 88 series for 1951 and beyond, with more horsepower as the years went by, along with increasingly bulky styling and more weight.

FOR

Power and performance ●Quality ●Looks ●Good club support ●Racing record ●Sure-fire investment

AGAINST

Some rust threat ●Body and trim parts scarce

SPECIFICATIONS

Length (in.) 202.0 **Wheelbase (in.)** 119.5
Weight (lbs.) 3455-3780 **Price (new)** $1878-3296

ENGINES

cid/type	bore x stroke	bhp	years
303.7/ohv V8	3.75×3.44	135	1949-50

PRICES/PROJECTION

Restorable $1000-2000 **Good** $2000-3000
Excellent $3500-5500 Add 60% for 2-door models, 90% for Holiday hardtop or wagon, 350% for convertible.
5-year projection +10%

Oldsmobile 98 Fiesta 1953

1953 Ninety-Eight Fiesta convertible

PRODUCTION

458

HISTORY

A special limited-edition luxury convertible based on the standard 98 bodyshell, one of three GM "show cars for the public" introduced this year (Buick Skylark and Cadillac Eldorado were the others). Predictive styling, with wraparound windshield, spinner hubcaps (widely copied as an aftermarket accessory), and flush-folding top. Cost a lot, but came with a special tuned version of the Rocket V8, a custom leather-lined interior, and just about every option in the book (including Hydra-Matic, power steering and brakes, and electric windows and seat). More a glamor item than a serious high-volume seller, it was withdrawn after a short production run (Buick and particularly Cadillac were more successful with their snazzy ragtops).

FOR

Rare, highly prized ●Advanced styling features ●Hot performer

AGAINST

Virtually impossible to find now ●Unique body parts and trim are replacement headaches ●Expensive to buy and restore

SPECIFICATIONS

Length (in.) 215.0 **Wheelbase (in.)** 124.0 **Weight (lbs.)** 4453
Price (new) $5717

ENGINES

cid/type	bore x stroke	bhp	years
303.7/ohv V8	3.75×3.44	170	1953

PRICES/PROJECTION

Restorable $5000-8000 **Good** $8000-15,000
Excellent $12,000-20,000 **5-year projection** +15%

Oldsmobile 1955

PRODUCTION

88 4d sedan 57,777 **2d sedan** 37,507
4d Holiday hardtop 41,310 **2d Holiday hardtop** 85,767
Super 88 4d sedan 111,316 **2d sedan** 11,950

1955 Ninety-Eight Starfire convertible

4d Holiday hardtop 47,385   **2d Holiday hardtop** 62,354
2d convertible 9007   **Ninety-Eight 4d sedan** 39,847
4d Holiday hardtop 31,267   **2d Holiday hardtop** 38,363
2d Starfire convertible 9149

HISTORY

A standout among mid- to late-'50s Oldsmobiles in most every way. Arguably the best combination of styling, performance, and craftsmanship Lansing had yet issued. The public reacted by helping Olds set a production record that put the division fourth behind Chevy, Ford, and Buick. A facelift on the new '54 bodyshell featured clean lines, jaunty two-toning, and plush interiors. Horsepower from the bored out Rocket V8 introduced for 1954 was up to 185 for 88 and up to a little over 200 for Super 88 and Ninety-Eight. This was also the first year for an Olds four-door hardtop (shared with Buick), beating the rest of the industry by a full year. In all, a very nice group of cars, and attractive collectibles now because of reasonable prices in addition to all that made them desirable when new.

FOR

Widely underrated, hence quite affordable • Performance • Good contemporary '50s styling • Fine construction quality

AGAINST

Surprisingly hard to find in good condition • Some body/trim parts scarce • Slow appreciation rate • Overchromed dash

SPECIFICATIONS

Length (in.) 203.4 (88s), 212.4 (98s)
Wheelbase (in.) 122.0 (88s), 126.0 (98s)
Weight (lbs.) 3707-4159   **Price (new)** $2297-3276

ENGINES

cid/type	bore x stroke	bhp	years
324.3/ohv V8	3.88×3.44	185/202	1955

PRICES/PROJECTION

SEDANS **Restorable** $1000-2000 **Good** $2000-3000
Excellent $3000-6000 Add 50% for Holiday coupe, 125% for convertible (10% additional for 98 convertible).
5-year projection +15%

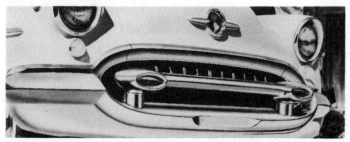

1955 Oldsmobile grille

Oldsmobile Starfire 1961-66

1961 Super 88 convertible (Starfire similar)

PRODUCTION

1961 2d convertible 7600		**1962 2d convertible** 7149	
2d hardtop 34,839	**1963 2d convertible** 4401		
Holiday 2d hardtop 21,148	**1964 2d convertible** 2410		
Holiday 2d hardtop 13,753	**1965 2d convertible** 2236		
Holiday 2d hardtop 13,024	**1966 Holiday 2d hardtop** 13,019		

HISTORY

Oldsmobile's full-size performance cars of the early '60s. Introduced in convertible-only form as a sub-model in the 1961 Super 88 series. Became a separate series from 1962 on, but was always built on Oldsmobile's shorter chassis, not the Ninety-Eight platform. Fitted with the most powerful Olds V8s through 1965. Has found a niche in today's collector market, the crisply styled 1962-63 models in particular being among the most desirable Oldsmobiles of these years. The rarer convertibles naturally lead the hardtops in value, but all Starfires are eminently collectible for their relatively low production, smooth highway cruising ability, and Ninety-Eight-level luxury interior with bucket seats, console, and high-grade trim.

FOR

Big, comfortable road-eater • Luxury • Distinctive styling • Strong performer

AGAINST

Thirsty • Starfire-only trim bits scarce now

SPECIFICATIONS

Length (in.) 212.0(1961), 213.9 (1962), 214.5 (1963), 215.3 (1964), 216.9 (1965-66)   **Wheelbase (in.)** 123.0
Weight (lbs.) 4013-4334   **Price (new)** $3564-4778

ENGINES

cid/type	bore x stroke	bhp	years
394/ohv V8	4.13×3.69	325/330/345	1961-64
425/ohv V8	4.13×3.98	370/375	1965-66

PRICES/PROJECTION

1962-63 CONVERTIBLE **Restorable** $1000-1250
Good $1750-3000 **Excellent** $4000-7000 1962-63 HARDTOP
Restorable $750-1000 **Good** $1500-2500
Excellent $3000-5200 Deduct 10% for 1961 and 1964-65 models, 50% for 1966 **5-year projection** +15% 1962-63 models, +10% others

Oldsmobile F-85 Deluxe Jetfire 1962-63

1962 F-85 Deluxe Jetfire 2-door hardtop

PRODUCTION

1962 3765   **1963** 5842

HISTORY

The most technically interesting and collectible version of Oldsmobile's early-'60s F-85 compacts, offered in limited numbers for these two years only. Based on the bucket-seat Cutlass coupe introduced for 1961, but powered by a turbocharged version of the Buick aluminum V8 available for the F-85/Skylark at the time. Though the turbo yielded one bhp per cubic inch, it caused reliability problems involving carbon buildup, not fully alleviated by Olds' alcohol-and-water injection, which was standard with the package. The Jetfire was quite rapid when working properly, however, with 0-60 mph available in 8.5 seconds from standstill and a top speed of 107 mph. But the old axiom "there's no substitute for cubic inches" was still very much in force in Detroit, and Olds abandoned this pocket powerhouse for 1964 in favor of a larger Cutlass with big-inch, conventional cast-iron V8s.

FOR

Technical, historical interest • Good go • Build quality • Practical size • Neat, slightly innocuous looks • Pretty affordable

AGAINST

Mechanical woes • Rust can attack undercarriage • Special parts in short supply • Modest appreciation rate

SPECIFICATIONS

Length (in.) 188.2 (1962), 192.2 (1963)   **Wheelbase (in.)** 112.0
Weight (lbs.) 2739-2774   **Price (new)** $3049-3048

ENGINES

cid/type	bore x stroke	bhp	years
215.0/ohv V8	3.50×2.50	215	1962-63

PRICES/PROJECTION

Restorable $750-1250 **Good** $1500-2750
Excellent $3000-4000 **5-year projection** +10%

Oldsmobile F-85 Cutlass 4-4-2 1964-65

1964 Cutlass Holiday 2-door hardtop (4-4-2 similar)

PRODUCTION

1964 Holiday 2d hardtop 2999
1965 Holiday 2d hardtop 21,535   **2d convertible** 3468

HISTORY

Oldsmobile's counterpart to the Pontiac GTO in the burgeoning mid-size muscle market. Not a separate model in these years but an option package usually ordered on the sporty Cutlass two-doors. An outgrowth of the "Police Apprehender Pursuit Package" (option B-09) that was theoretically available on any '64 F-85 or Cutlass. Renamed 4-4-2 to denote four-speed floorshift manual gearbox, four-barrel carburetor, and dual exhausts. The package also threw in heavy-duty suspension, wider wheels and tires, special rear axle and driveshaft, HD engine mounts/steering gear/frame, front and rear stabilizer bars, 11-inch clutch, 70-amp battery, and special nameplates. For 1965, the designation stood for a new standard 400-cid V8 with four-barrel carb and dual exhausts. The 4-4-2 package could be combined with any trim level from plain to fancy. Exhilarating performance was guaranteed: 0-60 mph came up in 7.5 seconds, the standing-start quarter-mile in 17 seconds, and top speed was around 125 mph. Road manners were a cut above its competitors'.

FOR

A stormer from the good old days • Capable handling • Reasonable size • Nice styling • Strong appreciation • Convertibles rare

AGAINST

Thirsty and doesn't like today's low-calorie gas • Most examples thrashed hard • Not as quick as a GTO

SPECIFICATIONS

Length (in.) 203.0 (1964), 204.3 (1965)   **Wheelbase (in.)** 115.0
Weight (lbs.) 3141-3338   **Price (new)** $2700-3200 (base; approx.)

ENGINES

cid/type	bore x stroke	bhp	years
330/ohv V8	3.94×3.38	310	1964
400/ohv V8	4.00×3.98	345	1965

PRICES/PROJECTION

Restorable $500-1000 **Good** $1000-2000
Excellent $2000-3000 Add 50% for convertible.
5-year projection +10%

5-year projection +50%

Oldsmobile Jetstar I
1964-65

1964 Jetstar 88 4-door sedan (Jetstar I similar)

PRODUCTION

1964 16,084   **1965** 6552

HISTORY

Sporty flagship for Oldsmobile's new low-priced Jetstar 88 series, and arriving with it for 1964. Curiously listed as part of the Dynamic 88 series in its debut year, then as a separate model for '65. Essentially the Starfire idea at a more popular price, but offered only as a two-door hardtop. Not as successful, probably because the market was turning to the lighter, more maneuverable intermediates packing similar big-inch engines. Powerplants were the same as Starfire's, but a bit less weight gave the Jetstar I better pickup. The Jetstar 88 series lasted through 1966, then was renamed Delmont.

FOR

Very low production; suggests possible appreciation rise ●Good performance ●Decent styling ●Nicely outfitted interiors

AGAINST

Not really collectible yet ●Low appreciation now ●Special trim parts hard to get

SPECIFICATIONS

Length (in.) 215.3 (1964), 216.9 (1965)   **Wheelbase (in.)** 123.0
Weight (lbs.) 4019-3982   **Price (new)** $3603-3602

ENGINES

cid/type	bore x stroke	bhp	years
394/ohv V8	4.13×3.69	345	1964
425/ohv V8	4.13×3.98	370	1965

PRICES/PROJECTION

Restorable $500-1250 **Good** $1500-2500
Excellent $3000-4500 **5-year projection** +10%

Oldsmobile 4-4-2
1966-70

PRODUCTION

1966* 2d coupe 1430   **2d Sport Coupe** 3937

1966 4-4-2 Holiday 2-door hardtop

Holiday 2d hardtop 10,053	**2d hardtop** 3827
2d convertible 2750	**1967*** 2d Sport Coupe 5215
Holiday 2d hardtop 16,514	**2d convertible** 3104
1968 2d Sport Coupe 4282	**Holiday 2d**
hardtop 24,183	**2d convertible** 5142
1969 2d Sport Coupe 2475	**Holiday 2d hardtop** 19,587
2d convertible 4295	**1970 2d Sport Coupe** 1688
Holiday 2d hardtop 14,709	**2d convertible** 2933

*proportioned from total Cutlass production. Total 4-4-2 production 1966: 21,997   1967: 24,833

HISTORY

Oldsmobile's mid-size muscle machine, listed as a separate series beginning 1966. Continued with the 115-inch wheelbase and square-rigged styling initiated with the 1964 Cutlass redesign. More flowing body contours and a shorter 112-inch chassis for two-doors arrived for '68, and continued through 1970. Horsepower generally went up in each of these years, and 1970 brought a big 455 V8 option following GM's decision to rescind its unwritten rule against cars this size with less than 10 pounds per horsepower. Styling and equipment changes usually paralleled those in the tamer Cutlass models, but beefed-up suspension, air-induction hood, sporty striping, and other performance mods were reserved strictly for 4-4-2. A rare tri-power option with 360 bhp was listed for '66, then disappeared, making cars so equipped a rare find. There were also various package models with identifying W-30 or W-31 (based on the 350 V8) decals and special paint. Not included here but surely worth exploring are the special Hurst/Olds conversions that began with a Force-Air 455 model in 1968 packing 380 bhp. Power and performance started to slide with the 1971 models. The 4-4-2 reverted to an option package for '72, and held on as a shadow of its former self for a few years after that.

FOR

Fast but never overstressed ●Big, easy-revving engines ●Good handling ●Aggressive looks ●Strong appreciation potential

AGAINST

Thirsty, of course ●Cop-baiting appearance add-ons on some models ●Indifferent fit and finish in later years

1967 4-4-2 Holiday 2-door hardtop

SPECIFICATIONS

Length (in.) 204.2 (1966-67), 201.6 (1968), 201.9 (1969), 203.2 (1970) **Wheelbase (in.)** 115.0 (1966-67), 112.0 (1968-70)
Weight (lbs.) 3502-3740 **Price (new)** $2604-3567

ENGINES

cid/type	bore x stroke	bhp	years
350/ohv V8	4.06×3.38	325	1968-70
400/ohv V8	4.00×3.98	350/360	1966-67
455/ohv V8	4.13×4.25	365/370	1970

PRICES/PROJECTION

Restorable $750-1500 **Good** $1500-2500
Excellent $3000-5200 Add 15-20% for convertible
5-year projection +10%

Oldsmobile Toronado 1966-67

1966 Toronado Deluxe 2-door hardtop

PRODUCTION

1966 2d hardtop 6333 **Deluxe 2d hardtop** 34,630
1967 2d hardtop 1770 **Deluxe 2d hardtop** 20,020

HISTORY

A bold idea combined with intriguing styling. The first attempt to apply front wheel drive to a full-size American car since the mid-'30s Cord, and one of the most desirable Oldsmobiles ever produced. The drive system featured a split transmission with the torque converter behind the V8 engine and the gearbox located remotely under its left cylinder bank; the two were connected by a chain drive and sprocket. This arrangement allowed the heavy engine to sit over the front wheels, which resulted in a favorable weight distribution (54/46 front/rear) for such a large fwd car. Styling changed only in detail in the Toro's first two years, and was exquisite — every detail beautifully executed by GM design chief William L. Mitchell. Jutting front fenders, hidden headlamps, muscularly flared wheelarches, and cropped tail trailing a smooth fastback roofline makes the first-generation models unmistakeable even now. As it should be, the original '66 is more desirable, but

1967 Toronado 2-door hardtop

there's nothing wrong with a '67 if you're less concerned about "first of its kind" status.

FOR

A technological success that's with us yet • Not a Milestone, but could be • Exceptional traction, handling, performance • Distinctive styling (evokes Cord comparisons for some) • Luxury • Comfort • Strong appreciation

AGAINST

Complicated mechanical restoration • Not cheap to run • Heavy front tire wear • Rust-prone

SPECIFICATIONS

Length (in.) 211.0 **Wheelbase (in.)** 119.0
Weight (lbs.) 4310-4366 **Price (new)** $4617-4869

ENGINES

cid/type	bore x stroke	bhp	years
425/ohv V8	4.13×3.98	385	1966-67

PRICES/PROJECTION

1966 Restorable $1000-2000 **Good** $2000-3500
Excellent $3500-5000 Deduct 35% for 1967 models, 5% for non-Deluxe model both years. **5-year projection** +10%

Oldsmobile Hurst-Olds 1968-72

1972 Hurst-Olds 2-door hardtop

PRODUCTION

1968 515 **1969** 906 **1972** 629

HISTORY

A series of low-production conversions carried out by Hurst Performance Products on the contemporary Oldsmobile Cutlass 4-4-2. Began life as a personal car for George H. Hurst, president of Hurst-Campbell, Inc. The main difference between the factory's 4-4-2 and the H/O (Hurst said the initials stood for "Hairy Olds") was in the engine. Until 1970, GM had an unwritten corporate ban against production models smaller than full-size with less than 10 pounds per horsepower. Hurst stepped in where the factory dared not tread, substituting Oldsmobile's big-block 455 V8 for the top 400-cid unit from the ordinary 4-4-2. To this was added a fiberglass

1972 Hurst-Olds convertible (Pace Car Replica)

1968 Toronado 2-door hardtop

hood with forced-air induction (by means of mean-looking twin hood scoops), special grey and black paint, appropriate emblems, and a modified Turbo-Hydramatic transmission with Hurst's Dual-Gate floor-mount shifter that allowed full manual hold in any of the three gears. The full range of Cutlass options was available for the H/O. The package proved successful from a promotional standpoint, and returned for 1969 with 10 fewer horses, revised gold and white paint, and a new rear deck spoiler. Most H/Os in these years were two-door hardtops, but a few fixed-pillar coupes may have been given the treatment as well. When Olds offered the 455 as a production option for 1970, the H/O vanished. It then resurfaced in 1972, this time based on the plusher, heavier Cutlass Supreme platform. This package was little more than fancy trim, but it was available in both hardtop and convertible styles, some with pace car regalia to celebrate the H/O's selection for that year's Indy 500. These cars also had the top W-30 engine, fiberglass hood with functional scoops, and snazzy wheels and tires, but offered no extra performance over a properly optioned factory 4-4-2. Desirable today primarily for their high performance and limited-production appeal.

FOR

As for 1966-70 Cutlass 4-4-2, plus more performance (1968-69 models) and greater rarity

AGAINST

As for 1966-70 Cutlass 4-4-2, but harder to find, and even thirstier

SPECIFICATIONS

Length (in.) 201.6 (1968), 201.9 (1969), 203.6 (1972)
Wheelbase (in.) 112.0 (1968-69) 121.0 (1972)
Weight (lbs.) approx. 3500-3800   **Price (new)** $4760 original list price in 1969

ENGINES

cid/type	bore x stroke	bhp	years
455/ohv V8	4.13×4.25	380/390*	1968-69

*SAE gross; rated at 300 bhp net for 1972

PRICES/PROJECTION

Add 40% to 1966-70 Cutlass 4-4-2 values
5-year projection +10%

Oldsmobile Toronado 1968-70

PRODUCTION

1968 2d hardtop 3957   **Custom 2d hardtop** 22,497

1969 2d hardtop 3421   **Custom 2d hardtop** 25,073
1970 2d hardtop 2351   **Custom 2d hardtop** 23,082

HISTORY

Continuation of Oldsmobile's big front-driver, still on a 119-inch wheelbase. Aside from greater engine displacement, the main difference between these models and the 1966-67 editions is styling, which became progressively more "formal" and therefore less distinctive. The original jutting front fenders were blunted for '68, and overlaid with a massive divided grille. This face was retained for '69, but the tail was lengthened and an optional vinyl roof was available to destroy the unbroken line from C-pillar to lower body. Headlights were exposed for 1970 (some owners complained the headlight doors acted up on earlier models) and trim rearranged just for the sake of change. Underneath all the glitter, though, Toronado was still the same fine car, but it's the retrograde appearance changes that make these versions less desirable now. Toronado would grow to unbelievable proportions for 1971 and beyond, and these are most definitely not collectible.

FOR

More affordable ● Others as for 1966-67 Toronado

AGAINST

Hamfisted styling alterations and slower appreciation ● Others as for 1966-67 Toronado

SPECIFICATIONS

Length (in.) 221.4 (1968), 214.8 (1969), 214.3 (1970)
Wheelbase (in.) 119.0   **Weight (lbs.)** 4316-4386
Price (new) $4750-5216

ENGINES

cid/type	bore x stroke	bhp	years
455/ohv V8	4.13×4.25	375/400	1968-70

PRICES/PROJECTION

Restorable $750-1500 **Good** $1500-2500
Excellent $3000-4000 **5-year projection** +10%

Oldsmobile Hurst-Olds 1973-75

PRODUCTION

1973 1097   **1974** 1800   **1975** 2535

1974 Hurst-Olds coupe (Pace Car Replica)

1974 Hurst-Olds coupe (Pace Car Replica)

HISTORY

Continuation of the specialty mid-size Oldsmobiles created and marketed by Hurst, now based on the "Colonnade" bodyshell introduced for 1973. As before, the powertrain was built around the 455 big-block V8 and Turbo-Hydramatic with Dual-Gate shifter, embellished with special paint schemes, color-keyed road wheels, radial tires, and special H/O regalia. You had your choice of two colors in '73: white or black with contrasting gold trim. The following year, the H/O was again chosen for Indy Pace Car duty, and was issued with appropriate decals for the owner to apply. For the first time, buyers could have either the "W-30" big-block or a smaller 350 V8 (option code Y-77), a sign of the move away from performance in the wake of the first fuel crisis. Of the year's total production, 1420 units had the smaller V8. Performance was de-emphasized even more for 1975 in favor of a new T-top roof treatment with removable glass panels, a business Hurst was beginning to get into to make up for the sag in its aftermarket speed equipment sales. The '75 was based on the heavier, formal-roof Cutlass Supreme model rather than the semi-fastback Cutlass S used for the 1973-74 H/Os. De-tuned engines necessitated by stiffening emissions controls make these cars less fiery than their predecessors. Nevertheless, they are interesting newer models that attempted to keep the performance spirit of the '60s alive in an age when everything seemed to be working against development and sale of enthusiast cars. This plus low production make the last Hurst-built H/Os possible collector-car comers down the road.

FOR

Scarcity • Decent performance for the period • Many amenities • Eye-catching appearance • Last of a type

AGAINST

Somewhat fuelish • Collectibility questionable at present • Fewer mechanical differences from stock models than earlier H/Os

SPECIFICATIONS

Length (in.) 207.0 (1973), 211.5 (1974), 211.7 (1975)
Wheelbase (in.) 112.0   **Weight (lbs.)** NA; approx. 3850
Price (new) NA

1975 Hurst-Olds coupe

ENGINES

cid/type	bore x stroke	bhp	years
350/ohv V8	4.06×3.38	200*	1974-75
455/ohv V8	4.13×4.25	250*	1973-75

*est. SAE net

PRICES/PROJECTION

Restorable $1000-1500 **Good** $2000-3000
Excellent $3000-5900 **5-year projection** +25%

Packard Eight 1930-32

1930 DeLuxe Eight Model 745 phaeton (Eastern Packard Club)

PRODUCTION

1930 726 15,731, **733** 12,531, **734 Spdstr** 113, **740 Custom** 6200, **745 DeLuxe** 1789. **1931 826** 6009, **833** 6096, **840 Custom** 2035, **845 DeLuxe** 1310. **1932 901** 3922, **902** 3737, **903 DeLuxe** 955, **904 DeLuxe** 700.

HISTORY

The quintessential Classic. Powered by Packard's by-then traditional big inline eights. Offered with magnificent closed body types plus phaeton, roadster, and convertible styles as well as the exotic Speedster (1930). Individual customs by Dietrich and Packard were available for the 833, 840 and 904 chassis. Styling was strictly evolutionary and bore the same hallmarks, with streamlining increasingly evident as the years passed. Bijur automatic chassis lube and more power in 1931, improved all-synchromesh transmission in 1932.

FOR

Not one is anything less than majestic • Plethora of parts suppliers • Strong club support

AGAINST

Expensive • Trucky handling • High operating costs

SPECIFICATIONS

Length (in.) NA **Wheelbase (in.)** 127.5-147.5
Weight (lbs.) 3935-5635 **Price (new)** $2385-7250

ENGINES

cid/type	bore x stroke	bhp	years
320.0/L8	3.19×5.00	90-110	1930-32[1]
384.8/L8	3.50×5.00	106-120	1930-31[2]
384.8/L8	3.50×5.00	125-145	1930[3]
384.8/L8	3.50×5.00	135	1932[4]

[1]726, 733, 826, 833, 900, 901
[2]740, 745, 840, 845
[3]734
[4]903, 904

PRICES/PROJECTION

726/826/901 **Restorable** $3000-6000 **Good** $8000-15,000
Excellent $15,000-25,000 733/833/902 OPEN
Restorable $15,000-25,000 **Good** $30,000-50,000
Excellent $60,000-80,000. CLOSED deduct 50% for coupes,
70% for others. 734 SPEEDSTER RUNABOUT (Boat-tail)
Restorable $35,000-60,000 **Good** $75,000-110,000
Excellent $125,000-200,000, PHAETON Deduct 50%, CLOSED
Deduct 70%. 740/745/840/845/903/904 STD LINE OPEN
Restorable $20,000-50,000 **Good** $60,000-100,000
Excellent $100,000-165,000. CLOSED Deduct 60%.
INDIVIDUAL CUSTOM add 25% to above figures. Appraisal
assistance strongly recommended. **5-year projection** open
+20%, closed +10%

Packard 900 Light Eight & 1001 Eight 1932-33

1933 Eight "1000" touring sedan (pre-production)

PRODUCTION

1932 (900) 6750 **1933 (1001)** 1882

HISTORY

Packard's first response to the Depression. An attempt to expand
volume upward by extending price downward. Built on its own

shorter wheelbase, the Light Eight weighed significantly less than
the standard Eight but used its engine and thus had better performance. Priced at the upper end of the medium bracket and a quality
car, though not as nice-looking as other Packards. A bargain for
customers but cost almost as much to build as other models and
stole some of their sales. The factory hardly broke even, so the Light
Eight was dropped after but one year. The 1001 of 1933 was its
spiritual successor.

FOR

Performance • Club support • Pioneer Junior luxury trial, preceding Cadillac's downpriced LaSalle by two years and Lincoln
Zephyr by four, thus historically important

AGAINST

Staid styling • Body parts scarce • Slower to appreciate than
senior linemates

SPECIFICATIONS

Length (in.) NA **Wheelbase (in.)** 127.8 (900); 127.5 (1001)
Weight (lbs.) 3930-4115 (900); 4150-4335 (1001)
Price (new) $1895-1940 (900); $2150-2250 (1001)

ENGINES

cid/type	bore x stroke	bhp	years
320.0/L8	3.19×5.00	110-120	1932-33

PRICES/PROJECTION

OPEN **Restorable** $6000-10,000 **Good** $12,000-20,000
Excellent $25,000-40,000 CLOSED **Restorable** $2000-6000
Good $7000-14,000 **Excellent** $14,000-22,000
5-year projection +10%

Packard Twin Six/Twelve 1932-39

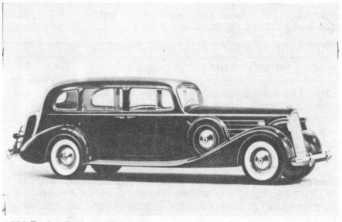

1936 Twelve 7-passenger sedan

PRODUCTION

1932 (Twin Six) 549 **1933** 520 **1934** 960 **1935** 721 **1936** 682
1937 1300 **1938** 566 **1939** 446

HISTORY

Initially conceived for a front-drive set-up that never happened. Had

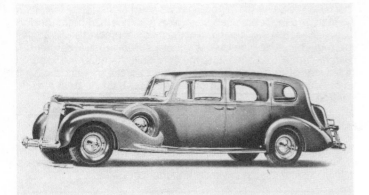

1938 Twelve 7-passenger limousine

to be massaged to give it superior performance to the Eights, since the original rationale was for a car below their rank. Nevertheless, whisper-quiet at 60-70 mph and smoothly refined at all except its flat-out 90 mph. Carried Packard's largest and lushest custom and semi-custom bodies on the longest wheelbases. Like the Super Eight, received independent front suspension and conventional (instead of Bijur) lube fittings in 1937, when it also commanded Packard's only wheelbase over 140 inches. Switched to the lighter Super Eight chassis in 1938 and lost the 144-inch chassis entirely. Shelved after 1939, when it was Packard's only custom-bodied line.

FOR

Unquestioned all-time Packard great • Smooth, satisfying performance • Outstanding quality, coachwork, engineering • A famous powerplant

AGAINST

Price • Limited availability • High restoration/operating costs

SPECIFICATIONS

Length (in.) NA **Wheelbase (in.)** 142.5, 147.5 (1932); 142.0, 147.0 (1933-34); 139.0, 144.0 (1935-37); 134.0, 139.0 (1938-39) **Weight (lbs.)** 4950-5950 **Price (new)** $3420-8510

ENGINES

cid/type	bore x stroke	bhp	years
445.5/V12	3.44×4.00	160	1932-34
473.0/V12	3.44×4.25	175	1935-39

PRICES/PROJECTION

Lack of frequent sales, often conducted privately between long-time collectors, prevents serious price guidelines model for model. The 1932-34 models are more desirable than later cars; among these, Dietrich phaetons and convertible victorias can approach $200,000 in authentic restored condition, and could cost $25,000 in "restorable" condition—providing there were any unrestored cars left, which is doubtful. Even standard open convertibles and phaetons will fetch $100,000 in fine condition. On the other hand, it should be possible to obtain a show-winning sedan or club sedan for as little as $35,000, although long-wheelbase sedans/limousines will be 30-40 percent higher. The minimum price for a closed car in restorable condition is about $4000.

Prices relax slightly for 1935-39, when individual customs largely disappeared from the ranks. Here, the most valuable Twelves are the sport phaeton and the later convertible victoria. The former can command $125,000, the latter $100,000 in prime condition. Neither could be had for much below $10,000, even in pieces. Other open models are 10-20 percent less, with even lower prices for 1938-39 models. Closed 1935-36 cars run from

$7500 (restorable) up to about $50,000 in top show condition. Later examples run from $5000 up to about $40,000.

As with Duesenbergs, there has been a moderate amount of body-swapping among Packards, so there may be more open cars now than the factory built. Pre-purchase appraisal is thus strongly recommended. **5-year projection** from +10% among closed cars up to +25% for the best open models.

Packard Super Eight 1933-36

1934 Super Eight Model 753 sedan (Eastern Packard Club)

PRODUCTION

1933 1300 **1934** 1920 **1935** 1392 **1936** 1330

HISTORY

A big, strong, beefy Classic. Shared much of the mighty Twelve's chassis and body componentry through 1936, then reduced to a much smaller, lighter, and more modern design. Gradually outdistanced by the Twelve in price, thus falls in a grey area among collectors. At the time, Packard increasingly concentrated on the medium-priced field exploited by the One Twenty. Individual customs offered 1933-34; wheelbases shrank in 1935 as Packard consolidated its senior models, although the LeBaron-built all-weather cabriolet was continued.

FOR

The Twelve's great looks for less money • Fine highway tourer • Excellent investment

AGAINST

Scarce and increasingly pricey • A lot of car to handle • Sadly, more often trailered than driven

SPECIFICATIONS

Length (in.) NA **Wheelbase (in.)** 135.0, 142.0 (1933); 135.0, 142.0, 147 (1934); 132.0, 139.0, 144.0 (1935-36) **Weight (lbs.)** 4490-5525 **Price (new)** $2750-7065

ENGINES

cid/type	bore x stroke	bhp	years
384.8/L8	3.50×5.00	145-150	1933-36

PRICES/PROJECTION

1933-34 OPEN **Restorable** $10,000-25,000 **Good** $35,000-50,000 **Excellent** $65,000-115,000 CLOSED

Deduct 50% INDIVIDUAL CUSTOM Add 15%. 1935-36 OPEN **Restorable** $8000-18,000 **Good** $25,000-35,000 **Excellent** $40,000-60,000 CLOSED Deduct 15% Appraisal and club expertise recommended. **5-year projection** +15%. See also general remarks under Packard Twelve.

Packard One Twenty/Eight 1935-39

1936 One Twenty 5-passenger sedan

PRODUCTION

1935 24,955 **1936** 55,042 **1937** 50,100 **1938** 22,624 **1939** 17,647

HISTORY

Historically the most important Packard of the 1930s. Saved the company at the time, though continuing emphasis on similar middle priced products in the postwar years ultimately cost Packard its life. Sold very well with traditional styling, straightforward specifications, and a modest but reliable and smooth L-head eight. Designated Eight for 1938 only. Interesting models include the post-1935 convertible sedan (called "Dietrich" but no relation), a wagon, and long-wheelbase sedans and customs (from 1937). Long subject to an unfair press as a "cheap Packard," but offered good value for money, excellent performance, and high quality. Without it, the company would have expired by 1936.

FOR

The best all-around touring Packard of the 1930s • The most affordable Packard Eight from the same period • Traditional PMCC styling • Plenty of parts suppliers • Very popular among collectors

AGAINST

Still haunted by the "cheap Packard" label • Lacks Classic status,

1940 One Twenty touring sedan (1939 similar)

save custom bodies • Closed models cannot be called beautiful

SPECIFICATIONS

Length (in.) NA **Wheelbase (in.)** 120.0 (1935-36); 120.0, 138.0 (1937); 127.0, 139.0, 148.0 (1938); 127.0, 148.0 (1939) **Weight (lbs.)** 3340-5225 **Price (new)** $945-5385

ENGINES

cid/type	bore x stroke	bhp	years
257.2/L8	3.25×3.88	110	1935
282.0/L8	3.25×4.35	120	1936-39

PRICES/PROJECTION

OPEN **Restorable** $3000-8000 **Good** $10,000-18,000 **Excellent** $18,000-32,000 WAGONS deduct 35% OTHER CLOSED **Restorable** $2000-4000 **Good** $4000-8000 **Excellent** $8000-16,000. ROLLSON CUSTOMS (1938) **Restorable** $5000-15,000 **Good** $20,000-35,000 **Excellent** $35,000-60,000. **5-year projection** +15%

Packard Super Eight 1937-39

1939 Super Eight touring sedan (Eastern Packard Club)

PRODUCTION

1937 5793 **1938** 2478 **1939** 3962

HISTORY

Far more successful than concurrent Twelves, probably because it sold for much less, and vastly downsized from early-Thirties models in both seen and unseen places. Independent front suspension, a smaller eight, grease nipples instead of Bijur lubrication, and hydraulic brakes were featured, and the old "suicide" front doors were eliminated. Also more streamlined in keeping with current trends (the radiator was raked 30 degrees now) but retained the "Packard look." Weight was cut almost as dramatically as on GM's smaller 1977 full-size cars.

FOR

Excellent driving machines • Strong club support—very popular • Parts and service not a problem • Almost affordable by mere mortals

AGAINST

Classic enthusiasts often look askance at the fact that they are not locomotives, like earlier Supers

SPECIFICATIONS

Length (in.) NA **Wheelbase (in.)** 127.0, 134.0, 139.0 (1937-38); 127.0, 148.0 (1939) **Weight (lbs.)** 3860-5360
Price (new) $1650-7475

ENGINES

cid/type	bore x stroke	bhp	years
320.0/L8	3.19×5.00	130-135	1937-39

PRICES/PROJECTION

OPEN **Restorable** $8000-15,000 **Good** $20,000-35,000
Excellent $35,000-50,000 LEBARONs add 10% CLOSED deduct 50%. **5-year projection** +10% See also general remarks under Packard Twelve.

Packard Custom Super Eight 180 by Darrin 1940-42

1940 Custom Super Eight 180 convertible sedan by Darrin

PRODUCTION

less than 200 (est.)

HISTORY

Howard A. "Dutch" Darrin began building rakish convertibles on the Packard Eight chassis in 1937. These became regular catalog items in the senior series for the years here, along with a sport sedan offered for 1940 only. A convertible sedan was available on the 138-inch wheelbase through 1941, and the 127-inch-wheelbase convertible victoria—the most exotic and desirable of these cars—was available in all three years.

FOR

One of the great Classics • Splendid styling • Super luxury

AGAINST

Formidable prices • Expensive to restore • Structural weaknesses

1940 Custom Super Eight 180 convertible victoria by Darrin

SPECIFICATIONS

Length (in.) NA **Wheelbase (in.)** 127.0/138.0
Weight (lbs.) 3920-4121 (victoria), 4050 (conv sedan), 4490 (sport sedan) **Price (new)** $4595 (victoria), 6332 (conv sedan), 4795 (sport sedan)

ENGINES

cid/type	bore x stroke	bhp	years
356/L8	3.50×4.63	160/165	1940-42

PRICES/PROJECTION

Restorable $10,000-20,000 **Good** $30,000-50,000
Excellent $50,000-80,000 Deduct 10% for convertible sedan, 20% for sport sedan **5-year projection** +5%

Packard Custom Super Eight 180 by Rollson 1940-42

1940 Custom Super Eight 180 town car by Rollson

PRODUCTION

less than 100 (est.)

HISTORY

Among the last Packards with custom coachwork—in this case an all-weather cabriolet on the 138-inch wheelbase and a town car on the 148-inch wheelbase by the Rollson (formerly Rollston) company. These senior Packards did not adopt the flush-sided Clipper styling in 1942 as did the One Eighty sedans. Their classic lines preserved traditional Packard appearance from the marque's golden age. Among closed Packards from this period, they were the most elegant and luxurious, selling for the equivalent of $50,000 and up in today's money.

FOR

Superb workmanship ●CCCA Classic status ●Rare and desirable

AGAINST

Expensive to acquire and maintain

SPECIFICATIONS

Length (in.) NA **Wheelbase (in.)** 138.0/148.0
Weight (lbs.) 4050-4075 (cabriolet), 4175-4200 (town car)
Price (new) $4473-4792 (cabriolet), $4599-4889 (town car)

ENGINES

cid/type	bore x stroke	bhp	years
356/L8	3.50×4.63	160/165	1940-42

PRICES/PROJECTION

Restorable $5000-10,000 **Good** $15,000-30,000
Excellent $45,000-60,000 **5-year projection** +5%

Packard One Ten (and equivalent) open models 1940-42

1941 One Ten convertible coupe

PRODUCTION

1940 750   **1941** 500   **1942** 500 (all est.)

HISTORY

The most prized model in the six-cylinder companion series of the One Twenty line, built on a 5-inch shorter wheelbase. Like the Eights, this convertible retained a traditional upright Packard appearance when other body styles went to the more streamlined "Clipper" styling for 1942. Unlike the One Twenty, no convertible sedan was offered.

FOR

More affordable than comparable One Twentys ●Others as for 1940-42 One Twenty

AGAINST

Far less masterful on the road than One Twenty ●Less impressive to look at, too

SPECIFICATIONS

Length (in.) NA **Wheelbase (in.)** 122.0
Weight (lbs.) 3200-3315 **Price (new)** (new) $1104-1375

ENGINES

cid/type	bore x stroke	bhp	years
245.3/L6	3.50×4.25	100/105	1940-42

PRICES/PROJECTION

Restorable $2500-5000 **Good** $6000-9000
Excellent $15,000-23,000 **5-year projection** +5%

Packard One Twenty (and equivalent) open models 1940-42

1942 One Twenty convertible coupe

PRODUCTION

1940 1500   **1941** 1000   **1942** 1000 (all est.)

HISTORY

The much sought-after open models in Packard's junior series. Offered as a standard or Deluxe convertible coupe and convertible sedan for 1940. The convertible sedan was dropped the following year. For 1942, the One Twenty designation disappeared and Clipper styling was applied to most of the Packard line, leaving a Deluxe convertible as the only small Packard Eight with "traditional" styling. The One Twenty was not, as is often assumed, a cheap car; in price it compared most closely with Buick and Chrysler. Its 282-cid straight eight was silky smooth in operation, and the car had performance and roadability of a high order.

FOR

The most affordable prewar Packard Eight convertibles ●Classic lines will always be in style ●Fine performance ●Traditional Packard quality

AGAINST

A bit pricey ●Lowly reputation among the uninitiated

1942 One Twenty convertible coupe

SPECIFICATIONS

Length (in.) NA   **Wheelbase (in.)** 127.0
Weight (lbs.) 3540-4000   **Price (new)** $1277-1753

ENGINES

cid/type	bore x stroke	bhp	years
282/L8	3.25×4.25	120/125	1940-42

PRICES/PROJECTION

Restorable $3000-6000   **Good** $7500-15,000
Excellent $20,000-25,000   **5-year projection** +10%

Packard Super Eight 160 open models 1940-41

1941 Super Eight 160 convertible sedan

PRODUCTION

less than 500 per year (est.)

HISTORY

The mildly less luxurious, standard-body series sold alongside the One Eighty in these years. Offered with the same choice of wheelbases and Packard's smooth, powerful nine-main-bearing 356-cid straight eight. Four open styles—standard and Deluxe convertible coupe and convertible sedan—were offered only on the 127-inch chassis in both years. Like One Eightys, all One Sixtys are highly desirable. The open versions naturally generate the greatest interest and command the highest prices on today's collector market.

FOR

Not designated Classics, but ought to be ●Traditional Packard four-square styling ●Smooth performance ●Convertible allure

AGAINST

More "standard" than the custom-body One Eightys ●Very costly

SPECIFICATIONS

Length (in.) NA   **Wheelbase (in.)** 127.0
Weight (lbs.) 3825-4140   **Price (new)** $1797-2225

ENGINES

cid/type	bore x stroke	bhp	years
356/L8	3.50×4.63	160	1940-41

PRICES/PROJECTION

Restorable $5000-7000   **Good** $12,000-20,000
Excellent $35,000-50,000   Add 10-20% for convertible sedan
5-year projection +10%

Packard Clipper 1941

1941 Clipper 4-door sedan

PRODUCTION

16,600

HISTORY

The first car to combine modern flush-sided styling with the Packard nameplate, replacing straight lines with curves. The original design seems to have come from Dutch Darrin, but detail development was the work of Packard's own Werner Gubitz. Offered only as a four-door sedan in its debut year on the 127-inch-wheelbase chassis, and was well-received by the public. The following year, most Packards from One Ten to One Eighty acquired similar styling. Convertibles were the notable exceptions (hence their collectibility today as preservers of the "old order") along with formal models and certain commercial bodies.

FOR

Historical importance ●Fine engineering ●Good performance ●Packard panache

AGAINST

Collector recognition still limited ● In short supply today

SPECIFICATIONS

Length (in.) 203.0   **Wheelbase (in.)** 127.0   **Weight (lbs.)** 3725
Price (new) $1420

ENGINES

cid/type	bore x stroke	bhp	years
282/L8	3.25×4.25	125	1941

PRICES/PROJECTION

Restorable $1500-2500 **Good** $3000-5000
Excellent $6000-8000 **5-year projection** +10%

Packard Clipper 180 1942

1942 Clipper 180 4-door sedan

PRODUCTION

600 (est.)

HISTORY

The top of the standard-body prewar Packard line. "Clipper" styling applied to this year's senior One Sixty and One Eighty sedans and club coupes resulted in handsome cars that are still enviable today. The One Eighty sedan was priced at $2196, making it considerably more expensive than its One Sixty linemate and about 50% costlier than the '41 Clipper. The interior offered fine carpeting, Bedford cord upholstery, and two types of woodgraining on side panels. The big 356 straight eight was as smooth and powerful as ever.

FOR

The most luxurious prewar Packard ●Smooth, comfortable tourer ●Elegant looks

AGAINST

Extremely scarce, but little else

SPECIFICATIONS

Length (in.) 212.0 **Wheelbase (in.)** 127.0
Weight (lbs.) 4010-4030 **Price (new)** $2099-2196

ENGINES

cid/type	bore x stroke	bhp	years
356/L8	3.50×4.63	165	1942

PRICES/PROJECTION

Restorable $2000-3000 **Good** $3500-5000
Excellent $7500-10,000 **5-year projection** +10%

Packard Custom Super Clipper 1946-47

1946 Custom Super Clipper 4-door sedan

PRODUCTION

Total sedans and coupes 7162
Total long-wheelbase models 3081

HISTORY

Postwar continuation of the elegant Clipper-based 1942 models at their most luxurious. The 127-inch-wheelbase four-door sedan and club coupe were now joined by a seven-passenger sedan and limousine built for Packard by the Henney body company on the long 148-inch chassis. Though these used basically stock mechanicals, their body panels were somewhat different. Many experts today think this well-balanced design could have carried Packard through to its first complete postwar restyle, which took place for the 1951 model year. But a modified, bloated look replaced it for 1948.

FOR

One of the few cars with both Classic and Milestone rankings ●Timeless design; seems to look better every year ●Superb quality ●Smooth performance

AGAINST

Henney body panels in short supply

SPECIFICATIONS

Length (in.) 204.0/225.0 **Wheelbase (in.)** 127.0/148.0
Weight (lbs.) 3384-4090/4870-4920
Price (new) $2913-3449/$4332-4668

1946 Custom Super Clipper 4-door sedan

ENGINES

cid/type	bore x stroke	bhp	years
356/L8	3.50×4.63	165	1946-47

PRICES/PROJECTION

STANDARD MODELS **Restorable** $1500-2250
Good $3000-4000 **Excellent** $5000-7000 HENNEY MODELS
Restorable $2000-3000 **Good** $4000-6000
Excellent $6000-9000 **5-year projection** +5%

Packard Custom Eight 1948-50

1948 Custom Eight 4-door sedan

PRODUCTION

1948 2d/4d sedans 5936   **2d convertible** 1105
long-wheelbase sedan/limo 230   **chassis** 1941
1949a 2d/4d sedans 2990   **2d convertible** 213
long-wheelbase sedan/limo 50   **1949b 2d/4d sedans** 973
2d convertible 68   **chassis** 160   **1950 2d/4d sedans** 707
2d convertible 77   **chassis** 244

HISTORY

Packard's top-line series during the "elephantine" styling era, benefiting greatly in appearance from its long wheelbase. Also the last Packards powered by the venerable 356-cid nine-main-bearing straight eight. A full range of typically Packard appointments was fitted here, including Amboyna burl woodgraining, leather-piped Bedford cord upholstery, Mosstred carpeting from New York's Shelton Looms, a unique fore/aft headliner on the Twenty-Second Series 1948-49a models, and "Ultramatic Drive" on the Twenty-Third Series 1949b-1950 cars. Initial 1948 production almost completely met demand, which suggests Packard's market had changed considerably from the luxury-only orientation of prewar times. The long sedans and limousines were dropped from the Twenty-Third Series, as was the fastback two-door club sedan.

FOR

Packard's best in this period ● Outstanding construction ● Comfort ● Smooth performance

AGAINST

The ugliest Packards of the postwar era (though Customs fared better than lesser models)

SPECIFICATIONS

Length (in.) 204.0/225.0 **Wheelbase (in.)** 127.0/148.0
Weight (lbs.) 4110-4530 (lwb: 4860-4880)
Price (new) $3700-4520 (lwb: $4704/4868)

ENGINES

cid/type	bore x stroke	bhp	years
356/L8	3.50×4.63	160	1948-50

PRICES/PROJECTION

Restorable $1200-1800 **Good** $2000-3800
Excellent $5000-7000 Add 100% for convertible, 25% for limousine **5-year projection** +5%

Packard Eight Station Sedan 1948-50

1948 Eight Station Sedan (wagon)

PRODUCTION

3864

HISTORY

An interesting sedan-like station wagon designed along the lines of the streamlined 1941-42 Chrysler Town & Country. Sheetmetal was shared with the standard Eight ahead of the firewall, and most of the rear body was metal. Ash framing on the bodysides was decorative, but it did have a structural purpose for the tailgate area. Priced just $300 below the Custom Eight, and didn't sell well. Most Station Sedans built were 1948s; those sold through 1950 were simply retitled leftovers.

FOR

The most desirable junior Packard of the period ● Fine construction quality ● Historically important ● Not too costly

AGAINST

"Pregnant elephant" styling ● Expensive to buy and maintain ● Not easy to find

SPECIFICATIONS

Length (in.) 204.6 **Wheelbase (in.)** 120.0 **Weight (lbs.)** 4075
Price (new) $3425-3449

ENGINES

cid/type	bore x stroke	bhp	years
288/L8	3.50×3.75	130/135	1948-50

PRICES/PROJECTION

PRICES/PROJECTION

Restorable $3000-4000 **Good** $4000-7000
Excellent $8000-12,000 **5-year projection** +15%

Packard Super Eight DeLuxe 1949-50

1949 Super Eight DeLuxe club sedan

PRODUCTION

1949 2d/4d sedans 3000 (est.) **2d convertible** 685
long-wheelbase sedan/limo 4 **1950 2d/4d sedans** 2000 (est.)
2d convertible 600

HISTORY

The big reason why Custom Eight sales dropped so drastically after 1948. Shared the grille style and wheelbase of the costlier Custom, and you could even order its cloisonné-decorated hubcaps from the dealer. The 1949-50 Customs were not as richly trimmed as the '48s, and the Super's 327-cid straight eight was almost as smooth as the big 356 unit. No wonder many buyers saw little reason to pick the Custom and pay $700-900 more.

FOR

Custom Eight looks at a lower price still its biggest attraction ● Better performance than heavier Custom despite smaller engine

AGAINST

As for 1948-50 Custom Eight

SPECIFICATIONS

Length (in.) 211.7/225.7 **Wheelbase (in.)** 127.0/141.0
Weight (lbs.) 3855-4260 (lwb: 4600-4620)
Price (new) $2894-2919 (lwb: $3950-4100)

ENGINES

cid/type	bore x stroke	bhp	years
327/L8	3.50×4.25	150	1949-50

PRICES/PROJECTION

Restorable $800-1500 **Good** $1500-3500
Excellent $4500-6000 Add 100% for convertible or long-wheelbase models **5-year projection** +10%

Packard Patrician 1951-54

1951 Patrician 400 4-door sedan

PRODUCTION

1951 9001 **1952** 3975 **1953** 7456 **1954** 2760

HISTORY

Packard's newly named top-line standard sedan in the early '50s. Along with other models, carried the firm's first complete redesign since the Clipper of a decade earlier. The shape, which designer John Reinhart named "high pockets," didn't wear particularly well, however. There was no criticizing the Patrician's integrity, though—it was beautifully built, comfortable in the Packard tradition, and surprisingly fast. Most buyers thought it dull and uninteresting next to the tailfinned Cadillac V8s and the very roadable Lincolns of these years, and spent their money accordingly.

FOR

Top-of-the-line ● Quality ● Luxury ● Another Packard Milestone

AGAINST

Rust-prone ● 1954 gear-start Ultramatic gave frequent trouble

SPECIFICATIONS

Length (in.) 218.0 **Wheelbase (in.)** 127.0
Weight (lbs.) 4100-4190 **Price (new)** $3662-3890

ENGINES

cid/type	bore x stroke	bhp	years
317/L8	3.50×4.25	155/180	1951-53
359/L8	3.56×4.50	212	1954

PRICES/PROJECTION

Restorable $1000-2000 **Good** $2500-4500
Excellent $4500-7000 **5-year projection** no change

Packard Patrician formal sedan by Derham 1951-54

PRODUCTION

approx. 25 per year

1953 Patrician formal sedan by Derham

HISTORY

Longtime Packard body builders Derham and Company of Rosemont, Pennsylvania answered PMCC president James Nance's call for a formal sedan by adapting a leather (occasionally canvas) padded top and a smaller rear window to the basic Patrician sedan. The result was a very "private" four-door that managed to capture the flavor of the old coachbuilding days before the war.

FOR

They made so few

AGAINST

And you'll pay accordingly

SPECIFICATIONS

Length (in.) 218.0   **Wheelbase (in.)** 127.0   **Weight (lbs.)** 4335
Price (new) $6531

ENGINES

cid/type	bore x stroke	bhp	years
317/L8	3.50×4.25	155/180	1951-53
359/L8	3.56×4.50	212	1954

PRICES/PROJECTION

Restorable $1000-1500 **Good** $3000-5000
Excellent $6000-8500 **5-year projection** +25%

Packard Caribbean 1953-54

1953 Caribbean convertible

PRODUCTION

1953 750   **1954** 400

1954 Caribbean convertible

HISTORY

Packard's answer to the Cadillac Eldorado, both in concept and marketing strategy. A limited-production, ultra-posh convertible styled by Richard A. Teague, who took as his inspiration the Henney-built Pan American show cars of 1952. Built on the 122-inch-wheelbase chassis and basic convertible body, but with a more rakish appearance thanks to full rear wheel cutouts and distinctive chrome trim. Powered by Packard's five-main-bearing 327 straight eight initially, then switched to the nine-main unit with displacement increased to 359 cid. The most luxurious and sporting Packards in a generation.

FOR

Dashing looks • Ample comfort • One of the most desirable postwar Packards • High appreciation potential

AGAINST

Hefty prices, and rising all the time

SPECIFICATIONS

Length (in.) 220.3   **Wheelbase (in.)** 122.0
Weight (lbs.) 4265-4660   **Price (new)** $5210-6100

ENGINES

cid/type	bore x stroke	bhp	years
327/L8	3.50×4.25	180	1953
359/L8	3.56×4.50	212	1954

PRICES/PROJECTION

Restorable $2000-4000 **Good** $5000-8000
Excellent $10,000-16,000 **5-year projection** +20%

Packard Clipper Sportster 1953-54

PRODUCTION

1336

HISTORY

An interesting member of the lower-priced Packard line. Offered hardtop-style appointments (two-tone paint and nice interior) without the pillarless roof at a reasonable price, only $185 above the basic Clipper DeLuxe club sedan. Eclipsed in its second year by a true pillarless model, the Panama, in the Clipper Super series.

FOR

Uncommon • Affordable

AGAINST

Trim on the plain side • Are there any left?

SPECIFICATIONS

Length (in.) 213.3   **Wheelbase (in.)** 122.0
Weight (lbs.) 3595-3720   **Price (new)** $2805-2830

ENGINES

cid/type	bore x stroke	bhp	years
327/L8	3.50×4.25	165	1954
288/L8	3.50×3.75	150	1953

PRICES/PROJECTION

Restorable $800-1500   **Good** $2000-3000
Excellent $3500-5500   **5-year projection** +10%

Packard Caribbean 1955-56

1956 Caribbean 2-door hardtop

PRODUCTION

1955 500   **1956 2d hardtop** 263   **2d convertible** 276

HISTORY

Continuation of the posh Packard sporty car, now based on the new 1955 platform with updated styling and revised chassis featuring torsion bar suspension. Also new: Packard's first overhead valve

1956 Caribbean convertible

V8, putting out an impressive 275 bhp in Caribbean tune from its 352 cid. A bore increase the following year brought output up to a rousing 310 bhp. Ultramatic Drive was improved for greater reliability. The last of the great open Packards, these models sported flashy three-tone paint jobs, reversible cloth or leather front seat covers (1956), a broad eggcrate grille, and distinctive "cathedral" taillights. Broken out into a separate series for '56, when a companion two-door hardtop was fielded in addition to the usual softtop. Remarkably, in view of the number built, these models are no costlier today than earlier Caribbeans, though styling may be a factor here.

FOR

High on the want list of postwar Packard fanciers • Satisfying road car • Low-production appeal • High-yield investment

AGAINST

Ultramatic and suspension know-how hard to find • Rust problems • Gaudy styling in some collectors' opinion

SPECIFICATIONS

Length (in.) 218.5   **Wheelbase (in.)** 127.0
Weight (lbs.) 4590-4755   **Price (new)** $5495-5995

ENGINES

cid/type	bore x stroke	bhp	years
352/ohv V8	4.00×3.50	275	1955
374/ohv V8	4.13×3.50	310	1956

PRICES/PROJECTION

Restorable $2500-5000   **Good** $6000-10,000
Excellent $10,000-17,000 Deduct 35% for 1956 hardtop.
5-year projection +15%

Packard Clipper Constellation 1955

1955 Clipper Constellation 2-door hardtop

PRODUCTION

6672

HISTORY

An attractive hardtop with the new ohv V8 and torsion-level suspension from the senior Packards. Engine output was discreetly rated at 15 bhp less, however. Offered this year in the new Clipper Custom series, which then became part of the lineup for the separate Clipper make for '56 (see Clipper). The most desirable of the smaller '55 Packards then and now.

FOR

Nice styling • Fine ride • Good performance • Rarity • Strong appreciation potential

AGAINST

Thirsty •Some body parts hard to find

SPECIFICATIONS

Length (in.) 214.8 **Wheelbase (in.)** 122.0 **Weight (lbs.)** 3865
Price (new) $3076

ENGINES

cid/type	bore x stroke	bhp	years
352/ohv V8	4.00×3.50	245	1955

PRICES/PROJECTION

Restorable $600-1000 **Good** $1000-2500
Excellent $3500-5800 **5-year projection** +15%

Packard Four Hundred 1955-56

1955 Four Hundred 2-door hardtop

PRODUCTION

1955 7206 **1956** 3224

HISTORY

New two-door hardtop derivative of the Patrician sedan, built on the longer of Packard's two wheelbases in these years. A pillarless roof and more frequent use of two-toning gave it a sportier look. Otherwise identical with the four-door.

FOR

As for 1955-56 Patrician, plus hardtop sportiness and stronger appreciation

AGAINST

As for 1955-56 Patrician

SPECIFICATIONS

Length (in.) 217.8 **Wheelbase (in.)** 127.0
Weight (lbs.) 4080-4250 **Price (new)** $3930-4190

ENGINES

cid/type	bore x stroke	bhp	years
352/ohv V8	4.00×3.50	260	1955
374/ohv V8	4.13×3.50	290	1956

PRICES/PROJECTION

Restorable $1500-3000 **Good** $4000-7000
Excellent $7500-9800 **5-year projection** +10%

Packard Patrician 1955-56

1956 Patrician 4-door sedan

PRODUCTION

1955 9127 **1956** 3775

HISTORY

Packard's top-line four-door, continuing from previous years with a clever facelift by Dick Teague. The result throughout the line was a Packard that managed to look less like the five-year-old design it was and more like the competition. Bold grillework, cathedral taillights, advanced torsion bar suspension with self-leveling, and a new ohv V8 were shared with the sporty Caribbeans, but exterior and interior trim were appropriately more muted in keeping with the Patrician's upper-class image.

FOR

Period styling •Smooth performance •Luxury •Widely sought today •Low production •Packard nameplate

AGAINST

Indifferent assembly quality •Occasionally suffers from rust

SPECIFICATIONS

Length (in.) 217.4 **Wheelbase (in.)** 127.0
Weight (lbs.) 4045-4275 **Price (new)** $3890-4160

ENGINES

cid/type	bore x stroke	bhp	years
352/ohv V8	4.00×3.50	260	1955
374/ohv V8	4.13×3.50	290	1956

PRICES/PROJECTION

Restorable $1000-2000 **Good** $2500-3500
Excellent $4000-7000 **5-year projection** +10%

Packard Executive
1956

1956 Executive 2-door hardtop

PRODUCTION

4d sedan 1784   **2d hardtop** 1031

HISTORY

New bottom-line series in the senior Packard line, intended to bridge a small price gap created when Clipper became a separate make this year. Built on the Clipper's shorter 122-inch wheelbase, but had senior front-end styling and decklid treatment. Power was provided by the top engine from '55, the 275-bhp 352 V8.

FOR

A genuine Packard that's still affordable • Clean period styling • Good performance • Exceptional torsion-level suspension • Strong appreciation potential

AGAINST

Low-line status • Tends to rust • Fuel thirst • Body parts now scarce

SPECIFICATIONS

Length (in.) 214.8   **Wheelbase (in.)** 122.0   **Weight (lbs.)** 4185 (either model)   **Price (new)** $3465/3560

ENGINES

cid/type	bore x stroke	bhp	years
352/ohv V8	4.00×3.50	275	1956

PRICES/PROJECTION

SEDAN **Restorable** $400-800 **Good** $800-2000
Excellent $2500-5000 Add 25% for hardtop
5-year projection +5%

Packard Clipper
1957

PRODUCTION

4d sedan 3940   **4d wagon** 869

HISTORY

The so-called "Packardbaker," based on this year's Studebaker President and built alongside it at South Bend following the deci-

1957 Clipper Country Sedan wagon

sion to close Packard's Detroit factory. These cars were issued partly to meet dealer franchise requirements and partly with the hope that demand for a big luxury Packard would eventually return. Styling, evolved by Dick Teague, made clever use of traditional Packard "cues," like '56 Clipper taillights and a dash similar in appearance to the 1955-56 control board. Body, chassis, and running gear were pure Studebaker, however. The once broad lineup was thinned to just two models, the four-door Town Sedan and four-door Country Sedan wagon, in an obvious effort to cut production costs. The only engine listed was the familiar Studebaker 289 with 275 bhp courtesy of a McCulloch supercharger, so performance was respectable despite the car's humble origins. These were not Packards in the true sense, though they were very good Studebakers.

FOR

An historical footnote • Good quality • Performance • Better-looking than comparable '58s • Scarce yet affordable

AGAINST

McCulloch supercharger notoriously fickle • Front fender rust • Badge-engineered character • Not likely to go up in value

SPECIFICATIONS

Length (in.) 211.8 (sedan), 204.8 (wagon)
Wheelbase (in.) 120.5 (sedan), 116.5 (wagon)
Weight (lbs.) 3570/3650   **Price (new)** $3212/3384

ENGINES

cid/type	bore x stroke	bhp	years
289/ohv V8	3.56×3.63	275	1957

PRICES/PROJECTION

Restorable $500-800 **Good** $800-1800
Excellent $2000-3500 Add 10% for wagon
5-year projection no change

Packard
Hawk
1958

PRODUCTION

588

HISTORY

One of four Studebaker-based models fielded in Packard's swansong year, and easily the most interesting and collectible. Styling

1958 Hawk 2-door hardtop

was a severe facelift, created by Duncan McCrae, of Studebaker's original 1953 "Loewy coupe" body. It consisted of a low, jutting "mouth" grille, sweeping mylar-adorned tailfins, simulated spare tire embossed into the trunklid, and padded section that some called armrests, on the exterior door panels. Inside, the Hawk was all business, with fine leather upholstery and a no-nonsense dash with full instrumentation. The bizarre styling was influenced by Roy Hurley of Curtiss-Wright, then Studebaker-Packard's benefactor. Power was supplied by the McCulloch-supercharged version of the Studebaker 289 V8. A four-door sedan and wagon and two-door hardtop were also offered halfheartedly before the decision was made to cease Packard production in June, 1958. In all, a sad ending for one of America's finest marques.

FOR

Much better than its looks suggest • Exceptional performance and luxury • Last of the line • Low-production appeal

AGAINST

Studebaker fender rust problem • Vacuum-cleaner frontal styling • Only modest appreciation potential

SPECIFICATIONS

Length (in.) 204.6 **Wheelbase (in.)** 120.5 **Weight (lbs.)** 3470
Price (new) $3995

ENGINES

cid/type	bore x stroke	bhp	years
289/ohv V8	3.56×3.63	275	1958

PRICES/PROJECTION

Restorable $1000-2500 **Good** $3000-5000
Excellent $5000-8000 **5-year projection** +20%

Pierce-Arrow Eight 1930-38

PRODUCTION

1930 6795* **1932** 2284* **1933** 1527 **1934** 1358* **1935** 523
1936 636 **1937** 121 **1938** 12* (*est.)

HISTORY

Acquired in 1928 by Studebaker, just in time for the Depression, Pierce spent most of the '30s in a rear-guard action for survival, a fight it didn't win. The company became independent with Studebaker's early-1933 bankruptcy, but had so heavily invested in the new Twelve that it was caught in a cash-flow vice. Nevertheless the straight-eight Pierce-Arrow was a fine product, deftly engineered to operate like a Swiss watch, though the bodies were on the ponderous side. The line was restyled and more streamlined in 1934 and again in 1936, but losses continued and production wound down. Pierce declared final bankruptcy in December 1937 and was liquidated the following year.

FOR

The panache of a blue-chip nameplate • Excellent support via Pierce-Arrow Society • Finely engineered high-speed touring cars • Strong investment potential

AGAINST

Expensive to acquire and operate • Scarce, particularly open models • Engine parts increasingly hard to come by.

SPECIFICATIONS

Length (in.) NA **Wheelbase (in.)** 132.0-144.0 (1930); 134.0-147.0 (1931); 137.0/142.0 (1932); 136.0/139.0 (1933); 136.0/139.0/144.0 (1934-38) **Weight (lbs.)** 4290-5600
Price (new) $2495-6400

ENGINES

cid/type	bore x stroke	bhp	years
340.0/L8	3.38×4.75	115	1930-31
366.0/L8	3.50×4.75	125/135	1930-35
385.0/L8	3.50×5.00	132/150	1930-31, 1934-38

PRICES/PROJECTION

1930-32 OPEN **Restorable** $12,500-25,000
Good $35,000-60,000 **Excellent** $50,000-95,000 Add 15% for Models A/41/54. CLOSED **Restorable** $7000-15,000
Good $20,000-35,000 **Excellent** $33,000-40,000 Add 10% for Models A/41/54. 1933-38 OPEN **Restorable** $9000-18,000
Good $20,000-45,000 **Excellent** $45,000-70,000 Deduct 30% for closed. **5-year projection** +20%

Pierce-Arrow Twelve 1932-38

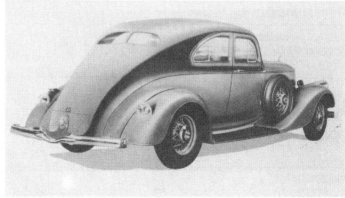

1934 Model 1240 Silver Arrow sedan

PRODUCTION

1932 199 **1933** 771 **1934** 377 **1935** 204 **1936** 206 **1937** 43
1938 12 (est. by Pierce-Arrow Society)

HISTORY

Engineered by Pierce's famous Karl M. Wise. Engine initially offered in two sizes, but the smaller version was quickly dropped owing to its lackluster performance. Enlarged in 1933 for more power (one averaged nearly 113 mph at Bonneville over 24 hours). Greatest among a flock of fine bodies was the Silver Arrow show car of 1933, of which only five were built. Sales had few good periods after 1931, and Pierce Motor Car Company foundered despite restyling in 1934 and 1936. Production was suspended in 1937 except for show models and spare parts. A 1938 line was announced, but the firm went bankrupt in December 1937 and was liquidated the following May.

FOR

The ultimate Classic-era Pierce-Arrow • Smooth performance from a gem of an engine • Posh coachwork of high quality • Relatively underpriced

AGAINST

Costly all the same • Scarcity • Mechanical complexity • High operating expenses

SPECIFICATIONS

Length (in.) NA **Wheelbase (in.)** 137.0/142.0/147.0 (1932); 136.0/139.0/137.0/142.0/147.0 (1933); 139.0/144.0/147.0 (1934-38) **Weight (lbs.)** 4620-5780 **Price (new)** $2785-7200

ENGINES

cid/type	bore x stroke	bhp	years
398.0/V12	3.25×4.00	140	1932
429.0/V12	3.38×4.00	150	1932-33
462.0/V12	3.50×4.00	175/185	1934-38

PRICES/PROJECTION

OPEN **Restorable** $12,000-20,000 **Good** $25,000-40,000 **Excellent** $50,000-85,000 CLOSED **Restorable** $7500-15,000 **Good** $15,000-30,000 **Excellent** $35,000-45,000 SILVER ARROW (production) **Restorable** $10,000-20,000 **Good** $30,000-45,000 **Excellent** $50,000-65,000 SILVER ARROW SHOW CAR Impossible to establish.
5-year projection closed +10%, open +25%

Plymouth 1930-32

PRODUCTION

1930-31 76,950 (approx. 57% in 1931) **1932** 83,910 **1932 open models:** roadster 4843, **phaeton** 787, **convertible** 7636

HISTORY

Long beloved by collectors (the Plymouth Club was originally devoted only to the four-cylinder models). Good-looking small cars with styling that followed general Chrysler trends, which were excellent in the early '30s. Mechanical features included four-wheel hydraulic brakes, "Floating Power" engine mounts in 1931 and more horsepower in 1932, the four-cylinder Plymouth's final year. There were also some attractive open body styles offered, including the now-scarce phaeton.

1932 Plymouth PB 2-door convertible sedan

FOR

Easy to acquire, own and run • Good club support • Parts readily available • Decent investment (open body styles)

AGAINST

Not as smooth or mechanically sophisticated as the Chevy six or '32 Ford V8 • Closed models slow to appreciate

SPECIFICATIONS

Length (in.) NA **Wheelbase (in.)** 109.0 (1930 Model U, 1930-31 Model 30U, 1932 PA); 112.0/121.0 (1932 PB) **Weight (lbs.)** 2280-3075 **Price (new)** $495-785

ENGINES

cid/type	bore x stroke	bhp	years
175.4/L4	3.63×4.25	45	1930*
196.1/L4	3.63×4.75	48	1930-32**

*Model U
**Model 30U, PA/PB

PRICES/PROJECTION

OPEN **Restorable** $2500-5500 **Good** $6000-15,000 **Excellent** $15,000-20,000 Add 10% for phaeton. CLOSED **Restorable** $1000-2500 **Excellent** $5000-8000 Deduct 10% for 2/4d sedans.
5-year projection open +15%, closed +10%

Plymouth Special DeLuxe convertible/ wagon 1941-49

PRODUCTION

1941 2d convertible coupe 10,545 **4d wagon** 5594
1942 2d convertible coupe 2806 **4d wagon** 1136
1946-49 2d convertible coupe 15,295 **4d wagon** 12,913

HISTORY

The most interesting body styles among '40s Plymouths, with un-

1942 Special DeLuxe convertible coupe

spectacular, rounded styling and the reliable, if ordinary, 87/95-bhp flathead six. Quite dull, but gave Chrysler a firm hold on third place in industry production. The upper-level Special DeLuxe series replaced the 1940 DeLuxe, and included these convertibles and woody wagons in all years. Nicely finished with quality materials, but built in fairly low numbers. The mildly restyled postwar carryovers remained unchanged from 1946 through the first part of the '49 model year, being replaced by the new boxy "second series" design that spring.

FOR

Solid construction • Relatively affordable

AGAINST

Ordinary styling and engineering • Not much performance

SPECIFICATIONS

Length (in.) 196.8 **Wheelbase (in.)** 117.0
Weight (lbs.) 3166-3402 **Price (new)** $1007-2068

ENGINES

cid/type	bore x stroke	bhp	years
201.3/L6	3.13×4.38	87	1941
217.8/L6	3.25×4.38	95	1942-49

PRICES/PROJECTION

CONVERTIBLE **Restorable** $3000-5000 **Good** $4000-9000
Excellent $9000-16,000 WAGON **Restorable** $2500-4500
Good $4000-7500 **Excellent** $7500-10,500
5-year projection +10%

1941 Special DeLuxe wood-body wagon

Plymouth DeLuxe Suburban 1949

1949 DeLuxe Suburban 2-door wagon

PRODUCTION

19,220

HISTORY

Here's an historically important model you can buy for little money and use as practical transportation to boot. Built on Plymouth's shorter DeLuxe chassis, the Suburban pioneered all-steel station wagon construction. In effect, it made this body style more practical and easier to live with. Beautiful though it was, the structural wood used in station wagons up to this time took a lot of work to keep in good condition. And keeping it up was critical for body rigidity. Collectors may bemoan their loss today, but the fact is that woody wagons were already on the way out by the late '40s. The Suburban and the wagons that followed were thus a logical and inevitable step that would make the wagon a permanent part of the American automotive scene in the '50s.

FOR

Inexpensive • Well-built • Historical interest • Practicality

AGAINST

Little collector recognition • Dullness • Slow to appreciate

SPECIFICATIONS

Length (in.) 185.3 **Wheelbase (in.)** 111.0 **Weight (lbs.)** 3105
Price (new) $1840

ENGINES

cid/type	bore x stroke	bhp	years
217.8/L6	3.25×4.38	97	1949

PRICES/PROJECTION

Restorable $500-1000 **Good** $1000-2500
Excellent $2500-4500 **5-year projection** +10%

Plymouth Cranbrook Belvedere 1951-52

PRODUCTION

51,266 (combined)

1951 Cranbrook Belvedere 2-door hardtop

1955 Belvedere 2-door hardtop

HISTORY

Plymouth's first pillarless hardtop, introduced in the top-line series, naturally. As was customary in Detroit at the time, the new body style was given its own distinct name. Arrived at about the same time as the Ford Victoria, but a year behind Chevy's Bel Air. Quite popular, however, with an interesting two-tone paint job and convertible-like interior adding some much needed spice to the very conservative design first seen in 1949. You'll have to look closely to tell the two model years apart, and there are no mechanical changes. Chrysler itself quotes only combined production figures for all its lines in these years, perhaps for this reason.

FOR

Important in Plymouth history • Solid build

AGAINST

Uninspired styling • Not much collector following

SPECIFICATIONS

Length (in.) 193.9 **Wheelbase (in.)** 118.5
Weight (lbs.) 3182/3105 **Price (new)** $2114-2216

ENGINES

cid/type	bore x stroke	bhp	years
217.8/L6	3.25×4.38	97	1951-52

PRICES/PROJECTION

Restorable $750-1250 **Good** $1500-2500
Excellent $3000-4000 Add 100% for convertible.
5-year projection no change

Plymouth Belvedere convertible & hardtops 1955-56

PRODUCTION

1955 2d hardtop 47,375	2d convertible 8473	
1956 2d hardtop 24,723	2d convertible 6735	
4d hardtop 17,515		

HISTORY

After years of staid boxiness, Plymouth got a healthy injection of pizzazz with a startlingly new 1955 line, part of Chrysler's wholesale design turnaround that year. Styling, by Virgil Exner's lieutenant Murray Baldwin, was clean and pleasing: peaked front fenders, wrapped windshield, shapely rear fenders. Belvedere, which had become the top-line series the previous year, featured an optional bodyside contrasting color sweep and nicely outfitted interior. Like Chevrolet, Plymouth also got its first V8 for '55 in 241- and 260-cid displacements. Hardtops could be had with the familiar L-head six, but the V8 was standard in the ragtop, and proved more popular in Belvederes by a factor of three. A mild facelift for '56 brought taller finned rear fenders housing slim vertical taillights, plus a chromier grille, pushbutton controls for the optional two-speed PowerFlite automatic, and larger V8s with power options up to 200 bhp.

FOR

Sharp looks • Fine V8 performance • An attractive buy • Just as good as contemporary Chevys

AGAINST

Limited appreciation potential • Lacks broad collector following • Slightly weird symmetrical dash layout

SPECIFICATIONS

Length (in.) 203.8 (1955), 204.8 (1956) **Wheelbase (in.)** 115.0
Weight (lbs.) 3261-3585 **Price (new)** $2217-2638

ENGINES

cid/type	bore x stroke	bhp	years
230.2/L6	3.25×4.63	117/125/131	1955-56
241/ohv V8	3.44×3.25	157	1955
260/ohv V8	3.56×3.25	167/177	1955
270/ohv V8	3.63×3.26	180	1956
277/ohv V8	3.75×3.13	187/200	1956

PRICES/PROJECTION

HARDTOP Restorable $750-1500 **Good** $1500-3000
Excellent $3000-5000 **CONVERTIBLE Restorable** $1500-3000
Good $3000-5000 **Excellent** $5000-7500
5-year projection +10%, convertible +10%

1956 Belvedere convertible

Plymouth Fury 1956

1956 Fury 2-door hardtop

PRODUCTION

4485

HISTORY

First of the limited-edition, high-performance Plymouths, a kind of junior version of the Chrysler 300. Available only as a two-door hardtop, painted off-white and bearing an anodized gold bodyside sweepspear. Standard power was provided by a 303-cid enlargement of Plymouth's "Hy-Fire" V8 packing 240 horses. Off the showroom floor, the car was capable of 0-60 mph in 10 seconds and 110 mph tops. A specially prepared Fury hit 145 mph in tests on the sands of Daytona Beach.

FOR

Rapid • Contemporary good looks • Nicely finished throughout • Not outrageously priced today for a low-production item • Strong value rise probable

AGAINST

Styling far from timeless • Rust bothers

SPECIFICATIONS

Length (in.) 204.8   **Wheelbase (in.)** 115.0   **Weight (lbs.)** 3650
Price (new) $2866

ENGINES

cid/type	bore x stroke	bhp	years
303/ohv V8	3.82×3.31	240	1956

PRICES/PROJECTION

Restorable $1500-2000 **Good** $2500-3500
Excellent $4500-5500 **5-year projection** +10%

Plymouth Belvedere convertible/hardtop coupe 1957-58

PRODUCTION

| **1957 2d hardtop** 67,268 | **2d convertible** 9866 |
| **1958 2d hardtop** 36,043 | **2d convertible** 9941 |

1958 Belvedere 2-door hardtop

HISTORY

Plymouth's top-of-the-line models (aside from the limited-production Fury), all-new again for '57 with "Suddenly It's 1960" styling, a 3-inch longer wheelbase and torsion bar front suspension, and newly available three-speed TorqueFlite automatic. As before, the convertible came only with a V8 engine, and there were hairier options available throughout the line, which also included the stripped Plaza and mid-priced Savoy models. Unfortunately, these dramatic new Plymouths were let down by noticeably poorer quality control, a problem that plagued all Chrysler products in this period and one that damaged the Corporation's fine engineering reputation. Styling was modestly revised for 1958, with the then-obligatory four-headlamp front end, horizontal bar grille, and shorter taillights residing in the '57 fins. Too easily attacked by the dreaded tinworm, these Plymouths have a lot to recommend them as collectibles, provided you can find a decent one.

FOR

A budget collectible • Important and striking design • Good V8 performance • Fine handling

AGAINST

Rust can be fatal • Smaller collector following than Chevrolet

SPECIFICATIONS

Length (in.) 206.1   **Wheelbase (in.)** 118.0
Weight (lbs.) 3325-3585   **Price (new)** $2349-2762

ENGINES

cid/type	bore x stroke	bhp	years
230.2/L6	3.25×4.63	132	1957-58
277/ohv V8	3.75×3.13	197/235	1957
301/ohv V8	3.91×3.13	215/235	1957
318/ohv V8	3.91×3.31	225/250	1958
350/ohv V8	4.06×3.38	305/315	1958

PRICES/PROJECTION

Restorable $400-800 **Good** $1000-1800
Excellent $2000-3200 **Add 100% for convertible**
5-year projection +10%

Plymouth Fury 1957-58

PRODUCTION

1957 7438   **1958** 5303

1958 Fury 2-door hardtop

HISTORY

Continuation of Plymouth's high-performance special, now clothed in Virgil Exner's swoopy, low-beltline styling with thin-section roof and hefty shark fin rear. Still available only as a hardtop in these years. Standard power came from a 318 V8. For 1958, a 350-cid unit was offered with 315 bhp courtesy of fuel injection. Very good-looking for its day, and still holding up well despite those fins. Only minor styling changes for '58, confined to quad headlamps, a more unified grille, and revised taillights. Chrysler construction quality took a nosedive beginning with the '57s, and its cars developed a reputation for early rust out. This means good-condition Fury survivors will be even harder to find than the low production figures suggest.

FOR

High style • Exceptional performance • Probably undervalued— a good investment

AGAINST

Very thirsty and demands high octane • Seriously rust-prone • Most not pampered

SPECIFICATIONS

Length (in.) 206.1 **Wheelbase (in.)** 118.0
Weight (lbs.) 3595/3510 **Price (new)** $2925/3067

ENGINES

cid/type	bore x stroke	bhp	years
318/ohv V8	3.91×3.31	290	1957-58
350/ohv V8	4.06×3.38	305/315	1958

PRICES/PROJECTION

Restorable $2000-3000 **Good** $3000-5000
Excellent $4500-6500 **5-year projection** no change

Plymouth Sport Fury 1959

PRODUCTION

2d hardtop 17,867   **2d convertible** 5990

HISTORY

Replacement for the Fury as Plymouth's high-performance cars this year (the Fury name was used for the top-line standard series, pushing Belvedere and Savoy down a notch and knocking out

1959 Sport Fury 2-door hardtop

Plaza). Now available as a convertible as well as the usual hardtop. Standard power was a 260-bhp 318 V8; Plymouth's "Golden Commando" 361 was optional. A heavy facelift on the 1957-58 bodyshell, shared with lesser models, featured a broad eggcrate grille, prominent headlamp eyelids, and longer, higher tailfins. Sport Fury also wore an embossed spare tire bulge on the trunklid. New for '59 was Chrysler's optional swivel front seats, semi-bucket affairs that turned outward when a door was opened to assist entry/exit. Handling and performance were as good as ever, and assembly quality as bad as ever. Not one of Plymouth's best years, but relative low cost today and spirited acceleration makes the Sport Fury an interesting addition to a car collector's stable.

FOR

Fast on straights and curves • Typical '50s gadgetry

AGAINST

Pug-ugly compared with the neat 1957-58 • Still too susceptible to early rust-out • Gadget gremlins

SPECIFICATIONS

Length (in.) 208.2 **Wheelbase (in.)** 118.0
Weight (lbs.) 3475/3670 **Price (new)** $2927/3125

ENGINES

cid/type	bore x stroke	bhp	years
318/ohv V8	3.91×3.31	260	1959
361/ohv V8	4.12×3.38	305	1959

PRICES/PROJECTION

Restorable $700-1000 **Good** $1250-2000
Excellent $2000-3200 Add 30% for convertible.
5-year projection +5%

Plymouth Valiant Signet 1962

PRODUCTION

28,586

HISTORY

Bucket-seat hardtop offering in the final year of the first-generation Valiant designed by Virgil Exner. The pillarless body style had debuted a year earlier in the V200 series along with a fixed-pillar two-door sedan and, if anything, enhanced the chunky lines Plymouth's compact wore in these `years. Listed as a separate model for '62, the Signet had an even cleaner appearance thanks

1962 Valiant Signet 2-door hardtop

to a black-painted grille and absence of the previous decklid tire bulge. With its posh appointments it was an obvious rival to the Corvair Monza and Falcon Futura. Available only with a six-cylinder engine in a choice of two displacements, but it was a good one— Chrysler's slant six, which was already renowned for the rugged dependability that would keep it in production into the 1980s.

FOR

Plenty still around • Attractive bucket-seat interior • Floorshift available • Good performance • Unburstable engine with parts still as close as your nearest dealer • Cheap to buy

AGAINST

Rust-prone (unit construction) unless carefully looked after • Limited appreciation potential • Debatable styling

SPECIFICATIONS

Length (in.) 184.2 **Wheelbase (in.)** 106.5 **Weight (lbs.)** 2515
Price (new) $2230

ENGINES

cid/type	bore x stroke	bhp	years
170/ohv I6	3.40×3.13	101	1962
225/ohv I6	3.40×4.13	145	1962

PRICES/PROJECTION

Restorable $250-1000 **Good** $1000-2000
Excellent $2000-3000 **5-year projection** +5%

Plymouth Barracuda 1964-66

1966 Barracuda 2-door fastback hardtop

PRODUCTION

1964 23,433   **1965** 64,596   **1966** 38,029

HISTORY

"Glassback" derivative of the compact Valiant, launched in early 1964 as part of the Signet 200 series. Appeared about the same time as Ford's Mustang, which was probably a coincidence, though most observers took it as Plymouth's direct reply to the Dearborn ponycar, which it probably wasn't. Retained the Valiant's lower body, but used a fastback superstructure with massive wraparound backlight and stubby trunklid. Equipped with the Signet's bucket-seat interior, plus a flip-down rear seatback and security panel that opened up the trunk area for carrying long items (the ads liked to show surfboards). Engine offerings were the same as Valiant's, with standard 225 slant six or a newly optional 273 V8. Horsepower options ran from 180 to 235 in these years, and a "Rallye" suspension and four-speed gearbox were also listed. Facelifted along with Valiant for '66, but got its own distinct grille. A special Formula S package was available beginning in 1965, and turned the Barracuda into a capable road machine.

FOR

Satisfying V8 performance • Excellent six-cylinder mileage and durability • "Hatchback" practicality • Affordable • Right at home in today's traffic conditions

AGAINST

Huge rear window lets interior cook on sunny days • Indifferent assembly quality • Can rust • Obviously Valiant-based

SPECIFICATIONS

Length (in.) 188.2 **Wheelbase (in.)** 106.0
Weight (lbs.) 2725-2865 **Price (new)** $2365-2556

ENGINES

cid/type	bore x stroke	bhp	years
225/ohv I6	3.40×4.13	145	1964-66
273/ohv V8	3.62×3.31	180/235	1964-66

PRICES/PROJECTION

Restorable $1000-2000 **Good** $2000-3500
Excellent $3500-5000 **5-year projection** +10%

Plymouth Satellite 426 1966

1966 Satellite 426 2-door hardtop

PRODUCTION

NA, but limited

HISTORY

The top-line hardtop and convertible in Plymouth's newly reconstituted intermediate Belvedere line equipped with the closest thing to a full-house racing engine you could buy for the street. Though the legendary hemi-head V8 had returned to the stock-car tracks and dragstrips in 1964, it wasn't a true production option before 1966 (available on any mid-size Plymouth). The Satellite was the sportiest of this year's Belvederes, with standard bucket seats and console, plus options like tachometer, stiff suspension, and wide tires. Its base engine was the little 273 V8, but the hemi made it something else. The Belvedere/Satellite body/chassis design was essentially a continuation of the "standard" 1964 Plymouth, which in turn evolved from the original "downsized" 1962 models that sold poorly against full-size Fords and Chevys. Quality control had improved considerably by the mid-'60s, however, and styling was much neater and trimmer. In all, the hemi-powered Satellite is mighty impressive for its blinding speed and, with the right chassis equipment, capable road manners.

FOR

Tremendous performance • Great looks • Rarity

AGAINST

High operating costs • High-octane diet • Watch out for rust

SPECIFICATIONS

Length (in.) 200.5 **Wheelbase (in.)** 116.0
Weight (lbs.) 3400-3520 (approx.)
Price (new) $2695-2910 (base V8)

ENGINES

cid/type	bore x stroke	bhp	years
426/ohv V8	4.25×3.75	425	1966

PRICES/PROJECTION

Restorable $1000-2500 **Good** $2500-4000
Excellent $4000-6000
5-year projection +10%

Plymouth Barracuda 1967-69

1967 Barracuda 2-door hardtop

1968 Barracuda Formula S 2-door fastback hardtop

PRODUCTION

1967 2d hardtop 28,196   **2d convertible** 4228
2d fastback hardtop 30,110   **1968 2d hardtop** 19,997
2d convertible 2840   **2d fastback hardtop** 22,575
1969 2d hardtop 12,757   **2d convertible** 1442
2d fastback hardtop 17,788

HISTORY

Plymouth's sporty compact, now a true ponycar with pretty, well-integrated new styling on a 2-inch longer wheelbase. Two V8s, a 273 and 383, were offered for '67, joined by a 340 unit for 1968-69. All could be coupled with the Formula S package consisting of heavy-duty suspension, tachometer, Wide-Oval tires, and special emblems and warpaint. The 225 Slant Six was standard for 1968-69. The original fastback was augmented by a handsome new convertible and a curiously styled notchback hardtop with a curved rear window. Styling changes were limited to grilles and minor trim in these years. All models came with a complete set of engine gauges set in a simple, no-nonsense dash. Collectors should note the production figures. Convertibles stand to become ultra-rare in the future, yet are currently priced not much higher than closed models.

FOR

Convertibles' rarity and strong appreciation • Smooth styling • Handy size • Roadability • Overall balance with smaller V8s

AGAINST

Rust potential • Body and some mechanical parts hard to find • 383's clumsier handling

SPECIFICATIONS

Length (in.) 193.0 **Wheelbase (in.)** 108.0
Weight (lbs.) 2793-2940   **Price (new)** $2449-3082

ENGINES

cid/type	bore x stroke	bhp	years
225/ohv I6	3.40×4.13	145	1968-69
273/ohv V8	3.62×3.31	180/235	1967
318/ohv V8	3.91×3.31	230	1968
340/ohv V8	4.04×3.31	275	1968-69
383/ohv V8	4.25×3.38	300/325/330	1967-69

PRICES/PROJECTION

Restorable $900-1200 **Good** $1500-3000
Excellent $3000-5000 Add 10% for convertible, 10% for Formula S model. **5-year projection** +10%; convertible +25%

Plymouth Belvedere GTX 1967

1967 Belvedere GTX 2-door hardtop

PRODUCTION

2d hardtop 2000 **2d convertible** 300 (both est.)

HISTORY

A more serious Plymouth muscle car, successor to the big-inch Satellite (which continued this year in lower-power form). Like other Belvederes, largely a repeat of the handsome 1966 package, but set off with special identification (silver and black grille and trunklid appliqué, simulated hood air scoops, quick-fill-style fuel cap, dual exhausts) to give plenty of warning to others at stoplights. The standard GTX engine was an enlarged version of Chrysler's wedgehead V8 with 440 cubes and 375 bhp. The hemi was the only option, still rated at its customary (and nominal) 425 bhp. Not stark, with full carpeting, vinyl upholstery, bucket seats, and plenty of sparkling interior accents. Offered in both hardtop and convertible body styles. Not a tremendous seller when new, so has a certain status now as a low-volume collectible.

FOR

As for 1966 Satellite 426 •440 V8 less temperamental • Rarity (especially convertibles)

AGAINST

As for 1966 Satellite 426

SPECIFICATIONS

Length (in.) 200.5 **Wheelbase (in.)** 116.0
Weight (lbs.) 3545/3615 **Price (new)** $3178-3418

ENGINES

cid/type	bore x stroke	bhp	years
426/ohv V8	4.25×3.75	425	1967
440/ohv V8	4.32×3.75	375	1967

1967 Belvedere GTX convertible

PRICES/PROJECTION

Restorable $1500-3400 **Good** $3400-5400
Excellent $4700-7000 Add 15% for convertible.
5-year projection +10%

Plymouth Road Runner 1968-70

1968 Road Runner convertible

PRODUCTION

1968 2d coupe 29,240		**2d hardtop** 15,359
1969 2d coupe 33,743		**2d hardtop** 48,549
2d convertible 2128	**1970 2d coupe** 15,716	
2d hardtop 24,944	**2d convertible** 824	

HISTORY

Plymouth's cleverly named budget bomb based on the intermediate Belvedere. Aimed squarely at younger buyers interested in high performance who couldn't afford a GTX or who thought that model too ritzy. With a base price below $3000, the Runner packed a standard 383 V8 with 335 bhp, plus four-speed transmission, heavy duty suspension, GTX-like hood bulges, a taxicab-basic interior, little cartoon bird decals on the doors, and a "beep-beep" horn. A fixed-pillar coupe with flip-out rear side windows was offered initially, joined during the '68 model year by a hardtop. A soft-top version was added for '69, along with dress-up options for those who weren't comfortable with the plain trim. The Road Runner continued as a Plymouth model after 1970, ultimately winding up as a package option for the 1976 Volaré compact.

FOR

Low-priced new, still so today •Convertibles' rarity and appreciation •High performance

AGAINST

Indifferent assembly quality • "Hotdogger" image

SPECIFICATIONS

Length (in.) 202.7 **Wheelbase (in.)** 116.0
Weight (lbs.) 3435-3790 **Price (new)** $2896-3313

ENGINES

cid/type	bore x stroke	bhp	years
383/ohv V8	4.25×3.38	335	1968-70
426/ohv V8	4.25×3.75	425	1968-70
440/ohv V8	4.32×3.75	375/390	1969-70

PRICES/PROJECTION

COUPE/HARDTOP **Restorable** $750-1500 **Good** $2000-3000 **Excellent** $3000-4000 CONVERTIBLE **Restorable** $1500-2500 **Good** $2500-3500 **Excellent** $3500-5000 **5-year projection** no change

Plymouth AAR 'Cuda & Hemi-Cuda 1970

1970 Hemi-Cuda 2-door hardtop

PRODUCTION

2500 (est.)

HISTORY

Strong collector potential in the two hottest editions of Plymouth's redesigned (lower, wider, and heavier) ponycar. The third-generation Barracuda had enough engine room to accommodate the hemi-head V8, and could storm off the line like a funny car dragster (complete with body shake and sideways "torque step") when so equipped. More intriguing and roadable was the AAR, named after Dan Gurney's All-American Racers operation, which ran a team of factory-backed Barracudas for the 1970 Trans-Am series. Included in this very limited-edition package was a tuned 340 V8 with triple two-barrel carbs, front and rear spoilers, fat wheels and tires, "strobe stripe" bodyside decals, and mean-looking side exhaust pipes. The AAR was canned after an unsuccessful racing season, but the hemi continued for another year. Barracuda lost most of its performance teeth after that, and production halted after the 1974 model year in the face of a rapidly declining ponycar market.

FOR

Values already leading those of lesser '70 Barracudas ● AAR's rarity and race history ● Clean styling ● Tremendous go

AGAINST

High-octane a must ● High running costs ● Subject to rust ● Hemi's suspect handling, roadholding

SPECIFICATIONS

Length (in.) 186.7   **Wheelbase (in.)** 108.0
Weight (lbs.) 3500-3800 (approx.)
Price (new) $3164-4000 (approx.)

ENGINES

cid/type	bore x stroke	bhp	years
340/ohv V8	4.04×3.31	290	1970
426/ohv V8	4.25×3.75	425	1970

PRICES/PROJECTION

Restorable $2000-3000 **Good** $3500-5500 **Excellent** $5000-8000 Add 50% for Hemi **5-year projection** +30%

Plymouth Barracuda convertible (exc. 'Cuda) 1970-71

1971 'Cuda convertible (Barracuda similar)

PRODUCTION

1970 2150   **1971** 1850

HISTORY

The short-lived convertibles in Plymouth's third-generation ponycar line, offered for these two model years only. Rebodied with very husky, yet clean, lines to accommodate Chrysler's big-block engines. The performance-oriented 'Cuda was made a separate series, offering a standard 375-bhp 383, with two versions of the big 440 available as options. But these heavy engines made for piggish handling, and the 'Cudas were a bit overdecorated even for muscle machines. More tasteful were the base and new Gran Coupe series, offered with standard slant six. V8 options of 318, 340, and 383 cid provided more than sufficient go in these relatively heavy cars. Few styling, mechanical, or equipment changes were made for '71, but production slipped. The convertibles were never high-demand items, making them quite scarce but potentially good collector investments today. The notchback Barracuda hardtops continued for 1973-74 minus most of the previous high-power engines. The model was dropped entirely for 1975, a victim of the energy crisis and changing public tastes.

FOR

Quite rare ● Good handling and performance ● Gran Coupe interior ● "Last convertible" interest

AGAINST

Six's poor pickup ● Rust potential ● Indifferent build quality ● True investment potential still unclear

SPECIFICATIONS

Length (in.) 186.7   **Wheelbase (in.)** 108.0
Weight (lbs.) 3071-3200   **Price (new)** $3034-3400

ENGINES

cid/type	bore x stroke	bhp	years
225/ohv I6	3.40×4.13	145	1970-71
318/ohv V8	3.91×3.31	230	1970-71
383/ohv V8	4.25×3.38	290/330	1970-71

ENGINES

cid/type	bore x stroke	bhp	years
440/ohv V8	4.32×3.75	375	1970
426/ohv V8	4.25×3.75	425	1970

PRICES/PROJECTION

Restorable $1000-2000 **Good** $2800-4500
Excellent $4000-6000 **5-year projection** +30%

PRICES/PROJECTION

Restorable $5000-7000 **Good** $6000-8500
Excellent $10,000-15,000 **5-year projection** +30%

Plymouth Road Runner Superbird 1970

Plymouth Sport Fury GT 1970-71

1970 Road Runner Superbird 2-door hardtop

1970 Sport Fury GT 2-door hardtop

PRODUCTION

1920

PRODUCTION

1970 NA **1971** 375

HISTORY

Plymouth's continuation of the limited-production Dodge Charger Daytona (1969), again offered for the public to satisfy production requirements for stock-car racing. Carried the same "droop snoot" nose with hidden headlamps and the high rear stabilizer wing mounted on tall struts. Competition versions could achieve over 220 mph. At the 1970 Daytona 500, Pete Hamilton beat the field with an average speed of nearly 150 mph, and the Superbird went on to take 21 of the 38 Grand National events that year. For the 1971 season, NASCAR changed its rules to bar these winged wonders, leaving the Superbird, like the Charger Daytona before it, a one-year-only special. The "street" model carried the 375-horsepower 440 wedgehead V8, and the fabled hemi was optional.

HISTORY

Plymouth's somewhat belated attempt at a high-performance full-size model, produced in very low numbers for these two model years only. Though a Sport Fury subseries had been offered previously as the top of Plymouth's big-car line and was available with the division's largest engines, the GT version was even more special. As part of Plymouth's 1970 "Rapid Transit System," this two-door hardtop was decked out with the big-block Super Commando 440 V8 with single quad-pot carb, good for 350 horses. A 390-bhp version with Plymouth's Six Pack carburetion (a trio of two-barrels) was optional. The package also included heavy-duty underpinnings and bodyside "strobe stripes." For 1970 only, a companion model, the S/23, was also listed, powered by the mild-mannered 318. Horsepower ratings for the basically similar '71 Sport Fury GT were 335 standard and 385 for the six-carb engine. Not an answer to a market trend, nor did it start one, but an interesting newer collectible for those interested in performance with big-car room and ride.

FOR

Growing collector following ●Special Daytona/Superbird club ●Tremendous performance ●Unique appearance ●Race record

FOR

Exclusivity ●Performance ●Interior room, luxury ●Burly looks ●Last of the big performance Plymouths

AGAINST

High running costs ●Indifferent construction quality ●Special body pieces may present restoration problems ●Not that many around

AGAINST

The usual unit-construction rust worries ●Very thirsty ●Hard to find in good condition ●Not in high demand, and not likely to be for awhile yet

SPECIFICATIONS

Length (in.) 220.0 **Wheelbase (in.)** 116.0 **Weight (lbs.)** 3785
Price (new) $4298

SPECIFICATIONS

Length (in.) 214.9 (1970) 215.1 (1971) **Wheelbase (in.)** 120.0
Weight (lbs.) 3950 (approx.) **Price (new)** $3898

ENGINES

cid/type	bore x stroke	bhp	years
440/ohv V8	4.32×3.75	335-390	1970-71

PRICES/PROJECTION

Restorable $500-1000 **Good** $1000-1500
Excellent $2000-3000 **5-year projection** +10%

Plymouth GTX & Road Runner 1971-75

1971 Road Runner 2-door hardtop

PRODUCTION

1971 Road Runner 2d hardtop 14,218
GTX 2d hardtop 2942   **1972 Road Runner 2d hardtop** 7628
1973 Road Runner 2d coupe 19,056
1974 Road Runner 2d coupe 11,555
1975 Road Runner 2d coupe 7183

HISTORY

Continuation of Plymouth's muscle cars, now with brand-new, handsome styling shared with the ordinary family models (the 115-inch-wheelbase Sebring/Sebring Plus coupes and the 117-inch-wheelbase Satellite sedans and wagons). Convertibles were dropped with the switch in platform, but there was still some semblance of performance for 1971. That year's Road Runner came with a 300-bhp 383 V8 that ran on regular gas. The GTX was powered by a four-barrel 440 V8 with 370 bhp. The 425-bhp hemi and the 440 Six Pack were optional for both. For 1972, the hemi was made a dealer option, a victim of tightening emissions controls and (as the production figures suggest) a dramatic drop in demand for high-performance intermediates. The GTX was cancelled, but the Runner lived on, offering a standard 400-cid V8, with the 440 optional. The Road Runner was continued with progressively less power through 1975, after which the concept was applied to the compact Volaré as an option package.

FOR

Handsome looks • Decent performance for the period • Fairly rare, yet still readily available today

1974 Road Runner 2-door hardtop

AGAINST

Rust-prone • Performance falls off greatly after '71 • Collectibility not yet firmly established

SPECIFICATIONS

Length (in.) 203.5 **Wheelbase (in.)** 115.0 **Weight (lbs.)** 3300 (approx.) **Price (new)** $3120-3973

ENGINES

cid/type	bore x stroke	bhp	years
318/ohv V8	3.91×3.31	150/170	1973-75
340/ohv V8	4.04×3.31	275/240[1]	1971-73
360/ohv V8	4.00×3.58	180/245	1973-75
383/ohv V8	4.25×3.38	300	1971
400/ohv V8	4.34×3.38	165-260[1]	1972-75
426/ohv V8	4.25×3.75	425	1971
440/ohv V8	4.32×3.75	370/385[2]	1971-75

1. SAE gross/net bhp
2. 1971 SAE gross bhp; 260-280 bhp SAE net 1972-75

PRICES/PROJECTION

Restorable $600-1200 **Good** $1000-2000
Excellent $2500-5600 **5-year projection** +30%

Pontiac Streamliner 1942-48

Streamliner Station Wagon

THE *FINE* CAR WITH THE *LOW* PRICE

1942 Streamliner Chieftain wood-body wagon

PRODUCTION

1942 Six 12,742 **Eight** 26,506 **1946 Six** 43,430 **Eight** 49,301
1947 Six 42,336 **Eight** 86,324 **1948 Six** 37,742 **Eight** 123,115

1946 Streamliner Six 4-door sedan

HISTORY

The last prewar Pontiac and its postwar continuations in the division's upper-priced series. Fresh pontoon-fender styling changed only in detail during these years. Top-line Chieftain models are the pick among the rare '42s; only 11,041 Eights and 2458 Sixes were built. Choicest of the choice would be the wood-body wagon and the slick sedan-coupe. Convertible was relegated to the Torpedo line (see entry). Postwar hallmarks are triple chrome fender strips and a full-width grille on '46s, a simpler grille on '47s, and an above-grille nameplate on '48s. The last appeared with "Silver Streak" chrome script, a term earlier applied to Pontiac styling. DeLuxe versions of the four-door sedan, wagon, and sedan-coupe were offered for '48 only.

FOR

Solid construction • Quality materials • Among GM's nicer-looking mid-'40s cars • Rarity of some models

AGAINST

Solid but stolid engines • '42s hard to find • High maintenance on woody wagons • Indifferent performance • Lacks appeal of concurrent Chevys

SPECIFICATIONS

Length (in.) 210.3 **Wheelbase (in.)** 122.0
Weight (lbs.) 3400-3870 **Price (new)** $1030-2490

ENGINES

cid/type	bore x stroke	bhp	years
239.2/L6	3.56×4.00	90	1942-48
248.9/L8	3.25×3.75	103	1942-48

PRICES/PROJECTION

1942 **Restorable** $750-1250 **Good** $2000-3500
Excellent $4000-5000 1946-48 **Restorable** $500-2000
Good $1500-2500 **Excellent** $2500-4500 Add 100% for wagons **5-year projection** +15% 1942, +10% 1946-48

Pontiac Torpedo convertible 1942-48

1946 Torpedo Eight convertible

PRODUCTION

1942 2500 **1946** 5000 **1947** 10,000 **1948** 10,000 (all est.; calendar year production 10,020 in 1947, 15,937 in 1948)

HISTORY

Pontiac's only convertible of the mid-'40s, built on the shorter-wheelbase chassis and available with the familiar six- and eight-cylinder engines like the Streamliners. A more elaborately trimmed

DeLuxe soft-top was offered for 1947-48 at about $50 extra. Styling changes parallel those made to Streamliners (see entry). Mechanical changes were almost nil in this period, however.

FOR

Convertible allure • Nicely finished inside and out • '42s' rarity • Others as for 1942-48 Streamliner

AGAINST

As for 1942-48 Streamliner

SPECIFICATIONS

Length (in.) 204.5 **Wheelbase (in.)** 119.0
Weight (lbs.) 3525-3605 **Price (new)** $1165-2072

ENGINES

cid/type	bore x stroke	bhp	years
239.2/L6	3.56×4.00	90	1942-48
248.9/L8	3.25×3.75	103	1942-48

PRICES/PROJECTION

Restorable $4000-6000 **Good** $7000-12,000
Excellent $12,000-18,000 **5-year projection** +10%

Pontiac Chieftain DeLuxe 1949

1949 Chieftain Eight DeLuxe 4-door sedan

PRODUCTION

50,000 (est.)

HISTORY

The cream of the crop in Pontiac's first new postwar generation. Clean, modern styling courtesy of Harley Earl's staff, and similar in general concept to that seen on GM's other new model lines this year. All Pontiacs now rode the same 120-inch-wheelbase chassis. The former top-line Streamliner series moved down to take over for the old Torpedo, while the new Chieftain moved in above it. Both series were offered with the familiar inline engines from earlier years, and there were DeLuxe trim models in each.

FOR

Good construction quality • First new postwar design • Good tourer

AGAINST

Lackluster engines

SPECIFICATIONS

Length (in.) 202.5 **Wheelbase (in.)** 120.0
Weight (lbs.) 3345-3670 **Price (new)** $1805-2206

ENGINES

cid/type	bore x stroke	bhp	years
239.2/L6	3.56×4.00	90/93	1949
248.9/L8	3.25×3.75	104/106	1949

PRICES/PROJECTION

Restorable $500-1000 **Good** $1250-2800
Excellent $2500-4000 Add 100% for convertible
5-year projection +25%

Pontiac Streamliner wood-body wagon 1949

1949 Streamliner Eight DeLuxe wood-body wagon

PRODUCTION

1000 (est.)

HISTORY

Last of the wood-bodied Pontiac cargo haulers. Offered as an alternative to a new all-steel wagon this year, though there was little difference in price. Both six- and eight-cylinder versions were available. A standard-trim eight-passenger model was offered, and there was a six-passenger equivalent with DeLuxe trim only.

FOR

Well ahead of contemporary all-steel wagons in value • Fine carpentry • Last of the breed

AGAINST

Wood care costly, time-consuming • Pricey • Same old engines

SPECIFICATIONS

Length (in.) 202.5 **Wheelbase (in.)** 120.0
Weight (lbs.) 3730/3835 (6/8) **Price (new)** $2543/2690 (6/8)

ENGINES

cid/type	bore x stroke	bhp	years
239.2/L6	3.56×4.00	90/93	1949
248.9/L8	3.25×3.75	104/106	1949

PRICES/PROJECTION

Restorable $1000-2000 **Good** $2500-4800
Excellent $6550-10,000 **5-year projection** +20%

Pontiac Chieftain Catalina 1950

1950 Chieftain Eight DeLuxe Catalina 2-door hardtop

PRODUCTION

40,000 est.

HISTORY

Pontiac's first pillarless hardtop, the first car to bear what would become one of the division's most familiar names. Introduced along with the Chevrolet Bel Air a year after Buick, Cadillac, and Oldsmobile had broken ground with this body type. Decked out with convertible-type interior fittings (including chrome headliner strips to simulate a true convertible's top ribs). Offered with either six- or eight-cylinder L-head engines, the Catalina was available in Pontiac's DeLuxe trim or as the even ritzier Super, the only model so designated through 1953. Styling throughout the 1950 line was a mild facelift of the all-new 1949 look. A small bore increase gave the hardy old straight eight a small boost in rated horsepower.

FOR

Historical interest • Smooth looks • Others as for 1949 Chieftain DeLuxe

AGAINST

Same dull old engines

SPECIFICATIONS

Length (in.) 202.5   **Wheelbase (in.)** 120.0
Weight (lbs.) 3469/3549 (6/8)   **Price (new)** $2000-2127

ENGINES

cid/type	bore x stroke	bhp	years
239.2/L6	3.56×4.00	90	1950
268.4/L6	3.38×3.75	108	1950

PRICES/PROJECTION

Restorable $1000-2500 **Good** $2500-4500
Excellent $4500-6500 **5-year projection** +10%

Pontiac Safari 1955-57

PRODUCTION

1955 3760   **1956** 4042   **1957** 1292

1956 Safari 2-door "hardtop" wagon

HISTORY

Pontiac's version of the two-door Chevrolet Nomad wagon, produced only in these years (the Safari name was applied to Pontiac's conventional four-door wagons beginning with the '57s). Powered by the Division's excellent new ohv V8, which increased in displacement and horsepower in each of these years. The exciting blend of hardtop and wagon styling developed at Chevrolet was so fascinating to Pontiac that the Division won permission from GM management (to Chevy's chagrin) to build its own version. Elegantly trimmed inside, flashy outside with bright two-tone paint treatment and chrome accents aplenty. Built on the shorter 122-in-wheelbase Chieftain 870 chassis, not the Star Chief's 124, but usually considered part of the top-line series because it was trimmed and equipped similarly. Interestingly, the 1955-56 wore no identifying series script. Like Nomad, the Safari didn't sell well because of its steep price and lack of full wagon practicality. Not many were made, so asking prices now are on the high side.

FOR

The only Milestone Pontiac • Styling • Good performance • Low-production appeal • High appreciation potential

AGAINST

Special Safari pieces hard to find • Like Nomad, subject to water leaks and some rust around tailgate

SPECIFICATIONS

Length (in.) 206.7 (1955-56), 207.7 (1957)
Wheelbase (in.) 122.0   **Weight (lbs.)** 3636-3750
Price (new) $2962-3481

ENGINES

cid/type	bore x stroke	bhp	years
287.2/ohv V8	3.75×3.25	180	1955
316/ohv V8	3.94×3.25	227	1956
347/ohv V8	3.94×3.56	270/290	1957

PRICES/PROJECTION

Restorable $3000-4000 **Good** $4000-7000
Excellent $7000-10,000 **5-year projection** +15%

Pontiac Star Chief convertible 1955-56

PRODUCTION

1955 19,726   **1956** 13,510

1955 Star Chief convertible

HISTORY

Among the more attractive soft-tops of the '50s. Offered only in Pontiac's top-line series, which had debuted the year before on a 2-inch longer wheelbase than the cheaper Chieftains. All-new styling for 1955 was typically Harley Earl, with a subtle beltline dip aft of the doors, bold combination bumper/grille, and rakish two-toning in eye-popping colors. A modest facelift the following year brought more and rearranged tinware and greater overall length, but Pontiac would never get into the fin game the way some other makes (notably Chrysler products) would. A modern, ohv V8 arrived for '55, Pontiac's first, and delivered fine performance. A bore increase for '56 brought standard Star Chief power up to 227.

FOR

Reasonably plentiful today • Solidly built • Attractiveness • Convertible appeal

AGAINST

Not cheap to run • Trim parts scarce

SPECIFICATIONS

Length (in.) 210.2 (1955), 212.6 (1956)   **Wheelbase (in.)** 124.0
Weight (lbs.) 3791/3860   **Price (new)** $2691/3105

ENGINES

cid/type	bore x stroke	bhp	years
287.2/ohv V8	3.75×3.25	173-200	1955
316.6/ohv V8	3.94×3.25	202-227	1956

PRICES/PROJECTION

Restorable $2000-3000 **Good** $3000-5000
Excellent $6000-10,000 **5-year projection** +15%

Pontiac Bonneville 1957-58

PRODUCTION

1957 2d convertible 630   **1958 2d hardtop** 9144
2d convertible 3096

HISTORY

The fastest Indians yet built. Began as a limited-production convertible launched during the 1957 model year, a product of performance enthusiast and division general manager S.E. "Bunkie" Knudsen. Based on the body/chassis design introduced with the 1955 models, then in its last year. Best remembered for introducing fuel injection (a mechanical system similar to, but not the same as,

1957 Bonneville convertible

Chevrolet's Ramjet) to Pontiac. Most '57s were painted white. All wore special Fuel Injection script on the front fenders. For 1958, Pontiac adopted what would turn out to be a one-year-only body-shell, which it shared with Chevrolet, thus making this year's Bonneville a counterpart to the Bel Air Impala. A two-door hardtop was added, and both offerings became a distinct series. Pontiac again bored out its V8 (from 347 to 370 cid), and offered the Bonneville with horsepower ranging from 255 up to 310 bhp with injection. Also available (introduced on lesser models the year before, actually) was a Tri-Power version, with three two-barrel carbs and 300 horses. Bonneville wheelbase shrank two inches, and curb weight was somewhat less than that of the hefty '57. Despite fairly low production, these cars put Pontiac on the performance map, so the name was spread across a full range of body styles for 1959 and beyond. Extremely rare when new, the '57 is the prize pick today, but there's nothing wrong with a '58 aside, perhaps, from its over-chromed front end.

FOR

'57 a should-be Milestone • Big, fast, good-looking • High appreciation • Pontiac image-makers • Rarity

AGAINST

High running costs • Styling not ageless • You'll need the high-calorie stuff to run them • '57s very scarce

SPECIFICATIONS

Length (in.) 213.8 (1957), 211.7 (1958)
Wheelbase (in.) 124.0 (1957), 122.0 (1958)
Weight (lbs.) 4285 (1957), 3710/3925 (1958)
Price (new) $5782 (1957), $3481-3586 (1958)

ENGINES

cid/type	bore × stroke	bhp	years
347/ohv V8	3.94 × 3.56	300+	1957
370/ohv V8	4.06 × 3.56	255-310	1958

PRICES/PROJECTION

1957 **Restorable** $3000-5000 **Good** $6000-8000
Excellent $9000-15,400 1958 **Restorable** $2000-3000
Good $4000-8000 **Excellent** $9000-13,000 Deduct 30% for hardtop. **5-year projection** +15%

1957 Bonneville convertible

Pontiac Grand Prix 1962-64

1962 Grand Prix 2-door hardtop

PRODUCTION

1962 30,195   **1963** 72,959   **1964** 63,810

HISTORY

One of the earliest and most popular personal cars of the '60s, and the first in a long line of posh Pontiacs that continue to this day. Introduced as a single hardtop model for 1962, built on the 120-inch-wheelbase Catalina platform, Pontiac's shorter big-car chassis. Elegantly decked out with the buckets-and-console interior so popular in those years, it offered cleaner looks than other Pontiacs, plus fine handling. The straight-lined '62 styling was replaced for 1963-64 with more flowing fender contours and an interesting concave rear window exclusive to the GP. Also special to it were grille treatment and a tail panel with concealed taillamps. Grand Prix continued as a full-size car and grew larger and heavier as the years went by. After 1968 it became a long-wheelbase intermediate based on the Tempest/LeMans series, which it still is today. The "classic" early-'60s GPs are the ones to look for, however. Engine options in this period were built around the 389 and 421 V8s, with horsepower as high as 370.

FOR

Desirable, collectible standard-size sportster • Crisp good looks • Performance • Posh interior

AGAINST

A natural hunger for high-octane gas • Limited appreciation potential

SPECIFICATIONS

Length (in.) 211.9 (1962), 213.6 (1963-64)
Wheelbase (in.) 120.0   **Weight (lbs.)** 3835-3930
Price (new) $3489-3499

ENGINES

cid/type	bore x stroke	bhp	years
389/ohv V8	4.06×3.75	303/370	1962-64
421/ohv V8	4.09×4.00	350/370	1963-64

PRICES/PROJECTION

Restorable $750-1500   **Good** $2000-3500
Excellent $3500-5000   **5-year projection** +10%

Pontiac Tempest LeMans 1962-63

1961 Tempest LeMans sport coupe (prototype)

PRODUCTION

1962 2d sport coupe 39,662   **2d convertible** 15,559
1963 2d sport coupe 45,701   **2d convertible** 15,957

HISTORY

Pontiac's compact, introduced for 1961, was technically interesting. It featured a radical flexible driveshaft and a rear-mounted transmission/differential combination (transaxle) with link-type suspension. This layout was not shared with the companion Buick Special and Oldsmobile F-85 (introduced the same year and using the same bodyshell as Tempest) or anything else. However, it was advanced, as shown by Porsche's much later adoption of the concept for its 924 and 928. The most sporting of the early Tempests were the LeMans fixed-pillar coupe and convertible. Introduced as a package option during the '61 model year, it became a full-fledged series from 1963 on (the name would eventually supplant Tempest for Pontiac's intermediate line). In these years, LeMans meant bucket seats, console, posh interior decor, and discreet exterior emblems. Power options had graduated to the hot 326 V8 by 1963. The standard Tempest engine in these years was a small four-cylinder unit.

FOR

Technical interest • Practical size • Sporty looks • Good performance with optional V8s

AGAINST

Tricky handling, especially in the wet • Mechanical complexity • Rust-prone • Some mechanical parts becoming scarce

SPECIFICATIONS

Length (in.) 189.3   **Wheelbase (in.)** 112.0
Weight (lbs.) 2800-3035   **Price (new)** $2294-2794

ENGINES

cid/type	bore x stroke	bhp	years
194.5/ohv I4	4.06×3.75	110-166	1962-63
215/ohv V8	3.50×2.80	185	1962
326/ohv V8	3.72×3.75	260	1963

PRICES/PROJECTION

COUPE Restorable $500-750   **Good** $1000-1500
Excellent $2000-2750   **CONVERTIBLE Restorable** $500-1250
Good $1500-2500   **Excellent** $3000-4500
5-year projection no change

Pontiac Tempest GTO 1964-67

1964 Tempest GTO sport coupe

PRODUCTION

1964 2d sport coupe 7384   **2d hardtop** 18,422
2d convertible 6644   **1965 2d sport coupe** 8319
2d hardtop 55,722   **2d convertible** 11,311
1966 2d sport coupe 10,363   **2d hardtop** 73,785
2d convertible 12,798   **1967 2d sport coupe** 7029
2d hardtop 65,176   **2d convertible** 9517

HISTORY

Virtually the originator of the "muscle car" concept, generally credited to ad man Jim Wangers. Introduced as a package option shortly after the start of the '64 model year; separated into a distinct series from 1966 on. The initial package consisted of floorshift, 389 V8, quick steering, stiffer suspension, dual exhausts, and premium tires—all for about $300. To this you could add a four-speed gearbox, sintered metallic brake linings, heavy-duty radiator, limited-slip differential, and power options that seemed to go up the scale every year. Shared basic Tempest/LeMans styling for the most part, identified specifically with discreet grille accents and those all-important "GTO" badges. All models in this generation were built on the 115-inch wheelbase introduced for '64. A mid-life facelift for 1966 brought more rounded "coke bottle" fender contours and tunneled rear roof/window treatment.

FOR

Milestone •Tremendous go •Fine handling •Widely sought-after, much admired

AGAINST

High operating costs •Mediocre construction quality •Pristine specimens hard to find

1966 Tempest GTO convertible

SPECIFICATIONS

Length (in.) 203.0 (1964-65), 206.4 (1966), 206.7 (1967)
Wheelbase (in.) 115.0 **Weight (lbs.)** 3000-3563
Price (new) $2751-3500

ENGINES

cid/type	bore x stroke	bhp	years
389/ohv V8	4.06×3.75	325-360	1964-66
400/ohv V8	4.12×3.75	255-360	1967

PRICES/PROJECTION

Restorable $1500-3000 **Good** $3000-5000
Excellent $5000-7000 Add 20% for convertible. Deduct 10% for 1965, 30% for 1966-67 models. **5-year projection** +10%

Pontiac Firebird 1967-69

1967 Firebird 2-door hardtop

PRODUCTION

1967 2d hardtop 67,032   **2d convertible** 15,526
1968 2d hardtop 90,152   **2d convertible** 16,960
1969 2d hardtop 76,059   **2d convertible** 11,649

HISTORY

Pontiac's somewhat more upmarket version of the Chevrolet Camaro, and very successful. Shared the same body/chassis design, but wore a distinctly Pontiac divided grille. Offered initially with five different engines, ranging from a base-tune version of the division's overhead cam six (introduced for 1966) to a 325-bhp 400 V8. Model designations reflected what was under the hood. The interesting Sprint model used a modified six, packing 215 horsepower from a Rochester Quadra-Jet carb, hot timing, and other tweaks. There were also Firebird 326s with 250 and (in H.O. form) 285 bhp. The 326 became the Firebird 350 for 1968. Styling was virtually unchanged in the first two years, then heavily facelifted for 1969, the year which saw the first of the mighty Trans Ams, powered by the big 400 with Ram-Air induction. In all, a broad and interesting ponycar lineup offering performance to suit most every taste.

FOR

Large following •Enjoyable to drive •Lots of variations to choose from •Nice styling •Still inexpensive •Trans Am's rarity •Sprint's technical interest •Strong appreciation potential

AGAINST

Cramped in back •Meager luggage space •Huge running costs with V8s •Hot models won't have been pampered

1969 Firebird Sprint convertible

SPECIFICATIONS

Length (in.) 188.4 (1967), 188.8 (1968), 191.1 (1969)
Wheelbase (in.) 108.1   **Weight (lbs.)** 2955-3346
Price (new) $2666-3045

ENGINES

cid/type	bore x stroke	bhp	years
230/ohc I6	3.88×3.26	165/215	1967
250/ohc I6	3.88×3.53	175/215/230	1968-69
326/ohv V8	3.72×3.75	250/285	1967
350/ohv V8	3.88 × 3.75	265-330	1968-69
400/ohv V8	4.13 × 3.75	335/345	1969

PRICES/PROJECTION

HARDTOP **Restorable** $700-1500 **Good** $1800-3000
Excellent $3000-5000 Add 100% for Trans Am CONVERTIBLE
Restorable $1500-2500 **Good** $3000-5000
Excellent $5000-7000 Add 300% for Trans Am.
5-year projection +50%, Trans Am convertible +30%

Pontiac GTO 1968-70

1969 GTO 2-door hardtop

PRODUCTION

1968 2d hardtop 77,704	**2d convertible** 9980		
1969 2d hardtop 64,851	**2d convertible** 7436		
1970 2d hardtop 36,366	**2d convertible** 3783		

HISTORY

Continuation of Pontiac's mid-size supercar. Based on GM's corporate "split wheelbase" intermediate body/chassis design that debuted this year, with two-door models mounted on the shorter 112-inch span. GTO maintained is familial resemblance to the big Pontiacs, particularly in front with an oversize bumper/grille covered in soft Endura body-color plastic. Beginning in 1969, Pontiac offered "The Judge" package, with 366-bhp Ram-Air V8 and Hurst shifter, plus identifying front-fender decals and low wing spoiler on the decklid. GM finally rescinded its edict against intermediates with fewer than 10 pounds per horsepower for the 1970 season, and Pontiac duly made its largest 455 V8 a GTO option. For 1971 and beyond, engine output declined in the face of emission controls and, later, the fuel crunch. The 1968 bodyshell lasted through '72. After that, GTO again became a package option. The 455 Super Duty V8 with 310 bhp was still available for '73. The next year, GTO became an option for the compact Pontiac Ventura. No models after 1970 are really collectible now.

FOR

More affordable than earlier GTOs, with the same qualities

AGAINST

Not as universally admired as earlier GTOs, although convertibles are rare and should pick up in value

SPECIFICATIONS

Length (in.) 200.7 (1968), 201.2 (1969), 202.9 (1970)
Wheelbase (in.) 112.0   **Weight (lbs.)** 3503-3691
Price (new) $3101-3492

ENGINES

cid/type	bore x stroke	bhp	years
400/ohv V8	4.12×3.75	265-370	1968-70
455/ohv V8	4.15×4.21	360	1970

PRICES/PROJECTION

Restorable $1000-1800 **Good** $2000-3700
Excellent $3500-5000 Add 40% for convertible
5-year projection no change

Pontiac Firebird 1970

1970 Firebird Formula 400 sport coupe

PRODUCTION

standard 18,874   **Formula 400** 7708   **Esprit** 18,961
Trans Am 3196

HISTORY

The second-generation Pontiac ponycar, introduced mid-way through the model year. Beautifully styled under the direction of Division studio chief Bill Porter, and distinctively Pontiac despite continued bodyshell sharing with Camaro. Increasingly tough Federal emissions and bumper-impact regulations were met successfully in later years without compromising the clean, pure shape too much. But as is often the case with collectible cars, these first-of-the-line models are the most desirable. Offered in four distinct variations of a single coupe body style (a convertible was never contemplated). Two, standard and Esprit, were mild; Formula 400 and the spoilered Trans Am were the wild ones. Worth having for styling and performance, but it's a bit premature to predict the ultimate collectibility of these models, not to mention the later ones.

FOR

One of the best designs anywhere ● Great performance ● Fine roadability ● Formula/Trans Am rarity ● Reasonable asking prices

AGAINST

Big engines thirsty ● Sixes anemic ● Limited back seat space ● Tiny trunk ● Performance versions won't have had an easy life ● Projected appreciation may not pan out

SPECIFICATIONS

Length (in.) 191.6 **Wheelbase (in.)** 108.0
Weight (lbs.) 3140-3550 **Price (new)** $2875-4305

ENGINES

cid/type	bore x stroke	bhp	years
250/ohv I6	3.88×3.53	155	1970
350/ohv V8	3.88×3.75	255	1970
400/ohv V8	4.13×3.75	330/345	1970

PRICES/PROJECTION

Restorable $500-1000 **Good** $1000-2000
Excellent $2500-3500 Add 100% for Trans Am, 20% for Ram-Air
5-year projection +10%

Pontiac Firebird Trans Am 1971-73

1971 Firebird Trans Am sport coupe

PRODUCTION

1971 2116 **1972** 1286 **1973** 4802

HISTORY

Pontiac's ripsnorting ponycar model, a continuation of the new second-generation design launched at mid-model year 1970. Each of these Trans Ams makes our collectibles roster on the basis of low production, particularly the '72s, which were in short supply because of the crippling auto workers strike at GM's Norwood, Ohio F-car plant that also affected Camaro Z-28 output. Styling and equipment remained relatively unchanged from 1970½, but the advent of low-compression engines at GM starting with the '71 model year robbed the Trans Am of some of its fire. Nevertheless, desirable for its macho styling and acceleration to match. The first of what would become known as the "screaming chicken" Firebird hood decals arrived as a $53 option for the '73s, but the once-functional shaker hood scoop was corked up. Trans Am power for 1971-72 was supplied exclusively by Pontiac's 455 H.O. V8 (factory order code LS-5). For 1973, a detuned version (L-75) became standard, and a new Super-Duty engine (installed in only 252 Trans Ams) was optional.

FOR

As for 1970 Firebird, plus Trans Am's performance appeal and greater exclusivity than other models in these years

AGAINST

As for 1970 Firebird, plus fuel thirst ● Also, difficult to find now in clean, original condition

SPECIFICATIONS

Length (in.) 191.6 **Wheelbase (in.)** 108.2 **Weight (lbs.)** 3700 (approx.) **Price (new)** $4103-4557

ENGINES

cid/type	bore x stroke	bhp	years
455/ohv V8	4.15×4.21	250-310*	1971-73

*SAE net bhp; rated at 335 bhp gross (305 SAE net) in 1971

PRICES/PROJECTION

As for 1970 Firebird Trans Am

Pontiac Grand Am 1973-75

1973 Grand Am "Colonnade" 2-door hardtop

PRODUCTION

1973 2d cpe 34,443 **4d sdn** 8691 **1974 2d cpe** 13,961
4d sdn 3122 **1975 2d cpe** 8786 **4d sdn** 1893

HISTORY

Pioneering American "Eurosedan," based on the workaday mid-size LeMans and sharing the new-for-'73 "Colonnade" styling common to all GM intermediates. Name derived from its presumed combination of Grand Prix luxury and Trans Am performance. Engineered by wizards John Seaton and Bill Collins, who tried to approximate the character and capabilities of comparable Mercedes-Benz and BMW models at a third or half their cost. Ride and handling not as good, but the differences were acceptable given the much lower price. Shorter-wheelbase coupe more able (and popular) than the longer, heavier sedan. Easily distinguished from other Pontiacs by a bulbous nose made of Endura deformable plastic.

FOR

Fine roadability and performance • Distinctive styling (especially in white) • Not a hot item now, thus inexpensive

AGAINST

Debatable styling to some • Interior strains to ape M-B design • Rust-prone • Body and soft-trim parts drying up; repros seem a long way off • Not much collector recognition now

SPECIFICATIONS

Length (in.) 208.0 (2d)/212.0 (4d) **Wheelbase (in.)** 112.0 (2d)/116.0 (4d) **Weight (lbs.)** 3992-4073 **Price (new)** $4264-4976

ENGINES

cid/type	bore x stroke	bhp*	years
400.0/ohv V8	4.12×3.75	170-225	1973-75
455.0/ohv V8	4.15×4.21	200	1975

*SAE net

PRICES/PROJECTION

TWO-DOOR Restorable $600-1000 **Good** $1200-2500 **Excellent** $2700-5000 **FOUR-DOOR Restorable** $600-800 **Good** $1000-2000 **Excellent** $2500-3400 **5-year projection** +40%

Pontiac Firebird Limited Edition Trans Am 1976

1976 Firebird Limited-Edition Trans Am coupe

PRODUCTION

2400

HISTORY

A special version of Pontiac's top ponycar, an outgrowth of an idea suggested by GM styling chief William L. Mitchell and executed by designer John R. Schinella. Introduced to commemorate Pontiac's 50th anniversary, the Limited Edition was mechanically the same as other Trans Ams. But you couldn't miss it on the street. It was all-black, highlighted by gold striping, grille insert and trim, and gold colored, honeycomb pattern polycast wheels. Inside was a gold-anodized instrument panel appliqué, gold steering wheel spokes, and special upholstery. A Hurst T-bar roof with smoke-tinted removable glass panels was offered as an extra, but leak problems led Pontiac to curtail installations to just 643. The deliberately restricted production run quickly sold out, which convinced Pontiac to offer a similar treatment under the name Special Edition for 1977-79. These are far more numerous and hence less desirable from the collector standpoint, though they're immensely desirable cars. The big-block 455-cid V8 vanished after 1976.

FOR

Looks still turn heads • Fine performance • Super handling • Low-production appeal

AGAINST

Collector prices not firmly established at present • Very thirsty • Difficult and expensive to insure • Sure-fire thief and cop bait

SPECIFICATIONS

Length (in.) 196.8 **Wheelbase (in.)** 108.2 **Weight (lbs.)** 3600 (approx.) **Price (new)** $8500

ENGINES

cid/type	bore x stroke	bhp	years
400/ohv V8	4.12×3.75	185*	1976
455/ohv V8	4.15×4.21	200*	1976

*SAE net

PRICES/PROJECTION

Restorable $1000-2000 **Good** $2500-4000 **Excellent** $5000-6500 **5-year projection** no change

Pontiac 10th Anniversary Trans Am 1979

1979 Firebird Tenth Anniversary Trans Am coupe

PRODUCTION

7500

HISTORY

Another commemorative Firebird, this one marking the first decade of Pontiac's still-successful ponycar. Officially priced at around

$10,600, but the announced low production and the model's perceived historical significance created a rash of speculation (classified ads appeared shortly after introduction listing $30,000 asking prices). Equipped with power everything, plus a distinctive silver and charcoal paint treatment, T-bar roof with silver-tint glass hatches, silver interior with leather upholstery, the heavy-duty WS-6 handling package, and "Turbo Alloy" wheels (designed by John Schinella and made by Appliance). The Tenth Anniversary Trans Am (TATA) came with the Oldsmobile built 403 V8 that was standard in the normal versions, but Pontiac had saved some of its own 400-cid V8s with higher horsepower just for this special birthday model, even though the engine had been dropped for '79. A very few 400s were teamed with four-speed manual gearbox, making this the most desirable drivetrain of the lot. Too new to be in wide circulation on the collector market, but a car that's sure to go up in value as the years pass and the brilliant second-generation Firebird becomes a more distant memory.

FOR

As for 1976 Firebird Limited Edition Trans Am

AGAINST

As for 1976 Firebird Limited Edition Trans Am

SPECIFICATIONS

Length (in.) 196.8 **Wheelbase (in.)** 108.2 **Weight (lbs.)** 3600 (approx.) **Price (new)** $10,619 original list price

ENGINES

cid/type	bore x stroke	bhp	years
400/ohv V8	4.12×3.75	220*	1979
403/ohv V8	4.35×3.36	185*	1979
*SAE net			

PRICES/PROJECTION

Difficult to establish with much accuracy at this writing. As an estimate, add 50% to 1976 Firebird Limited Edition Trans Am prices **5-year projection** no change

Rambler Rebel 1957

HISTORY

A specially trimmed four-door hardtop in the Custom series, introduced as a mid-1957 offering. Belied Rambler's conservative economy image because of its 327 V8 (from the last of the Big Nash and Hudson cars) and 9.5:1 compression ratio, good for 255 bhp and a 0-60 mph time of about seven seconds. A beefed-up driveline was matched by heavy-duty Gabriel adjustable shocks. A Bendix electric fuel injection unit was supposed to be offered as an option later, but never materialized. Styling was attractive and sporty, a mild facelift of the all-new '56 look. The Rebel had a chrome bodyside sweepspear filled with gold-colored anodized aluminum—not unlike the Plymouth Fury's, in fact. As a Rambler, this Rebel was a contradiction in terms, however, and went against the grain of George Romney's plans for sensible products. For 1958 all V8-equipped Ramblers were called Rebel, but the biggest engine listed was a 250. The 327 came only in the longer-wheelbase Ambassador, which sold only in very limited numbers.

FOR

AMC's first performance car • Not yet noticed much by the hobby, thus still quite affordable • Unique one-year-only model • Low production • Plenty of zip

AGAINST

Thirsty • Special trim pieces in short supply • Rust-prone unless properly cared for • Not easily found

SPECIFICATIONS

Length (in.) 191.1 **Wheelbase (in.)** 108.0 **Weight (lbs.)** 3353 **Price (new)** $2786

ENGINES

cid/type	bore x stroke	bhp	years
327/ohv V8	4.00×3.25	255	1957

PRICES/PROJECTION

Restorable $750-1500 **Good** $1500-2500 **Excellent** $2500-3500 **5-year projection** no change

Rambler Marlin 1965

1957 Rebel 4-door hardtop

1965 Marlin 2-door fastback hardtop

PRODUCTION

1500

PRODUCTION

10,327

HISTORY

American Motors' attempt to cash in on the sporty fastback craze of the mid-'60s. Essentially a re-roofed version of the intermediate Rambler Classic. Styling, created by Richard A. Teague, was first seen on a 1964 show car, the Tarpon, based on the smaller Rambler American platform. While its sweeping fastback looked good, it didn't suit the larger-scale Classic at all, aggravated by that car's nose, which looked too short and stubby in relation. Came out shortly after the Plymouth Barracuda, so comparisons were inevitable. Though the Marlin had a nice bucket-seat interior, it lacked the Plymouth's fold-down rear seat. The Rambler nameplate was removed for the carryover '66 version. For '67, Marlin was switched to the longer Ambassador chassis, which yielded more pleasing overall proportions. But it was too late. Marlin never really picked up enough buyer support to warrant continuing. Besides, AMC had a more attractive sporty car ready in the '68 Javelin.

FOR

Plush, bucket-seat interior •Decent performance with optional drivetrains •Historical oddity •Priced low today

AGAINST

Rust a constant worry •"Distinctive" styling •Slow to appreciate

SPECIFICATIONS

Length (in.) 195.0 **Wheelbase (in.)** 112.0 **Weight (lbs.)** 3234
Price (new) $3100

ENGINES

cid/type	bore x stroke	bhp	years
232/ohv I6	3.75×3.25	155	1965
287/ohv V8	3.75×3.25	198	1965
327/ohv V8	4.00×3.25	270	1965

PRICES/PROJECTION

Restorable $500-1000 **Good** $1000-2500
Excellent $2500-3500 **5-year projection** +10%

Rambler Rogue
1966-69

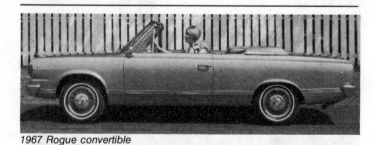

1967 Rogue convertible

PRODUCTION

NA (1969: 5055)

HISTORY

Dick Teague's pretty little Rambler American hardtop in its buckets-and console trim. Replaced the 1964-65 440-H as AMC's sporty compact for '66. Offered with six-cylinder engines only that

1969 Rogue 2-door hardtop

year, and afterwards with AMC's efficient 290 V8 in two stages of tune. These nicely trimmed little runabouts didn't change much in these years, though the '69 version is interesting historically as this was the last year for the Rambler nameplate. A Rogue convertible was offered for one year only, 1967, the last soft-top in the American series. It would be an extremely rare bird today. Still quite up to date in size, performance, and mileage, and quite affordable. And to our eyes, one of the nicest styling jobs ever done in Kenosha.

FOR

Quite affordable •Styling •Sportiness •Mileage and low running costs

AGAINST

Unit construction rust worries •Little appreciation potential

SPECIFICATIONS

Length (in.) 181.0 **Wheelbase (in.)** 106.0
Weight (lbs.) 2630-2821 **Price (new)** $2244-2611

ENGINES

cid/type	bore x stroke	bhp	years
199/ohv I6	3.75×3.00	128	1966-67
232/ohv I6	3.75×3.25	145	1967-69
290/ohv V8	3.75×3.28	200/225	1967-69

PRICES/PROJECTION

Restorable $500-1000 **Good** $1000-2000
Excellent $2000-3000 All 50% for convertible.
5-year projection no change

Rambler SC/Rambler
1969

PRODUCTION

1512

HISTORY

A limited-edition hardtop, mid-model year addition to the Rambler American line built under the aegis of the Hurst shifter people. The fastest car ever produced with the Rambler nameplate, it packed AMC's 390 V8 and Borg-Warner four-speed gearbox with (naturally) Hurst linkage. Outlandishly adorned with a bold functional hood scoop, red white and blue paint job, tri-color headrests, styled steel wheels, wider tires, and hood lock pins. One magazine

1969 SC/Rambler 2-door hardtop

clocked the "Scrambler" at just over six seconds in the 0-60 mph test, with the quarter-mile timed at a hair over 14 seconds at better than 100 mph. Only a very few were made—a dozen more in fact than 1957 Rambler Rebels—and this plus its high performance makes this pretentious little stormer a nice collectible that's also reasonably affordable.

FOR

High performance • Very low production • Budget collectible

AGAINST

Tacky "hi-po" add-ons ruin a clean basic shape • Thirsty • Rust-prone

SPECIFICATIONS

Length (in.) 181.0 **Wheelbase (in.)** 106.0 **Weight (lbs.)** 3160
Price (new) $2998

ENGINES

cid/type	bore x stroke	bhp	years
390/ohv V8	4.17×3.57	315	1969

PRICES/PROJECTION

Restorable $1000-2000 **Good** $2000-3000
Excellent $3000-4500 **5-year projection** no change

Reo Royale 1931-34

PRODUCTION

1931 830 926 **831** 707 **8-35** 2711 **1932 8-31** 126 **8-35** 176
RYL 6654 **Custom** 5128 **1933 Eight** 1300 (est.) **Custom Eight** 127 **1934 N-1 Custom Eight and N-2 Eight** NA

HISTORY

Underrated luxury car styled by Amos Northup, with pioneer streamlined bodywork featuring fashionable skirted fenders, a long hood, and dignified radiator. An immense 152-inch-wheelbase chassis was used for a seven-passenger sedan and limo in the 8-35 range of 1932. With its big nine-bearing straight eight and Northup's glamorous bodies, the Royale was a splendid car but entirely wrong for the times. The cars we cite are the only Reos ranked as Classics by the CCCA, and deservedly so.

1931-32 Royale 8-35 4-door sedan

FOR

Splendid, ahead-of-its-time coachwork • Smooth straight-eight performance • Luxury and quality • Some good buys still to be found

AGAINST

Parts scarce • A bit out of the ordinary and not as well recognized as they should be

SPECIFICATIONS

Length (in.) NA **Wheelbase (in.)** 131.0, 135.0 (1931-34); 152.0 (1932-34) **Weight (lbs.)** 4310-5075 **Price (new)** $1500-3895

ENGINES

cid/type	bore x stroke	bhp	years
358.0/L8	3.00×4.75	125	1931-34

PRICES/PROJECTION

Restorable $4000-8000 **Good** $12,000-20,000
Excellent $20,000-30,000. Add 40% for convertible coupe (available 1932-33 only). **5-year projection** +25%

Ruxton 1930

1930 4-door sedan

PRODUCTION

Approx. 500

HISTORY

Technically unique and aesthetically memorable, created under the aegis of colorful and controversial promoter Archie Andrews. Early example of front-wheel drive, chosen mainly for the lower-slung looks it conferred. All models were without conventional running boards, had ultra-low fenders, and were often equipped with impractical but eye-catching Woodlite headlamps. Production ended almost as soon as it started, thus making this an early casualty of the Depression.

FOR

Technically interesting • Important historically • Svelte, low bodywork • Always a novelty and widely admired

AGAINST

Extremely scarce • Fairly expensive, though not as much as you'd think • Parts of all kinds impossible

SPECIFICATIONS

Length (in.) NA **Wheelbase (in.)** 130.0 **Weight (lbs.)** 4670
Price (new) $4550 (sedan)

ENGINES

cid/type	bore x stroke	bhp	years
268.6/L8	3.00×4.75	85	1930

PRICES/PROJECTION

SEDAN/TOWN CAR **Restorable** $12,000-25,000
Good $30,000-45,000 **Excellent** $50,000-75,000 ROADSTER/
PHAETON **Restorable** $20,000-35,000 **Good** $50,000-80,000
Excellent $85,000-110,000. **5-year projection** +10%

Shelby GT-350
1965-67

PRODUCTION

1965 562 **1966** 2380 **1967** 1175

HISTORY

Carroll Shelby's high-performance conversion of the Ford Mustang. Aimed at capturing the Sports Car Club of America class B-production road racing title, which it did in 1965-67. Starting with a specially assembled Mustang fastback, the Shelby factory added a warmed-up Ford 289 V8 hooked to an aluminum-case Borg-Warner T-10 four-speed gearbox driving a hefty Galaxie rear axle. Metallic-lined rear brake drums, metal-based pads for the Kelsey-Hayes front disc brakes, Koni shocks, cast-aluminum wheels, and distinctive rocker panel and topside striping were all standard. The

1966 GT-350 fastback coupe

1965-model cars came without the Mustang's rear seat, using the space to house the spare tire (a Shelby trick to qualify the GT-350 as a sports car). Later, a fold-down rear seat was offered. Amazingly fast on turns or straights, the first GT-350 was one of the great road machines of the '60s.

FOR

Historical significance •Huge collector interest •Superb performance •High appreciation potential

AGAINST

Indifferent assembly quality, though Shelby components were well-built •High operating costs • Asking prices can vary wildly (see above)

SPECIFICATIONS

Length (in.) 181.6 **Wheelbase (in.)** 108.0 **Weight (lbs.)** 2800
Price (new) $3995-4547

ENGINES

cid/type	bore x stroke	bhp	years
289/ohv V8	4.00×2.87	290/306	1965-67

PRICES/PROJECTION

Restorable $5000-8000 **Good** $10,000-15,000
Excellent $15,000-20,000 Deduct $1000 for 1966-67 models
5-year projection +30%

Shelby GT-500
1967

PRODUCTION

2050

HISTORY

When Ford offered a 390-cid V8 as an option for the 1967 production Mustang, Carroll Shelby decided to one-up the factory by offering Ford's big-block 428 engine in his sharp GT. The result was the GT-500, packing an advertised 355 bhp, though actual output was closer to 400. Mustang was reskinned from the beltline down for '67, and fastbacks got a full-sweep roofline to replace the previous semi-fastback shape. The '67 Shelbys (both 350 and 500) changed accordingly, but were set even more apart from their mass-market cousins. This was accomplished with a specially styled fiberglass front end with a plain, open grille housing two small driving lights in its center, plus add-on scoops ahead of the rear wheel openings and on the rear roof quarters, a prominent trunklid spoiler, and wide taillight assemblies. Interiors were dominated by a thick, black-painted rollbar to which inertia-reel lap/shoulder belts were attached. A new emblem (a coiled cobra snake in anodized gold) was much in evidence. Prices were about $600 lower than the year before.

FOR

Staggering acceleration from Shelby-modified 428

AGAINST

A handful for all but highly skilled drivers •High operating costs •May cost a bundle to insure

SPECIFICATIONS

Length (in.) 181.6 **Wheelbase (in.)** 108.0 **Weight (lbs.)** 3000
Price (new) $4195

ENGINES

cid/type	bore x stroke	bhp	years
428/ohv V8	4.13×3.98	355*	1967

*advertised; actual estimated output 400 bhp

PRICES/PROJECTION

Restorable $4000-6000 **Good** $6000-10,000
Excellent $12,000-16,000 **5-year projection** +30%

Shelby GT-350
1968-70

PRODUCTION

1968 2d fastback coupe 1253 **2d convertible** 404
1969 2d fastback coupe 1085 **2d convertible** 194
1970 total 350

HISTORY

Further refinements of the earlier, smaller-engine Shelby-Mustangs, but closer in appearance and (1969-70) mechanical specs to the mass-production models. The Shelbys were modestly facelifted, with wide hood nostrils as air intakes, revised grille, and sequential turn signals for the taillights. The 302 version of the Ford small-block replaced the 289 V8 for the '68 GT-350. For 1969, the 351-cid extension of this unit was listed. Mustang was rebodied for '69 (though on the same wheelbase), so the Shelby was, too. Again there was a special front end and hood plus scoops and scallops almost everywhere stylists could put them. Beginning with the '68 models, the Shelby GTs were assembled in Michigan by the A.O. Smith company under contract to Ford. (This was reflected in availability of a first-ever convertible model in both GT-350 and 500 versions beginning this year.) Production ended with the '69s, though a few leftovers were given new serial numbers and sold as '70s. Government regulations, high insurance rates, and the beginning of the decline in buyer demand for thirsty, big-inch supercars are the factors that led Ford to drop its Shelby sideline.

FOR

Shelby performance at relatively lower prices ● Good investment potential, especially convertibles ● Rarity

AGAINST

Not as distinctive as earlier models ● High running costs ● More contrived '69 styling

SPECIFICATIONS

Length (in.) 183.6 (1968), 187.4 (1969-70)
Wheelbase (in.) 108.0 **Weight (lbs.)** 3000/3100
Price (new) $4117-4800

ENGINES

cid/type	bore x stroke	bhp	years
302/ohv V8	4.00×3.00	250	1968
351/ohv V8	4.00×3.50	290	1969

PRICES/PROJECTION

1968 Restorable $4000-7000 **Good** $8000-10,000
Excellent $10,000-15,000 **1969-70 Restorable** $3000-6000
Good $7000-9000 **Excellent** $9000-14,000 **Add 25% for convertible 5-year projection** +30%

Shelby GT-500
1968-70

1968 GT-500 convertible

PRODUCTION

1968 2d fastback coupe 1140 **2d convertible** 402
1969 2d fastback coupe 1536 **2d convertible** 335
1970 total 286

HISTORY

Continuation of the big-block Shelby GTs, more Mustang-like in appearance and mechanical specifications. Comments about the GT-350 in this period also apply here, apart from the engine, of course, which continued to be Ford's 428 Cobra Jet offering 335 to 375 advertised horsepower.

FOR

As for 1968-70 GT-350, 1967 GT-500

AGAINST

As for GT-350, 1967 GT-500

SPECIFICATIONS

Length (in.) 183.6 (1968), 187.4 (1969-70)
Wheelbase (in.) 108.0 **Weight (lbs.)** 3100/3200
Price (new) $4317-5100

ENGINES

cid/type	bore x stroke	bhp	years
428/ohv V8	4.13×3.98	335/360/375	1968-70

1969 GT-500 fastback coupe

Restorable $4000-6000 **Good** $7000-10,000
Excellent $10,000-15,000 Add 20% for convertible
5-year projection +30%

Shelby GT-500KR 1968

1968 GT-500KR fastback coupe

PRODUCTION

2d fastback coupe 933   **2d convertible** 318

HISTORY

A special version of the big-engine Shelby, offered only in this model year. "KR" stood for "King of the Road." Power was supplied by Ford's Cobra Jet 428 with oversize heads and intake manifold and a Holley 735-cfm carburetor. Identical in other respects to the "milder" GT-500 except for appropriate model name on the rocker panel tape stripes.

FOR

One of the hottest Shelby-Mustangs • Others as for 1968-70 GT-500, GT-350

AGAINST

As for 1968-70 GT-500, GT-350

SPECIFICATIONS

Length (in.) 183.6 **Wheelbase (in.)** 108.0
Weight (lbs.) 3200/3300 **Price (new)** $4473/4594

ENGINES

cid/type	bore x stroke	bhp	years
428/ohv V8	4.13×3.98	400*	1968

*estimated; advertised output lower

1968 GT-500KR fastback coupe

Add 20% to 1968 GT-500 prices **5-year projection** +30%

Studebaker President Eight 1930-33

1932 President Eight St. Regis brougham

PRODUCTION

1930 15,000 (est.) **1931** 4000 (est.) **1932** 2399 **1933** 1829

HISTORY

Studebaker's most impressive car of the early Depression years, built between 1929 and 1933 and engineered by the legendary Delmar G. "Barney" Roos. The President turned a leisurely 2800 rpm at 60 mph, was improved in 1931 when its engine was switched from five to nine main bearings and got more horsepower. The crankshaft, derived from the Liberty aircraft engine, was partly responsible for this powerplant's well-known durability and low-end stamina. Offered on two wheelbases for most of its life and with a wide variety of handsome body styles. The basis for Studebaker's most successful racers in this period and probably the best overall automobile ever produced at South Bend.

FOR

For years the most protested omission on the CCCA list, now a full Classic • Style and stamina

AGAINST

Growing parts shortage • Open bodies not cheap • Classic status will inevitably exert upward price pressure

SPECIFICATIONS

Length (in.) NA **Wheelbase (in.)** 125.0/135.0 (1930, 1933); 130.0/136.0 (1931); 135.0 (1932) **Weight (lbs.)** 3480-4605
Price (new) $1325-2595

ENGINES

cid/type	bore x stroke	bhp	years
337.0/L8	3.50×4.38	115-132	1930-33
250.0/L8	3.06×4.25	110	1933*

*Series 82

PRICES/PROJECTION

ROADSTERS **Restorable** $7000-15,000 **Good** $20,000-30,000
Excellent $35,000-50,000 OTHER OPEN deduct 25%. CLOSED
Restorable $4000-7000 **Good** $8000-15,000
Excellent $15,000-25,000. **5-year projection** +10%

Studebaker President Eight 1934-39

1938 State President 4-door Cruising Sedan

PRODUCTION

1934 3698 **1935** 2305 **1936** 7297 **1937** 9000 **1938** 5474
1939 8205

HISTORY

Continuation of Studebaker's top-of-the-line series, increasingly
streamlined through the late 1930s, gaining pontoon fenders and
rounded grillework but retaining a crisp, individual appearance.
Warner overdrive and "planar" independent front suspension in
1935 (transverse leaf spring with upper/lower links and rotary
shocks); "Hill Holder" in 1936. Automatic choke, vacuum-assisted
brakes, rotary door latches, all-steel bodies also arrived in late '30s.
Restyled by Raymond Loewy in 1938, and from that point they just
kept getting better, with prow-front motif, flush headlamps. All
models this period powered by Studebaker's 250-cid L-head eight
with up to 115 horsepower, which was more than adequate.

FOR

Superb road performer • High quality and style • Huge array of
bodies including the "Year Ahead" streamliners beginning July 1934

AGAINST

Not nearly as widely recognized and sought after as earlier
Presidents

SPECIFICATIONS

Length (in.) NA **Wheelbase (in.)** 123.0 (1934); 124.0 (1935);
125.0 (1936-37); 122.0 (1938-39) **Weight (lbs.)** 3300-3970
Price (new) $1015-1555

ENGINES

cid/type	bore x stroke	bhp	years
250.0/L8	3.06×4.25	110-115	1934/39

PRICES/PROJECTION

OPEN **Restorable** $4000-8000 **Good** $10,000-15,000
Excellent $15,000-22,000. Add 10% for convertible sedans.
CLOSED **Restorable** $1500-4000 **Good** $4000-7500
Excellent $7500-10,000. Add 10% for coupes & Custom
berlines. **5-year projection** open cars +10%; closed cars +5%

Studebaker President 1940-42

1941 President Skyway Land Cruiser sedan

PRODUCTION

1940 6444 **1941** 6994 **1942** 3500

HISTORY

The largest and most luxurious of the Raymond Loewy-styled
Studebakers in the years before World War II, priced in Buick Century and Chrysler Windsor territory. Improving finances allowed
Studebaker to offer three separate trim stages in 1941-42, and nine
different '42 models. The various permutations were all based on
only three closed body styles. A coupe, club sedan, and four-door
Cruising Sedan were offered for 1940. A sedan-coupe, Cruising
Sedan, and new Land Cruiser four-door were the 1941-42 offerings. A smooth L-head straight eight delivering 110/117 bhp provided the power. The President name did not return to Studebaker
until 1955. However, the long-wheelbase Land Cruisers were revived for the interim 1946 model year, an attempt to continue a car
this size with a more economical six-cylinder engine.

FOR

Relative rarity • Smooth open-road performance • Quality
construction

AGAINST

Limited body types • Unexciting styling

1942 President DeLuxstyle sedan-coupe

SPECIFICATIONS

Length (in.) 211.3 **Wheelbase (in.)** 122.0 (1940), 124.5 (1941-42) **Weight (lbs.)** 3280-3540 **Price (new)** $1025-1276

ENGINES

cid/type	bore x stroke	bhp	years
250.4/L8	3.06×4.25	110/117	1940-42

PRICES/PROJECTION

Restorable $2000-4000 **Good** $4000-6000
Excellent $6000-8000 Add 20% for sedan-coupe, 25% for Land Cruiser. **5-year projection** no change

Studebaker Skyway Champion 1946

1946 Skyway Champion 3-passenger coupe

PRODUCTION

3-pass. coupe 2465 **5-pass. coupe** 1285
2d club sedan 5000 **4d sedan** 10,525

HISTORY

Temporarily after the war, Studebaker built a limited number of Champions with prewar body dies and the well-proven 80-bhp L-head six. Alterations from 1942 were minimal: the upper grille molding was extended under the headlamps, side hood moldings were eliminated. As in '42, optional auxiliary lamps were available for the front fender tops.

FOR

Quite rare, especially coupes • The end of a design era • Well built

AGAINST

Now quite pricey for a Champion • Hard to find • Certain body parts now in short supply

SPECIFICATIONS

Length (in.) 197.8 **Wheelbase (in.)** 110.0
Weight (lbs.) 2491-2566 **Price (new)** $1002-1097

ENGINES

cid/type	bore x stroke	bhp	years
169.6/L6	3.00×4.00	80	1946

PRICES/PROJECTION

Restorable $500-1500 **Good** $2000-3000
Excellent $4000-5000 **5-year projection** no change

Studebaker Champion coupe/convertible 1947-49

1947 Champion Regal DeLuxe Starlight coupe

PRODUCTION

1947 Starlight 5-pass. coupe 16,731	**2d convertible** 2251
1948 Starlight 5-pass. coupe 14,481	**2d convertible** 9996
1949 Starlight 5-pass. coupe 15,746	**2d convertible** 7035

HISTORY

The same interesting, all-new postwar styling as the 1947-49 Commander in Studebaker's lower-priced series. Rode a 7-inch shorter wheelbase than Commander, and had a smaller (169.6-cid) L-head six. Less impressive-looking and with less performance, too, but includes all the same design qualities that make Studebakers of these years so noteworthy. Model offerings duplicate those in the Commander line, but with correspondingly lower prices then and now.

FOR

Trend-setting styling • Economical operation • Good parts supplies

AGAINST

As for 1947-49 Commander

SPECIFICATIONS

Length (in.) 190.6 (1947-48), 191.9 (1949)
Wheelbase (in.) 112.0 **Weight (lbs.)** 2670-2895
Price (new) $1472-2086

ENGINES

cid/type	bore x stroke	bhp	years
169.6/L6	3.00×4.00	80	1947-49

PRICES/PROJECTION

Approximately 10-15% below comparable Commanders
5-year projection no change

Studebaker Commander
coupe/convertible
1947-49

1948 Commander convertible

PRODUCTION

1947 Starlight 5-pass. coupe 13,299 **2d convertible** 1503
1948 Starlight 5-pass. coupe 14,441 **2d convertible** 7982
1949 Starlight 5-pass. coupe 8990 **2d convertible** 1702

HISTORY

The all-new postwar Studebaker in its most glamorous guises. Announced well in advance of the 1947 model year in early '46. A styling sensation that, to some extent, predicted design trends not only at Studebaker but also for the auto industry as a whole — particularly the flow-through front fenders and the low hood/deck height. The work mainly of Loewy Associates with input from Virgil Exner. The Starlight coupe featured an impressively large wraparound rear window, and was truly individual-looking. It was available in DeLuxe and Regal DeLuxe trim. The Commander convertible was offered only in Regal DeLuxe form. Though not as important as the Starlight, the soft-top is notable for its smooth lines and jaunty top-down character.

FOR

An outstanding industrial design • Good performance

AGAINST

Not cheap or easy to find anymore • Rust-prone, especially front fenders

SPECIFICATIONS

Length (in.) 204.3 (1947-48), 205.4 (1949)
Wheelbase (in.) 119.0 **Weight (lbs.)** 3200-3420
Price (new) $1755-2468

ENGINES

cid/type	bore x stroke	bhp	years
226.2/L6	3.31×4.38	94	1947-48
245.6/L6	3.31×4.75	100	1949

PRICES/PROJECTION

STARLIGHT **Restorable** $750-1500 **Good** $2500-3500
Excellent $4000-5500
CONVERTIBLE **Restorable** $2000-3000 **Good** $3000-4500
Excellent $5500-8000 **5-year projection** +no change

Studebaker Commander
1951

1951 Commander State Starlight coupe

PRODUCTION

124,329

HISTORY

The most important collector items among 1950-51 "bullet nose" Studebakers. The main reason is that this was the first year for the firm's pioneering 232 V8, really the first of the small-block engines (though Chevy and Ford usually get the credit). Though conventionally engineered and heavy compared to later small V8s, this reliable powerplant could deliver surprising economy with good performance. Coupled with the Studebaker/Detroit Gear three-speed automatic announced the previous year, the V8 made the '51 Commander very attractive, and sales were high. The most collectible models are the Starlight 5-passenger coupe, the convertible, and the long-wheelbase Land Cruiser four-door. Two- and four-door sedans were also available in this year's Commander line. Nomenclature for trim levels was revised, with Regal denoting the lower coupe and sedans and State applied to the upper-level sedans, coupe, and convertible in the Commander series. This was the next-to-last year for the 1947 "which way is it going?" design, a problem the more defined bullet nose front helped alleviate.

FOR

Notable historically • Good performance/economy balance • Nicely trimmed • Solid construction

AGAINST

Debatable styling (especially the front) • Traditional rust problems • An oil-leaker, though not usually an oil-burner

SPECIFICATIONS

Length (in.) 197.5 (Land Cruiser: 201.5) **Wheelbase (in.)** 115.0 (Land Cruiser: 119.0) **Weight (lbs.)** 3030-3240
Price (new) $1997-2381

ENGINES

cid/type	bore x stroke	bhp	years
232.6/ohv V8	3.38×3.25	120	1951

PRICES/PROJECTION

Restorable $500-1000 **Good** $1250-2000
Excellent $2500-4000 Add 25% for Land Cruiser, 30% for Starlight, 150% for convertible **5-year projection** no change

Studebaker Commander State Starliner 1952

1952 Commander State Starliner 2-door hardtop

PRODUCTION

14,548

HISTORY

New addition to Studebaker's upper series in the last year of the 1947 body design. The bullet nose was eliminated in favor of a "shovel" snout (sometimes dubbed clam digger), which some designers found less appealing. (The bullet nose has received a lot of flak over the years, but somehow looks less bizarre now than it did then; could it be the many blunt fronts we've seen in the years since?) The Starliner is significant in that it was Studebaker's first "hardtop convertible," with top-quality interior and pillarless roof. A companion Regal Starliner was also offered in the six-cylinder Champion line as well, which had been moved up to the Commander's 115-inch wheelbase the previous year. South Bend was the last major manufacturer to introduce a hardtop, but in the following year would carry this body type to its ultimate.

FOR

Historical interest ● Good performance from small-block V8

AGAINST

Underwhelming looks ● Rust susceptibility ● Poor-quality chrome

SPECIFICATIONS

Length (in.) 197.5 **Wheelbase (in.)** 115.0 **Weight (lbs.)** 3220 **Price (new)** $2488

1952 Commander State Starliner at South Bend ceremony

ENGINES

cid/type	bore x stroke	bhp	years
232.6/ohv V8	3.38×3.25	120	1952

PRICES/PROJECTION

Restorable $1000-1500 **Good** $2250-3000
Excellent $3500-5000 **5-year projection** +10%

Studebaker Champion Regal Starlight/Starliner 1953-54

1953 Champion Starliner 2-door hardtop

PRODUCTION

1953 Starliner 2d hardtop 13,058
Starlight 2d coupe 25,488   **1954 Starliner 2d hardtop** 4302
Starlight 2d coupe 12,167

HISTORY

Probably the outstanding American automotive design of the '50s, certainly one of the all-time greats. The smooth Starliner hardtop and companion Starlight fixed-pillar coupe were mainly the work of Robert E. Bourke, chief of the Raymond Loewy studios at South Bend. The styling was about as perfect as it could be: nothing out of place, nothing contrived or unnatural. The Starliner is the purer of the two in styling, but the Starlight holds together better because of the extra body rigidity conferred by its fixed roof pillar. Vertical grille teeth distinguish the '54s from the toothless '53s. As in past years, these Champion versions were six-cylinder cars, identifiable externally by an S-in-a-circle emblem on hood and deck in place of the V8 emblem found on the costlier Commanders. Studebaker's side-valve six was lighter than the V8, providing better balance and less final understeer. It was capable of notable economy, though far less performance than the V8. The '53 Champion dashboards differed from Commander dashes, grouping instruments under a single panel instead of housing them in hooded pods.

FOR

Landmark American styling ● Still very affordable considering design merit ● Less numerous but cheaper than Commanders ● Strong appreciation potential

AGAINST

A serious ruster ● Indifferent brakes ● Only fair construction quality, mainly '53s

SPECIFICATIONS

Length (in.) 201.9 **Wheelbase (in.)** 120.5
Weight (lbs.) 2700-2825 **Price (new)** $1955-2241

ENGINES

cid/type	bore x stroke	bhp	years
169.6/L6	3.00×4.00	85	1953-54

PRICES/PROJECTION

STARLINER Restorable $1000-1500 **Good** $2000-3000
Excellent $3000-4500 **STARLIGHT Restorable** $800-1200
Good $1200-2000 **Excellent** $2400-4000
5-year projection +10%

Studebaker Commander Regal Starlight/Starliner 1953-54

1953 Commander Starliner 2-door hardtop

PRODUCTION

1953 Starliner 2d hardtop 19,326
Starlight 2d coupe 20,859   **1954 Starliner 2d hardtop** 5040
Starlight 2d coupe 6019

HISTORY

The V8 version of the daring and enduring "Loewy coupe" design, similar in most other respects to the six-cylinder Champion models. The sleek European styling was matched by equally nice interiors, trimmed mainly in vinyl or (for 1954 only) cloth, both color-keyed. (There was also a slightly less posh DeLuxe-trim version of the fixed pillar Starlight offered in both years.) These could have been

1954 Commander Regal Starliner 2-door hardtop

the cars that would have assured Studebaker's future, but, as the production figures suggest, they didn't. One reason was spotty assembly quality on the '53s, a result of the rush to get the design into production. Another was the company's miscalculation about the sales of the coupes versus those of other body styles. Had Studebaker geared up to build more coupes, more would undoubtedly have been sold. As it was, the company thought the shorter-wheelbase sedans and wagons, with scrunched-up lines based on the coupe styling, would sell better. Despite their greater rarity, the '54s seem to trail the '53s in value right now, but that seems likely to reverse itself in time.

FOR

As for 1953-54 Champion models, plus good performance

AGAINST

As for 1953-54 Champion models, but more expensive even though more survive

SPECIFICATIONS

Length (in.) 201.9 **Wheelbase (in.)** 120.5
Weight (lbs.) 3040-3175 **Price (new)** $2213-2502

ENGINES

cid/type	bore x stroke	bhp	years
232.6/ohv V8	3.38×3.25	120	1953-54

PRICES/PROJECTION

Restorable $800-1500 **Good** $2000-3500
Excellent $3500-5500 **5-year projection** +10%

Studebaker President Speedster 1955

1955 President Speedster 2-door hardtop

PRODUCTION

2215

HISTORY

Studebaker's first step toward the sporty car, and forerunner to the memorable Hawks. The most expensive offering in this year's revived top-line President series, this two-door hardtop featured a special interior with quilted-pattern leather and vinyl upholstery and a full complement of white-on-black instruments set into a dash with tooled-metal appliqué. A high-performance rendition of the Studebaker small-block V8, now bored out to 259.2 cid, was standard. Speedsters shared the heavy, more chrome-laden front-end styling adopted this year across the line. All Speedsters wore two- or three-tone paint jobs in garish color combinations like the unforgettable "lemon and lime."

FOR

Rarity ●Historical interest ●Excellent performance ●A driver's cockpit ●Equipment

AGAINST

Retrograde facelift of the clean 1953-54 ●Significant rust problems ●Oil leaks

SPECIFICATIONS

Length (in.) 204.4 **Wheelbase (in.)** 120.5 **Weight (lbs.)** 3301
Price (new) $3253

ENGINES

cid/type	bore x stroke	bhp	years
259.2/ohv V8	3.56×3.25	185	1955

PRICES/PROJECTION

Restorable $1500-3000 **Good** $3000-5000
Excellent $5000-8500 **5-year projection** no change

Studebaker Golden Hawk 1956

1956 Golden Hawk 2-door hardtop

PRODUCTION

4071

HISTORY

The last Studebaker until the Avanti with styling influenced by the Loewy Studios. An evolution of the original 1953 Starliner/Starlight, distinguished by a squared-off eggcrate grille and raised trunklid. The Golden Hawk was the most luxurious, expensive, and powerful member of a four-model Hawk family for '56, and stood apart as a separate offering not directly tied to a regular series (the Flight, Power, and Sky Hawks were listed in the Champion, Commander, and President series, respectively). Available in pillarless form only, it was distinguished by grafted-on fiberglass tailfins. Standard power came from the big 352-cid Packard V8 with 275 bhp. A

heavy engine, it had a very negative effect on handling, but gave brilliant straightline pickup. Interestingly enough, Studebaker was able to price the Golden Hawk $200 below its 1955 President Speedster predecessor because of fewer standard accessories and a correspondingly longer options list.

FOR

Strong appreciation potential ●Flashy looks ●Impressive acceleration and high-speed cruising ability

AGAINST

Thirsty ●Don't take on better-balanced sports cars on a winding road

SPECIFICATIONS

Length (in.) 203.9 **Wheelbase (in.)** 120.5 **Weight (lbs.)** 3360
Price (new) $3061

ENGINES

cid/type	bore x stroke	bhp	years
352/ohv V8	4.00×3.50	275	1956

PRICES/PROJECTION

Restorable $2000-4000 **Good** $4000-6000
Excellent $7000-9500 **5-year projection** +10%

Studebaker Sky Hawk 1956

1956 Sky Hawk 2-door hardtop

PRODUCTION

3610

HISTORY

A less garish relative of this year's Golden Hawk, also with hardtop styling but without the tailfins or Packard engine. Part of the President series, and powered by the 210- or 225-bhp versions of Studebaker's V8, now stroked to 289 cid.

FOR

Good styling for the '50s ●Reasonably good handling ●Fine performance ●Low-production appeal ●Highly sought-after

AGAINST

Stude's usual rust and oil leak problems

SPECIFICATIONS

Length (in.) 203.9 **Wheelbase (in.)** 120.5 **Weight (lbs.)** 3215
Price (new) $2477

ENGINES

cid/type	bore x stroke	bhp	years
289/ohv V8	3.56×3.63	225	1956

PRICES/PROJECTION

Restorable $1000-2000 **Good** $2500-4000
Excellent $4500-6000 **5-year projection** +10%

Studebaker Golden Hawk 1957-58

1957 Golden Hawk 2-door hardtop

PRODUCTION

1957 4356 **1958** 878 (figures include 400 sub-model)

HISTORY

Continuation of the 1956 Golden Hawk, with the Packard V8 now replaced by a Studebaker 289 fortified by a McCulloch supercharger to develop the same 275 bhp. Styling differences in these years were confined to larger concave steel fins, usually carrying the contrasting color when two-tone paint was ordered. A variation introduced in April 1957 was the 400, featuring a leather-trimmed interior, upholstered trunk, and special trim details.

FOR

The best Hawks of the '50s for handling and performance

AGAINST

As for 1956 Sky Hawk

SPECIFICATIONS

Length (in.) 204.0 **Wheelbase (in.)** 120.5
Weight (lbs.) 3185/3470 **Price (new)** $3182/2382

ENGINES

cid/type	bore x stroke	bhp	years
289/ohv V8	3.56×3.63	275	1957-58

PRICES/PROJECTION

1957 Restorable $1500-2500 **Good** $2500-4000
Excellent $4000-7000 Add 25% for 1958 model, 50% for Golden Hawk 400. **5-year projection** +10%

Studebaker Silver Hawk & Hawk 1959-61

1959 Silver Hawk 2-door coupe

PRODUCTION

1959 V8 5371 **six** 2417 **1960** 4280 **1961** 3663 (figures do not include some 1960-61 Hawk six-cylinder export models)

HISTORY

Simplified successor to the Golden Hawk, a result of continued low 1957-58 sales. Listed simply as Hawk after 1959, when only a V8 engine was offered, Studebaker's 289, in two stages of tune and without the previous supercharger. Styling became cleaner, and an optional four-speed gearbox was made available for 1961. Note that Hawks in these years were all fixed-pillar coupes, not the pillarless hardtop style.

FOR

Good-looking ●Lively performance ●More reasonably priced than earlier "blown" models

AGAINST

As for 1956 Sky Hawk

1961 Hawk 2-door coupe

SPECIFICATIONS

Length (in.) 204.0 **Wheelbase (in.)** 120.5
Weight (lbs.) 2795-3207 **Price (new)** $2360-2650

ENGINES

cid/type	bore x stroke	bhp	years
169.6/L6	3.00×4.00	90	1959
259.2/ohv V8	3.56×3.25	180/195	1959
289/ohv V8	3.56×3.63	210/225	1960-61

PRICES/PROJECTION

Restorable $1000-1500 **Good** $2000-4000
Excellent $4500-5500 Add 20% for four-speed 1961 model,
deduct 20% for 1959 six. **5-year projection** +10%

Studebaker Gran Turismo Hawk 1962-64

1962 Gran Turismo Hawk 2-door hardtop (prototype)

PRODUCTION

1962 8388   **1963** 4634   **1964** 1767   (figures do not include six-cylinder export models)

HISTORY

Updated continuation of Studebaker's four-seat sporty car, now wearing a heavy but astonishingly successful facelift by designer Brooks Stevens. Still built on the old "Loewy coupe" bodyshell and 120.5-inch wheelbase from 1953 minus the 1957-61 tailfins. Stevens added a Thunderbird-like formal roof with broad C-pillars, removed needless trim from the bodysides and outlined them in bright metal, and introduced a new three-element dash design with room enough for a big tach and clock. Studebaker's 289 V8 in 210- and 225-bhp tune was carried over from '61 for the GT Hawk's first year. For 1963-64 it was supplemented with Avanti R-series versions packing up to 335 bhp by 1964. Despite good press and ideal packaging in the personal-car idiom, the GT Hawk was a sales disappointment, and was accordingly dropped after Studebaker consolidated production in Canada in January 1964.

FOR

Milestone status • Styling • Outstanding performance • Deft interior

AGAINST

Terrifically rust-prone • Poor component accessibility • All-vinyl 1962 upholstery not very durable

SPECIFICATIONS

Length (in.) 204.0 **Wheelbase (in.)** 120.5
Weight (lbs.) 3120-3280 **Price (new)** $2966-3095

ENGINES

cid/type	bore x stroke	bhp	years
289/ohv V8	3.54×3.63	210-290	1962-64

PRICES/PROJECTION

Restorable $1000-1250 **Good** $2000-4500
Excellent $5500-6500 Add 20% for 1964 models, 20% for R-series engines 1963-64 **5-year projection** +10%

Studebaker Lark Daytona hardtop/convertible 1962-64

1963 Lark Daytona 2-door hardtop

PRODUCTION

1962 2d hardtop 8480*		**2d convertible** 2681	
1963 2d hardtop 3763		**2d convertible** 1015	
1964 2d hardtop 2414		**2d convertible** 703	

*includes Regal models

HISTORY

The sportiest models in Studebaker's aging compact line. Introduced for 1962 along with a major reskinning by stylist Brooks Stevens, who again accomplished wonders for South Bend on a minimal budget. More flowing body lines for 1962-63 were set off by a Mercedes-style square grille. For 1964, styling became more straight-edged and crisper, and a neat inverted-trapezoid grille was used. Underneath it all, however, was the basic bodyshell first seen in the 1953 Champion/Commander series. The top-line Daytona offered front bucket seats, center console, and (from 1963 on) full instrumentation. Reclining front backrests and floor-mounted stickshift were optional, as was an interesting folding cloth sunroof for 1962-63. Offered with both six- and eight-cylinder engines, everything from the ancient L-head six to the hot R-series versions of the 289 V8 (though very few found their way into Larks). Studebaker's declining sales volume make these models quite rare today—and they're quite good cars at that, with a useful combination of performance and economy.

FOR

Economical collector-car buy •Size, character still appropriate •Ragtops' low production

AGAINST

Usual Stude rust propensity •Spotty fit and finish on '62s •Somewhat hard to find

SPECIFICATIONS

Length (in.) 188.0 (1962), 184.0 (1963), 190.0 (1964)
Wheelbase (in.) 109.0 **Weight (lbs.)** 2765-3320
Price (new) $2308-2843

ENGINES

cid/type	bore x stroke	bhp	years
169.6/ohv I6	3.00×4.00	112	1962-64
259/ohv V8	3.56×3.25	180/195	1962-64
289/ohv V8	3.56×3.63	210-335	1962-64

PRICES/PROJECTION

HARDTOP Restorable $900-1250 **Good** $1500-3000
Excellent $3000-4300 Add 45% for convertible, 20-40% for R-series engine. **5-year projection** +10%

Studebaker Avanti 1963-64

1963 Avanti sport coupe

PRODUCTION

1963 3834 **1964** 809

HISTORY

Eleventh-hour attempt by Studebaker president Sherwood Egbert to rejuvenate his company's staid image. A four-place *gran turismo* with a fiberglass body styled by a team working under Raymond Loewy. The result was advanced in several ways: coke bottle fender contours, grille-less front end, asymmetrically placed hood bulge, distinctive window shaping and large glass area, and a short, rounded tail. Inside were aircraft-like instrumentation and controls (some mounted overhead), slim-section bucket seats, and a built-in padded roll bar. Based on a shortened, modified Lark convertible chassis, with Bendix disc brakes and anti-sway bars front and rear. Powered by a standard 240-bhp 289 V8, but available with R-series engine options that raised output considerably. An experimental 304.5-cid R-5 engine used twin Paxton blowers and fuel injection to develop an alleged 575 bhp. An R-3 Avanti broke 29 speed records at the Bonneville Salt Flats. But production problems put the damper on the initial high enthusiasm for the car, and very few were actually delivered. Faltering finances caused Studebaker to consolidate its family-car operations in Canada in early 1964, which

1964 Avanti sport coupe

spelled the end of Avanti. But it was only temporary as the model was revived as a separate make by two Studebaker dealers in South Bend. It continues today as the Avanti II (see entry).

FOR

A truly important postwar car •High performance •High desirability •Always a show stopper •No-rust body (one of the few Studebakers so blessed)

AGAINST

Variable fiberglass finish •Not cheap on today's collector market •A little fuelish

SPECIFICATIONS

Length (in.) 192.5 **Wheelbase (in.)** 109.0
Weight (lbs.) 3140/3195 **Price (new)** $4445

ENGINES

cid/type	bore x stroke	bhp	years
289/ohv V8	3.56×3.63	240-335	1963-64

PRICES/PROJECTION

Restorable $3000-6000 **Good** $6000-12,000
Excellent $12,000-18,000 Add 20% for 1964 model, at least 20% for R2/3/4 engine. **5-year projection** +10%

Studebaker Lark Daytona Wagonaire 1963-64

1963 Lark Daytona Wagonaire wagon

PRODUCTION

NA

HISTORY

Another novel—and practical—styling idea by design consultant Brooks Stevens. Named for its sliding rear roof section that could be moved forward leaving unlimited "headroom" for carrying tall objects. Offered in standard and Regal trim for 1963, but the sportier Daytona models in both years are more collectible today. A fixed-roof standard model came along for mid-1963 priced about $100 lower, then was made an option for '64. The Wagonaire was ostensibly continued as part of the abbreviated Studebaker line built in Hamilton, Ontario, Canada following closure of the South Bend factory in early 1964, but the '63s are far more numerous. Listed with both six and V8 engines, including the Avanti R-series versions of the 289, though it's likely very few were actually bolted into these wagons.

FOR

A unique idea, never quite duplicated • Comparative rarity

AGAINST

We know of one that doesn't leak • Stude tinworm infestation

SPECIFICATIONS

Length (in.) 187.0 (1963), 193.0 (1964) **Wheelbase (in.)** 113.0 **Weight (lbs.)** 3245-3555 **Price (new)** $2700-2843

ENGINES

cid/type	bore x stroke	bhp	years
169.6/ohv I6	3.00×4.00	112	1963-64
259.2/ohv V8	3.56×3.25	180/195	1963-64
289/ohv V8	3.56×3.63	210-290	1963-64

PRICES/PROJECTION

Restorable $700-1000 **Good** $900-1300 **Excellent** $2000-3300 Deduct 15% for six-cylinder engine. Add 20% for R-series engine **5-year projection** +10%

Studebaker Daytona/ Wagonaire V8 1965-66

1965 Daytona 2-door sport sedan

PRODUCTION

NA

HISTORY

The last Studebakers, built at Hamilton, Ontario, Canada after closure of the old South Bend plant. The '65s were essentially a carry-over of the heavily revised '64 series, with the singular exception of engines—Studebaker now switched to Chevrolet power, six and V8. In the case of the latter, it was the famous 283 small-block, mildly tuned in this application, though capable of far more. A Daytona Sport two-door sedan and sliding-roof wagon were offered with V8 only for '65. For 1966, a single Wagonaire and Daytona two-door were listed, but now also available with the six. Styling in Studebaker's farewell model year was marked by single headlamps instead of quads and a new grille composed of four slim rectangles. On Daytonas, air extractor vents appeared where backup lamps (now mounted lower) had been. The Wagonaire was also available in less luxurious Commander trim in these years, and a Cruiser four-door sedan was still offered as in 1961-64. A fixed-roof wagon returned for '66 after a one-year absence. None of these, however, is as collectible as the last of the sporty Daytonas and practical Wagonaires with Chevy's evergreen, lightweight V8.

FOR

They didn't make any more, and these were the best of the last • Chevy engines more durable than Stude units • Attractive package size • Fine performance

AGAINST

Even DaVinci couldn't have done much with the basic styling • Some body parts almost unobtainable

SPECIFICATIONS

Length (in.) 193.0 **Wheelbase (in.)** 109.0 (Daytona), 113.0 (Wagonaire) **Weight (lbs.)** 2970-3505 **Price (new)** $2500-2695

ENGINES

cid/type	bore x stroke	bhp	years
194/ohv I6	3.56×3.25	120	1966
283/ohv V8	3.88×3.00	195	1965-66

PRICES/PROJECTION

Restorable $500-1000 **Good** $1000-2000 **Excellent** $2000-3000 **5-year projection** +10%

Stutz DV32 1932-36

1932 DV32 Continental coupe by Waterhouse

PRODUCTION

Under 200

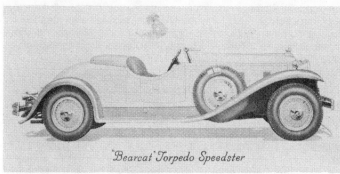
1931 DV32 Bearcat Torpedo Speedster

HISTORY

Stutz couldn't afford a multi-cylinder engine, so it mounted a super-charger on its eight, designed a new 32-valve head with double overhead cams, deleted the eight's twin ignition, and wrung 43 extra horsepower out of the 322 cubic inches. High-priced coachwork soon included the short-wheelbase Super Bearcat, initially fitted with artificial leather Weymann body. It would do 100 mph with ease, but even sedans could cruise effortlessly at 70. In 1932 the previous four-speed gearbox was replaced with a three-speed Muncie and freewheeling. This is found on all DV-32s.

FOR

The great name of Stutz • The heritage of a thoroughbred • Engineering exotica • Splendid coachwork

AGAINST

Extremely scarce • Very expensive • Mechanically complex • Very difficult engine parts situation

SPECIFICATIONS

Length (in.) NA Wheelbase (in.) 116.0/134.5/145.0
Weight (lbs.) 4538-5420 Price (new) $3795-5895

ENGINES

cid/type	bore x stroke	bhp	years
322.0/L8*	3.38×4.50	156	1932-36

*Supercharged

PRICES/PROJECTION

OPEN Restorable $30,000-50,000 Good $65,000-100,000 Excellent $100,000-135,000. CLOSED Restorable $9000-20,000 Good $20,000-40,000 Excellent $40,000-60,000. 5-year projection +10%

Stutz SV16 1932-36

PRODUCTION

Under 300

HISTORY

Smaller of the two Stutz Eights during the final years of the company, the SV16 pumped out only 113 horsepower, but its two long chassis carried the same plush bodies as the more famous DV32, including the last of the Stutz Bearcat two-passenger speedsters. A twin-ignition engine like the contemporary Nash unit, but not particularly lively. The bodies, however, were magnificent. All Stutzes are CCCA Classics.

FOR

Svelte coachwork, open and closed • The existence of a Bearcat model

AGAINST

Underpowered • Mechanically complex • Parts impossible • Any left to find?

SPECIFICATIONS

Length (in.) NA Wheelbase (in.) 116.0/134.5/145.0
Weight (lbs.) 4488-5346 Price (new) $1895-5095

ENGINES

cid/type	bore x stroke	bhp	years
322.0/L8	3.38×4.50	113	1932-36

PRICES/PROJECTION

BEARCAT Restorable $20,000-35,500 Good $40,000-75,000 Excellent $80,000-120,000. OTHER OPEN deduct 25%. CLOSED Restorable $8000-15,000 Good $20,000-30,000 Excellent $35,000-50,000. Add 15% for Versailles model, 10% for close-coupled coupes. 5-year projection +10%

Terraplane open models 1934-37

1937 Super convertible coupe

PRODUCTION

Open models comprised a small fraction—perhaps 2000 per year—of total Terraplane production, which was as follows:
1934 51,084 **1935** 51,134 **1936** 86,791 **1937** 90,253

HISTORY

Replaced the Essex Terraplane as a make in its own right for four years, after which it became a Hudson series. These years saw the most interesting styling, a major powerplant change—a new, larger six with more bhp than the old Essex eight—longer wheelbases, sleeker body styling and more performance. A 1936 sedan tested in

Britain did 0-60 mph in 26.6 seconds and delivered 82 mph top speed—highly creditable for a 2800-pound car at that time. Open body styles are, as usual, the most desirable. Convertible models numbered two per year except in 1935, when there was only the DeLuxe Six convertible. A six-passenger convertible brougham was added to the DeLuxe and Super lines in 1937. Independent front suspension added in 1934.

FOR

Handsome 1934-35 styling • Excellent performance • Strong club support

AGAINST

Unlovely 1936-37 "fencer's mask" grille • Difficult to find • Increasing scarcity of body parts

SPECIFICATIONS

Length (in.) NA **Wheelbase (in.)** 112.0 (1934-35); 115.0 (1936); 116.0 (1934); 117.0 (1937) **Weight (lbs.)** 2590-2915
Price (new) $695-845

ENGINES

cid/type	bore x stroke	bhp	years
212.0/L6	3.00×5.00	80-102	1934-37

PRICES/PROJECTION

1934 **Restorable** $4400-8800 **Good** $8800-13,500
Excellent $15,000-20,000 1935-37 **Restorable** $2200-5500
Good $5500-$10,000 **Excellent** $10,000-16,000
5-year projection +20%

Tucker "48" 1948

1948 Tucker "48" 4-door sedan

PRODUCTION

51

HISTORY

The most futuristic of the many advanced cars promised for the immediate postwar period, now almost legendary. Contrary to what you may have heard, was not done in by General Motors or Michigan's congressional delegation. Preston Tucker hired noted stylist Alex Tremulis to design this "torpedo" four-door sedan. Power was supplied by an unusual 335-cid aluminum-alloy flat six, mounted at the rear for a claimed benefit to weight distribution. Four-wheel

independent suspension, a central headlight that pivoted in the same direction as the front wheels, and a padded safety dash were other uncommon features trumpeted in Tucker advertising. Performance was excellent: 0-60 mph in 10 seconds, a top speed of about 120 mph.

FOR

An intriguing concept with an interesting history •Good appreciation potential •Outstanding performance

AGAINST

Forbiddingly expensive today •Scarce parts •Very few left on the market

SPECIFICATIONS

Length (in.) 219.0 **Wheelbase (in.)** 128.0 **Weight (lbs.)** NA
Price (new) $2450 (projected)

ENGINES

cid/type	bore x stroke	bhp	years
335/ohv flat 6	4.50×3.50	166	1948

PRICES/PROJECTION

Restorable $30,000-45,000 **Good** $45,000-60,000
Excellent $50,000-100,000 **5-year projection** +20%

Willys Americar 1941-42

PRODUCTION

1941 approx. 22,000 **1942** approx. 7000

HISTORY

Ordinary but well-built passenger cars produced under the presidency of Joseph W. Frazer (later of Kaiser-Frazer) and engineered by Barney Roos. The L-head four-cylinder engine and ladder chassis were conventional, while the sharp-nosed body styling owed a little to previous Hudsons and Nashes. Prices as low as $634 made the Americar competitive, but production had hardly begun when the company regrouped to build the immortal Jeep. Three variations — Speedway, DeLuxe and Plainsman — were offered, each with coupe and sedan, plus a DeLuxe four-door woody wagon.

FOR

Inexpensive now •The last Willys cars until 1952

AGAINST

Styling •Conventional specs •Body parts scarce now •Slow to appreciate

SPECIFICATIONS

Length (in.) 170.0 **Wheelbase (in.)** 104.0
Weight (lbs.) 2116-2512 **Price (new)** $634-978

ENGINES

cid/type	bore x stroke	bhp	years
134.2/L4	3.13×4.38	63	1941-42

PRICES/PROJECTION

Restorable $1000-3000 **Good** $3000-5000
Excellent $5000-8000 Add 25% for wagon.
5-year projection no change

Willys Jeepster
1948-51

1950 Jeepster phaeton convertible

PRODUCTION

1948 4-cylinder 10,326   **1949 4-cylinder** 2307
6-cylinder 653   **1950-51 4-cylinder** 4066   **6-cylinder** 1778

HISTORY

Sprightly touring car with styling by Brooks Stevens in the World War II Jeep vein. Could have had tremendous appeal in the early postwar years, but proved uncomfortable and clumsy to drive and too expensive. It was accordingly dropped as Willys' "passenger car." Engines were converted to overhead valve heads in mid-1949. The 1948-49 Jeepsters, with upright instead of eggcrate grilles, are finished to a higher standard than the later models. Though unsuccessful in these years, the Jeepster concept was revived about 15 years later for the Commando line of jaunty Jeep-based recreational vehicles.

FOR

Fair collector following • Many parts still available • Interesting styling and concept

AGAINST

Slow appreciation • Noisy • Uncomfortable

SPECIFICATIONS

Length (in.) 174.8   **Wheelbase (in.)** 104.0
Weight (lbs.) 2392-2485   **Price (new)** $1390-1765

ENGINES

cid/type	bore x stroke	bhp	years
134.3/L4	3.13×4.38	63	1948-49
134.3/ohv I4	3.13×4.38	72	1949-51
148.5/L6	3.00×3.50	72	1949-50
161/ohv I6	3.13×4.38	75	1950-51

PRICES/PROJECTION

Restorable $1500-2500 **Good** $3000-5000
Excellent $5000-7000 **5-year projection** +10%

Willys Aero-Eagle
1952-54

1952 Aero-Eagle 2-door hardtop

PRODUCTION

1952 2364   **1953** 7018   **1954 226 cid** 973 (inc. 11 Customs)
161 cid 583 (inc. 499 Customs)

HISTORY

Willys' return to a "proper" passenger car, engineered by Clyde Paton and styled by Phil Wright. Built with monocoque construction, the clean-lined Aero Willys was practical in size and one of the best-riding compacts of the early '50s. Unfortunately, price was too high to wean many buyers away from Ford, Chevy, and Plymouth models, even the cheaper ones. The Aero-Eagle two-door hardtop was the costliest and most luxurious of the various models offered, which also included Wing, Lark, Ace, and Falcon two- and four-door sedans. Kaiser acquired Willys in 1954, and the 226-cid Kaiser six was offered as an optional alternative to the Willys F-head four and 161-cid six. The Custom designation was introduced that year to denote an exterior or "continental" style spare tire mount.

FOR

Nice looks • Fine ride/handling combination • 226-cid models have good performance • Reasonable economy even today

AGAINST

Slow appreciation • Early rust-out threat • Body parts scarce

SPECIFICATIONS

Length (in.) 180.9 (1952-53), 183.0 (1954)
Wheelbase (in.) 108.0   **Weight (lbs.)** 2575-2847
Price (new) $2155-2904

ENGINES

cid/type	bore x stroke	bhp	years
134.2/L4	3.13×4.38	75/90	1952-54
161/ohv I6	3.13×4.38	72	1953-54
226.2/L6	3.31×4.38	115	1954

PRICES/PROJECTION

Restorable $750-1500 **Good** $1500-2500
Excellent $2500-3800 Add 10% for 1954 226-cid engine, 10% for Eagle Custom (continental spare). **5-year projection** +10%

Willys Bermuda
1955

1955 Bermuda 2-door hardtop

PRODUCTION

226 cid 2156   **161 cid** 59

HISTORY

Renamed successor to the Aero-Eagle hardtop in Willys' last-ditch attempt to improve its meager sales. A modest facelift performed by Kaiser on the Aero-Willys bodyshell brought a vertical bar grille, bodyside two-toning, and new ornamentation and taillights. Hardtop prices were cut to below the $2000 level in an effort to stimulate showroom traffic. But it wasn't enough, and only a few Bermudas were produced, along with an equally modest number of Ace and Custom sedans. Rarity, top-line status, and the marque's final model year make the Bermuda the most collectible of all the Aero-Willys models. Willys passenger cars continued to be built for several years in Brazil following the end of Kaiser-Willys' U.S. operations.

FOR

Scarcity • Good investment • Others as for 1952-54 Aero-Eagle

AGAINST

Styling • Others as for 1952-54 Aero-Eagle

SPECIFICATIONS

Length (in.) 189.9   **Wheelbase (in.)** 108.0   **Weight (lbs.)** 2831
Price (new) $1997

ENGINES

cid/type	bore x stroke	bhp	years
161/ohv I6	3.13×4.38	90	1955
226.2/L6	3.13×4.38	115	1955

PRICES/PROJECTION

Restorable $750-1500   **Good** $1500-3000
Excellent $3000-5000   **5-year projection** no change

Foreign Collectible Cars

AC Ace
1954-63

PRODUCTION

225

HISTORY

Superlative forerunner of the fabulous Cobra, designed by John Tojeiro with not a little inspiration from the contemporary Ferrari Barchetta. One of the classic postwar English roadsters: all-independent suspension; spartan leather upholstered cockpit; full instrumentation; four-speed gearbox; lithe and lean lines. Minimal weather protection in the English tradition. Excellent performance (100-plus mph, 0-60 mph in 11.5 seconds). Prominent in production-car racing in both Europe and America in its day, but considered an "exotic" even when new.

FOR

Magnificent styling • High performance • High investment potential • Cheaper than a Cobra • Low-production appeal

AGAINST

Hard-to-restore aluminum body • Some parts now scarce • Limited U.S. club activity

SPECIFICATIONS

Length (in.) 149.5   **Wheelbase (in.)** 90.0   **Weight (lbs.)** 1680
Price (new) $4000-5500 (U.S.)

ENGINES

cc/type (cid)	bore x stroke (mm)	bhp	years
1991/ohc I6 (121)	65×100	85/90/103	1954-63

PRICES/PROJECTION

Restorable $6000-10,000   **Good** $11,500-13,500
Excellent $14,000-22,000   **5-year projection** +10%

AC Aceca
1955-63

PRODUCTION

154

HISTORY

A smooth GT version of the Ace roadster. One of the great design triumphs, with lines that are faultless from any angle. Composite steel-tube-and-ash body construction was coupled with thick insulation, roll-up windows, and walnut and leather interior.

FOR

Landmark styling •Faster and smoother than Ace •Others as for 1954-63 Ace

AGAINST

As for 1954-63 Ace

SPECIFICATIONS

Length (in.) 149.5 **Wheelbase (in.)** 90.0 **Weight (lbs.)** 1680
Price (new) $4000-5500 (U.S.)

ENGINES

cc/type (cid)	bore x stroke (mm)	bhp	years
1991/ohc I6 (121)	65×100	85/90/103	1955-63

PRICES/PROJECTION

Restorable $4000-7000 **Good** $7000-11,000
Excellent $12,500-18,000 **5-year projection** +10%

AC Ace-Bristol 1957-63

PRODUCTION

463

HISTORY

AC's long-running traditional roadster with an engine transplant. To provide more power for the Ace, racing driver and engine specialist Ken Rudd suggested AC fit the Bristol 100D2 engine, which yielded a 115-mph top speed and a 0-60 mph time of 8.5 seconds. Rudd later developed three higher stages of tune. The top Stage 4 produced 148 bhp. The clean and nimble Ace-Bristols dominated the Sports Car Club of America's class E-production, and one took the 2.0-liter GT class win at Le Mans in 1958.

FOR

The ultimate version of the Ace, with stupendous performance for a 2.0-liter sports car •Very high appreciation

AGAINST

Very costly now •Engine parts increasingly scarce •Others as for standard Ace

SPECIFICATIONS

Length (in.) 149.5 **Wheelbase (in.)** 90.0 **Weight (lbs.)** 1700
Price (new) $4700-6000 (U.S.)

ENGINES

cc/type (cid)	bore x stroke (mm)	bhp	years
1971/ohv I6 (120)	66×96	105-148	1957-63

PRICES/PROJECTION

Restorable $8000-10,000 **Good** $12,500-16,000
Excellent $18,000-25,000 **5-year projection** +20%

1955-63 Aceca coupe

AC Aceca-Bristol 1957-63

PRODUCTION

172

HISTORY

The grandly styled Aceca with the superior Bristol 100D2 engine.

FOR

The most desirable AC next to a Cobra •Others as for 1957-63 Ace-Bristol

AGAINST

As for 1957-63 Ace-Bristol

SPECIFICATIONS

Length (in.) 149.5 **Wheelbase (in.)** 90.0 **Weight (lbs.)** 1700
Price (new) $4700-6000 (U.S.)

ENGINES

cc/type (cid)	bore x stroke (mm)	bhp	years
1971/ohv I6 (120)	66×96	105-148	1957-63

PRICES/PROJECTION

Restorable $7250-9250 **Good** $12,000-15,500
Excellent $17,000-24,000 **5-year projection** +20%

AC Cobra 289 1962-65

PRODUCTION

654 (including 75 260-cid models, 39 competition roadsters, 6 coupes)

1963-65 Cobra 289 roadster

HISTORY

The first of the high-powered transatlantic hybrids created by Texas chicken rancher and ex-race car driver Carroll Shelby. Ford's light, efficient small-block V8 was a natural for the low and lean AC Ace roadster, and was accommodated with only a modest lengthening of the nose. Took over completely at AC's Thames-Ditton premises, which shipped body and chassis to California where Shelby American dropped in the engine and completed assembly. Like the Ace/Aceca, used a sturdy tubular chassis with all-independent transverse leaf spring suspension—very hard but superbly controllable. Immense performance at low cost. The first 75 production models had the 260-cid engine; others used the 289. AC also built 29 "late" examples with the wider, fender-flared 427 body developed for the big-block version of the Cobra that was produced starting in 1965. These "AC 289s" were sold only in Europe.

FOR

Flashing acceleration ● Rarity and consequent high desirability ● American-made mechanicals ● Strong club support

AGAINST

Flimsy light-alloy body ● Thirsty ● British-made parts in short supply ● Costs a bundle ● Skimpy weather protection ● Has almost disappeared from the market

SPECIFICATIONS

Length (in.) 158.0   **Wheelbase (in.)** 90.0   **Weight (lbs.)** 2315
Price (new) $5995 (1962 U.S. base)

ENGINES

cid/type	bore x stroke	bhp	years
260/ohv V8	3.80×2.87	164	1962
289/ohv V8	4.00×2.87	260/271/306	1962-65

PRICES/PROJECTION

Restorable $10,000-25,000 **Good** $25,000-40,000
Excellent $45,000-60,000 Expert appraisal recommended.
5-year projection +15%

AC Cobra 427
1965-67

PRODUCTION

348 (numbered chassis)

Cobra 427 roadster (ERA replica)

HISTORY

The fastest street sports car ever produced, with mind-boggling acceleration courtesy of Ford's big-inch 427 mill slotted into the light AC Ace roadster. Off the showroom floor, this speed demon was capable of 0-100-0 mph in 14 seconds. Similar to the Cobra 289 except for a beefed-up frame to handle the engine's huge torque output, plus coil springs in place of leafs and fatter tires and wheels residing under the bulgier fenders needed to accommodate them. More exclusive than the 289 model, and like it a sure-fire investment, provided you can find one and have the considerable "scratch" it takes to purchase it. Not for unskilled drivers, and a real handful even for an expert, but there's just nothing to touch it for sheer speed and excitement.

FOR

As for 1962-65 Cobra 289, but more of it

AGAINST

As for 1962-65 Cobra 289, but even costlier and rarer ● Extremely thirsty

SPECIFICATIONS

Length (in.) 158.0   **Wheelbase (in.)** 90.0   **Weight (lbs.)** 2600
(approx.)   **Price (new)** $7000 (approx.)

ENGINES

cid/type	bore x stroke	bhp	years
427/ohv V8	4.23×3.78	345/425	1965-67

1965-67 Cobra 427 roadster

PRICES/PROJECTION

Restorable $20,000-40,000 **Good** $35,000-60,000
Excellent $65,000-90,000 **5-year projection** +10%

AC 428
1966-73

PRODUCTION

2d coupe 51 **2d convertible** 29

HISTORY

A rare combination of Cobra chassis engineering, lazy Ford V8 power, and Italian high style. The tubular Ace/Cobra chassis was lengthened 6 inches and topped by a brand-new hatchback coupe body styled by Pietro Frua. Overall appearance was quite close to the contemporary Maserati Mistrale. As the designation suggests, powered by Ford's slow-revving 428 V8 in very "soft" tune. In spite of its considerable size and weight, this car offered 140 mph and 0-60 mph acceleration of about 6.2 seconds. Virtually all examples were fitted with the Ford C-6 three-speed automatic transmission. Strictly a two-seater. Very high-priced when new, so production was low, both of which make the AC 428 quite desirable now. Collector prices are reasonable all things considered; it's far cheaper than a Cobra despite its greater rarity.

FOR

Frua styling • Simple mechanical layout • Cheap Ford drivetrains • Priced lower than a Cobra • Real exclusivity; very few reached the U.S.

AGAINST

Body parts impossible to find (hand-built coachwork here) • Looks too much like concurrent Maseratis • Only two seats • High fuel consumption • You'll look long and hard to find one

SPECIFICATIONS

Length (in.) 177.5 **Wheelbase (in.)** 96.0 **Weight (lbs.)** 3265
Price (new) NA

ENGINES

cid/type	bore x stroke	bhp	years
428/ohv V8	4.13×3.98	345	1966-73

PRICES/PROJECTION

Restorable $4000-5000 **Good** $8000-12,000
Excellent $15,000-20,000 **5-year projection** +100%

1967 428 convertible

Alfa Romeo
8C2300/8C2600
1931-34

PRODUCTION

188

HISTORY

Vittorio Jano's masterpiece, a followup to the very successful 6C1750 competition car. New 142-bhp supercharged twincam straight eight, four-speed gearbox, and torque-tube rear axle. Rock-hard leaf-spring front and rear suspension, massive drum brakes, high but narrow wire-spoke wheels, and several peerless body styles made for a sensational car—the Ferrari Boxer of its day. Long and short wheelbases, two-seat sports cars, coupes and cabriolets. Did 110 mph maximum from the start, even faster in ultra-rare 2.6-litre "Monza" form. Many still race in historic events today.

FOR

Amazing performance for the period • Looks, panache • Lovely supercharged engine • Roadholding, response • Rarity

AGAINST

Extremely expensive • Cramped, noisy, and stark, a no-compromise "road-racing" car • Parts no longer obtainable

SPECIFICATIONS

Length (in.) 153.0-169.0 **Wheelbase (in.)** 104/108/122
Weight (lbs.) 2200-2650 (approx.) **Price (new)** NA

ENGINES

cc/type (cid)	bore x stroke (mm)	bhp	years
2336/dohc I8 (143)	65×88	142-180	1931-34
2556/dohc I8 (156)	68×88	180	1933-34

PRICES/PROJECTION

Restorable $30,000-40,000 **Good** $120,000-140,000
Excellent $140,000-160,000 **5-year projection** +20%

Alfa Romeo 6C2300
1934-39

PRODUCTION

1606

HISTORY

Replacement for the long-running and successful 1500/1750/1900 range. The "volume" Alfa of these years. Not as fast, yet more civilized, than the firm's contemporary eight-cylinder monster. Styling was strictly derivative of other Alfas and concurrent Italians, though many sedans had distinctly U.S. lines. Early models had

1937 6C2300 Mille Miglia Berlinetta

1938 8C2900B Spider Corsa by Touring

beam front axles. Coil spring independent front suspension from 1935 (a first for Alfa) allied to swing-axle (Alfa said "Porsche type") independent rear. Twincam engines, but no "blowers" now that racing regulations had changed, so top speed less than 80 mph in most cases. Many wheelbase, power, and body style variations. Gave rise to the 6C-2500 of postwar fame.

FOR

Less complex than 8C, but still an Alfa • Good body style choice • Still a feasible rebuild bet • Not too rare

AGAINST

Not a fashionable Alfa • Disappointing performance • Sedans' stodgy looks • Bodies rot badly and no parts exist

SPECIFICATIONS

Length (in.) 160.0-175.0 **Wheelbase (in.)** 115.0/118.0/128.0
Weight (lbs.) 2820-3450 (approx.) **Price (new)** NA

ENGINES

cc/type (cid)	bore x stroke (mm)	bhp	years
2309/dohc I6 (141)	70×100	68-95	1934-39

PRICES/PROJECTION

Restorable $10,000-15,000 **Good** $30,000-35,000
Excellent $40,000-50,000 (depending on coachwork)
5-year projection no change

Alfa Romeo 8C2900 1935-39

PRODUCTION

41

HISTORY

Unquestionably the most desirable—and the rarest—prewar Alfa. Engine developed from the 8C2300/2600 unit and single-seat racing-car practice. Independent front and rear suspension but still with right-hand steering. More supple ride, but the fastest "over-the-counter" car in Europe. Up to 140 mph claimed—120-125 mph for most "customer" cars—ahead of everyone else. Various hand-built

styles, all with rounded lines and partly recessed headlamps but individually tailored. As scarce as nickel hamburgers now, but not at that price! Sold with "Corto" (short) and "Lungo" (long) chassis. Most were lightweight sports racers, but a few sumptuous coupes or cabriolets were also built.

FOR

Outstanding performance • Superb race-bred engineering • The sound, the charisma, the response • Ultra rare

AGAINST

Rarity makes restoration difficult • So specialized • Function before comfort

SPECIFICATIONS

Length (in.) 153.0-165.0 **Wheelbase (in.)** 108/110/118
Weight (lbs.) 1900-2750 **Price (new)** NA

ENGINES

cc/type (cid)	bore x stroke (mm)	bhp	years
2905 dohc I8 (177)	68×100	180/220	1935-39

PRICES/PROJECTION

Restorable $50,000-70,000 **Good** $200,000-250,000
Excellent $250,000-300,000 Values vary with coachwork.
5-year projection +20%

Alfa Romeo 6C-2500 1946-52

PRODUCTION

1947 486 **1948** 451 **1949** 414 **1950-52** 100 (approx.) (All figures are for calendar year production)

HISTORY

Last of the coachbuilt Alfas, descended from the Vittorio Jano-designed prewar 2300/2500. Featured light-alloy detachable cylinder heads, double overhead cams, hemispherical combustion chambers, plus four-speed all-synchro transmission. Most models would do 95 mph, the SS 10 mph more. Styles included the SS three-seat coupe, the Sports cabriolet, the lovely Freccia d'Oro

1947-52 6C-2500 "Freccia D'Oro" (Golden Arrow) coupe

1946-52 1900 Berlina (4-door sedan)

(Golden Arrow) coupe, and a Sports sedan offered in later years. SS coachwork was by Carrozzeria Touring; others were built by Alfa.

FOR

Usually good styling • Reasonable performance • Quality construction • Unique even in Alfa Romeo circles

AGAINST

Chancey parts supplies • Fuel thirst • Tricky aluminum bodywork • Unreliable electrics • Some dumpy-looking bodies

SPECIFICATIONS

Length (in.) NA   **Wheelbase (in.)** 118.0 (SS: 106.0)
Weight (lbs.) 3000-3500   **Price (new)** NA

ENGINES

cc/type (cid)	bore x stroke (mm)	bhp	years
2500/dohc I6 (153)	NA	90/105	1946-52

PRICES/PROJECTION

Restorable $10,000-15,000   **Good** $20,000-35,000
Excellent $35,000-90,000 Add 10-15% for SS or Freccia d'Oro.
5-year projection no change

Alfa Romeo 1900 1950-58

PRODUCTION

21,304 (includes 949 Sprints, 854 Super Sprints)

HISTORY

Alfa's first new postwar generation pioneered a number of firsts for the Italian automaker: unit steel construction, a twincam four-cylinder engine, and engineering specifically with quantity production in mind. Most built were four-door sedans, but Sprints (to 1953) and Super Sprints (from 1953 on) were offered in Touring coupe and Pininfarina convertible bodies. Less exclusive compared to previous Alfas, but cheaper and simpler to buy and operate. The TI versions of the sedan would top 100 mph; the special-bodied models were even faster. These were also the first Alfas to reach North America in significant numbers.

FOR

Rugged, high-class Italian twincam engineering • Simple layout • Not too highly tuned

AGAINST

Some parts nearly unobtainable now • Little factory support • Bodies rust badly • Dated styling • Few survivors

SPECIFICATIONS

Length (in.) Variable with body style   **Wheelbase (in.)** 98.5
Weight (lbs.) 2205 (coupe), 2425 (convertible)   **Price (new)** NA

ENGINES

cc/type (cid)	bore x stroke (mm)	bhp[1]	years
1884/dohc I4 (115)	83×88	100[2]	1950-53
1975/dohc I4 (121)	85×88	115[3]	1953-58

1. Net   2. Sprint   3. Super Sprint

PRICES/PROJECTION

Restorable $1000-2000   **Good** $3000-6000
Excellent $7000-14,000   **5-year projection** +15%

Alfa Romeo Giulietta 1954-65

1954-65 Giulietta Sprint Speciale coupe by Bertone

PRODUCTION

177,690 (incl. 27,142 Sprint, 17,096 Spider, 1576 special Sprint)

1954-65 Giulietta Sprint coupe by Bertone

1958-62 2000 Spider (convertible) by Touring

HISTORY

The first "small" Alfa, and phenomenally successful. Offered as a conventional four-door sedan styled by Alfa, plus the pretty Sprint coupe from Bertone and the Spider convertible by Pininfarina. There were also short-wheelbase, special lightweight models, the Bertone-styled SS and the SZ by Zagato. Specifications and engine tune were altered to suit the various applications. All Giuliettas had a twincam four-cylinder engine with wet liners, plus four- or five-speed gearboxes and an excellent-handling chassis. Successful in racing and rallying, and sold in the U.S. in huge numbers by Alfa standards. A typically raspy Italian exhaust note made them sound faster than they were, though the Sprints were capable of a genuine 100 mph, and the lightweight specials could see the right side of 120 mph.

FOR

Matchless styling (except sedans) • Sturdy engine • Great gearbox • Fine handling • Lots of model variations • No real problems with mechanical parts or rebuilds

AGAINST

Rust-prone Italian bodies • Little factory service or parts support • Overly complex mechanicals for the performance

SPECIFICATIONS

Length (in.) 153.5-162.2   **Wheelbase (in.)** 93.7 (Spider and SS/SZ: 88.6)   **Weight (lbs.)** 1700 (SZ)-2015 (sedan) **Price (new)** NA

ENGINES

cc/type (cid)	bore x stroke (mm)	bhp	years
1290/dohc I4 (79)	74×75	80/90/100	1954-65

PRICES/PROJECTION

Restorable $750-1500 **Good** $2000-3000 **Excellent** $4000-7000 Add 100% for special Zagato and Bertone body types **5-year projection** +10%

Alfa Romeo 2000
1958-62

PRODUCTION

4d sedan 2804   **2d Spider convertible** 3443 **2d Sprint coupe** 700

HISTORY

Successor to the long-running 1900 range, available in sedan, convertible (Spider), and coupe (Sprint) body types. Retained the 1975cc double overhead cam four from the last of the 1900s, but housed it in a new unit body/chassis. Sedans were built by Alfa, the Sprint by Bertone, and the Spider by Touring. The faster versions were capable of 110 mph, but these models were overshadowed by the smaller Giuliettas for performance and overall value. Replaced in 1962 by the six-cylinder 2600 series that used the same bodies.

FOR

Fashionable Italian looks • Rugged engine • Simple chassis

AGAINST

No factory service support any more • Parts difficult to find • Rust-prone • Spartan trim, furnishings • Somewhat heavy

SPECIFICATIONS

Length (in.) 185.6 (sedan), 180.3 (Sprint), 177.2 (Spider) **Wheelbase (in.)** 107.0 (sedan), 101.6 (Sprint), 98.5 (Spider) **Weight (lbs.)** 2600-2955   **Price (new)** NA

ENGINES

cc/type (cid)	bore x stroke (mm)	bhp	years
1975/dohc I4 (121)	85×88	115	1958-62

PRICES/PROJECTION

Restorable $500-800 **Good** $3000-3500 **Excellent** $4000-6000 Add $2000 for Spiders and special styles **5-year projection** +10%

1958-62 2000 Spider (convertible) by Touring

Alfa Romeo 2600
1962-68

PRODUCTION

4d sedan 2092 **2d Sprint coupe** 6999
2d Spider convertible 2255 **2d SZ coupe** 105

HISTORY

Continuation of the previous 2000 series as the "senior" Alfa offerings, now with twincam 2.6-liter six-cylinder engine. Same styling, but more performance and higher sales in these years. Performance boosted to the 120-mph level in some versions. New to the range was a special lightweight coupe styled and built by Zagato, of which only 105 were built.

FOR

As for 1958-62 2000, but better performance •Zagato's rarity

AGAINST

As for 1958-62 2000, but engine is more rare and thus more difficult to rebuild

SPECIFICATIONS

Length (in.) 185.0 (sedan), 180.3 (Sprint), 177.2 (Spider), 173.2 (SZ) **Wheelbase (in.)** 106.7 (sedan), 101.6 (Sprint), 98.4 (Spider, SZ) **Weight (lbs.)** 2690-2998 **Price (new)** NA

ENGINES

cc/type (cid)	bore x stroke (mm)	bhp	years
2584/dohc I6 (158)	83×80	130	1962-68

PRICES/PROJECTION

Restorable $1000-2000 **Good** $2000-3000
Excellent $4000-6500 Add 50% for special coachwork or Spiders 100% for SZ **5-year projection** no change

Alfa Romeo Giulia
1962-79

PRODUCTION

Over 400,000; more than 100,000 are Sprint coupe, Spider convertible, and special-body models

1970 Giulia Duetto convertible by Pininfarina

1972 Giulia Berlina (4-door sedan)

HISTORY

Alfa's brilliant, long-lived smaller series. Engine was the twincam four from the previous Giulietta, and went through a number of displacement and tuning changes through the years spanning 1.3 to 2.0 liters. Remarkably, it's still in production today. Many interesting models here besides the plain-looking Alfa-built sedans. Among the more notable are the Sprint coupe (built by Bertone and one of the earliest of Giorgetto Giugiaro's efforts) and the Spider two-seat roadster styled by Pininfarina (marketed initially as the Duetto with a long, tapering tail; later versions had a chopped Kamm-style tail and no specific name). There were also Zagato's usual lightweight types with that coachbuilder's oddly rounded lines. A special GTA version of the Sprint with light-alloy body and hopped-up engine was created for racing. Giulias were sold in fair numbers stateside through the '70s despite our emissions and bumper impact regulations. Too many permutations to describe here, but every one had character and the kind of surprising performance for which Italian cars are noted.

FOR

Popular, versatile design •Numerous • A model for every taste and pocketbook •Light, nimble, quick •Many body parts still available

AGAINST

Steel-body models rust badly •Not very exclusive •Italianate driving position won't suit everyone •Body construction doesn't match robust engine •Engine parts a bit scarce •Engine rebuild demands more than usual knowledge and skill

SPECIFICATIONS

Length (in.) 163.7 (sedan), 160.6 (Sprint), 167.9 161.1 (Spider) **Wheelbase (in.)** 98.8 (sedan), 92.5 (Sprint), 88.6 (Spider) **Weight (lbs.)** 2180-2300 **Price (new)** $4700 U.S. for 1750 Spider Veloce in 1971; $5600 for 2000 GTV in 1972

ENGINES

cc/type (cid)	bore x stroke (mm)	bhp*	years**
1290/dohc I4 (79)	74×75	90	1962-68
1570/odhc I4 (96)	78×82	110	1968-70
1779/dohc I4 (108)	80×89	120	1970-75
1962/dohc I4 (120)	84×90	130	1975-79

*figures approximate; output varies according to application and, in U.S. market, emission controls
**calendar year availability in U.S.

1974 2000 GT Veloce coupe by Bertone

PRICES/PROJECTION

As for Alfa Romeo Giulietta

Alfa Romeo Montreal 1971-75

PRODUCTION

3925

HISTORY

The production version of Alfa Romeo's "dream car" first seen at Expo '67 in Montreal. Distinctive, Bertone-designed body sat on a Giulia floorpan and suspension. Besides its looks, a 2.6-liter twin-cam V8 (a detuned version of Alfa's 3.0-liter racing unit) made this a very special machine. Not quite in the supercar class (top speed was 137 mph in European trim), it was nevertheless as fast as a Porsche 911, its main price competitor. Not heavily promoted, and not a profit-maker for a firm that was beset by financial and labor troubles at the turn of the decade. All models were equipped with a ZF five-speed gearbox, and the engine was tuned to 200 bhp only.

There were no other variations, and Alfa didn't even bother to replace this unique top-of-the-line model after production quietly ended.

FOR

Unique styling ●Excellent performance ●Low-production appeal ●Sturdy Giulia underpinnings ●Not that expensive now for what it is

AGAINST

Complex engine nearly hand-built, parts now very scarce, rebuilds tricky ●Bodyshell quite rust-prone ●Suspension doesn't match straightline performance ●Little importer interest

SPECIFICATIONS

Length (in.) 156.0   **Wheelbase (in.)** 92.5   **Weight (lbs.)** 2830
Price (new) NA

ENGINES

cc/type (cid)	bore x stroke (mm)	bhp	years
2593/dohc V8 (158)	80×65	200*	1971-75

*DIN

PRICES/PROJECTION

Restorable $3000-5000   **Good** $5000-10,000
Excellent $14,000-18,000   **5-year projection** +10%

Allard K1 1946-49

PRODUCTION

151

HISTORY

The first series-built British Allard, not counting the limited-production, 100-inch-wheelbase J1. Like the J1, a two-seat sports

1971-75 Montreal coupe by Bertone

roadster, but on a 106-inch wheelbase. Like all early Allards, rode a special box-section chassis with transverse leaf spring suspension front and rear. Wheel location was provided by swing axles in front and by a torque tube/beam axle at the rear. The Allard-built body was constructed of wood framing overlaid with steel paneling, and featured a full-width nose with the characteristic waterfall-style grille. A few K1s were sold without engines (mainly in the U.S.), but the majority were equipped with British Ford or Canadian Mercury flathead V8s. Not very refined, and expensive new, but there was no mistaking its individual personality.

FOR

Mechanical simplicity •Lively performance •Rarity

AGAINST

Bodies deteriorate badly •Crude detailing •Except for engine, parts very hard to find

SPECIFICATIONS

Length (in.) 168.0 **Wheelbase (in.)** 106.0 **Weight (lbs.)** 2460
Price (new) NA

ENGINES

cc/type (cid)	bore x stroke (mm)	bhp	years
3622/LV8 (221)	78×93	85/95	1946-49
3917/LV8 (239)	81×98	95/100	1946-49

PRICES/PROJECTION

Restorable $800-1500 **Good** $2000-3000
Excellent $4800-6000 **5-year projection** +10%

Allard J2
1950-51

PRODUCTION

90

HISTORY

Stark, two-seat open sports car built with U.S. exports in mind by the small English concern headed by former racing driver Sydney Allard. Simple box-section frame had coil spring and swing axle front suspension, De Dion rear suspension. Light-alloy, cigar-shape body design (somewhat similar to the Healey Silverstone's), with separate cycle-type front fenders. No full-width windshield provided unless you insisted; no weather protection or heater, either. Often supplied without engine or gearbox, which owner would then have installed. The fastest J2s were fitted with Cadillac ohv V8s, others with contemporary Ford V8s or the flathead Lincoln V12 engine. A high power-to-weight ratio made the J2 quite a stormer, but it was a short-lived model even so. Replaced by the J2X.

FOR

Performance • Simple mechanical layout • U.S. mechanicals • Active club • Very rare

AGAINST

Crude in detail • Little in the way of comfort • No weather protection

•British-made parts very scarce • Are there any left on the market?

SPECIFICATIONS

Length (in.) 148.0 **Wheelbase (in.)** 100.0 **Weight (lbs.)** 2500
(depending on engine) **Price (new)** NA

ENGINES

cid/type	bore x stroke	bhp	years
331/ohv V8[1]	3.81×3.63	160	1950-51
239.4/V8[2]	3.19×3.75	100	1950-51
292/LV12[3]	2.88×3.75	125	1950-51
1. Cadillac 2. Ford 3. Lincoln			

PRICES/PROJECTION

Restorable $1200-2500 **Good** $4500-6000
Excellent $6000-7200 **5-year projection** +10%

Allard K2
1950-52

1952 K2 roadster

PRODUCTION

119

HISTORY

Running mate to the J2 of these years, and basically similar to its K1 predecessor. Still with Ford-style transverse leaf spring rear suspension design, but front suspension now by coil springs. Unchanged in appearance except for a smaller grille replacing the K1's "waterfall."

FOR

As for 1946-49 K1

AGAINST

As for 1946-49 K1

SPECIFICATIONS

Length (in.) 168.0 **Wheelbase (in.)** 106.0 **Weight (lbs.)** 2460
Price (new) NA

ENGINES

cc/type (cid)	bore x stroke (mm)	bhp*	years
3622/LV8 (221)	78×93	85/95	1950-52

cc/type (cid)	bore x stroke (mm)	bhp	years
3917/LV8 (239) *gross	81×98	95/100	1950-52

PRICES/PROJECTION

As for 1946-49 Allard K1

Allard K3
1952-54

PRODUCTION

62

HISTORY

Another of Sydney Allard's low-production series sports roadsters, retaining many components from the K2. Revised chassis now with tubular construction, similar to that of the J2X in most respects. De Dion linkage was used for the rear suspension. A major restyle brought a simple, slab-sided, full-width body; an oval grille with horizontal slats; a vee'd windshield; and better-quality trim and fittings. Like all production Allards, built at the firm's small London workshops. Offered with a choice of Ford or Mercury V8s. Some visual similarity with the Palm Beach (see entry), but very different mechanically.

FOR

As for 1946-49 K1, 1950-52 K2

AGAINST

As for 1946-49 K1, 1950-52 K2

SPECIFICATIONS

Length (in.) 177.0 **Wheelbase (in.)** 100.0 **Weight (lbs.)** 2580
Price (new) NA

ENGINES

cc/type (cid)	bore x stroke (mm)	bhp	years
3622/LV8 (221)	78×93	85/95	1952-54
3917/LV8 (239)	81×98	100/110	1952-54

PRICES/PROJECTION

As for 1946-49 K1 and 1950-52 K2

Allard J2X
1952-54

PRODUCTION

83

HISTORY

A re-engineered derivative of the J2, and perhaps the best remem-

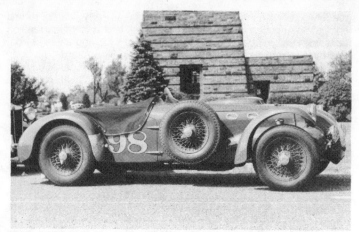

1952 J2X roadster

bered of Allard's transatlantic hybrids. Powered by Cadillac's modern, high-compression, 331-cid overhead valve V8 set seven inches further back in the tubular chassis than J2 engines. Otherwise, little changed from its predecessor, with the same cigar-style body shape, separate cycle-type front fenders, and sparse creature comforts. More rigid yet lighter frame, however, so roadholding was improved to match the higher performance potential of the Caddy engine.

FOR

As for 1950-52 J2, but more thoroughly engineered

AGAINST

As for 1950-52 J2

SPECIFICATIONS

Length (in.) 148.0 **Wheelbase (in.)** 100.0 **Weight (lbs.)** 2500
Price (new) NA

ENGINES

cid/type	bore x stroke	bhp	years
331/ohv V8	3.81×3.63	160	1952-54

PRICES/PROJECTION

Restorable $5000-10,000 **Good** $10,000-25,000
Excellent $30,000-40,000 **5-year projection** +20%

Allard Palm Beach
1952-59

PRODUCTION

1.5 Litre 8 **2.2 Litre** 65 **Mark II** 7

HISTORY

Allard's unsuccessful try at a smaller, lighter, cheaper model to replace its V8 powered roadsters. Built around a tubular frame and a shorter 96-inch wheelbase. The body was much like the K3's, a full-width roadster style with one-piece windshield and oval grille. Offered initially with British Ford four- and six-cylinder powerplants. Looking in many ways like the Swallow Doretti, the Palm Beach proved no more popular than that car. A redesign was accordingly instituted for 1956, bringing a more shapely form reminiscent of the Austin-Healey. Ford, Jaguar, and even Chrysler V8 engines were listed, but only seven of these Mark II cars were built. Never a

1958 Palm Beach Mk II convertible

high-volume manufacturer, Allard had already peaked in the early '50s. The company closed its doors in 1959.

FOR

Mechanical simplicity • Neat styling

AGAINST

Very few built • No parts available • Crude and less lively compared with concurrent Austin-Healeys and Triumph TRs

SPECIFICATIONS

Length (in.) 156.0 **Wheelbase (in.)** 96.0
Weight (lbs.) 1850/1950 **Price (new)** NA

ENGINES

cc/type (cid)	bore x stroke (mm)	bhp*	years
1508/ohv I4 (92)	79×76	47	1952-59
2262/ohv I6 (138)	79×76	68	1952-59

*gross

PRICES/PROJECTION

Restorable $800-1500 **Good** $2000-4000
Excellent $4000-6000 **5-year projection** +20%

1956 Palm Beach convertible

Alvis 3½ Litre/ Speed 25/4.3 Litre 1935-40

PRODUCTION

3½ Litre 61 **Speed 25** 536 **4.3 Litre** 198

HISTORY

Alvis of Coventry began after World War I and made its name with the 12/50. Its first inline six-cylinder model appeared in 1927. Engines grew larger and more powerful over the years while chassis grew more rigid and took on independent front suspension and an all-synchromesh gearbox. The ultimate developments were these late-'30s models, all with triple SU carburetors, high performance (maxima of 92, 97 and 104 mph, respectively), and elegant, coach-built bodies crafted by various specialists. At a time when Bentley was strictly hoi-polloi, Alvis was the one to buy for real grand touring. The Speed 25 had more power and better handling than the 3½, while the 4.3 Litre was the fastest six-cylinder British car of the day. None of these models reappeared after the war—German bombing saw to that—which makes the survivors more desirable than ever.

FOR

Elegance • High performance • Excellent transmission • Fine craftsmanship allied to great road manners

AGAINST

Parts no longer available • Most bodies rotted badly • Complex engines • Marque little known here

SPECIFICATIONS

Length (in.) 185.0/190.0/191.0 **Wheelbase (in.)** 124.0/127.0 (all chassis) **Weight (lbs.)** 3700-4300 **Price (new)** NA

ENGINES

cc/type (cid)	bore x stroke (mm)	bhp	years
3571/I6 (218)	83×110	102/106*	1935-40
4387/I6 (268)	92×110	137	1936-40

*Speed 25

PRICES/PROJECTION

Restorable $4000-5000 **Good** $10,000-13,000
Excellent $15,000-20,000 **5-year projection** +10%

Alvis TA21 1950-53

PRODUCTION

1310

HISTORY

The first cars on what would be the only new postwar chassis

1953 TA21 4-door sedan by H.J. Mulliner

design from this small English manufacturer. Was used for several model generations from 1950 through 1967, when it was finally withdrawn. The TA21 series comprised a four-door sedan with bodywork by H.J. Mulliner and a two-door convertible by Tickford. The chassis were separate from the bodies, and had coil-spring independent front suspension. Rather old-fashioned styling was matched by a sturdy but hardly modern cast-iron six-cylinder engine. Alvis was more interested in building aircraft engines than cars, though aviation standards of engineering and workmanship were applied to its automobile chassis. Still a staid, dignified car for the British middle-class in these years as it had been previously. Evident quality, but little performance. A car for the "gentleman" and his companions.

FOR

Traditional British styling • Strong separate frame • Understressed engine • Exclusive; few sold in U.S.

AGAINST

Wood-framed bodies rot badly if neglected • Parts now unobtainable except through Red Triangle in GB

SPECIFICATIONS

Length (in.) 182.5   **Wheelbase (in.)** 111.5   **Weight (lbs.)** 3250
Price (new) NA

ENGINES

cc/type (cid)	bore x stroke (mm)	bhp*	years
2993/ohv I6 (183)	84×90	85/90	1950-53

*net

PRICES/PROJECTION

Restorable $1000-1500 **Good** $4000-5000
Excellent $5500-6500 **5-year projection** +10%

Alvis TC21 & TC21/100 1953-56

PRODUCTION

TC21 250   **TC21/100** 475

HISTORY

The mildly restyled successor to the TA21, also sold in sedan or drophead (convertible) form. The TC21/100 was named for its

1953-56 TC21/100 convertible

100-bhp engine, which gave it a maximum speed around the "ton."

FOR

As for 1950-53 TA21, plus more performance

AGAINST

As for 1950-53 TA21

SPECIFICATIONS

Length (in.) 182.5   **Wheelbase (in.)** 111.5   **Weight (lbs.)** 3250
Price (new) NA

ENGINES

cc/type (cid)	bore x stroke (mm)	bhp*	years
2993/ohv I6 (183)	84×90	85/100	1953-56

*net

PRICES/PROJECTION

Restorable $2000-3000 **Good** $4000-5000
Excellent $5000-7000 **5-year projection** +10%

1953-56 TC21/100 "Grey Lady" 4-door sedan

Alvis TC108/G Graber 1956-58

PRODUCTION

30

HISTORY

A successful (from the design standpoint) new body style by Graber of Switzerland on the existing TC21/100 chassis. This two-door, four-seat coupe was built by Willowbrook of Loughborough, and embodied an unusual blend of traditional chassis behavior allied to contemporary looks. The model's commercial success was held back by the coachbuilder's inability to make enough cars. Top speed was well over 100 mph. Almost every one of these was sold in Britain, though a few may have wandered into the U.S. Replaced in 1958 by the Park Ward-bodied TD21.

FOR

Unmistakable Graber body •Solid separate chassis •Quality engineering •Good appreciation

AGAINST

Body parts have vanished •Body deteriorates rapidly •Archaic handling, roadholding •Heavy steering •Where do you look?

SPECIFICATIONS

Length (in.) 189.0 **Wheelbase (in.)** 111.5 **Weight (lbs.)** 3285
Price (new) NA

ENGINES

cc/type (cid)	bore x stroke (mm)	bhp*	years
2993/ohv I6 (183)	84×90	104	1956-58
*net			

PRICES/PROJECTION

Restorable $1500-2500 **Good** $3500-4500
Excellent $5000-6000 **5-year projection** +10%

Alvis TD21 1958-63

PRODUCTION

1060

HISTORY

Mildly restyled TC108/G with new bodywork by Park Ward of London (best known as purveyors of special Rolls-Royces). The most successful "Graber" derivative, now also offered in convertible form for the first time. Became faster and acquired disc brakes and an optional automatic transmission as the years progressed. A ZF five-speed manual gearbox was offered from 1963 on. Power from the well-tried straight six was boosted to 120 bhp during 1959.

FOR

As for TC108/G, but better Park Ward body •More performance •Availability of automatic, 5-speed

AGAINST

As for TC108/G, though body less prone to fall apart •Ancient chassis

SPECIFICATIONS

Length (in.) 189.0 **Wheelbase (in.)** 111.5 **Weight (lbs.)** 3285
Price (new) NA

ENGINES

cc/type (cid)	bore x stroke (mm)	bhp	years
2993/ohv I6 *net	84×90	104/120*	1958-63

PRICES/PROJECTION

Restorable $1800-2800 **Good** $3800-5000
Excellent $5500-6800 Add $1500 for convertible

Alvis TE21 1963-66

1963-66 TE21 coupe by Park Ward

PRODUCTION

350

HISTORY

A continuation of the TD21 series, but now wearing vertically stacked quad headlamps on either side of the upright Alvis grille. Revised steering and suspension in these years, plus another horsepower boost for the straight six engine.

FOR

As for 1958-63 TD21

AGAINST

As for 1958-63 TD21

SPECIFICATIONS

Length (in.) 189.0 **Wheelbase (in.)** 111.5 **Weight (lbs.)** 3450
Price (new) NA

ENGINES

cc/type (cid)	bore x stroke (mm)	bhp*	years
2993/ohv I6 (183)	84×90	130	1963-66

*net

PRICES/PROJECTION

As for TC-108G Graber, but add $1500 for convertible

Alvis TF21
1966-67

1966-67 TF21 coupe by Park Ward

PRODUCTION

105

HISTORY

The last of the Alvis "Graber" styles, and the last cars bearing this marque. Alvis had merged with Rover in 1965, and the make would be dropped once Rover became part of the Leyland (later British Leyland) group. Compared with the TE21, these models had improved controls (including power steering) and a new cylinder head for the long-lived six-cylinder engine that gave an extra 20 bhp and 110-mph performance.

FOR

As for TD21 and TE21

AGAINST

As for TD21 and TE21

SPECIFICATIONS

Length (in.) 189.0 **Wheelbase (in.)** 111.5 **Weight (lbs.)** 3475
Price (new) NA

ENGINES

cc/type (cid)	bore x stroke (mm)	bhp*	years
2993/ohv I6 (183)	84×90	150	1966-67

*net

PRICES/PROJECTION

As for 1963-66 TE21

Amphicar
1961-68

1960-68 convertible

PRODUCTION

3500 (approx.)

HISTORY

Superb neither on water or land, but nonetheless the world's only amphibious passenger car. Designed by Hans Trippel and powered by a Triumph Herald four-cylinder engine, it did what its maker claimed: run on the road (68 mph tops), sail on water (7 knots maximum) without sinking (rubber gaskets seal the doors; a bilge pump is available if the scupper-level rises.) A transfer case handles the drive to twin props, and water navigation is via the steering wheel (the front wheels act as rudders). The sure cure for marina fees, yacht club sharks, and people who want to borrow your boat.

FOR

Absolutely unique ● Engine parts readily available ● Perfect for antique boat meets or drive-in pool parties

AGAINST

Underpowered and cramped as a car ● Drippy '50s styling cliches ● A serious ruster (if only it were fiberglass!) ● Body parts in short supply.

SPECIFICATIONS

Length (in.) 157.5 **Wheelbase (in.)** 83.0 **Weight (lbs.)** 2292
Price (new) $3395

ENGINES

cc/type (cid)	bore x stroke (mm)	bhp*	years
1147/ohv I4 (66)	69×76	43	1961-68

*net

Arnolt-Bristol
1954-61

1956 roadster

PRODUCTION

142 (130 sold; 12 lost to warehouse fire)

HISTORY

A hybrid sports car created especially for the North American market, the product of Chicago foreign car entrepreneur Stanley H. "Wacky" Arnolt. Combined the rolling chassis of the British Bristol 404 with a sleek, two-seat body styled by Nuccio Bertone of Italy. Mechanically not a "pure" 404 (transmission and brakes were from the earlier 403), but had a tuned version of Bristol's BS1 Mark II engine with more power than the 404. The sturdy box-section chassis had transverse-leaf front suspension and a carefully located live rear axle. Light weight gave a good power-to-weight ratio, and acceleration was quick: 0-60 mph in 8.7 seconds, a top end of 110 mph. Offered in three versions: a starkly outfitted "Bolide" roadster, a more completely equipped DeLuxe roadster, and a fixed-roof coupe with roll-up windows (only three of the latter were built). Excellent weight distribution and fine road manners made the A-B a racing natural, and it competed with distinction at Sebring in 1955 and '56. Of the total number built, five were aluminum-bodied semi-racers; another four were fitted with 283-cid Corvette V8s. Expensive now, but body and engine parts are still available through Arnolt's son.

FOR

High-quality Bristol engineering • Great handling/roadholding • Punchy, tuneable engine • Low-production exclusivity

AGAINST

Engine parts running out now • Rust-prone • Not cheap to restore or maintain • Spartan furnishings • A rarity on the market

SPECIFICATIONS

Length (in.) 168.0 **Wheelbase (in.)** 96.0
Weight (lbs.) 2050-2315 **Price (new)** $3995-5995

1958 roadster

ENGINES

cc/type (cid)	bore x stroke (mm)	bhp*	years
1971/ohv I6 (120)	66×96	130	1955-61

*net

Aston Martin
1½-Litre/2-Litre
1927-39

PRODUCTION

599

HISTORY

The famous "Bertelli" series built at Feltham and powered by the same overhead-cam four. Vintage British, which means a willowy chassis, skimpy wooden-framed bodywork, cycle-type fenders, and a very noble radiator style. Very sporting. Enjoyed a measure of racing success through a succession of owners and recurring financial crises. Various power ratings and model names. International, Le Mans, and Ulster are the most famous ones. No functional connection with the postwar Astons, built under different owners and quite different in their engineering.

FOR

Great "vintage" character • A sports car above all • Super engine • Fine roadholding

AGAINST

Rare these days • Parts difficult • Cramped cockpit • Minimal weather protection • Little U.S. expertise available

SPECIFICATIONS

Length (in.) 144-168 **Wheelbase (in.)** 102/120 (1½); 99/116 (2.0) **Weight (lbs.)** 2000-3100 **Price (new)** NA

ENGINES

cc/type (cid)	bore x stroke (mm)	bhp*	years
1495/sohc I4 (91)	69.3×99	56-85	1927-35
1950/sohc I4 (119)	78×102	98/110	1936-39

*net

PRICES/PROJECTION

Restorable $5000-8000 **Good** $17,000-20,000
Excellent $20,000-25,000 **5-year projection** +30%

Aston Martin DB2
1950-53

1950-53 DB2 coupe

PRODUCTION

410

HISTORY

A millionaire British industrialist's "bit o' fun" that started a long and famous line of sports cars. David Brown's inspired amalgamation of a stillborn Aston Martin chassis design with a twincam six-cylinder engine developed by W. O. Bentley for the by-then bankrupt Lagonda concern. Multi-tubular frame, independent front suspension, and 100-mph performance from 2.6-liter engine. Prototypes raced with honor in 1949 and '50, and later production models continued to benefit from race-proved improvements. Two-seater fastback coupe and convertible were offered, both with light-alloy bodywork. Unmistakable styling, great charisma, and excellent road manners all add up to a fine automotive collectible.

FOR

Racing pedigree ●Impeccable road manners ●Flexible engine ●Not as common as contemporary Jaguar XK120

AGAINST

Mechanical parts hard to come by, but still around ●No body parts any more ●Construction quality not as high as you'd think ●Not as quick, either (early Triumph TRs and Austin-Healeys beat it)

SPECIFICATIONS

Length (in.) 169.5 **Wheelbase (in.)** 99.0 **Weight (lbs.)** 2660
Price (new) NA

ENGINES

cc/type (cid)	bore x stroke (mm)	bhp*	years
2580/dohc I6 (157)	78×90	105/125	1950-53

*net

PRICES/PROJECTION

Restorable $4000-8000 **Good** $8000-10,000
Excellent $12,000-18,000 **5-year projection** +30%

Aston Martin DB2/4
1953-57

PRODUCTION

763

HISTORY

Revised version of the DB2, with 2+2 seating and an early form of hatchback coupe body, now supplied by Mulliner (the convertible's was by Tickford). Engine capacity increased to 2922cc in 1954, giving a needed gain in power and torque to move these heavier models. The small rear seat made the car more versatile and therefore more attractive to a wider number of buyers, and construction quality was notably better in these years.

FOR

As for 1950-53 DB2, plus greater practicality

AGAINST

As for 1950-53 DB2 except for improved construction quality

SPECIFICATIONS

Length (in.) 169.5 **Wheelbase (in.)** 99.0 **Weight (lbs.)** 2730
Price (new) NA

ENGINES

cc/type (cid)	bore x stroke (mm)	bhp*	years
2580/dohc I6 (157)	78×90	125	1953-54
2922/dohc I6 (178)	83×90	140	1954-57

*net

PRICES/PROJECTION

As for 1950-53 DB2

Aston Martin DB Mark III
1957-59

PRODUCTION

550

1953-57 DB2/4 coupe

HISTORY

The final—and best—version of the original DB2 design. Offered in the same 2+2 hatchback style as the DB2/4, but given a restyled nose, more power, and (on most examples) front disc brakes. Overshadowed from 1958 on by the new and larger DB4. Model designation here was used to avoid confusion with the 1952 sports-racing DB3. The best quality and fittings of any of the early so-called "W.O." Astons.

FOR

As for 1953-57 DB2/4 but more so, plus good disc brakes and 120-mph performance

AGAINST

As for 1953-57 DB2/4

SPECIFICATIONS

Length (in.) 169.5 **Wheelbase (in.)** 99.0 **Weight (lbs.)** 2800
Price (new) NA

ENGINES

cc/type (cid)	bore x stroke (mm)	bhp*	years
2922/dohc I6 (178)	83×90	162/178/195	1957-59

*net

PRICES/PROJECTION

As for 1950-53 DB2, but add 20-50% for convertible

Aston Martin DB4 1958-63

PRODUCTION

1119

HISTORY

The first all-new Aston Martin since the David Brown regime took over in 1950. Offered as a full four-seater coupe with Superleggera (super-light) construction by Touring of Italy. There was also a new platform-style frame and a splendid light-alloy twincam six of great power. Not an easy car to drive well, but very quick (140 mph with standard engine) and reassuringly solid on the road. Convertible and hardtop derivatives were also built. The DB4 went through five distinct "series" in these years, each faster, better equipped, and more luxurious than the last. A five-speed manual and three-speed automatic transmissions were listed by 1963, along with a choice of two engine tunes.

FOR

Very fast Italian-style coupe (who needs a Ferrari?) ● Magnificent engine, splendid chassis if properly maintained ● Solid and safe if cared for ● A real thoroughbred

AGAINST

Very rust-prone ● Heavy steering ● Fuel thirst ● Parts available, but costly ● Not cheap to buy ● High maintenance demands and costs

SPECIFICATIONS

Length (in.) 176.0 **Wheelbase (in.)** 98.0 **Weight (lbs.)** 2885
Price (new) NA

ENGINES

cc/type (cid)	bore x stroke (mm)	bhp*	years
3670/dohc I6 (224)	92×92	240/266	1958-63

*net

1963 DB4 coupe

Aston Martin DB4GT & Zagato 1959-61

PRODUCTION

GT 75   **Zagato** 25

1960 DB4GT coupe

HISTORY

Short-wheelbase, two-seat derivatives of the DB4, with lightweight construction for possible racing duty. The GT looked much like the standard DB4, right down to its faired-in headlamps. The Zagato had a more distinctive appearance, with a rounded fastback body and the curious combination of curves and angles associated with this Italian coachbuilder's styling. Less weight, arguably superior aerodynamics, and careful engine tuning all contributed to improved performance, and these Astons were quite fast by any standard. Two more highly sought-after, if prohibitively expensive, collectibles from Newport Pagnell.

FOR

Fast (Zagato runs to 150 mph) ● Prime investment ● Others as for 1958-63 DB4

1960 DB4GT coupe by Zagato

AGAINST

Very flimsy Zagato aluminum body ● Highly tuned engine demands much care and attention ● Others as for 1958-63 DB4

SPECIFICATIONS

Length (in.) 171.8 (GT), 168.0 (Zagato)   **Wheelbase (in.)** 93.0
Weight (lbs.) 2705 (approx.)   **Price (new)** NA

ENGINES

cc/type (cid)	bore x stroke (mm)	bhp*	years
3670/dohc I6 (224)	92×92	302/314	1959-61

*net

Aston Martin DB5 1963-65

1964 DB5 coupe

PRODUCTION

1187

HISTORY

Successor to the DB4, but retained its chassis, basic running gear, and bodyshell (with a minor styling update). A bore increase brought displacement on Aston's twincam six to near 4 liters. As with the last DB4s, a choice of engine tunes was available, either 282 or 325 bhp, depending on how much the customer thought he or she could handle. Four transmission choices were offered, including 5-speed ZF manual and Borg-Warner automatic. A much-modified DB5 put this model on the map in the U.S. and elsewhere when it was used as James Bond's spy car in the film *Goldfinger*.

FOR

As for 1958-63 DB4

AGAINST

As for 1958-63 DB4

SPECIFICATIONS

Length (in.) 180.0   **Wheelbase (in.)** 98.0   **Weight (lbs.)** 3235
Price (new) $13,200 U.S. in 1964

ENGINES

cc/type (cid)	bore x stroke (mm)	bhp*	years
3995/dohc I6 (244)	96×92	282/325	1963-65

*net

PRICES/PROJECTION

Restorable $5000-10,000 **Good** $11,000-14,000
Excellent $15,000-20,000 Add 50% for convertible
5-year projection +30%

Aston Martin DB6 1965-71

1970 DB6 coupe

PRODUCTION

1753

HISTORY

Reworked replacement for the DB5, with a longer wheelbase, more rear seat space, Kamm-style spoilered tail, and greater weight. Not as fast as earlier DBs, but more practical. Fastback coupe and two-door convertible (called Volante) body styles continued as before. Beginning at the end of 1969 a Mark II version was offered with DBS-type wheels and tires, flared wheel openings, and an optional fuel injection system. Normal engine tune delivered a 140-mph maximum speed, the Vantage version 148 mph.

FOR

As for DB4 and DB5, plus more interior room

AGAINST

As for DB4 and DB5 • Fuel injection troublesome and best avoided

SPECIFICATIONS

Length (in.) 182.0 **Wheelbase (in.)** 101.7 **Weight (lbs.)** 3250
Price (new) $15,400 U.S. list in 1966

ENGINES

cc/type (cid)	bore x stroke (mm)	bhp	years
3995/dohc I6 (244)	96×92	282/335	1965-71

PRICES/PROJECTION

As for DB5

1969 DBS coupe

Aston Martin DBS & Vantage 1967-73

PRODUCTION

857

HISTORY

Newly styled four-seat GT supplement to the DB6, revealed in 1967. Designed expressly for a new V8 engine, but powered initially by Aston's well-tried twincam six. Chassis design was a wider and longer development of the DB6 platform, but fitted with De Dion rear suspension. Dramatically handsome fastback styling by William Towns (then working for AM). British to the core, and literally hand-built at Newport Pagnell, but looked and sounded Italian. Available in normal and 325-bhp Vantage tune (in which form the car would nudge 150 mph). Somewhat bulky, and handling ponderous unless optional power steering was ordered, but very desirable. After a change of company ownership (David Brown sold his Aston Martin Lagonda interests in 1969), the designation was changed to Aston Martin Vantage and minor styling changes (including a switch from quad to dual headlamps) instituted. The model continued in V8 form into the 1980s. At one time, a long-wheelbase sedan derivative of this design was rumored for the Lagonda badge, and a prototype was built and widely shown in the British press. However, the revived Lagonda that ultimately emerged was a far different machine (though again styled by Towns).

FOR

Proven powertrain and chassis • Solid, reassuring road manners • Great performance • Six cheaper and easier to maintain than later V8 • Clean styling • Traditional British GT appointments

AGAINST

Steel understructure rusts badly if neglected • Costly to restore • Overshadowed for sheer speed by DBS V8

SPECIFICATIONS

Length (in.) 180.5 **Wheelbase (in.)** 102.8 **Weight (lbs.)** 3760
Price (new) $12,650 FOB factory list in 1969

ENGINES

cc/type (cid)	bore x stroke (mm)	bhp	years
3995/dohc I6 (244)	96×92	282/325	1967-73

PRICES/PROJECTION

Restorable $8000-10,000 **Good** $12,000-14,000
Excellent $14,000-17,000 **5-year projection** +30%

Aston Martin DBS V8 & (AM) V8 1969-80

1971 DBS V8 coupe

PRODUCTION

DBS V8 405 (1969-72) **AM V8** 2000+ since 1972

HISTORY

Aston Martin's Italianate GT, now with the V8 originally intended (though it did not immediately replace the six-cylinder DBS). Power output for this all-aluminum twincam engine was never quoted (an AM policy similar to that of Rolls-Royce), but most British writers estimated it at around 400 bhp (SAE gross). The result was blistering performance despite considerable heft, with a top end of 160 mph plus. More silky and refined than the six-cylinder DBS and appointments similar, but a big beast for all that. A higher-output Vantage model was added later, sporting deep front spoiler, wider wheels and tires, and various chassis modifications. Available with a no-cost choice of five-speed manual or three-speed automatic. No convertible until the late '70s, when the Volante (not considered here) was fielded. Cars designated DBS V8 had Bosch fuel injection. After David Brown sold his AML interests, the model reverted to four two-barrel Weber carbs, which actually increased power output and performance, and the designation was changed to simply Aston Martin V8. Still in production at this writing.

FOR

As for 1967-73 DBS, but even more performance • Parts no problem (model still in production) • Not expensive right now • Strong appreciator

AGAINST

Injection engine finicky to keep in tune • Parts very costly • Limited U.S. dealer network and parts supplies • Others as for 1967-73 DBS

SPECIFICATIONS

Length (in.) 180.5 **Wheelbase (in.)** 102.8 **Weight (lbs.)** 3850
Price (new) $47,500 in 1978

ENGINES

cc/type (cid)	bore x stroke (mm)	bhp*	years
5340/dohc V8 (326)	100×85	400/450	1969-80

*estimated SAE gross

PRICES/PROJECTION

Restorable $10,000-15,000 **Good** $16,000-25,000
Excellent $20,000-37,000 **5-year projection** +20%

Austin-Healey 100 (BN1/BN2) 1953-56

1954 100 (BN1) roadster

PRODUCTION

BN1 10,688 **BN2** 3924

HISTORY

First of the smooth-lined British roadsters designed by Donald Healey. Based on running gear from the Austin A90 sedan, and adopted by British Motor Corporation (BMC) for quantity production. Rugged ladder-style chassis with steel-and-alloy body welded up to it. Beautiful, and mostly practical for a two-seat open sports car, but let down by comparatively scant ground clearance and excessive engine heat seeping into the cockpit. The first BN1 models used the A90 four-speed gearbox with top simply blanked off. The later BN2s had four forward speeds, plus Laycock overdrive. Well received in the U.S., where enthusiasts found it offered everything contemporary MGs didn't, including a good deal more speed. The early models were predictably the lightest; the later ones were heavier but more civilized and better equipped. The A-H quickly earned a reputation for being virtually unbreakable in anything short of a complete crack-up. Styling wore well, and evolved with remarkably few changes through the six-cylinder Healey 3000s of the '60s.

FOR

Simple, rugged mechanicals • Easy to service and restore • Most parts still available • Styling • Open-air allure

AGAINST

Bodies rot badly in wet climates • Minimal ground clearance

● Cockpit heat (no cure) ● Rather basic equipment

SPECIFICATIONS

Length (in.) 151.0 **Wheelbase (in.)** 90.0
Weight (lbs.) 2015-2150 **Price (new)** NA

ENGINES

cc/type (cid)	bore x stroke (mm)	bhp*	years
2660/ohv I4 (162)	87×111	90	1953-56

*net

PRICES/PROJECTION

Restorable $3000-5000 **Good** $6000-8000
Excellent $8000-15,000 **5-year projection** +10%

Austin-Healey 100S 1955

PRODUCTION

50

HISTORY

Racing derivative of the first-series BN1 A-H. Differences from the mass-production version included a different cylinder head and internal engine modifications for more power, plus a light-alloy bodyshell, four-speed gearbox without overdrive, and standard Dunlop disc brakes on all four wheels. Not as practical for daily driving as the tamer four-cylinder Healeys, but a worthwhile collectible for its rarity and mechanical specification.

FOR

As for 1953-55 BN1, plus rarity (yet reasonably affordable despite that) and strong appreciation potential

AGAINST

More fragile than production models ● Engine parts mostly gone ● Aluminum body restoration difficult ● Seldom seen on the market

SPECIFICATIONS

Length (in.) 151.0 **Wheelbase (in.)** 90.0 **Weight (lbs.)** 1925
Price (new) NA

1956-59 100-6 (BN4) roadster

ENGINES

cc/type (cid)	bore x stroke (mm)	bhp*	years
2660/ohv I4 (162)	87×111	132	1955

*net

PRICES/PROJECTION

Restorable $6000-10,000 **Good** $12,000-16,000
Excellent $16,000-24,000 **5-year projection** +50%

Austin-Healey 100-6 (BN4/BN6) 1956-59

PRODUCTION

BN4 10,246   **BN6** 4150

HISTORY

The revised and expanded Healey series of the late '50s, with svelte styling similar to the original's. A longer wheelbase allowed BMC to offer a choice of two-seat (BN6) or four-seat (BN4) layouts, and a detachable hardtop was offered as a new factory accessory. The main item of interest was a new 2.6-liter six-cylinder engine. From November 1957, this gained a more efficient cylinder head for greater power and performance. All BN6s had it as this model was introduced after the BN4 following customer requests for the return of the "pure" two-seat Healey.

FOR

As for 1953-56 BN1/BN2 100 models, plus more readily available spare parts

AGAINST

As for 1953-56 BN1/BN2 100 models, but heavier and less lively despite bigger engine ● Some compromises on original styling

SPECIFICATIONS

Length (in.) 157.5 **Wheelbase (in.)** 92.0 **Weight (lbs.)** 2435
Price (new) NA

ENGINES

cc/type (cid)	bore x stroke (mm)	bhp*	years
2639/ohv I6 (161)	79×89	102/117	1956-59

*net

PRICES/PROJECTION

Restorable $3000-4000 **Good** $4500-6000
Excellent $7000-11,500 2-seaters 10-50% higher
5-year projection +10%

Austin-Healey Sprite 1958-61

PRODUCTION

48,999

1958-61 Sprite "Mk I" roadster

Austin-Healey 3000 1959-68

1962 3000 Mk II convertible

PRODUCTION

Mark I 13,650   **Mark II** 5450   **Mark II Convertible** 6113   **Mark III** 17,712

HISTORY

The Healey family's follow-up to successful collaboration with British Motor Corporation (BMC) on the Healey 100. This new low-priced sports car, patterned after the old MG Midget, featured unitized steel construction on tiny overall dimensions. Running gear and front suspension were borrowed from the Austin A35 sedan. Rear suspension was by cantilever quarter-elliptic springs supporting a solid axle, about as simple as could be. The original plan to give the Sprite hidden headlamps was abandoned for cost reasons, which resulted in fixed lamps that gave the rounded front end a quaintly cute "frog eye" appearance. The entire front sheetmetal section, including the fenders, was hinged at the front, and lifted up for superb engine access. At the opposite end of the car, there was no trunklid, and only modest storage space in the tail (accessible only from behind the hinged front seat backrests). Performance was less than expected (top speed only 80 mph), but handling was predictably sprightly and fuel economy great. Assembly was actually carried out at MG's Abingdon factory, which may explain why a Midget version followed with the Sprite's Mark II restyle. Equipment was very basic initially (rubber floormats, clip-on side curtains) but loads of extras were available from the factory and various accessory and performance-parts makers. Proved enormously popular and, when heated up, able to best 100 mph.

FOR

Mechanical simplicity ●Great character ●Light and frugal ●Parts (except body) still in good supply ●Cheap to buy ●Fun to drive ●Easy to work on

AGAINST

Rudimentary ride and equipment ●Rusts out easily ●Worn chassis prone to oversteer handling behavior

SPECIFICATIONS

Length (in.) 137.2   **Wheelbase (in.)** 80.0   **Weight (lbs.)** 1460
Price (new) NA

ENGINES

cc/type (cid)	bore x stroke (mm)	bhp*	years
948/ohv I4 (58)	63×76	43	1958-61

*net

PRICES/PROJECTION

Restorable $800-1200   **Good** $2500-3500
Excellent $4000-6500   **5-year projection** +10%

HISTORY

Final development of the Austin-Healey theme. Basic layout of the previous 100-6 retained, but with enlarged engine capacity and standard front disc brakes. The Mark II series gained more power and a new "Convertible" model, with the same basic styling plus fold-away top and roll-up door windows. The final Mark III versions had more power still, plus a restyled wood-covered dash and revised rear suspension incorporating radius arms for better axle location. These last Healeys also had 120-mph capability. A factory detachable hardtop was available for all 3000s, though few Convertibles were so equipped. All Convertibles had 2+2 seating, but Mark I and II were offered as two-seaters as well. Mark II introduced spring 1961, the Convertible in summer 1962, and Mark III in spring 1964. Impending U.S. safety and emissions regulations scheduled to take effect after the 1967 model year effectively killed the big Healey in its biggest export market. To continue, it would have had to be redesigned at prohibitive cost. A few leftover '67s may have been sold here as '68s. BMC attempted to fill the gap in both the U.S. and Europe with the six-cylinder MGC, which proved a marketing disaster. Donald Healey would make one more try at building a well-balanced two-seat roadster, the short-lived Jensen-Healey of the early '70s. As our prices indicate, the Mark IIIs have a slight lead on the collector market as the last of the A-Hs and because of their more complete equipment and the best Healey performance.

1966 3000 Mk III convertible

FOR

Performance gets better on successive versions • Better braking than 100/6 • Better equipment, too • Same rugged chassis and rugged good looks • Parts easier to obtain now than for earlier models • Last of the breed • Mark III's better ground clearance and equipment

AGAINST

As for 1953-56 BN1/BN2

SPECIFICATIONS

Length (in.) 157.5   **Wheelbase (in.)** 92.0
Weight (lbs.) 2460-2550   **Price (new)** $3565 U.S. in 1966

ENGINES

cc/type (cid)	bore x stroke (mm)	bhp*	years
2912/ohv I6 (178)	83×89	124/132/148	1959-67

*net

PRICES/PROJECTION

Restorable $3000-4000 **Good** $6000-8000
Excellent $9000-15,000 **5-year projection** +10%

Austin-Healey Sprite (& MG Midget) 1961-71

1964 Sprite Mk III roadster

PRODUCTION

Mark II 31,665   **Mark III** 25,905   **Mark IV** 22,793

HISTORY

Restyled successor to the Mark I "bugeye" Sprite, with a squared-up nose and tail grafted onto the original main body section. Retained diminutive 80 inch wheelbase chassis and suspension of its predecessor, though rear springing was changed from quarter- to half-elliptics beginning in spring 1964. Also at that time BMC changed from sliding sidescreens to proper wind-up windows for the doors. The lift-up nose section and lidless tail on early models gave way to a conventional hood and opening trunklid. Engines progressed through several displacements, but all were based on BMC's rugged A-series four-cylinder unit (still in production as the modified A-plus) that had been around since the war.

1967 Midget Mk III roadster

Trim and equipment were gradually upgraded over the years. Following the end of Donald and Geoff Healey's association with BMC, their name was removed from the last 1971 models, known simply as Austin Sprite. Also sold with the MG badge as the near-identical Midget, which continued beyond the end of Sprite production through 1979 (a total of 226,526 built). A very basic sports car, the Sprite taught a lot of young Americans what British-style motoring was all about. It's still enjoyable as economical everyday transport, providing you can put up with its very cramped cockpit, hard ride, and crude controls. Offsetting these drawbacks are nimble handling, open-air flair, and sturdy mechanicals just right for novice mechanics. The 1961-67 cars are preferred as federal safety and emissions controls somewhat robbed later models of power and, to an extent, agility.

FOR

Better equipped, more practical than "frogeye" • Progressively more (though always modest) performance • Cheap to buy and run • Production (Midget) recently ended, so parts plentiful

AGAINST

Cramped accommodations • Low-geared, buzzy engine • Rust-prone • Oxcart ride

SPECIFICATIONS

Length (in.) 137.5   **Wheelbase (in.)** 80.0
Weight (lbs.) 1550-1650   **Price (new)** $2000-3000 (U.S.)

1965-68 Midget MK III roadster

ENGINES

cc/type (cid)	bore x stroke (mm)	bhp	years
948/ohv I4 (58)	63×76	46	1961-65
1098/ohv I4 (67)	65×83	56/59	1965-68
1275/ohv I4 (78)	71×81	65	1968-71

PRICES/PROJECTION

Restorable $750-1500 **Good** $1700-2500
Excellent $3000-4500 **5-year projection** +10%

Austin Seven 1930-39

1930 BMW Dixi 3/15 roadster (Seven similar)

PRODUCTION

290,861

HISTORY

The tiny car that helped save Austin from bankruptcy in the 1920s and made motoring affordable for thousands. Unlike any previous Austin, with a flexible frame, beam axles, and transverse-leaf front springing. A nominal four-seater in sedan form but hardly spacious. Some open two-seaters quite sporting though never very fast. Gutless little side-valve engine, abrupt in/out clutch, and spidery mechanicals provided lots of character for masochists and contortionists. Built under license in the U.S. as the American Austin/Bantam (see entries). Also in Germany as the Dixi by BMW, in Japan as the first Datsun, and several other countries.

FOR

A tiny oddity • Great charm

AGAINST

Negligible performance • Cramped, rugged, uncomfortable

• Difficult parts supply

SPECIFICATIONS

Length (in.) 118.0 **Wheelbase (in.)** 81.0
Weight (lbs.) 1100-1200 **Price (new)** NA

ENGINES

cc/type (cid)	bore x stroke (mm)	bhp	years
696/L4 (42.5)	54.0×76.2	NA	1922-39
747/L4 (45.6)	56.0×76.2	NA	1922-39

PRICES/PROJECTION

Restorable $500-1000 **Good** $2500-3500
Excellent $3500-7000 **5-year projection** no change

Bentley 8 Litre 1930-31

PRODUCTION

100

HISTORY

Largest, last, and greatest member of the original "W.O." Bentley family, with huge overhead-cam inline six in massive chassis spanning a choice of wheelbases. Directly descended from the 6½-litre/Speed Six, and so powerful and smooth that it challenged Rolls-Royce for a very small market sector. Fixed-head engine, separate non-synchro gearbox, and hypoid rear axles, plus beam front, of course. All built with special coachwork, mostly sedans, though roadsters were offered in later years. Whatever the body, capable of 100 mph in grand locomotive-like style and with great reliability. They truly don't make 'em like this any more.

FOR

Rarity • Enormous 1920s-style character • Impressive engineering for the period • High performance • Massive build

AGAINST

Very costly to rebuild • Only remanufactured parts available • Heavy and difficult to drive until you get the knack

SPECIFICATIONS

Length (in.) 201.0-213.0 **Wheelbase (in.)** 144.0/156.0
Weight (lbs.) 5400-5600 **Price (new)** NA

ENGINES

cc/type (cid)	bore x stroke (mm)	bhp	years
7982/sohc I6 (487)	110×140	180*	1930-31

*net

PRICES/PROJECTION

Restorable $50,000-60,000 **Good** $115,000-135,000
Excellent $145,000-175,000 **5-year projection** +20%

Bentley 3½ Litre 1933-37

PRODUCTION

1177

HISTORY

The first Bentley after the original "W.O." firm crashed in 1931 and was taken over by Rolls-Royce. Modified Rolls-Royce 20/25 engine and entirely new chassis were featured. Compared with earlier Bentleys, this was the "Silent Sports Car," softer in character, more refined, and even better built. Really a quasi-Rolls; many now call it a "Rolls-Bentley." Power outputs unstated, and a synchro gearbox with right-hand gearchange restated the pedigree. Built at Derby, not Cricklewood, as rolling chassis only, so bodies came from outside coachbuilders. Though capable of more than 90 mph in fine style and comfort, still backward, with leaf springs and beam axles front and rear, plus very British styling.

FOR

Great elegance and style • Rolls-Royce build quality • High performance for the period • Sporting but comfortable

AGAINST

Very costly to buy • Even more costly to restore • Wood-body rot • Few parts • 1930s UK styling?

SPECIFICATIONS

Length (in.) 174.0 **Wheelbase (in.)** 126.0 **Weight (lbs.)** 3400-3500 **Price (new)** NA

ENGINES

cc/type (cid)	bore x stroke (mm)	bhp	years
3669/ohv I6 (224)	82.5×114	NA	1933-37

PRICES/PROJECTION

Restorable $4800-6000 **Good** $15,000-18,000 **Excellent** $15,000-20,000 **5-year projection** +20%

Bentley 4¼ Litre 1936-39

PRODUCTION

1234

HISTORY

Lineal descendant of the 3½-Litre, with the same chassis, suspensions, and choice of custom bodies. Larger engine's extra power and torque (neither ever revealed) made up for the heavier coachwork and equipment that always came along. As before, a Rolls-Royce with a Bentley badge and 90+mph performance, but no independent front suspension. From late 1938, an "overdrive" transmission with geared-up top was fitted to make the car better

1939 4¼-Litre sedan

suited to fast roads. Many with Park Ward bodies, now without wooden framing, so they've lasted better.

FOR

A real aristocrat • Top-drawer build quality • Comfortable, dignified, yet sporting • Parts supply still OK

AGAINST

Costly to buy, very costly to run • Wood bodies still rot • Inferior to contemporary Americans in ride • Styling a bit traditional

SPECIFICATIONS

Length (in.) 192.0 **Wheelbase (in.)** 126.0 **Weight (lbs.)** 3750 **Price (new)** NA

ENGINES

cc/type (cid)	bore x stroke (mm)	bhp	years
4257/ohv I6 (260)	88.9×114	NA	1936-39

PRICES/PROJECTION

As for 3½ Litre

Bentley Mark VI 1946-52

PRODUCTION

4946

HISTORY

The first postwar Bentley of Rolls-Royce design, powered by a new six-cylinder F-head engine (overhead intake, side-mounted exhaust valves). Also the first Bentley with standard, factory-designed bodywork (built by Pressed Steel Co.), reflecting a change in Rolls-Royce policy from strictly hand-built to "standardized" bodies that could be produced in greater numbers at the firm's new factory at Crewe. Like prewar Bentleys, the Mark VI was large, stately, and impressive. It rode a massive separate chassis featuring coil-spring independent front suspension, quite an advance for the marque in this period. Most Mark VI cars were the "standard" four-door sedan with semi-traditional lines including separate front fenders. However, a number were built with custom sedan and convertible (drophead) coachwork by such R-R specialists as H.J. Mulliner, Park Ward, and James Young.

1949 Mark VI drophead (convertible) coupe by Park Ward

FOR

Cachet of Rolls ownership ● Mechanical parts still readily available ● Extensive club interest and restoration assistance

AGAINST

Standard bodies rot-prone ● Custom body replacement panels unobtainable ● Costly to maintain, acquire, and restore

SPECIFICATIONS

Length (in.) 204.0 **Wheelbase (in.)** 120.0
Weight (lbs.) 4090 (standard sedan) **Price (new)** NA

ENGINES

cc/type (cid)	bore x stroke (mm)	bhp*	years
4256/F6 (260)	89×114	120/130	1946-52

*estimated net; actual output not quoted

PRICES/PROJECTION

Restorable $8000-12,000 **Good** $14,500-19,000
Excellent $20,000-27,000 +30-60% for good/excellent special bodywork **5-year projection** +20%

Bentley R-Type 1952-55

1951-55 R-Type 4-door sedan

PRODUCTION

2320

HISTORY

Revised version of the Mark VI with greater engine displacement and a longer tail for the standard-body sedan. Offered with optional Rolls-Royce/GM Hydra-Matic automatic transmission beginning in 1952, which became instantly more popular than the manual gearbox. Styling and mechanical changes parallel those made to the lookalike Rolls-Royce Silver Dawn. Maximum speed now over 100 mph, but not that much faster than the Mark VI.

FOR

More luggage space than Mark VI ● Optional automatic convenience ● Others as for 1946-55 Mark VI

AGAINST

As for 1946-55 Mark VI

SPECIFICATIONS

Length (in.) 210.0 **Wheelbase (in.)** 120.0 **Weight (lbs.)** 4200
Price (new) NA

ENGINES

cc/type (cid)	bore x stroke (mm)	bhp*	years
4566/F6 (279)	92×114	130	1952-55

*Actual output not quoted; estimated net bhp

PRICES/PROJECTION

Restorable $7200-9600 **Good** $20,000-24,000
Excellent $35,000-42,000 **5-year projection** +20%

Bentley R-Type Continental 1952-55

PRODUCTION

208

1952-55 R-Type Continental fastback coupe by H.J. Mulliner

HISTORY

Perhaps the most exciting Bentley of the postwar period. A sensationally styled, lightweight fastback coupe built on the R-Type sedan chassis. Only a small number were built, all two-door four-seaters, most with bodywork by H.J. Mulliner. Originally powered by the Bentley six as fitted to the sedans, but a larger-capacity 4887cc version was specified beginning in 1954. A true GT with handling that belied its massive size and still considerable weight. Just the thing for blasting across the continent at easy three-figure speeds (up to 115 mph). Rare, but worth seeking out, and a true classic even among classic Bentleys.

FOR

Distinctive styling •Rot-free light-alloy body •Higher top speed than other R-Types •Others as for Mark VI and R-Type

AGAINST

Body panel replacements hopeless • Rare and costly to buy • Others as for R-Type

SPECIFICATIONS

Length (in.) 206.5 **Wheelbase (in.)** 120.0 **Weight (lbs.)** 3740
Price (new) NA

ENGINES

cc/type (cid)	bore x stroke (mm)	bhp*	years
4566/F6 (279)	92×114	145	1952-53
4887/F6 (298)	95×114	155	1954-55

*Actual output not quoted: estimated net bhp

PRICES/PROJECTION

Restorable $7200-9600 **Good** $20,000-24,000
Excellent $35,000-42,000 **5-year projection** +20%

1952 R-Type Continental fastback coupe by H.J. Mulliner

Bentley S-Type 1955-65

1955-62 S-Type 4-door sedan (Series I/II)

PRODUCTION

S-1 3107 (inc. 35 limousine)   **S-2 V8** 1954   **S-3 V8** 1286
(S-2/S-3 inc. 89 limousine)

HISTORY

Essentially a "grille engineered" version of the concurrent Rolls-Royce Silver Cloud of these years, sharing the same all-new chassis, suspension design, and styling for the standard sedan body. Most of those built were the "factory" four-doors, but a few limousine types were also built on a 4-inch longer wheelbase. As before, chassis were supplied to approved coachbuilders, who created custom sedan and convertible bodies. Powered by the carryover 4.9-liter straight six from the R-Type through the fall of 1959 (Series I or S-1), after which Rolls-Royce's new light-alloy, short-stroke 6.2-liter V8 (said to have been cribbed from the 1949 Cadillac design) took over for the Series II (S-2). A restyled Series III (S-3) was announced in the autumn of 1962 and was mostly unchanged mechanically. It was marked by quad headlamps and a lower hoodline (as was the parallel Cloud III) much to the consternation of traditionalists. Replaced in 1965 by the unit-construction Rolls-Royce Silver Cloud and its T-Type Bentley equivalent.

FOR

Superb luxury •Rolls construction quality •Dignified styling with loads of snob appeal •Excellent club support •Body and mechanical parts still available •Good V8 performance •Many had GM automatic transmission •Cheaper than a new one

AGAINST

Not very fast with six •Rust-prone •Costly to maintain and restore •Low mpg

SPECIFICATIONS

Length (in.) 212.0 (limo: 216.0) **Wheelbase (in.)** 123.0 (limo: 127.0) **Weight (lbs.)** 4480-4650 (limo: 4650-4815)
Price (new) NA

ENGINES

cc/type (cid)	bore x stroke (mm)	bhp*	years
4887/F6 (298)	95×114	NA	1955-59
6230/ohv V8 (380)	104×91	NA	1959-65

*Rolls-Royce/Bentley does not quote horsepower

PRICES/PROJECTION

Restorable $3600-4800 **Good** $8500-10,000
Excellent $10,000-18,000 +25-50% for good/excellent special
bodywork **5-year projection** +20%

Bentley S-Type Continental 1955-65

1962-65 S-Type Continental "Flying Spur" sedan by Park Ward

PRODUCTION

S-1 431   **S-2 V8** 388   **S-3 V8** 312

HISTORY

Continuation of the sporting special-bodied Bentleys aimed at the gentleman-enthusiast, but on the more modern S-Type/Silver Cloud chassis. As with the preceding R-Type models, custom light-alloy bodies were available mainly from H.J. Mulliner and Park Ward. Two-door coupes accounted for most of the very limited production, but a few convertibles were built along with a new four-door sedan dubbed "Flying Spur." Mechanical and appearance changes were the same as for concurrent S-Type sedans, including adoption of the new Rolls-Royce V8 for Series II models and the "mod" quad-headlamp front end for the Series III. Virtually all Continentals in this period had the R-R/GM Hydra-Matic transmission, which allowed a top speed in the area of 100-115 mph. Conspicuously absent from the specification was disc brakes.

FOR

As for R-Type Continental, plus new four-door and more performance ● Others as for S-Type sedans

AGAINST

As for R-Type Continental and S-Type sedans

SPECIFICATIONS

Length (in.) 210.5   **Wheelbase (in.)** 123.0
Weight (lbs.) 3980-4450   **Price (new)** NA

1962-65 S-Type Continental convertible by Park Ward

ENGINES

cc/type (cid)	bore x stroke (mm)	bhp*	years
4887/F6 (298)	95×114	NA	1955-59
6230/ohv V8 (380)	104×91	NA	1959-65

*Rolls-Royce/Bentley does not quote horsepower

PRICES/PROJECTION

As for R-Type Continental

BMC Mini-Cooper S 1963-71

1968 Mini-Cooper S 2-door sedan

PRODUCTION

45,442

HISTORY

Inspired "homologation special" based on British Motor Corporation's front-drive minicar designed by Alex Issigonis. Main differences between this production hot rod and the more basic Minis were higher Cooper-tuned versions of the BMC A-series four, beefed-up driveline components, front disc brakes, and discreet exterior emblems. Offered initially in 1071cc form (modified version of the Formula Junior engine provided to Cooper). There were also 970cc and 1275cc versions listed from 1964 aimed at 1.0- and

1.3-liter racing classes. Retained the regular Mini's wheel-at-each-corner box-body, only 120 inches long, with full four-seat accommodation. Coopers had slightly better instrumentation and a more businesslike interior. The Mini, but not the Cooper, is still in production after more than 25 years, and a huge variety of bolt-on performance and dress-up accessories is available from both domestic and overseas suppliers. With the right equipment, the little engine could pump out at least 50 percent more power. The Cooper S carried BMC's rally colors in the early '60s, and did quite well against larger, more powerful opposition. Minis of any kind were never sold widely in the U.S., and the advent of federal emissions/safety standards banned the Cooper S from our market after 1967. Some were sold in Canada until the new Leyland regime dropped the model in 1971.

FOR

Cheeky charm unmatched by other cars • Still rare in North America • Wonderfully nimble front-drive handling • Many non-mechanical parts still available • Not expensive

AGAINST

Engine parts in short supply • Undercarriage (especially subframe) rust-prone • Noisy • No match for Detroit iron in traffic • Make sure you fit

SPECIFICATIONS

Length (in.) 120.2 **Wheelbase (in.)** 80.0 **Weight (lbs.)** 1440
Price (new) NA

ENGINES

cc/type (cid)	bore x stroke (mm)	bhp*	years
970/ohv I4 (59)	71×62	65	1964-65
1071/ohv I4 (65)	71×68	70	1963-64
1275/ohv I4 (78)	71×81	76	1964-71

PRICES/PROJECTION

Restorable $1000-2000 **Good** $2000-4000
Excellent $4000-6000 **5-year projection** +10%

1937-41 Type 327 coupe

BMW 327/328
1936-41

PRODUCTION

327 461 **328** 1396

HISTORY

Based on the six-cylinder 315/319 of 1934-37, the 328 was a sleek, efficient, two-seat sports roadster with a tubular frame and transverse-leaf-spring independent front suspension. The engine was the cleverly detailed straight six from the 326, with opposed valves and cross-pushrod valvegear. Offered 90+ mph flat out, and its great style and comfort rendered most other middle-price sports cars crudely old-fashioned. The longer, wider, and heavier 327 coupe and convertible followed with less power but simpler inline valvegear, plus genuine four-passenger capacity. Appearance of all remarkably similar (aped by the postwar Bristol 400), with trademark "twin-kidney" grille, recessed headlamps, and flowing lines. The 327 was also available with the 328 engine in 1937-41 as the confusingly named 327/28. Up to anything produced by Italy or the U.S. in this period and likely more sought-after now than they were then.

FOR

The most charismatic prewar Bimmers • Advanced chassis • Fine handling • Good performance (328) • Period styling • Durability

AGAINST

328s very expensive • Restoration difficult

SPECIFICATIONS

Length (in.) 176.0 (327), 156.0 (328) **Wheelbase (in.)** 108.3 (327), 94.5 (328) **Weight (lbs.)** 2425/1830 **Price (new)** NA

ENGINES

cc/type (cid)	bore x stroke (mm)	bhp	years
1971/ohv I6 (120)	66×96	55	1937-41
1971/ohv I6 (120)	66×96	80	1936-40

PRICES/PROJECTION

327 Restorable $4000-6000 **Good** $14,000-16,000
Excellent $17,000-20,000 **328 Restorable** $8000-10,000
Good $30,000-35,000 **Excellent** $35,000-40,000
5-year projection +20%

BMW Type 503
1956-59

PRODUCTION

412

HISTORY

The first postwar sporting car from Bavarian Motor Works. Based on the Type 502 sedan box- and tubular-section chassis, and also shared its 3.2-liter V8 engine. Offered in sleek coupe or cabriolet (convertible) body styles designed by Count Albrecht Goertz, both with 2+2 accommodations. An expensive indulgence but a great image builder for BMW, still recovering from wartime damage and facing many financial problems in these years. Relatively heavy, in the German manner, so performance was limited to about 118 mph maximum. Offered a civilized interior and assured (if not nimble) handling. The four-speed manual gearbox was mounted remotely on early models, as on the 502, but was placed in unit with the engine from late 1957. The original steering column gearchange gave way to a floor-mounted mechanism on later examples.

FOR

Exclusive '50s BMW • Robust chassis and engine • Rarity • Good appreciation

AGAINST

Parts impossible to obtain nowadays • Overshadowed by 507, and not as nice to drive • Hard to find • Expensive if you do

SPECIFICATIONS

Length (in.) 187.0   **Wheelbase (in.)** 111.6   **Weight (lbs.)** 3310
Price (new) NA

ENGINES

cc/type (cid)	bore x stroke (mm)	bhp*	years
3168/ohv V8 (193)	82×75	140	1956-59

*net

PRICES/PROJECTION

Restorable $1000-1500   **Good** $3500-4500
Excellent $5000-6000   **5-year projection** +50%

BMW Type 507
1956-59

1956-59 Type 507 cabriolet

PRODUCTION

253

HISTORY

Two-seat running mate to the Type 503 in this period. Sensational styling, again by Albrecht Goertz, was years ahead of its time, and unrivaled by any other European of the day. It was notable for the lack of BMW's traditional "twin kidney" grille treatment. Running gear was shared with the 503, but higher tune gave the V8 engine 10 more horsepower, good for a top speed of nearly 130 mph. Basic chassis design was also shared, except for the two-seater's shorter wheelbase. Lighter and better-handling than the 503, the 507 was virtually handbuilt at Munich, and therefore much too expensive for all but a small number of Europeans. Offered in both coupe and cabriolet (convertible) body styles, and brought into the U.S. in very small numbers. That plus its fine engineering and

still-eye-catching looks makes this probably the most desirable collector BMW of all.

FOR

Exclusive and charismatic • Sensational looks • Performance • Beautiful engineering • Rare and highly coveted • Strong club • High-appreciation investment

AGAINST

Body and engine parts virtually extinct • Little factory back-up • Expensive

SPECIFICATIONS

Length (in.) 172.4   **Wheelbase (in.)** 97.6   **Weight (lbs.)** 2935
Price (new) NA

ENGINES

cc/type (cid)	bore x stroke (mm)	bhp*	years
3168/ohv V8 (193)	82×75	150	1956-59

*net

PRICES/PROJECTION

Restorable $10,000-15,000   **Good** $25,000-30,000
Excellent $30,000-40,000   **5-year projection** no change

BMW 3200CS
1962-65

1962-65 3200CS coupe by Bertone

PRODUCTION

603

HISTORY

Interim sporting BMW bridging the gap between the Type 503/507 of the '50s and the 2000/2800CS of the '60s. A close-coupled four-seat coupe based on the Type 503 chassis, sharing the same wheelbase, suspension layout, and powertrain. Styling was courtesy of Bertone of Italy, which also supplied finished bodies to BMW for final assembly in Munich. In overall appearance the 3200CS was similar to the later 2000/2800CS, particularly the thin-section roof, notched rear side window shape, and slim B-pillars, indicating that Bertone probably influenced BMW's own designers through this model. The Germans' trusty V8 was tweaked once again to produce 160 bhp, sufficient to give this car a 125-mph top speed. Like the 503/507, mostly handbuilt and quite costly as a result. However, an aging chassis and running gear rendered it behind the times almost as soon as it was introduced.

FOR

Fast, sturdy, and nicely furnished • Pleasant Bertone styling • Good accommodations • Rarity (especially in U.S.)

AGAINST

Quite rust-prone • Scarce body and engine parts • Heavy and thirsty

SPECIFICATIONS

Length (in.) 190.0 **Wheelbase (in.)** 111.6 **Weight (lbs.)** 3310
Price (new) NA

ENGINES

cc/type (cid)	bore x stroke (mm)	bhp*	years
3168/ohv V8 (193)	82×75	160	1962-65

*DIN

PRICES/PROJECTION

Restorable $3000-5000 **Good** $5000-7000
Excellent $7000-9000 **5-year projection** +10%

BMW 2000CS
1965-68

1965-68 2000CS coupe by Karmann

PRODUCTION

11,720

HISTORY

Coupe derivative of BMW's successful "comeback" early-'60s sedan series designed around the firm's new overhead cam inline four. Shared underpan and running gear with the 2000 four-door, but wore a distinctive pillarless hardtop body built by Karmann and incorporating BMW's then-current styling themes. Its only flaw was a snubbed snout that awkwardly tried to blend BMW's trademark kidney grille into a rounded shape accentuated by wide wraparound headlamp/parking light units. Offered in two versions, a lower-powered automatic model and a faster manual car capable of 110 mph. Not space efficient (only passable 2+2 seating in a package longer than the sedan), but was intended more to lend some sportiness to the lineup than to be strictly practical. With new sheetmetal ahead of the cowl and a brilliant six-cylinder engine, the 2000CS would be transformed into the much nicer-looking and more capable 2800CS.

FOR

Unique model • Powerful and reliable ohc engine • Fine handling • German craftsmanship • Good appreciation potential • Not costly • Strong club support

AGAINST

Beware of unit body/chassis rust • Body parts now hard to acquire • Overshadowed in collector circles by 2800CS • Front end spoils otherwise pleasant styling

SPECIFICATIONS

Length (in.) 178.3 **Wheelbase (in.)** 100.4 **Weight (lbs.)** 2630
Price (new) $5185 U.S. in 1966

ENGINES

cc/type (cid)	bore x stroke (mm)	bhp*	years
1990/ohc I4	89×90	100/120	1965-68

*DIN

PRICES/PROJECTION

Restorable $2000-3000 **Good** $4000-6000
Excellent $6000-8000 **5-year projection** +30%

BMW 1600
1966-75

1966-67 1600 2-door sedan ("Coupe")

PRODUCTION

277,320

HISTORY

The second new mass-production BMW sedan of the '60s, slightly smaller than the earlier four-doors and wrongly called "Coupe" in some markets. Production for Europe lasted a decade, with convertibles (conversions by Baur) and a three-door "Touring" (hatchback) offered in addition to the basic two-door notchback. However, only the two-door 1600 made it to the U.S., and was replaced here after 1970 by the 2002 and its various derivatives mainly to satisfy performance buyers in the face of the strangling effects of emissions and safety rules. The cars covered here were powered by the 1573cc version of BMW's neat overhead-cam four introduced in the early '60s, and which survives today. Thoroughly practical four-seat interior, 100-mph performance, typical Teutonic thoroughness in engineering and construction, and nimble handling made it a hit here and abroad. It also brought the pleasures of owning a Bimmer within reach of a greater range of buyers than ever before.

FOR

Straightforward mechanical layout ● Sedan practicality with sports-car verve ● Reasonably good parts supplies even now ● Familiar to U.S. BMW dealers and many specialists ● Strong club ● Bargain prices; may be undervalued at present

AGAINST

Unitized, so rust a worry ● Plain styling, interior decor ● Good-condition examples hard to find ● Parts expensive ● Overshadowed in performance and collector interest by 2002s

SPECIFICATIONS

Length (in.) 164.5 **Wheelbase (in.)** 98.4 **Weight (lbs.)** 2070
Price (new) $2658 U.S. list price in 1967

ENGINES

cc/type (cid)	bore x stroke (mm)	bhp*	years
1573/ohc I4 (96)	84×71	85/105	1966-75

*DIN; standard/TI models, respectively

PRICES/PROJECTION

Restorable $400-700 **Good** $1500-2000
Excellent $2000-3000 **5-year projection** no change

BMW 2800CS
1968-71

1968 2800CS coupe by Karmann

PRODUCTION

9399

HISTORY

A brilliant development of the four-cylinder 2000CS coupe, made possible by BMW's remarkably smooth and eager new ohc six launched earlier in the upmarket 2800/Bavaria sedan. Shared the 2000CS body/chassis aft of the firewall, but had a longer front end to accommodate the six, a revised front suspension, and a neat new "face" with quad headlamps. Performance was much higher (128 mph tops), and smoother and less fussed as well. Handling and roadholding were of a high order, too. Bodies were still supplied by Karmann, and were trimmed neatly though not luxuriously with high-quality materials in the German manner. Eventually supplanted by the 3.0CS. A special lightweight version, with aluminum body panels and various wings and fins, designated CSL

was active and successful on the long-distance "sedan" racing circuits in both Europe and America. A nearly irresistible BMW and a prime collector's item.

FOR

Much better balanced styling ● Delightful BMW six ● Top-drawer construction quality, materials ● Superb tourer ● Brisk acceleration ● Good coupe accommodations ● Strong club interest ● Not expensive now ● Certain to appreciate in value

AGAINST

As for 2000CS, but parts more readily available (engine still in production) ● Also, handling trickier due to greater power

SPECIFICATIONS

Length (in.) 183.4 **Wheelbase (in.)** 103.3 **Weight (lbs.)** 2845
Price (new) approx. $8100 (U.S.)

ENGINES

cc/type (cid)	bore x stroke (mm)	bhp*	years
2788/ohc I6 (170)	86×80	170	1968-71

*DIN

PRICES/PROJECTION

Restorable $4000-5000 **Good** $5000-6000
Excellent $7000-10,000 **5-year projection** no change

BMW 2002
1968-76

1976 2002 2-door sedan (U.S. model)

PRODUCTION

2d sedan 339,084 **2d cabriolet by Baur** 4199
2d ti sedan 16,448 **2d tii sedan** 38,703
3d Touring sedan 11,488

HISTORY

The well-loved and highly successful 2.0-liter version of BMW's smaller sedan, unchanged in dimensions or basic appearance from the original 1600. Offered variously in three different stages of engine tune, not all of which were available in the U.S. because of then-current emissions regulations. Also not available here were custom targa convertible conversions carried out by the Baur coachworks of Stuttgart or the neat "Touring" hatchback derivative of this bodyshell. Carbureted standard and ti models were offered through 1974, the fuel-injected tii beginning for 1972. The mainstay of BMW's American and European lineups in these years, and remarkably little changed. Quite fast (110 mph standard, 120 mph tii in European trim) for such a practical design (full four-seat capacity, roomy trunk, well-chosen driving stance, and great outward visibility), yet could beat the socks off many a so-called sports car in a handling duel. Its most oft-criticized shortcomings were no provision for fresh-air ventilation and steadily escalating prices. Replaced by the more refined, more expensive 3-series based on similar mechanicals and suspension, but to many BMW fans the 2002 is the best car ever to come from Munich.

FOR

Gutsy character •Great performance •Surprising mileage •High-demand item •Others as for 1966-75 1600

AGAINST

As for 1966-76 1600, plus detrimental effects of U.S. emissions controls compared to European versions

SPECIFICATIONS

Length (in.) 166.5 (1968-73), 176.0 (1974-76)
Wheelbase (in.) 98.4   **Weight (lbs.)** 2150-2450
Price (new) $5500-8500 (U.S.)

ENGINES

cc/type (cid)	bore x stroke (mm)	bhp	years
1990/ohv I4	89×80	100-130*	1968-76
(121)		113-140**	1971-76

*DIN; European models   **SAE net, U.S. models

PRICES/PROJECTION

Restorable $600-800 **Good** $1700-3000
Excellent $3000-6000 **5-year projection** +10%

Bristol Type 400 1947-49

1947-49 Type 400 coupe

PRODUCTION

700

HISTORY

The first model of a new postwar British marque, a sideline operation of the Bristol Aeroplane Company. Born out of BMW designs purloined as "war reparations," and redeveloped with help from ex-BMW designer Dr. Fritz Fiedler. The 400 was a combination of the Type 326 chassis and Type 328 engine plus a BMW-like (right

down to its slim twin-kidney grille) four-seat coupe body. It offered creditable performance (perhaps near 90 mph maximum), and its chassis was modern by contemporary standards, so handling and roadholding were excellent. Bristol's standards for quality control and materials were at least as good as, and probably even higher than, Rolls-Royce's. Despite all this, the 400 was hampered by lack of development (shown in its high curb weight) and cramped interior. Nevertheless, an interesting car because of the way it came about — rather like Boeing deciding to make a better car than Porsche or Mercedes-Benz today.

FOR

Individuality combined with British hand-built quality •First of the line •Fine chassis and road manners •Great club interest (especially in Britain)

AGAINST

Body parts unavailable •Engine parts almost gone •Cramped interior •Limited outward visibility •Hard to find in U.S.

SPECIFICATIONS

Length (in.) 183.0   **Wheelbase (in.)** 114.0   **Weight (lbs.)** 2830
Price (new) $6000 (U.S. equivalent)

ENGINES

cc/type (cid)	bore x stroke (mm)	bhp*	years
1971/ohv I6	66×96	80	1947-49
(120)			

*net bhp

PRICES/PROJECTION

Restorable $2000-3000 **Good** $4000-5000
Excellent $5500-10,000 **5-year projection** +50%

Bristol Type 401 1949-53

PRODUCTION

650

1949-53 Type 401 coupe

1949-53 Type 401 coupe

HISTORY

The rebodied successor to the Type 400, with a little more power and a 100-mph top speed. The new four-seat, two-door fastback body was styled by Touring of Italy and built by Bristol, and used light-alloy panels. The front-end treatment was still clearly linked to that of prewar BMWs. Competed in European rallies, but was hampered by its still considerable weight. Like the 400, the engine used in the 401 was a complex "cross-pushrod" design, which makes it a difficult rebuild job for even expert restorers today.

FOR

As for Type 400, but more distinctive styling for a body less likely to deteriorate

AGAINST

As for Type 400

SPECIFICATIONS

Length (in.) 190.0 **Wheelbase (in.)** 114.0 **Weight (lbs.)** 2670 **Price (new)** NA

ENGINES

cc/type (cid)	bore x stroke (mm)	bhp*	years
1971/ohv I6 (120)	66×96	85	1949-53

*net

PRICES/PROJECTION

As for Type 400

Bristol Type 402
1949-51

PRODUCTION

24

HISTORY

An open-air derivative of the Bristol Type 401, using the same chassis and running gear. Pininfarina had a hand in modifying the basic lines to accommodate the folding top, but the result was less elegant—not to mention less rigid—than the coupe.

FOR

As for 1949-53 Type 401, plus much greater exclusivity and open-air appeal

AGAINST

As for 1949-53 Type 401, but body deterioration much more rapid

SPECIFICATIONS

Length (in.) 190.0 **Wheelbase (in.)** 114.0 **Weight (lbs.)** 2800 (approx.) **Price (new)** NA

ENGINES

cc/type (cid)	bore x stroke (mm)	bhp*	years
1971/ohv I6 (120)	66×96	85	1949-51

*net

PRICES/PROJECTION

Restorable $2000-4000 **Good** $6000-8000
Excellent $10,000-12,000 **5-year projection** no change

Bristol Type 403
1953-55

1953-55 Type 403 coupe

PRODUCTION

300

HISTORY

Mildly revised version of the Type 401, with improved chassis details and greater power and performance (top speed up to 106 mph). Styling was unchanged from the 401, and no convertible body style was offered, following demise of the 402.

FOR

As for 1949-53 Type 401, plus better performance

AGAINST

As for 1949-53 Type 401

SPECIFICATIONS

Length (in.) 190.0 **Wheelbase (in.)** 114.0 **Weight (lbs.)** 2670
Price (new) NA

ENGINES

cc/type (cid)	bore x stroke (mm)	bhp*	years
1971/ohv I6 (120)	66×96	100	1953-55

*net

PRICES/PROJECTION

As for 1949-53 Type 401

Bristol Type 404 1953-56

PRODUCTION

40

HISTORY

A short-wheelbase two-seat coupe based on the familiar Bristol chassis design. This 96-inch-wheelbase platform was also used for the Italian-styled Arnolt-Bristol sports car. Sleek fastback styling earned the Type 404 the nickname Businessman's Express, but only very rich executives could afford it, which helped keep sales extremely low. Besides, most Bristol customers wanted something more than two-passenger seating. The 404's basic lines, however, would later be applied to the longer and more practical Type 405 sedan. The familiar 2.0-liter inline six-cylinder engine from the '40s continued with yet another horsepower boost (up to 125 bhp in the higher of the two available tunes).

FOR

Unique (to Bristol) short-wheelbase chassis • Nice styling • Fine performance • Very exclusive • High appreciation • Others as for 1953-55 Type 403

AGAINST

Body corrosion • Limited interior room • Rather costly • Where do you find one?

SPECIFICATIONS

Length (in.) 171.2 **Wheelbase (in.)** 96.0 **Weight (lbs.)** 2265
Price (new) NA

ENGINES

cc/type (cid)	bore x stroke (mm)	bhp*	years
1971/ohv I6 (120)	66×96	105/125	1954-56

*net

PRICES/PROJECTION

Similar to Type 402 prices

Bristol Type 405 1954-58

PRODUCTION

340 (including 43 convertibles)

HISTORY

The replacement for the Type 401/403, and the only four-door Bristol ever built. Styling derived from the neat 96-inch-wheelbase Type 404 Coupe on the original 114-inch-wheelbase chassis. Sedan bodywork was designed and made by Bristol, but a rare convertible model with coachwork by Abbotts of Farnham was also offered in these years.

FOR

As for 1953-55 Type 403, but better entry/exit and interesting styling

AGAINST

Body rots easily if neglected • Limited performance despite sleek looks • Others as for 1953-55 Type 403

1953-56 Type 404 2-seat coupe

SPECIFICATIONS

Length (in.) 185.2 **Wheelbase (in.)** 114.0 **Weight (lbs.)** 2675
Price (new) $10,000 U.S. equivalent in 1954

ENGINES

cc/type (cid)	bore x stroke (mm)	bhp*	years
1971/ohv I6 (120)	66×96	105	1954-58

*net

PRICES/PROJECTION

Restorable $2000-3000 **Good** $5000-6000
Excellent $6000-8000 **5-year projection** +30%

Bristol Type 406 1958-61

1958-61 Type 406 coupe

PRODUCTION

300

HISTORY

A further revision of the basic Type 401/403/405 chassis, this time with an enlarged version of the Bristol straight six and all-disc brakes. The firm reverted to two doors for an all-new notchback coupe body, which set the style for succeeding models of the '60s and '70s. By now, the aging chasis and excess curb weight of what was basically prewar engineering were catching up with Bristol, and its comparatively poor performance was becoming a distinct draw-back. That would be rectified with the 407. Cars were still a sideline operation for this aircraft manufacturer, so production was as meager as in previous years, a reflection of the painstaking, hand-built construction methods employed. Most 406s were built by Bristol, but a handful featured special coachwork (and somewhat bizarre looks) by Zagato of Italy.

FOR

As for 1954-58 Type 405, plus crisper appearance and better brakes • Also, surprisingly affordable

AGAINST

Too heavy • Disappointing performance • Others as for 1954-58 Type 405

SPECIFICATIONS

Length (in.) 198.0 **Wheelbase (in.)** 114.0 **Weight (lbs.)** 3010
Price (new) $8400 U.S. equivalent base price

ENGINES

cc/type (cid)	bore x stroke (mm)	bhp*	years
2216/OHV I6 (135)	69×100	105/130	1958-61

*net

PRICES/PROJECTION

Restorable $1800-2500 **Good** $4400-6000
Excellent $6000-7500 **5-year projection** +25%

Bristol Type 407 1961-63

1961-63 Type 407 coupe

PRODUCTION

300

HISTORY

The model that marked Bristol's first major mechanical change since the marque appeared in late '40s. Replacing the old BMW-based six-cylinder engine was a special 5.1-liter (313-cid) export version of the Chrysler hemi-head V8. The U.S. company's fine TorqueFlite automatic transmission was also specified. At one stroke, this substitution transformed what had been a milquetoast, conservative tourer into a high-performance GT. Except for minor trim and ornamentation changes, the four-seat Type 406 bodyshell was left alone, and the chassis (still prewar BMW, remember), suspension, and brakes were not seriously altered.

FOR

Very fast • Well-known Detroit drivetrain • Neat lines • Body durability better than before • Top-flight construction, materials • Chassis parts still available • Not costly for a low-production item

AGAINST

Expensive to rebuild (except drivetrain) and run • Not easy to find in U.S., and not much restoration help available • Modest appreciation potential

SPECIFICATIONS

Length (in.) 199.0 **Wheelbase (in.)** 114.0 **Weight (lbs.)** 3585
Price (new) NA

ENGINES

cc/type (cid)	bore x stroke (mm)	bhp*	years
5130/ohv V8 (313)	98×84	250	1961-63

*SAE gross

PRICES/PROJECTION

Restorable $2500-3800 **Good** $6500-7500
Excellent $8500-12,500 **5-year projection** +25%

Bristol Type 408
1963-65

PRODUCTION

300 (est.)

HISTORY

A slightly restyled Type 407, with a squared-up nose and somewhat taller and more narrow overall shape. Still built only as a two-door notchback coupe. The last few models were equipped with mechanical components from the successor Type 409 (see entry).

FOR

As for 1961-63 Type 407

AGAINST

As for 1961-63 Type 407, plus less pleasant styling

SPECIFICATIONS

Length (in.) 199.0 **Wheelbase (in.)** 114.0 **Weight (lbs.)** 3600
Price (new) approx. $12,000 U.S. equivalent

ENGINES

cc/type (cid)	bore x stroke (mm)	bhp*	years
5130/ohv V8 (313)	98×84	250	1963-65

*SAE gross

As for 1961-63 Type 407

Bristol Type 409
1965-67

1965-67 Type 409 coupe

PRODUCTION

300 (est.)

HISTORY

An updated continuation of the Type 407/408, with fairly extensive (for Bristol) mechanical modifications. These included a larger Chrysler V8 with the same power as the previous 313-cid unit, plus softer suspension settings and Girling instead of Dunlop disc brakes. Cars built from the autumn of 1966 were available with ZF power steering as an optional extra. These were the last Bristols that could be legally imported into the U.S. before the advent of Federal emissions controls, though few actually were.

FOR

See 1961-63 Type 407 and 1963-65 Type 408

AGAINST

See 1961-63 Type 407 and 1963-65 Type 408

1963-65 Type 408 coupe

SPECIFICATIONS

Length (in.) 193.5 **Wheelbase (in.)** 114.0 **Weight (lbs.)** 3528
Price (new) NA

ENGINES

cc/type (cid)	bore x stroke (mm)	bhp*	years
5211/ohv V8 (318)	99×84.1	250	1965-67

*gross

PRICES/PROJECTION

See 1961-63 Type 407

Bristol Type 410 1967-69

1967-69 Type 410 coupe

PRODUCTION

300 (est.)

HISTORY

The last Bristol of the '60s, included here because it marked the end of the hemi-engine models and also because it is easier to bring into compliance with applicable U.S. safety and emissions regulations than the later 411/412 models. Mechanically, the 410 was exactly like the 408/409 except for the use of 15-inch instead of 16-inch-diameter wheels. A minor nose job resulted in small sheetmetal scallops under the headlights for a bit smoother look. The standard TorqueFlite automatic was now controlled by a tunnel-mounted stick instead of the previous column lever. The 410 continued previous (and current) Bristol practice of carrying the spare tire under a lift-up flap in the left front fender aft of the wheel opening; a storage compartment was provided on the opposite side. This arrangement contributed to the car's long-hood/short-deck proportions.

FOR

As for Type 407/408/409, plus better styling details • Last of the hemis

AGAINST

As for Type 407/408/409

SPECIFICATIONS

Length (in.) 193.5 **Wheelbase (in.)** 114.0 **Weight (lbs.)** 3600
Price (new) NA

ENGINES

cc/type (cid)	bore x stroke (mm)	bhp*	years
5211/ohv V8 (318)	99×84.1	250	1967-69

*SAE gross

PRICES/PROJECTION

Restorable $2500-3800 **Good** $6500-7500
Excellent $8500-12,500 **5-year projection** +25%

Bugatti Type 43/43A 1930-31

PRODUCTION

approx. 150 (began 1927)

HISTORY

Ettore Bugatti's cars had been around since 1910, and by the mid-1920s had become famous in European competition. Built at Molsheim in eastern France, all "Bugs" had flexible chassis, rock-hard suspensions, and either four- or eight-cylinder engines. Generally considered one of Bugatti's four greatest creations, the straight-eight Type 43 offered a 100-mph top speed but MGA/Triumph TR3 acceleration. Really a long-chassis Type 35/38 with a larger supercharged engine. Most built with narrow torpedo-style sports bodies, but some four-seat roadsters are known. The 43A had American-style rumble-seat bodywork.

FOR

Impeccable vintage racing pedigree • Eight-cylinder smoothness • High-quality design • Charisma

AGAINST

Rock-hard ride • Crude suspension • Floppy chassis • Few creature comforts • Very costly to buy and restore

SPECIFICATIONS

Length (in.) 154.0 **Wheelbase (in.)** 117 **Weight (lbs.)** 2300 (approx.) **Price (new)** NA

ENGINES

cc/type (cid)	bore x stroke (mm)	bhp	years
2262/ohc I8 (138)	60×100	115	1930-31

PRICES/PROJECTION

Restorable $48,000-60,000 **Good** $120,000-160,000
Excellent $160,000-190,000 **5-year projection** +20%

Bugatti Type 49 1930-34

PRODUCTION

470

HISTORY

The last—and best—of the single-cam eight-cylinder Bugattis. A larger engine made a more flexible, refined tourer than the Type 43. Bodies tended to be bigger, plusher, and more civilized. Alloy or wire wheels were specified. "Only" 80 mph allied to Bugatti's habitually hard suspension, but pinpoint-accurate controls and great French character. Practical and versatile by Bugatti standards and not really intended for competition.

FOR

Bugatti engineering with a measure of reliability • Character • Relatively well-known "Bug" • Styling

AGAINST

Function before luxury • Hard ride • "Traditional" detailing • Expensive to buy and run • High restoration costs

SPECIFICATIONS

Length (in.) 165.0 **Wheelbase (in.)** 127.0 **Weight (lbs.)** 3000 (approx.) **Price (new)** NA

ENGINES

cc/type (cid)	bore x stroke (mm)	bhp	years
3257/ohc I8 (199)	72×100	NA	1930-34

PRICES/PROJECTION

Restorable $36,000-48,000 **Good** $96,000-120,000
Excellent $120,000-160,000 **5-year projection** +20%

Bugatti Type 50 1930-34

PRODUCTION

65

HISTORY

A "derivative" Bugatti built on a scaled-down Type 46 Royale chassis. Gearbox in unit with the rear axle. Up front was the new, large twincam eight allegedly patterned on the U.S. Miller racing unit. A direct replacement for the Type 46 and big and luxurious by any standards. Choice of two wheelbases and several sumptuous bodies. Sold in small numbers because of Rolls-Royce prices, spine-numbing roadholding, lots of engine noise, and definite "mechanical" character. A very desirable Bugatti for the sportsman rather than the sybarite.

FOR

Peerless Bugatti character • Trend-setting twincam eight • Big and impressive • Easy to drive

AGAINST

Expensive to buy and restore • Mechanically complex • Not many around today • Lacks refinement

SPECIFICATIONS

Length (in.) 178.0+ **Wheelbase (in.)** 122/138
Weight (lbs.) 4000+ **Price (new)** NA

ENGINES

cc/type (cid)	bore x stroke (mm)	bhp	years
4972/dohc I8 (303.5)	86×107	200*	1930-34

*net

PRICES/PROJECTION

Restorable $36,000-48,000 **Good** $110,000-120,000
Excellent $140,000-180,000 **5-year projection** +20%

Bugatti Type 55 1932-35

1932 Type 55 Supersport roadster

PRODUCTION

35

HISTORY

A *very* exclusive roadgoing version of the small-engined, supercharged Type 51 Grand Prix car. Expect the fierce character of a blown twincam eight and a chassis almost exactly the same as that of the GP car. Like the Type 43 in many ways, yet considerably faster: some say the standard-bodied two-seat roadster could exceed 112 mph when new, comparable to Ferrari Boxer/Lamborghini Countach performance today. Offers all the usual joys and heartaches of a true thoroughbred Bugatti plus greater exclusivity.

FOR

High performance • Grand Prix heritage • Styling, of course • "Animal" charm • Rarity

AGAINST

Ludicrous prices • Extremely expensive to own • Chassis old-fashioned even for the mid-'30s • Are there any left to find?

SPECIFICATIONS

Length (in.) 162.0 **Wheelbase (in.)** 108.0 **Weight (lbs.)** 2050 **Price (new)** NA

1933 Type 55 Supersport roadster

ENGINES

cc/type (cid)	bore x stroke (mm)	bhp	years
2262/dohc I8	60×100	135*	1932-35

*net; supercharged

PRICES/PROJECTION

Restorable $60,000-95,000 **Good** $215,000-240,000
Excellent $240,000-300,000 **5-year projection** +20%

Bugatti Type 57/57C 1933-40

1938 Type 57 Ventoux coupe

PRODUCTION

630

HISTORY

The final statement of Bugatti's design philosophy, combining a fine, modern engine with an uncompromisingly "vintage" chassis and a great variety of startlingly styled bodywork. Still no independent front suspension or synchronized gearbox, but hydraulic brakes from 1938. Splendidly detailed center-lock wire wheels are worth $10,000 just to look at! The supercharged 57C (*Compresseur*) of 1937-39 could easily best the 57 in top speed, 110 versus 95 mph. Pure 1930s supercar apart from the old-fashioned road manners and immensely desirable now.

FOR

Magnificent engine • Performance, especially 57C • Styling,

especially coupes and cabriolets • Character and sound • Good value today compared with other Bugattis

AGAINST

Complex and costly to restore • Archaic handling/roadholding • Not readily available

SPECIFICATIONS

Length (in.) 172.0 **Wheelbase (in.)** 130.0 **Weight (lbs.)** 3000 (approx.) **Price (new)** NA

ENGINES

cc/type (cid)	bore x stroke (mm)	bhp*	years
3257/dohc I8 (199)	72×100	135*/160**	1933-40

*net
**supercharged (1937-39)

PRICES/PROJECTION

Restorable $24,000-36,000 **Good** $65,000-72,000
Excellent $72,000-95,000 **5-year projection** +20%

Bugatti Type 57S/57SC 1935-38

1936 Type 57SC Atlantique Electron coupe

PRODUCTION

approx. 40

HISTORY

Even better than the Type 57. The more sporting short-chassis version. Sold with the same normally aspirated (S) or supercharged (SC) engines with dry-sump lubrication and a higher state of tune for more power. Mechanically the same otherwise. Quite startling coachwork, still with the unmistakable "horseshoe" radiator. Irresistible to the very rich then as now. The best 57SCs could top 120 mph, unbelievable by late-1930s standards. Today, very few are ever bought or sold.

FOR

Very high performance • Styling, especially coupes • Mechanical elegance • Sexy charisma

continued on page 297

△1936 Hudson Custom Eight   ▽1954 Hudson Italia by Touring

△1955 Imperial　　▽1940 Jaguar SS100

△1958 Jaguar XK150 ▽1954 Kaiser Manhattan

△1954 Kaiser-Darrin DFK-161   ▽1930 LaSalle Series 340

△1940 LaSalle Series 52   ▽1941 Lincoln Continental

△1951 Lincoln Cosmopolitan   ▽1936 Mercedes-Benz 500K

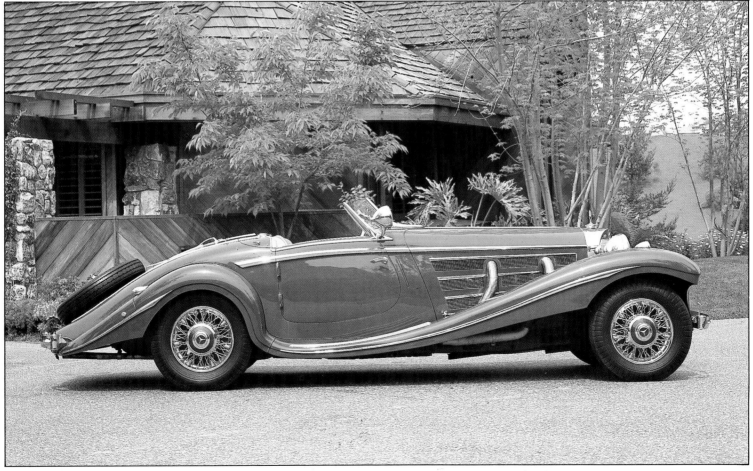

△1955 Mercedes-Benz 300SL   ▽1954 Mercury Monterey

△1968 Mercury Cougar XR-7   ▽1952 Muntz Jet

△1948 Nash Ambassador Custom ▽1953 Nash-Healey

△1950 Oldsmobile Futuramic 88 Holiday ▽1966 Oldsmobile Toronado

△1933 Packard V12 by Dietrich   ▽1955 Packard Clipper Custom Constellation

△1933 Pierce-Arrow Model 1242 V12   ▽1941 Plymouth Special DeLuxe

△1966 Pontiac GTO   ▽1969 Pontiac Firebird 400

△1963 Porsche Carrera 2   ▽1931 Reo Royale Eight Model 8-35

△1941 Studebaker President Skyway   ▽1957 Studebaker Golden Hawk

△1948 Tucker "48"   ▽1949 Willys Jeepster

AGAINST

Archaic chassis • Noisy to drive fast • Enormously costly to buy, run, and restore

SPECIFICATIONS

Length (in.) 159.0 **Wheelbase (in.)** 118.0 **Weight (lbs.)** 2700 (approx.) **Price (new)** NA

ENGINES

cc/type (cid)	bore x stroke (mm)	bhp*	years
3257/dohc I8 (199)	72×100	175/200**	1935-38

*net
**supercharged (1937-38)

PRICES/PROJECTION

Restorable $36,000-60,000 **Good** $110,000-130,000
Excellent $140,000-180,000 **5-year projection** +20%

Cisitalia Type 202 Gran Sport 1947-52

1947-52 Type 202 Gran Sport coupe by Pinin Farina

PRODUCTION

approx. 170, incl. 60 cabriolets

HISTORY

The car best remembered for its critically acclaimed Pinin Farina styling, one of the designer's landmarks. The brainchild of wealthy Italian industrialist Piero Dusio, Cisitalia started by building single-seat racing cars. The Type 202 was a roadgoing version of that design, and like it was based on contemporary Fiat 1100 (Type 508) mechanical components. The complex multi-tubular chassis was the product of Dr. Dante Giacosa of Fiat. While the drivetrains were cheap and familiar, the coachbuilt bodies were not. Cisitalia was soon overtaken by cheaper and more modern competitors, and the firm ran out of funds before a Grand Prix car project was completed. Dusio moved his operations to Argentina, but the cars built there under the Cisitalia name were far different. In 1950, production of the Type 202 was supposed to resume in Italy under new ownership, but though a few cars were built through 1965, they

appeared sporadically. Most were simply cobbled-up amalgamations of mass-produced chassis and drivetrains with special bodies. The trend-setting 202 Gran Sport is the only truly collectible model. A convertible version was offered in addition to Farina's beautifully contoured coupe (which has since been enshrined in New York's Museum of Modern Art).

FOR

Timeless Pinin Farina styling • Unique chassis design • Simple running gear • Very rare, highly prized

AGAINST

Virtually none left • Not quick (maybe 80 mph tops) • Chassis difficult to restore • Fragile, light-alloy bodywork • Body and mechanical parts extinct

SPECIFICATIONS

Length (in.) NA **Wheelbase (in.)** NA **Weight (lbs.)** 1760
Price (new) $6800 U.S. list price

ENGINES

cc/type (cid)	bore x stroke (mm)	bhp*	years
1089/ohv I4 (66)	68×75	51-70	1947-52

*gross

PRICES/PROJECTION

Restorable $5000-10,000 **Good** $20,000-25,000
Excellent $25,000-30,000 **5-year projection** no change

Citroën DS19/20/21/23 1955-75

1970 DS23 4-door sedan (U.S. model)

PRODUCTION

1,456,115 of all types

HISTORY

Futuristic design from French pioneer of front-wheel drive, and still quite advanced next to most competitors when it was replaced 20

1970 DS21 Safari wagon

years later by the current CX series. The mainstay of the Citroen line for many years, the "Goddess" was the first car reflecting the firm's interest and expertise in the art of aerodynamics. The monocoque body/chassis featured fully detachable skin panels; the car could even be driven in "skeleton" form. The DS also introduced Citroen's unique hydraulic (actually gas/oil) all-independent suspension system run from an engine-driven pump that also provided assistance for steering and brakes. The suspension incorporated a variable height adjustment that could be used for clearing road hazards, fording streams, or even jacking up the car when changing a flat. (U.S. advertising tauted this as the only car you could ride going up and down.) The low-drag body put the wheels at the "corners" of the car, resulting in a spacious interior. Model designations reflect engine size. Through 1966, the DS used Citroen's ancient four-cylinder engine, but this was replaced by a more modern design in later models. A confusing succession of tuning and equipment changes marked this series through the years, but while it sold fairly well in Europe, the DS was never a high-volume item in the U.S. Most of the ones sold here were four-door sedans, but an even longer wagon was also sold in modest numbers. The hydraulic suspension gave a cloud-like ride that made the DS unmatched in this area by almost any other car, although certain surface irregularities would upset the car strangely. Leech-like roadholding was another virtue, but the performance wasn't. The engines were considered under-powered for really brisk standing-start acceleration, although top speed was high, a benefit of the slippery body. Not the sort of car that stood up well to American driving conditions and owner habits, but a fairly rare and distinctive collectible with the advantage that production ended only a short time ago.

FOR

Unique design in all respects • Ride and handling still up to current standards • Parts still available from overseas • Budget buy • High appreciation potential

AGAINST

Mechanically complex, so expect restoration and maintenance headaches • Disappointing acceleration • Strange dash and minor control layout • Brakes demand driver practice • Rust-prone

SPECIFICATIONS

Length (in.) 190.5 (sedan), 198.0 (wagon)
Wheelbase (in.) 123.0   **Weight (lbs.)** 2690-3100
Price (new) NA

ENGINES

cc/type (cid)	bore x stroke (mm)	bhp*	years
1911/ohv I4 (117)	78×100	60	1955-66
1985/ohv I4 (121)	86×86	103	1966-75
2175/ohv I4 (133)	90×86	115	1968-75
2347/ohv I4 (143)	93.5×86	125	1971-75

*DIN

PRICES/PROJECTION

Restorable $800-1200 **Good** $2000-3000
Excellent $3000-5100 Add 100% for convertible
5-year projection +10%

Citroën Chapron DS19/20/21/23 1957-75

1968 DS21 convertible by Chapron

PRODUCTION

approx. 100 per year

HISTORY

Rare and expensive convertible conversion of the front-drive Citroen DS-series sedans carried out by the French coachbuilders, Henri Chapron. Built in very small numbers to customer order, mostly for very wealthy private buyers and the French government. Most had two-door bodywork, but some four-door convertible sedans were also built. Chapron still carries out this work on Citroen's current CX models, but like these earlier DS examples most are not exported. Thus, finding a DS ragtop in the U.S. will, needless to say, be akin to the old needle-in-a-haystack exercise.

FOR

As for DS19/20/21/23 plus convertible appeal and great scarcity

AGAINST

As for DS19/20/21/23, but few body parts available, and body not as rigid

SPECIFICATIONS

Length (in.) 190.5 **Wheelbase (in.)** 123.0 **Weight (lbs.)** 3200 (approx.) **Price (new)** NA

ENGINES

cc/type (cid)	bore x stroke (mm)	bhp*	years
1911/ohv I4 (117)	78×100	60	1955-66
1985/ohv I4 (121)	86×86	103	1966-75
2175/ohv I4 (133)	90×86	115	1968-75
2347/ohv I4 (143)	93.5×86	125	1971-75

*DIN

PRICES/PROJECTION

Restorable $3000-5000 **Good** $4500-6000
Excellent $5500-7500 **5-year projection** +20%

Citroën SM 1972-74

1972 SM coupe (European model)

PRODUCTION

NA, but limited; probably no more than 5000 total (Note: years shown are for U.S. importation only)

1972 SM coupe (European model)

HISTORY

The most spectacular postwar Citroën, and a car with strong collector potential despite its mechanical complexity and attendant reliability problems. The result of a temporary corporate marriage between the French concern and Maserati, the SM was powered by a four-cam V6 engine designed by the Italians, and which also found its way into the mid-engine Maserati Merak. Styling was recognizably Citroën and quite stunning, a sort of sports interpretation of DS-series themes. It undoubtedly had good aerodynamics (long a Citroën passion) as the car's 135-mph top speed suggests. Like the DS, the SM used Citroën's fully pressurized hydraulics for brakes and as a suspension medium, but here it also powered the steering, which was lightning quick (2 turns lock-to-lock) and would self-center without any driver assist with the car at rest. Another novel touch on European models was a six-headlamp system with the inboard units linked to the steering so they'd turn in the same direction as the front wheels—shades of Tucker! Unfortunately, the SM bowed almost on the eve of the first energy crisis, which made fast tourers like this almost unsaleable in Europe and put both Citroën and Maserati in serious financial trouble. Citroën withdrew from the American market after 1974. SM production limped along for about another year, then ceased following Peugeot's acquisition of the firm. Named "one of the ten best cars in the world" in 1971 by *Road & Track* magazine, a debatable accolade, perhaps, in view of subsequent events. Not a strong collector comer at present, but unique design and comparative rarity should start to tell further down the road.

FOR

Unique design • Splendid performance • Citroën ride • Rarity

AGAINST

Engines subject to cam-drive problems • Parts supplies dicey • Hydraulics a bear if something breaks

SPECIFICATIONS

Length (in.) 160.6 **Wheelbase (in.)** 95.0 **Weight (lbs.)** 2130 **Price (new)** $9000 U.S. in 1972

ENGINES

cc/type (cid)	bore x stroke (mm)	bhp*	years
2965/dohc V6 (181)	92×75	190	1972-74

*SAE net

PRICES/PROJECTION

Restorable $3000-6000 **Good** $6500-9000
Excellent $10,000-14,000 **5-year projection** +10%

Daimler SP250
1959-64

1959-64 SP250 roadster with hardtop

PRODUCTION

2465

HISTORY

Daimler's second stab at a sporting model, approved following a company shakeup in the mid-'50s. Ex-motorcycle engine designer Edward Turner became managing director, and laid out a splendid new pushrod V8 that was first seen in this two-seat roadster. The SP250 chassis and suspension were much like those of the Triumph TR3A (even some parts were shared), as was the gearbox. Styling for the fiberglass body was instantly recognizable: a broad, oval, eggcrate grille; sloping domed hood; curved character lines on front and rear fenders; and even modest fins. Originally displayed at the New York Auto Show as the Dart, but Dodge complained, so the designation was changed to reflect engine capacity (in ccs divided by 10). Good performance (120 mph-plus top speed), but rather loose body construction (not cured until 1963). Some cars were equipped with Borg-Warner automatic, and a few fixed-roof hardtops were also built. The 2.5-liter V8 was also used in Daimler's version of the Jaguar Mark II sedan through 1969.

FOR

Efficient engine and high performance •Reasonable economy •Simple-to-maintain chassis •Rust-free, easy-to-repair fiberglass body

AGAINST

Spare parts are gone except for TR3A-shared chassis pieces •Controversial styling •Flimsy body (early models) •Don't call Jaguar Rover Triumph with problems

SPECIFICATIONS

Length (in.) 160.5 **Wheelbase (in.)** 92.0 **Weight (lbs.)** 2220
Price (new) NA

ENGINES

cc/type (cid)	bore x stroke (mm)	bhp*	years
2548/ohv V8 (156)	76×70	140	1959-64

*net

PRICES/PROJECTION

Restorable $1500-2000 **Good** $4000-5000
Excellent $5000-7500 **5-year projection** +10%

Datsun 240Z
1970-73

1970 240Z coupe

PRODUCTION

1970 16,215 **1971** 33,684 **1972** 52,658 (U.S. calendar year exports)
Total U.S. exports 1970-73: 130,000+

HISTORY

The first Japanese car with definite collectibility apart from the extremely rare Toyota 2000GT, Datsun's hot-selling Z-car already commands a large and fanatical following. A sensation when it hit the market at an astoundingly low $3526 base price, with a combination of style, performance, and equipment that sent auto writers into gales of praise and buyers streaming into Datsun showrooms. Though the original bodyshell would be continued through larger engine displacements as the 260Z and 280Z, these first 2.4-liter models are the ones to have. They're less affected by emissions and safety rules than the 1974-77 Zs, and Datsun's fine overhead cam six was never smoother or freer-revving. Handling, too, is better here than in later years when clumsy and heavy bumpers added extra weight, particularly to the front end, and made power steering almost mandatory. In all, a marvelous blend of Jaguar E-Type styling and a character not unlike that of the late, lamented Austin-Healey 3000. A definite comer among late-model collectibles.

FOR

Reasonably priced (though values fluctuate) •Great blend of performance, rugged engineering, decent mileage •Well equipped •Still looks great •Fine road manners •Parts supplies still ample

AGAINST

Rust-prone, especially lower fenders and rockers •Most were driven hard •Many modified with juvenile add-ons •'73s prone to vapor lock

SPECIFICATIONS

Length (in.) 161.3 **Wheelbase (in.)** 90.7 **Weight (lbs.)** 2355
Price (new) $3526 (original U.S. P.O.E.)

1970 240Z coupe

ENGINES

cc/type (cid)	bore x stroke (mm)	bhp	years
146/ohc I6 (2393)	3.26×2.90	139-151*	1970-73

*SAE net

PRICES/PROJECTION

Restorable $500-800 **Good** $2000-3000
Excellent $3000-4700 **5-year projection** +20%

Delage D8
1930-35

PRODUCTION

NA

HISTORY

Delage had built GP and record cars as well as memorable road machines in the 1920s. The firm excelled itself in the hard-pressed 1930s with this splendidly flashy long-distance straight-eight tourer, the type the French called a *grand routier*. Inevitably, it helped to bankrupt Delage, which was then forced to merge with Delahaye. The D8 had everything: smooth engine, sexy styling, near-vintage chassis and handling, and thus great character. The D8S and D8SS variations introduced in 1932 had dropped frames and even more performance (100 mph maximum). Predictably, none of these cars survived the merger or World War II which makes them very rare today.

FOR

Famous name • Great French elegance • Silky engine • Solid engineering+high gearing = fine performance

AGAINST

Expensive to restore • Too "continental" for some • Rather backward chassis design • High ownership costs

SPECIFICATIONS

Length (in.) 192.0-205.0 **Wheelbase (in.)** 130.0/143.0
Weight (lbs.) 4400+ **Price (new)** NA

ENGINES

cc/type (cid)	bore x stroke (mm)	bhp*	years
4050/ohv I8 (247)	77×109	120/145**	1930-35

*gross
**145 bhp on D8S/D8SS

PRICES/PROJECTION

Restorable $6000-8000 **Good** $18,000-20,000
Excellent $25,000-35,000 **5-year projection** +30%

Delahaye Type 135
1935-50

1947 Type 135M close-coupled by Guillaré

PRODUCTION

approx. 200

HISTORY

Delahaye's fine, modern grand touring car, which took over from Delage in the hearts of sporting drivers. Powered by a very refined truck engine and, like the Delage, distinguished by a variety of typical French shapes. Most were built with sedan and sporting two-door bodywork, but a few serious competition cars were also completed. Chassis strictly conventional apart from independent

1947 Type 135M close-coupled coupe by Guillaré

front suspension and synchromesh gearbox, though with supple and advanced road behavior and 100-mph performance. Some cars were fitted with the Cotal electromagnetic gearbox, a real French specialty.

FOR

High performance • Excellent roadholding • Styling of sports versions • Simple to maintain • Not frightfully expensive

AGAINST

Obsolete now, so no parts • No restoration expertise • Few bodies have survived intact • Not widely appreciated in U.S.

SPECIFICATIONS

Length (in.) 180.0+ **Wheelbase (in.)** 116.0
Weight (lbs.) 2800+ **Price (new)** NA

ENGINES

cc/type (cid)	bore x stroke (mm)	bhp*	years
3237/ohv I6 (198)	80×107	130	1935-36
3557/ohv I6 (217)	84×107	160**	1935-39

*gross
**competition model only

PRICES/PROJECTION

Restorable $6000-8000 **Good** $18,000-20,000
Excellent $25,000-35,000 **5-year projection** +20%

De Tomaso Mangusta 1967-71

PRODUCTION

NA

HISTORY

Striking Italian supercar, the first serious production-car effort from motorcycle magnate Alejandro de Tomaso. A mid-engine layout tied a small-block Ford V8 to a ZF transmission within a steel backbone chassis not unlike Lotus. Chunky, muscular styling by Ghia, then recently acquired by De Tomaso. Very much a detuned sports-racing car, with considerable rear weight bias, very little luggage space, accommodation for two only, and superb performance. A top speed of 155 mph was claimed, but handling was tricky, particularly in poor weather when the limited visibility afforded by the low-slung body didn't help matters. Built in very small numbers, and sold to a fortunate few. Great for rushing along twisty back roads on sunny days, though, and an admirable piece of sculpture standing still.

FOR

Performance • Styling • Familiar Detroit iron • Mid-engine panache • Rarity

AGAINST

Cramped interior • Suspect wet-road handling • Rust-prone body • Not likely to go up in value soon

SPECIFICATIONS

Length (in.) 168.0 **Wheelbase (in.)** 98.4 **Weight (lbs.)** 3050
Price (new) $11,150 U.S. list price in 1969

ENGINES

cid/type	bore x stroke	bhp	years
302/ohv V8	4.00×3.00	230*	1967-71

*DIN

PRICES/PROJECTION

Restorable $3500-4800 **Good** $9500-13,000
Excellent $14,500-18,000 **5-year projection** +20%

De Tomaso Pantera 1971-80

1971 Pantera coupe by Ghia

PRODUCTION

1971-74 5629 **1975-80** approximately 25 per year

HISTORY

Alejandro de Tomaso's "volume" sports car, and successor to the Mangusta. An outcome of Ford's acquisition of De Tomaso's operations, and sold in the U.S. through selected Lincoln-Mercury dealers. Like its predecessor, a mid-engine GT with dramatic wedge-shaped lines by Ghia and a tuned version of Ford's domestic 351-cid "Cleveland" V8. Also featured a pressed-steel underpan, all-independent suspension, and four-wheel disc brakes. More practical than the Mangusta, though lack of cabin space, excess cockpit heat, a peculiar driving position, and indifferent quality control came in for criticism. Nevertheless, something of a bargain for an Italian exotic at its initial U.S. price of around $10,000. Sold here with Ford's normal new-car warranty, a good thing as the electrical system frequently packed up and engine overheating was a common problem. Ford rebuilt many of those imported to the States just to keep customers happy. By 1973, the Pantera had acquired a rubber-covered nose to meet bumper standards, but they got tougher for 1974 models and effectively spelled the end of U.S. sales. Production continued for the European market (the car was especially popular in Germany), but at much-reduced levels. Reintroduced to the U.S. on a very limited basis in 1981 by two Americans operating under the Panteramerica banner. The newer cars are remarkably little changed from the early-'70s versions apart from a switch to Ford of Australia powertrains and a much higher price (close to $60,000, the cost of federal certification for a low-volume, hand-built supercar). Great looks and effortless performance with a 150-mph top end plus Italian *brio* make this one of the most fabulous "world cars" ever powered by Ford.

1971 Pantera coupe by Ghia

FOR

High performance • Styling • Reliable U.S. engine • Strong club interest • Most parts and accessories still available

AGAINST

Indifferent construction quality (1971-74s) • Innate mid-engine shortcomings • Rust-prone body/chassis • Parts expensive • Not a profitable investment

SPECIFICATIONS

Length (in.) 168.0 **Wheelbase (in.)** 99.0 **Weight (lbs.)** 3100
Price (new) $10,295 (approx. U.S. base)

ENGINES

cid/type	bore x stroke	bhp	years
351/ohv V8	4.00×3.50	310*	1971-74**

*SAE gross
**Models built after 1974 and sold in Europe were changed to a similar 351 V8 built by Ford of Australia, offering similar power output. Up to 350 bhp (SAE gross) available for GTS model not sold in U.S.

PRICES/PROJECTION

Restorable $3500-6000 **Good** $8300-12,000
Excellent $12,000-21,000 **5-year projection** +15%

Facel Vega & FV 1954-59

PRODUCTION

352 (incl. 11 convertibles)

HISTORY

Classy Franco-American hybrid GT. Power by Chrysler, designed and built by Facel Metallon, previously known as a body supplier to other manufacturers. Styling was probably influenced by the Simca Sport and other cars built by Facel in the late '40s and early '50s. Engineered in limited-production Italian style, with a large-tube fabricated chassis carrying independent front suspension and a conventional live axle rear end. The separate bodyshells were built by Facel. Costly but very fast thanks to Chrysler hemi-head V8s, which were supplied with increased displacement in 1956 and again in '58. Top speed was at least 130 mph, more on later models with the larger engines. Usually recognized by a distinctive "face" with ver-

1954-59 FVS coupe

tical eggcrate grille flanked by oval head/parking lamp clusters. Usually carried wire wheels. Most FVs were thin-pillar two-door coupes, but a few convertibles were also constructed.

FOR

Individual French styling • Performance • Reliable Detroit engines • Low-production appeal

AGAINST

Heavy and thirsty • Few parts available now • Drum brakes • Only modest appreciation

SPECIFICATIONS

Length (in.) 179.0-181.0 **Wheelbase (in.)** 103.5/104.7
Weight (lbs.) 3585-4105 **Price (new)** $7000 U.S. (Vega),
$7500/9750 (FV)

ENGINES

cc/type (cid)	bore x stroke (mm)	bhp*	years
4528/ohv V8 (276)	92×85	170	1954-55
4768/ohv V8 (291)	95×85	180	1954-55
5407/ohv V8 (330)	95×97	250	1956-57
5801/ohv V8 (354)	100×92	325	1958-59

*SAE gross

PRICES/PROJECTION

Restorable $2000-5000 **Good** $5000-7000
Excellent $9000-11,500 **5-year projection** +10%

Facel Vega Excellence 1957-64

PRODUCTION

156

HISTORY

A long-wheelbase four-door hardtop derivative of the FV-series coupe, with standard automatic transmission and Chrysler V8 power. Styling was an interesting blend of then-current Detroit and European themes, including the formal Facel "face," wraparound windshield, and rear-hinged back doors. A very heavy car in appearance and on the scale. Engine displacement and output were generally the same as for other Facel models of the period. Another very low-production, almost limousine-type model intended more as a car of state than a private owner-driver vehicle.

FOR

As for 1954-59 FVS, plus greater rarity and unique body style

AGAINST

As for 1954-59 FVS, plus trouble-prone bodywork

SPECIFICATIONS

Length (in.) 207.0   **Wheelbase (in.)** 125.0   **Weight (lbs.)** 4315
Price (new) NA

ENGINES

cc/type (cid)	bore x stroke (mm)	bhp*	years
5407/ohv V8 (330)	94×97	250	1957
5801/ohv V8 (354)	100×92	325	1958-59
6276/ohv V8 (383)	108×86	360	1959-64

*SAE gross

PRICES/PROJECTION

Restorable $4500-6000   **Good** $6000-7500
Excellent $8000-12,000   **5-year projection** +20%

Facel Vega HK500 1959-62

1959-62 HK500 2-door hardtop

PRODUCTION

490

HISTORY

A rebodied version of the original FV-series Facel Vega with a larger Chrysler V8 engine. Notable for having a full wraparound windshield in the best Detroit style, but otherwise quite Italian-looking. More massive and impressive than the FV, and probably more controllable due to standard power steering and four-wheel disc brakes (by Dunlop). The HK500 engine was Chrysler's wedgehead 383-cid unit, able to push this hefty GT to a top of 140 mph. Chrysler's TorqueFlite automatic transmission was offered as an option to the French Pont-a-Mousson four-speed manual gearbox (also offered as an option on the 1960 Chrysler 300F). Identifi-

cation points include HK500 script on the trunklid and stacked quad headlamps.

FOR

As for 1954-59 FVS

AGAINST

As for 1954-59 FVS, but better brakes

SPECIFICATIONS

Length (in.) 181.0   **Wheelbase (in.)** 105.0   **Weight (lbs.)** 4035
Price (new) NA

ENGINES

cid/type	bore x stroke	bhp	years
383/ohv V8	4.03×3.75	360*	1959-62

*SAE gross

PRICES/PROJECTION

As for 1954-59 FVS

Facel Vega Facel II 1962-64

1964 Facel II coupe

PRODUCTION

180

HISTORY

The second complete restyle on the original FV-series Facel chassis, and successor to the HK500. Tubular chassis construction, a live rear axle, four-wheel disc brakes, and Chrysler 383 V8 were all continued. The more square-cut body lines were set off by vertical quad headlamps covered by bulging lenses. A taller, non-wrapped windshield and slimmer roof pillars were also featured. Top speed was now up to about 150 mph, making this a real Ferrari competitor in its day. However, Facel went bankrupt during 1964, a result of too-few sales and high tooling costs for the smaller four-cylinder Facellia model that didn't prove successful.

FOR

As for FVS and HK500 models, plus last of the line and great rarity

1962-64 Facel II coupe

AGAINST

As for FVS and HK500 models

SPECIFICATIONS

Length (in.) 185.5   **Wheelbase (in.)** 105.0   **Weight (lbs.)** 4035
Price (new) NA

ENGINES

cid/type	bore x stroke	bhp	years
383/ohv V8	4.03×3.75	355/390*	1962-64

*SAE gross, with automatic and manual transmission, respectively

PRICES/PROJECTION

Restorable $5000-6500 **Good** $6500-9000
Excellent $8500-13,000 **5-year projection** +10%

Ferrari Type 166 1948-51

1950 Type 166 berlinetta by Pinin Farina

PRODUCTION

38

HISTORY

Ferrari's first road car following the 166 Sports of 1947, and the model that established the firm's design pattern for the next ten years. Major highlights included an oval-section large-tube chassis, independent front suspension, live rear axle, and the first of the legendary "Colombo" single-cam V12 engines. Bodywork was supplied to order by Italian coachbuilders like Vignale, Ghia, and Pinin Farina, never Ferrari itself, on a choice of two wheelbases. At this time, the firm wasn't really interested in selling road cars, so all these 166s were essentially hand-built, and not far removed from Ferrari's racing machines. Rarity, Italian style, and status as

Ferrari's first "production" series are the main attractions for collectors.

FOR

Rarity ●First "production" Ferrari ●Simplest type of Ferrari engineering ●High club and collector interest ●Strong appreciation

AGAINST

Body parts no longer available, most other parts nearly gone ●Less performance than expected ●Very expensive ●Hard to find

SPECIFICATIONS

Length (in.) 146.2 (variable with body)
Wheelbase (in.) 98.4/103.1 (per customer choice)
Weight (lbs.) 2000 (average)   **Price (new)** NA

ENGINES

cc/type (cid)	bore x stroke (mm)	bhp	years
1995/sohc V12 (122)	60×59	110	1948-51

PRICES/PROJECTION

Restorable $10,000-15,000 **Good** $35,000-40,000
Excellent $50,000-60,000 **5-year projection** +10% Values vary greatly with coachwork

Ferrari Type 195/212 1948-53

1949 Type 195 2-seat convertible by Vignale

PRODUCTION

195 series 25   **212 series** 80   (estimates)

HISTORY

Larger-engine derivatives of the 166 Inter offered in a greater array of coachbuilt body styles. Most were created for touring or sports-racing use, and all were two-seaters. Typical top-end speed was 110 mph for the 195s and 120 for the 212s.

FOR

As for 1948-51 Type 166, though not the first roadgoing Ferraris

AGAINST

As for 1948-51 Type 166

1952 Type 212 Inter convertible by Pinin Farina

SPECIFICATIONS

Length (in.) 146.2 (variable with body)
Wheelbase (in.) 98.4/103.1 (per customer choice)
Weight (lbs.) 2100 (approx. average)   **Price (new)** NA

ENGINES

cc/type (cid)	bore x stroke (mm)	bhp	years
2340/ohv V12[1] (143)	65×59	130[3]	1948-53
2562/ohv V12[2] (156)	68×59	140/170[3]	1948-53

1. 195 Inter   2. 212 Inter   3. net

PRICES/PROJECTION

As for 1948-51 166

Ferrari Type 340/342/375 America 1951-55

1952 Type 340 Mexico berlinetta

PRODUCTION

Type 340 22   **Type 342** 6   **Type 375** 12

HISTORY

A new Ferrari combination: the Type 166/195/212 chassis engineering plus the more massive long-block V12 engine designed by Aurelio Lampredi and first raced in 1950. Very fast, and built in extremely limited quantity with custom Italian bodywork. The top speed capability on most examples was in the region of 140 mph.

FOR

As for 166/195/212

AGAINST

As for 166/195/212, plus virtually unobtainable parts for "Lampredi" engines

SPECIFICATIONS

Length (in.) 170.0 (approx.; variable with body style)
Wheelbase (in.) 104.3 (Type 340/342), 110.2 (Type 375)
Weight (lbs.) 2650 (average)   **Price (new)** NA

ENGINES

cc/type (cid)	bore x stroke (mm)	bhp	years
4101/sohc V12[1] (250)	80×68	220[3]	1951-55
4522/sohc V12[2] (276)	84×68	300[3]	1951-55

1. Type 340/342   2. Type 375   3. net

PRICES/PROJECTION

As for Type 166/195/212

Ferrari Type 250 Europa 1954-55

PRODUCTION

21

HISTORY

The final development of the Type 166 platform, this time with a smaller version of the big Lampredi engine, the only Ferrari 250 to use this type. With suitable gearing, top speed could be as high as 130 mph. Again, Italian coachbuilders provided sleekly styled bodies. Pinin Farina supplied most in the form of a high-waisted semi-fastback coupe, but some cabriolets (convertibles) came from Vignale. Nearly all Europas were sold in the U.S.

FOR

As for Type 166/195/212, plus distinctive bodywork and more performance

AGAINST

As for Type 166/195/212

SPECIFICATIONS

Length (in.) 170.0   **Wheelbase (in.)** 110.2   **Weight (lbs.)** 2650
Price (new) NA

ENGINES

cc/type (cid)	bore x stroke (mm)	bhp*	years
2963/ohc V12 (181)	68×68	200	1954-55

*net

PRICES/PROJECTION

As for Type 166/195/212, but deduct 25% for Farina coupe

Ferrari Type 250GT 1954-64

1957 Type 250GT coupe

PRODUCTION

Approx. total 2500   **GTB (Berlinetta)** 80   **GTO** 42
Spider California 104   **Lusso** 350

HISTORY

Ferrari's first true "production" series, Enzo's standard products that continued successfully for 10 years. All shared the same large diameter tube frame, coil-spring independent front suspension, and live rear axle, plus the delightful and powerful 3.0-liter "Colombo" V12 engine, with power progressively increased as the years went on. Disc brakes were added to the specification in 1959. There were several distinct series or families based primarily on body type, all with two-passenger seating. As before, all bodies were built and designed by Italian coachwork suppliers, never at the Maranello factory. The Pininfarina coupes of 1958-60 are well-known, as is the sleek Berlinetta Lusso of 1962-64, probably the prettiest of the group. The series also includes the mean GTO (Gran Turismo Omologato), Ferrari's interpretation of the dual-purpose race-and-ride sports car, plus Farina's handsome Spider California roadsters. Some competition 250GTs were also built, equipped with five-speed gearboxes. Despite careful hand construction, workmanship on these cars was variable and not always satisfactory. But there was no mistaking what would come to be frequently described as the banshee wail of the Ferrari V12 or the thrilling performance it delivered (up to 130-140 mph). Despite limited numbers, this is a diverse group, so collector prices today span a wide range.

FOR

Best-known thoroughbred Ferrari two-seaters •Fierce performance •Some mechanical parts still available, along with restoration help •Limited-production appeal •Period Italian styling

AGAINST

No body parts around, and construction quality spotty •Corrosion a severe problem generally •Very costly to acquire and restore

1962-64 Type 250GTO sports/racing coupe

1959 Type 250GT short-wheelbase berlinetta

•Limited number on the market •May be expensive to insure

SPECIFICATIONS

Length (in.) 185.0 (GTB: 164.0; GTO: 173.2)
Wheelbase (in.) 102.3 (94.5 Spider California, GTB, GTO)
Weight (lbs.) 2100-2815   **Price (new)** NA; variable

ENGINES

cc/type (cid)	bore x stroke (mm)	bhp*	years
2953/sohc V12 (180)	73×59	220-300	1956-64

*net; output variable depending on application and state of tune

PRICES/PROJECTION

Restorable $6000-12,000   **Good** $16,000-43,000
Excellent $19,000-60,000   **5-year projection** +20%

Ferrari Type 410 Superamerica 1956-59

1957-58 Type 410 Superamerica coupe by Pinin Farina

PRODUCTION

Series I 15   **Series II** 8   **Series III** 15

HISTORY

A further refinement of the "ultimate street Ferrari" concept initiated with the 340/342/375 America. Chassis modified by the coil-spring front suspension design from the concurrent 250GT series. Like its predecessors, the Superamericas were monstrously powerful and blindingly fast (up to 165 mph in top tune). The aggressively styled bodies were almost always executed by Pininfarina and were offered in open and closed form. Wheelbase initially was 110.2 inches, later shortened to 102.3. A very desirable group of cars even among Ferraris.

FOR

As for all early Ferraris, plus phenomenal speed and power • Great exclusivity • Wonderful styling

AGAINST

As for earlier Ferraris, but brakes not really up to the performance • Indifferent construction quality

SPECIFICATIONS

Length (in.) 175.0 (variable with coachbuilder)
Wheelbase (in.) 110.2 (1956), 102.3 (1957-59)
Weight (lbs.) 2400-2500 **Price (new)** NA

ENGINES

cc/type (cid)	bore x stroke (mm)	bhp*	years
4961/sohc V12 (303)	88×68	340/400	1956-59

*net; Series I & II/Series III

PRICES/PROJECTION

Restorable $15,000-20,000 **Good** $45,000-55,000
Excellent $65,000-80,000 **5-year projection** +20% Values vary with coachwork

Ferrari Type 400 Superamerica/Type 500 Superfast 1960-66

1965 Type 500 Superfast 2+2 coupe by Pininfarina

PRODUCTION

Type 400 48 **Type 500** 37

HISTORY

Final developments of the earlier America/Superamerica series. Still two-seaters with custom-crafted bodywork styled and built by Pininfarina, mostly two-door coupes. Powered by the largest of Ferrari's then-current single cam V12s. The main difference between the two types (apart from bodywork) was in engine displacement and output, wheelbase, and overall length, the Type 500 being longer, heavier, and more powerful than the 400. During its

production life, the Type 400 chassis was shortened by seven inches. Both series also used more powerful disc brakes instead of the drums on earlier models.

FOR

As for Type 410 Superamerica, plus better (disc) brakes

AGAINST

As for Type 410 Superamerica

SPECIFICATIONS

Length (in.) 172.0 (Type 400), 190.0 (Type 500) depending on body **Wheelbase (in.)** 95.3/102.3 (Type 400), 104.3 (Type 500)
Weight (lbs.) 2860 (Type 400), 3100 (Type 500) **Price (new)** NA

ENGINES

cc/type (cid)	bore x stroke (mm)	bhp	years
3967/sohc V12[1] (242)	77×71	340[3]	1960-66
4961/sohc V12[2] (303)	88×68	400[3]	1960-66

1. Type 400   2. Type 500   3. net

PRICES/PROJECTION

As for 1956-59 Type 410 Superamerica

Ferrari Type 250/330GT 2+2 1960-68

1965 Type 330GT 2+2 coupe by Pininfarina

PRODUCTION

250GT 2+2 950 **330GT** 1000

HISTORY

Ferrari's first four-seaters. Built on the 250GT chassis from the late '50s with coil-spring front suspension and live rear axle. Wheelbase remained as before (about 102 inches), but pedals and front floorboard were moved forward along with the front seats, leaving a marginal but still useful rear seat area. Sold initially as the 250GTE 2+2 with twin headlamps and notchback two-door coupe bodywork, later offered as the 330GT "America." Another 330 variant had four headlamps at first, then reverted to twin lights and acquired a new jutting snout. The 3.0-liter 250s were equipped with a four-speed-plus overdrive transmission, the 4.0-liter 330s with a five-speed gearbox. Like Ford's Thunderbird, proved to be much more popular than Ferrari's two-seat models.

FOR

Traditional Ferrari virtues • More practical accommodations • Good supply (by Ferrari standards) • Most mechanical parts still available • Active club

AGAINST

Bodies rust badly ●Early overdrive transmissions troublesome ●Heavier and slower than two-seaters ●Body parts gone ●Mechanical parts cost a mint ●Not very strong appreciation

SPECIFICATIONS

Length (in.) 185.0 **Wheelbase (in.)** 102.4
Weight (lbs.) 2820-3040 **Price (new)** $14,200 U.S. in 1967

ENGINES

cc/type (cid)	bore x stroke (mm)	bhp	years
2953/sohc V12[1] (180)	73×59	240[3]	1960-68
3967/sohc V12[2] (242)	77×71	300[3]	1960-68

1.250GT 2+2 2.330GT 2+2 3. net

PRICES/PROJECTION

Restorable $4000-6000 **Good** $12,000-15,000
Excellent $20,000-25,000 **5-year projection** +10% Values vary with coachwork.

Ferrari Type 250/275LM 1963-65

PRODUCTION

40

HISTORY

The first mid-engine Ferrari road car, though actually more of a racing machine. Derived from the 250P racing prototype, with the usual type of Ferrari multi-tube chassis, "Colombo" engine mounted aft of the driver, and all-independent coil-spring suspension. The two-seat closed coupe body was built by Scaglietti, and a few open versions were also seen in racing. Very fast, indeed—170 mph with the proper gearing. All but the first example had the 3.3-liter Ferrari V12. Extremely rare and desirable, and not really related to any other roadgoing Ferrari. That it ever got off the track at all was probably because the firm wanted to qualify it for production-class events.

FOR

Very exclusive and exotic ●Superb roadholding and agility ●Race-level performance from well-known "street" components ●Unmistakable styling ●Great Ferrari club interest

AGAINST

Not on the market much and very costly ●No spare parts available ●Too high-strung for everyday traffic ●Cramped accommodation

SPECIFICATIONS

Length (in.) 161.0 **Wheelbase (in.)** 95.0 **Weight (lbs.)** 1880
Price (new) NA

ENGINES

cc/type (cid)	bore x stroke (mm)	bhp*	years
3286/sohc V12 (200)	77×59	320	1963-65

*net

PRICES/PROJECTION

Restorable $50,000-100,000 **Good** $180,000-200,000
Excellent up to $250,000 **5-year projection** no change

Ferrari Type 275GTB & GTB/4 1964-68

1966-68 Type 275GTB/4 coupe

PRODUCTION

GTB 450 **GTB/4** 280 **GTS (convertible)** 200

HISTORY

An important forerunner of several later '60s Ferraris because of its rear transaxle (gearbox in unit with the final drive). The chassis was the usual multi-tube affair with the by-now customary all-independent suspension. Power was supplied by the 3.3-liter Ferrari V12, initially with single-cam head. From the fall of 1966, however, a new twincam head was applied for the derivative GTB/4. The GTB had the famous "rope drive" propshaft, a very slim unit carried in center bearings, while the GTB/4 had engine, propshaft cover, transmission, and differential all bolted up in one solid unit. Bodywork was by Scaglietti as on the concurrent LM, all two-seat coupes with long hood/short deck proportions. A convertible version called GTS (for Spider) was also available.

FOR

More modern handling than other Ferraris of the period ●Great performance (155 mph for GTB/4) ●Chassis/suspension components still available ●Great club backup

AGAINST

Overshadowed by its Daytona successor ●Styling not as popular as on earlier or later models ●Very costly to buy, restore, and run

SPECIFICATIONS

Length (in.) 171.3 **Wheelbase (in.)** 94.5 **Weight (lbs.)** 2490
Price (new) $14,500 U.S. in 1966

ENGINES

cc/type (cid)	bore x stroke (mm)	bhp	years
3286/sohc V12[1] (201)	77×69	280/300[2]	1964-68

1. dohc on GTB/4 2. DIN bhp; GTB and GTB/4 respectively

PRICES/PROJECTION

Restorable $8000-10,000 **Good** $25,000-30,000
Excellent $32,000-44,000 **5-year projection** +10%

Ferrari Type 330/365 GTC & GTS 1966-70

1966 Type 330GTC 2+2 coupe by Pininfarina

PRODUCTION

330GTC 600 **330GTS** 100 **365GTC** 200 **365GTS** 20

HISTORY

Essentially larger-engine versions of the 275GTB/GTS powered by single cam V12 engines of 3967cc (330) or 4390cc (365). The Spider convertible was mostly the same as the corresponding 275GTS. The 330/365GTCs shared a new, but less rakish, two-seat coupe bodyshell designed by Pininfarina. All models in this series featured a front engine/rear transaxle drivetrain arrangement plus all-independent suspension.

FOR

As for 1964-68 275 series, plus more performance

AGAINST

As for 1964-68 275 series, plus GTC styling more pedestrian

SPECIFICATIONS

Length (in.) 173.2 **Wheelbase (in.)** 94.5
Weight (lbs.) 2650-3195 **Price (new)** NA

ENGINES

cc/type (cid)	bore x stroke (mm)	bhp	years
3967/sohc V12[1] (242)	77×71	300[3]	1966-68
4390/sohc V12[2] (268)	81×71	320[3]	1968-70

1. 330GTC/GTS 2. 330GTC/GTS 3. net

PRICES/PROJECTION

As for 275GTB, but add 50-100% for GTS (spider)
5-year projection no change

Ferrari Type 365GT 2+2 1967-71

1967-71 Type 365GT 2-door coupe

PRODUCTION

800

HISTORY

Almost all of Ferrari's then-current GT ideas wrapped up in one package, a replacement for the 330GT 2+2. Carried the firm's typical multi-tubular chassis design, but with new all-independent suspension. Engine was the big-displacement V12 mated to a front-mounted gearbox and 275GTB-type rigid driveline. Had the distinction of being Ferrari's largest car to date, with long, classically refined styling by the masterful house of Pininfarina. Despite fairly hefty weight and size, could top 150 mph. Criticized at the time for limited rear seat room for so large a package, but who ever said a Ferrari must meet the standards applied to lesser cars? Early-production examples ran on disc wheels with knock-off hubs, but later cars had Daytona five-spoke alloy wheels. Not the most famous Ferrari of the '60s, but one of the most numerous and one of the easiest to acquire today.

FOR

As for 1960-68 330GT 2+2

AGAINST

As for 1960-68 300GT 2+2

SPECIFICATIONS

Length (in.) 196.0 **Wheelbase (in.)** 104.2 **Weight (lbs.)** 3500
Price (new) $18,900 U.S. in 1969

ENGINES

cc/type (cid)	bore x stroke (mm)	bhp*	years
4390/sohc V12 (268)	81×71	320	1967-71

*DIN

PRICES/PROJECTION

As for 1961-67 250GT/330GT

Ferrari Dino 206GT 1967-69

1968 Dino 206GT coupe by Pininfarina

PRODUCTION

150

HISTORY

Another landmark Ferrari—Maranello's first car with the Dino twin-cam V6, and the first with a transverse mid-engine layout. The all-alloy engine was actually built by Fiat, however, and was aimed at Formula Two racing. The Dino also marked Ferrari's attempt at starting a companion marque. The model did not wear the famous prancing horse badge, and the factory referred to it strictly as a Dino. But nobody was fooled: this was a true Ferrari, even if it didn't have 12 cylinders. It certainly acted and sounded like one: same delightful exhaust snarl, plus extremely deft handling thanks to the balanced weight distribution made possible by the mid-engine placement. It was even styled by Ferrari's by-now favored design house, Pininfarina. Curvaceous yet compact, the body was marked by headlights set back deeply in the front fenders, plus a short, sloping nose and an upright back window set in between flowing rear quarters or flying buttresses. Not much luggage room, but who cared? This car was—and still is—for enthusiasts who just can't resist the temptation to tear along a winding two-lane blacktop when nobody's looking.

FOR

Small and nimble, a delight to drive • Still in good supply despite low production • Parts still available • Great performance (140 mph tops) from 2.0-liter engine • You're welcome at Ferrari meets

AGAINST

Rust-prone body • Limited accommodation • Pricey parts and service • Not cheap to buy

SPECIFICATIONS

Length (in.) 165.0 **Wheelbase (in.)** 90.0 **Weight (lbs.)** 2380
Price (new) NA

ENGINES

cc/type (cid)	bore x stroke (mm)	bhp*	years
1987/dohc V6 (121)	86×57	180	1967-69

*DIN

1967 Dino 206GT coupe by Pininfarina

PRICES/PROJECTION

Restorable $6000-10,000 **Good** $12,000-15,000
Excellent $15,000-20,000 **5-year projection** +10%

Ferrari Type 365GTB/4 Daytona 1968-74

1968-74 Type 365GTB/4 Daytona coupe by Pininfarina

PRODUCTION

coupe 1285 **spider** 127

HISTORY

The last, greatest, and most popular of the front-engine, two-seat production Ferraris. Arguably the prettiest, too, with sensational fastback coupe styling by Pininfarina. Scaglietti built the bodies, including some Spider convertibles, which rested on the basic 275GTB/4 chassis. Suspension and mechanical layout were also similar, but the Daytona had a near-new 4.4-liter twincam V12 that gave phenomenal performance for a road car (up to 175 mph if you were brave enough). European models sported a full-width plastic lens with the headlights mounted outboard behind it; since this was illegal in the U.S., cars imported here were given hidden headlights (later used in other markets, too). Competed successfully and with surprising effectiveness. Perhaps the ultimate in sex appeal aside from the later mid-engine Berlinetta Boxer. Unfortunately, you won't find one for sale every day. Some coupes have been turned into roadsters by aftermarket conversion companies, a point to keep in mind if authenticity is of prime importance.

FOR

Everything: mind-boggling speed, great looks, superb road manners •Parts and service still available •Active Ferrari club support •Relatively good U.S. supply

AGAINST

Not cheap, and expensive to own •Our 55-mph speed limit; where could you really drive it? •Body rot worries •Real thief-bait •Can you afford the insurance?

SPECIFICATIONS

Length (in.) 174.0 **Wheelbase (in.)** 94.5 **Weight (lbs.)** 3530
Price (new) $19,500 U.S. in 1970

ENGINES

cc/type (cid)	bore x stroke (mm)	bhp*	years
4390/dohc V12 (268)	81×71	362	1968-73

*DIN

PRICES/PROJECTION

Restorable $15,000-20,000 **Good** $35,000-40,000
Excellent $40,000-56,000 Add up to 50% for factory-built Spider or convertible. **5-year projection** +10%

Ferrari Dino 246GT/GTS 1969-73

1973 Dino 246GT coupe by Pininfarina

PRODUCTION

GT 2732 **GTS** 1180

HISTORY

A re-engineered successor to the Dino 206, now with a more reliable 2.4-liter iron-block V6 engine and (from 1972) a new targa-top Spider (GTS) alternative. Built in greater numbers, but otherwise mostly the same as the 206GT in styling and mechanical specifications. Replaced by the 3.0-liter Dino 308 V8 series beginning in 1973.

FOR

As for 1967-69 Dino 206GT, but more reliable and more available

AGAINST

As for 1967-69 Dino 206GT

SPECIFICATIONS

Length (in.) 165.0 **Wheelbase (in.)** 90.0 **Weight (lbs.)** 2380
Price (new) approx. $15,000 U.S. in 1972

ENGINES

cc/type (cid)	bore x stroke (mm)	bhp*	years
2418/dohc V6 (148)	93×60	195	1969-73

*DIN

PRICES/PROJECTION

As for Dino 206GT, but add up to 100% for GTS (spider)

Fiat 8V 1952-54

1952 8V 2-seat coupe

PRODUCTION

114

HISTORY

A classic case of engineers "thinking aloud", and a very specialized product from a firm whose main business is mostly four-cylinder economy models. Typical limited-production Italian sports car usable on the road, but really intended for "production" racing. The chassis featured all-independent suspension as well as some transmission components borrowed from the four-wheel-drive Fiat Campagnola. The narrow-angle (70-degree) V8 was never used in any other Fiat. Neither were the narrow, hand-built two-seat bodies (supplied by Fiat, Ghia, and Zagato), often with staggered seats to leave sufficient working room for the driver. Enjoyed some competition success against Alfa Romeo, but never intended for volume sale. Expensive when new, and its limited-production nature means that replacement parts of all kinds are virtually unobtainable today, as is the car itself.

FOR

Unique design •Distinctive styling •Rapid for its day •Very rare •High appreciation

AGAINST

Parts virtually extinct •Survivors very rust-prone •Factory would rather not remember it •Almost impossible to find

SPECIFICATIONS

Length (in.) 158.6 **Wheelbase (in.)** 94.5 **Weight (lbs.)** 2340
Price (new) NA

ENGINES

cc/type (cid)	bore x stroke (mm)	bhp*	years
1996/ohv V8 (122)	72×61	105/115	1952-54

*net

PRICES/PROJECTION

Restorable $5000-10,000 **Good** $22,000-27,000
Excellent $25,000-35,000 **5-year projection** +10%

Fiat 1100TV
1953-62

PRODUCTION

Not available

HISTORY

The sporty, higher-power version of Fiat's small-to-medium market family sedan line of these years, with 53 bhp instead of the base 36-bhp 1100cc engine. The "TV" designation stands for "Touring Veloce"—lively touring car. Many variations were tried through the series' decade of production. Most were based on the boxy, upright four-door sedan bodyshell, but there was also a quaintly styled open two-seat roadster, which is the body style to have today. Stark trim and equipment, but very sporting road manners made the 1100TV a natural in its day as a platform for rally use. Sedans featured an identifying "cyclops" auxiliary center headlight in the grille. The basic 1100 design continued to be built in other countries after its phaseout in Italy. These included India, where production lasted until the mid-'70s.

FOR

No-nonsense engineering • Quite lively • Unbreakable engine if cared for • Some parts still available

AGAINST

Unexciting styling, even on roadster • Monocoque construction rust worries • Limited performance (80 mph tops) • Not very refined

SPECIFICATIONS

Length (in.) 148.0 **Wheelbase (in.)** 92.0 **Weight (lbs.)** 1865
Price (new) NA

ENGINES

cc/type (cid)	bore x stroke (mm)	bhp*	years
1089/ohv I4 (66)	68×75	53	1953-62

*gross

PRICES/PROJECTION

Restorable $200-500 **Good** $600-800 **Excellent** $2000-3000
5-year projection +10%

Fiat 1200/1500/1500S/1600S Cabriolet 1959-66

1963-66 1500 (left) & 1600S cabriolet by Pininfarina

PRODUCTION

43,000

HISTORY

Fiat's first high-volume in-house sports car, based on mass-production components. Steel monocoque body engineered by Fiat but styled by Pininfarina, with square, sleek lines reminiscent of the contemporary Innocenti Spider (the rebodied, license-built Italian version of the Austin-Healey Sprite). Suspension and manual gearbox (no automatic available) were borrowed initially from the Fiat 1200 sedan. Offered in base form with an overhead-valve four and as the faster, more expensive "S" with an OSCA-designed twincam unit. Both versions acquired more displacement and power in 1963. The twincam was as good as any Alfa engine of the day, but was never used in any other Fiat. Practical two-seaters all and the true forerunners of the even more successful 124 Sport Spider.

FOR

Neat, timeless styling • Good road manners • Simple engine and mechanical equipment • Much easier top conversion than contemporary Brit roadsters • Twincam models' brisk performance

AGAINST

Ohv models' limited top speed (90 mph at best) • No factory support or interest now • Not a "fashionable" collector's item • Twincam engine parts extinct • Latin rust habit

SPECIFICATIONS

Length (in.) 159.0 **Wheelbase (in.)** 92.0
Weight (lbs.) 1985-2000 (approx.) **Price (new)** NA

ENGINES

cc/type (cid)	bore x stroke (mm)	bhp*	years
1221/ohv I4 (75)	72×75	63	1959-63
1491/dohc I4 (91)	78×78	90	1959-63

| 1481/ohv I4 (90) | 77×80 | 80 | 1963-66 |
| 1568/dohc I4 (96) | 80×78 | 100 | 1963-66 |

*gross

ENGINES

cc/type (cid)	bore x stroke (mm)	bhp*	years
2279/ohv I6 (139)	78×80	117/150	1961-68

*gross

PRICES/PROJECTION

Restorable $1200-2000 Good $2500-3000
Excellent $4000-5000 5-year projection +10%

PRICES/PROJECTION

Restorable $500-800 Good $2000-3000
Excellent $5000-6200 5-year projection +10%

Fiat 2300S
1961-68

1961-68 2300S coupe by Ghia

PRODUCTION

NA

HISTORY

Here's a remarkable case of a silk purse being made from a sow's ear. Began life as a one-off design study that was then adopted by Fiat as a regular model. The neat four-seat semi-fastback coupe styling was from the house of Ghia, which also supplied finished bodyshells to Fiat for mounting on chassis from the firm's 2300 sedan. The complicated six-cylinder engine developed 150 bhp (good for a top end of 120 mph), and four-wheel disc brakes were unique to this specification at Fiat. Also produced in base (non-S) form with a 117-bhp version of the same engine. The firm's sporting flagship in these years until the advent of the Ferrari-engine Fiat Dinos of 1967-68. Styling was typical of Ghia coupes in this period, with a high grille and tail, reverse-slant C-pillar, and a wraparound backlight with two chrome vertical divider bars forming triangular-shaped outer sections.

FOR

Ghia styling • Fine performance • Four-seat accommodation • Good appreciation • Not expensive

AGAINST

Very rust-prone • Few mechanical parts now available • Replacement body panels extinct • Not plentiful in U.S. • Dubious collector merit

SPECIFICATIONS

Length (in.) 182.0 Wheelbase (in.) 104.3 Weight (lbs.) 2790
Price (new) NA

Fiat 850 Coupe & Spider
1965-74

1965-67 850 Spider & Coupe (above) with 850 sedan

PRODUCTION

coupe 342,873 spider 124,660

HISTORY

Two more special-bodied Fiat sports cars based on mundane sedan components. In this case, the basis was the rear-engine 850, which donated its floorpan, drivetrain, and all-independent suspension to a neat little Fiat-designed four-seat fastback coupe and a Bertone-bodied two-seat roadster. Not quick by any means (85-90 mph top speed) and quite noisy and cramped, but great fun to drive (except perhaps in a strong crosswind) because of Lilliputian size and light weight. Both models were popular (by European sales standards) in the U.S., particularly the Spider, which was seen as the Italian entry in the basic sports car market against such traditionalists as the Triumph Spitfire and A-H Sprite/MG Midget. Engine size was increased to 903cc for 1969, partly to compensate for U.S. emissions rules, but 1968 American-spec models used an even smaller 817cc engine to get under the minimum displacement limit for desmogging. Safety laws also took their toll, particularly on the Spider, which lost its covered headlights in favor of a more "frogeye" look with exposed units. It also acquired heavier, more ungainly bumpers. The Spider continued longer than the coupe, and was eventually succeeded by the mid-engine X1/9. The Italian tuning firm Abarth offered hotted up versions of both models, some with twincam engines, but only a relative few made it to the U.S., where most were used for racing in SCCA and similar events. Notable for being the last of Fiat's rear engine sports models.

1968-74 850 Spider convertible by Bertone (U.S. model)

FOR

Styling (especially early Spiders) •Simple chassis •Great character •Sprightly handling

AGAINST

Parts now difficult to obtain, especially for body •Fiat's well-known tinworm propensities •U.S. importer not much help •Cramped •Noisy •Indifferent construction quality

SPECIFICATIONS

Length (in.) 149.0 (Spider), 141.0 (Coupe)
Wheelbase (in.) 80.0 **Weight (lbs.)** 1620 (Spider), 1610 (Coupe) (approx.) **Price (new)** $2500 (approx. U.S. P.O.E.)

ENGINES

cc/type (cid)	bore x stroke (mm)	bhp*	years
843/ohv I4 (51)	65×64	54	1965-68
903/ohv I4 (55)	65×68	60	1969-74

*gross

PRICES/PROJECTION

Restorable $1000-2000 **Good** $2000-3000
Excellent $3000-4000 Add 30% for Spider **5-year projection** no change

1968-71 850 coupe

Fiat 124 Sport 1968-72

PRODUCTION

1.4/1.6-liter spiders 60,233 **1.8-liter spiders** 69,208 **2.0-liter spiders** 48,998 **coupes** 279,672

HISTORY

The most successful of the Fiat sports cars, based on the suspen-

1972-74 124 Sport Coupe (U.S. model)

sion and running gear of the 124 sedan introduced in 1966. The dohc Fiat-designed four-cylinder engine (derived from the pushrod sedan unit) was built in huge numbers, and survived into the '80s. So did the Pininfarina-bodied Spider, which outlasted the factory-styled four-seat coupe (dropped after 1974). As with Fiat's other volume sports cars, these were built on shorter wheelbases, and had less space but better handling and performance than their sedan cousins. Engine displacement was increased to 1608cc for 1971, later to 1756 and then to 1995 in the face of tighter U.S. emissions controls and added weight from our impact-protection rules as the decade progressed. We have arbitrarily limited "collectibility to these five model years as these cars are least affected by our regulations. However, later Spiders may also achieve high desireability in the future. Now made by Pininfarina (with remarkably little styling change).

FOR

Styling •Simple engineering •Spirited performance (100 mph) •Good U.S. supply •Most parts still available •Spider's convenient soft top mechanism •Italian *brio* •Good trunk space for sports cars •Good appreciation •Not costly to buy •Good mileage

AGAINST

Premature rust-out •Dubious mechanical and electrical reliability

SPECIFICATIONS

Length (in.) 156.0 (Spider), 162.0 (Coupe) **Wheelbase (in.)** 89.8 (Spider), 95.3 (Coupe) **Weight (lbs.)** 2100 (Spider), 2005 (Coupe) **Price (new)** $2924-3694 (original U.S. base prices 1968-72)

ENGINES

cc/type (cid)	bore x stroke (mm)	bhp*	years
1438/dohc I4 (88)	80×72	96	1968-70
1608/dohc I4 (98)	80×80	104	1971-72

*net

1968-72 124 Sport Spider (European model)

PRICES/PROJECTION

COUPE **Restorable** $400-500 **Good** $1000-1500
Excellent $1500-2500 SPIDER **Restorable** $1000-1200
Good $2000-3000 **Excellent** $3000-4000 **5-year projection** no change

Fiat Dino Spider & Coupe 1967-73

1967-73 Dino Spider convertible by Pininfarina

PRODUCTION

2000 Spider 1163 **2000 Coupe** 3670 **2400 Spider** 420
2400 Coupe 2398

HISTORY

An exciting collaboration between Fiat and Ferrari, and mutually beneficial. The former gained a glamorous line leader; the latter was able to qualify its twincam Dino V6 for Formula Two through Fiat, which built the engines for this application. A mass-production effort for Ferrari (which took over assembly toward the end of the run), a low-volume sideline for Fiat. Offered as a clean-lined two-door fastback styled by Bertone and as a roadster designed by Pininfarina. Both coachworks also built the monocoque body/chassis, though engineering was Fiat's. Cars built up to late 1969 had a 2.0-liter displacement and a live rear axle; after this, capacity was boosted to 2.4 liters (with iron replacing aluminum for the block) and independent rear suspension. The coupe had four seats and a longer wheelbase than the two-seat Spider. Later models are preferred for their bigger engine, better suspension, five-speed ZF gearbox, and more "practiced" construction. Never officially sold as part of the U.S. Fiat line; most were brought in privately before government regulations made such things difficult.

FOR

Panache of Ferrari-designed engine • High performance • Simpler in design than equivalent Ferraris and much cheaper

AGAINST

Limited U.S. availability • Notorious body corrosion • Crude rear suspension (2.0-liter models) • Body parts no longer stocked • Running gear difficult to rebuild and maintain

SPECIFICATIONS

Length (in.) 161.7 (Spider), 177.7 (Coupe) **Wheelbase (in.)** 88.8 (Spider), 100.4 (Coupe) **Weight (lbs.)** 2600 (Spider), 2825 (Coupe) **Price (new)** NA

1967-73 Dino fastback coupe by Bertone

ENGINES

cc/type (cid)	bore x stroke (mm)	bhp*	years
1987/dohc V6 (121)	86×57	160	1967-69
2418/dohc V6 (148)	93×60	180	1969-73

*DIN

PRICES/PROJECTION

Restorable $1500-2000 **Good** $6000-8000
Excellent $10,000-13,000 **5-year projection** +10%

Ford (GB) Lotus-Cortina 1963-70

1963-65 Lotus-Cortina 2-door sedan

PRODUCTION

"Mark I" 2927 **"Mark II"** approx. 4000 (Ford-built)

HISTORY

The brilliant "homologation special" based on Ford of England's mass-market Cortina sedan, created by Colin Chapman for racing and rallying duty. The main difference between the bread-and-butter models and this "production" flyer (offered only in two-door form) was the engine, a conversion of the sturdy Ford GB four-cylinder unit with a Lotus-designed twincam cylinder head. Lightweight body panels and a rather complicated rear suspension (which proved unreliable and was later simplified) were also featured. The first-generation "Mark I" models were assembled by Lotus with Ford-supplied components, and retained the current Cortina's angular styling. The situation was reversed beginning with the restyled Mark II Cortina introduced in 1967, and the Lotus variant was put together at Dagenham with far fewer special components. Both series were identified by a black grille, Lotus emblems, distinctive green bodyside striping against white body paint, a lower ride height, and wider-than-stock wheels and tires. The interiors were basically the same as for concurrent Cortina GTs, with full instrumentation, bucket seats, and all-black color scheme, but a wood-rimmed, Lotus-badged steering wheel was fitted to most examples. The Lotus-Cortina was quite fast for a 1.6-liter sedan of the '60s (105 mph top speed), and was Ford's main weapon on the international rally circuit until it was succeeded by the smaller Escort Twin-Cam in 1969. The Mark I model was sold in limited numbers through Ford import dealers in the U.S. The Mark II was never officially brought in, but a few may have sneaked across our borders before the regulatory curtain fell on cars that couldn't meet federal emissions and safety standards.

FOR

Great performance (a real pocket rocket) •Lotus image rub-off •Terrific handling •Many body parts and some mechanical pieces still available •Active Lotus club •Race history •High appreciation potential •Pretty rare in U.S. •Not expensive

AGAINST

Non-aluminum body panels rust badly •Engine demands careful tuning •Mark I models fragile •Mark II models less distinctive •Limited U.S. availability •Hard to find in good, unmodified condition

SPECIFICATIONS

Length (in.) 168.0 **Wheelbase (in.)** 98.0 **Weight (lbs.)** 1820 (Mark I), 2010 (Mark II) **Price (new)** $2548 U.S. equivalent in 1964

ENGINES

cc/type (cid)	bore x stroke (mm)	bhp*	years
1558/dohc I4 (95)	83×73	105/110	1963-70

*net bhp, Mark I/Mark II

PRICES/PROJECTION

Restorable $1000-1500 **Good** $2500-3000
Excellent $3000-4000 **5-year projection** +50%

Ford (Europe) Capri/ Capri II 1970-77

1975-76 Capri II 2.8 Ghia hatchback coupe (U.S. model)

PRODUCTION

Capri I 1,169,088 **Capri II** 404,169 through 1977

1972 Capri 1600 coupe (U.S. model)

HISTORY

A European ponycar built by Ford's subsidiaries in both England and Germany, where it proved as popular (comparatively speaking) as the original Mustang. Introduced in 1969, the Capri was brought to the U.S. in late 1970 under the Mercury nameplate, though it never bore that badge. While European customers could choose from a vast array of power and trim options (the personalizing with options concept that had proved so successful here), U.S. buyers initially got a German-built coupe in one state of trim, powered by the British Ford 1600cc crossflow "Kent" engine as used in the Cortina. There were reasons for this: German construction quality was superior and the Cortina four was already emissions-legal. Buyers took to the Capri in sufficient numbers to encourage Ford to broaden power and trim choices. Thus, a larger 2.0-liter four was added shortly (along with more complete engine instrumentation), followed by a V6. In 1974, the car was treated to a mild frontal redo and a new dashboard, then was more extensively redesigned with revised outer panels and a hatchback rear as the Capri II, introduced late in the 1975 model year and officially designated a '76. Base, luxury Ghia, and sporty "S" models were now listed, the last available with a striking black-and-gold color scheme reminiscent of the John Player Lotus Grand Prix cars. Unfavorable currency exchange rates were rendering German goods quite costly by 1977, by which time Ford was well along with a more civilized domestic ponycar to replace the modestly successful Mustang II. It was decided to give Mercury a Capri version of this car for 1979, and imports of "the sexy European" were halted. Production ceased in 1987. Collectibility still arguable at this point, but the potential is there.

FOR

Easy parts connections via Lincoln-Mercury •Nice performance/ economy balance •Good handler •Inexpensive to buy and maintain

AGAINST

Seriously rust-prone •Indifferent body and interior trim quality •V6 valvetrain and oil leak problems •Little collector interest at present

SPECIFICATIONS

Length (in.) 167.8 (1970) to 174.8 (1977)
Wheelbase (in.) 100.8 **Weight (lbs.)** 2150 (1970) to 2571 (1977 Ghia) **Price (new)** $2445 (1970) to $4373 (1977); $4585 (1977 Ghia)

ENGINES

cc/type (cid)	bore x stroke (mm)	bhp	years
1599/ohv I4 (98)	81×78	64	1971-72
1993/sohc I4 (122)	91×77	85	1971-74
2550/ohv V6 (156)	90×67	107/120	1972-73
2792/ohv V6 (171)	93×69	119/110	1974-77

Note: Not officially imported for 1975 model year and after 1977.

PRICES/PROJECTION

Restorable $500-1000 **Good** $2000-3000
Excellent $3000-4000 Add 20% for V6 or Ghia models.
5-year projection +30%

Frazer-Nash chain-drive models 1930-39

PRODUCTION

350

HISTORY

The Frazer-Nash marque grew out of the GN design, and was always related in philosophy to the HRG (see entry). F-N's claims to fame were a simple chassis with cart-spring suspension and chain-drive transmission. Characterized by stark vintage-style bodies with cycle-type fenders that gave them an uncompromisingly sporty nature. Traction (with no differential) was remarkable, as was the animal-like handling response, but creature comforts and accommodation were nearly non-existent. Maximum speeds ranged from 70 to 90 mph depending on engine and coachwork. Over the years, a variety of 1½-liter four- and six-cylinder engines were used. Specifications are for the popular Meadows-engine TT (Tourist Trophy) Replica model.

FOR

Prewar Brit sports car appeal • Handling • Rugged durability • Active (UK) club • Simple to rebuild

AGAINST

Poor weather protection • Frail transmission (but easy to repair) • Very hard suspension • Cramped interiors

SPECIFICATIONS

Length (in.) 150.0 **Wheelbase (in.)** 102.0 **Weight (lbs.)** 1800
Price (new) NA

ENGINES

cc/type (cid)	bore x stroke (mm)	bhp*	years
1496/ohv I4 (91)	69×100	62	1931-39

*gross

PRICES/PROJECTION

Restorable $8000-10,000 **Good** $20,000-25,000
Excellent $25,000-30,000 **5-year projection** +30%

Frazer-Nash 1948-56

PRODUCTION

95

1948-56 Le Mans Replica roadster

HISTORY

A hand-built British sports car of the old school, powered by the contemporary Bristol six-cylinder engine based on prewar BMW engineering. A variety of body styles from closed coupe to single-seat Formula 2 racer was available for the tubular ladder-style chassis featuring independent front suspension and live rear axle. All bodies were made of aluminum. Several engine tunes were also offered, with output ranging from 105 to 130 bhp. In fact, there was no such thing as a "standard" Frazer-Nash, as the production total suggests, each one being made to special order. The best-known models were the cycle-fender High Speed/Le Mans Replicas. Envelope-body cars included the colorfully named Mille Miglia, Targa Florio, Sebring, and Fast Tourer. Costly when new despite minimal trim and equipment, mostly because of expensive, painstaking construction techniques. A thoroughbred driving machine all the way, with no concessions to comfort or modern engineering.

FOR

Excellent handling • High performance (up to 120 mph) • Very rare • Rustproof body

AGAINST

Supply restricted, to say the least • Very expensive to buy • Few outside UK • No body, chassis parts now • Expensive to restore and maintain

SPECIFICATIONS

Length (in.) 150.0 (variable with body) **Wheelbase (in.)** 96.0
Weight (lbs.) 1800-1950 **Price (new)** NA

ENGINES

cc/type (cid)	bore x stroke (mm)	bhp*	years
1971/ohv I6 (120)	66×96	105-130	1948-56

*net

PRICES/PROJECTION

Restorable $7000-10,000 **Good** $28,000-35,000
Excellent $40,000-50,000 **5-year projection** +20%

Glas 1300/1700/1600GT 1963-68

1963-67 1300GT coupe

PRODUCTION

1300/1700GT (1963-67): approx. 800 **BMW 1600GT** (1967-68): 1255

HISTORY

A brave attempt at a sporting product by an old-line German independent in its final years. All are 2+2 fastback coupes with unit construction and shapely styling by Frua of Italy, which also built a few convertibles with similar lines beginning in 1965. Model designations reflect displacement of the sohc four-cylinder engines. The 1300 and (from 1965) 1700 units were Glas' own, borrowed from its "volume" sedans and notable for the first cogged belt for the cam drive. The 1700GT was briefly offered in the U.S. before Glas was absorbed by BMW, which attempted to boost sales by substituting the engine, transmission, and rear suspension from its 1600ti sedan.

FOR

Distinctive Italianate styling • Advanced Glas engine (1300/1700) • More powerful and reliable BMW engine (1600) • Rare in U.S.

AGAINST

Parts of all kinds are gone • BMW can't help much • Very rust-prone • Serious handling flaws on 1300/1700

SPECIFICATIONS

Length (in.) 161.4 **Wheelbase (in.)** 91.4
Weight (lbs.) 2010/2115 (1700/1600) **Price (new)** $3695 in U.S for 1700GT in 1966

ENGINES

cc/type (cid)	bore x stroke (mm)	bhp*	years
1289/sohc I4 (79)	75×73	75	1963-67
1682 sohc I4 (103)	78×88	100	1965-67
1573 sohc I4 (96)	84×71	105	1967-68
*DIN			

PRICES/PROJECTION

Restorable $500-1000 **Good** $2000-2500
Excellent $3000-4000 **5-year projection** +10%

Glas 2600/3000GT 1965-68

1967 3000GT V8 coupe by Frua

PRODUCTION

NA

HISTORY

A last desperate move by Glas to change its image as a maker of stodgy family cars. Italian stylist Pietro Frua designed the conservative but clean semi-fastback four-seat coupe body, which rested on a special platform chassis with De Dion rear suspension. Power was supplied by a V8, effectively two four-cylinder units from the 1300GT on a common crankcase, and a surprisingly successful piece of quick production engineering. Following the takeover of Glas by BMW in 1966, engine size was uprated to 3.0 liters for 1967 in an attempt to broaden the model's market appeal. It also acquired circular blue-and-white BMW logos on hood, trunklid, and hubcaps. Styling had much in common with the Frua-designed Maseratis of the period, though there was also some family resemblance to the smaller 1300/1700GT. The front end was marked by a fussy grille with large, high-set square headlamps.

FOR

Interesting styling • U.S. rarity • Effective engine and performance (125 mph maximum)

AGAINST

Few built • Engine, chassis components unavailable • Hard to find now

SPECIFICATIONS

Length (in.) 182.0 **Wheelbase (in.)** 98.4 **Weight (lbs.)** 2485
Price (new) NA

ENGINES

cc/type (cid)	bore x stroke (mm)	bhp*	years
2576/dohc V8 (157)	75×73	140	1965-66
2982/dohc V8 (182)	78×78	160	1967-68
*DIN			

PRICES/PROJECTION

Restorable $600-800 **Good** $3500-4000
Excellent $7000-8000 **5-year projection** +10%

Gordon-Keeble GK1 & IT
1964-66

1965 GK1 coupe by Bertone

PRODUCTION

GK1 series 80   **IT series** 19

HISTORY

A feeble attempt to combine Chevrolet V8 power with British chassis engineering and Bertone styling. This smart, close-coupled four-seat coupe featured a fiberglass body set on a separate multi-tubular chassis. Very fast thanks to the 300-bhp Chevy 327 V8, and also offered good handling and running refinement. The Bertone styling dated from 1960, and was a more elegant forerunner of the Iso Rivolta shape. The G-K was distinguished by a four-headlamp front end (with the lamps mounted in slant-eye formation). Considered as desirable as a Ferrari at the time, but lacked the cachet of a famous name. Ultimately, the Gordon-Keeble was a commercial failure because it was underpriced. A very sought-after car today because of its rot-free body, but not common or widely known outside its home country.

FOR

Rustproof fiberglass body • High performance from easily serviced Detroit iron • Styling • Exclusivity • Active British club

AGAINST

No chassis or body parts any more • Extremely costly to buy • Not as refined as equivalent Ferraris • Are there any in the States?

SPECIFICATIONS

Length (in.) 189.5   **Wheelbase (in.)** 102.0   **Weight (lbs.)** 3165
Price (new) NA

ENGINES

cc/type (cid)	bore x stroke (mm)	bhp*	years
5355/ohv V8 (327)	102×83	300	1964-66

*gross

PRICES/PROJECTION

Restorable $3000-4000 **Good** $7000-9000
Excellent $10,000-13,000 **5-year projection** no change

Healey
1946-54

1946-54 coupe by Tickford

PRODUCTION

Silverstone 105   **Tickford** 225   **Elliott** 101   **Convertible** 25
Total 781

HISTORY

Donald Healey's initial offerings as an independent manufacturer in Warwick, England. The models here were all built on the same newly designed box-section chassis featuring a trailing-arm type of independent front suspension. Up to the early '50s, Healey specified the 2.4-liter Riley four-cylinder engine and corresponding transmission, but some 25 cars were equipped with the 3.0-liter Alvis six-cylinder engine from 1951 to '54. Roadster and coupe bodies for both "series" were supplied by various English coachbuilders. The open models were known as Westland, Sportsmobile, Abbott, and Alvis-Healey; the closed versions had bodywork by Elliott, Duncan, and Tickford. The Tickford coupe was perhaps the most stylish of the lot, but the Silverstone (named after the famous British automobile race course) was undoubtedly the most romantic, with a stark roadster body, freestanding cycle-type fenders, headlamps mounted behind a tall vertical grille, low-cut windscreen, and large slotted-disc wheels. By 1950, Donald Healey had become involved with Nash, and most of his firm's efforts went into the Nash-Healey hybrid. Then in 1953, he became more closely involved with British Motor Corporation in design and production of the BMC-built Austin-Healey 100. As a result, few of his "independent" products were built in these years or sold outside England.

FOR

Famous name • Hand-built appeal • Relatively fast (100-105 mph) • Good road manners • Silverstone's stark functionalism, Milestone status • Not difficult to rebuild or maintain

AGAINST

Body and chassis parts are no more • Poor body quality • Styling of some models • Not a high-demand collectible despite current steep values

SPECIFICATIONS

Length (in.) 174.0 (average, depending on body style)
Wheelbase (in.) 102.0 **Weight (lbs.)** 2400-3000 (depending on body style) **Price (new)** NA

ENGINES

cc/type (cid)	bore x stroke (mm)	bhp*	years
2443/ohv I4 (149)	81×120	104	1946-51**
2993/ohv I6 (183)	84×90	106	1951-54**

*gross
**approximate calendar years, based on extant vehicles

PRICES/PROJECTION

Restorable $1000-2500 **Good** $3000-4500
Excellent $4000-6000 **5-year projection** +10%

Hispano-Suiza H6C 1930-34

PRODUCTION

264 (began 1924)

HISTORY

Massive six-cylinder machine from the renowned Franco-Spanish concern and one of its best. Built in both France and Spain like most "Hissos." Like Rolls-Royce, offered only as a rolling chassis. French specialists supplied most of the coachwork. High weight limited top speed to 90 mph for all except the very rare short-chassis Boulognes. All French-built examples had right-hand-drive. Strictly vintage-style chassis engineering with beam axles on leaf springs at both ends. The engine was the jewel in this particular crown, and the name did the rest. Like a vintage Bentley, you bought it for what it said about you rather than what it was—plus, of course, its locomotive-like reliability.

FOR

Advanced engine • Very high build quality • French coachbuilt elegance • Performance (short-chassis models)

AGAINST

Old-fashioned chassis for the '30s • Expensive to buy and restore • Rather truck-like • No new parts anymore

1932 V12 sedan by Van Vouren of Paris

SPECIFICATIONS

Length (in.) 165.0/178.0 **Wheelbase (in.)** 133.5/146
Weight (lbs.) 4000 (approx.) **Price (new)** NA

ENGINES

cc/type (cid)	bore x stroke (mm)	bhp*	years
7982/ohc I6 (487)	110×140	150	1930-34

*gross

PRICES/PROJECTION

Restorable $30,000-35,000 **Good** $95,000-110,000
Excellent $110,000-145,000 **5-year projection** +20%

Hispano-Suiza Type 68 V12 1931-38

PRODUCTION

NA

HISTORY

Hispano-Suiza brought together Swiss design, Spanish capital and French production facilities to create what many consider the world's best automobile of the mid-1930s, Rolls-Royces and the *Grosser* Mercedes notwithstanding. Offered only as a rolling chassis, with massive construction and a choice of four wheelbases. Huge "square" V12 was an engineering masterpiece but burned fuel as rapidly as you'd expect in an enormously heavy car. Bodywork, of course, was to customer choice, and most examples carried every luxury and convenience feature imaginable at the time. A very few were built with sporty styles, those by Saoutchik being the most memorable and striking. A genuine international Classic of interest today only to a very fortunate few.

FOR

Exclusivity • Magnificent V12 performance • Styling • Hispano quality and snob appeal

AGAINST

Too costly for mere mortals • Old-fashioned chassis • Parts nearly impossible • Very thirsty

SPECIFICATIONS

Length (in.) 192+ **Wheelbase (in.)** 135/146/150/158
Weight (lbs.) 4900-6500 **Price (new)** NA

ENGINES

cc/type (cid)	bore x stroke (mm)	bhp	years
9424/ohv V12 (575)	100×100	220*	1931-38

*gross

PRICES/PROJECTION

Restorable $35,000-48,000 **Good** $144,000-180,000
Excellent $180,000-240,000 **5-year projection** +30%

HRG 1100/1500 1935-56

1948 roadster

PRODUCTION

240

HISTORY

Stark, hard-riding vintage British sports car, continued with few changes into the postwar world. The cramped two-seat cockpit featured creature comforts notable by their absence. Except for the unsuccessful envelope-body "Aerodynamic" model (of which only 30 were built in 1946-48), all HRGs had the same styling, including the traditional vertical radiator, cycle-type front fenders, and Bugatti-type exposed front quarter-elliptic leaf springs. Powered by a choice of two four-cylinder engines from the Singer Motor Company of Coventry. The HRG was slower than it looked (73 mph tops for the 1100, 83 mph for the 1500), but very nimble. A real driver's car, and quite reliable for rallying and other competition, but incredibly uncomfortable. Like a cold shower, invigorating but painful.

FOR

Low-production appeal • British "trad" style • Strong, simple • More exclusive than a postwar MG • Active British club

AGAINST

Very hard suspension • No parts available now • Little weather protection • Prewar engineering • Virtually unkown in U.S.

SPECIFICATIONS

Length (in.) 144.0 **Wheelbase (in.)** 99.5/103.5
Weight (lbs.) 1510-1750 **Price (new)** $NA

ENGINES

cc/type (cid)	bore x stroke (mm)	bhp	years
1074/ohc I4 (65)	60×95	40	1935-56
1496/ohc I4 (91)	68×103	61	1935-56

*net

PRICES/PROJECTION

Restorable $4000-6000 **Good** $13,000-16,000
Excellent $15,000-20,000 **5-year projection** +10%

Humber Super Snipe 1959-67

1965 Super Snipe Estate Car (wagon)

PRODUCTION

1959-60 Series I/II 7500 (est.) **1961-62 Series III** 7257 **1963-64 Series IV** 6495 **1965-67 Series V** 3000 (est.)

HISTORY

Britain's Buick, exported to America in small quantities. Built by the Rootes Group, once part of Chrysler, these cars have since found a small but enthusiastic stateside following. Monocoque four-door body shared initially with the cheaper Hawk model and styled by Raymond Loewy. Offered smooth six-cylinder performance—but not much acceleration—plus scads of walnut, leather and wool in the best English tradition and many no-cost accessories. Series V updated with a crisper greenhouse that made it look a lot like the R-R Silver Shadow from the rear—or a Checker taxi from the side! Ventwings at all four corners, twin Zenith carbs and slightly more bhp also marked Series Vs. A nifty wagon was also offered, as was a division-window limousine hand-built from stock sedan bodies.

FOR

Quality construction • Smooth highway cruiser • Unbreakable engine • High equipment level • Low cost

AGAINST

Dumpy looks • Unit construction rust worries • Horrible mileage • Low appreciation • Hard to find in U.S.

SPECIFICATIONS

Length (in.) 184.5 **Wheelbase (in.)** 110.0 **Weight (lbs.)** 3100 (approx.) **Price (new)** $3800-4895

ENGINES

cc/type (cid)	bore x stroke (mm)	bhp	years
2651/ohv I6 (161.7)	83×83	105	1959

2965/ohv I6 (180.9) *net	87×83	121-129	1960-67

ENGINES

cc/type (cid)	bore x stroke (mm)	bhp*	years
2965/ohv I6 (180.9) *net	87×83	128.5	1965-67

PRICES/PROJECTION

Restorable $1000-2000 **Good** $2000-3000
Excellent $3000-5000 Add 10% for wagon.
5-year projection no change

PRICES/PROJECTION

Restorable $1500-2500 **Good** $2000-3500
Excellent $4000-5500 **5-year projection** no change

Humber Imperial 1965-67

1965-67 Imperial 4-door sedan by Thrupp & Maberly

Iso Rivolta 1963-70

1963-70 Rivolta coupe by Bertone

PRODUCTION

Series V 1200 (est.)   **Series Va** 1125

PRODUCTION

NA, but very limited

HISTORY

A custom version of the Super Snipe by the Thrupp and Maberly works. Easily distinguished by a black vinyl roof, "Imperial" script on front doors, standard fog and driving lights (one each), and T&M badges on the door sills. Rootes Group (now with substantial financial backing from Chrysler Corporation) made every conceivable accessory standard on this model: automatic transmission, power steering, power front disc brakes, front and rear heaters and radio speakers, rear window defroster, passenger compartment reading lamps, door-open warning lights, and Armstrong Selectaride adjustable rear shock absorbers. All Imperials were assembled by T&M in London, and finished with top-quality Connolly leather, West of England cloth, and Wilton carpeting. The division-window limousine was continued as in previous years. Not really part of the slow-selling Rootes line in the U.S., but in the days before federal regulations you could get one through your local dealer with enough persuasion.

HISTORY

Italo-American hybrid from a company whose main business was refrigerators. Power was supplied by the familiar Chevrolet 327 V8 mounted in a steel platform chassis designed by ex-Ferrari engineer Giotto Bizzarrini. The steel notchback coupe body was styled by Bertone, and offered full four-passenger seating. A very roadable machine thanks partly to the De Dion rear suspension, and quite fast — up to 142 mph. Some models were fitted with ZF five-speed gearbox, others with the Chevy four-speed manual or three-speed automatic. Rather "soft" for a high-performance Latin, designed with an eye to American sales, which were never high. Not as sleek as contemporary Ferraris, but roomier. A more practical proposition for mechanical rebuilds and routine servicing on this side of the Atlantic, too, due to mass-production drivetrains. Replaced by the S4 Fidia sedan at the end of the decade.

FOR

Last and best of the big Humbers •Many interesting equipment items •Superbly built •Fine materials •Good ride

FOR

Simple, sturdy Detroit powertrains •Fine chassis •Cheaper to buy than other Italian exotics •Nice Bertone styling

AGAINST

A ruster •Poor mileage •Parts now scarce •Electrical goodies can and do pack up •A rare commodity in America

AGAINST

Lacks pedigree of a Ferrari or Maserati •Rust-prone •No body/chassis parts any more

SPECIFICATIONS

Length (in.) 184.5 **Wheelbase (in.)** 110.0 **Weight (lbs.)** 3200 (approx.) **Price (new)** NA

SPECIFICATIONS

Length (in.) 187.4 **Wheelbase (in.)** 106.0 **Weight (lbs.)** 3420
Price (new) approx. $9200 (U.S.)

ENGINES

cid/type	bore x stroke	bhp	years
327/ohv V8	4.00×3.25	300/335*	1962-70
*gross			

PRICES/PROJECTION

Restorable $1000-1500 **Good** $5000-7000
Excellent $9000-12,500 **5-year projection** +10%

Iso Grifo
1965-74

1965-74 Grifo coupe by Bertone

PRODUCTION

NA, but very limited

HISTORY

A short-wheelbase, two-seat fastback derivative of the Iso Rivolta. Handsome, muscular styling again by Bertone, with a low greenhouse and large windshield and backlight. Four headlamps were used at the outer ends of a split grille. Some cars had a hood bulge to provide clearance for the air cleaners of the Chevy-built V8 engines, offered variously in 327- and 427-cid sizes. Late in the model run, the nose was modified to look more Ferrari-like, and hooded headlamps were adopted. Built in very limited numbers.

FOR

As for 1962-70 Rivolta, plus more performance with larger engines and more distinctive styling

AGAINST

As for 1962-70 Rivolta

SPECIFICATIONS

Length (in.) 175.0 **Wheelbase (in.)** 98.5
Weight (lbs.) 3180-3520 **Price (new)** NA

ENGINES

cid/type	bore x stroke	bhp	years
327/ohv V8	4.00×3.25	300/335*	1965-74
427/ohv V8	4.25×3.76	385/400*	1968-74
*gross			

PRICES/PROJECTION

Restorable $5000-10,000 **Good** $13,000-16,000
Excellent $18,000-25,000 **5-year projection** +20%

Iso S4 Fidia
1967-74

PRODUCTION

NA, but very limited

HISTORY

Four-door successor to the Rivolta coupe, using the same basic chassis design on a 6-inch longer wheelbase. Styling by Ghia featured a blunt nose with quad square headlamps, a fairly short tail, and flowing "coke bottle" fender lines. The plain but well-appointed interior featured standard air conditioning, an impressively instrumented dash, center console, and front bucket seats. Big and heavy, but quite quick (over 130 mph top speed).

FOR

As for 1962-70 Rivolta, plus better equipment and four-door practicality

AGAINST

As for 1962-70 Rivolta

SPECIFICATIONS

Length (in.) 195.7 **Wheelbase (in.)** 112.2 **Weight (lbs.)** 3700
Price (new) $14,300 (U.S. base price in 1969)

ENGINES

cid/type	bore x stroke	bhp	years
327/ohv V8	4.00×3.25	300*	1967-74
*gross			

PRICES/PROJECTION

As for 1962-70 Rivolta

Jaguar Mark IV
1945-48

1945-48 Mark IV 1.5-Litre 4-door sedan

PRODUCTION

1.5 Litre 5761 **2.5 Litre** 1861 **3.5 Litre** 4420
Convertibles 104 (2.5 Litre) and 560 (3.5 Litre)

HISTORY

Jaguar's first cars after World War II, essentially continuations of the 1938-39 models. Most were four-door sedans and shared the same bodyshell, but the 1.5 Litre model rode a 6-inch shorter wheelbase and had a four- instead of six-cylinder engine made by the Standard Motor Car Company. Appearance was marked by a long hood, upright radiator capped by the Jaguar mascot, large freestanding headlamps, flowing separate front fenders, and a narrow, close-coupled body. An archaic (even by the late '40s) leaf-spring/live-axle suspension was used both front and rear. High-quality interior furnishings included a traditional British wood dash with large, plainly marked dials. Top speed for the 1.5 Litre was about 70 mph; the 3.5 Litre could reach a bit over 90 mph. Most Mark IVs were built with right-hand drive for the British market as Jaguar's export drive didn't begin in earnest until a few years later.

FOR

Classic lines • Rugged simplicity • Rare in U.S. • Convertibles very desirable • Good appreciation ·

AGAINST

Parts supplies dried up long ago • Limited performance • Poor body quality • Old-fashioned chassis

SPECIFICATIONS

Length (in.) 173.0 (1.5), 186.0 (2.5/3.5) **Wheelbase (in.)** 112.5 (1.5), 120.0 (2.5/3.5) **Weight (lbs.)** 2970 (1.5), 3585 (2.5), 3670 (3.5) **Price (new)** NA

ENGINES

cc/type (cid)	bore x stroke (mm)	bhp*	years
1776/ohv I4 (108)	73×106	65	1945-48
2663/ohv I6 (163)	73×106	105	1945-48
3485/ohv I6 (213)	82×110	125	1945-48

*gross

PRICES/PROJECTION

Restorable $2500-5000 **Good** $5000-7500
Excellent $10,000-15,000 **5-year projection** +10%

Jaguar Mark V
1948-51

PRODUCTION

2.5 Litre Saloon 1661 **2.5 Litre Drophead** 29
3.5 Litre Saloon 7831 **3.5 Litre Drophead** 972

HISTORY

The first true postwar Jaguars, with an all-new chassis featuring independent front suspension. This platform would be used for the later Mark VII sedans and, in shortened form, for the pace-setting XK sports cars beginning in 1949. Styling was an updated version of the Mark IV, still with a traditional vertical radiator and sweeping separate fenders, but headlamps were now partially integral with the fenders. Roomy four-door saloons (sedans) were most common, but many 3.5 Litre chassis were built with dignified two-door drophead (convertible) coupe bodywork, and are considerably

more collectible today. Engines were essentially holdovers of the prewar six-cylinder units. Like all such Jaguars, fast for the period (more than 90 mph for the 3.5 Litre models), and trimmed with lots of real wood cappings and plush upholstery.

FOR

As for 1945-48 Mark IV, plus better handling

AGAINST

As for 1945-48 Mark IV

SPECIFICATIONS

Length (in.) 187.0 **Wheelbase (in.)** 120.0 **Weight (lbs.)** 3700 (sedan), 3860 (convertible) **Price (new)** NA

ENGINES

cc/type (cid)	bore x stroke (mm)	bhp*	years
2663/ohv I6 (163)	73×106	105	1948-51
3485/ohv I6 (213)	82×110	125	1948-51

*gross bhp

PRICES/PROJECTION

Restorable $1000-3000 **Good** $5000-8000
Excellent $10,000-14,000 Add 100% for convertible.
5-year projection +15%

Jaguar XK120
1948-54

1949-58 XK120 roadster

PRODUCTION

Roadster 7631 **Coupe** 2678 **Convertible** 1769

HISTORY

One of the most important Milestones from either side of the Atlantic, a trend-setting sports car that became a legend in its own time. A modern envelope body with integral fenders was new for Jaguar, and was mounted on a massive, newly designed chassis with torsion bar front suspension. The sleek, flowing lines were created by Jaguar's William Lyons, and would have wide industry influence. A vee'd windshield rode above a long hood that tapered to a narrow, oval grille flanked by large headlamps nestled in the "catwalk" areas between the fender tops and the grille. Delicate-looking bumpers front and rear were connected by curvaceous, perfectly proportioned fenders. This was the car that introduced the remarkable XK-series twincam six, which would prove amazingly adaptable and long-lived. The XK120 (the designation stemmed from the top speed recorded by prototypes) was offered as an open roadster, drophead (convertible), and fixed head (steel top) coupe. Bodies were constructed initially of light alloy, then switched to conventional pressed steel. Incredible value for the money when new, and amazingly successful despite heavy handling and marginal brakes (later improved). Still commands a huge and loyal following nearly 30 years after it went out of production.

FOR

Classic styling • Legendary performance • Rugged, long-life engine • Most mechanical parts still available • Active club support

AGAINST

Body rusts badly if neglected • Heavy steering • Dodgy brakes • Poor driving position • Not cheap to buy • Always in demand

SPECIFICATIONS

Length (in.) 174.0 **Wheelbase (in.)** 102.0
Weight (lbs.) 2855-3080 **Price (new)** approx. $3500 in 1951

ENGINES

cc/type (cid)	bore x stroke (mm)	bhp*	years
3442/dohc I6 (210)	83×106	160/180	1948-54

*gross

PRICES/PROJECTION

Restorable $4000-8000 **Good** $9500-12,000
Excellent $14,000-23,000 **5-year projection** +10%

Jaguar Mark VII/VIIM 1950-57

1954-57 Mark VIIM 4-door sedan

PRODUCTION

Mark VII 20,939 **Mark VIIM** 9261

HISTORY

Hot on the heels of the stunning XK120 sports car came Jaguar's first all-new postwar sedan, combining the previous Mark V chassis with the magnificent XK twincam six. The bulbous envelope body

retained a distinctive Jaguar vertical grille and a trace of the traditional separate fenderlines. The leading front fender tips, rear fenders, roof, tail, and side window shapes were all gently rounded. Roomy compared to previous Jaguars, with all the usual wood and leather fittings. This was also the first car from Coventry offered with an optional automatic transmission, supplied by Borg-Warner. The Mark VII had 160 bhp and foglamps recessed into the front fender valences. The Mark VIIM replaced it in 1954 with a 190-bhp version of the XK six and freestanding foglights. All models were equipped with drum brakes, and power steering was not available. Succeeded by the Mark VIII series in 1957.

FOR

Six passenger room combined with near XK120 performance • Graceful "period" styling • Not expensive now for a collectible

AGAINST

Rust-prone • Body parts no longer around • Marginal brakes • Construction quality doesn't match looks

SPECIFICATIONS

Length (in.) 196.5 **Wheelbase (in.)** 120.0 **Weight (lbs.)** 3865
Price (new) approx. $4000-4600 in U.S.

ENGINES

cc/type (cid)	bore x stroke (mm)	bhp*	years
3442/dohc I6	83×106	160/190	1950-57

*gross bhp, Mark VII/VIIM

PRICES/PROJECTION

Restorable $2000-4000 **Good** $4500-6000
Excellent $7000-10,000 **5-year projection** +15%

Jaguar C-Type 1951-53

1951-53 C-Type sports/racing roadster

PRODUCTION

43 (plus 11 race versions)

HISTORY

A very specialized car developed by Jaguar primarily for racing, but could also be used on the road (as many were). Borrowed many XK120 components (twincam engine, gearbox, rear axle), but had its own multi-tubular chassis and distinctive aerodynamic light-alloy open roadster body. Styling was unmistakably Jaguar, with a touch of the XK120's lines in profile, but the oval, vertical bar grille was shorter and wider. No concession was made to weather protection or comfort. There was no heater and little in the way of exhaust muffling or sound deadening; they would have only added weight, undesirable in a racing machine. A successful competitor at Le Mans (scoring outright wins in 1951 and '53), with a top speed comfortably over 140 mph.

FOR

Significance to Jaguar racing history • Rugged reliability • Restoration help still available • Low-production scarcity

AGAINST

A sunny-days-only machine • Flimsy body • A noisy extrovert • Exorbitant asking prices • Virtually off the market

SPECIFICATIONS

Length (in.) 157.0 **Wheelbase (in.)** 96.0 **Weight (lbs.)** 2075
Price (new) approx. $6000 U.S. equivalent

ENGINES

cc/type (cid)	bore x stroke (mm)	bhp*	years
3442/dohc I6 (210)	83×106	200	1951-53

*gross

PRICES/PROJECTION

Restorable $25,000-30,000 **Good** $80,000-100,000
Excellent $120,000-150,000 **5-year projection** +30%

Jaguar D-Type & XKSS 1954-57

1957 D-Type sports/racing roadster

PRODUCTION

D-Type 71 (incl. 18 team race cars) **XKSS** 16

HISTORY

The D-Type succeeded the C-Type as Jaguar's "factory racer" in these years, but was less practical as a road car. The XKSS was essentially a street version of it, with minimal bumpers, two opening doors (instead of one), a full windshield, and a rudimentary folding top. A disastrous fire at the Jaguar plant cut short production, which was never resumed afterward. The aerodynamic shape of these cars predicted the styling of the production E-Type (XKE) introduced in 1961. A small oval front air intake, highly arched fenders, and considerable bodyside tuck-under were complemented on some cars by a faired-in headrest for the driver (a few had a vertical fin trailing from this). Power was supplied by a race-tuned XK engine hooked to an all-synchromesh gearbox. A complex multi-tubular front frame was used, with separate monocoque center and tail sections. A dozen factory racers were built in 1955-56 with long noses and integral tailfins. Top speed was over 150 mph with suitable gearing. The XKSS was built only in 1957.

FOR

The ultimate in "macho" • Sturdy production Jaguar components • High-performance • Predictive styling

AGAINST

Impractical on the road • Terrifically expensive today • Expensive to restore, maintain • None really left on the market • Appeal diluted by modern replicas

SPECIFICATIONS

Length (in.) 154.0 **Wheelbase (in.)** 90.6 **Weight (lbs.)** 1930 (D-Type), 2015 (XKSS) **Price (new)** approx. $5600 (XKSS), $9900 (D-Type) in U.S.

ENGINES

cc/type (cid)	bore x stroke (mm)	bhp*	years
3442/dohc I6 (210)	83×106	250	1954-57

*gross

PRICES/PROJECTION

Restorable $25,000-30,000 **Good** $100,000-130,000
Excellent $120,000-150,000 **5-year projection** +20%

Jaguar XK140 1954-57

PRODUCTION

Roadster 3347 **Coupe** 2797 **Convertible** 2740

HISTORY

A re-engineered version of the XK120 intended specifically for the increasingly important North American export market. Styling was basically the same except for a "wide stripe" grille. The fixed-roof coupe and soft-top convertible models now offered +2 rear seating. Mechanical changes included an improved cooling system and steering (now by rack and pinion), and sturdier bumpers. Automatic transmission became available late in the model run except for the roadster.

FOR

As for XK120, plus better performance and sturdier body

AGAINST

As for XK120, except for improved brakes and handling

SPECIFICATIONS

Length (in.) 176.0 **Wheelbase (in.)** 102.0
Weight (lbs.) 3135-3250 **Price (new)** approx. $3600 U.S. in 1955

ENGINES

cc/type (cid)	bore x stroke (mm)	bhp*	years
3442/dohc I6 (210)	83×106	190/210	1954-57

*gross

PRICES/PROJECTION

Restorable $3000-6000 **Good** $7000-10,000
Excellent $15,000-22,000 **5-year projection** +10%

Jaguar Mark VIII
1956-59

PRODUCTION

6332

HISTORY

Slightly heavier replacement for the Mark VII/VIIM sedans. Minor styling changes and more power, but otherwise the same. Identification points include a one-piece instead of split windshield, two-tone paint, a bolder grille, reshaped seats, and more luxurious interior trim. Output of the XK twincam six was boosted from 190 to 210 bhp for this application, about 1 horsepower per cubic inch. Still with drum brakes. Most examples were fitted with Borg-Warner automatic transmission.

FOR

As for 1950-57 Mark VII/VIIM

AGAINST

As for 1950-57 Mark VII/VIIM

SPECIFICATIONS

Length (in.) 196.5 **Wheelbase (in.)** 120.0 **Weight (lbs.)** 4030
Price (new) approx. $5000 U.S.

ENGINES

cc/type (cid)	bore x stroke (mm)	bhp*	years
3442/dohc I6 (210)	83×106	210	1956-59

*gross

PRICES/PROJECTION

As for 1950-57 Mark VII/VIIM

Jaguar XK150
1957-61

1957-61 XK150 3.4-Litre coupe

PRODUCTION

3.4 Litre Roadster 1297 **3.4 Litre Coupe** 3445
3.4 Litre Convertible 1903 **3.8 Litre Roadster** 42
3.8 Litre Coupe 656 **3.8 Litre Convertible** 586

HISTORY

The final derivative of the XK120, but more "matronly" in appearance. The basic XK120/140 bodyshell was substantially restyled with higher front fenders, a wider grille, and a curved, one-piece windshield. The heavier look was matched by a gain in curb weight, though it didn't spoil the good overall balance of previous models. The basic XK chassis was retained, updated with Dunlop disc brakes at each wheel. The 210-bhp version of the 3.4-liter twincam inline six was standardized, and beginning in the fall of 1959 a 3.8-liter bored-out enlargement with 20 extra horses was offered as an optional extra. Many were sold with the Borg-Warner automatic transmission. Replaced by the sensational E-Type during 1961.

FOR

As for 1954-57 XK140, plus better brakes and more restful performance

AGAINST

As for 1954-57 XK140, but less pleasant lines and extra weight

SPECIFICATIONS

Length (in.) 177.0 **Wheelbase (in.)** 102.0
Weight (lbs.) 3220-3520 **Price (new)** approx. $4500-5200 U.S.

ENGINES

cc/type (cid)	bore x stroke (mm)	bhp	years
3442/dohc I6 (210)	83×106	210	1957-61
3781/dohc I6 (231)	87×106	220	1959-61

PRICES/PROJECTION

As for 1954-57 XK140

Jaguar XK150S
1958-61

PRODUCTION

3.4 Litre Roadster 888   **3.4 Litre Coupe** 199
3.4 Litre Convertible 104   **3.8 Litre Roadster** 36
3.8 Litre Coupe 150   **3.8 Litre Convertible** 89

HISTORY

The fiercest of all the early XKs thanks to a more highly tuned twincam engine with a different cylinder head and three SU carburetors. Not available with automatic transmission, the "S" version boasted a top speed of well over 135 mph. Identified from the outside by discreet badges and from under the hood by the triple carburetors.

FOR

As for 1957-61 XK150, plus more performance and greater rarity

AGAINST

As for 1957-61 XK150, but more difficult to find

SPECIFICATIONS

Length (in.) 177.0   **Wheelbase (in.)** 102.0
Weight (lbs.) 3220-3520   **Price (new)** approx. $5600 U.S. in 1958

ENGINES

cc/type (cid)	bore x stroke (mm)	bhp*	years
3442/dohc I6 (210)	82×106	250	1958-61
3781/dohc I6 (231)	87×106	265	1959-61

*gross

PRICES/PROJECTION

As for XK120, but add 5-20% for 3.8-liter engine

Jaguar Mark IX
1959-61

PRODUCTION

10,005

HISTORY

The last of the original 1950 Mark VII design, now with four-wheel disc brakes, power steering, and the bored-out 3.8-liter twincam engine as standard equipment. Virtually all were equipped with Borg-Warner automatic transmission. The only appearance change of note compared to the previous Mark VIII was a change in the identifying nameplate on the trunklid.

FOR

As for Mark VII/VIIM and Mark VIII, plus better brakes

AGAINST

As for Mark VII/VIIM and Mark VIII

SPECIFICATIONS

Length (in.) 196.5   **Wheelbase (in.)** 120.0   **Weight (lbs.)** 4000
Price (new) approx. $6500 U.S. in 1961

ENGINES

cc/type (cid)	bore x stroke (mm)	bhp*	years
3781/dohc I6 (231)	87×106	220	1959-61

*gross

PRICES/PROJECTION

As for 1950-57 Mark VII/VIIM

Jaguar Mark II
1960-69

1960-67 Mark II 3.8-Litre 4-door sedan

PRODUCTION

2.4 Litre 25,173   **3.4 Litre** 28,666   **3.8 Litre** 30,141
240 4446   **340** 2800

HISTORY

The restyled and more attractive successor to Jaguar's smaller sedan line introduced in 1956. The monocoque bodyshell was given a more open greenhouse and minor exterior trim changes, but stayed dimensionally the same. Powered by the workhorse XK twincam six in a choice of three displacements and power ratings, and available with both manual and automatic transmission. Numerous other extra-cost items were listed, including handsome knock-off-center wire wheels. All these are good-handling cars and, in the case of the 3.8-liter versions, quick (up to 135 mph maximum). This series had live-axle rear suspension, unlike later models that had an independent setup. Sold fairly widely in the U.S. through 1967, after which the 3.8-liter engine was dropped to make room in the lineup for the new XJ6 and the remaining models were renamed 240 and 340. In England, the latter were replaced by the long-tailed S-Type and 420 derivatives of this basic design.

FOR

Compact size • Fine handling • Legendary XK performance • Wide choice of specs • Many parts still available • Conservative British appearance

AGAINST

Unit construction rust problem • Limited performance (2.4 liter) • Not as much room as you'd think

SPECIFICATIONS

Length (in.) 181.0   **Wheelbase (in.)** 107.4
Weight (lbs.) 3200-3360   **Price (new)** $4800 U.S. for 3.8-Litre in 1960

ENGINES

cc/type (cid)	bore x stroke (mm)	bhp*	years
2443/dohc I6 (149)	83×77	120	1960-69
3442/dohc I6 (210)	83×106	210	1960-69
3781/dohc I6 (231)	87×106	220	1960-67

*gross

PRICES/PROJECTION

Restorable $1500-3000   **Good** $3000-5000
Excellent $5000-8000   **5-year projection** +30%

Jaguar E-Type (XKE) 1961-71

1966 E-Type 4.2-Litre 2-seat coupe

PRODUCTION

3.8 Litre Roadster 7820   **3.8 Litre Coupe** 7670
4.2 Litre Roadster 18,180   **4.2 Litre Coupe** 12,630
4.2 Litre 2+2 Coupe 10,930

HISTORY

Jaguar's sexy, sensational '60s sports car, successor to the XK150 but sharing a good many styling and technical details first seen on the racing D-Type. Like that car, the E-Type's construction used a multi-tube front end bolted to a "bathtub" steel bodyshell. The long, low hood and front fenders were welded as one assembly, and hinged at the front to lift up for almost unrestricted engine access. The 3.8-liter version of the venerable twincam XK engine was marketed first, along with a manual gearbox with non-synchro first gear. Beginning in 1965, the larger 4.2-liter engine and an all-synchro transmission were specified, which improved low-speed driving ease. Initial body styles were the traditional two-seat road-

1970 E-Type 4.2-Litre 2+2 coupe (U.S. model)

1969 E-Type 4.2-Litre roadster (U.S. model)

ster and a sleek new fastback coupe with side-hinged rear door. These were joined in 1966 by a stretched-wheelbase coupe with 2+2 seating and somewhat less lithe appearance, offered only with the larger six. U.S. models were sold as the XKE, and differed little from British-market versions through 1967. After that, styling suffered due to federal safety standards, which brought side marker lights, clumsier bumpers, and more upright exposed headlights (previously mounted behind smoothly shaped plastic covers). Independent suspension and disc brakes were found at each wheel, and the E-Type quickly earned fame for its terrific roadability matched with brisk performance. The basic design continued into the early '70s in much-modified form with Jaguar's then-new V12. That ultimately gave way to the current XJS, which was more a GT than a true sports-car successor. Still a head-turner even today, and one of the most desirable collector's items you can have. Prices are reasonable now, but don't buy with dollar appreciation in mind.

FOR

Fantasy styling, still looks good ●Great performance (140+ mph) ●Parts and service still plentiful ●Good U.S. supply ●The last Jaguar roadsters ●Milestone status ●Strong club support

AGAINST

Bodies attract the tinworm ● Costly to restore and maintain ● Limited cockpit, luggage space ● Marginal cooling capacity for warm weather areas ● English electrical gremlins ● Not a profit-maker investment

SPECIFICATIONS

Length (in.) 175.0 (2-seaters), 184.5 (2+2)
Wheelbase (in.) 96.0 (2-seaters), 105.0 (2+2)
Weight (lbs.) 2690/2800 (2-seaters), 3100 (2+2)
Price (new) approx. $5600-6500 U.S.

ENGINES

cc/type (cid)	bore x stroke (mm)	bhp*	years
3781/dohc I6 (231)	87×106	265	1961-65
4235/dohc I6 (258)	92×106	265	1965-71

*gross

PRICES/PROJECTION

Restorable $3000-5000   **Good** $7000-9000
Excellent $11,000-16,000   Add 10-25% for good/excellent roadster
5-year projection +30%

Jaguar Mark X
1961-65

1961 Mark X 4-door sedan

PRODUCTION

12,977

HISTORY

The largest Jaguar sedan ever, and completely different from its Mark IX predecessor in styling and chassis design. Body-on-frame construction was replaced by a massive unitized structure with coil-spring independent rear suspension like that of the then-new E-Type sports car. Offered in these years with the middle-size version of the famous twincam XK engine, and came equipped with power steering and Borg-Warner automatic transmission. Almost as large as some full-size American cars of the period, but managed to look smaller because of the traditionally graceful Jaguar styling. Its appearance was much more modern than the Mark IX's, too, with straight-through fenders (no hint of separate "wings" remained), a tapering tail, and a sloping front end with a more shallow grille. The interior had all the usual Jaguar accoutrements: wood-faced dash bristling with switches and dials and comfy seats upholstered in genuine leather. A few Mark Xs were fitted with a division window and sold as limousines. Despite its size, this big cat could reach 120 mph, though it was not quick off the line. Not many were sold in the U.S.

FOR

Roomy, comfortable highway car • Nice blend of modern and traditional styling • Lovely XK engine • Well-equipped • Handling (despite size) • Not costly to buy

AGAINST

Rusts easily if neglected • Trim and body parts now in short supply • Poor mileage • Underpowered for give-and-take traffic • May be too large for some

SPECIFICATIONS

Length (in.) 202.0 **Wheelbase (in.)** 120.0 **Weight (lbs.)** 4175
Price (new) Approx. $7,000 (U.S.)

ENGINES

cc/type (cid)	bore x stroke (mm)	bhp*	years
3781/dohc I6 (231)	87×106	265	1961-65
*gross			

PRICES/PROJECTION

Restorable $1500-2500 **Good** $3000-5000
Excellent $5000-8000 **5-year projection** no change

Jaguar S-Type/420
1963-69

1965 S-Type 3.4-Litre 4-door sedan

PRODUCTION

3.4S 10,036   **3.8S** 15,135   **420** 9801

HISTORY

Literal extensions of Jaguar's original Mark II sedan series first seen in 1956. The S-Type, introduced for 1963, featured a longer, Mark X-like tail grafted onto the original unitized body/chassis structure. To go with it, Jaguar added a coil-spring independent rear suspension similar to that of the E-Type. To provide even closer family resemblance with the Mark X, renamed 420G in 1966, Jaguar announced the 420, which was the S-Type with squared-up Mark X nose including a square grille and four headlamps. By this time, there was little of the original 2.4-liter Mark II left. All these models carried the by-now familiar twincam XK engine, with model designation reflecting displacement. Typical Jaguar interior appointments were featured, and both manual and automatic transmissions were available. Each version was slightly heavier and less nimble than the one before it. The 420, capable of 125 mph, was also sold in England as the badge-engineered Daimler Sovereign with a different grille and trim details. This series can be considered the direct predecessor of the sterling XJ6, which arrived for the 1969 model year.

FOR

As for 1960-69 Mark II series, plus better ride and handling and more luggage space

AGAINST

As for 1960-69 Mark II series, but mileage hurt by increasing weight and U.S. emissions/safety concessions

SPECIFICATIONS

Length (in.) 187.0   **Wheelbase (in.)** 107.7
Weight (lbs.) 3585-3700   **Price (new)** $6300 U.S. for 3.8S in 1964; $7000 for 420 in 1967

ENGINES

cc/type (cid)	bore x stroke (mm)	bhp*	years
3442/dohc I6 (210)	83×106	210	1963-66
3781/dohc I6 (231)	87×106	220	1963-66
4235/dohc I6 (258)	92×106	245	1966-69

*gross

PRICES/PROJECTION

As for 1960-69 Mark II series

Jaguar Mark X & 420G 1965-70

1966-70 420G 4-door sedan

PRODUCTION

Mark X 5680   **420G** 5554

HISTORY

Continuations of Jaguar's larger sedan, now with the larger 4.2-liter version of the faithful dohc six specified for the E-Type beginning in 1965. Though manual gearbox was available, most of these cars had Borg-Warner three-speed automatic. The standard power steering system was also revised. There were no visual changes compared to the "Series I" Mark X. The result was a more torquey and flexible limousine-like Jaguar. The model was renamed 420G beginning in 1966 to bring nomenclature into line with that of the smaller 240/340/420 sedans based on the Mark II platform. Appearance changes were confined to thin chrome side moldings and a more formal upright grille. After 1967, the 420G was effectively withdrawn from the U.S. market (though it continued overseas until about 1970), leaving Jaguar without a prestige offering until the arrival of the XJ6, which replaced both the Mark X and the compact S-Type/420 series.

FOR

As for 1961-64 Mark X, but greater low-end torque for easier city driving

AGAINST

As for 1961-64 Mark X

SPECIFICATIONS

Length (in.) 202.0   **Wheelbase (in.)** 120.0   **Weight (lbs.)** 4300
Price (new) NA

ENGINES

cc/type (cid)	bore x stroke (mm)	bhp*	years
4235/dohc I6 (258)	92×106	265	1965-70

*gross

PRICES/PROJECTION

As for Mark X, but add 10-30% for division limousine

Jaguar E-Type V12 1972-75

1972 E-Type V12 convertible (U.S. model)

PRODUCTION

9382 (U.S. sales only)

HISTORY

Continuation of Jaguar's sexy '60s sports car, but considerably hammed up by size increases, safety bumpers, and emissions equipment. The main attraction was Jaguar's powerful (but thirsty) new V12 engine, which was also offered in the XJ sedan. To accommodate the longer powerplant, Jaguar adopted the 6.7-inch longer wheelbase previously used for the Series I/II 2+2 coupe. Body modifications included a larger hood bulge, wider tires mounted on slotted wheels adorned with disc wheel covers, cross-hatch grille insert, and more ungainly bumpers. Offered only as a 2+2 convertible and roadster, effectively replacing all six-cylinder E-Types. Quite fast (0-60 mph in 7.5 seconds and a 15.4-second quarter mile were reported by *Road & Track* magazine), and the least expensive 12-cylinder sports cars on the market. Ultimately doomed by the energy crisis because of its fuelishness, as well as buyer preference for GT-like refinement and safety. Jaguar obliged with the XJS four-seat coupe in 1976.

FOR

Traditional E-Type looks • Plush yet all-business cockpit • Electrifying getaway • Mechanical parts still available • Last of the breed

AGAINST

Thirsty • Mechanically unreliable • Expensive to fix • Very rust-prone

SPECIFICATIONS

Length (in.) 184.4 (1972-74), 189.6 (1975)

Wheelbase (in.) 104.7   **Weight (lbs.)** 3380-3450
Price (new) Convertible: $6950 (1972) to $9200 (1975)

ENGINES

cc/type (cid)	bore x stroke (mm)	bhp*	years
5343/sohc V12 (326)	90×70	244-272	1972-75

*SAE net

PRICES/PROJECTION

Restorable $4000-8000 **Good** $10,000-12,000
Excellent $14,500-21,000 Add 10-25% for good/excellent
roadster **5-year projection** +30%

Jaguar XJC
1975-78

1975 XJ6C 2-door hardtop (U.S. model)

PRODUCTION

Six 1794 **V12** 686 (U.S. sales only)

HISTORY

A neat-looking hardtop derivative of the superlative Jaguar XJ sedan, built only on the original short-wheelbase Series I platform. Called "the corporate sports car" by Jaguar's U.S. advertising agency, and "the corpulent sports car" by one agency wag. Originally scheduled to be launched along with the Series II sedans in late 1973, but actual production was considerably delayed because of structural rigidity bothers. A rival in concept for the "New Generation" Mercedes-Benz hardtops of the day, the XJC didn't sell well, perhaps because of its restricted rear seat space, the very thing that led to adoption of a longer wheelbase for the sedans. Plush leather and walnut interior, neat styling, and smooth, powerful engines (your choice of the traditional dohc six or the new V12) combine with low production to make the XJC a high-potential collectible. One of the few cars of the '70s that looked great and performed beautifully despite safety and emissions regulations. UK production continued through 1978, after which the "C" was dropped and the sedans updated to current Series III specifications.

FOR

Low-production appeal ●High investment potential long term ●Luxury and full amenities ●Scintillating to sizzling performance ●Unique Jaguar body style ●Mechanical parts still plentiful, especially for the six

AGAINST

The usual Jag reliability headaches ●Expensive to repair and maintain ●Somewhat rust-prone

SPECIFICATIONS

Length (in.) 195.0   **Wheelbase (in.)** 108.8   **Weight (lbs.)** 4195
Price (new) $17,000 U.S. in 1976

ENGINES

cc/type (cid)	bore x stroke (mm)	bhp*	years
4235/dohc I6 (258)	92×106	162	1975-78
5343/sohc V12 (326)	90×70	244	1976

*SAE net

PRICES/PROJECTION

Restorable $3000-4000 **Good** $5000-7000
Excellent $8000-11,000 Add 15-30% for V12 engine
5-year projection +20%

Jaguar XJS
1976-80

1979 XJS coupe (U.S. model)

PRODUCTION

Over 30,000 to date

HISTORY

The apparent successor to the E-Type as Jaguar's sporting model, this four-seat coupe emerged with a vastly different character. It was bigger, heavier, quieter, and more luxurious—clearly aimed at the GT market rather than the wind-in-the-hair set. Chassis design was broadly similar to that of the XJ-series sedans, and power was provided exclusively by Jaguar's superlative V12. Despite its heft, the XJS was no slouch, able to leap to 60 mph from rest in about 8.5 seconds and able to see the far side of 130 mph flat out. The snug cabin was sumptuously trimmed, and featured first-class ergonomics. In fact, everything about it was terrific—except the styling, which was roundly criticized as lacking cohesion. Though Jaguar founder Sir Williams Lyons had a hand in the original shape (with help from his friend Malcolm Sayer), it was compromised by the "committee think" approach to design that was becoming characteristic of British Leyland, not to mention the inevitable concessions to safety regulations. At least the design shunned the contemporary "tab A into slot B" approach being popularized by Giugiaro and others, and was smoothly curvaceous and recognizably Jaguar. As Sir William's last design project, the XJS has some historical importance, and reflects his long-time emphasis on "grace, pace, space." It wasn't the incredible bargain the XK sports cars were, however. Produced later as the XJS H.E. (High Efficiency) with "Fireball" cylinder head claimed to yield a 20 percent gain in fuel economy. Low production and its Jaguar pedigree suggest the XJS is a collectible, though it's too early to predict its ultimate position on the value scale.

FOR

Opulent and refined GT • Fine performance • Not that common, yet readily available • Rewarding driver's car • Twelve-cylinder appeal

AGAINST

Looks? • Stupefyingly complicated, an absolute animal to maintain, though those who want one probably know this already

SPECIFICATIONS

Length (in.) 191.7 (1976), 200.5 (1977), 192.3 (1978-80)
Wheelbase (in.) 102.0 **Weight (lbs.)** 3830-3960
Price (new) $19,600 U.S. in 1976, rising to $25,000 by 1979

ENGINES

cc/type (cid)	bore x stroke (mm)	bhp*	years
5343/sohc V12 (326)	90×70	244	1976-80

*SAE net

PRICES/PROJECTION

Governed more by used-car market valuations than by collector valuations. Average retail price is currently $15,000 for good-condition examples; model year maker less difference than condition.

Jensen CV8
1962-66

1965 CV8 coupe

PRODUCTION

Mark I/II 314   **Mark III** 182

HISTORY

Low-production Anglo-American hybrid built by the small, West Bromwich coachworks run by Richard and Alan Jensen, successful purveyors of custom bodies for various British chassis in the '30s. The CV8 was the last—and regrettably the ugliest—of Jensen's own fiberglass-body production models descended from the original 541 design first seen in 1953. The four-seat, close-coupled coupe body rested on a very strong tubular chassis, with the tubes sealed to act as vacuum reservoirs for the brakes. The styling, which had evolved through several previous models, was marked by a controversial front end with slant-eye quad headlamps flanking a jutting, eggcrate grille. Wheel openings were accented with sharp horizontal creases above, and the gently curved tail had three small circular lights. Power was supplied by contemporary Chrysler wedgehead V8s, initially 361 cid, then 383. The Mark I became the

Mark II in 1963, followed by the Mark III in 1965. More aerodynamic than it looked, the CV8 could reach 130 mph, and was fairly quick from standstill. Almost all examples had right-hand drive, and few were sold in the U.S. Expensive when new, mostly a function of Jensen's small production capacity and semi-handbuilt construction methods.

FOR

Torquey, reliable Chrysler power • Rot-free fiberglass body • Rare in U.S. • Mechanical parts plentiful yet • Body panels still available in Britain

AGAINST

Love-it-or-leave-it styling • Burly handling • Fuel thirst • Modest rear-seat accommodation

SPECIFICATIONS

Length (in.) 184.5   **Wheelbase (in.)** 105.0
Weight (lbs.) 3360-3515   **Price (new)** NA

ENGINES

cid/type	bore x stroke	bhp	years
361/ohv V8	4.12×3.38	305*	1962-63
383/ohv V8	4.25×3.38	330*	1963-65

*gross

PRICES/PROJECTION

Restorable $2000-4000 **Good** $4000-7500
Excellent $8000-9000 **5-year projection** +10%

Jensen Interceptor
1966-76

1971-76 Interceptor Series III coupe

PRODUCTION

6387

HISTORY

The handsome successor to the CV8, reviving a name first used in 1949. Retained its predecessor's sturdy tubular chassis with conventional A-arm/coil spring front suspension, live axle/leaf spring rear suspension, and Chrysler drivetrain mounted well back for good weight distribution. The brutish but clean all-steel body was designed by Touring of Italy, but built by Vignale, then Jensen itself. The smart two-door coupe featured square-cut lines except for a gently rounded tail with an enormous wraparound window that doubled as a luggage compartment hatch. No serious U.S. import efforts before the 1971 Series III models. The Series II, announced in 1969, differed from the Series I mainly in having standard power steering and minor trim and mechanical alterations. San Francisco sports car baron Kjell Qvale became involved in Jensen's management in the early '70s, and it was through him that the Interceptor was officially certified for U.S. sale. At that point, the previous 383-cid Chrysler engine gave way to the 440 unit, and a reworked dashboard was slotted in. Also new was a convertible version sold in very low quantity. A special SP model was offered on the British market, with a three-carburetor version of the Series III power unit, which delivered a top end of about 140 mph. A very exclusive executive express of enduring style, the Interceptor was ultimately doomed by Jensen's collapse in 1976 following the ill-fated Jensen-Healey sports car project.

FOR

Italian grace • American pace • Fairly plentiful here, yet has low-production appeal • Ubiquitous, easily serviced drivetrains • Some body parts still available in UK

AGAINST

Change to steel construction brings rust worries • Very heavy on fuel • Low appreciation potential

SPECIFICATIONS

Length (in.) 186.0 **Wheelbase (in.)** 105.0
Weight (lbs.) 3500-4000 **Price (new)** $15,500 (U.S. list price, 1973)

ENGINES

cid/type	bore x stroke	bhp	years
383/ohv V8	4.25×3.38	325/330*	1966-71
440/ohv V8	4.32×3.75	350/385*	1971-76
*gross			

PRICES/PROJECTION

Restorable $4000-10,000 **Good** $8000-25,000
Excellent $10,000-30,000 **5-year projection** +30%

Jensen FF
1966-71

1966-71 FF coupe

PRODUCTION

HISTORY

A trail-blazing high-performance GT closely related to the contemporary Interceptor, but featuring Ferguson Formula four-wheel drive and Dunlop "Maxaret" anti-skid braking system. Differed from the Interceptor in appearance only in a 4-inch longer wheelbase (all ahead of the cowl) and an extra vertical cooling louver in the front fenders. Very complex, and very expensive to build—too costly, in fact, to be continued once the Interceptor was reworked to Series III specifications. Offered only with Chrysler TorqueFlite automatic transmission and power steering. The FF drive system worked via a center differential, and was full-time. Never officially sold in the U.S., though a few early examples were likely imported privately. Built on an as-needed basis, which along with the unique specification guarantees collectibility. However, finding one won't be easy.

FOR

Unique concept (the world's first 4WD supercar) • Real exclusivity • Terrific traction • Others as for 1966-76 Interceptor

AGAINST

FF drivetrain parts in short supply, as are longer hood and fenders • Limited appreciation • Restoration costly and complex

SPECIFICATIONS

Length (in.) 191.0 **Wheelbase (in.)** 109.0 **Weight (lbs.)** 4030
Price (new) NA

ENGINES

cid/type	bore x stroke	bhp	years
383/ohv V8	4.25×3.38	325/330*	1966-71
*gross			

PRICES/PROJECTION

Restorable $4000-5000 **Good** $8000-10,000
Excellent $10,000-15,000 **5-year projection** +50%

Jensen-Healey
1972-77

PRODUCTION

1972 705	**1973** 3846	**1974** 4550			
1975 1301	**1976** 51	**U.S. imports** 7709			

HISTORY

The brainchild of Jensen's U.S. distributor, Kjell Qvale, this two-seat sports car was seen as a way for the small British manufacturer to crack the mass market and return to profitability in the face of declining demand for its large Interceptor. Launched after a protracted gestation period, the J-H was either a challenge to the trends of the '70s or an answer to a question nobody asked, depending on your point of view. In an age of closed GTs, it was a traditional open roadster; at a time when the mid-engine layout was all the rage, it had a conventional front-mounted engine—and a live rear axle and rear drum brakes. The general styling was suggested by the indomitable Donald Healey, and was clean but certainly not eye-catching. Handling was good, but cowl shake and a clumsy-to-put-up soft top were throwbacks to the good/bad old days. The engine was a dohc four supplied by Lotus, a development of a Vauxhall (British GM) unit. Suspension pieces and steering were also borrowed from Vauxhall, the four-speed all-synchro gearbox from Chrysler UK's Sunbeam Rapier HK120. Engine problems

1972-77 roadster

1937 4½-Litre Rapide roadster

surfaced early, and along with the uninspired design kept sales far below expectations. Donald Healey disassociated himself from the venture, which is why a 2+2 coupe derivative was called Jensen GT. It didn't help. Production ground to a halt in early 1977. Because the company had so much of its assets tied up in the project, the J-H's demise effectively spelled the end of Jensen as well. The J-H will never rank with its Austin-Healey predecessor among the truly great British sports cars. Whether collectors ultimately view it as desirable or a mere aberration has yet to be determined.

FOR

Sprightly performance (up to 125 mph) and reasonable economy (24 mpg) • Traditional sports car virtues in a newer package • Rarity interest

AGAINST

Parts supplies variable • A questionable investment • Little organized club support at present • Rust-prone

SPECIFICATIONS

Length (in.) 162-166 **Wheelbase (in.)** 92.0
Weight (lbs.) approx. 2200 (roadster), 2400 (GT coupe)
Price (new) $4795 original U.S. list price

ENGINES

cc/type (cid)	bore x stroke (mm)	bhp	years
1973/dohc I4 (120)	95×69	140	1973-77

PRICES/PROJECTION

Restorable $1000-2000 **Good** $2500-3000
Excellent $4000-8000 **5-year projection** +15%

Lagonda 4½-Litre 1934-39

PRODUCTION

841 (incl. 78 Rapide)

HISTORY

A series of big, beefy traditional cars produced by the oh-so-British company named for a river in Ohio. Power was supplied by Meadows and was sufficient to propel all models past 90 mph. The more powerful (120-130 bhp) and aptly named Rapide versions actually

managed the magic 100 mph, which was *fast* for the time. Like early Bentleys, these were large, truck-like cars at first, but improvements came for '36 when W.O. Bentley was on board as a Lagonda designer. The smoothest was the LG6 of 1938-39, which borrowed chassis and styling from the contemporary Lagonda V12 (see entry). Synchromesh for '36 on, and late LG6s even had independent front suspension. Heavy and thirsty, but massively built and lots of character. The spiritual descendant of the grand "W.O." Bentleys and thus a good alternative for those who missed out on one.

FOR

A handbuilt rarity • Rugged British style and build • Good performance from unstressed engine • Thriving (UK) club

AGAINST

Restoration near-impossible due to parts famine • Little appreciated in U.S. • "Trucky" and "fuelish"

SPECIFICATIONS

Length (in.) 184.0-188.0 **Wheelbase (in.)** 129.0-135.0
Weight (lbs.) 4300-4600 **Price (new)** NA

ENGINES

cc/type (cid)	bore x stroke (mm)	bhp*	years
4467/ohv I6 (272)	88.5×120.6	110-130	1934-39

*gross

PRICES/PROJECTION

Restorable $4000-5000 **Good** $11,000-14,000
Excellent $15,000-20,000 Add 25-100% for Rapide.
5-year projection +20%

Lagonda V12 1938-39

PRODUCTION

189

HISTORY

The second-generation "Bentley," produced under the aegis of W.O.

Bentley after he joined Lagonda in 1935. In the same heroic mold as his earlier cars but with a magnificent single-cam 60-degree V12. Solid separate chassis, torsion-bar independent front suspension, and a huge choice of bodies from tourers to limousines. Though the engine is a problem for today's restorers—parts for it simply don't exist anymore—this was one of the '30s fastest British cars, with a brave and well-executed basic concept that made it altogether more sporting and exciting than a contemporary Rolls/Bentley. Silky smooth performance up to 105 mph top speed in a 5000-pound car was—and is—formidable.

FOR

High performance from splendid engine • Rarity • Smooth and sophisticated • Styling

AGAINST

Engine parts not available • Complex to maintain • Heavy and thirsty • Ownership costs very high • Little U.S. interest

SPECIFICATIONS

Length (in.) 200.0-212.0 **Wheelbase (in.)** 124.0-138.0
Weight (lbs.) 4400-5000 **Price (new)** NA

ENGINES

cc/type (cid)	bore x stroke (mm)	bhp	years
4480/sohc V12 (273)	75×84.5	180	1938-39

*gross

PRICES/PROJECTION

Restorable $10,000-15,000 **Good** $30,000-35,000
Excellent $40,000-50,000 **5-year projection** no change

Lagonda 2.6/3.0 Litre 1949-58

1950 2.6-Litre convertible by Tickford

PRODUCTION

2.6 Litre (1949-53) 550 **3.0 Litre (1953-58)** 420

1953-58 3.0-Litre Rapide 4-door sedan by Tickford

HISTORY

First postwar Lagonda, designed under W.O. Bentley but produced by David Brown of Aston Martin, Lagonda's new owner. Engine was the same as used in Aston Martin DB2 and DB2/4. Rigid cruciform chassis with independent rear suspension was clothed in semi-classical sedan and convertible bodywork by Tickford. Top speed of the 2.6 was only 90 mph, but the 3.0 could reach the magic "ton" (100 mph). Handbuilt cars aimed at the wealthy and priced accordingly.

FOR

Aston Martin powertrain • Many mechanical parts still available • Advanced chassis for the period

AGAINST

Limited performance (2.6) • Old-fogey styling • Body parts extinct • Bodies deteriorate rapidly • Not plentiful in the U.S.

SPECIFICATIONS

Length (in.) 188.0 (2.6), 196.0 (3.0) **Wheelbase (in.)** 113.5
Weight (lbs.) 3345/3410 (2.6 sedan/convertible); 3615/3660 (3.0 sedan/convertible) **Price (new)** NA

ENGINES

cc/type (cid)	bore x stroke (mm)	bhp	years
2580/dohc I6 (158)	83 × 90	105*	1949-53
2922/dohc I6 (178)		140**	1953-58

*net (2.6 Litre)
**gross (3.0 Litre)

PRICES/PROJECTION

Restorable $1000-2000 **Good** $2000-3000
Excellent $3000-5000 Add 10% for 3.0-Litre.
5-year projection +50%

Lagonda Rapide 1961-64

PRODUCTION

55

HISTORY

After a three-year hiatus, the Lagonda marque returned on a high-performance sedan as Aston Martin again tried the four-door GT

1961-64 Rapide 4-door sedan

formula. The Rapide used a longer-wheelbase version of the DB4 platform, with a De Dion rear suspension and the same dohc six in a lower state of tune. Sleek body styling was spoiled by a clumsy front-end treatment, with four headlamps (two large and two small) and an unfortunate Edsel-like vertical grille. More massive than the DB4, too much so to qualify as an Aston Martin product in the mind of prospective buyers, though the car lived up to its name with a top speed of approaching 130 mph. Production was an on-again, off-again proposition, and virtually all the handful of cars actually completed remained in England.

FOR

Very rare • Aston performance with four-door convenience • Many mechanical parts still stocked • Nice lines despite front end

AGAINST

Where do you begin to look? • Big, heavy, and thirsty • Body parts extinct

SPECIFICATIONS

Length (in.) 195.5 **Wheelbase (in.)** 114.0 **Weight (lbs.)** 3780 **Price (new)** NA

ENGINES

cc/type (cid)	bore x stroke (mm)	bhp*	years
3995/dohc I6 (244)	96×92	236	1961-64

*net

PRICES/PROJECTION

Restorable $3000-5000 **Good** $7000-8000
Excellent $8000-10,000 **5-year projection** +20%

Lamborghini 350/400GT 1964-68

PRODUCTION

380

HISTORY

The first of the Ferrari-fighting high-performance GTs backed by Italian tractor king Ferruccio Lamborghini. The engine and chassis design was mostly the work of ex-Ferrari engineer Giotto Bizzarrini. The former was an intricate, jewel-like four-cam V12. The latter was a typical low-volume Italian tubular frame with all-independent coil-spring suspension system. The 350GT was a two-seater

1964-68 350GT coupe by Touring

notchback coupe with a 3.5-liter engine. The 400GT was basically the same car with +2 rear seating shoehorned in and a larger 4.0-liter displacement. Styling was curiously rounded, and though it had the right proportions it lacked the grace and panache of Maranello's Pininfarina-shaped cars in these years. Significant as the progenitor of the later and more famous Lamborghinis. Replaced by the Islero in 1968.

FOR

First edition Italian exotic • 150-mph-plus performance • Magnificent engine

AGAINST

Styling • Poor body construction • Body panels aren't to be found • Expensive to restore, run, and insure • Most survivors already spoken for

SPECIFICATIONS

Length (in.) 184.5 **Wheelbase (in.)** 100.4 **Weight (lbs.)** 2650 (350GT), 3200 (400GT) **Price (new)** $14,250 U.S. for 400GT in 1966

ENGINES

cc/type (cid)	bore x stroke (mm)	bhp*	years
3464/dohc V12 (211)	77×62	280	1964-68
3929/dohc V12 (240)	82×62	330	1964-68

*DIN

PRICES/PROJECTION

Restorable $7000-10,000 **Good** $16,000-20,000
Excellent $20,000-27,000 **5-year projection** +30%

Lamborghini Miura 1966-72

PRODUCTION

760

HISTORY

The sensational mid-engine Lamborghini that started life as a

Lamborghini Espada 1968-78

1966-70 P400 Miura coupe by Bertone

1968-79 Espada 2+2 coupe by Bertone

dream car, and was "forced" into production by public demand. Apart from the Ferrari 275LM, the first production mid-engine exotic. Powered by Lamborghini's renowned 4.0-liter quad-cam V12 mounted just aft of the two-seat cabin and situated transversely instead of longitudinally as in the front engine Lamborghinis. Taking drive to the rear wheels was a five-speed manual gearbox, the only one offered. The separate chassis was big and brawny but light, and boasted the all-independent suspension expected in cars of this class. The aggressive, low-slung body was styled by Bertone, and consisted of a steel structure overlaid with unstressed aluminum panels. Body contours were curvy and sensual. When not in use, the exposed headlamps reclined into recesses in the front fenders. The front fenders/hood and engine/wheel/tail cover lifted up as complete assemblies for service access. No Spider version was officially sold, though a few of the closed cars may have been converted, and an open car was seen briefly at auto shows. Sold in three forms throughout its life: the P400, the higher-powered 400S in 1970, and the ultra-rapid Miura SV from 1971. Billed as the fastest production car in the world at the time, and the SV's claimed 180-mph top speed seemed to back that up. Not for those to whom considerations like luggage space and noise control are important, but surely the fastest way to travel on land short of a surface-to-surface missile.

FOR

Unique styling •Monstrous performance •Technical interest •Trend-setter

AGAINST

Incredibly costly to buy and run •Highly impractical •Rust-prone •Body parts hard to find

SPECIFICATIONS

Length (in.) 171.5 **Wheelbase (in.)** 98.5 **Weight (lbs.)** 2850 **Price (new)** $19,250 U.S. in 1969

ENGINES

cc/type (cid)	bore x stroke (mm)	bhp*	years
3929/dohc V12 (240)	82×62	350-385	1966-72

*DIN

PRICES/PROJECTION

Restorable $10,000-20,000 **Good** $30,000-40,000 **Excellent** $41,000-60,000 **5-year projection** +30%

PRODUCTION

1000 (est.)

HISTORY

The long-lived four-seat Lamborghini with styling inspired by Bertone's Marzal show car of 1966. The magnificent 4.0-liter V12 engine was front-mounted in a steel platform chassis with all-independent suspension, and drove the rear wheels through a five-speed gearbox or (on some mid-'70s specimens) a Chrysler TorqueFlite automatic. (The same basic chassis layout was also used in short-wheelbase form for the Jarama 2+2 coupe.) The Espada looked like no other car on the road: a low, wide front end with quad headlamps flanking a simple blacked-out grille; large inset hood scoops; huge windshield; a low beltline kicked up at the rear; and a near-horizontal fastback roofline terminating in a chopped tail with a glass panel between the taillights to assist rearward vision. A large and heavy car, it offered marginal four-place seating and a top speed of "only" 150 mph. One of the most exotic of the limited-production Latin flyers, and surprisingly practical despite that.

FOR

One-of-a-kind styling •Near four-seat layout •Delectable engine •All the amenities you could want •Low-production snob appeal

AGAINST

Hardly cheap today •Costly to restore and run •Most survivors have rusted badly •Body parts have vanished •Gas guzzler •A rare commodity

SPECIFICATIONS

Length (in.) 184.0 **Wheelbase (in.)** 104.5 **Weight (lbs.)** 3750 **Price (new)** $21,000 U.S. in 1969

ENGINES

cc/type (cid)	bore x stroke (mm)	bhp*	years
3929/dohc V12 (240)	82×62	325-365	1968-78

*DIN

PRICES/PROJECTION

Restorable $10,000-15,000 **Good** $17,000-20,000 **Excellent** $25,000-29,000 **5-year projection** +30%

Lamborghini Islero 1968-69

1968-70 Islero coupe by Marazzi

PRODUCTION

225

HISTORY

The rebodied replacement for the original 350GT/400GT. Used the same chassis, but was offered only with the 4.0-liter version of the quad-cam V12. The more angular body styling was the work of Marazzi of Milan, but paled next to the Bertone-designed Espada and mid-engine Miura sold alongside it. Seating was still strictly 2+2, and the Islero was quite fast—more than 140 mph available. Replaced as the least exotic Lambo by the Jarama in 1970.

FOR

As for 1964-68 350GT/400GT, plus neater (if more bland) looks

AGAINST

Undistinguished for a supercar ●Others as for 1964-68 350GT/400GT

SPECIFICATIONS

Length (in.) 178.0 **Wheelbase (in.)** 100.4 **Weight (lbs.)** 2795
Price (new) approx. $18,000 U.S.

ENGINES

cc/type (cid)	bore x stroke (mm)	bhp*	years
3929/dohc V12 (240)	82×62	330	1968-69

*DIN

PRICES/PROJECTION

As for 1964-68 350GT/400GT

Lamborghini Jarama 400GT 1970-76

PRODUCTION

NA

HISTORY

The last member of Lamborghini's 400GT series, successor to the short-lived Islero. The Jarama was essentially the same mechanical package (front-mounted quad-cam V12 driving the rear wheels through a five-speed gearbox) wrapped in a newly designed, very angular 2+2 coupe bodyshell styled by Bertone. Unlike its predecessors, though, the Jarama featured unit-steel construction instead of a separate tubular chassis. Wheelbase was even shorter than on the original 350GT, but clever use of interior space allowed Lamborghini to claim marginal 2+2 seating, even if the rear passengers had to adopt the lotus position to fit. Suspension was the same at both ends: unequal-length A-arms, coil springs, and anti-roll bar. A terrific performer in a straight line (100 mph was only 18 seconds away from standstill), the Jarama was also a delightful handler, no doubt due as much to its ultra-wide tires and low center of gravity as to the suspension. Not the most practical Lambo from the standpoint of packaging and interior design, but the aggressive styling has aged well. A victim of Lamborghini's roller-coaster financial fortunes in the mid- to late '70s. Most of those brought to the U.S. are 1972-spec models (sold through the 1974 model year), though some later versions may have been brought in and certified privately.

FOR

Supercar performance ●Bertone styling ●Sumptuous appointments ●Pedigree road manners

AGAINST

Thirsty ●Expensive to run ●Limited accommodations ●Erratic construction quality ●Too new to be firmly established as a collectible

SPECIFICATIONS

Length (in.) 176.5 **Wheelbase (in.)** 93.5 **Weight (lbs.)** approx. 3600 **Price (new)** $23,500 U.S. in 1972, rising to $28,000 in 1975

ENGINES

cc/type (cid)	bore x stroke (mm)	bhp*	years
3929/dohc V12 (240)	82×62	350	1970-76

*net

PRICES/PROJECTION

Restorable $8000-15,000 **Good** $15,000-20,000
Excellent $20,000-25,000 **5-year projection** +30%

Lamborghini Urraco 1972-79

PRODUCTION

P250 520 **P300** 190 **P200** 66

HISTORY

Lamborghini's reply to Ferrari's V6 Dino, not a successor to the mighty Miura. Powered by a brand-new all-aluminum V8 with "only" one overhead camshaft per cylinder bank, mounted crosswise behind a nominal four-place cockpit and driving the rear wheels through a five-speed gearbox. Unit construction with all-independent MacPherson-strut suspension (aided by transverse arms and anti-roll bars) gave the leech-like handling/roadholding expected in a "midi." Low and wide 2+2 coupe by Bertone, marked by Miura-like slats over the fastback rear window, plus a short pointy front and large wheels and tires. Initially sloppy dash design improved as production progressed, but not the oft-criticized "Italian ape" major control spacings. Offered with three different engine displacements, the 2.0-liter version being a home-market "tax dodge" not sold in the U.S. Effectively replaced by a restyled targa-top derivative called Silhouette, which in turn led to the current Jalpa powered by the basic Urraco engine

FOR

A supercar in everything but size • Delightful engine • Superb road manners • Quick • Parts still available if you're patient

AGAINST

Unit-construction rust worries • Limited passenger and luggage space • Odd driving stance • Messy dash • Rather piggish (about 13 mpg) • Spotty parts/service support

SPECIFICATIONS

Length (in.) 167.3 **Wheelbase (in.)** 96.3
Weight (lbs.) 2420-2820 **Price (new)** $22,500 U.S. in 1975 (P250), rising to $24,150 in 1977 (P300)

ENGINES

cc/type (cid)	bore x stroke (mm)	bhp	years
2463/sohc V8 (152)	86×53	220[1]	1971-76
2996/sohc V8 (183)	86×65	265[2]	1975-79
1994/sohc V8 (122)	77×53	182[3]	1975-77

*net 1:P250   2: P300   3: P200

PRICES/PROJECTION

Restorable $10,000-12,000 **Good** $14,000-18,000
Excellent $19,500-24,000 **5-year projection** +30%

Lamborghini Countach 1973-date

PRODUCTION

NA, but limited; no more than 50 per year through 1979

HISTORY

The wildest-looking Italian supercar ever, the spiritual successor to the Miura. Drivetrain layout is unusual, with a quad-cam V12 as in the Miura, but mounted longitudinally with the 5-speed gearbox ahead of it. Drive to the rear wheels is via a power takeoff through the engine sump to a ZF limited-slip differential. Body styling is by Bertone, marked by an almost pyramidal shape. Wide doors are

1978 LP400S Countach

hinged at the front, but swing upwards to provide somewhat clumsy access to a wide but snug-feeling cockpit dominated by a large central tunnel and aircraft-like dashboard. Construction consists of an advanced tubular space-frame chassis clothed by aluminum panels only a millimeter thick. Suspension is very sophisticated, with unequal-length A-arms, coil springs, and anti-roll bar in front; at the rear, upper lateral links, A-arms, upper and lower trailing arms, two coil springs per side, dual shocks, and anti-roll bar. Specifications were slightly changed for the Countach S, announced in 1978, with revised suspension geometry to accommodate wider wheels and tires. Tack-on fender flares were added, giving the car an even more menacing appearance. A change in the type of Weber carburetors used (still six two-barrel units, though) brought horsepower down, but this was still one of the world's fastest production cars. There's some doubt, however, as to whether the Countach or its Ferrari rival, the 512 Berlinetta Boxer, can lay absolute claim to being *the* fastest. Certified briefly for U.S. sale in the mid-'70s. Thereafter, modified and certified independently by an American firm. Still in production at this writing; Lamborghini was bought out by Chrysler Corporation in 1987.

FOR

Exotic looks, specifications • Fantastic performance (at least 150 mph) • Rarity • Great charisma ensures collectibility

AGAINST

Thirsty • Costly to acquire • Horrendous upkeep costs • Restricted accommodations for persons over about 5 ft. 10 in. • Not at home in urban traffic • Collector values (as distinct from used car values) not yet established

SPECIFICATIONS

Length (in.) 163.0 **Wheelbase (in.)** 96.5
Weight (lbs.) 3020-3200 **Price (new)** $52,000 U.S. in 1976, rising to $102,500 in 1981 (includes safety and emissions certification)

ENGINES

cc/type (cid)	bore x stroke (mm)	bhp	years
3929/dohc V12 (239.7)	82×62	325-375	1973-date

PRICES/PROJECTION

LP400 Restorable $10,000-15,000 **Good** $25,000-30,000
Excellent $30,000-45,000 **5-year projection** +50% Post-1975 model values currently governed more by the used "exoticar" market than by collector-market forces.

Lancia Aprilia 1937-49

1937 Aprilia 4-door sedan

PRODUCTION

14,704

HISTORY

One of the most advanced of all 1930s European light cars, built by the Italian concern famous for innovation. Featured unit body/chassis, all-independent suspension, hydraulic brakes, and a narrow-angle overhead-cam V4. Remarkably efficient styling; it could beat 80 mph, which suggests good aerodynamics, a necessity with less than 50 horsepower. Most of those built were four-door sedans, but a few long-wheelbase sporty models are known. Rust has sent most of these cars to that great scrapheap in the sky.

FOR

Inimitable Lancia character • Advanced engineering • Interest value as a sort of baby Airflow/Zephyr

AGAINST

Small interior • Rust-prone, so few survivors • Few parts, too • Little support in U.S.

SPECIFICATIONS

Length (in.) 157.0 **Wheelbase (in.)** 112.2 **Weight (lbs.)** 1950
Price (new) NA

ENGINES

cc/type (cid)	bore x stroke (mm)	bhp*	years
1352/ohc V4 (82)	72×83	47	1937-39
1486/ohc V4 (91)	74.6×85	48	1939-49

*gross

PRICES/PROJECTION

Restorable $2000-3500 **Good** $3000-4000
Excellent $4000-6000 **5-year projection** no change

Lancia Aurelia Coupe & Spider 1951-58

1952 Aurelia B20 GT coupe by Pinin Farina

PRODUCTION

Coupe 3871 **Spider** 761

HISTORY

Hailed by many as the first "true" GT, the Aurelia coupe was a two-door fastback based on the chassis and drivetrains of the Aurelia sedan. Styling by Pinin Farina was distinguished by a proud, distinctively shaped Lancia grille and a smooth, sloping roofline. Like all contemporary Lancias, the coupe had a sliding-pillar front suspension, and shared its V6 engine and rear-mounted gearbox with the sedan. Two engine sizes were offered through six marginally different "series" in the model's life, 1991cc (1951-53) and 2451cc (1953-58). Available beginning in 1954 was a pretty Farina-styled open roadster (Spider) on a shorter wheelbase. The first 240 built had a trendy wraparound windshield and no door windows. After that a conventional windshield and roll-up glass appeared. A major chassis change occurred in 1954, when the semi-trailing link independent rear suspension was exchanged for a De Dion layout on coupes. Spiders used the De Dion arrangement exclusively.

FOR

Significant modern Lancia • Milestone status • Agile handling • Styling (especially Spider) • Engineering • Performance

AGAINST

Rust-prone • Parts now hard to obtain • Not numerous any more

SPECIFICATIONS

Length (in.) 172.0 (Coupe), 165.4 (Spider)
Wheelbase (in.) 104.7 (Coupe), 96.5 (Spider) **Weight (lbs.)** 2630 (Coupe), 2500 (Spider) **Price (new)** approx. $5500 U.S. for Spider in 1956; $5800 for GT coupe in 1958

ENGINES

cc/type (cid)	bore x stroke (mm)	bhp*	years
1991/ohv V6 (121)	72×81.5	75/80	1951-53
2451/ohv V6 (150)	78×85.5	118/122	1953-58

*net

1953-58 Aurelia B24 spider (convertible) by Pinin Farina

PRICES/PROJECTION

Restorable $1000-2000 **Good** $2500-4000
Excellent $4000-5000 Add 60-100% for good/excellent Spider
5-year projection no change

Lancia Flaminia Coupe & Spider 1959-62

1956-59 Flaminia sports coupe by Zagato

PRODUCTION

2.5-Litre Coupe 4151   **2.8-Litre Coupe** 1133
2.5-Litre special-bodied units 2593
2.8-Litre special-bodied units 868

HISTORY

Introduced in 1956 as the eventual replacement for the Aurelia, the all-new Flaminia also featured a V6 engine (though of a different type). It also had a similar rear transaxle but a much more modern coil spring front suspension. The "volume" model in this series was the Pininfarina-styled four-seat notchback coupe. There were also various special-bodied coupes and Spider roadsters offered on a shortened version of the Flaminia sedan chassis designed by the likes of Touring, Zagato, and Ghia. Engine displacement was raised from 2.5 to 2.8 liters in 1963, and four-wheel disc brakes were used from the beginning. By the early '60s, the Flaminia had become overshadowed by the smaller and more saleable Fulvia and Flavia series. The most striking of the coachbuilt cars was probably the Zagato fastback, with sleek Alfa-type lines and headlamps deeply set into housings covered by clear lenses.

FOR

Italian *brio* and style • Fine brakes • Capable road manners • Zagato's distinctive looks

AGAINST

Body rot problems • Parts difficult to find now • Mediocre styling on Farina notchback coupe

SPECIFICATIONS

Length (in.) 184.5 (Coupe), 177.0 (Zagato)
Wheelbase (in.) 108.3 (Coupe), 99.2 (Zagato)
Weight (lbs.) 3265 (Coupe), 2670 (Zagato) **Price (new)** approx. $6500 U.S. in 1960

ENGINES

cc/type (cid)	bore x stroke (mm)	bhp*	years
2458/ohv V6 (150)	80×82	119/140	1959-63
2775/ohv V6 (169)	85×82	150	1963-69

*net

PRICES/PROJECTION

Restorable $1000-2000 **Good** $2000-3000
Excellent $3000-5000 Add 50-100% for good/excellent special coachwork models. **5-year projection** no change

Lancia Flavia/2000 Coupe/ Convertible/Zagato 1962-75

1969-75 2000 coupe by Pininfarina

PRODUCTION

Flavia 1500 Coupe /Convertible 4449
Flavia Zagato 1500 Sport 98
Flavia 1800 Coupe/Convertible 16,445
Flavia Zagato 1800 Sport 628   **2000 Coupe** 6791

HISTORY

The first Italian car with front-wheel drive, and the first Lancia to make use of a horizontally opposed engine. As with other Lancia series, a humdrum sedan (not included here) was introduced first, followed by these more desirable sporty models. These consist of a smart Pininfarina-styled notchback coupe with four headlamps and four seats, plus a convertible and an "ugly/beautiful" Zagato fastback with lightweight body. Engine displacement rose to 1.8 liters in 1963, and the lineup continued mostly unchanged until 1969. At that point, everything but the notchback was dropped. The coupe was given a restyled nose and reintroduced without the Flavia appellation as the 2000, denoting its enlarged 2.0-liter flat four. Fuel injection was offered as well as carburetors during the lengthy model run. Most examples weren't as fast as their styling implied, but the injected Zagato could reach 120 mph given enough space. Production gradually tapered off beginning around 1969, when Fiat took over Lancia.

FOR

Lancia prestige and engineering • Neat Pininfarina styling • "Distinctive" Zagato styling • Front-drive pace-setter

AGAINST

Rust-prone • Drivetrain parts have dried up

SPECIFICATIONS

Length (in.) 176.5 (Coupe), 175.6 (Zagato)
Wheelbase (in.) 97.6 **Weight (lbs.)** 2550-2800 (Coupe), 2340 (Zagato) **Price (new)** NA

ENGINES

cc/type (cid)	bore x stroke (mm)	bhp*	years
1500/ohv flat 4 (92)	81×71		1962-63
1800/ohv flat 4 (110)	88×74		1963-69
1990/ohv flat 4 (121)	89×80		1969-75

*90 bhp (net) to 140 bhp (gross) depending on displacement and fuel delivery (injection or carburetors)

PRICES/PROJECTION

Restorable $2000-3000 **Good** $2500-4000
Excellent $4000-6000 **5-year projection** +10%

Lancia Fulvia Coupe & Zagato 1965-76

1971-76 Fulvia 1.3 coupe

PRODUCTION

1.2-Litre Coupe 20,436	**1.2-Litre HF Coupe** 490
1.3-Litre Zagato 202	**1.3-Litre Coupe** 113,599
1.3-Litre HF Coupe 2239	**1.3-Litre Zagato** 6100
1.6-Litre HF Coupe 3690	**1.6-Litre Zagato** 800

HISTORY

The last Lancia wholly designed by the old-line Italian automaker before it was acquired by Fiat (which then took increasing responsibility for engineering and styling of subsequent Lancias). New from end to end, with front-wheel drive and a narrow-angle overhead cam V4 engine inclined at 45 degrees in the nose. Besides a dull-looking four-door sedan (not considered here), the Fulvia was offered as a deliciously cute 2+2 notchback coupe and as a longer two-seat Sports coupe styled by Zagato in its typical fashion. The latter featured extensive use of aluminum body panels, as did the special high-performance HF coupe. Engine displacement was increased from 1.2 to 1.3 liters in 1967, the last year these cars were legally imported into the U.S. An extensively revised 1.6-liter version of the V4 was optional for 1969 and later HFs and the last 1971 Zagatos. All models featured four-wheel disc brakes and splendid front-drive handling. The HF earned its stripes in European rallying, and hung around after the Fiat-based Beta series arrived to replace other Fulvia models in the early '70s.

FOR

Neat styling • Handling • Performance (110 mph for 1.6) • Brakes

AGAINST

Meager parts supplies • Bodies rust-prone • Most slower than they look • Crowded cabin

SPECIFICATIONS

Length (in.) 156.0 (Coupe), 161.0 (Zagato)
Wheelbase (in.) 91.7 **Weight (lbs.)** 1975-2110 (Coupe), 1820 (HF), 2060 (Zagato) **Price (new)** $3520 (1.3 Coupe), $4520 (1.3 Zagato) in U.S. in 1967

ENGINES

cc/type (cid)	bore x stroke (mm)	bhp*	years
1216/dohc V4 (74)	76×67	80	1965-67
1298/dohc V4 (79)	77×70	90	1967-76
1584/dohc V4 (97)	82×75	115	1969-76

*DIN

PRICES/PROJECTION

Restorable $2000-3000 **Good** $2500-4000
Excellent $4000-6000 Add up to 50% for Zagato or HF.
5-year projection +10%

Land-Rover Series I-III 1948-80

PRODUCTION

761,000 (Series I, II, IIA)

HISTORY

British reply to the American Army's go-anywhere four-wheel-drive vehicle that proved so valuable in World War II, but introduced in the postwar period. Very different in appearance, with fully enclosed front wheels and severe, angular body lines. Early models had inboard headlamps mounted behind a mesh-screen grille guard. Later models had exposed lamps that ultimately were moved into the front fenders. Offered in a bewildering choice of models—short and long wheelbases, gasoline and diesel engines, various body styles (pickup truck, van, station wagon, special-purpose coachwork). Like most 4x4s, the Land-Rover affords two- or four-wheel drive with high and low ranges, and has front and rear differential locking for the ultimate in traction on low-friction surfaces and difficult terrain. Bodies are made of light alloy to keep weight down. The passenger compartment is spartan but very

1949 Series I pickup

functional. Never intended to double as a passenger car (the more stylish and luxurious Range Rover introduced in 1970 fills that role), the Land-Rover is built and sold strictly for hard work in conditions that would stop other vehicles cold. It's still in production today (available with a detuned version of the ex-Buick 3.5-liter aluminum V8), and remains a mainstay of the British Army, fire departments, and seekers of high adventure from tropical jungles to frozen tundra. Not imported to the U.S. in any significant volume, though not difficult to find.

FOR

Rugged durability • Supreme all-terrain capability • Rust-free body • Wide choice of sizes, types, specifications • Still in production

AGAINST

Hard springing, mountain-goat ride • Spartan • Not very fast (about 60 mph) • Early body and mechanical parts questionable now

SPECIFICATIONS

Length (in.) 132.0-175.0 (depending on body)
Wheelbase (in.) 80/86/107/109   **Weight (lbs.)** 2500-3600 (depending on specifications)   **Price (new)** NA

ENGINES

cc/type (cid)	bore x stroke (mm)	bhp*	years
1596/ohv I4 (97)	70×105	50	1948-51
1997/ohv I4 (122)	78×105	52	1952-58
2286/ohv I4 (140)	91×89	77	1958-date
2625/ohv I6 (160)	79×92	85	1967-date
2052/ohv I4D (125)	NA	55	1958-61
2286/ohv I4D (140)	91×89	62	1958-date
3528/ohv V8 (215)	89×71	100**	1980-date

*net **est.

PRICES/PROJECTION

Restorable $500-1500 **Good** $2000-3000
Excellent $3000-5000 **5-year projection** +10%

Lotus Seven
1957-80

1957-70 Seven sports/racing roadster

PRODUCTION

S1 242 **S2** 1350 **S3** 350 **S4** 1000 **Caterham S3** 850+

HISTORY

The original British "club racer," about as pure a sports car as you'll ever see. Introduced in 1957 as a kit to get around home market purchase tax, later sold by Lotus fully assembled, and today built by Caterham Cars of South London with few changes to the original Colin Chapman design. Intended as a low-cost way to enjoy sporty motoring and/or to go racing, and its kit-car heritage shows in the wide variety of proprietary engines that will fit in the lightweight square-rigged body. The Seven is about as spartan as they come —even side curtains and rudimentary soft top were options—and its tiny size makes the cockpit extremely confining for anyone larger than a munchkin. It's like driving a motorized roller skate. Performance depends on what engine/transmission is used, but can range from brisk to sensational. Wonderful on twisty, lightly traveled back roads because of marvelously precise handling and cornering abilities, but worrisome in traffic because the low build makes you invisible to most other drivers. The stark, functional styling—free-standing headlamps and flowing, separate front fenders, upright windshield that can be folded flat, a bobtail rear—has been widely imitated. Most Sevens had light-alloy bodies, but the early-'70s Mark IV versions used fiberglass. Lotus relied most heavily on British Ford engines, including the Chapman-modified dohc unit, which is the one to look for on the collector market. In all, an extremely versatile platform every bit as popular today as it was some 30 years ago, providing only the basics required for high-spirited driving fun.

FOR

Handling • Simplicity • Individuality • Entertainment value

AGAINST

Somewhat fragile • Lacks refinement and modern amenities • Not for all-round use

SPECIFICATIONS

Length (in.) 132.0 **Wheelbase (in.)** 88.0 **Weight (lbs.)** 1655 (average) **Price (new)** approx. $5500 U.S. in 1970 (variable with drivetrain components specified)

ENGINES

cc/type (cid)	bore x stroke (mm)	bhp	years

Most examples fitted with four-cylinder Ford of Britain engines of 1000-1600cc. Output ranges from 40 bhp to 125 bhp (DIN). Valve-train configurations include side valve, overhead valve, and twin overhead cam (Chapman-modified 1588cc unit only).

PRICES/PROJECTION

Restorable $2000-4000 **Good** $4000-6000
Excellent $5000-7000 **5-year projection** no change

Lotus Elite
1959-63

1959-63 Elite coupe

PRODUCTION

988

HISTORY

Lotus' first serious road car. A fiberglass, monocoque two-seat coupe with virtually no steel body reinforcement. Smooth styling was marked by a low-set oval air intake, sloping hood, fixed door glass, and a neat, cut-off tail. The chassis featured fully independent suspension and four-wheel disc brakes. Power was supplied by an all-aluminum overhead cam four made by Coventry Climax and offered in various states of tune (71/83/95/105 bhp). British BMC or German ZF manual transmissions were used. The initial Series I models had a MacPherson-type rear suspension layout (called "Chapman strut" by Lotus). The Series II had revised lower wishbone geometry, and was built in greater numbers. A somewhat fragile car that was expensive for Lotus to build and customers to buy, but gave the firm valuable "volume" production experience. Costly to keep on the road and not all that refined, but a high-appreciation investment of ageless beauty.

FOR

Styling ● Technical sophistication ● Handling ● Performance (up to 120 mph) ● Good economy ● High appreciation potential

AGAINST

Engine, suspension breakdowns common ● Fiberglass deteriorates ● Noisy ● Parts now in short supply

SPECIFICATIONS

Length (in.) 148.0 **Wheelbase (in.)** 88.0 **Weight (lbs.)** 1460 **Price (new)** NA

ENGINES

cc/type (cid)	bore x stroke (mm)	bhp*	years
1216/ohc I4 (74)	76×67	71-105	1959-63

*net

PRICES/PROJECTION

Restorable $4000-6000 **Good** $8000-10,000
Excellent $10,000-13,000 **5-year projection** +10%

Lotus Elan
1962-73

1970 Elan S4 coupe

PRODUCTION

9659

HISTORY

If the Elite was Lotus' first serious road car, the Elan was the first practical one. It also introduced what would become a Lotus design trademark, a folded-steel "backbone" chassis. The diminutive fiberglass body was available in open and closed styles, distinguished by neat lines and pop-up headlamps. Power was supplied by the 1558cc twincam Lotus four based on the British Ford push-rod unit. The Elan progressed through five different series, designated S1 to S4 through 1971, followed by the Elan Sprint. Power went from 105 bhp at first to 115, (net) then to 126 (DIN) for the Sprint. Trim and equipment were also steadily upgraded. Tiny size, light weight, all-independent suspension, and fast rack-and-pinion steering made the Elan the standard for sports car handling and roadholding in its day. Passenger and cargo space were both very restricted, but ideal for those young-at-heart types small enough to fit. Quite quick, too—up to 120 mph, which is excellent zing for a 1.6-liter car. Imported to the U.S. in relatively small numbers.

FOR

Performance ● Roadability ● Mechanically simple (apart from engine) ● Surprising mileage ● Neat styling ● High fun quotient ● Good investment

AGAINST

Engine not reliable ● Cramped interior ● Roadster's old-fashioned top ● Very vulnerable to crash damage ● Size works against you in heavy traffic ● Body parts now impossible to come by

SPECIFICATIONS

Length (in.) 145.0   **Wheelbase (in.)** 84.0   **Weight (lbs.)** 1515
Price (new) approx. $5600 U.S. for S/E roadster in 1967

ENGINES

cc/type (cid)	bore x stroke (mm)	bhp*	years
1558/dohc I4 (95)	83×73	105-126	1962-73

*See text

PRICES/PROJECTION

Restorable $2000-3000   **Good** $4000-5000
Excellent $5000-9000 Add up to 50% for late-model "Big Valve"
engine   **5-year projection** +10%

Lotus Elan+2
1967-74

1967-70 Elan +2 coupe

PRODUCTION

4798

HISTORY

Essentially a stretched version of the Elan, sharing the same chassis layout and drivetrain. As the name suggests, the +2 rode a longer wheelbase that was supposed to provide enough cabin space for an extra pair of passengers, but in reality this was still only a two-seater, albeit less cramped than its smaller sister. The graceful fiberglass bodyshell was styled along similar lines, but was trimmed and equipped to a higher standard. Unlike the Elan, the +2 was never available in kit form. Beginning in 1971, a revised model appeared, called the +2S 130, with more horsepower. In the fall of 1972, a five-speed gearbox became available for the +2S 130/5. All models were capable of reaching about 120 mph.

FOR

As for 1962-73 Elan, plus roomier interior and greater U.S. rarity
• High-value appreciation

AGAINST

As for 1962-73 Elan, but harder to find in U.S.

SPECIFICATIONS

Length (in.) 169.0   **Wheelbase (in.)** 96.0   **Weight (lbs.)** 2085
Price (new) approx. $6800 U.S. for +2S 130 in 1972

ENGINES

cc/type (cid)	bore x stroke (mm)	bhp*	years
1558/dohc I4 (95)	83×73	115/126	1967-74

*net/DIN

PRICES/PROJECTION

Restorable $1500-2500   **Good** $3500-5000
Excellent $5000-10,000 Add up to 50% for late-model "Big Valve"
engine   **5-year projection** +10%

Lotus Europa
1967-72

1967-71 Europa coupe

PRODUCTION

9230

HISTORY

Lotus' first mid-engine car, intended as a running mate to the front-engine Elan (and possibly as its eventual successor). Less expensive to build, however, because of proprietary drivetrain borrowed from the front-drive Renault 16 sedan. In the Europa, the engine was turned around back-to-front and mounted behind the tiny two-seat cockpit to drive the rear wheels. The separate bodyshell was made of fiberglass as on other Lotus models, but featured broad, high sail panels aft of the doors that earned the nickname "breadvan." The front end was reminiscent of the Elite's, with a low nose, small oval air intake, and scooped headlight recesses. The result was a lightweight car with impeccable handling but the same cramped interior and dubious construction quality that were limiting the Elan's market appeal. Because of Lotus' desire to crack the Common Market (one reason for using the Renault drivetrain), all Series I models were sold outside England. The Series II arrived in 1970 with bolt-on, instead of bonded, body attachment and the larger 1565cc version of the Renault four from the 16TS. In 1972, Lotus fitted its own twincam 1558cc four (based on the British Ford ohv "Kent" engine) to produce the Series III, which also got slightly lower sail panels for a marginal visibility improvement. In the U.S., this model was known as the Europa Special, and was equipped with the "Big Valve" Lotus dohc engine. A 5-speed gearbox was optional. U.S. imports were sporadic up to late 1969, after which the Europa was officially certified for U.S. sale. This means most of the ones you'll find for sale here will be late Series II and Special models.

FOR

Technical interest • Marvelous roadability • Good mileage • Fine twincam performance • Lotus pedigree • Strong appreciation

AGAINST

Dubious spare parts supplies now • Very cramped cockpit • Wicked rear vision • Fragile in a crack-up • Spotty construction quality

SPECIFICATIONS

Length (in.) 156.5   **Wheelbase (in.)** 91.0   **Weight (lbs.)** 1350
Price (new) $4695 U.S. in 1969; approx. $6000 U.S. in 1973

ENGINES

cc/type (cid)	bore x stroke (mm)	bhp	years
1470/ohv I4 (90)	76×81	78[1]	1967-70
1565/ohv I4 (95.5)	77×84	87[2]	1970-72
1558/dohc I4 (95.1)	83×73	113[3]	1973-74

1. net
2. SAE net
3. SAE net for U.S. model

PRICES/PROJECTION

Restorable $1500-3000 **Good** $3000-4000
Excellent $4000-5000 Add 25% for late-model Special
5-year projection +30%

Lotus Esprit 1976-80

1980 Esprit S2 coupe by Ital Design

PRODUCTION

S1 1060 **S2** 88

HISTORY

One of Colin Chapman's best, and among current Lotus cars the one with the best chance for long-term acclaim among collectors. Originated as a design exercise from Giorgetto Giugiaro's Ital Design firm as shown at the 1972 Turin auto show. It made the transition to production reality with remarkably few changes — even Giugiaro's suggested name for it was retained. Beautifully chiseled styling of the "flying doorstop" school looks futuristic and has exceptionally good aerodynamics. As on other '70s Lotus cars, the body is executed in fiberglass with color impregnated into the plastic by a closely guarded Lotus process. An all-business cockpit encourages serious driving, and performance is ample: 0-60 mph in about 9 seconds, a top (fifth) gear speed of 120 mph. Yet fuel economy from the Lotus designed dohc four, mounted amidships, is excellent: 27-28 mpg at moderate cruising speeds. Despite a rear end weight bias, the Esprit's road manners are in the Lotus tradition, which is to say excellent, going from moderate understeer to final oversteer when pressed. Progressed from Series I to Series II specifications in 1980, and a companion Turbo model was intro-

duced with even more performance. Still more of an "elite car" than a collectible at this writing because of newness, but if you've got one now, hang onto it: we think it can't miss as a future treasure.

FOR

Styling • Performance • Handling • Economy • Rot-free fiberglass body • Great fun on twisty two-lanes

AGAINST

Typical mid-engine sacrifices in people and luggage space • Quality-control problems • Poor ventilation • Apt to remain costly for a long while yet • Limited parts and service backup

SPECIFICATIONS

Length (in.) 167.7   **Wheelbase (in.)** 96.0   **Weight (lbs.)** 2350
Price (new) $15,990 U.S. in 1976

ENGINES

cc/type (cid)	bore x stroke (mm)	bhp*	years
1973/dohc I4 (120)	95×69	125-140	1976-80

*SAE net

PRICES/PROJECTION

Restorable $5000-7000 **Good** $8000-12,000
Excellent $14,000-24,000 **5-year projection** +15%

Maserati A6/1500 1946-50

PRODUCTION

60

HISTORY

The first road-going Maserati, built and sold in small numbers. Offered in two-seat closed coupe or open cabriolet body styles designed by Pinin Farina. The front end on both was smooth, marked by a radiator similar to that of Maserati's racing machines. In overall shape, there was a slight resemblance to the Lancia Aurelia coupe. The A6/1500 naturally owed much to the competition Masers, including its large-diameter-tube chassis with coil spring independent front suspension and conventional live axle rear suspension. The engine was an sohc six developed from a late-'30s racing unit. It was very small for a six, and produced only 65 horsepower, so the car was not very fast (the factory claimed only 94 mph tops). Not very exciting to drive, either, and expensive when new, but a high-interest collectible as the first of the great Maserati road cars.

FOR

Historical interest • Reliable engine • Solid chassis • Rarity

AGAINST

Parts nonexistent today • Not very fast • Crudely finished • Difficult to find

SPECIFICATIONS

Length (in.) 160.0   **Wheelbase (in.)** 100.4   **Weight (lbs.)** 1765
Price (new) NA

ENGINES

cc/type (cid)	bore x stroke (mm)	bhp*	years
1488/sohc I6 (91)	66×73	65	1946-50

*net

PRICES/PROJECTION

Restorable $5000-20,000 **Good** $20,000-25,000
Excellent $25,000-30,000 **5-year projection** no change

Maserati AG6 & AG6/2000 1951-57

PRODUCTION

sohc engine 16 **dohc engine** 59

HISTORY

Successor to the A6/1500 as Maserati's "production" model, and based on a similar chassis and mechanical layout. Powered initially by a larger single overhead cam six, later revised with a dohc engine that was essentially a detuned version of Maserati's sports-racing/Grand Prix unit. All models featured two-seat custom-built bodies. Design work was handled by Vignale, Frua, Zagato, Allemano, and (with sohc engine only) Pinin Farina. Styling differed according to coachbuilder, the only common link being the grille.

FOR

As for 1946-50 A6/1500, plus more performance with twincam engine

AGAINST

As for A6/1500

SPECIFICATIONS

Length (in.) 154.0 (average; variable with body)
Wheelbase (in.) 100.4 **Weight (lbs.)** 1900 (average)
Price (new) NA

ENGINES

cc/type (cid)	bore x stroke (mm)	bhp*	years
1954/sohc I6 (119)	72×80	100	1951-53
1985/dohc I6 (121)	77×72	150	1953-57

*net

PRICES/PROJECTION

Restorable $10,000-30,000 **Good** $30,000-50,000
Excellent $50,000-60,000 **5-year projection** +10%

Maserati 3500GT/GTI 1957-64

PRODUCTION

2223

1958-62 3500GT coupe by Touring

HISTORY

The first Maserati produced in any significant numbers. Like many Italian exotics of the day, built on a simple, robust chassis composed of large-diameter tubes. Despite their fairly long wheelbase, these were two-seat cars only. All bodies were custom made in the Italian tradition, and the maximum production rate was just 10 cars per week. A coupe (supplied mostly by Touring) and a Spider roadster (by Vignale) were offered. The former was marked by straight-through fenderlines and the characteristic air vents in the front fenders behind the wheel openings. Power was supplied by an enlarged version of Maserati's famous dohc Grand Prix engine of the '50s, with mechanical fuel injection (GTI) from 1962 on. Also at that time, all cars got four-wheel disc brakes. As befits a small specialist manufacturer, no two 3500GTs were exactly the same, customers being able to specify changes from the "standard" spec to suit their individual needs and tastes.

FOR

High performance (130 mph maximum) ●Strong, reliable engine ●Fine brakes ●Handsome styling ●Roadability ●Racing heritage

AGAINST

Factory now out of parts ●Most survivors have seen hard lives ●Only two seats ●Injection tricky to service

SPECIFICATIONS

Length (in.) 180.0 **Wheelbase (in.)** 102.3 **Weight (lbs.)** 3400
Price (new) $11,400 U.S. list price in 1960

ENGINES

cc/type (cid)	bore x stroke (mm)	bhp*	years
3485/dohc I6 (213)	86×100	220/235	1957-64

*net bhp for carbureted/injected engine

PRICES/PROJECTION

Restorable $2000-3000 **Good** $9000-10,000
Excellent $10,000-12,000 **5-year projection** +10%

Maserati Sebring 1962-66

PRODUCTION

Series I 348 **Series II** 98

HISTORY

Rebodied, modernized successor to the 3500GTI, sharing the same chassis and drivetrain. Built exclusively with Vignale coachwork, a ruggedly styled two-seat notchback coupe marked by quad headlamps and an eggcrate grille incorporating a prominent Maserati trident emblem.

FOR

As for 1958-64 3500GT/GTI

AGAINST

As for 1958-64 3500GT/GTI

SPECIFICATIONS

Length (in.) 176.0   **Wheelbase (in.)** 102.3   **Weight (lbs.)** 3330
Price (new) NA

ENGINES

cid/type	bore x stroke	bhp*	years
3694/dohc I6	86 × 106	245	1962-66
*net			

PRICES/PROJECTION

Restorable $3000-5000 **Good** $7000-10,000
Excellent $10,000-12,000 **5-year projection** +10%

Maserati Mistral 1963-70

1963-70 Mistrale coupe by Frua

PRODUCTION

Coupe 828   **Spider** 120

HISTORY

A more sporty-looking running mate to the Sebring coupe, with sleek styling by Pietro Frua and better performance from extra displacement for Maserati's twincam engine. Both the fastback coupe and Spider roadster bore Frua's characteristic design themes: long, sloping hood leading down to a blade-like front bumper surmounting the grille; a tall, glassy greenhouse; rounded corners; and a high, short tail. The Coupe featured a lift-up wraparound rear window/hatch, and the Spider was quite close to Frua's later AC 428 in overall appearance. Acceleration was electrifying, yet the Mistrale (named for a hot desert wind) was at its best on the open road, which it could devour with prodigious ease.

FOR

As for 1962-66 Sebring, plus handsome Frua lines, more go

AGAINST

As for 1962-66 Sebring

SPECIFICATIONS

Length (in.) 177.0   **Wheelbase (in.)** 94.4   **Weight (lbs.)** 2800
(approx.)   **Price (new)** $14,700 U.S. in 1968

ENGINES

cc/type (cid)	bore x stroke (mm)	bhp*	years
3964/dohc I6 (225)	86 × 106	245	1963-70
4012/dohc I6 (245)	88 × 110	255	1963-70
*net			

PRICES/PROJECTION

Restorable $4000-8000 **Good** $8000-10,000
Excellent $12,000-15,000 Add 20% for 1969 models, 50% for convertible **5-year projection** +20%

Maserati Quattroporte 1963-69

1963-69 Quattroporte (4-door sedan) by Frua

PRODUCTION

759

HISTORY

A four-seat Italian supercar with four-door convenience was a rarity in the '60s. It still is, which makes the Quattroporte (Italian for "four doors") an unusual collectible for high-performance enthusiasts. Once again, Maserati gave its styling brief to Pietro Frua, who devised an interesting mix of curves and angles for this very large GT. As on his Mistral, the sedan's greenhouse was tall, very glassy, and showed noticeable curvature. A jutting "mouth" carrying the Maserati trident was flanked by twin rectangular headlamps (changed to four round units on later European and all U.S. models). The chassis was a combination of tubular and box-section elements, and incorporated disc brakes for all wheels. A De Dion rear suspension was used initially, but was later discarded in favor of a less troublesome, bog-simple live axle on semi-elliptic leaf springs. Power was supplied by a four-cam V8, essentially a "pro-dified" version of the mighty 450S racing engine of the late '50s. This would continue as Maserati's main powerplant well into the '70s. For the Quattroporte, it was destroked to 4.2 liters, then upped a bit to 4.7 with the switch in rear suspension. Of the total number built, approximately 500 cars have the larger power unit. Aside from Iso's unsuccessful S4 Fidia, no other producer of high-performance GTs tried the GT sedan idea, though Aston Martin thought about it. Maserati gave up on it for a few years, partly due to financial troubles, but brought out another Quattroporte for the European market in 1979. It's on sale in the U.S. at this writing.

FOR

Supercar go with four-door convenience •Distinctive design •Sumptuous, spacious cabin •Fast (130 mph) •Reliable engine, and still in production •Not costly, all things considered

AGAINST

Thirsty •Questionable body construction •Trouble-prone De Dion suspension •Costly to restore and run •Not likely to go up in value soon

SPECIFICATIONS

Length (in.) 196.0 **Wheelbase (in.)** 108.0 **Weight (lbs.)** 3810
Price (new) $15,000 (U.S.)

ENGINES

cc/type (cid)	bore x stroke (mm)	bhp*	years
4136/dohc V8 (253)	88×85	260	1963-68
4719/dohc V8 (288)	94×85	290	1968-69

*net

PRICES/PROJECTION

Restorable $4000-6000 **Good** $6000-8000
Excellent $8000-9000 **5-year projection** +10%

Maserati Mexico 1965-68

1966 Mexico coupe by Vignale

PRODUCTION

250

HISTORY

A high-style, four-seat notchback coupe built on a short-wheelbase version of the Quattroporte sedan's platform chassis. Styling and body construction were by the Vignale coachworks, marked by a low beltline, slim roof pillars, a broad hood, wide grille, four headlamps, and squared-up rear wheel openings. Fitted exclusively with the Quattroporte's leaf-spring rear suspension, not the earlier De Dion arrangement, and genuine wire wheels. The larger-displacement rendition of Maserati's quad-cam V8 was tuned to produce 330 bhp in this application. Like the sedan, the Mexico was fitted with ZF five-speed manual transmission.

FOR

As for 1963-70 Quattroporte (but two doors and less passenger room) •Clean looks •Greater scarcity

AGAINST

As for 1963-70 Quattroporte

SPECIFICATIONS

Length (in.) 187.4 **Wheelbase (in.)** 103.5 **Weight (lbs.)** 3640
Price (new) NA

ENGINES

cc/type (cid)	bore x stroke (mm)	bhp*	years
4136/dohc V8 (253)	88×85	260	1965-68
4719/dohc V8 (288)	94×85	330	1965-68

net bhp

PRICES/PROJECTION

As for Mistral

Maserati Ghibli 1967-73

1967-73 Ghibli coupe by Ghia

PRODUCTION

Coupe 1149 **Spider** 125

HISTORY

Replacement for the Mistrale as Maserati's premium two-seat GT. The most memorable thing about the Ghibli is its styling — masculine yet sensuously curvy, with perfect proportions and adroit detailing courtesy of Giorgetto Giugiaro. The long snout sported flip-up headlamps at its leading edge, and the full-fastback roofline swept right back to a short, cropped trail panel. The low, ground-hugging appearance suggested considerable heft, and the steel-body Ghibli was indeed quite weighty (nearly two tons). Yet, it was capable of up to 160 mph thanks to extra displacement and output from the Maserati four-cam V8. The chassis was basically the same as that of the Quattroporte/Mexico, still with leaf-spring rear suspension, but wheelbase was shorter. Maserati's best until it was replaced by the mid-engine Bora, and a rival for Ferrari's 375GTB/4 and the Lamborghini Miura in its heyday. Buying, restoring, and then running one will take an understanding banker, but even after 10 years a Ghibli is one of the sexiest collectibles you can have in your garage.

FOR

Beautiful styling (less so on street-legal U.S. models after 1970) ●Amazing performance ●Fine furnishings ●Marvelous Maserati engine ●Good appreciation potential

AGAINST

As for 1965-68 Mexico, plus early rust-out if body neglected ●Fuelishness ●Mixed assembly quality

SPECIFICATIONS

Length (in.) 180.7 **Wheelbase (in.)** 100.4 **Weight (lbs.)** 3745
Price (new) $20,000 (1971 U.S. list price)

ENGINES

cc/type (cid)	bore x stroke (mm)	bhp*	years
4719/dohc V8 (288)	94×85	330	1967-70
4930/dohc V8 (301)	94×89	355	1970-72

*net

PRICES/PROJECTION

Restorable $7000-12,000 **Good** $13,000-17,000
Excellent $17,000-21,000 Add 55% for convertible
5-year projection +20%

Maserati Indy
1969-74

1969-74 Indy coupe by Vignale

PRODUCTION

1136

HISTORY

Replaced the Mexico as Maserati's four-seat GT, and differed from the firm's other front engine V8 cars in using steel unit body/chassis construction. Styling, by Vignale, was completely different in detail from that of the Ghia-bodied Ghibli, yet the two cars had some

familial relationship, particularly in the long, shark-like nose with hidden headlamps. The Indy sported a longer greenhouse with a prominent B-pillar, however, and rode a longer 102.5-inch wheelbase. More a 2+2 than a genuine four-seater, yet proved popular nonetheless, and offered the bonus of generous (for the class) luggage space under a large rear hatch. Available with ZF manual or an optional automatic transmission like other V8 Maseratis. The Indy was dropped during an ownership change in 1975-76 when Maserati was taken over (briefly as it turned out) by Citroen.

FOR

Neat, trim lines ●Four-seat accommodation ●High flyer (155 mph) ●Engine parts still available

AGAINST

Unit-construction rust worries ●Body panels difficult to find ●Thirsty ●Costly to restore and insure

SPECIFICATIONS

Length (in.) 186.6 **Wheelbase (in.)** 102.5 **Weight (lbs.)** 3640
Price (new) $18,500 (1970 U.S. list price)

ENGINES

cc/type (cid)	bore x stroke (mm)	bhp*	years
4136/dohc V8 (253)	88×85	260	1969-72
4719/dohc V8 (288)	94×85	330	1972-73
4930/dohc V8 (301)	94×89	355	1973-74

*net

PRICES/PROJECTION

Restorable $6000-10,000 **Good** $12,000-15,000
Excellent $17,000-24,000 **5-year projection** +20%

Maserati Bora
1971-80

1971-80 Bora coupe by Ital Design (U.S. model)

PRODUCTION

571

HISTORY

The first evidence of what would be a fairly brief Citroën/Maserati alliance. Introduced at the 1971 Geneva salon, with production beginning the following year. Unusual in using Citroën's high-pressure hydraulics to power its brakes. The same system also actuated the standard power seats, and unusually the pedals were adjustable as well. Powered by Maserati's well-proven quad-cam

V8 mounted longitudinally amidships and driving the rear wheels through a ZF 5-speed gearbox. Initially, displacement was 4.7 liters for the European market, but U.S. models used the larger 4.9-liter version as in the Ghibli and, later, the Khamsin. The mid-engine layout afforded a natural rear weight bias that obviated the need for power steering. Aggressively muscular styling by Giorgetto Giugiaro featured a short, pointy nose, bulging bodysides, a full fastback roof tapering to a sharply cut off tail, neatly upswept door windows, and a squat, powerful-looking stance. Roomy for a mid-engine two-seater, and surprisingly refined. Naturally, it was fast, with 0-60 mph coming up in about 7.5 seconds from rest and a top end of 160 mph available for those who could indulge such things. Maserati's up-and-down financial fortunes in the '70s, aggravated by a sudden drop in the supercar market following the 1973-74 Arab oil embargo, made the Bora a very expensive commodity. Ultimately, high price and high fuel consumption forced the end of production. Not a high-appreciation item at the moment, but seems certain to gain in stature.

FOR

Powerful looks • Powerful performance • Surprisingly light and easy to drive • Phenomenal roadability • Engine parts still readily available • Dash like a 747's

AGAINST

Easily confused with tamer Merak cousin • Thirsty • Costly to acquire and maintain • Brakes take getting used to

SPECIFICATIONS

Length (in.) 181.0 **Wheelbase (in.)** 102.3
Weight (lbs.) approx. 3800 **Price (new)** $26,900 U.S. in 1973, rising to $39,900 in 1978

ENGINES

cc/type (cid)	bore x stroke (mm)	bhp*	years
4930/dohc V8 (301)	94×89	280-335	1971-80

*net

PRICES/PROJECTION

Restorable $10,000-18,000 **Good** $20,000-23,000
Excellent $23,000-30,000 **5-year projection** +20%

Maserati Merak 1972-80

1977-79 Merak/SS coupe by Ital Design (U.S. model)

PRODUCTION

1666

HISTORY

Very much a little brother to the V8 Bora, sharing its wheelbase, forward body structure, and mid-engine configuration. But the Merak was arguably more Citroën than Maserati, borrowing the Maserati-designed dohc V6 engine, 5-speed transmission, and even the dashboard from the Citroën SM. The Merak also differed from the Bora in rear structure, having a flat rear deck and non-structural "flying buttresses" that carried the roofline down to the tail panel instead of a hatch and glassed-in rear quarters. Also made use of Citroën hydraulics for its all-disc braking system, but lacked the Bora's hydraulically adjustable seats. The 90-degree V6 was shorter than it was wide, so it was mounted fore/aft instead of transversely as in Ferrari's 308 series. In fact, the Merak used the SM's entire front-wheel-drive package turned around 180 degrees, which left room for a pair of tiny rear seats suitable only for infants. Lighter and a bit more economical than the Bora, but not as fast—though 0-60 mph in around 9 seconds is hardly loafing. Meraks sent to the U.S. up through 1977 suffered compared to their Italian counterparts in having unsightly bulges in the rear decklid to provide air cleaner clearance. Following dissolution of the Citroën/Maserati "marriage" and Maserati's subsequent takeover by Alejandro de Tomaso, a revised version called the Merak/SS was issued, which did away with this as well as the SM dash (replaced by fittings from the by-now discontinued Bora). Withdrawn from the U.S. market after 1979, a victim of surging fuel prices and inflation.

FOR

Giugiaro styling • Splendid roadability • Marginal +2 seating, unusual for a mid-engine GT • Comfortable, well-appointed cockpit • Still in production, so parts no hassle

AGAINST

Looks outsized now • Not that thrifty with fuel • Same cam-drive problems and hydraulic system worries that plague the SM • Odd Citroën dash in early models • Little collector following at present

SPECIFICATIONS

Length (in.) 180.0 **Wheelbase (in.)** 102.3
Weight (lbs.) approx. 3200 **Price (new)** $19,975 U.S. in 1974, rising to $40,550 in 1981

ENGINES

cc/type (cid)	bore x stroke (mm)	bhp*	years
2965/dohc V6 (181)	92×75	180-182	1972-80

*SAE net

PRICES/PROJECTION

Restorable $8000-12,000 **Good** $14,000-17,000
Excellent $17,000-23,000 **5-year projection** +15%

Maserati Khamsin 1974-80

PRODUCTION

412

1974-80 Khamsin coupe by Bertone

Mercedes-Benz Type 770 Grosser 1930-37

1930-31 Type 770 Grosser *Cabriolet F*

PRODUCTION

117

HISTORY

It wasn't easy to follow a styling masterwork like the Ghibli, but Bertone succeeded with its show-stopping successor. Following Maserati's practice of naming its cars after fierce desert winds, it was dubbed Khamsin, and debuted at the 1972 Turin show to replace the Giugiaro-designed car as Maserati's big front-engine GT. Its dashing contours were highlighted by marked tumblehome on a low greenhouse, a very long hood with asymmetrically placed lateral cooling louvers, hidden headlamps, and a Kamm-style tail panel with a glass insert between the taillamps to assist rearward vision in what was a fairly low car. The snug cabin afforded a low seating position up front and occasional rear accommodation on a none-too-comfortable, thinly padded bench. Like its predecessor, the Khamsin utilized a front-engine/rear-drive configuration and the powerful Maserati quad-cam V8. Unlike the Ghibli, though, it had fully independent rear suspension — A-arms and coil springs — instead of a solid axle on leaf springs. Reflecting Maserati's then-current partnership with Citroën, the Khamsin used the French firm's high-pressure hydraulic system for power assistance to the steering and brakes, and even the clutch. The result was a driving feel unique among Italian supercars. The steering, for instance, required only two turns lock-to-lock, and would automatically self-center with the vehicle at standstill. A ZF 5-speed manual gearbox put the power to the road (automatic was optional), which meant about 7 seconds to 60 mph for a determined driver and easy three-figure cruising speeds. Withdrawn from the U.S. market after 1979, but produced through 1981 for Europe and other areas.

HISTORY

D-B's self-indulgent Depression-era flagship, announced four years after the merger between Daimler and Benz. Massive, powerful, and ponderous, it was intended for heads of state and certain political leaders, hence the use of the name "Grand." Smooth and dignified by German standards and easy to drive slowly as well as quickly. Newly designed overhead-valve straight eight. Supercharger, plus vacuum-servo brakes and optional Maybach pre-selector gearbox, but ordinary beam axles front and rear and rather undistinguished, though lavishly furnished, bodywork. Some survivors are erroneously billed as the "Hitler Mercedes," though it's doubtful *Der Fuhrer* had only one as his personal car. Emperor Hirohito of Japan bought seven, which he used into the 1960s.

FOR

Sex appeal •High performance, Italian-style •Finely balanced handling/roadholding •Light controls •Ride still firm, but more comfortable than Ghibli's •Parts still available.

FOR

Period M-B flagship • Exclusivity • Cost-no-object engineering

AGAINST

Thirsty (12 mpg or so) •Complex mechanicals, so frequent (and costly) service a must •Dealers aren't everywhere •Erratic construction quality

AGAINST

Heavy styling • Heavy to drive (no power steering) • No parts for restoration • Very expensive • Too much historical hype keeps them that way

SPECIFICATIONS

Length (in.) 180.0 **Wheelbase (in.)** 100.3
Weight (lbs.) approx. 3800 **Price (new)** $32,975 U.S. list in 1975; $42,600 in 1978

SPECIFICATIONS

Length (in.) 210.0 **Wheelbase (in.)** 136.0 **Weight (lbs.)** 6000+
Price (new) NA

ENGINES

cc/type (cid)	bore x stroke (mm)	bhp*	years
4930/dohc V8 (301)	94×89	280-315	1974-80

*SAE net

ENGINES

cc/type (cid)	bore x stroke (mm)	bhp*	years
7655/ohv I8 (467)	95×135	150/200	1930-37

*net; supercharger out/in

PRICES/PROJECTION

Similar to Bora prices **5-year projection** +20%

PRICES/PROJECTION

Restorable $50,000-70,000 **Good** $80,000-250,000
Excellent $150,000-300,000 Values vary somewhat with coachwork. **5-year projection** +20%

Mercedes-Benz 380K/500K/540K 1933-39

1935 Type 500K Special Roadster

PRODUCTION

380K (1933-34) 114 **500K (1934-36)** 354 **540K (1936-39)** 447

HISTORY

Streamlined 1930s followup to the massive Porsche-designed S/SS/SSK of the late '20s. Supercharged straight eight with clutch-in blower as before, but all-independent suspension and more touring than sports car in character. New engine design by Hans Nibel, one of his last works, progressively enlarged. D-B's Sindelfingen works supplied the vulgar but impressive and comfortable bodies. Top speed was 90 mph for the 380K up to 105 mph+ for the 540K. D-B's ultimate in this period apart from the *Grossers* and priced accordingly, hence the low production. Ideal for swishing along Hitler's new *autobahnen* but harder work on twisting roads (no power steering, but hydraulic brakes on later cars). Styling was the great selling point, especially on the beautifully streamlined 500/540 Special Roadster. Has distinction now as among the most expensive of collector cars.

FOR

German period styling • 500/540 performance • Mercedes reliability • Latter-day charisma/value

AGAINST

Very expensive to buy and restore • Heavy fuel consumption

1935 Type 500K 2-seat coupe

1936 Type 540K 2-seat coupe

• Hard work to drive • No body and few mechanical parts to be found

SPECIFICATIONS

Length (in.) 185-205 **Wheelbase (in.)** 123.5 (380K); 129.5 (500/540K) **Weight (lbs.)** 4500-5100 **Price (new)** $12,000 U.S. (1936-39)

ENGINES

cc/type (cid)	bore x stroke (mm)	bhp*	years
3823/ohv I8 (233)	75×100	90/120	1933-34[1]
5019/ohv I8 (306)	86×108	100/160	1934-36[2]
5401/ohv I8 (330)	88×111	115/180	1936-39[3]

*net; supercharger out/in
[1] 380
[2] 500
[3] 540

PRICES/PROJECTION

Restorable $44,000-55,000 **Good** $99,000-220,000 **Excellent** $220,000-275,000 **5-year projection** +20%

Mercedes-Benz Type 770 Grosser 1938-40

PRODUCTION

88

HISTORY

Titanic successor to the original *Grosser*, built largely for the greater glory of the Third Reich. Heavier and more ostentatious, with a slightly more powerful version of the previous straight eight. More up to date, with oval-tube chassis, coil-spring independent front suspension, and De Dion rear suspension, all as per D-B's most recent Grand Prix racers. As with the earlier model, production was strictly to special order. Predictably, most were reserved for Adolf Hitler and his cronies and had gargantuan bodies with armor plating.

1939 Type 770 Grosser limousine

FOR

Rarity • Presence • More modern styling, engineering • Most of M-B's best in this period

AGAINST

As big and heavy as they come—and as impractical • No parts for restoration • Amazingly expensive to buy and own • Little to excite the enthusiast

SPECIFICATIONS

Length (in.) 246.0 **Wheelbase (in.)** 155.0
Weight (lbs.) 7600-8100 **Price (new)** NA

ENGINES

cc/type (cid)	bore x stroke (mm)	bhp	years
7655/ohv I8 (467)	95×135	155/230	1938-40

*net; supercharger out/in

PRICES/PROJECTION

Restorable $110,000-165,000 **Good** $300,000-350,000
Excellent $380,000-440,000 **5-year projection** +20%

Mercedes-Benz Type 300 1951-62

PRODUCTION

1951-55 300/300b 6214 **1955-57 300c** 1432
1957-62 300d 3077

HISTORY

The first completely new offering from Daimler-Benz following World War II, with the emphasis mainly on engineering. A big car for big occasions, the 300 featured new running gear from end to end, including an overhead cam 3.0-liter inline six that would later gain fame in the 300SL racing and road-going sports cars. The chassis was an oval-tube affair with independent suspension all around. Rear ride height was electrically adjustable from inside by means of auxiliary torsion bars. Massive for a European car, with "transition" styling that marked M-B's move to more modern full-width envelope body lines. Remained in production for a decade, but in its last

1951-55 Type 300/300b 4-door sedan

years was mostly an indulgence for the firm. The design went through four distinct phases. More horsepower, optional automatic transmission, and a higher final drive were offered beginning with the 300c in 1955. The 300d introduced in 1957 was more powerful still. Offered as pillared and pillarless four-door sedans plus a limousine model, all with upright, traditional lines featuring a tall Mercedes grille, semi-integrated front fenders, and a short, rounded rump. Ponderous to drive, but meticulously engineered and beautifully finished.

FOR

Solid separate chassis • Thorough, somewhat advanced engineering for the time • "Gothic" styling for those who like it • Spaciousness • Well-equipped

AGAINST

Bulky and tedious in tight spots • Parts impossible to find • Pricey now, and not cheap to restore or maintain

SPECIFICATIONS

Length (in.) 195.0 (limo: 204.0) **Wheelbase (in.)** 120.0 (limo: 124.0) **Weight (lbs.)** 3860-4400 **Price (new)** NA

ENGINES

cc/type (cid)	bore x stroke (mm)	bhp*	years
2996/ohc I6 (183)	85×88	115/125/160	1951-62

*DIN

PRICES/PROJECTION

Restorable $5000-8000 **Good** $8000-10,000
Excellent $10,000-15,000 **5-year projection** +10%

Mercedes-Benz Type 300S/Sc 1952-58

PRODUCTION

300S: coupe 216 **convertible** 203 **roadster** 141
300Sc: coupe 98 **convertible** 49 **roadster** 53

HISTORY

Massive but tremendously impressive short-wheelbase derivatives of Mercedes' flagship sedan series, offering greater engine power and even better equipment. The initial 300S had a 150-bhp version of the normal 3.0-liter straight six. The later Sc switched from carburetors to fuel injection (related to the 300SL system) to obtain an

1955-58 Type 300Sc coupe

extra 50 horses. Styling was very much in the late '30s mold. Open versions were offered both with and without roll-down windows and folding top, and the fixed-roof coupe had very broad rear quarters and a small rear window.

FOR

As for 1951-62 Type 300, plus more power and performance, and more manageable

AGAINST

As for 1951-62 Type 300

SPECIFICATIONS

Length (in.) 186.0 **Wheelbase (in.)** 114.0 **Weight (lbs.)** 3600 (average) **Price (new)** NA

ENGINES

cc/type (cid)	bore x stroke (mm)	bhp*	years
2996/ohc I6 (183)	85×88	150/220	1952-58

*gross

PRICES/PROJECTION

Restorable $10,000-15,000 **Good** $30,000-35,000
Excellent $40,000-50,000 **5-year projection** +10%

Mercedes-Benz 190SL 1955-63

1955-63 190SL convertible with hardtop

PRODUCTION

25,881

HISTORY

The first high-volume Daimler-Benz sports car, and one of the firm's best-known U.S. models in the '50s. Followed Austin-Healey/Triumph TR practice in using mass-production components, in this case the four-cylinder engine, running gear, and (shortened) floorpan from the Type 180 sedan series. Styling was deliberately chosen for close identification with the exotic 300SL, and featured a similar low grille, long hood, wheel opening eyebrows, and generally rounded contours. Not really intended for competition use, and too heavy for its engine anyway, but a pleasant tourer with a top speed capability of slightly more than 105 mph. Many left the factory with a removable steel top in addition to the normal folding fabric roof. Easier to maintain and cheaper to own than a 300SL then and now. Built with all the solid integrity for which Mercedes had long been famous. Overlooked for many years because of its stolid performance, the 190SL is still reasonably priced on the collector market and fairly available, as a good many made their way to the States. In all, an unbeatable combination of open-air driving appeal and the magic of the three-pointed star.

FOR

Mercedes cachet • Solid construction • Simple engineering means fairly easy upkeep • Some mechanical parts still available

AGAINST

Limited performance • Tricky swing-axle handling/roadholding • Rust-prone • Expensive upkeep

SPECIFICATIONS

Length (in.) 169.0 **Wheelbase (in.)** 94.5 **Weight (lbs.)** 2515
Price (new) $4000 (original U.S. list price)

ENGINES

cc/type (cid)	bore x stroke (mm)	bhp*	years
1897/ohc I4 (116)	85×84	120	1955-63

*gross

PRICES/PROJECTION

Restorable $5000-8000 **Good** $8000-12,000
Excellent $13,000-20,000 **5-year projection** +15%

Mercedes-Benz 300SL 1954-63

1957-63 300SL roadster

PRODUCTION

1954-57 Coupe 1400 **1957-63 Roadster** 1858

1954-57 300SL "Gullwing" coupe

Mercedes-Benz 220SE
Coupe & Cabriolet 1959-65

1961-65 220SE cabriolet

PRODUCTION

16,902

HISTORY

The imposing "panzerwagen" sports car from Germany, a direct development of the racing M-B SL prototypes fielded for GT endurance events starting in 1952. Offered initially as a closed coupe with unique, upward-opening doors that earned it the nickname Gullwing. In appearance, the 300SL was quite modern compared to other current Mercedes, with a horizontal grille dominated by a big three-pointed star, twin longitudinal bulges in the hood, rounded front fenders and trunklid, prominent eyebrows over the wheel openings, and a heavy, ground-hugging look that belied its SL ("super leicht" or "super light") designation. The 300SL was a pioneer of the multi-tube "space frame" approach to chassis construction. All-independent suspension (the rear by treacherous swing axles) and direct fuel injection were other features. The Gullwing's doors left wide, high sills that made clambering in or out a chore for some, but the cockpit was snug and businesslike in the German manner. In 1957, the coupe was replaced by a two-seat roadster with conventional front-hinged, side-opening doors. A detachable steel top was offered as an option. M-B offered a choice of final drive ratios, which allowed a maximum speed of up to 165 mph from the 3.0-liter straight six shared with the flagship Type 300 sedan models. A car that required regular, expensive servicing, but a highly desirable grand tourer then, even more so today. Replaced by a smaller-engine SL series with more angular styling beginning in 1963.

The sporty pillarless hardtop and convertible models in Mercedes' midrange series introduced in 1958. Following typical Daimler-Benz practice, the four-door sedan was introduced first, followed somewhat later by these two-door models. The 220s were powered by a 2.2-liter overhead cam straight six, notable for its standard fuel injection (the "E" part of the designation), one of the first mass-production applications at Mercedes (as opposed to special models like the 300SL). An unmistakably Mercedes vertical radiator grille was flanked by pod-mounted headlamp/parking lamp units (U.S. versions had stacked round quad headlamps). Fenderlines flowed straight back past a mildly wrapped windshield and gently rounded rear roof to a fairly short rear deck that lacked the sharp tailfins of the early sedans. Chassis featured Mercedes' customary low-pivot swing-axle rear suspension. The interior was furnished in top-quality materials carefully applied, and offered sufficient, if not sumptuous accommodations for four. In all, worthy successors to the 300S/Sc coupe/cabriolet. The basic 220SE design was continued beyond 1965 with a different powerplant, a new 3.5-liter V8.

FOR

Timeless, unmistakable looks ● Performance aplenty ● Thorough Germanic engineering (except rear suspension) ● Will always be in demand ● A Milestone, and rightly so

Nice styling (still looks good) ● Engineering and mechanicals the same as for the more numerous sedans ● M-B construction quality, snob appeal ● Some mechanical parts still available

AGAINST

Tricky swing-axle handling (though better on roadster) ● Costly to acquire and maintain ● Parts hard to come by ● Most examples were spoken for long ago

Special body parts now in short supply ● Big and heavy, so mileage nothing special ● Swing-axle handling/roadholding bothers

SPECIFICATIONS

Length (in.) 180.0 **Wheelbase (in.)** 94.5 **Weight (lbs.)** 2750 (coupe), 3000 (roadster) **Price (new)** approx. $7300 U.S. in 1956; approx. $11,400 in 1960

Length (in.) 192.0 **Wheelbase (in.)** 108.0 **Weight (lbs.)** 3450 (Coupe), 3330 (Cabriolet) **Price (new)** approx. $5200 U.S. in 1962

ENGINES

cc/type (cid)	bore x stroke (mm)	bhp*	years
2996/ohc I6 (183)	85×88	240/250	1954-63

*gross

cc/type (cid)	bore x stroke (mm)	bhp*	years
2195/ohc I6 (134)	80×73	134	1959-65

*gross

PRICES/PROJECTION

Restorable $20,000-40,000 **Good** $50,000-75,000
Excellent $75,000-110,000 **5-year projection** +10%

Restorable $1500-2000 **Good** $4000-9000
Excellent $6000-12,000 Add for Cabriolet
5-year projection +100%

Mercedes-Benz Type 600 1963-80

1963-80 Type 600 standard-wheelbase sedan

PRODUCTION

2677

HISTORY

The "Grosser" Mercedes—the car of popes, potentates, and pop singers. Crafted only by hand on an as-needed basis, the 600 was notable for its great bulk, unprecedented by European standards and as large as anything Cadillac ever made. Three "production" models were listed, all with Mercedes' four-square styling that related to lesser models of the period. There were a standard-wheelbase four-door, a longer-wheelbase "Pullman" four-door, and an even longer sedan with six doors. A very few were also built with a "landaulette" type of rear passenger compartment, complete with fold-down fabric section, for parades and functions of state. All models featured a division window to separate the chauffeur from his "retainers." The first Mercedes to use the firm's massive 6.3-liter V8, which later powered the incredibly fast 300SEL 6.3 sedan of 1968. The enormously complex chassis featured air suspension and electro-hydraulic controls. Surprisingly fast for its size, and not all that bad for handling, either. A direct match for the upper Rolls-Royce models in concept, mechanical sophistication, and equipment if not in image. Production continued through the end of 1981, by which time the 600 had been left behind by technical advances made to lower-line models. Frequently seen in motion pictures whenever a big, impressive, slightly sinister limo was called for.

FOR

Exclusivity ●Grandeur ●Top-flight engineering and construction quality ●Ballroom-size interior ●Beautiful ride ●The most imposing Mercedes you can own

AGAINST

Too big for the city ●Hardly economical ●Costly to buy ●Complex, so parts and service cost a bundle ●Demands specialized service knowledge

SPECIFICATIONS

Length (in.) 218.0 (standard), 246.0 (Pullman)
Wheelbase (in.) 126.0 (standard), 153.5 (Pullman)
Weight (lbs.) 5445 (standard), 5820 (Pullman)
Price (new) approx. $60,000 U.S. in 1963

ENGINES

cc/type (cid)	bore x stroke (mm)	bhp*	years
6332/ohc V8 (387)	103×95	250	1963-80

*DIN

PRICES/PROJECTION

Restorable $20,000-28,000 **Good** $25,000-40,000
Excellent $35,500-50,000 Add 10% for long-wheelbase Pullman.
5-year projection +10%

Mercedes-Benz 230SL 1963-67

1965 230SL roadster with hardtop

PRODUCTION

19,831

HISTORY

Mercedes' sports car of the '60s, successor to both the 190SL and 300SL. More advanced than the former, much slower but more practical than the latter. Like the 190SL, based on the floorpan and running gear of a volume sedan, in this case the 220SE. Styling was unique to the SL, however, marked by square-cut lines, vertical headlamp pods and the typical low SL grille bearing a large three-pointed star. Offered initially with a 2.3-liter version of Mercedes fuel-injected dohc six (which would later be enlarged to 2.5 and then to 2.8 liters). Also available with automatic transmission and an optional steel hardtop with a depressed center section that earned it the title of "pagoda roof." The cockpit was designed strictly for two, but a small package shelf behind the seats could take two smaller riders in a pinch. The rear suspension continued with M-B's usual low-pivot swing axle arrangement. Even though this SL generation is fairly common in the U.S., the cars stand to appreciate strongly in the future. They're also lighter and (some say) nicer to drive than their 450SL successors.

FOR

Engineering ●Styling ●Open-air allure ●Active club interest ●Strong appreciator ●Some mechanical parts still available

AGAINST

Heavy and a bit fuelish ●Monocoque construction means rust potential ●Modest handling limits ●Middling performance ●Parts and service costly

SPECIFICATIONS

Length (in.) 169.5 **Wheelbase (in.)** 94.5 **Weight (lbs.)** 2855
Price (new) approx. $6500 U.S. in 1967

ENGINES

cc/type (cid)	bore x stroke (mm)	bhp*	years
2308/dohc I6 (141)	82×73	150	1963-67

*net

PRICES/PROJECTION

Restorable $3500-4000 **Good** $7000-8000
Excellent $12,000-15,000 **5-year projection** +10%

Mercedes-Benz 250SL 1967-68

PRODUCTION

5196

1968 250SL roadster with hardtop (U.S. model)

HISTORY

Essentially the 230SL but with a different engine—a seven-bearing 2.5-liter stroked version of Mercedes' dohc six, replacing the original four-bearing 2.3-liter unit. Rated horsepower stayed the same, but increased torque benefited driving ease and refinement. Otherwise the same as the 230SL.

FOR

As for 1963-67 230SL, and may also be considered a Milestone

AGAINST

As for 1963-67 230SL

SPECIFICATIONS

Length (in.) 169.5 **Wheelbase (in.)** 94.5 **Weight (lbs.)** 2870
Price (new) approx. $7000 U.S. in 1968

ENGINES

cc/type (cid)	bore x stroke (mm)	bhp*	years
2496/dohc I6 (152)	82 × 79	150	1967-68

*net

PRICES/PROJECTION

As for 1963-67 230SL except **Excellent** $13,000-18,000

Mercedes-Benz 280SL 1968-71

PRODUCTION

23,885

HISTORY

Continuation of the original 230SL, and difficult to identify without reading the emblems on the trunklid. This time, Mercedes bored out its dohc six slightly to near 2.8 liters, which brought a 20-bhp gain in output. Daimler-Benz was now beginning to respond to U.S. safety and emissions regulations, which were sapping power and performance of its American-market models, hence the larger engine to compensate. The 280SL was a bit faster and easier to drive than the 250SL, but its tricky handling that resulted from the swing-axle rear suspension was looking quite dated by 1970. Replaced in Europe by the V8-engine 350SL beginning in 1972. For

the U.S. market, a larger 4.5-liter V8 was offered as the 450SL, which arrived here late that year.

FOR

As for 1963-67 230SL and 1967-68 250SL, plus "last of the line" status

AGAINST

More numerous (but easier to find) than earlier models ● Others as for 1963-67 230SL and 1967-68 250SL

SPECIFICATIONS

Length (in.) 169.5 **Wheelbase (in.)** 94.5 **Weight (lbs.)** 2900
Price (new) approx. $8000 U.S. in 1969

ENGINES

cc/type (cid)	bore x stroke (mm)	bhp*	years
2778/dohc I6 (170)	87 × 79	170	1968-71

*net

PRICES/PROJECTION

Restorable $4000-7000 **Good** $8000-12,000
Excellent $15,000-20,000 **5-year projection** +15%

Mercedes-Benz 300SEL 6.3 1967-72

PRODUCTION

1840 (U.S. sales incl. European deliveries)

HISTORY

German-built freeway flyer with electrifying performance. Created by slotting the big quad-cam V8 engine from the massive 600 limousine into the smaller, lighter type W109 bodyshell ordinarily propelled by M-B's 3.0-liter six. As in the 600, Bosch timed-flow fuel injection was used, good for a rousing 250 bhp (DIN) and a solid 369 ft-lbs of torque. The result, according to factory figures, was 0-100 kph (62 mph) in 6.5 seconds and a top end of 130 mph plus, making this the world's fastest luxury sedan. Air suspension with built-in self-leveling was exclusive to the 6.3 among Mercedes' "mass-market" models. Other features included standard air con-

1968-72 300SEL 6.3 4-door sedan (U.S. model)

ditioning, leather upholstery, M-B's 4-speed automatic transmission, AM/FM radio, and central locking system. Impossible to tell from an ordinary 300SEL except by the discreet "6.3" badge on the right of the trunklid, and many owners removed that to avoid suspicious glances from the law. A goodly proportion of the deliberately limited production run made its way to the U.S. Withdrawn in the aftermath of the first energy crisis, and also to make way for the new-generation W116 series S-class sedans introduced for 1973. Succeeded in the lineup by the 450SEL 6.9 in 1976.

FOR

Prestige with punch •Four-door convenience •Superlative construction quality •Solid handling •Rarity

AGAINST

Air suspension leak problems •Thirsty •Some mechanical parts in short supply

SPECIFICATIONS

Length (in.) 196.9 **Wheelbase (in.)** 112.8 **Weight (lbs.)** 4010
Price (new) approx. $14,500 U.S. in 1969

ENGINES

cc/type (cid)	bore x stroke (mm)	bhp*	years
6332/dohc V8 (387)	103×95	250	1967-72

*DIN

PRICES/PROJECTION

Restorable $6000-10,000 **Good** $8000-11,000
Excellent $12,000-15,000 **5-year projection** +10%

Mercedes-Benz 450SEL 6.9 1975-80

PRODUCTION

1816 (U.S. sales incl. European deliveries)

HISTORY

Continuation of the big-engine S-class sedan, now built on the W116 platform introduced for 1973. Considerably changed from its 6.3 predecessor, with somewhat lower and sleeker lines that were still distinctly Mercedes. A bore increase brought up displacement

on the big quad-cam V8 engine, still related to the original 600 limousine unit, and there were numerous modifications such as Bosch K-Jetronic fuel injection, breakerless electronic ignition, dry-sump lubrication, and hydraulic valve gear actuation. Suspension was shared with lesser-powered S-class models (lower A-arms, upper transverse links, and anti-roll bar in front, semi-trailing arms and anti-roll bar at the rear), but springing was now provided by hydropneumatic oil/nitrogen struts instead of air bags as on the 6.3. As before, rear end self-leveling was incorporated to compensate for a heavy load of luggage or passengers. The revised chassis gave even better handling and roadholding than the already capable 6.3, plus a softer ride. Equipped with most every conceivable luxury feature, the 6.9 was slightly slower than the 6.3 off the line, but had a bit more available in top speed, now about 140 mph. Equipped only with 3-speed torque-converter automatic transmission, replacing the previous 4-speed fluid-coupling unit. Fast but thirsty, the 6.9 was launched a good three years after the rest of the W116 range because of Mercedes' sense of propriety in the wake of the 1973-74 Arab oil embargo. When fuel prices "destabilized" again in 1979, U.S. fuel economy standards were in force, which made the 6.9 something of a liability here. Accordingly, the model was dropped after 1979. The fastest version of what was widely considered "the best sedan in the world," argument enough for its status as a collectible.

FOR

As for 1968-72 300SEL 6.3, plus greater refinement and better ride and handling

AGAINST

As for 1968-72 300SEL 6.3 but U.S. versions more affected by desmogging and bumper rules than corresponding 6.3s •Also, very pricey and likely to remain so

SPECIFICATIONS

Length (in.) 205.5 **Wheelbase (in.)** 116.5
Weight (lbs.) approx. 4500 **Price (new)** $35,000 U.S. in 1976; $50,000 in 1979

ENGINES

cc/type (cid)	bore x stroke (mm)	bhp*	years
6834/dohc V8 (417)	107×95	250	1975-80

*SAE net, U.S. model

PRICES/PROJECTION

Difficult to establish accureately at present; consider the following as estimates only. **Restorable** $8000-10,000
Good $15,000-20,000 **Excellent** $25,000-30,000
5-year projection +10%

1976-79 450SEL 6.9 4-door sedan (U.S. model)

MG M-Type Midget 1930-32

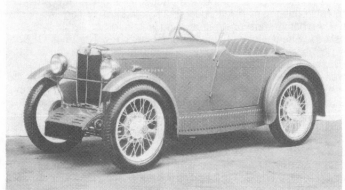

1930 M-Type Midget roadster

PRODUCTION

3235 (began 1928)

HISTORY

Abingdon's first small sports car, now a real collector's item despite running gear borrowed from the contemporary—and more mundane—Morris Minor sedan. Little overhead-cam engine was advanced for the day (the cam drive doubled as the generator drive), but most everything else was cheap and cheerful. In typical period British fashion, a narrow two-seater with a flexible chassis, ox-cart springs, and anvil-like beam axles front and rear. Skimpy wood-framed bodywork, some fabric-covered, with boattail rear-end styling, two-piece vee'd windshield, and freestanding cycle-type fenders. Very perky character but no more than 60 mph flat out despite low weight. As with so many prewar (and postwar) British sportsters, image mattered more than guts, so weather protection is minimal, cockpit appointments spartan. Also offered as the close-coupled Sportsman's Coupe, but it's the roadster everyone remembers.

FOR

Classic looks • Cheeky character • Small size, great heart • Uncomplicated • Rare nowadays

AGAINST

Negligible performance • Tight cockpit • Spindly engineering, build • Parts almost impossible to get anymore • No value appreciation at present

SPECIFICATIONS

Length (in.) 123.0 **Wheelbase (in.)** 78.0 **Weight (lbs.)** 1120
Price (new) NA

ENGINES

cc/type (cid)	bore x stroke (mm)	bhp	years
847/ohc I4 (52)	57×83	20/27*	1928-32

*net

PRICES/PROJECTION

Restorable $3000-6000 **Good** $6000-8000
Excellent $9000-12,000 **5-year projection** +10%

MG J-Type Midget 1932-34

1933 J2 Midget roadster

PRODUCTION

J1 380 **J2** 2083

HISTORY

Successor to the M-Type and its dumpy four-seat D-Type companion. Retained their basic ohc four with a new head that delivered more power. Wheelbase was extended eight inches, and there was new body styling that forecast the shape of MGs all the way through the TD of the early Fifties. All J2s were open two-seaters. Early examples had cycle-type fenders, which later gave way to clamshell-type "swept wings." The four-seat J1 was offered in both open and closed form. Cutaway doors and wood-framed bodies were common to both J-Types. Maintained MG practice with a very hard leaf-spring suspension, solid front and rear axles, non-synchromesh gearbox, and precious little weather protection, but performance was improved to a best of a bit over 80 mph.

FOR

Sweet, almost feminine character • Creditable go and handy size in a vintage Brit sportster • Rare and valuable

AGAINST

Not much value for money in today's terms • Crude "crashbox" • Cramped cockpit • Antediluvian ride, handling

SPECIFICATIONS

Length (in.) 124.0 **Wheelbase (in.)** 86.0 **Weight (lbs.)** 1260
Price (new) NA

ENGINES

cc/type (cid)	bore x stroke (mm)	bhp	years
847/ohc I4 (52)	57×83	36*	1932-34

*net

PRICES/PROJECTION

As for 1928-32 M-Type

MG K3 Midget
1932-34

PRODUCTION

33

HISTORY

The fiercest of all 1930s MGs and one of the rarest—if not *the* rarest—today. If you find one, buy first and then ask questions. An open two-seater with typical MG styling, lightweight construction, and no-compromise equipment, but intended for competition. Powered by a larger, supercharged version of MG's overhead-cam four mated to a pre-select four-speed gearbox. One of several K-Type models (including open-body Magnettes) that shared this chassis, but none have the same appeal. Many first and second owners modified the bodies, though most surviving examples still have the original cycle-type fenders. Absolutely no protection from the weather or anything else, though a couple of small "aero" screens help keep bugs out of your teeth. Most were raced at one time or another and, as a group, were very successful in the 1.1-liter class.

FOR

Very rare mighty mite • Every one has a story • Fascinating pre-selector gearbox

AGAINST

Only a fair-weather friend • Too specialized for road use • Parts supplies long extinct • Requires frequent attention

SPECIFICATIONS

Length (in.) 136.0 **Wheelbase (in.)** 94.0 **Weight (lbs.)** NA
Price (new) NA

ENGINES

cc/type (cid)	bore x stroke (mm)	bhp	years
1087/ohc I4 (66)	57×71	80-100*	1932-34

*net

PRICES/PROJECTION

Restorable $20,000-40,000 **Good** $45,000-60,000
Excellent $60,000-85,000 **5-year projection** +20%

MG PA/PB
1934-36

PRODUCTION

PA (1934-35) 1973 **PB (1935-36)** 526

HISTORY

Smoother and marginally more sophisticated than the J2 it replaced, but still mainly for masochists with narrow shoulders. Retained MG's unmistakable design hallmarks: proud radiator, freestanding headlamps, classic clamshell fenders, and "slab-back" fuel tank. PA retained the existing 847cc displacement, while the PB had a bored-

1936-39 PB roadster

out 939cc version with eight extra horsepower. Three body styles were offered: two-seat roadster (the most sought-after today), a four-seater, and the unusual, gracefully shaped "Airline" fastback coupe. All featured center-lock wire wheels, real leather upholstery, and MG's customary wood-framed body construction, plus fold-down windshields on the open models. Capable of 70+ mph, but a hard ride and lack of gearbox synchronization made this a rugged driving experience.

FOR

Last MGs in the original Cecil Kimber mold • Rarity • Small, light, and handy • Excellent club support

AGAINST

Performance still limited • Rot-prone bodies • Parts now scarce and pricey • Cramped • Bone-crusher ride • Not an everyday find

SPECIFICATIONS

Length (in.) 131.0 **Wheelbase (in.)** 87.5 **Weight (lbs.)** 1510
Price (new) NA

ENGINES

cc/type (cid)	bore x stroke (mm)	bhp	years
847/ohc I4 (52)	57×83	35*	1934-35
939/ohc I4 (57)	60×83	43*	1935-36

*net

PRICES/PROJECTION

Restorable $2000-4000 **Good** $6000-8000
Excellent $8000-11,000 **5-year projection** +15%

MG TA/TB
1936-39

PRODUCTION

TA (1936-39) 3003 **TB (1939 only)** 379

HISTORY

Abingdon's first offering after MG merged with the Nuffield organiza-

1936-39 TA roadster

tion. Rather different from the superseded P-Types and less distinctly MG. Transmission (with synchromesh phased in as a running change after the first few months of production) and pushrod engine both based on Wolseley components; no other important mechanical changes. Styling very familiar and similar to the P-Type's, though bodies were longer and a touch wider. Rakish roadster was joined in 1938 by a new drophead (convertible) coupe with full-height doors, crafted by Tickford. TA's old-fashioned long-stroke engine was replaced on the 1939-only TB models by the new shorter-stroke (but still markedly undersquare) XPAG unit, which would run into the mid-1950s. Important as the direct ancestors of the romantic postwar TC, which was essentially a carryover TB.

FOR

Rarity, especially TB • More space than PB • Simple engineering • Many parts common with TC • 1930s MG appeal • Ample club support

AGAINST

Hard ride • Still cramped despite larger bodies • Bodies still rot-prone • Not much go or refinement • Slow to appreciate

SPECIFICATIONS

Length (in.) 140.0 **Wheelbase (in.)** 94.0 **Weight (lbs.)** 1960
Price (new) NA

ENGINES

cc/type (cid)	bore x stroke (mm)	bhp	years
1292/ohv L4 (79)	63.5×102.0	52*	1936-39**
1250/ohv L4 (76)	66.5×90.0	54*	1939***

*net
**TA
***TB

PRICES/PROJECTION

Restorable $3000-5000 **Good** $7500-11,000
Excellent $12,000-14,000 **5-year projection** +10%

MG TC 1945-49

1945-49 TC roadster

PRODUCTION

10,000

HISTORY

Archetypal prewar British sports car design carried over into the early postwar period. But the TC was different: somehow it turned Americans onto European sports cars. Its Milestone status derives partly from that, and partly from its classic 1930s lines — free-standing headlamps, upright radiator shell, sweeping front fenders, rakish cutaway doors, fold-down windshield, abbreviated tail (housing fuel tank and spare tire), and spindly 19-inch-diameter wire wheels (with knockoff hubs, of course). A very old-fashioned car even before the war, with a flexible ladder-type chassis and crude solid axle suspension front and rear. The TC's ride was joggly and stiff, but its agility was a revelation to Yankees raised on workaday Fords and Chevys. Not very fast, with a top speed well under 80 mph and acceleration to match, but its simple 1250cc four wore like the cast iron it was made of. Despite rumors to the contrary, no left-hand-drive models were built. Still a cult car, and a prime collectible best reserved for top-down, sunny-days driving.

FOR

Very desirable even now • Simple, rugged engineering • Huge following • Good number of mechanical and body parts, many reproduction, still available

AGAINST

Costly for what it is and does • Dreadful ride • Body rots easily • Cramped accommodations • Appeal diluted now by mass of replicas • Amazing price spread

SPECIFICATIONS

Length (in.) 139.5 **Wheelbase (in.)** 94.0 **Weight (lbs.)** 1735
Price (new) $1895 U.S. in 1949

ENGINES

cc/type (cid)	bore x stroke (mm)	bhp*	years
1250/ohv I4 (76)	67 × 90	54	1945-49

*net

PRICES/PROJECTION

Restorable $4000-6500 **Good** $7000-12,000
Excellent $12,000-18,000 **5-year projection** +10%

MG TD
1949-53

1950-53 TD roadster

PRODUCTION

29,664

HISTORY

A more modern version of the TC with the same irresistible charm. The engine and transmission were not changed, but everything else was. A new box-section chassis with coil-spring independent front suspension was concealed by a wider, more squat body, still in traditional British-roadster style. The separate headlamps and flowing front fenders were retained as were the classic TC overall proportions, but the large-diameter wire wheels gave way to smaller steel disc wheels. The TD was built with left-hand drive for the U.S., which eagerly took most exports. Still a crude car, with a

primitive and frustrating folding top and snap-in side curtains. The TDII appeared in 1951 with more standard equipment and detail styling changes. This was followed by a TD "Mark II" with a little more horsepower. TDs were actively raced by Americans learning about things like road courses and rallying, and MG assisted with tuning kits for the little four-cylinder engine. In all, a much better car than the TC, but not as pure in styling, which may be why it's considered less desirable by collectors today.

FOR

Better ride and handling than TC • Simple to work on • Chassis and engine parts still around • Still in great demand

AGAINST

Same limited performance as TC • Wood-framed bodies don't hold up well • Body parts very costly now • Horribly old-fashioned, even when new • Is it overpriced today?

SPECIFICATIONS

Length (in.) 145.0 **Wheelbase (in.)** 94.0 **Weight (lbs.)** 1930
Price (new) NA

ENGINES

cc/type (cid)	bore x stroke (mm)	bhp*	years
1250/ohv I4 (76)	67 × 90	54-57	1949-53

*net

PRICES/PROJECTION

Restorable $3000-6000 **Good** $7000-10,000
Excellent $11,000-17,000 **5-year projection** +10%

MG TF/TF-1500
1953-55

1954-55 TF1500 roadster

PRODUCTION

9600 total; **TF1500** 3400

HISTORY

A hastily revamped TD, built for less than two years. The most noticeable difference in the TF was its appearance, a kind of streamlined update of the TC/TD. The nose was reworked to accommodate a raked-back radiator shell, headlamps were faired into the front fenders, the tail was revised, and instruments were given octagonal housings echoing the MG badge. The drivetrain was taken straight from the TD, but beginning in the autumn of 1954 an enlarged, more powerful four was substituted and model designation changed to TF1500.

FOR

As for 1950-53 TD

AGAINST

As for 1950-53 TD and less "classic" appearance

SPECIFICATIONS

Length (in.) 147.0 **Wheelbase (in.)** 94.0 **Weight (lbs.)** 1930
Price (new) NA

ENGINES

cc/type (cid)	bore x stroke (mm)	bhp*	years
1250/ohv I4 (76)	67×90	57	1953-54
1466/ohv I4 (89)	72×90	63	1954-55

*net

PRICES/PROJECTION

As for 1945-49 TC

MG MGA 1955-62

1961-62 1600 Mk II roadster

PRODUCTION

1500 58,750   **1600** 31,501   **1600 Mark II** 8719

HISTORY

MG's late-'50s sports car, considered almost shockingly modern compared to its T-series predecessors. Styling was sleek and up to date. The long hood terminated in a rounded front end bearing a squat, MG-style radiator/grille. Front fenders were semi-integrated with the envelope body, and swept back and downward into the doors, then kicked up into the curvy rear fenders. The sloping tail was bereft of an outside spare tire. Offered in both the traditional roadster with side curtains and (later) a fixed-roof coupe with wraparound rear window and (horrors!) roll-up door glass. The wood framing for the body gave way to modern all-steel construction. The initial specification was basically as for the TF1500. In 1960 the sturdy four was bored out to just under 1.6 liters, and the all-drum brakes were changed to a front-disc/rear-drum system. The 1600 Mark II sported more upright vertical grille bars and a displacement a bit over 1.6 liters for more power. The smooth bodywork aided top speed, which was in the vicinity of 100 mph (slightly more on the Mark II). With this model, MG was firmly established as part of the American scene. The MGA is considered by some to be the last MG faithful to "true" sports-car precepts (stark appointments, minimal weather protection), and marked a transition between the "vintage" (T-series) and "modern" (MGB) eras for the marque.

FOR

Styling •Strong chassis •Mechanically simple, easy to work on •Many parts still available •Open-air fun (roadster) •Good U.S. supply •Still commands intense interest

AGAINST

Steel-body rust worries •Limited luggage space

SPECIFICATIONS

Length (in.) 156.0 **Wheelbase (in.)** 94.0 **Weight (lbs.)** 1985 (roadster), 2050 (coupe) **Price (new)** approx. $2500 U.S. in 1960

ENGINES

cc/type (cid)	bore x stroke (mm)	bhp*	years
1489/ohv I4 (91)	73×89	72	1955-57
1588/ohv I4 (97)	75×89	80	1957-60
1622/ohv I4 (99)	76×89	86	1961-62

*net

PRICES/PROJECTION

Restorable $1000-2000 **Good** $3000-5500
Excellent $6000-8000 **5-year projection** +10%

MG MGA Twin-Cam & DeLuxe 1958-62

1958-60 Twin-Cam roadster

PRODUCTION

2111 (plus 388 "1600 DeLuxe" models)

HISTORY

An extensively revised version of the MGA, and sold alongside the regular models. The main distinction, as the name implies, was its four-cylinder engine with double-overhead-cam head. This power unit was finicky to tune, and wouldn't tolerate low-grade fuel, but most surviving cars have been modified to run on today's low-calorie stuff. Also equipped with four-wheel disc brakes and steel, center-lock disc wheels. Much faster than the "cooking" MGAs, the Twin-Cam could reach 115 mph, but was quite a bit more expensive. Produced in limited numbers primarily for competition duty. It was dropped sometime before the MGA itself, replaced by the "1600 DeLuxe", which retained the all-disc brakes but reverted to the normal 1.6-liter (1588 and 1622cc) pushrod engines from the standard models.

FOR

As for 1955-62 MGA, plus more performance and exclusivity

AGAINST

Few parts left now for complex dohc engine • Hard to find in reasonable condition • Not as easily found as regular MGA • Others as for 1955-62 MGA

SPECIFICATIONS

Length (in.) 156.0 **Wheelbase (in.)** 94.0 **Weight (lbs.)** 2185 (roadster), 2245 (coupe) **Price (new)** approx. $3200 U.S. in 1960

ENGINES

cc/type (cid)	bore x stroke (mm)	bhp*	years
1588/dohc I4 (97)	75×89	108	1958-60
1588/ohv I4 (97)	75×89	80	1960
1622/ohv I4 (99)	76×89	86	1961-62

*net

PRICES/PROJECTION

Similar prices to MGA, but add 25-50% for good/excellent examples with recently rebuilt engine

MG MGB 1962-80

1966 GT coupe

PRODUCTION

Approximately 515,000 (incl. approx. 150,000 GT coupes)

HISTORY

One of the longest-running models in recent history and, as it would turn out, the last "real" MGs to be built. Introduced in two-seat roadster form, then supplemented by a closed 2+2 GT coupe at the start of the 1966 model year. Powered by BMC's sturdy B-series four-cylinder engine, essentially the MGA unit bored out to near 1.8 liters. The 1962-64 models had three-main-bearing engines; five mains were adopted with the '65s. The monocoque bodyshell was cleanly styled if a bit plain, marked by a wide MG vertical bar grille and headlamps residing in front fender "scoops." In British fashion, the roadster's top was still infuriatingly difficult to put up or take down, but purists cringed at the "modern" roll-up door windows and proper heater. A Mark II version arrived for the 1968 model year with an all-synchromesh gearbox (earlier cars had a non-synchro first gear), and automatic transmission was made an extra-cost item. A good many manual cars were fitted with Laycock de Normanville overdrive, a worthwhile extra to look for. Styling and equipment changed little through 1968. After that, however, things got worse, particularly on "federalized" MGBs. Beginning in 1969, BMC took the cheapest and least imaginative ways to meet U.S. safety and emissions requirements, including a hastily contrived padded overlay that hid the normal glovebox and engines that were progressively detuned, dropping in both horsepower and torque every year. U.S. models also got uglier rubber-covered bumpers in the early '70s, then were cranked up on their suspensions to meet headlight height requirements. This was accompanied by a protruding black "bra" that simply ruined the original tidy front end appearance. Already eclipsed by more modern competitors by the late '60s, the B was probably kept on too long. For us, the most desirable models are the 1962-67 roadsters and the pretty little BGTs that were sold in the U.S. through 1975.

FOR

Parts and service everywhere • Solid engineering • Sturdy and simple to maintain • Fine handling (to 1974) • Extensive club support • Cheap to buy and run • Traditional MG virtues (and vices)

AGAINST

Too common for high appreciation • Very rust-prone • Slower than it looks (100 mph tops) • GT body panels scarce in U.S. • Typically suspect British construction quality

SPECIFICATIONS

Length (in.) 153.3 **Wheelbase (in.)** 91.0
Weight (lbs.) 2030-2600 (roadster), 2190 (GT)
Price (new) $2500-8000 U.S.

1979 roadster (U.S. model)

ENGINES

cc/type (cid)	bore x stroke (mm)	bhp*	years
1798/ohv I4 (110)	80×89	60-95	1962-80

*net

PRICES/PROJECTION

Restorable $1000-2500 **Good** $2500-3500
Excellent $3000-6800 **5-year projection** +10%

MG MGC
1967-69

1967-68 roadster

PRODUCTION

8999 (incl. 4449 GT coupes)

HISTORY

A short-lived and unsuccessful attempt at making the MGB a successor to the late Austin-Healey 3000. The normal four-cylinder engine was replaced by a 3.0-liter inline six completely different in detail from the Healey unit. Torsion bars were substituted for the B's front coil springs, 15-inch wheels replaced 14-inchers, and the hood grew a prominent bulge to clear the bulkier powerplant. In other respects, the C was much like the B — except in the way it drove. It suffered ponderous understeer, and didn't have as much snap as it should have due to a conspicuous lack of torque. Nevertheless, it was fast in a straight line (120 mph available) and reasonably economical. The motoring press turned up its collective nose, as did most potential buyers, and the C was withdrawn after only about two years. Offered in both roadster and GT coupe body styles with standard all-synchromesh manual gearbox or optional automatic. Not very popular in the U.S. for the obvious reasons, including a somewhat steeper price than that of the much more pleasant MGB.

FOR

Some parts still available in UK • Better performance and equipment than MGB

AGAINST

Heavy steering and stodgy handling • Engine parts becoming scarce • Poor reputation among non-MG enthusiasts

SPECIFICATIONS

Length (in.) 153.2 **Wheelbase (in.)** 91.0 **Weight (lbs.)** 2460 (roadster), 2610 (GT) **Price (new)** approx. $3700 U.S. in 1969

ENGINES

cc/type (cid)	bore x stroke (mm)	bhp*	years
2912/ohv I6 (178)	83×89	145	1967-69

*net

PRICES/PROJECTION

Restorable $1000-2500 **Good** $3000-4000
Excellent $5000-7000 **5-year projection** +10%

MG Midget Mark III/1500
1971-79

1977 Midget Mk IV roadster (U.S. model)

PRODUCTION

approx. 60,000

HISTORY

Continuation of the "Spridget" following departure of the Austin-Healey Sprite in 1970, but still based on the Mark II platform dating back to 1961. Updated by a minor restyle and extra equipment as the Mark III from 1971-74, still powered by the venerable BMC A-series four in 1275cc form. U.S. safety and emissions regulations began adding weight and draining power as the decade wore on, and the new British Leyland regime needed to meet even stiffer forthcoming regulations as economically as possible in its biggest export market. The result was the 1500, which arrived for the 1975 model year sporting ugly black "rubber baby buggy bumpers" and the entirely different 1.5-liter engine from corporate stablemate Triumph Spitfire. Despite production economies that dictated relatively crude solutions to meeting the standards, the Midget retained its appeal as a low-cost "learner's" sports car, an old-fashioned machine you could buy new to experience what traditional open-air motoring was all about. Sold in modest numbers until its phase-out after the 1979 season, by which time financially troubled BL had more or less decided to abandon the sports car market. Midget collectibility is still very much a question mark right now, but the car will probably always have its advocates, which means it should hold its value fairly well in coming years.

FOR

Inexpensive • Economical • Perhaps the cheapest way to get into topless driving • Others as for 1961-71 Austin-Healey Sprite

AGAINST

British construction quality problems • Very cramped cockpit • Noisy at speed • Hard ride • Archaic specs

SPECIFICATIONS

Length (in.) 137.6 (1971-74), 141.0 (1975-76), 143.0 (1977-79)
Wheelbase (in.) 80.0 **Weight (lbs.)** 1560-1826
Price (new) $2395 U.S. in 1971, rising to $5200 by 1979

ENGINES

cc/type (cid)	bore x stroke (mm)	bhp*	years
1275/ohv I4 (78)	71×81	55-62	1971-74
1493/ohv V4 (91)	74×87	50-55	1975-79
*SAE net			

PRICES/PROJECTION

Restorable $750-1000 **Good** $1500-2500 **Excellent** $2900-4100
5-year projection +10%

Morgan 4/4 Series I 1936-50

1948 4/4 Series I roadster

PRODUCTION

1980 (824 prewar, 578 postwar)

HISTORY

Malvern Link's first four-wheel sports car, introduced after 26 years of building nothing but three-wheelers (with the single wheel at the rear). Very much an extension of the original design, with the same sliding-pillar independent front suspension and Z-section frame side members, both still found on today's "Moggies." Much like the early MG T-Type in concept and character, though not as fast or agile. Offered in roadster and convertible (full top) body styles, both with wood-framed bodywork built by Morgan. Early examples carried Coventry-Climax power before Morgan switched to engines from Standard Motor Car Company, used exclusively postwar. Top speed was only about 70 mph, but that was enough thanks to the spine-jarring ride, lack of creature comforts, and slow-synchro gearbox. As usual, the two-seat roadsters are more desirable, but all these cars have immense charm.

FOR

Period British sports car appeal • Simple to maintain • More exclusive than concurrent MGs • Company still in business • Good factory and club support

AGAINST

Amazingly hard ride • Wood-frame bodies rot badly • Cramped cockpit • Few mechanical parts left and no body items

SPECIFICATIONS

Length (in.) 136.0/139.0 (roadster/convertible)
Wheelbase (in.) 92.0 **Weight (lbs.)** 1625-1735
Price (new) NA

ENGINES

cc/type (cid)	bore x stroke (mm)	bhp	years
1098/F4 (67)	62.3×90.0	45	1938-39
1122/F4 (68)	63.0×90.0	34	1936-39
1267/ohv I4 (77)	64.0×100.0	40	1939-50
*gross			

PRICES/PROJECTION

Restorable $2500-5000 **Good** $5000-7000
Excellent $8000-15,000 **5-year projection** no change

Morgan Plus 4 1950-68

1957 Plus 4 roadster

PRODUCTION

2088cc 893 **1991cc** 2237 **2138cc** 1523 **Supersport** 101

HISTORY

Replacement for the 4/4, with the same basic body and chassis engineering on a 4-inch longer wheelbase. Still with sliding-pillar front suspension and separately mounted Moss gearbox. The longer chassis enabled an extra pair of "occasional" seats to be stuffed into the cockpit. Styling and engineering gradually changed over the years, with a sloping nose and faired-in headlamps by the mid-'50s. But even in 1968, a Morgan was still like Morgans always had been — modified 1930s styling, louvered hood, rudimentary equipment, nice handling, and a rock-hard ride. Mechanical changes included adoption of front disc brakes in 1960, a switch to the 1991cc Triumph TR2 engine in 1954, then adoption of the 2138cc TR4 powerplant in 1962. A Supersport version was offered with souped-up TR engines by the British Lawrencetune firm. Most had light-alloy bodies.

FOR

As for 1939-50 4/4 Series I, plus more performance and better mechanical parts availability

AGAINST

As for 1939-50 4/4 Series I

SPECIFICATIONS

Length (in.) 144.0 **Wheelbase (in.)** 96.0 **Weight (lbs.)** 1915 (average) **Price (new)** NA

ENGINES

cc/type (cid)	bore x stroke (mm)	bhp*	years
2088/ohv I4 (127)	85×92	68	1950-54
1991/ohv I4 (122)	83×92	90	1954-62
2138/ohv I4 (131)	86×92	100	1962-68

*gross

PRICES/PROJECTION

As for 4/4 Series I, but add up to 50% for light-alloy body

Morgan 4/4 Series II/III/IV 1955-68

1955-59 4/4 Series II roadster

PRODUCTION

Series II 387   **Series III** 59   **Series IV** 206   **Series V** 639

HISTORY

A reborn 4/4 Morgan built on a lengthened Plus 4 chassis. Engines and gearboxes were supplied by Ford of Britain, not Standard-Triumph. The 1172cc side valve four-cylinder unit was used on Series II cars. Later models were fitted with the overhead valve "Kent" engine introduced in 1959 (and still in production) with displacement varying with series. Offered in only one body style, a two-seat roadster, quite similar in appearance with concurrent Plus 4s. Lighter but not as fast as the Plus 4, though 1.5-liter 4/4s could reach 100 mph. Replaced in 1968 by the 4/4 1600, unchanged in appearance, powered by the familiar Cortina version of the Kent four with crossflow head. This model is still in production at this writing.

FOR

As for 1950-68 Plus 4

AGAINST

As for 1950-68 Plus 4, but less performance

SPECIFICATIONS

Length (in.) 144.0 **Wheelbase (in.)** 96.0 **Weight (lbs.)** 1570 (average) **Price (new)** NA

ENGINES

cc/type (cid)	bore x stroke (mm)	bhp	years
1172/L4 (71)	64×93	36-39	1955-59
997/ohv I4 (91)	81×48	54	1959-61
1340/ohv I4 (82)	81×65	60	1962-63
1498/ohv I4 (92)	81×73	78	1963-68

PRICES/PROJECTION

As for 1950-68 Plus 4

Morgan Plus Four Plus 1963-67

1963-67 Plus Four Plus coupe

PRODUCTION

26

HISTORY

A strange bird, this — the only Morgan with anything close to "modern" styling. Atop an unaltered Plus 4 frame with 2.2-liter Triumph TR4 engine was a bubble-top fixed-roof coupe body made of fiberglass. The almost bell-shaped roof contrasted with the rather four-square lower body with straight-through fenderlines and a flat rear deck. Seating was strictly for two, and the side windows were fixed. Not a commercial success, either because Morgan misjudged its customers or the car's styling appeal (or lack thereof). A very desirable rarity, though it's doubtful many made it to the U.S.

FOR

Extreme scarcity ● Interesting appearance ● Greater comfort and refinement ● Others as for 1950-68 Plus 4

AGAINST

Impossible to find any more • Body parts extinct • Others as for 1950-68 Plus 4

SPECIFICATIONS

Length (in.) 152.0 **Wheelbase (in.)** 96.0 **Weight (lbs.)** 1820
Price (new) NA

ENGINES

cc/type (cid)	bore x stroke (mm)	bhp*	years
2138/ohv I4 (131)	86×92	100	1963-67

*gross

PRICES/PROJECTION

As for 1950-68 Plus 4

Morgan Plus 8 1968-80

PRODUCTION

Over 2600 to date

HISTORY

A continuation of the Plus 4 design, but heavily modified. Morgan's antiquated sliding-pillar front suspension and rugged ladder chassis were retained, but wheelbase grew by 2 inches. The rakish two-seat roadster body, still with cutaway doors and crude folding top, continued to rely on wood framing to support its steel panels. The big change was under the hood. In place of the previous Triumph four was a light-alloy V8, the 3.5-liter Rover powerplant that British Leyland had acquired from Buick in the early '60s. Despite the awful aerodynamics of the traditional styling, top speed moved up to an impressive 125 mph, with similar gains in acceleration. Some Plus 8s were fitted with light-alloy body panels, but all wore cast-alloy wheels. Beginning in mid-1972, the antediluvian Moss gearbox finally gave way to a Rover transmission mounted in unit with the engine. A few cars were converted to run on propane and imported to the U.S. by a California firm. This was before the V8 was certified for U.S. sale in the Rover 3500 sedan, however, which means owning a Plus 8 now depends mainly on whether you can get around federal bumper and side-impact rules. Production continues at this writing, and there's a long waiting list, so older examples are also much in demand.

FOR

The only replicar that never went out of production • Very fast • Lovely ex-GM engine • Traditional roadster appeal • Rare in U.S.

AGAINST

Wood still rots • Few creature comforts • Unyielding ride • Mechanical parts increasingly difficult to come by outside UK

SPECIFICATIONS

Length (in.) 147.0 **Wheelbase (in.)** 98.0 **Weight (lbs.)** 1875
Price (new) $2800 at factory in 1969

ENGINES

cc/type (cid)	bore x stroke (mm)	bhp*	years
3528/ohv V8 (215)	89×71	151	1968-date

*net

PRICES/PROJECTION

Restorable $8000-12,000 **Good** $13,000-17,000
Excellent $17,000-19,000 **5-year projection** +15%

Morris Minor 1000 1956-71

PRODUCTION

948cc 544,048   **1098cc** 303,443

HISTORY

The final development of the original 1948 small car designed by the innovative Alex Issigonis, later of Mini fame. Once considered the car that could have done for Britain what the VW Beetle did for Germany, and more respected now than it ever was when in production. One of the first all-new postwar British models, the Minor was intended to provide low-cost motoring for the masses, and remained largely unchanged throughout its long life. Light in weight, it utilized all-steel unit body/chassis construction and an unusual (for the day) torsion bar front suspension. Styling was quaintly

1968-80 Plus 8 roadster

rounded, but provided a roomy interior within a fairly short wheelbase. Two- and four-door sedans and a two-door Traveler wagon with "Olde English" wood trim and twin side-hinged rear doors were offered. Intended as a minimal car in keeping with the "less is more" philosophy, so trim and equipment were very basic. The engine was BMC's A-series four, a rugged, almost unbreakable engine offered variously in two displacements. The Minor was far from exciting, however (top speed only around 75 mph), but its quick steering and capable chassis made it a surprisingly good-handling car. Although it was supposed to be replaced in the early '60s by the advanced front-drive BMC 1100 family (an Issigonis creation based on Mini design principles) the Minor continued in production due to steady, healthy customer demand. A good deal of its engineering was used in other, later BMC/British Leyland cars, so parts are surprisingly plentiful today through UK sources.

FOR

Great character and thoroughly British • Fine handling • Bulletproof engines • Engine and chassis parts still around • Easy to work on • Good accommodation for size • A cheap collectible that's cheap to run

AGAINST

Body/chassis very rust-prone • Front suspension often falls apart • Woodie wagon trim a bear to restore • Sparse trim and equipment • Slow by most standards and not very refined

SPECIFICATIONS

Length (in.) 148.0 **Wheelbase (in.)** 86.0 **Weight (lbs.)** 1755 (average) **Price (new)** NA

ENGINES

cc/type (cid)	bore x stroke (mm)	bhp	years
948/ohv I4 (58)	63×76	37	1956-65
1098/ohv I4 (67)	65×84	48	1965-71

PRICES/PROJECTION

Restorable $500-1000 **Good** $1200-1600 **Excellent** $2000-4000 **5-year projection** +10%

NSU Wankel Spider
1963-66

PRODUCTION

Approx. 5000

HISTORY

The first production car powered by Felix Wankel's rotary engine, produced in limited numbers by this old-line German firm to test public reaction. Unlike the later twin-rotor, front-drive Ro80 sedan, the Wankel Spider used a single-rotor engine mounted in its tail to drive the back wheels. The unit body/chassis was based on that of the ugly little Prinz sedan, but styling was created by Bertone. Accommodation was for two only, and there was no external clue as to the nature of the engine or its location. Unfortunately, the Wankel hadn't been completely perfected, and the one-rotor configuration proved less reliable and refined than predicted. Nonetheless, the Spider was quite quick for its displacement (equivalent to a 500cc reciprocating engine), with up to 92 mph at

1963-66 Wankel Spider convertible by Bertone

the top end. More a toy than a serious production effort, though it undoubtedly gave NSU valuable experience in manufacturing this new kind of engine and information about how it would stand up to typical owner use.

FOR

Curiosity value • Historical interest • Cuteness • Comparative rarity • High appreciation potential

AGAINST

Unreliable engine • Indifferent body construction • Not plentiful

SPECIFICATIONS

Length (in.) 143.0 **Wheelbase (in.)** 79.0 **Weight (lbs.)** 1545 **Price (new)** $2487 U.S. in 1967

ENGINES

cc/type (cid)	bore x stroke (mm)	bhp*	years
500/1-rotor Wankel (30.5)	not applicable	50	1963-66

*DIN

PRICES/PROJECTION

Restorable $1500-3000 **Good** $3000-5000 **Excellent** $4000-6000 **5-year projection** +20%

NSU Ro80
1967-77

1967-72 Ro80 4-door sedan

PRODUCTION

47,400

HISTORY

Second-generation Wankel-engine car from by-now faltering NSU, the firm's flagship model. The new twin-chamber engine was linked to a clutchless (semi-automatic) gearbox driving the front wheels. This mechanical package was clothed in a wind-cheating four-door sedan body featuring a very high, curved windshield; low rectangular grille; flowing fender contours; rounded "six light" greenhouse; and a short, high tail. Critically acclaimed when introduced for its advanced engineering, the Ro80 was just as much condemned when its engine proved cantakerously unreliable. Disgruntled owners, especially Britons, often resorted to substituting Ford V4 or V6 engines once the Wankel gave up the ghost. Like the Wankel Spider, it was the engine that spoiled an otherwise capable and interesting car. The main problem was short-lived rotor tip seals and resulting oil leaks when they wore out, plus chamber-wall distortion and other problems that usually necessitated a replacement engine or a complete rebuild before 30,000 miles. NSU lost its shirt on this car, partly because it tried to bolster the Wankel's reputation by honoring all warranty claims. NSU was absorbed by VW in 1969, which continued the car through 1977, after which it was unceremoniously dropped. By then, production of NSU's tiny rear-engine models had ceased, and the firm was folded in with VW's recently acquired (from Mercedes-Benz) Audi subsidiary, which ultimately took over NSU's Neckarsulm production facilities. It would be left to Toyo Kogyo (Mazda) of Japan to work out the bugs in Felix Wankel's engine, which it eventually did, but not before almost going the same way as NSU.

FOR

Trend-setter • Unique styling • Smooth road manners • Engine marvelous when it's whole

AGAINST

Premature rotor tip wear and oil leaks • Engine parts in short supply • Bad body corrosion problems

SPECIFICATIONS

Length (in.) 188.0 **Wheelbase (in.)** 112.5 **Weight (lbs.)** 2670
Price (new) NA

ENGINES

cc/type cid	bore x stroke*	bhp**	years
995/2-rotor (60)		113	1967-72

*not applicable; rotary engine
**DIN

PRICES/PROJECTION

Restorable $500-1000 **Good** $2000-3000
Excellent $3000-4000 **5-year projection** no change

Opel GT 1969-73

PRODUCTION

1969 11,880 **1970** 21,240 **1971** 13,696 **1972** 12,055
1973 11,693 (all figures for U.S. calendar year sales)

HISTORY

The curvy little "mini-Corvette" designed by GM's Clare MacKichan while on duty at Opel in Russelsheim, Germany. Developed from the Opel GT show car of a few years earlier, but not as exciting, mainly because wind tunnel tests decreed a sharper Kamm-style

1971 GT coupe

back, less smooth-looking front end, and a rounder profile. Chassis and running gear were shared with the contemporary Kadett, Opel's smallest model line. Bodies were built by Brissonneau & Lotz in France, then shipped to Germany for final assembly. The GT was strictly a two-seater, and like the 1968 Corvette had no external trunklid (cargo had to be wedged in behind the seatbacks and pushed into a small hold, hidden by a simple curtain). The driver sat quite low relative to the beltline, and faced an impressive-looking dashboard with full instrumentation. The hidden headlights rotated (by means of a manually controlled cockpit lever) upward out of their recesses, giving the car a kind of "frogeye" look. The GT has only recently emerged as a collectible, and examples may still be had for reasonable prices. Offered initially in the U.S. with two engines as in Europe. It's important to look for the reliable 1900 cam-in-head engine rather than the base 1.1-liter ohv unit. The latter was frugal with gas, but its pistons tended to seek daylight, especially near the redline. Dropped from the U.S. Opel lineup after 1973, but production continued in Europe for a short while.

FOR

A definite "comer" with good appreciation likely • Superb handling • Decent performance with 1900 engine • Styling • Sportiness

AGAINST

Seriously rust-prone (check potential buys carefully underneath) • Noisy, underpowered, somewhat questionable 1100 engine • Hard to find in clean, original condition

SPECIFICATIONS

Length (in.) 162.0 **Wheelbase (in.)** 95.7 **Weight (lbs.)** 2105
Price (new) $3395 (original U.S. list)

ENGINES

cc/type (cid)	bore x stroke (mm)	bhp	years
1078/ohv I4 (65.8)	75×61	67	1969-70
1897/ohv I4 (115.8)	93×70	75-90	1969-73

PRICES/PROJECTION

Restorable $1200-1800 **Good** $1800-2400
Excellent $2500-3200 **Deduct** 25% for 1100 engine
5-year projection +25%

Opel 1900/Manta Coupe/ Rallye/Luxus 1971-75

1971 1900 Rallye coupe

1973 Manta Luxus coupe

the German T-car design also used for the Chevy Chevette. Lowered compression for 1972-74, so the '71s and '75s have the best go.

PRODUCTION

1971 8378 **1972** 10,647 **1973 Rallye** 8360 **Luxus** 17,536 **1974 Rallye** 7959 **Luxus** 14,026 **1975** 15,118 (U.S. sales)

FOR

Amazingly rust-resistant • Ultra-strong engine • Neat looks, though aging now • Terrific handling • Class-leading passenger/trunk room • German build quality • Cheap

HISTORY

Smooth Euro-ponycar styled by Chuck Jordan, now GM Director of Design. Competed for pizzazz and practicality with the Mustang-like Capri from Ford Europe, but larger and not as quick despite less weight. All U.S. export models carried Opel's robust 1.9-liter cam-in-head four, still in production. The coupes were always called Manta in Europe and shared chassis, all-coil suspension, and drivetrain with the more upright Ascona sedans and wagons. All were initially marketed in America (through Buick dealers as per previous Opels from 1958) as the 1900; Manta name (but not Ascona) was applied from 1973. Rallye version had extra instruments, foglamps, matte-black hood, bodyside striping, stiffer suspension, slotted wheels, and a shorter final drive. Luxus had cord cloth upholstery, four-spoke wheels, and none of the Rallye's "boy-racer" goodies, but was quieter and more comfy. Also, a vinyl-trimmed base coupe all years. "Crash" bumpers for 1974-75, Bosch fuel injection for '75 only. Withdrawn from the U.S. market due to the unfavorable dollar-to-Deutschmark ratio at the time and resulting price escalation. Not to be confused with the later Isuzu-built "Opels" from Japan, based on

AGAINST

Parts tough to find through original sources, but some aftermarket suppliers are starting up • Driveability problems on '72s • Fuel injection woes on '75s • Original Luxus cloth upholstery wears out fast • Undergeared and noisy • Slow to appreciate

SPECIFICATIONS

Length (in.) 162.0 **Wheelbase (in.)** 95.7
Weight (lbs.) 2105-2225 **Price (new)** $2490 in 1971, $2800 (Luxus) 1973, $3800 (Manta) 1975

ENGINES

cid/type	bore x stroke	bhp	years
1897/ohv I4	93×70	90*/70**	1971-74
1897/ohv I4	93×70	77**	1975

*SAE gross
**SAE net

PRICES/PROJECTION

Restorable $500-1000 **Good** $750-1750 **Excellent** $1500-2500
Add $1000 for superb low-mileage original.
5-year projection no change

1973 Manta Luxus coupe

1975 Manta coupe

Pegaso Z102
1951-58

1952 Z102 sports coupe

PRODUCTION

110

HISTORY

A hand-built prestige product of ENASA, the state-owned Spanish truck and bus company. Designed for high-performance grand touring by Wilfredo Ricart, former Alfa Romeo technical director. A semi-monocoque steel underbody was used to mount standard factory-styled or custom bodies from specialist coachbuilders, including some Italian designs. Powered by a four-cam V8 variously offered in different displacements and states of tune; the largest version was available with a supercharger at extra cost. In its day, the Z102 was the fastest "production" car in the world, able to beat even contemporary Ferraris. No two were exactly alike, and because carmaking was only a sideline operation for the factory, there were few agents to handle sales and service. The company has since gone out of business.

FOR

Very rare and exotic • Fast (140-150 mph) • Engineering • Distinctive appearance

AGAINST

Forget restoration: parts are long extinct • Quite expensive

SPECIFICATIONS

Length (in.) 161.5 (average; variable with body fitted)
Wheelbase (in.) 92.0 **Weight (lbs.)** 2180 (average; variable with body and equipment) **Price (new)** NA

ENGINES

cc/type (cid)	bore x stroke (mm)	bhp*	years
2474/dohc V8 (151)	75×70	140	1951-58
2816/dohc V8 (172)	80×70	180	1951-58
3178/dohc V8 (194)	85×70	210/275	1951-58

*gross

PRICES/PROJECTION

Restorable $10,000-20,000 **Good** $25,000-35,000
Excellent $40,000-50,000 Values vary with type and style of coachwork. **5-year projection** +20%

Porsche 356
1950-55

PRODUCTION

10,678

HISTORY

Essentially a sports version of Dr. Ferdinand Porsche's Volkswagen Type 1 (Beetle) design, and the first production model from his independent carmaking firm. Based closely at first on the VW's platform chassis and running gear, including its rear-mounted air-cooled flat four engine and swing-axle rear suspension. Gradually became more distinct mechanically, stronger, faster, and more versatile. Offered in several body types, of which the 2+2 coupe with squat, stubby, rounded lines was most numerous. A cabriolet and an open roadster, called Speedster, were added later. Early 356s (through late 1951) are identifiable by their divided, slightly vee'd windshield. Generally top-quality construction, but handling was tricky near the limit. High-geared for flat-out cruising like the Beetle.

FOR

First of the Porsches • Good economy and roadability • Compact and manageable • Fine construction quality

AGAINST

Controversial styling (most like it, though) • Handling • Limited performance • Mechanical and body parts now in short supply

SPECIFICATIONS

Length (in.) 152.0-156.0 **Wheelbase (in.)** 82.7
Weight (lbs.) 1675-1830 **Price (new)** $4200 U.S. for 1952 coupe; $4400 for 1954 Super; $3500 for 1955 1500S Speedster

ENGINES

cc/type (cid)	bore x stroke (mm)	bhp	years
1086/ohv flat 4 (66)	74×64	40	1950-54
1286/ohv flat 4 (79)	80×64	44	1951-54
1290/ohv flat 4 (79)	75×74	55	1953-55
1488/ohv flat 4 (91)	80×74	55/70	1952-55

*DIN

PRICES/PROJECTION

Restorable $4000-6000 **Good** $6000-10,000
Excellent $12,000-21,000 Add up 50% for Speedster.
5-year projection +20%

Porsche 356A
1956-59

PRODUCTION

20,626

1956 356A Speedster roadster

HISTORY

A modified version of the original 356, with a curved one-piece windshield, more specialized Porsche components, and a greater choice of engines. A new powerplant was the race-bred, dohc Carrera unit, intended mainly for competition or flat-out high-speed on-road use.

FOR

As for Type 356

AGAINST

As for Type 356

SPECIFICATIONS

Length (in.) 152.0-156.0 **Wheelbase (in.)** 82.7
Weight (lbs.) 1800-2000 **Price (new)** approx. $3700-3950 U.S. for 1600 models; Carrera approx. $6000 in 1956

ENGINES

cc/type (cid)	bore x stroke (mm)	bhp*	years
1290/ohv flat 4 (79)	75×74	44/60	1956-57
1582/ohv flat 4 (97)	83×74	50/75	1956-59
1498/dohc flat 4 (91)	85×66	90/100	1956-58

*DIN

PRICES/PROJECTION

Restorable $5000-7000 **Good** $7000-10,000
Excellent $10,000-16,000 **5-year projection** +10%

1957-58 365A coupe

Porsche 356B/356C 1960-65

1959-61 356B hardtop coupe

PRODUCTION

1959-63 356B 25,834   **1963-65 356C** 16,674

HISTORY

Further developments of the original Type 356 design, identified by raised headlights and bumpers. A bit more interior room was found for the 356B by modifying the floorpan. Engine displacement now centered around 1.6 liters, and as before the air-cooled horizontally opposed four was offered in several stages of tune from the standard 60-bhp version on up through the 90-bhp Super 90 model and the dohc 115-bhp Carrera. A larger rear window and suspension refinements were also instituted. A hardtop coupe was briefly offered through 1961. For the 356C, disc brakes were fitted at each wheel, and equipment was again upgraded to keep pace with escalating prices. Top speeds were up to 110 mph for the 90-bhp overhead-valve engine, while the Carrera could see 120 mph. In its final year, the 356 was built alongside its eventual successor, the 911.

FOR

As for 1949-55 Type 356 and 1955-59 Type 356A, plus more performance and refinement, better equipment and handling

AGAINST

As for 1949-55 Type 356 and 1955-59 Type 356A

SPECIFICATIONS

Length (in.) 152.0-156.0 **Wheelbase (in.)** 82.7
Weight (lbs.) 1950-2080 **Price (new)** approx. $4100-4300 U.S. for "Normal" and Super 90 models

ENGINES

cc/type (cid)	bore x stroke (mm)	bhp*	years
1582/ohv flat 4 (97)	83×74	50-95	1960-65
1588/dohc flat 4 (97)	88×66	105/115	1960-61

*DIN

PRICES/PROJECTION

As for 1950-55 Type 356

Porsche Carrera 2
1962-64

PRODUCTION

1962-63 Type 356B 1810 **1963-65 Type 356C** 2134

HISTORY

The special high-performance race-and-rally version of the Type 356B/C, powered by a 2.0-liter enlargement of the dohc Carrera engine, hence the model designation. Very fast, with a top speed of up to 130 mph, and its beefed-up disc brakes helped keep the performance in check. Built with various body types, including some with styling by Zagato of Italy. Noisy, temperamental, and not meant for everyday road use.

FOR

As for 1959-65 Type 356B/356C, plus race-car specifications

AGAINST

As for 1959-65 Type 356B/356C, but more a racer than a road car and expensive to acquire and maintain

SPECIFICATIONS

Length (in.) 152.0-156.0 **Wheelbase (in.)** 82.7
Weight (lbs.) 2230 **Price (new)** approx. $7600 U.S. in 1962

ENGINES

cc/type (cid)	bore x stroke (mm)	bhp*	years
1966/dohc flat 4 (120)	92×74	130	1962-64

*DIN

PRICES/PROJECTION

Restorable $5000-6000 **Good** $8000-10,000
Excellent $12,000-16,000 Add 200% for Zagato Body (Abarth-Carrera GTL). **5-year projection** +15%

Porsche 911
1964-69

1969 911T coupe

PRODUCTION

36,533

HISTORY

The all-new second-generation Porsche, originally announced as the Type 901. Retained the 356-series chassis layout, with all-independent suspension, four-wheel disc brakes, and rear-mounted air-cooled engine with horizontally opposed cylinders. However, everything was new, including the all-steel monocoque body/chassis construction and thoroughly modern styling marked by a hood sloping down between prominent headlamps, ovoid side window shape, full-fastback roof, and sloping tail. Powered by a six instead of a four, the 911 was initially offered as a 2+2 coupe. For the 1967 model year it was supplemented by the "Targa," with a removable roof panel over the cockpit and take-out rear window that converted it into an open roadster with a fixed rollbar. Also for '67, a more powerful "S" model was added with 160 instead of 130 bhp. A detuned 911T (Touring) appeared the following year with 110 bhp, and the standard 911 was renamed 911L (Luxe). Much faster than the 356s, with 130 mph available right from the first, more on later versions. The rear seat backrests were split, and could be folded down for additional luggage space, a good thing as there wasn't much in the nose. Noisier but more exciting than its predecessor, the 911 was still plagued by sudden oversteer in tight corners, a function of hanging the engine out back beyond the rear axle centerline. Besides five-speed manual gearbox, a three-speed semi-automatic (dubbed "Sportomatic") was offered beginning with the '68 models. Updated for 1969 by a slight increase in wheelbase (achieved by moving the rear wheels further back) and adoption of wider wheels and tires to improve handling, which necessitated greater flare for the wheel openings. Mechanical fuel-injection replaced carburetors on the 911L and 911S to meet U.S. emissions requirements, and the 911L was redesignated 911E. The '69s were designated the B-series, superseding the A-series '68s.

FOR

Timeless styling ●Fast (especially 911S) ●Still in production, so parts no problem ●Active Porsche club ●Top-class construction and engineering ●Wonderful driver's car ●Good economy

AGAINST

Engine noise ●Tricky handling ●Minimal storage space

SPECIFICATIONS

Length (in.) 164.0 **Wheelbase (in.)** 87.0 (1964-68), 89.3 (1969)
Weight (lbs.) 2200-2300 **Price (new)** approx. $7000 U.S. base price in 1967

ENGINES

cc/type (cid)	bore x stroke (mm)	bhp*	years
1991/ohc flat-6 (122)	80×66	110-180	1965-68

*DIN

PRICES/PROJECTION

Restorable $3000-4000 **Good** $5000-6000
Excellent $7000-12,000 Add 10% for Targa model.
5-year projection +10%

Porsche 912
1965-69

PRODUCTION

30,300

1966 912 coupe

HISTORY

Porsche's "economy" model in these years. Shared the 911 body/chassis with simplified furnishings, but powered by the air-cooled flat-four from the Type 356C 1600SC. A good performer despite its low 102-bhp rating, the 912 could exceed 120 mph given enough room. Discontinued with introduction of the C-series 911s in late 1969, and effectively replaced in the lineup by the mid-engine, VW-powered 914 introduced in 1970.

FOR

As for 1964-69 911, plus engine somewhat more simple ● Better mileage ● Priced less than a 911

AGAINST

As for 1964-69 911, but slower and overshadowed by its more powerful linemates

SPECIFICATIONS

Length (in.) 164.0   **Wheelbase (in.)** 87.0   **Weight (lbs.)** 2135
Price (new) $4700 U.S. in 1966

ENGINES

cc/type (cid)	bore x stroke (mm)	bhp*	years
1582/ohv flat-4 (97)	83×74	102	1965-69

*DIN

PRICES/PROJECTION

Restorable $1000-30-00 **Good** $3000-4000
Excellent $5000-9000 Add 10% for Targa model.
5-year projection +10%

Porsche 911 1969-71

PRODUCTION

24,700

HISTORY

The "C-series" 911 produced from August 1969. Its main distinc-

1970 911E coupe

tion was a larger-bore engine giving a capacity of close to 2.2 liters and somewhat more power across the board. The main benefit, however, was increased torque that made the 911 easier and more relaxing to drive, especially in give-and-take city/suburban conditions. Brakes were also improved, and there were many detail mechanical and equipment changes. A ZF limited-slip differential was added as an option. As before, the low-power 911T used carburetors (now Zeniths instead of the previous Webers, however) while the 911E and S used fuel injection. The Targa body style was still available in each variation. Continued with a 2.4-liter version of the overhead cam flat-six after 1971.

FOR

As for 1965-69 911, plus better equipment and easier driveability

AGAINST

As for 1965-69 911

SPECIFICATIONS

Length (in.) 164.0   **Wheelbase (in.)** 89.3
Weight (lbs.) 2250-2350   **Price (new)** approx. $7000 U.S. list for 911E in 1969

ENGINES

cc/type (cid)	bore x stroke (mm)	bhp*	years
2195/ohc flat-6 (134)	84×66	125-180	1969-71

*DIN

PRICES/PROJECTION

As for 1964-69 911. **5-year projection** +10%

Porsche 914 1970-76

PRODUCTION

115,596

HISTORY

A semi-successful attempt by Porsche to crack the mass market, marking a return to its early close collaboration with Volkswagen. Designed by Porsche, the 914 was powered by the air-cooled 1.7-liter pushrod flat-four from VW's 411 sedan series. It was mounted just behind the two-seat cockpit ahead of a 911 gearbox, which was turned around 180 degrees for this application. The unit steel body/chassis made some use of 911 pieces for its all-independent

1970 914 coupe

1970-71 914/6 coupe (European model)

suspension, but styling and body panels were unique. Only one body style was offered, a notchback coupe with liftoff targa-style roof panel. The grille-less front end featured flip-up headlamps. The cabin was wide but rather short, so seating was a bit cramped for larger persons. The interior bore some resemblance to the 911's, but made extensive use of VW bits (instruments, door hardware, and the like). For 1973, the engine was enlarged to 1971cc as on the VW 412, and offered more power and torque for greater low-speed flexibility. The balanced weight distribution from the mid-engine layout provided excellent handling and roadholding, and performance was good (102 mph initially, 120 mph on later versions). Marketed in Europe as a "VW-Porsche" but sold exclusively as a Porsche in the U.S. Final assembly was done by the Karmann coachworks in Osnabrück, West Germany. Sales never lived up to expectations (though the 914 was popular in the States), perhaps because it was not viewed as a "real" Porsche by potential buyers. Replaced by the front-engine, water-cooled 924 beginning with the 1976 model year.

FOR

Mid-engine layout • Decent sports car stowage space • Road manners • Open-air versatility • Good supply in U.S.

AGAINST

Horrible engine access • Middling performance for a Porsche • Limited cabin space • Rust-prone • Engine parts drying up in U.S.

SPECIFICATIONS

Length (in.) 158.0 **Wheelbase (in.)** 96.5 **Weight (lbs.)** 2100
Price (new) $3595 original U.S. list, rising to $5300 in 1973

ENGINES

cc/type (cid)	bore x stroke (mm)	bhp*	years
1679/ohv flat-4 (102)	90 × 66	80	1970-73
1971/ohv flat-4 (120)	94 × 71	100	1973-76
1795/ohv flat-4 (110)	93 × 66	75	1974-75

*DIN

PRICES/PROJECTION

As for Porsche 912

Porsche 914/6 1970-71

PRODUCTION

3351

HISTORY

A six-cylinder version of the "VW-Porsche" 914, and built by Porsche at Zuffenhausen. Powered by the 2.0-liter carbureted flat-six from the previous 911T, but mounted amidships. Wider light-alloy wheels and fatter tires were standard equipment to suit the larger engine's greater performance potential. Other differences compared to the four-cylinder model included slightly larger vented disc brakes, deluxe trim, and more complete instrumentation. Priced quite a bit higher than the 914 and almost as much as a 911T, which had the advantage of "true" Porsche status in the eyes of many, a factor that undoubtedly hurt 914/6 sales. Dropped after only two years.

FOR

As for 1970-75 914, plus more performance and better equipment • Also more rare than 914 in U.S.

AGAINST

As for 1970-72 914, plus confused image from "mixed" parentage

SPECIFICATIONS

Length (in.) 158.0 **Wheelbase (in.)** 96.5 **Weight (lbs.)** 2070
Price (new) approx. $6100 U.S. in 1970

ENGINES

cc/type (cid)	bore x stroke (mm)	bhp*	years
1991/ohc flat-6 (122)	80 × 66	110	1970-71

*DIN; 125 bhp gross in U.S. tune

PRICES/PROJECTION

Restorable $1500-4500 **Good** $4500-6000
Excellent $6500-10,000 **5-year projection** +10%

Porsche 911 1972-73

PRODUCTION

1972 5120   **1973** 5836 (U.S. calendar year sales)

HISTORY

Continuation of Porsche's durable rear-engine sports car design, now with enlarged (via more stroke) version of familiar air-cooled flat six and fuel injection for all models. Length went up slightly for 1973 as Porsche successfully met U.S. bumper impact regulations

1972 911S coupe

1975 911 Carrera coupe (U.S. model)

with comparatively little change to overall appearance. Other changes for '73 included a small under-bumper front spoiler for the E and S models, and a rearranged shift pattern for the 911S 5-speed gearbox. Also offered as the Carrera RS, a street version of the racing Carrera that appeared in 1973, but not legally saleable in the U.S.

FOR

As for 1969-71 Type 911

AGAINST

As for 1969-71 Type 911

SPECIFICATIONS

Length (in.) 163.9 (1972), 168.4 (1973) **Wheelbase (in.)** 89.4
Weight (lbs.) approx. 2600 **Price (new)** $10,160 U.S. for 911S in 1973

ENGINES

cc/type (cid)	bore x stroke (mm)	bhp*	years
2341/sohc flat-6 (143)	84 ×70	134-181	1972-73

*DIN

PRICES/PROJECTION

Restorable $4000-6000 **Good** $7000-9000
Excellent $10,000-13,000 Add 10% for Targa.
5-year projection +30%

Porsche 911 1974-77

PRODUCTION

1974 5120 (incl. 548 Carrera models) **1975** 5480 (incl. 576 Carrera models) **1976** 6486 (incl. 626 Turbo Carrera)
1977 6226 (incl. 517 Turbo Carrera) (all figures for U.S. calendar year sales)

HISTORY

Again confounding those pundits who thought the 911 would have been retired by the mid-'70s, Porsche successfully updated the model for 1974 by another bore increase and a switch from Bosch mechanical to Bosch electronic fuel injection. The result was a modest gain in horsepower and acceleration with only a small penalty in fuel economy, both achieved while meeting the strictest ever U.S. emissions laws. Bumpers became more prominent starting

with the '74s, basically the same style seen on the current 911. Model offerings were shuffled, with a base 911 replacing the previous T, the 911S substituting for the former midrange E, and a new Carrera (with wider wheels and tires, modest tail spoiler, and bold bodyside lettering) taking over for the previous 911S. This non-turbocharged Carrera was essentially a U.S. version of the European RS minus its extra performance. For 1975, the line was pared to 911S and Carrera only. From then on, only the S remained as Porsche introduced its Type 930 Turbo Carrera (later called simply Porsche Turbo) for 1976. Still very much the same car it was in earlier years, but cornering power and handling predictability both gradually improved.

FOR

As for 1969-71 Type 911, plus parts and service more easily available

AGAINST

As for 1969-71 Type 911

SPECIFICATIONS

Length (in.) 168.9 **Wheelbase (in.)** 89.4 **Weight (lbs.)** approx. 2600 **Price (new)** $9950 U.S. in 1974, rising to $14,395 in 1977 for 911S

ENGINES

cc/type (cid)	bore x stroke (mm)	bhp*	years
2687/sohc flat 6 (164)	90×70	143-167	1974-77

*SAE net

PRICES/PROJECTION

Restorable $6000-7000 **Good** $9000-12,000
Excellent $13,000-16,000 Add 10% for Targa.
5-year projection +10%

Porsche 930 1976-79

PRODUCTION

1976* 626 **1977*** 517 **1978**** 566 **1979**** 849 (U.S. calendar year sales)
*Turbo Carrera **Turbo

HISTORY

Exciting, prestigious turbocharged version of Porsche's rear-engine

1979 930 Turbo coupe (U.S. model)

911, but so heavily re-engineered it was given a different type number. Marked externally by bulging wheelarch flares over wide tires mounted on cast-aluminum wheels, plus prominent tray-like rear spoiler, usually referred to as the whale tail. Initially, the 2.7-liter 911 engine was bored out to near 3.0-liter capacity, and featured a KKK turbocharger. A displacement increase followed for 1978, along with the addition of an air-to-air intercooler to provide a denser fuel/air mixture and consequently more power. Also differed from 911 in having a special wide-ratio 4-speed gearbox (instead of a close-ratio 5-speed) to take advantage of the engine's prodigious torque spread. Phenomenally fast *(Road & Track* magazine reported 0-60 mph at 5.0 seconds, with a 13.7-second quarter mile clocking at 106.5 mph), the 930 proved to be the most roadable Porsche ever, thereby refuting the argument that the tail-heavy rear-engine layout couldn't be made to work well with such power. A fantastically successful road racer, and continues so at this writing. Importation halted in 1979 in the wake of escalating fuel prices that made selling a car like this seem anti-social; returned to the U.S. market for the 1986 model year. Low production, sizzling acceleration, Porsche's high level of engineering expertise and craftsmanship, and a long string of competition wins virtually guarantee collectibility in future years for this German slingshot.

FOR

Rarity • High performance with civilized road manners and surprising fuel economy • Luxurious cabin appointments • Race prowess • Distinctive looks

AGAINST

Performance demands respect and quick reflexes • Costly to maintain or restore • You'll dig deep to put one in your driveway

SPECIFICATIONS

Length (in.) 168.9 **Wheelbase (in.)** 89.4

1978 930 Turbo coupe (U.S. model)

Weight (lbs.) 2700-2850 **Price (new)** $26,000 U.S. in 1976, rising to $38,500 in 1979

ENGINES

cc/type (cid)	bore x stroke (mm)	bhp*	years
2993/sohc flat 6T (183)	95×70	234	1976-77
3299/sohc flat 6T (201)	97×74	253	1978-79

*SAE net

PRICES/PROJECTION

Restorable $10,000-18,000 **Good** $20,000-25,000
Excellent $27,000-36,000 **5-year projection** +15%

Renault Caravelle 1962-68

1962-68 Caravelle convertible

PRODUCTION

NA

HISTORY

Successor to the Floride, a sporty derivative of Renault's air-cooled rear-engine Dauphine sedan. Renamed to suit Californians, and restyled with a squared-up nose. As before, convertible and close-coupled 2+2 hardtop (now with longer roof), built to an original Allemano design by Brissonneau & Lotz, which also carried out final assembly. Radiator resited toward the rear for more back seat space, and performance improved with substitution of the larger and more modern R8 sedan unit for the Dauphine's old long-stroke, 40-bhp 854cc four. Initial 956cc unit replaced by a bored-out enlargement from 1964 to give up to 90 mph, accompanied by all-synchromesh gearbox. Still Renault's answer to the Volkswagen Karmann-Ghia (just as Dauphine and R8 were Beetle competitors) but far less successful in the U.S. and never a big seller even by the French company's standards. U.S. imports doubtful after 1967, when Renault's big push here was with the front-drive 16.

FOR

Stying • Somewhat rare • Cheap • Economical

AGAINST

1-liter engine's performance • Running gear not all that reliable • Rust-prone • Hard to find

SPECIFICATIONS

Length (in.) 167.7 **Wheelbase (in.)** 89.0
Weight (lbs.) 1720/1780 (hardtop/convertible)
Price (new) $2199 U.S. in 1967

ENGINES

cc/type (cid)	bore x stroke (mm)	bhp	years
956/ohv I4 (58)	65×72	51	1962-63
1108/ohv I4 (68)	70×72	55-58	1964-68

PRICES/PROJECTION

As for 1959-62 Floride

Renault 8 Gordini 1100/1300   1964-69

1966-69 8 Gordini 1300 4-door sedan

PRODUCTION

NA

HISTORY

Limited-production "homologation special" based on the mass-market R8 sedan, intended as Renault's race-and-rally competitor against the BMW Mini-Cooper S. The rear-mounted, air-cooled engine used the normal R8 block, with a cross-pushrod cylinder head designed by the Amadee Gordini tuning firm. The original 1108cc displacement was boosted to 1255cc in mid-1966. Shared the standard R8's boxy, undistinguished four-door body. Almost all Gordinis were painted French Racing Blue with white "go faster" tape stripes on hood, roof, and rear deck. The 1300 version had four instead of two headlamps and an auxiliary fuel tank. Like the R8, had all-independent suspension and four-wheel disc brakes, the latter an unusual feature for a European small car of those days. The 1100s had a four-speed center-control gearbox, replaced by a five-speed Gordini box on 1300s. Noisy and crude, but very eager, with up to 110 mph in normal tune and even more possible with special tuning. Not seriously imported to the States.

FOR

Performance • Gutsy character • Gordini engine and brakes • Most body and chassis parts still available • Cheap collectible with high appreciation potential

AGAINST

Hard to find in U.S. • Dodgy handling • Rust-prone body • Lacking in refinement

SPECIFICATIONS

Length (in.) 157.5 **Wheelbase (in.)** 89.3
Weight (lbs.) 1755/1875 (1100/1300) **Price (new)** NA

ENGINES

cc/type (cid)	bore x stroke (mm)	bhp*	years
1108/ohv I4 (68)	70×72	95	1964-66
1255/ohv I4 (77)	75×72	103	1966-69

*gross

PRICES/PROJECTION

Restorable $400-500 **Good** $1600-2000
Excellent $3500-4000 **5-year projection** +10%

Riley MPH/ Sprite 1934-38

PRODUCTION

MPH 15 **Sprite** 50

HISTORY

Riley of England developed a series of fine sporting cars with modern engines in the 1920s and '30s. The most collectible today—if you can find one—are the related MPH and Sprite two-seaters. Both have the same solid chassis with a very tight all-leaf-spring suspension. The main difference is in engines, a straight six for MPH, a four for Sprite. The main attractions for Americans are the Wilson pre-selector gearbox (used by Cord among others) and styling that was a bit more graceful than MG's and a bit less florid than the SS100 (Jaguar). The Sprite's 85-mph top speed was creditable for the period. MPH was produced through 1935. Sprite ran 1936-38.

FOR

Styling • Novel pre-select gearbox • Solid reliability • Parts still around • Club support in both U.S. and UK

AGAINST

Very scarce • Hard ride • Cramped driving position • Not for rainy days

SPECIFICATIONS

Length (in.) 148.0 **Wheelbase (in.)** 97.5
Weight (lbs.) 2000/2200 **Price (new)** NA

ENGINES

cc/type (cid)	bore x stroke (mm)	bhp	years
1458/ohv I6 (89)	57.0×95.2	NA	1934-35*
1633/ohv I6 (100)	60.3×95.2	NA	1934-35*
1726/ohv I6	69.0×100.0	NA	1934-35*

(105)				
1496/ohv I4	69.0×100.0	NA	1936-38**	
(91)				

*MPH
**Sprite

PRICES/PROJECTION

Restorable $8000-10,000 **Good** $17,000-20,000
Excellent $20,000-25,000 **5-year projection** +10%

Rolls-Royce Phantom II 1930-35

1934 Phantom II Continental convertible coupe

PRODUCTION

1672 (some sources list 1767; began 1929)

HISTORY

An updated version of the original New Phantom (Phantom I) of 1925, with a new chassis (on two long wheelbases) and a much-modified engine and transmission. Typical of between-the-wars Royces in every way. All have stately hand-built coachwork, by Brewster on most left-hand-drive export models. Massive, heavy and predictably expensive. Performance and economy took a back seat to build quality and sumptuous fittings, lending credence to R-R's claim that this was "The Best Car in the World." Lower chassis featured four-wheel hydraulic brakes and more modern Hotchkiss drive and hypoid rear end instead of the torque tube used on Silver Ghost/Phantom I, but retention of beam-axle suspension front and rear (on semi-elliptic leaf springs) made it somewhat old-fashioned toward the end of the model's life. Numerous changes in these years, including smaller wheel/tire diameter, one-shot lube system, and synchromesh gearing on third and fourth (from 1932) and on second (1935 models). Significant as the last R-R designed by Henry Royce. Special Continental models (280 built) are the most coveted today.

FOR

R-R panache, prestige • Cost-no-object engineering • Exquisite looks • Restoration still possible from factory parts supplies • Extremely reliable

AGAINST

Very expensive • You'll need a mortgage to restore one • Archaic road manners and heavy to drive

SPECIFICATIONS

Length (in.) Variable with body style
Wheelbase (in.) 144.0/150.0 **Weight (lbs.)** 5000-6500 (est.)
Price (new) NA

ENGINES

cc/type (cid)	bore x stroke (mm)	bhp	years
7668/ohv I6	108.0×139.7	120*	1930-35
(468)			

*not officially quoted

PRICES/PROJECTION

Restorable $10,000-20,000 **Good** $22,000-30,000
Excellent $30,000-38,000 Values vary greatly with coachwork.
5-year projection +20%

Rolls-Royce 20/25 1930-36

PRODUCTION

3827

HISTORY

The second-generation "small" Rolls-Royce, the direct replacement for the original "20." Unlike the Phantoms, there was no Springfield equivalent built in the U.S. As with all such prewar Rolls-Royces, offered only as a rolling chassis for coachbuilt bodywork, so a huge variety of styles still exists. Beautifully and carefully crafted but surprisingly slow even for the period, about 70 mph tops. Synchro-mesh gearbox from 1932, complete centralized chassis lubrication from 1934. The British at their best, so no excuse—and surprisingly little cash—needed to buy one.

FOR

Magnificent construction • Mechanical parts still available • Silky controls • Luxurious British fittings

AGAINST

Very high parts and restoration costs • Stodgy performance • Body restoration difficult

SPECIFICATIONS

Length (in.) 180.0 (average) **Wheelbase (in.)** 129.0
Weight (lbs.) 3800 (approx.) **Price (new)** NA

ENGINES

cc/type (cid)	bore x stroke (mm)	bhp	years
3680/ohv I6	82.6×114.3	65*	1930-36
(224)			

*not officially quoted

Rolls-Royce Phantom III 1935-39

PRICES/PROJECTION

Restorable $6000-9500 **Good** $11,000-15,000
Excellent $15,000-18,000 **5-year projection** +20%

1937 Phantom III 4-door sedan

PRODUCTION

710

HISTORY

R-R's response to multi-cylinder giants from America and Europe and the first Royce with a V-configuration engine. Complex and released before it was fully developed, so not entirely successful. Much more modern than the PII, with a GM-type coil-spring independent front suspension. Long-stroke, seven-main-bearing V12 featured hydraulic valve lifters, twin-coil ignition, triple-pressure lubrication, wet liners, and marine-type conrods. Unfortunately, interesting iron/alloy construction was corrosion-prone, which led to cooling problems. Shorter than the PII in wheelbase and overall length, but only a little lighter yet surprisingly rapid. Incomparable specialist coachwork on all examples, mostly limousines and sedans. Survival rates have not been high, as many engines suffered neglect in middle age. Arguably the world's best prewar car. A high-status item today but best tackled only by serious collectors.

FOR

Advanced V12 engineering • High-quality period coachwork • Smooth, silent, serene, dignified • Marque and model magic

AGAINST

Extremely expensive to buy and restore • Nightmarish body rebuilds • More for passengers than drivers • Hard to find now, as is restoration expertise

SPECIFICATIONS

Length (in.) 191.0 (average) **Wheelbase (in.)** 142.0
Weight (lbs.) 5800 (approx.) **Price (new)** NA

ENGINES

cc/type (cid)	bore x stroke (mm)	bhp	years
7338/ohv V12 (448)	82.5×114.3 *not officially quoted	165-180*	1935-39

Rolls-Royce 25/30 1936-38

PRICES/PROJECTION

Restorable $10,000-20,000 **Good** $22,000-30,000
Excellent $30,000-38,000 Values vary with coachwork
5-year projection +20%

PRODUCTION

1201

HISTORY

Interim replacement for the 20/25 (see entry) as the "small" R-R, with a larger engine and more modern late-prewar styling. As before, solid-axle front suspension and a wide choice of coachbuilt body styles. A tad quicker than the 20/25, though weights rose almost as quickly as horsepower in this period. A "junior edition" but every inch a Rolls-Royce and built with infinite care.

FOR

As for 1930-36 Model 20/25

AGAINST

Stodgy performance • Not that expensive, but costly to restore • Less status than senior models

SPECIFICATIONS

Length (in.) 180.0 (average) **Wheelbase (in.)** 132.0
Weight (lbs.) 4000 (approx.) **Price (new)** NA

ENGINES

cc/type (cid)	bore x stroke (mm)	bhp	years
4257/ohv I6 (260)	88.9×114.0	85*	1936-38

*not officially quoted

PRICES/PROJECTION

As for 1929-36 Model 20/25

Rolls-Royce Wraith 1938-39

PRODUCTION

491

HISTORY

The last and most modern junior Royce of the prewar period, taking over for the 25/30 (see entry). Wheelbase was extended four inches over that of its predecessor for a chassis thoroughly revised along Phantom III lines, featuring GM-like independent front suspension with enclosed coil springs. Semi-elliptic leaf-sprung solid rear axle, servo-assisted four-wheel hydraulic brakes as before. More graceful though still very stately bodywork supplied by specialists per R-R

1938 Wraith 4-door sedan by Park Ward

1947-55 Silver Wraith coupe by James Young

tradition. Most were sedans with razor-edge lines, but a few, more flowing coupes and convertibles were also completed. Development was cut off by the outbreak of World War II and the model would not be revived postwar, making this effectively a one-year-only offering and thus among the rarest prewar Royces today. Bears no mechanical relationship with post-1945 models.

FOR

High-quality build • Pleasant, up-to-date handling • Magnificent furnishings and detailing • Marque's customary snob appeal • Exclusivity

AGAINST

Generally "heavier" styling than earlier R-R juniors • Still not fast (about 80 mph tops) • Costly to buy and restore • Rot-prone wood-frame bodywork a real headache

SPECIFICATIONS

Length (in.) Variable with body **Wheelbase (in.)** 136.0
Weight (lbs.) 5200 (approx.) **Price (new)** NA

ENGINES

cc/type (cid)	bore x stroke (mm)	bhp	years
4257/ohv I6 (260)	88.9×144.0	90*	1938-39

*not officially quoted

PRICES/PROJECTION

As for 20/25 and 25/30 models (see entries)

Rolls-Royce Silver Wraith 1946-59

PRODUCTION

127-in. wb 1144   **133-in. wb** 639

HISTORY

The custom-bodied Rolls-Royce series in the postwar years, continuing a famous name of the '30s. R-R built the chassis, essentially a stretched-wheelbase version (127 or 133 inches) of the contemporary 120-inch Silver Dawn/Bentley Mark VI platform, with the same suspension design and drivetrains. Bodywork was supplied by traditional R-R specialists — Park Ward, H.J. Mulliner, Hooper, and others—most with wood framing and light-alloy or steel panels. Many had "classic" lines, with freestanding headlamps, separate

front fenders, division window between passengers and chauffeur, and the characteristic Rolls-Royce "parthenon" grille. Complete luxury equipment was expected, and interiors were decked out with leather upholstery, wood trim, and, in a few cases, cut-glass ornaments. Displacement of R-R's F-head six was increased to 4.5 liters in 1951, then 4.9 liters in 1955; otherwise, few mechanical changes in these years. In this era there was no doubt: these were "The Best Cars in the World."

FOR

Handcrafted bodies, individual detailing • Superb workmanship • Opulence on a grand scale • Unbeatable Rolls-Royce cachet and exclusivity • Strong club support

AGAINST

Limited performance • Thirsty • Ponderous to drive • Body parts extinct • Now very costly to buy, restore, and own

SPECIFICATIONS

Length (in.) 200.0-206.0 **Wheelbase (in.)** 127.0/133.0
Weight (lbs.) 4735-5405 **Price (new)** NA

ENGINES

cc/type (cid)	bore x stroke (mm)	bhp*	years
4257/F6 (260)	89×114		1947-51
4566/F6 (279)	92×114		1951-55
4887/F6 (298)	95×114		1955-59

*NA; Rolls-Royce customarily does not quote power or torque output

PRICES/PROJECTION

Restorable $5000-8000 **Good** $10,000-20,000
Excellent $20,000-25,000 Add 30-50% for good/excellent individual custom bodies. **5-year projection** +15%

Rolls-Royce Silver Dawn 1949-1955

PRODUCTION

4¼-liter 170 **4½-liter short tail** 110 **4½-liter long tail** 481

HISTORY

The first Rolls-Royce model ever based on a Bentley; usually it's the other way around. Shared the "standard steel" bodyshell, chassis, and all running gear with the Bentley Mark VI of these years, though engine output was rumored to be lower. Marked, of course, by the distinctive R-R grille. Unlike the Bentley, models with left-hand drive featured a steering-column gearchange. Engine displacement was increased in 1951, followed shortly afterwards by a long-tail "B7" body style. Automatic transmission was made standard beginning in 1953. Styling followed the British "razor edge" school, with semi-integrated headlamps; separate, sweeping fenderlines; and semi-enclosed rear wheels (covered by "spats"). As expected from Rolls, interiors were plushly outfitted with leather upholstery, wood cappings for dash and doors, and lots of detail conveniences. A good many were sent to North America, as the model was never sold in Britian.

FOR

The Rolls-Royce name •Silence and refinement •Dignified styling •Many mechanical parts still available •Comfortable, well-furnished cabin

AGAINST

Not very fast (85-90 mph tops) •Rust-prone •Body parts extinct •Too much like a Bentley?

SPECIFICATIONS

Length (in.) 192.0 (1949-51), 199.5 (1951-55)
Wheelbase (in.) 120.0 **Weight (lbs.)** 4100 (average)
Price (new) NA

ENGINES

cc/type (cid)	bore x stroke (mm)	bhp*	years
4257/F6 (260)	89×114		1949-51
4566/F6 (279)	92×114		1951-55

*NA; Rolls-Royce customarily does not quote power or torque output

PRICES/PROJECTION

Restorable $4000-5000 **Good** $12,000-15,000
Excellent $15,000-20,000 Add 30-50% for good/excellent individual custom bodies. **5-year projection** +20%

Rolls-Royce Phantom IV 1950-56

PRODUCTION

18

HISTORY

The most exclusive of all postwar Rolls-Royce models, and not one you're apt to see any day of the week. Built on a longer Silver Wraith chassis and powered by the R-R straight six with two extra cylinders tacked on. Each Phantom IV was built to special order, and went to royalty or heads of state only. Each was fitted with a special handcrafted limousine body with wood framing, and offered seven-passenger seating capacity. In appearance, it was "British formal," with a very upright stance. Some models were fitted with freestanding headlamps; most had razor edge styling. R-R spared no expense on the Phantoms, the pride of its fleet, and apart from the chassis and suspension they shared nothing with the more "common" Wraith and Dawn models.

FOR

Tremendously scarce and desirable •Magnificent coachbuilt

bodywork •Superb craftsmanship throughout •Famous first owners

AGAINST

Most mechanical and all body parts now unobtainable •Extremely costly to buy, restore, and own •Ponderous to drive

SPECIFICATIONS

Length (in.) 229.0 (variable) **Wheelbase (in.)** 145.0
Weight (lbs.) 5500 (approx.) **Price (new)** NA

ENGINES

cc/type (cid)	bore x stroke (mm)	bhp*	years
5675/F8 (346)	89×114		1950-56

*NA; Rolls-Royce customarily does not quote power or torque output

PRICES/PROJECTION

Restorable $40,000-60,000 **Good** $80,000-100,000
Excellent $110,000-150,000 **5-year projection** +10%

Rolls-Royce Silver Cloud I 1955-59

1955-59 Silver Cloud I limousine

PRODUCTION

standard body 2238 **limo** 121

HISTORY

A near-identical twin to the Bentley S-Type (see entry) introduced concurrently with it, except for the distinctive, more expensive Rolls-Royce radiator and flying lady mascot. There was supposed to be a slight difference in engine power in 1955 and '56, though it would be hard to prove given R-R's nondisclosure policy. Offered as the "standard steel" four-door sedan, which is naturally the most numerous model today, as well as in long-wheelbase limousine form. Special coachbuilt bodies, mostly coupes and convertibles, were also available through Rolls-Royce's usual suppliers.

FOR

As for 1955-59 Bentley S-Type, plus R-R snob appeal

AGAINST

As for 1955-59 Bentley S-Type

SPECIFICATIONS

Length (in.) 212.0/216.0 (sedan/limo)
Wheelbase (in.) 123.0/127.0 (sedan/limo)
Weight (lbs.) 4370/4650 (sedan/limo)   **Price (new)** NA

ENGINES

cc/type (cid)	bore x stroke (mm)	bhp*	years
4887/F6 (298)	95×114		1955-59

*NA; Rolls-Royce customarily does not quote power or torque output

PRICES/PROJECTION

Restorable $8000-10,000 **Good** $15,000-20,000
Excellent $30,000-35,000 Addd up to 100% for custom coachbuilt body styles. **5-year projection** +10%

Rolls-Royce Phantom V 1959-68

1967 Phantom V limousine

PRODUCTION

793

HISTORY

Successor to the Silver Wraith, this massive limousine shared the chassis and running gear of the Series II Bentley S-Type/R-R Silver Cloud, but used an appropriately longer wheelbase. The chassis was the familiar, old-fashioned affair (beam axle, drum brakes, mechanical brake servo) that had been around for years, but was thoroughly developed and very reliable. Power was provided by the firm's new light-alloy V8 engine with what the factory described as "adequate" output, though R-R continued to refuse stating precisely what "adequate" meant. All Phantom Vs had custom-crafted bodies by "approved suppliers," mainly Mulliner and Park Ward. Rolls-Royce built the rolling chassis only. Similar in general appearance to, but much larger than, the Silver Cloud. Almost all had seven-passenger seating, division window, and chauffeur equipment; many had air conditioning and all were equipped with a General Motors-based Hydra-matic transmission. Lofty, stately, and extremely dignified, yet capable of 100-plus mph. Produced in greater numbers than the Phantom IV, but still the ultimate in "arrival impact" for pop singers and ruling monarchs.

FOR

Best of the best • Unmistakably Rolls-Royce, with prestige to match

• Enormous carrying capacity •Smooth, silent, luxurious • Active club support in U.S. and Britain

AGAINST

Expensive •Costs a bundle to buy and run • Big and ponderous to drive, let alone park •Body parts difficult to find at the right price

SPECIFICATIONS

Length (in.) 238.0   **Wheelbase (in.)** 144.0
Weight (lbs.) 5600-5800   **Price (new)** NA

ENGINES

cc/type (cid)	bore x stroke (mm)	bhp*	years
6230/ohv V8 (380)	104×91		1959-68

*NA; Rolls-Royce does not customarily quote power or torque output

PRICES/PROJECTION

Restorable $10,000-15,000 **Good** $30,000-40,000
Excellent $50,000-60,000 Add 50-100% for good/excellent Landaulette. **5-year projection** +10%

Rolls-Royce Silver Cloud II 1959-62

PRODUCTION

standard body 2417   **limo** 299

HISTORY

Essentially the original Silver Cloud with a different engine, R-R's new 6.2-liter light-alloy V8 said to have been inspired by Cadillac's 1949 ohv unit. Identical with the companion Bentley S-Type Series II of these years except for nameplates and, of course, the Rolls-Royce radiator and mascot. As with its predecessor, most of these cars had the "standard steel" sedan body, but 299 examples were long-wheelbase limousines with division window and handcrafted coachwork. Arguably, still the "Best Car in the World" at this time, but falling behind rising standards of chassis refinement.

FOR

As for 1955-59 Silver Cloud, plus more performance and smoother, quieter operation

AGAINST

As for 1955-59 Silver Cloud

SPECIFICATIONS

Length (in.) 212.0/216.0 (sedan/limo)
Wheelbase (in.) 123.0/127.0 (sedan/limo)
Weight (lbs.) 4550/4650 (sedan/limo)   **Price (new)** NA

ENGINES

cc/type (cid)	bore x stroke (mm)	bhp*	years
6230/ohv V8 (380)	104×91		1959-62

*NA; Rolls-Royce customarily does not quote power or torque output

PRICES/PROJECTION

As for 1955-59 Silver Cloud.

Rolls-Royce Silver Cloud III 1962-65

1962-65 Silver Cloud III standard sedan

PRODUCTION

standard body 2044   **limousine** 253   **custom body** 79

HISTORY

Last of the Silver Clouds, with changes both for the better and the worse. In the latter category was the styling, marked (like that of the Bentley S-Type Series III) by a lower hood and radiator and quad headlamps mounted in oval nacelles. Most purists thought this a shocking violation of R-R tradition at the time. Still mounted on a separate chassis (by now looking quite dated), with drum brakes and a live rear axle. In the "better" column was seven percent more power (not disclosed, but probably up to about 220 bhp net) from the aluminum 6.2-liter V8. Again identical to its Bentley stablemate apart from the obvious grille and nameplate differences. Replaced in late 1965 by the monocoque Silver Shadow series with more modern engineering and less distinctive appearance.

FOR

As for 1959-62 Silver Cloud II

AGAINST

As for 1959-62 Silver Cloud II, plus dubious front end restyle

SPECIFICATIONS

Length (in.) 211.0/216.0 (sedan/limo)
Wheelbase (in.) 123.0/127.0 (sedan/limo)
Weight (lbs.) 4480/4650 (sedan/limo)   **Price (new)** NA

ENGINES

cc/type (cid)	bore x stroke (mm)	bhp*	years
6230/ohv V8 (380)	104×91		1959-62

*220 bhp net (est); Rolls-Royce customarily does not quote power or torque output

PRICES/PROJECTION

As for 1959-62 Silver Cloud II

Rolls-Royce Phantom VI 1968-80

1976 Phantom VI limousine

PRODUCTION

311 (through spring 1978)

HISTORY

Continuation of the imposing Phantom V, with quad headlamps as the only obvious change. Chassis and running gear were carried over intact, but separate air conditioning units for the front and rear compartments were now fitted. Beginning in early 1978, an enlarged version of the Rolls-Royce V8 engine was specified, along with a differently designed automatic transmission. Production of these stately limousines averages only about 20 per year, and continues at this writing, still with time-honored hand-assembly methods and individually crafted bodies.

FOR

As for 1959-68 Phantom V

AGAINST

As for 1959-68 Phantom V

SPECIFICATIONS

Length (in.) 238.0   **Wheelbase (in.)** 145.0   **Weight (lbs.)** 6000
Price (new) NA

ENGINES

cc/type (cid)	bore x stroke (mm)	bhp*	years
6230/ohv V8 (380)	104×91		1968-78
6750/ohv V8 (412)	104×99		1978-date

*NA; Rolls-Royce customarily does not quote power or torque output

PRICES/PROJECTION

Restorable $10,000-15,000 **Good** $25,000-50,000
Excellent $50,000-75,000 Add 50-75% for good/excellent Landaulette. **5-year projection** +10%

1976 Phantom VI limousine

Rover P5/P5B Series 1959-73

PRODUCTION

NA

HISTORY

The second-generation postwar design from the British Rover company. All were four-door sedans featuring semi-unitized construction. A massive front subframe attached to the welded main body/floorpan structure carried the engine and transmission. Originally known as the 3-Litre, and powered by Rover's trusty F-head inline six. Following its acquisition by the parent British Leyland company, the Buick aluminum V8 engine was substituted for the 1967 model year, and the factory code designation changed to P5B. Automatic transmission was optional in all years, and power steering was made standard with the engine swap. Styling was rounded, staid, and conservative. A large square grille with vertical bars and rounded corners, split by a heavy chrome divider bearing the Rover emblem, dominated the front end. A low-roof four-door oddly called "Coupe" was also offered, and continued after introduction of the P6 series, when the standard-roof P5 models disappeared. Interiors featured lots of real wood, leather, fine-quality carpet, and traditional British fittings. More agile than its P4 predecessor, with better brakes and considerably more performance. The six-cylinder cars could reach 105 mph; with V8 the top end was around 115 mph despite the bluff shape. A good many of these Rovers survive in their homeland today, and the model is reasonably available in the U.S.

FOR

Engineering integrity • Well-built • Durable • Fine furnishings • Power steering, automatic on many examples

AGAINST

Heavy and gas-hungry • Ponderous handling • Dubious parts supplies

SPECIFICATIONS

Length (in.) 186.0 **Wheelbase (in.)** 110.5
Weight (lbs.) 3500-3610 **Price (new)** NA

ENGINES

cc/type (cid)	bore x stroke (mm)	bhp*	years
2995/F6 (183)	78×105	105/121	1959-67
3528/ohv V8 (215)	89×71	161	1967-73
*net bhp			

PRICES/PROJECTION

Restorable $500-700 **Good** $2000-2500 **Excellent** $4000-5000
5-year projection +30%

Rover 2000/2000TC 1963-73

PRODUCTION

NA

1968-69 2000TC 4-door sedan (U.S. model)

HISTORY

Dramatically more modern than any previous Rover, the new P6-series sedans were advanced enough to continue for a decade. Construction featured a monocoque "skeleton" structure (like the Citroën DS) to which outer skin panels were bolted. This had the advantage of making body repairs easier and cheaper. Suspension was independent in front (by coil springs and twin control arms), and De Dion linkage was used at the rear. Powered by a new four-cylinder overhead cam engine with single and dual (TC) carburetors. Styling was a complete departure for Rover, with a subtle wedge profile, a full-width grille containing quad headlamps, a squared-off trunklid, and a fairly low beltline. The interior featured a "modular" instrument cluster and huge gloveboxes that doubled as knee crash pads under a full-width dash rail. On the road, the Rover delivered a soft ride, aided by super-comfortable seating, and was remarkably stable at higher speeds. Top speed was 100-plus mph in basic form; the TC (introduced in 1966) could see 110 mph. Imported to the U.S. in modest numbers, but proved fragile for North American conditions and was notoriously trouble-prone. Succeeded in England by the more conventionally engineered SD1 fastback sedan series (sold here only for 1980 as the Rover 3500).

FOR

Styling • Roadability • Engineering sophistication • Comfort • Ergonomics • Quite affordable

AGAINST

Rust-prone • Unrefined engine • Parts running out now • Not that many left in U.S.

1966 Rover 2000TC 4-door sedan

SPECIFICATIONS

Length (in.) 178.5 **Wheelbase (in.)** 103.4
Weight (lbs.) 2770/2810 (2000/2000TC) **Price (new)** approx.
$4000 U.S. in 1964; approx. $4500 for TC in 1969

ENGINES

cc/type (cid)	bore x stroke (mm)	bhp*	years
1978/ohc I4 (121)	86×86	90/114	1963-73

*net, 2000/2000TC

PRICES/PROJECTION

Restorable $600-1200 **Good** $1700-2500
Excellent $2500-3200 **5-year projection** +10%

Rover 3500/3500S 1968-75

1968-69 3500 4-door sedan

PRODUCTION

NA

HISTORY

A clever engine transplant for the Rover 2000 sedan, made
possible by British Leyland's acquiring the tooling and production
rights for the aluminum small-block V8 engine first seen in the 1961
Buick Special. The model designation reflects engine displacement, about 3500cc (though for some reason the Brits referred to
the model as the "Three Thousand Five"). Except for this, the basic
P6 platform was surprisingly little changed. The V8 weighed about
the same as the 2.0-liter four, so steering and suspension balance
were as good as before. Performance, however, was vastly improved and top speed moved up to 120 mph. Introduced with
Borg-Warner three-speed automatic transmission; later, an uprated
2000 manual gearbox was made available for the 3500S. Sold in
the U.S. for a time, but Americans got a somewhat detuned engine,
and very ugly wheels and triple hood scoops cluttered up the exterior. Other P6 virtues and vices remained, the main drawback
being the erratic construction quality that had all but eliminated
British cars as serious American market contenders by 1970.
Withdrawn from the U.S. market at about that time, the Rover name
wouldn't be seen here again (and then only briefly) for another
decade.

FOR

Effortless, high-geared performance ● V8 still in production and a
known commodity here ● Compact size with comfortable four-seat
accommodation ● Fine ride ● Excellent roadability

AGAINST

Rust-prone ● Mechanically troublesome ● Parts supply diminishing
● Jaguar Rover Triumph would rather forget this car

SPECIFICATIONS

Length (in.) 180.0 **Wheelbase (in.)** 103.4 **Weight (lbs.)** 2865
Price (new) approx. $5400 U.S. list price for 3500S in 1969

ENGINES

cc/type (cid)	bore x stroke (mm)	bhp*	years
3528/ohv V8 (215)	89×71	143	1968-75

*DIN; U.S. net bhp for 3500S: 184

PRICES/PROJECTION

Restorable $800-1700 **Good** $2000-2700
Excellent $2900-5500 **5-year projection** +10%

Saab 750GT/850GT 1958-62

PRODUCTION

NA

HISTORY

The early Saab sedan in its hottest form. Introduced in 1958 with a
more powerful (45 vs. 38 bhp) version of the 746cc two-stroke,
three-cylinder engine from the then-current 93 model. Styling was
marked by the aerodynamic "humpback" look introduced with the
original Saab 92 of the late '40s. Construction was unitized, and the
very strong body/chassis had unusually good corrosion resistance.
Front wheel drive was a novelty for the day. When Saab replaced
the 93 with the 96 in the early '60s, engine size went up to 841cc,
and the GT version continued, still with more horsepower (57 vs.
48). Through 1960 a rather clumsy three-speed steering column
gearshift was fitted, but later models had a four-speed floorshift
transmission. Features on both 750 and 850 GTs were more complete instrumentation, including tachometer, plus foglamps and
special seats. Quite quick all things considered, the engine emitting
the distinctive "popcorn popper" sounds characteristic of two-
stroke units. Like other Saabs of the day, quite roomy for its size.
The 850 model was briefly marketed under the Montecarlo name in
recognition of the car's rally successes at the hands of Erik
Carlsson. The GT was discontinued once Saab adopted the German Ford V4 engine for the 95/96 models in the late '60s.

FOR

Front-drive handling/roadholding ● Durability ● Good accommodation ● Comparatively rare now ● Affordable

AGAINST

Noisy, smoky two-stroke engine ● Parts now hard to come by
● Styling?

SPECIFICATIONS

Length (in.) 159.0 **Wheelbase (in.)** 98.0
Weight (lbs.) 1800-1900 **Price (new)** approx. $2800 U.S. for
850GT in 1964

ENGINES

cc/type (cid)	bore x stroke (mm)	bhp	years
748/ohv I3 (46)	66×73	45	1958-62
841/ohv I3 (51.3)	70×73	57	1962-67

PRICES/PROJECTION

As for 1966-70 Sonett II

Saab Sonett II 1966-70

1966-70 Sonett II coupe

PRODUCTION

1868

HISTORY

Limited-production two-seat sporty coupe by Sweden's pioneer of front wheel drive. Chassis and suspension came from the normal Saab 96 sedan, but the body was completely different. Made of fiberglass, it featured a large wraparound rear window, minimal rear overhang, a fairly long snout with prominent hood bulge, a protruding lower bumper/grille, and stubby overall proportions. The hood and front fenders were a single unit, hinged at the front to provide engine access. Originally powered by the three-cylinder Saab two-stroke engine from the 96, but followed the sedans when the German Ford four-stroke V4 was adopted for 1968. The sleek shape allowed the Sonett to achieve up to 100 mph while delivering good economy. However, the model was more a prestige item for Saab than a serious attempt at a volume sports car. Replaced by the restyled Sonett III in 1970.

FOR

Front-drive tenacity and traction ●Rust-free fiberglass body ●Entertainment value ●Rarity

AGAINST

Unrefined two-stroke engine ●Body hardware and trim impossible to find now ●Parts for both engines becoming scarce ●Not plentiful anywhere

SPECIFICATIONS

Length (in.) 149.0   **Wheelbase (in.)** 85.0
Weight (lbs.) 1565-1700   **Price (new)** NA

ENGINES

cc/type (cid)	bore x stroke (mm)	bhp*	years
841/I3 (51)	70×73	60	1966-67
1498/ohv V4 (91)	90×59	65	1968-70

*net

PRICES/PROJECTION

Restorable $800-1000 **Good** $2500-3000
Excellent $3000-4000 **5-year projection** +10%

Saab Sonett III 1970-74

1970-74 Sonett III coupe

PRODUCTION

8350

HISTORY

A continuation of Saab's low-volume sports two-seater with much prettier new styling created by Sergio Coggiola of Italy. A longer, smoother nose terminated in a wide, shallow grille, with driving lights mounted behind its thin horizontal bars. Headlamps popped up from the nose. The tail was extended slightly, the Sonett II's wraparound backlight discarded, and a proper fastback roofline with lift-up hatch window substituted. Suspension and chassis still came from the Saab 96, but mounted a larger-displacement version of the German Ford V4 engine to drive the front wheels. The body was still made of fiberglass, and featured an integral rollover bar. In all, a unique piece from Sweden. Saab's planned phaseout of the 96 (in favor of the 99) doomed the Sonett in the North American market.

FOR

As for 1966-70 Sonett II, plus more handsome, practical styling and better performance

AGAINST

As for 1966-70 Sonett II

SPECIFICATIONS

Length (in.) 154.0 **Wheelbase (in.)** 85.0 **Weight (lbs.)** 1785
Price (new) approx. $4000 U.S. in 1970

ENGINES

cc/type (cid)	bore x stroke (mm)	bhp*	years
1699/ohv V4 (104)	90×67	75	1970-74

*DIN

PRICES/PROJECTION

As for 1966-70 Sonett II

SS I
1931-36

PRODUCTION

4254

HISTORY

The cars that marked the emergence of William Lyons' Swallow Sidecars coachbuilding company as an automaker in its own right and historically significant as the direct ancestors of the first Jaguar. Originally offered as a closed coupe in two versions, the 2054cc Sixteen and 2552cc Twenty, both with side-valve engines and underslung chassis from Standard Motor Co. Bodies were built by Swallow to Lyons' designs. Early models had cycle-type front fenders, later ones the "clamshell" style. All had long hoods. A touring convertible appeared in 1933, followed by a sedan in 1934-35. Undistinguished chassis featured beam axles at each end and cable-operated mechanical brakes. Synchromesh added to transmission in 1934. Long, low, and unmistakeable but not very fast; top end was barely 80 mph. Some versions had cramped cabins and small windows. But the sexy looks, wood-and-leather interior luxury, and amazingly low prices was a winning formula. Led directly to the SS100 produced under the renamed SS Jaguar marque (see entry).

FOR

Historical importance • Racy styling • Reasonably priced today • Enthusiastic worldwide club interest/support

AGAINST

Wood-framed—and thus rot-prone—bodies • Parts shortages makes restoration difficult • Slower than they look • Hard ride • Uncertain handling

SPECIFICATIONS

Length (in.) 174.0-186.0 **Wheelbase (in.)** 112.0 (1931-32), 119.0 (1933-36) **Weight (lbs.)** 2400-3000 **Price (new)** NA

ENGINES

cc/type (cid)	bore x stroke (mm)	bhp	years
2054/L6 (125)	65.6×101.6	45	1931-36
2552/L6 (156)	73.0×101.6	55/62	1931-36
2143/L6 (131)	65.6×106.0	53/62	1933-36

cc/type (cid)	bore x stroke (mm)	bhp	years
2664/L6 (163)	73.0×106.0	68/70	1933-36

*net

PRICES/PROJECTION

Restorable $3000-6000 **Good** $9000-11,000
Excellent $12,000-14,000 **5-year projection** +10%

SS100
1936-40

1936 SS100 3½-Litre roadster

PRODUCTION

2½ Litre 198 **3½ Litre** 116

HISTORY

Successor to the SS90, a short-wheelbase two-seater powered by the 2664cc side-valve Standard six and based on SS I chassis engineering. Only 23 were built in 1935. The SS100 retained the 90's basic 104-inch-wheelbase platform but mounted overhead-valve engines straight out of SS Jaguar's sedans. Initial 2.5-liter version was supplemented by a 3.5-liter unit in 1938. Though cramped even for a two-seater, the roadster styling was a sensation. Ride was hard and the steering quite vague, yet this was about the sexiest car on British roads and amazing value for money. The larger-engine model could do a genuine 100 mph, and even more power was obtainable via fairly simple tuning tweaks. Rare then and even scarcer now. You'll need a bundle of bucks to put one in your garage.

1938 SS100 2½-Litre roadster

FOR

Sensual, widely applauded styling • Zippy performance • Handy size • Uncommon today

AGAINST

Pricey, and becoming more so • Cramped cockpit • SS I road manners • Body parts scarce

SPECIFICATIONS

Length (in.) 150.0 **Wheelbase (in.)** 104.0 **Weight (lbs.)** 2600 **Price (new)** NA

ENGINES

cc/type (cid)	bore x stroke (mm)	bhp*	years
2664/ohv I6 (163)	73.0 × 106.0	105	1936-40
3485/ohv I6 (213)	82.0 × 110.0	125	1938-40

*gross

PRICES/PROJECTION

Restorable $10,000-15,000 **Good** $45,000-50,000
Excellent $50,000-60,000 **5-year projection** +10%

SS Jaguar
2½ Litre/3½ Litre
1936-40

1937 SS Jaguar 2½-Litre 4-door sedan

PRODUCTION

2½ Litre 5369 **3½ Litre** 1304

HISTORY

The four-seat running mates to the romantic SS100 roadster and the first cars to carry the Jaguar label. Chassis and bodywork from SS Cars, Ltd. Standard supplied transmissions and engines, the latter converted from side-valve to overhead-valve layout. Still with mechanical brakes and solid-axle front suspension, but great style and roomy interiors in four-door sedans and two-door convertible coupes. Massive headlamps and wire-spoke wheels handsomely set off the flowing William Lyons' lines, and cabins were trimmed in the expected wood and leather. As with the SS100, a larger 3.5-liter engine was offered beginning in 1938, at which time bodies were switched from wood-framed to all-steel construction and wheelbase

was stretched an inch. Also offered as a very similar short-wheelbase (108 inches) 1½ Litre with a 1608cc (later 1776cc) side-valve Standard six, but these are nowhere nearly as desirable today. Quicker than previous SS four-seaters. The rare 3.5-liter models could do at least 90 mph.

FOR

The first genuine Jags • Fleet and fleet-looking • Extra-desirable "dropheads" • Sporting sedans • Simple, easy mechanical rebuild • Ample club support and interest

AGAINST

Pre-1938 body rot • No body parts available • Marginal brakes • Old-fashioned road manners

SPECIFICATIONS

Length (in.) 186.0 **Wheelbase (in.)** 119.0 (1936-37), 120.0 (1938-40) **Weight (lbs.)** 3500-3650 **Price (new)** NA

ENGINES

cc/type (cid)	bore x stroke (mm)	bhp*	years
2664/ohv I6 (163)	73 × 106	105	1936-40
3485/ohv I6 (213)	82 × 110	125	1938-40

*gross

PRICES/PROJECTION

Restorable $3000-4000 **Good** $11,000-13,000
Excellent $13,000-16,000 **5-year projection** +10%

Sunbeam-Talbot 80
1948-57

PRODUCTION

3500

HISTORY

The original small-displacement edition of the Sunbeam-Talbot 90, powered by an 1185cc engine similar to that of the contemporary Hillman Minx (also made by Rootes Group). Offered only for two years. All models used the solid axle front suspension; in other respects, it was identical to the S-T 90. Performance was predictably much less, however: no more than 70-75 mph maximum

FOR

As for 1948-57 S-T 90

AGAINST

As for 1948-57 S-T 90, but much less performance

SPECIFICATIONS

Length (in.) 168.0 **Wheelbase (in.)** 97.5 **Weight (lbs.)** 2525 **Price (new)** NA

ENGINES

cc/type (cid)	bore x stroke (mm)	bhp*	years
1185/ohv I4 (72)	63×95	47	1948-50

*gross

PRICES/PROJECTION

Restorable $400-500 **Good** $1300-1500
Excellent $2000-2500 **5-year projection** no change

Sunbeam-Talbot 90 1948-57

PRODUCTION

Mark I 4000 **Mark II/IIA** 15,000 **Mark III** 4000

HISTORY

A solid, graceful, British-built sports sedan using many Humber components. The massive separate chassis had solid-axle front suspension through the end of the 1950 model year, after which it was changed to an independent design. The body was a modern envelope in four-door sedan form, with vertical grille, sweeping semi-integral front fenders, flush rear sides, and rounded contours. The original 1944cc overhead valve four was enlarged to near 2.3 liters for 1951, and its power was boosted in later years. Most cars had a column-mounted gearshift, but a floor-control conversion was offered later along with optional overdrive transmission. A product of the Rootes Group, which campaigned it very successfully on the European rally circuit in the '50s.

FOR

Solid chassis engineering •Rally-winner image •Neat, inoffensive styling •Stability and road manners

AGAINST

Not very fast •Parts in short supply •Seldom seen in U.S.

SPECIFICATIONS

Length (in.) 168.0 **Wheelbase (in.)** 97.5
Weight (lbs.) 2725-2925 **Price (new)** NA

ENGINES

cc/type (cid)	bore x stroke (mm)	bhp*	years
1944/ohv I4 (119)	75×110	64	1948-51
2267/ohv I4 (138)	81×110	70-85	1951-57

*gross

PRICES/PROJECTION

Restorable $1000-2000 **Good** $2000-3000
Excellent $4000-5000 **5-year projection** +20%

Sunbeam Alpine 1953-55

PRODUCTION

3000

HISTORY

Elegant two-seat open roadster based on the Sunbeam-Talbot 90 platform. Front end styling was unchanged from the sedan's, but a long downswept tail made the Alpine look considerably more rakish, particularly with the top down. Available in 1954 with optional overdrive, which was then made standard for the 1955 models. Intended mainly for export to North America, the Alpine had a minor supporting role in the Cary Grant/Grace Kelly film "To Catch a Thief."

FOR

As for 1948-57 S-T 90, plus open-air appeal and trimmer looks

AGAINST

As for 1948-57 S-T 90

1953 Alpine 2-seat roadster

SPECIFICATIONS

Length (in.) 168.0 **Wheelbase (in.)** 97.5 **Weight (lbs.)** 2965
Price (new) NA

ENGINES

cc/type (cid)	bore x stroke (mm)	bhp*	years
2267/ohv I4 (138)	81×110	80	1953-55

*gross

PRICES/PROJECTION

Restorable $1500-2000 **Good** $3000-4000
Excellent $4000-6000 **5-year projection** +10%

Sunbeam Rapier 1958-67

1959-65 Rapier 2-door hardtop

PRODUCTION

75,000 (est.)

HISTORY

A British-built two-door hardtop based on the mid-'50s Hillman Minx sedan platform. Won international laurels in tough rally competition for its maker, Rootes Group, and this experience showed in improvements that came thick and fast (at least by British industry standards). The Rapier progressed from the twitchy-handling, underpowered, chunky-looking 1956-58 Series I (not recommended as a collectible) to the Series II, with better styling and a larger engine, introduced for the 1959 model year. The Series III brought still-cleaner looks, a polished walnut dash, more horsepower, and standard front disc brakes. Engine displacement and power went up again for the interim Series IIIa of 1962. The Series IV received synchromesh for all gears of the standard four-speed manual gearbox. The last Series V Rapier was equipped with a larger five-main-bearing engine, but was not officially imported to the U.S. Despite its sporty character and fine rally record, the Rapier was overshadowed both here and overseas by the rakish Alpine two-seat sports car of the '60s, and sales were far below those of the more mundane Rootes models. Nevertheless, the Rapier is an unusual collectible for British-car fans, one of the few true hardtops from England.

FOR

Great rally heritage • Nicely trimmed four-seat interior • Good performance from 1.5/1.6-liter engines

AGAINST

Rusts out early and easily • Chunky "transatlantic" styling

SPECIFICATIONS

Length (in.) 162.5 **Wheelbase (in.)** 96.0 **Weight (lbs.)** approx. 2200 **Price (new)** $2499/2649 (hardtop/convertible) original U.S. list

ENGINES

cc/type (cid)	bore x stroke (mm)	bhp*	years
1390/ohv I4 (84.8)	76×76	62-68	1956-58
1494/ohv I4 (91)	79×76	68/78	1959-61
1592/ohv I4 (97.1)	82×76	75-78	1962-65
1725/ohv I4 (105.2)	82×83	85	1966-67**

*gross
**Series V not officially offered in U.S.

PRICES/PROJECTION

Restorable $300-500 **Good** $1500-2000
Excellent $2000-3000 **5-year projection** no change

Sunbeam Alpine 1960-68

1960 Alpine (Series I) convertible

PRODUCTION

1960 Series I 11,904 **1961-63 Series II** 19,956
1963-64 Series III 5863 **1964-65 Series IV** 12,406
1966-68 Series V 19,122

HISTORY

Rootes Group's sports car for the '60s, but seemed more a sporty tourer to many because of its "modern" creature comforts. Included were such niceties as roll-up windows, an easily erected top, a proper heater, and fully outfitted dash. A factory bolt-on hardtop was also available for year-round weather protection. About the same size as a Triumph TR3 or MGA, the Alpine had contemporary good looks, including a broad hood that dipped low between the headlights, and upswept tailfins housing large oval vertical taillights. The fins were mercifully shorn after the 1963-64 Series III, which gained a GT model with slightly detuned engine, walnut-trimmed dash, and a removable hardtop but, curiously, no standard soft top. Not a great track competitor, the Alpine provided a good ride and sparkling performance for very little money, along with decent (though a bit soft) handling. U.S. imports ended after the 1968 Series V, which had a stronger, smoother five-main-bearing engine.

FOR

Costs less now than Triumphs and MGs •Good looks •Well-built •Well-equipped •Parts supplies still good

AGAINST

Monocoque-construction rust worries •Pre-1966 engines not known for longevity

SPECIFICATIONS

Length (in.) 156.0 **Wheelbase (in.)** 86.0 **Weight (lbs.)** 2255 **Price (new)** $2595 U.S.; 1963 GT: $2749

ENGINES

cc/type (cid)	bore x stroke (mm)	bhp	years
1494/ohv I4 (91)	79×76	78	1959
1592/ohv I4 (97.1)	82×76	77-82	1961-65
1725/ohv I4 (105.2)	82×83	92	1966-68

PRICES/PROJECTION

Restorable $1000-2000 **Good** $2200-3200 **Excellent** $3500-6000 **5-year projection** +15%

Sunbeam LeMans by Harrington 1962-63

1962-63 LeMans coupe by Harrington

PRODUCTION

250

HISTORY

One of the first GT conversions of an open sports car. A Series II Alpine *sans* tailfins, with a smooth, fiberglass fastback roof running from windshield header to rear deck, where it ended in a reverse-canted "ducktail." The seams where fiberglass met the metal Alpine body toward the rear were covered by discreet "coachlines" (pinstripes) giving the finished product a very unified look—almost as if this had been the car's original design. The engine was Rootes Group's 1592cc inline four as found in contemporary Alpines and Rapiers, but tuned to "Stage 2" specifications related to those that had won Sunbeam the Index of Thermal Efficiency at the 24 Hours of Le Mans in 1961. "Harringtons" (Sunbeam didn't use this name in the U.S.) were luxuriously trimmed in leather or vinyl (trim varied

from one car to the next), and had the traditional British walnut-faced dash. Though other conversions were carried out by the Harrington firm, this was the best-selling one they did, though sales were limited by the car's high price.

FOR

Rare and highly sought-after •Fine styling •Good performance •Overdrive standard •Strong appreciation potential

AGAINST

Le Mans body parts now very scarce •A bit fidgety at low rpm

SPECIFICATIONS

Length (in.) 156.0 **Wheelbase (in.)** 86.0 **Weight (lbs.)** approx. 2300 **Price (new)** $3995 U.S.

ENGINES

cc/type (cid)	bore x stroke (mm)	bhp	years
1592/ohv I4 (97.1)	82×76	104	1962-63

PRICES/PROJECTION

Restorable $2000-4000 **Good** $3000-4000 **Excellent** $4000-6000 **5-year projection** +10%

Sunbeam Venezia by Superleggera 1964-65

1964-65 Venezia coupe by Superleggera

PRODUCTION

approx. 200

HISTORY

Anglo-Italian sports coupe based on the British Humber Sceptre sedan (some Hillman Super Minx platforms were also used in 1965), designed and constructed by the Turin coachbuilders, Superleggera. A tubular steel framework and unstressed aluminum body panels made the Venezia light, and gave it a considerable performance advantage over its Humber/Hillman parents, but high price kept sales very low. Several were imported to the U.S. by enthusiasts, though the model was never officially sold here.

FOR

Rarity and desirability •Fine Italian styling •Plush interior

AGAINST

Body parts virtually extinct •Variable construction quality

SPECIFICATIONS

Length (in.) 177.0 **Wheelbase (in.)** 101.0 **Weight (lbs.)** NA
Price (new) approx. $4000 (U.S. equivalent)

ENGINES

cc/type (cid)	bore x stroke (mm)	bhp	years
1592/ohv I4 (97.1)	82×76	88	1964-65

PRICES/PROJECTION

As for 1962-63 Sunbeam Le Mans by Harrington

Sunbeam Tiger 1965-67

1966 Tiger (Series I/Ia) convertible with hardtop

PRODUCTION

1964 Series I 1649   **1965-66 Series I** 3020
1966 Series Ia 1826   **1967 Series II** 421   **1968 Series II** 151

HISTORY

An intriguing Anglo-American hybrid. The brainchild of Rootes Group's West Coast sales manager Ian Garrad, who asked Carroll Shelby to drop a small-block Ford V8 into a suitably modified Alpine roadster. The result was electrifying enough to convince even Lord "Willy" Rootes that it should go into production. The Tiger received a "good press," but never bowled the public over. One reason was high price, not much less than a Corvette's at the time. Another was that it was not that obviously different from its four-cylinder sibling. Then Chrysler Corporation complicated matters by acquiring Rootes Group (and Simca in France), which put the American firm in the awkward position of selling (and providing warranty for) an engine built by its nearest competitor. And as usually happens with "captive imports," the Tiger never got the promotion it deserved in the U.S. No matter: word spread quickly among the knowledgeable that the Tiger was a terror. The car remained mostly the same throughout its rather short life. The Series I models all had the Ford 260 powerplant. On Series Ia cars, Rootes introduced pleated door panels and a new fresh-air ventilation system for top-up driving. The Series II (called "Tiger II" in the U.S.) was upgraded to the 289-cid small-block and got an egg-crate grille and twin rocker panel stripes for visual distinction from the Alpine. A terrific performer with all the Alpine's good qualities, and widely respected in sports car circles. Unfortunately, Chrysler didn't have a substitute engine for the car and could stand the embarassment no longer, so it halted Tiger imports after 1968. And without the lucrative U.S. market, there was little point in continuing it for British customers, so production ceased shortly afterwards.

FOR

Happy on regular gas • Dynamite performance • Good construction quality • High appreciation potential • Clean styling (Series I) • Well-known Ford engine easy and cheap to maintain

AGAINST

Rust-prone • Can be a handful for the uninitiated (rear traction bars a must to get power to the ground) • Retrograde Series II styling

SPECIFICATIONS

Length (in.) 156.0 **Wheelbase (in.)** 86.0 **Weight (lbs.)** 2550
Price (new) $3499-3797 U.S.

ENGINES

cid/type	bore x stroke	bhp	years
260/ohv V8	3.80×2.87	164	1965-66
289/ohv V8	4.00×2.87	200	1967-68

PRICES/PROJECTION

Restorable $2500-4000 **Good** $4800-7000
Excellent $7500-12,000 **5-year projection** +15%

Sunbeam Alpine GT 1969-70

1970 Alpine fastback hardtop (British model; U.S. GT similar)

PRODUCTION

5000 (est. U.S. sales)

HISTORY

A very different Alpine, this four-seat fastback coupe was sold in England as the Rapier. Based on the chassis and running gear of Rootes Group's answer to the British Ford Cortina, the Hillman Hunter (sold here as the Sunbeam Arrow), and deadly conventional. Front suspension was by MacPherson struts, coil springs, lower transverse arms, and drag struts. The rear end was simply a live axle tied down by leaf springs. Powered by the workhorse Rootes four in its 1725cc size, benefiting from the recent adoption of five (instead of three) main bearings. In appearance, the Alpine/Rapier resembled a scaled-down Plymouth Barracuda: slightly stubby front end (but with a horizontal bar grille and quad headlamps), pillarless roof, and large backlight (though not one-piece as on the American car). The interior featured nice high-back bucket seats, adequate space for four, polished-walnut dash with complete instrumentation, center console, floorshift, and full carpeting. Performance and handling were reasonably good, but construction quality was not the same as Rootes cars of yore. This plus erratic deliveries caused by worker walkoffs hurt the car's sales appeal (as it did the Arrow sedan's), and Chrysler began turning more strongly to its new Japanese partner, Mitsubishi, for its "captive imports." The Rapier continued in England for several more years, however, and was even offered as a hot Holbay-tuned model, the H120. A cheaper Alpine with simplified trim and equipment was also sold in the U.S., but the GT is the one to have.

FOR

A bargain fastback with the respected Sunbeam name • Good mileage • Adequate performance • Nicely furnished

AGAINST

Unexciting styling • Indifferent construction quality • Rust-prone • Not that numerous in U.S. • Parts scarce outside England • Questionable appreciation potential

SPECIFICATIONS

Length (in.) 174.5 **Wheelbase (in.)** 98.5 **Weight (lbs.)** 2360
Price (new) $2535 U.S. list

ENGINES

cc/type (cid)	bore x stroke (mm)	bhp	years
1725/ohv I4 (105.2)	82×82	94	1969-70

PRICES/PROJECTION

Restorable $500-1000 **Good** $1000-1500 **Excellent** $1500-2500
5-year projection no change

Swallow Doretti 1954-55

1954-55 Doretti roadster

PRODUCTION

approx. 250

HISTORY

A short-lived attempt at a competitor for the Triumph TR2. Production was undertaken in Britain by a subsidiary of the giant Tube Investments Group. The branch was descended from the original Swallow coachworks of the '30s from which Jaguar evolved, but was not connected with the latter-day Jaguar firm. The Doretti borrowed much from its intended rival, using the TR2 engine, transmission, and front suspension. The chassis was a box-section/tubular-member affair, and was topped by a smart, two-seat roadster body. Bigger, heavier, and slower than the TR2, yet top speed was comparable at about 100 mph. However, the Doretti was very costly, and failed to sell for that reason. Production ended almost as soon as it began, marking the first—and last—attempt by this Swallow company at carmaking.

FOR

Well-known Triumph running gear • Pleasant styling • Individual and exclusive

AGAINST

Body and chassis parts all gone now • Extremely rare and hard to find, even in Britain

SPECIFICATIONS

Length (in.) 156.0 **Wheelbase (in.)** 95.0 **Weight (lbs.)** 2155
Price (new) NA

ENGINES

cc/type (cid)	bore x stroke (mm)	bhp*	years
1991/ohv I4 (122)	83×92	90	1954-55

*gross

PRICES/PROJECTION

Restorable $2000-3000 **Good** $3000-5000
Excellent $5000-6000 **5-year projection** +10%

Talbot 90/105 1930-35

PRODUCTION

90 (1930-33) 216 **105 (1931-35)** 335

HISTORY

In the mid-1920s, Swiss-born Georges Roesch began transforming the British-built Talbots with a splendid series of overhead-valve sixes. By the 1930s, mechanical reliability had turned into sporting prowess. The 2.3-liter "90" raced with honor at LeMans, and the 3.0-liter "105" that followed it proved a great rally car and endurance racer. Both were marked by sturdy rather than advanced engineering, with simple carburetion for their deep-breathing power units. Some think of these as "vintage" cars, i.e. with a 1920s character, which is confirmed by their hard ride and lack of independent front suspension. After the French parent company went belly-up in 1935, the British subsidiary was acquired by Lord Willy Rootes and its cars became much more pedestrian.

FOR

Engine's rugged simplicity • Vintage Brit character • Reliable, sporting, and masculine

AGAINST

Old-fashioned for its day • Hard to find in ours, especially in the U.S. • Parts supplies nonexistent

SPECIFICATIONS

Length (in.) 182.0 (average) **Wheelbase (in.)** 111.0 (90); 114.0 (105) **Weight (lbs.)** 3900-4100 **Price (new)** NA

ENGINES

cc/type (cid)	bore x stroke (mm)	bhp*	years
2276/ohv I6 (139)	69.5×100	90	1930-33
2969/ohv I6 (181)	75.0×112.0	105	1931-35

*gross

PRICES/PROJECTION

Restorable $4000-7000 **Good** $9000-11,000
Excellent $12,000-15,000 **5-year projection** +10%

Triumph Dolomite 1936-39

1963-69 Dolomite roadster

PRODUCTION

NA

HISTORY

As an independent company, Triumph's finances sagged in the '30s yet its cars became more and more elegant. For 1937, its stylists took a long look at the SS Jaguars being built only hundreds of yards away, adopted similar lines, then grafted on a Hudson-like waterfall grille sometimes unflatteringly referred to as the "fencer's mask." Lifting the Dolomite name from its Alfa-inspired supercharged straight-eight roadster of 1935, the firm offered a choice of four or six cylinders and three different wheelbases on these successors to the previous Gloria and Vitesse models, which were similar in engine and chassis design. All the middle-class British virtues, including wire-spoke wheels, "tasteful" interiors and, at last, gearbox synchronization, but no independent front suspension, typical of the UK in this period. Body styles included the Foursome convertible coupe with three-position folding top, and the rumble-seat Roadster Coupe plus various close-coupled sedans. The Roadster was a fine rally car, and all Dolomites could be considered useful alternatives to equivalent Rileys and SS Jaguars. Alas, Triumph went broke in mid-1939. The company was revived after the war, but not these cars.

FOR

A famous name in its heyday • Real British elegance • Handsome styling • Simple engineering

AGAINST

Limited performance • Rot-prone coachbuilt bodies • Parts almost impossible to find

SPECIFICATIONS

Length (in.) 168.0-181.5 **Wheelbase (in.)** 108.0/110.0/116.0 **Weight (lbs.)** 2800-3300 **Price (new)** NA

ENGINES

cc/type (cid)	bore x stroke (mm)	bhp*	years
1496/ohv I4 (91)	69×100	50	1938-39
1767/ohv I4 (108)	75×100	60/65	1936-39
1991/ohv I6 (122)	65×100	72/75	1936-39

*gross

PRICES/PROJECTION

OPEN **Restorable** $2000-4000 **Good** $5000-7500
Excellent $7500-15,000 Deduct 50% for closed models.
5-year projection +20%

Triumph 1800 Town & Country 1946-49

1946-49 1800 Town & Country sedan

PRODUCTION

4000

HISTORY

The only prominent postwar make apart from Rolls-Royce to offer sedans with "knife-edged" styling, Triumph built the Town & Country to a beautiful design by Walter Belgrove. A luxurious leather and walnut interior and big, freestanding Lucas headlamps distinguished this attractive four-door. Front suspension was independent with a transverse leaf spring. The chassis was made up of steel tubes. The engine was built by Standard, hooked to a four-speed gearbox with column shift.

FOR

Often mistaken for a Rolls, which doesn't hurt • Fine construction quality • Classy looks

AGAINST

Wood-framed body tends to rot ● All have right-hand drive

SPECIFICATIONS

Length (in.) 175.0 **Wheelbase (in.)** 108.0 **Weight (lbs.)** 2828
Price (new) $3150

ENGINES

cc/type (cid)	bore x stroke (mm)	bhp*	years
1776/ohv I4 (107)	73×106	63	1946-49

*net

PRICES/PROJECTION

Restorable $1000-2000 **Good** $3000-4500
Excellent $5000-9000 **5-year projection** +10%

Triumph 1800 Roadster 1946-48

1946-48 1800 Roadster

PRODUCTION

2501

HISTORY

Triumph's Sir John Black was determined to compete with Jaguar with this car, but he didn't know about the forthcoming XK-120. A Jaguar it wasn't, though it did have its own appeal. The bizarre styling was the work of two different designers (the ideas meet at the cowl), and included a rumble seat with a flip-up windshield. Mechanically identical with the 1800 sedan, and stylistically unique, with freestanding Lucas lights and bulging front fenders engulfing the Triumph radiator.

FOR

Few open British cars of the early postwar years can be had for its price ● Definitely unique looks ● Good construction quality

AGAINST

Hardly a classic piece of styling ● Aluminum bodywork subject to corrosion ● Some rot may beset body's wooden framing

SPECIFICATIONS

Length (in.) 168.1 **Wheelbase (in.)** 108.0 **Weight (lbs.)** 2541
Price (new) $3025 (original U.S. equivalent)

ENGINES

cc/type (cid)	bore x stroke (mm)	bhp*	years
1776/ohv I4 (107)	73×106	63	1946-48

*net

PRICES/PROJECTION

Restorable $2000-5000 **Good** $5000-8000
Excellent $8000-14,000 **5-year projection** +10%

Triumph Mayflower 1949-53

1949-53 Mayflower 2-door sedan

PRODUCTION

2d sedan 34,990 **2d convertible** 10

HISTORY

Triumph's managing director, Sir John Black, liked the looks of his 1800/2000 sedans, and ordered his designers to apply the same razor-edge lines to a smaller economy model. As General Motors' former styling chief, William L. Mitchell, might say, this was like trying to tailor a dwarf. The result was named Mayflower to appeal to Americans, which it didn't (do you suppose they got the inspiration from Plymouth?). It was cute, but hardly elegant: the scale and proportions were all wrong. Nonetheless, the boxy body did offer an incredible amount of space for its overall size. Invariably a cause for smiles, and amusing to the collector with a sense of humor. A winsome little car that will grow on you, and it doesn't cost a mint to buy or restore.

FOR

Nothing quite like it ● Big interior ● Active club interest ● Squint hard and pretend it's a Rolls

AGAINST

No power • Tricky aluminum-head engine • Many parts now scarce

SPECIFICATIONS

Length (in.) 154.0 **Wheelbase (in.)** 84.0 **Weight (lbs.)** 2016
Price (new) $1695 (U.S. equivalent)

ENGINES

cc/type (cid)	bore x stroke (mm)	bhp*	years
1247/L4 (76)	63×100	38	1949-53

*net

PRICES/PROJECTION

Restorable $500-1000 **Good** $1500-2000
Good $2000-3000
Excellent $2000-3000 Add 200% for convertible
5-year projection +10%

Triumph 2000
1949

1949 2000 sedan

PRODUCTION

2000

HISTORY

Successor to the 1946-48 1800 sedan, and unchanged in appearance. Specifications were identical also, except that a relaxation in British horsepower tax encouraged Triumph to install the 2.0-liter engine and gearbox from Standard's Vanguard series. Unfortunately, the 2000 used a three- instead of four-speed transmission (although fully synchronized), and the shifter was still mounted on the steering column rather than on the floor.

FOR

As for 1946-48 1800 Town & Country

AGAINST

As for 1946-48 1800 Town & Country, plus less flexible gearbox

SPECIFICATIONS

Length (in.) 175.0 **Wheelbase (in.)** 108.0 **Weight (lbs.)** 2828
Price (new) $2950 (original U.S. equivalent)

ENGINES

cc/type (cid)	bore x stroke (mm)	bhp*	years
2088/ohv I4 (128)	85×92	68	1949

*net

PRICES/PROJECTION

As for 1946-48 1800 Town & Country

Triumph 2000 Roadster
1949

1949 2000 Roadster

PRODUCTION

2000

HISTORY

Continuation of the 1800 Roadster, still on a tubular-steel chassis. Like its 2000 sedan counterpart, adopted the drivetrain from the Standard Vanguard. With a high price and mediocre performance, this Roadster was outflanked by MG on one side and Jaguar on the other. By 1950, Standard-Triumph would drop this model and concentrate its attention on a brand-new and faster sports car to be known as the TR2.

FOR

As for 1946-48 1800 Roadster

AGAINST

As for 1946-48 1800 Roadster

SPECIFICATIONS

Length (in.) 168.1 **Wheelbase (in.)** 108.0 **Weight (lbs.)** 2540
Price (new) $2950 (original U.S. equivalent)

ENGINES

cc/type (cid)	bore x stroke (mm)	bhp*	years
2088/ohv I4 (128)	85×92	68	1949

*net

Triumph Renown
1950-54

1950 Renown sedan

PRODUCTION

4d sedan (108-inch wb) 6501   **4d sedan (111-inch wb)** 2800
Limousine (111-inch wb) 190

HISTORY

The final development of the razor-edge Triumph 1800/2000, now based on the Standard Vanguard pressed steel chassis and coil spring independent front suspension. In late 1951, a limousine with division window was produced on a 3-inch longer wheelbase, and beginning in 1952 all models adopted the longer chassis. While the Renown sedan is the most available razor-edge Triumph, the low-production limo is conversely the hardest to come by—extremely rare and desirable.

FOR

Overdrive was an option ● Same well-balanced styling as on 1800/2000 ● More up-to-date layout ● Quality materials and assembly

AGAINST

As for 1946-48 1800 and 1949 2000, plus likely high limousine asking prices

SPECIFICATIONS

Length (in.) 175.0 (1950-52), 181 (1952-54)
Wheelbase (in.) 108.0 (1950-52), 111.0 (limousine and 1952-54)
Weight (lbs.) 2800-3024   **Price (new)** $3150 (sedan), $3400 (limo) (U.S. equivalent)

ENGINES

cc/type (cid)	bore x stroke (mm)	bhp*	years
2088/ohv I4 (128)	85×92	68	1950-54

*net

Triumph TR2
1953-55

1953-55 TR2 roadster

PRODUCTION

8628

HISTORY

The first in the long-lived series of production Triumph two-seaters. The TR2 was developed from the 20TS or "TR1" prototype first shown at Earls Court, and evolved into a rapid machine selling at an attractive price. Body design by Triumph's Walter Belgrove featured a grille-less radiator opening, cutaway doors, flowing fenders integral with the body, and a relatively roomy trunk (one of the areas where the production car differed most from the prototype). TR2s began winning rallies and races, beginning a victory streak that would make TRs famous and respected. 100-mph performance was available from the four-cylinder engine (with "wet" cylinder liners), virtually unbreakable provided you observed the redline.

FOR

Rugged construction ● Strong engine ● Large following ● Plentiful new-old-stock and remanufactured parts

AGAINST

Dumpy styling ● Rusts easily ● A hundred rain leaks ● Some poor-quality interior trim

SPECIFICATIONS

Length (in.) 151.0   **Wheelbase (in.)** 88.0   **Weight (lbs.)** 1848
Price (new) $2499 in U.S.

ENGINES

cc/type (cid)	bore x stroke (mm)	bhp*	years
1991/ohv I4 (121.5)	83×92	90	1953-55

*gross

PRICES/PROJECTION

Restorable $3000-5000 **Good** $5000-6500
Excellent $7000-9000 **5-year projection** +10%

Triumph TR3
1955-57

1955-57 TR3 roadster

PRODUCTION

13,377

HISTORY

Mildly restyled successor to the TR2, easily distinguished by a proper grille with large eggcrates built into the front air intake. No major dimensional or mechanical changes except for introduction of front disc brakes early in the production run. Introduced with a small horsepower gain over the TR2, later increased to an even 100 bhp. Remarkably, the TR3 (like the TR2) does not enjoy the huge following of the "wide-mouth" TR3A. This translates into a lower price despite its greater rarity.

FOR

Costs less than TR3A, yet is scarcer • Others as for 1953-55 TR2

AGAINST

As for 1953-55 TR2

SPECIFICATIONS

Length (in.) 151.0   **Wheelbase (in.)** 88.0   **Weight (lbs.)** 1988
Price (new) $2625 original U.S. list

ENGINES

cc/type (cid)	bore x stroke (mm)	bhp*	years
1991/ohv I4 (121.5)	83×92	95/100	1955-57

*net

PRICES/PROJECTION

As for 1953-55 TR2

Triumph TR3A
1958-62

PRODUCTION

58,236

HISTORY

Continuation of the TR3, and one of the most ubiquitous sports cars of the late '50s/early '60s. More civilized than its predecessors thanks to better seats, proper door handles, and other interior refinements. Marked by a full-width stamped grille that earned it the name "wide mouth" in contrast to the "small mouth" TR3. The TR3A offered sparkling performance, unsophisticated handling (particularly on wet roads), and jaunty if slightly chubby styling, all at a highly competitive price. It enjoyed a long production run, and people continued clamoring for it even after the TR4 arrived. A long string of competition successes and its thoroughly British character helped win it an avid following that continues to this day.

1959 TR3A roadster (with non-standard windshield)

1958-62 TR3A roadster

FOR

Right now, your best TR investment ●Greater comfort, refinement than TR2/3 ●Others as for 1953-55 TR2

AGAINST

As for 1953-55 TR2, and still a devil in the wet

SPECIFICATIONS

Length (in.) 152.0   **Wheelbase (in.)** 88.0   **Weight (lbs.)** 2050
Price (new) $2675 original U.S. list

ENGINES

cc/type (cid)	bore x stroke (mm)	bhp*	years
1991/ohv I4 (121.5)	83×92	100	1958-62

*net

PRICES/PROJECTION

Restorable $2500-4000 **Good** $4000-6000
Excellent $7500-10,000 **5-year projection** +10%

1958-62 TR3A roadster with hardtop

Triumph TR3B
1962-63

PRODUCTION

3331

HISTORY

Not an official "factory" model and produced only for the U.S. market. What Triumph referred to as the "3B" comprised leftover TR3As, some equipped with the 2138cc engine and all-synchro gearbox from the successor TR4. Later 3Bs could be distinguished by a vinyl-covered central instrument panel, but were otherwise identical in looks to the TR3A.

FOR

As for 1953-55 TR2 and 1958-62 TR3A, plus low-production appeal

AGAINST

As for 1953-55 TR2

SPECIFICATIONS

Length (in.) 152.0   **Wheelbase (in.)** 88.0   **Weight (lbs.)** 2100
Price (new) $2365 original U.S. list

ENGINES

cc/type (cid)	bore x stroke (mm)	bhp*	years
1991/ohv I4[1] (121.5)	83×92	100	1962
2138/ohv I4[2] (130.4)	86×92	100	1963

1. Cars with TSF commission numbers only
2. Cars with TCF commission numbers only
*net

PRICES/PROJECTION

Add 10% to TR3A prices

Triumph TR4/TR4A
1961-68

1961-64 TR4 roadster

PRODUCTION

1961-64 TR4 40,253   **1965-68 TR4A** 28,465

1967 TR4A roadster (competition modified)

HISTORY

Triumph's new-generation sports car with body design by Italy's Giovanni Michelotti. Originally based on the TR3A chassis and running gear with a larger engine (though the 1991cc unit was available optionally to qualify for 2.0-liter class racing) and new all-synchromesh gearbox. The TR4A brought a tubular grille to replace the rather cheap stamped original item, and you could have independent rear suspension (by coil springs and semi-trailing arms) at extra cost. The TR4A also had a "quick-erect" top whereas the TR4's came off altogether and was the usual tedious, British "Erector-set" affair. However, the 4A top took up more space when folded. Michelotti's styling was contemporary and good-looking, with a squared tail and a curvaceous nose featuring high-set headlamps with "eyelids" formed by humps in the hood. A "power blister" offset to the right on the hood provided clearance for the air cleaner/carburetor.

FOR

Styling seems to look better as time passes • Very soundly built • Plush leather buckets and walnut dash in all but very early models

• Strong appreciation potential

AGAINST

Rust a continuing worry • IRS TR4As sometimes require costly suspension work

SPECIFICATIONS

Length (in.) 153.6 **Wheelbase (in.)** 88.0 **Weight (lbs.)** 2128 (TR4), 2240 (TR4A) **Price (new)** $2849 original U.S. list

ENGINES

cc/type (cid)	bore x stroke (mm)	bhp*	years
2138/ohv I4 (130.4)	86×92	100/104	1961-67

*net, TR4/TR4A

PRICES/PROJECTION

Restorable $700-1000 **Good** $3000-4500
Excellent $6000-7000 **5-year projection** +10%

Triumph GT6 Mark I/II 1966-70

PRODUCTION

1966-68 Mark I 15,818 **1969-70 Mark II (GT6+)** 12,066

HISTORY

A smooth-looking fastback derivative of the Triumph Spitfire roadster with the same general styling below the beltline. Styling on both was done by Giovanni Michelotti. The main difference was the engine. While the Spitfire had a pedestrian four, the GT6 (as the

1969-70 GT6 Mk II (GT6+) (British model)

name suggested) was powered by a small-displacement straight six shared with the contemporary Triumph 2000 sedan. Better equipped and more nicely trimmed than the Spitfire, the GT6 used the same basic instrument panel and tilt-up hood/front fenders assembly that provided unmatched drivetrain access. Able to leap tall Interstates in a single bound thanks to its easy-revving engine and long-legged gearing (a basic four-speed with Laycock de Normanville overdrive). For the 1969 model year, Triumph abandoned the Spitfire's tricky swing-axle rear suspension for double-jointed half-shafts located by A-arms below and a transverse leaf spring above. The result was safer handling less prone to sudden oversteer caused by the rear end "jacking up" in corners. This model was sold as the Mark II overseas and as the GT6+ in the U.S. Like its open cousin, the 1969-70 GT6 acquired higher front bumpers (bisecting the grille) and other changes to meet U.S. safety standards. Prices are still in the doldrums today, so the GT6 is an attractive alternative for Triumph fans appalled at the asking prices for TRs. Continued in Mark III form through the 1973 model year, but these are less desirable because of steadily declining horsepower in the face of stiffening American emissions controls.

FOR

One of the sweetest, smoothest small sixes ever built ●Good looks ●Hatchback convenience ●Comfortable long-haul tourer ●Superb engine access ●Nicely equipped

AGAINST

Pretty small inside and out ●Indifferent construction quality ●A fierce ruster ●Styling suffers on Mark II/GT6+

SPECIFICATIONS

Length (in.) 145.1 **Wheelbase (in.)** 83.0 **Weight (lbs.)** 1904
Price (new) $2895 original U.S. list; $3045 for GT6+ in 1969

ENGINES

cc/type (cid)	bore x stroke (mm)	bhp*	years
1998/ohv I6 (121.9)	75×76	95/104	1966-70

*net Mark I/Mark II (95 bhp net for 1969-70 U.S. model)

PRICES/PROJECTION

Restorable $500-1500 **Good** $2000-3000
Excellent $3000-4000 **5-year projection** +10%

Triumph TR250 1968

PRODUCTION

8484

HISTORY

The federalized equivalent to the British-market TR5 (not sold here), offered for this model year only. Both carried a new 2.5-liter straight six, but the 250 had only about the same power output as the TR4A thanks to twin Stromberg carburetors used to meet the new U.S. emissions standards (the TR5's Lucas fuel injection gave 150 bhp net). Nevertheless, the 250's smoother engine won buyers over, and set the stage for the restyled TR6 to follow. Some unwelcome compromises with TR4 tradition were vinyl instead of leather bucket seats, imitation instead of genuine wood for the dash, and a broad, reflective tape stripe on the hood and front fenders.

1968 TR250 roadster

FOR

Smooth, willing performance ●Still not widely collected by the TR crowd ●Others as for 1961-68 TR4/TR4A

AGAINST

Specification and design not up to TR tradition ●Rust-prone ●Some body parts now in short supply

SPECIFICATIONS

Length (in.) 153.5 **Wheelbase (in.)** 88.0 **Weight (lbs.)** 2268
Price (new) $3175 original U.S. list

ENGINES

cc/type (cid)	bore x stroke (mm)	bhp*	years
2498/ohv I6 (152.4)	75×95	104	1968

*net

PRICES/PROJECTION

Restorable $500-1000 **Good** $2500-3000
Excellent $3000-4000 **5-year projection** +10%

Triumph TR6 1969-76

PRODUCTION

94,619

HISTORY

The smoothly redesigned successor to the TR5/250, facelifted by Karmann of Osnabrück, the German coachbuilders. Essentially, the rework involved only the front and rear ends. The former had headlights moved outboard to the fender tips and a neat new grille. The rear was lengthened and squared off, adopting a Kamm-style chop and wraparound horizontal taillights. While these cosmetic changes gave the car a new lease on life, there was still no gain in performance, and the American version remained much less lively than its British counterpart. Though we include only the first two model years here, the TR6 continued in production through 1975, with U.S. sales extending into 1976 (mostly leftovers already in the export pipeline). Replaced by the four-cylinder TR7 coupe as Triumph's sporting two-seater in 1975. As with so many other cars of the '70s, bumpers became uglier and engines weaker on later

1969 TR6 roadster

TR6s. While it's a bit early to assess the TR6's ultimate value as a collectible, the recent demise of Triumph sports cars (and the TR6's acceptance among enthusiasts as a "true" TR) suggests it has potential.

FOR

As for 1968 TR250, plus better looks

AGAINST

Still a ruster • Others as for 1968 TR250

SPECIFICATIONS

Length (in.) 156.0 (1969-72), 162.1 (1973-74), 163.6 (1975-76)
Wheelbase (in.) 88.0   **Weight (lbs.)** 2390 (1971-74), 2438 (1975-76)   **Price (new)** $3275 original U.S. list; $6050 in 1976

ENGINES

cc/type (cid)	bore x stroke (mm)	bhp*	years
2498/ohv I6 (152.4)	75×95	104-106	1969-76

*net

PRICES/PROJECTION

Restorable $1500-2000 **Good** $3000-4500
Excellent $4500-7000 **5-year projection** +10%

TVR Grantura 1958-67

1961 Grantura coupe

PRODUCTION

1958 Mark I 100   **1959-62 Mark II/IIA** 400
1962-65 Mark III 90   **1800S** 206

HISTORY

Fastback, fiberglass-body two-seat sports car built by the Blackpool, England firm started by Trevor Wilkinson (hence the initials TVR). Sold both as a kit and fully assembled, powered by a variety of proprietary engines. The most familiar of these was the BMC (British Motor Corporation) 1.8-liter B-series four as used in the MGB. All TVRs were built on a short-wheelbase tubular backbone chassis. The Mark I through Mark IIA models had an all-trailing-link, VW Beetle-type suspension. This was replaced by a

1969 TR6 roadster

more up to date coil-spring-and-wishbone arrangement derived from Triumph Herald components. These early TVRs bear some styling resemblance to the Lotus Elite. The 1800S, introduced initially as the Mark III, had a much larger rear window and a severely chopped tail that gave it a stubby, truncated look. Very light and built low to the ground, these were hard-riding sports machines with excellent roadholding. Equipment levels were pretty complete, too, and included wind-up door windows. As one of Britain's numerous "cottage industry" specialist makers, TVR was a small firm that went through several management changes in its early years, so it's difficult to pinpoint precise model changes; improvements were usually instituted as needed, without regard for the calendar. The Grantura was a relation to the Ford V8-powered Griffiths.

FOR

Light, rust-free fiberglass body •Fierce handling/roadholding •Many parts still stocked •Good appreciation potential

AGAINST

Fragile construction quality •Cramped interior

SPECIFICATIONS

Length (in.) 138.0 **Wheelbase (in.)** 84.0-85.5
Weight (lbs.) 1455-1790 **Price (new)** NA

ENGINES

cc/type (cid)	bore x stroke (mm)	bhp	years
1172/F4 (71.5)	93×64	36	1957-59
1098/ohc I4 (67)	67×72	85	1957-59
1588/ohv I4 (97)	89×75	80	1959-62
1216/ohc I4 (74.2)	76×67	83	1959-63
1622/ohv I4 (99)	76×89	90	1962-63
1340/ohv I4 (81.8)	81×65	54	1962-63
1798/ohv I4 (109.7)	81×89	88/95	1963-67

PRICES/PROJECTION

Restorable $1500-3000 **Good** $3000-5000
Excellent $6000-7000 **5-year projection** no change

TVR Griffith 1963-67

PRODUCTION

300

HISTORY

Based closely on the four-cylinder TVR Grantura, the Griffith featured an American Ford 289-cid V8 and transmission, installed by Griffith Motors in the U.S. The result was shattering performance coupled to the Grantura's small size and nimble road manners. Identical in appearance with the Grantura 1800S, with a cutoff tail and large, wraparound rear window (though the first few cars differed slightly). Not a big seller here due to overheating problems

and disappointing construction quality. Replaced by a reengineered version, the Tuscan V8, powered by Ford's enlarged 302-cid small-block.

FOR

As for 1958-67 Grantura, plus much greater performance from easily serviced, well-known Ford V8

AGAINST

As for 1958-67 Grantura

SPECIFICATIONS

Length (in.) 138.0 **Wheelbase (in.)** 85.5 **Weight (lbs.)** 1905
Price (new) NA

ENGINES

cid/type	bore x stroke	bhp	years
289/ohv V8	4.00×2.87	195/271*	1963-67
*gross			

PRICES/PROJECTION

Restorable $2000-4000 **Good** $5000-8000
Excellent $8000-10,000 **5-year projection** no change

TVR Tuscan 1967-71

1967-71 Tuscan V6 coupe

PRODUCTION

V8 28 **long-wheelbase V8** 24 **"wide-body" V8** 21 **V6** 101

HISTORY

Further development of the TVR Grantura/Griffith, still with a fiberglass body atop a tubular steel chassis with all-independent suspension. The Tuscan continued to use American Ford V8 power like the abortive Griffith. After the first 28 were completed at the small shop in Blackpool, England, TVR lengthened the wheelbase and smoothed out the stubby tail a bit. There were also 21 special "wide-body" cars built from 1968 to '70, with a shape that predicted the firm's later M-series models. Tuscans were imported to America sporadically and in very small numbers during these years. Because of TVR's small production, the cars were exempt from U.S. safety standards, though engines had to be detoxed to meet then-current pollution standards. A V6 version was also offered, basically the same car but powered by the "Essex" 3.0-liter unit fitted to upmarket British Ford models. It's doubtful any of these were officially sold here due to the cost of certifying that engine for U.S. emissions compliance. The Tuscan came with nicer fittings than the Grantura or Griffith, including a polished wood dash and high-quality trim. Both models were swept away before the end of 1972.

FOR

Performance ● Better styling ● Equipment ● Others as for 1963-67 Griffith

AGAINST

As for 1963-67 Griffith, but overshadowed by M-series successors

SPECIFICATIONS

Length (in.) 138.0/145.0 **Wheelbase (in.)** 85.5/90.0
Weight (lbs.) 2000-2240 **Price (new)** $6250 in U.S. for 1969 Tuscan V8

ENGINES

cc/type (cid)	bore x stroke (mm)	bhp	years
2994/ohv V6 (183)	94×72	128*	1967-71
4727/ohv V8 (289)	102×73	195/271**	1967
4949/ohv V8 (302)	102×76	220**	1968-71
*DIN **gross			

PRICES/PROJECTION

Restorable $2000-4000 **Good** $4000-5000
Excellent $6000-8000 **5-year projection** no change

TVR 2500M
1972-77

PRODUCTION

947

HISTORY

Replacement for the Tuscan V8 and four-cylinder Vixen models, issued under the aegis of TVR's then new owner, Martin Lilley. Used the longer and more smoothly styled Tuscan bodyshell, but power was switched on this American-market model to the 2.5-liter straight six from Triumph's TR6 (in Europe the car continued with the British Ford "Essex" 3.0-liter V6). TVR also adopted a "space frame" type of chassis for this model, replacing the previous tubular-steel platform affair. Suspension at each end was by means of twin A-arms, and this plus mounting the engine well back in the chassis for near-even weight distribution gave terrific cornering grip and eager handling. Unfortunately, ride remained as bouncy as ever. Sold in very small numbers Stateside through a very few dealers. Replaced by the hatchback Taimar and Taimar roadster for 1978.

FOR

Fine performance ● Good road car ● Distinctive looks ● Rarity ● Engine parts still in good supply ● Rot-free, easy to repair fiberglass body ● Traditional British furnishings

AGAINST

Cramped cockpit ● Meager luggage space ● Variable construction quality ● Difficult to locate in good condition

SPECIFICATIONS

Length (in.) 154.0 **Wheelbase (in.)** 90.0 **Weight (lbs.)** approx. 2300 **Price (new)** $5450 U.S. in 1973, rising to $8900 in 1977

ENGINES

cc/type (cid)	bore x stroke (mm)	bhp	years
2498/ohv I6 (152)	75×95	106	1972-77

PRICES/PROJECTION

As for 1967-71 Tuscan V8 **5-year projection** +10%

TVR Taimar
1978-80

PRODUCTION

coupe 395 **roadster** 258

HISTORY

A final, short-lived variation of the original TVR design dating from the '50s, and arguably the best. Introduced at the 1976 London Motor Show as the familiar coupe, but with a more pleasingly styled nose, and—at last—the big wraparound rear window functioned as a hatch. Followed shortly by a roadster, not a convertible, with removable side curtains and an easy to convert soft top. Because of its small production volume, TVR obtained a waiver on meeting U.S. smog laws, so the Taimar was imported here with the same 3.0-liter overhead-valve British Ford V6 it carried in its native land.

FOR

As for 1972-77 TVR 2500M, plus roadster's open-air allure ● Also better built and better all-round performance

AGAINST

As for 1972-77 2500M

SPECIFICATIONS

Length (in.) 155.0 **Wheelbase (in.)** 90.0 **Weight (lbs.)** 2335
Price (new) $15,900 original U.S. list price (either model)

ENGINES

cc/type (cid)	bore x stroke (mm)	bhp*	years
2994/ohv V6 (183)	94×72	142	1978-80
*SAE net			

PRICES/PROJECTION

Restorable $3000-5000 **Good** $6000-8000
Excellent $8000-10,000 Add 50% for roadster.
5-year projection +10%

Vanden Plas Princess 3 Litre 1959-64

1962-64 Princess 3-Litre Mk II sedan

PRODUCTION

Mark I 4719   **Mark II** 7984

HISTORY

A carefully reworked, upper-crust version of a mass-market sedan, the familiar British Motor Corporation (BMC) mid-range series introduced in 1958 and styled by Pininfarina. Like the cheaper Austin A99/A110 variations, the V-P featured prominent fins and rather boxy overall contours, but the front had a distinctive square grille with vertical bars. Construction was monocoque, and the rear suspension was a simple beam-axle affair. Powered by BMC's old but sturdy 3.0-liter ohv straight six, which gave moderately good performance (around 100 mph tops). Unlike its corporate relatives, the Princess was trimmed at the Vanden Plas works, which installed plush carpeting, walnut-covered dash, a good deal of extra sound deadening, and other equipment to set this model apart. Rather like what GM would do two decades later when it offered the J-car both as a Chevrolet and a Cadillac.

FOR

Quality trim and furnishings ● Mechanically simple ● British-traditional appeal ● Vanden Plas name a plus for some ● Good appreciator

AGAINST

Indifferent road manners ● Modest performance ● Many parts no longer available

SPECIFICATIONS

Length (in.) 188.0   **Wheelbase (in.)** 108.0/110.0
Weight (lbs.) 3480-3540   **Price (new)** NA

ENGINES

cc/type (cid)	bore x stroke (mm)	bhp*	years
2912/ohv I6 (178)	83×89	105/120	1959-64

*net

PRICES/PROJECTION

Restorable $1000-2000 **Good** $2000-3000
Excellent $2500-4000 **5-year projection** +10%

Vanden Plas Princess 1100/1300 1963-75

1963-67 Princess 1100 sedan

PRODUCTION

39,000 (approx.)

HISTORY

Another "badge engineering" job from BMC, in this case the plushest and most expensive derivative of the front-drive 1100/1300 series designed by Alex Issigonis along the lines of his trend-setting Mini. Like the larger Farina-based Princess models, final assembly and trim application was carried out by Vanden Plas, but there was little difference in appearance or mechanical specifications from those of the downmarket models. Features included all-independent suspension by BMC's innovative (and extremely troublesome) "Hydrolastic" gas "springs," interconnected front-to-rear on each side, plus transversely mounted A-series four-cylinder engine and space-saving front-drive body design. Small but roomy for its size and nicely equipped in this form, with walnut veneer dash, leather upholstery, and full equipment. Marked by the traditional V-P stand-up vertical bar grille. The Princess was sold briefly in the U.S., but most of the emphasis was given to an MG version. Later, the same basic car was sold here as the Austin America. Though the 1100/1300 series was extremely successful in Britain, it bombed in the States, and imports effectively ended after 1969.

FOR

Quality furnishings ● Nimbleness ● A certain cuteness ● Good economy

AGAINST

Meager performance ● A bit small for some ● A rare bird in U.S. ● Parts now difficult to obtain ● Poor suspension reliability ● Rust-prone

SPECIFICATIONS

Length (in.) 147.0   **Wheelbase (in.)** 93.5   **Weight (lbs.)** 2000
Price (new) NA

ENGINES

cc/type (cid)	bore x stroke (mm)	bhp*	years
1098/ohv I4 (67)	65×84	55/58	1963-67
1275/ohv I4 (78)	71×81	65	1968-75

*net

PRICES/PROJECTION

Restorable $500-1500 **Good** $1500-2500
Excellent $2500-3000 **5-year projection** +25%

Vanden Plas Princess 4 Litre R 1964-68

1964 Princess 4-Litre R sedan

PRODUCTION

7087

HISTORY

Reworked replacement for BMC's prestige medium-size sedan. The "R" in the designation stands for Rolls-Royce, which supplied the light-alloy F-head six-cylinder engine, a relative of the Silver Cloud unit. Borg-Warner automatic transmission was standard, and all the luxury touches from the previous BMC-engined Princess 3 Litre were retained. By now, the trendy mid-'50s fins of the original Farina body were becoming dated, so they were sheared off. Other spotter's points include horizontal taillamps and smaller-diameter wheels. Not widely seen in the U.S. even before the advent of federal regulations, and only a modest seller at home.

FOR

As for 1959-64 Princess 3 Litre, plus slightly better performance (top speed up to 106 mph) and Rolls engine snob appeal

AGAINST

Engine costly to maintain • The same crashing boredom of the Princess 3 Litre

SPECIFICATIONS

Length (in.) 188.0 **Wheelbase (in.)** 110.0 **Weight (lbs.)** 3570
Price (new) NA

ENGINES

cc/type (cid)	bore x stroke (mm)	bhp*	years
3909/F6 (239)	95×91	175	1964-68

*gross

PRICES/PROJECTION

Restorable $1000-2500 **Good** $2500-3000
Excellent $5000-6000 **5-year projection** +20%

Volkswagen Beetle (split window) 1946-52

1952 Beetle split-window sedan

PRODUCTION

1946-48 91,921 **1949** 43,633 **1950** 81,917 **1951** 93,358
1952 114,327 (calendar year production)

HISTORY

The phenomenal "People's Car," designed by Dr. Ferdinand Porsche before World War II, though serious production began only gradually in a ravaged postwar Germany. By now, everyone is familiar with the formula: steel platform chassis with all-independent torsion bar suspension and an understressed, air-cooled flat four mounted at the rear. Styling needs no description: it's what earned the Type I the "Bug" or "Beetle" nickname in the U.S., where Volkswagen almost singlehandedly put imports on the map to stay. The Beetle's future as a collectible is assured. In time, the only car to exceed the Model T in production volume will be as ubiquitous—and prized—as the Tin Lizzy is today. For now, the pre-1953 models with the split rear window are the ones to look for. Model years were not formally observed until 1955, with detail changes being made almost continuously. The last split-window Beetles of 1952 received synchromesh on the upper gears, plus door vent wing windows, twin taillights, wider tires, and the famous (or infamous) rotary heater knob. Though the Beetle remains in production today in various third-world countries (including Nigeria and Mexico), the car was changed so much through the '50s, '60s, and '70s that virtually nothing is interchangeable between early and late models. Perhaps the things that haven't changed are the Bug's virtues and vices. It has strange oversteer handling characteristics, it's far from quick (especially these early cars), crosswind stability leaves a lot to be desired, and creature comforts are notable by their absence. On the other hand, traction is terrific, steering light, the engine reliable, and the general charm irresistible. Except for convertibles, it's too early to predict the exact course of later Beetles as collector's items, though there's evidence some upward movement in interest and prices has already begun.

FOR

Landmark historical importance • Great nostalgia car • Low-mileage originals have high appreciation potential

AGAINST

Underpowered • Tricky handling • Meager trunk space • Feeble heater • Older-model parts not as easy to obtain as you'd think

SPECIFICATIONS

Length (in.) 160.0 **Wheelbase (in.)** 94.5 **Weight (lbs.)** approx. 1700 **Price (new)** $1280 original U.S. list in 1949

ENGINES

cc/type (cid)	bore x stroke (mm)	bhp	years
1131/ohv flat 4 (69)	2.95×2.50	27.5-30	1946-52

PRICES/PROJECTION

Restorable $750-1250 **Good** $3000-4000
Excellent $4000-6000 **5-year projection** +10%

Volkswagen Beetle convertible 1953-79

PRODUCTION

20,000 per year (est. average)

HISTORY

In light of the current Great Convertible Revival in Detroit, it's impossible to overlook Volkswagen's Type 1 cabriolet as a collectible. Beetle ragtops of all years are already in strong demand. Karmann of Osnabrück carried out the assembly work, including installation of the typically Teutonic folding top. When buttoned up, the convertible was as tight and quiet as the sedan thanks to its thick "sandwich" top construction and glass (not plastic) rear window. When folded down, the top created an enormous "bustle," giving the car a look like that of no other. Styling and mechanical refinements followed those made to sedan models over the years, so let your taste and pocketbook be your guide. The parts situation naturally gets progressively better the newer the model you're talking about. The last Beetle convertibles were built in 1979, and by that time had become quite expensive in the U.S. owing to inflation and the relative value of the dollar versus the Deutschmark. These will no doubt command the highest collector prices as time goes on as "last of the line" models. In all, an automobile with permanent appeal, a piece of history you can drive every day.

1975 Beetle convertible

FOR

Strong appreciation ● A coast-to-coast network of dealers still happy to provide service ● High-quality materials and finish ● Beetle reliability, simplicity

AGAINST

All the Beetle's well-known infuriations, plus somewhat greater rust susceptibility and high rebuild costs for soft top

SPECIFICATIONS

Length (in.) 160.0 (1953-71), 165.0 (1972-79)
Wheelbase (in.) 94.5 (1953-72), 95.3 (1973-79)
Weight (lbs.) 2000 (average) **Price (new)** $1995 (1953), $6800 (1979) in U.S.

ENGINES

cc/type (cid)	bore x stroke (mm)	bhp*	years
1192/ohv flat 4 (72.7)	77×64	36/40	1953-65
1289/ohv flat 4 (78.4)	78×70	50	1966
1493/ohv flat 4 (91.1)	83×69	53-57	1967-7
1583/ohv flat 4 (96.6)	85×69	60**	1971

*gross **46-48 net

PRICES/PROJECTION

1953-67 MODELS **Restorable** $900-2000 **Good** $2000-3500
Excellent $4000-6000 More recent models considerably higher, depending on condition **5-year projection** +20% for early models with 1970-79s depreciating slightly, but never going below $5000 in prime condition

1977 Beetle convertible

Volkswagen Karmann-Ghia 1956-74

1973 Karmann-Ghia convertible

1968 Karmann-Ghia coupe

PRODUCTION

1956 2452   **1957** 4130   **1958 coupe** 4700   **conv.** 1325
1959 coupe 6265   **conv.** 1770   **1960 coupe** 7247
conv. 2044   **1961 coupe** 6706   **conv.** 1891
1962 coupe 9656   **conv.** 2723   **1963 coupe** 12,010
conv. 3387   **1964 coupe** 13,084   **conv.** 3691
1965 coupe 14,191   **conv.** 4003   **1966 coupe** 17,112
conv. 4827   **1967 coupe** 16,107   **conv.** 3174
1968 coupe 19,177   **conv.** 4157   **1969 coupe** 21,100
conv. 4584   **1970 coupe** 32,952   **conv.** 5873
1971 coupe 17,816   **conv.** 5567   **1972 coupe** 11,208
conv. 3076   **1973 coupe** 10,271   **conv.** 2650
1974 coupe 5779   **conv.** 1926   (U.S. sales; 1958-66
breakdowns estimated)

HISTORY

Volkswagen's sporty, two-seat alternative to the Beetle. Based on the stock Type 1 platform with a specially crafted body built by the Karmann coachworks of Osnabrück, West Germany. Styling was the work of Luigi Segre of the Ghia studios in Italy, and was patterned after the Chrysler d'Elegance show car by Virgil Exner. The combination of swoopy, rounded looks, impeccable construction, and the ordinary but sturdy and economical Beetle drivetrain proved irresistible, and led to a long production run and many admirers for the K-G. The new body also brought two beneficial side effects: slightly better crosswind resistance on the highway and a bit better cornering ability compared to the Beetle. The convertible model's top was constructed similarly to that of the Beetle cabriolet: several layers of top material and insulation and a glass, not plastic, rear window. The K-G ragtop was great for sunny days, but the very wide rear quarters made for hellish visibility with the top up. But compared to contemporary British roadsters, converting the K-G cabriolet from open to closed (or vice versa) was simplicity itself. VW advertising made much about Karmann's almost hand construction methods, which included filling, filing, and sanding all seams before painting. It was great for appearance, but made for costly repairs if you ever had to replace a panel. In all, a very pleasant little tourer, and so numerous that finding one presents no problem. Most mechanical parts are still available, too, through the large chain of VW dealers that helped make this marque so successful in the U.S. Of all the models, the 1500cc 1967 version is probably the most desirable as the peppiest. It was also the last K-G unaffected by U.S. safety and emissions rules.

FOR

Superb styling for its day, and aging gracefully • Fine construction quality • No mechanical parts shortages • Thrifty

AGAINST

Rust-prone • Early body parts becoming scarce • Not as fast as it ought to be • Only two-passenger accommodation • Post-1967 models suffer from U.S. safety/emissions equipment

SPECIFICATIONS

Length (in.) 163.0   **Wheelbase (in.)** 94.5   **Weight (lbs.)** approx. 2300   **Price (new)** $2395 (1956), $2725 (1958 convertible), $3500-4000 by 1974 (all U.S. list prices)

ENGINES

cc/type (cid)	bore x stroke (mm)	bhp*	years
1192/ohv flat 4 (72.7)	77×64	36/40	1956-65
1289/ohv flat 4 (78.4)	78×70	50	1966
1493/ohv flat 4 (91.1)	83×69	53-57	1967-70
1583/ohv flat 4 (96.6)	85×69	60**	1970-74

*gross   **45-48 bhp net

PRICES/PROJECTION

COUPE **Restorable** $500-1000   **Good** $1000-2000
Excellent $2300-4000 Add up to 40% for convertible.
5-year projection +20%

Volkswagen Karmann-Ghia Type 3 1500/1600 1962-67

PRODUCTION

NA

HISTORY

The Karmann-Ghia idea applied to Volkswagen's boxy, new-generation design of the early '60s, the Type 3. Although Type 3s were sold here as the Fastback and Squareback (three-door wagon) "sedans," the K-G models were never officially imported. Those few that did seep in did so privately, some through Canada, others from abroad directly, all well before the Type 3's formal U.S. introduction. The styling was not as successful here as on the Type 1 Karmann-Ghia, with rather angular lines and an awkwardly shaped front end with sheetmetal creases curling around the headlamps. Virtually all those built were coupes, but a few convertibles were also constructed. Though the Type 3 was superficially similar in layout to the Type 1, its engine was completely different, having a flatter "pancake" block and initially more displacement. The Type 3s first brought to the U.S. all used the 1600cc version of this unit instead of the original 1500cc size. Like the Type 1, the Type 3 mounted its air-cooled engine in the rear of a steel platform chassis with all-independent torsion bar suspension.

FOR

Uniqueness •Roomier than Type 1 K-G •Somewhat better performance

AGAINST

Parts scarce •Suspect construction quality •Low appreciation potential •Rust-prone

SPECIFICATIONS

Length (in.) 168.5 **Wheelbase (in.)** 94.5 **Weight (lbs.)** approx. 2200 **Price (new)** $2875 (coupe), $3300 (convertible) U.S. equivalent

ENGINES

cc/type (cid)	bore x stroke (mm)	bhp	years
1493/ohv flat 4 (91.1)	83×67	53	1962-65
1583/ohv flat 4 (96.6)	85×69	60	1966-67

PRICES/PROJECTION

As for 1956-74 Karmann-Ghia

Volvo PV 544 1958-65

1964 PV544 sedan

PRODUCTION

243,995

HISTORY

The final version of the first postwar design by Sweden's long-time automaker. Introduced as the PV444 in 1944. The first Volvo to have any significant impact on the American market, the PV544 differed from its predecessor in having a one-piece (instead of divided) windshield, a larger rear window, revised interior, and minor trim changes. In appearance, however, the car remained nothing so much as a scaled-down version of the 1946 Ford, with rounded fastback body (in two-door form only), tapering hood, distinct front and rear fenderlines, rectangular grille, and low-mounted integral headlamps. Powered by Volvo's own four-cylinder engine, available in standard and more powerful "S" tune. Built to last indefinitely and reliably even in severe climates, the PV544 established Volvo's reputation for sturdiness and solid construction. This model was also surprisingly quick for its day, and saw sporadic competition success in the U.S. Succeeded by the more stylish Amazon/120 series notchbacks, which borrowed much from it mechanically. The two lines ran side by side for several years.

FOR

Rugged Swedish reliability •Good handling, performance •Adequately roomy •Some parts still available

AGAINST

1940s styling •Not numerous any more

SPECIFICATIONS

Length (in.) 177.0 **Wheelbase (in.)** 102.5 **Weight (lbs.)** 2100-2200 **Price (new)** NA

ENGINES

cc/type (cid)	bore x stroke (mm)	bhp*	years
1583/ohv I4 (97)	79×80	60/75	1958-60
1778/ohv I4 (109)	84×80	90/95	1961-65

*gross

PRICES/PROJECTION

Restorable $500-1000 **Good** $1500-2500 **Excellent** $2500-3800 **5-year projection** +10%

Volvo P1800/1800S/ 1800E/1800ES 1962-73

1968 1800S coupe

PRODUCTION

1962-63 P1800 6000		**1963-68 1800S** 23,993	
1969-72 1800E 9414		**1973-74 1800ES** 8078	

HISTORY

Volvo's sports car, a rakish 2+2 sports coupe introduced as a 1962 model in late '61. Bodies were initially supplied by Jensen in England, which also assembled the first cars, designated P1800. Production was transferred to Sweden in late 1964, and the designation changed to P1800S. For the 1969 model year, the original 1.8-liter four-cylinder engine got a displacement boost to a full 2.0

injected 1800E and ES are probably the most desirable models in this bunch, having four wheel disc brakes, aluminum alloy wheels, a beefed-up gearbox, and nicer furnishings than earlier models. A good many 1800s were equipped with manual four-speed transmission with electric overdrive effective on top gear.

1973 1800ES wagon

liters plus Bosch fuel injection to become the 1800E. All these cars used the chassis and running gear of Volvo's 120/Amazon sedans of the mid-'50s to mid-'60s, clothed in styling that was rather dated by the time the 1800 was announced. The lines were curvy, marked by a jutting nose carrying an oval eggcrate grille. Out back were modest little fins and bullet-shaped pod taillights. The roof was quite low, but so was the driving position, which gave a real bathtub effect. The rear seat was virtually useless for anyone larger than kids, but the 1800 shone as a two-seater with ample luggage space for a sporty car. For 1973, Volvo re-roofed the basic body-shell to convert it into the 1800ES, a sports/GT wagon with a deep frameless glass hatch. The coupe was discontinued, and the 1800ES continued for a short while before Volvo decided to abandon the market. Not very fast or terribly refined, but a good-handling car offering comfortable accommodations (Volvo's orthopedically designed seats were famous by now) and great durability. The

FOR

Pleasant touring car • Good mileage • Nicely equipped • Robust Volvo construction • 1800ES a Swedish Chevy Nomad

AGAINST

Buried driving position • Crowded interior • Body parts now difficult to find • Somewhat rust-prone • Throbby engine

SPECIFICATIONS

Length (in.) 172.6 **Wheelbase (in.)** 96.5
Weight (lbs.) 2400-3000 **Price (new)** $6000 U.S. list for 1800ES in 1972

ENGINES

cc/type (cid)	bore x stroke (mm)	bhp*	years
1778/ohv I4 (109)	84×80	100-115	1962-68
1986/ohv I4 (121)	89×80	118-135	1969-73
*gross			

PRICES/PROJECTION

Restorable $1000-2000 **Good** $2500-4000
Excellent $3800-7100 **5-year projection** no change

Milestone Cars Roster

To learn how the Milestone Car Society selects its Milestone Cars, please consult the Introduction under "Selection Criteria." Since the Milestone roster is added to periodically, contact the MCS for up-to-date listings.

DeSoto Adventurer 1956-58
Devon S/S 1958-62
Dodge Coronet R/T. 1967-70
Dodge Charger R/T &
   Daytona. 1968-70
Dual-Ghia 1956-58
Excalibur Series I 1965-69
Facel Vega V-8 1954-64
Ferrari V-12 (All Front
   Engined) 1947-67
Ford Sportsman. 1946-48
Ford Crestline Skyliner 1954
Ford Skyliner 1957-59
Ford Crown Victoria
   Skyliner 1955-56
Ford Mustang GT/GTA
   V8. 1965-67
Ford Mustang Boss
   302/Mach 1. 1969-70
Ford Thunderbird 1955-60
Frazer Manhattan 1947-50
Gaylord 1955-57
Healey Silverstone 1949-50
Hudson (all) 1948-49
Hudson Hornet. 1951-54
Imperial 1955-56
Jaguar XK120 1945-54
Jaguar Mark V Drophead . . 1951
Jaguar Mark VII/VII M . . .1951-54
Jaguar XK140 1954-57
Jaguar Mark VIII 1956-57
Jaguar Mark IX 1958-61
Jaguar Mark X 1962-64
Jaguar XK150 1958-61
Jaguar 3.4/3.8 sedans . . .1957-64
Jaguar E-Type 1961-67
Kaiser-Darrin 161 1954
Kaiser Deluxe/Deluxe
   Virginian 1951-52
Kaiser Dragon 1951-53
Kaiser Manhattan 1954-55
Kaiser Vagabond 1949-50
Kaiser Virginian
   (hardtop) 1949-50
Lagonda V12 1948-49
Lagonda 2.5-Liter drophead
   coupe 1949-53
Lancia Flaminia
   Zagato 1959-64
Lancia Flaminia GT. 1961-63
Lancia Flavia Coupe . . . 1962-66
Lancia Aurelia B.20 and B.20
   coupe 1951-59
Lancia Aurelia B.24 spyder &
   convertible 1953-59
Lea-Francis 2.5-Liter Eighteen
   Sports 1950-54

Lincoln Capri 1952-54
Lincoln
   Continental . . 1946-48, 1961-64
Lincoln Continental
   convertible . . 1958-60, 1965-67
Lincoln Continental Custom
   Limos (Lehmann
   Peterson) 1961-67
Lotus Elite 1958-63
Maserati 3500/3700
   GT 1957-64
MG TC. 1946-49
MG TD. 1950-53
Mercedes-Benz
   190 SL 1955-62
Mercedes-Benz 220A coupe &
   convertible 1951-54
Mercedes-Benz 220/220SE
   coupe & convertible . . .1956-65
Mercedes-Benz 230SL coupe &
   convertible 1963-67
Mercedes-Benz 250SE coupe &
   convertible 1965-67
Mercedes-Benz 250 SL . .1965-67
Mercedes-Benz 280SL . 1969-70
Mercedes-Benz 300SE coupe &
   convertible 1965-67
Mercedes-Benz 300 (S, SL, SE,
   300 coupe &
   convertible). 1952-64
Mercedes-Benz 600 1964-70
Mercury Cougar XR-7 . . .1967-68
Mercury Sportsman 1946
Mercury Sun Valley. 1954-55
Morgan Plus Four 1950-64
Muntz Jet 1950-54
Nash-Healey. 1951-54
NSU Wankel Spyder. 1964
OSCA MT-4 1948-56
Oldsmobile 88 (coupe,
   convertible, Holiday). . .1949-50
Oldsmobile 98 Holiday 1949
Oldsmobile Fiesta 1953
Oldsmobile 4-4-2. 1964-70
Oldsmobile Toronado 1966-67
Packard Caribbean 1953-56
Packard Custom (Clipper &
   Custom Eight) 1946-50
Packard
   Pacific/convertible 1954
Packard Panther Daytona . . 1954
Packard Patrician/400 . . .1951-56
Panhard Dyna 1946-67
Pegaso (all) 1951-58
Plymouth Fury 1956-58
Plymouth Satellite SS &
   GTX 1965-70

Plymouth Barracuda
   Formula S 1965-69
Plymouth Road Runner &
   Superbird 1968-70
Pontiac Safari. 1955-57
Pontiac GTO 1964-69
Porsche 356. 1949-64
Porsche 356C 1965
Riley 2.5 (RMA, RME) . . .1945-55
Rolls-Royce (All) 1947-67
Shelby GT-350 &
   GT-500 1965-67
Sunbeam Tiger 1965-67
Studebaker Avanti 1963-64

1964 Studebaker Avanti

Studebaker Gran Turismo
   Hawk 1962-64
Studebaker Starlight
   (all) 1947-49
Studebaker convertible
   (all) 1947-49
Studebaker Starlight
   (Six & V8) 1953-54
Studebaker Starliner
   (Six & V8) 1953-54
Studebaker President
   Speedster 1955
Talbot-Lago 4.5 (all) 1946-54
Triump TR2/TR3 1953-63
Tucker 1948
Volvo P1800S. 1961-67
Willys Jeepster. 1948-51
Woodill Wildfire 1952-58

Milestone Car Society
P.O. Box 50850
Indianapolis, IN 46250